THE COLLECTED WORKS OF
KEN WILBER

The Collected Works of Ken Wilber

THE COLLECTED WORKS OF

KEN WILBER

VOLUME SEVEN

A BRIEF HISTORY
OF EVERYTHING

THE EYE OF
SPIRIT

SHAMBHALA
Boston
2000

SHAMBHALA PUBLICATIONS, INC.
Horticultural Hall
300 Massachusetts Avenue
Boston, Massachusetts 02115
www.shambhala.com

9 8 7 6 5 4 3 2 1

First Edition
Printed in the United States of America
⊗ This edition is printed on acid-free paper that meets the
American National Standards Institute z39.48 Standard.
Distributed in the United States by Random House, Inc.,
and in Canada by Random House of Canada Ltd

Library of Congress Cataloging-in-Publication Data
Wilber, Ken.
[Works. 1998]
The collected works of Ken Wilber.—1st ed.
p. cm.
Includes bibliographical references and indexes.
Contents: v. 1. The spectrum of consciousness; No boundary.—
v. 2. The Atman project; Up from Eden—
v. 3. A sociable god; Eye to eye.
ISBN 1-57062-501-8 (v. 1: cloth: alk. paper).—
ISBN 1-57062-502-6 (v. 2: cloth: alk. paper).—
ISBN 1-57062-503-4 (v. 3: cloth: alk. paper)
1. Consciousness. 2. Subconsciousness. 3. Self-perception.
4. Psychology—Philosophy. 5. East and West. I. Title.
BF311.W576 1999 97-45928
191—DC21 CIP
ISBN 1-57062-504-2 (v. 4: cloth: alk. paper)
ISBN 1-57062-505-0 (v. 5: cloth: alk. paper)
ISBN 1-57062-506-9 (v. 6: cloth: alk. paper)
ISBN 1-57062-507-7 (v. 7: cloth: alk. paper)

CONTENTS

INTRODUCTION
TO VOLUME SEVEN

THE INTEGRAL VISION AT THE MILLENNIUM

W E LIVE IN AN EXTRAORDINARY TIME: all of the world's cultures, past and present, are to some degree available to us, either in historical records or as living entities. In the history of the planet earth, this has never happened before.

It seems hard to imagine, but for humanity's entire stay on this planet—for some million years up to the present—a person was born into a culture that knew virtually nothing about any other. You were, for example, born a Chinese, were raised a Chinese, married a Chinese, and followed a Chinese religion—often living in the same hut for your entire life, on a spot of land that your ancestors settled for centuries. From isolated tribes and bands, to small farming villages, to ancient nations, to conquering feudal empires, to international corporate states, to global village: the extraordinary growth toward an integral village that seems humanity's destiny.

So it is that the leading edge of consciousness evolution stands today on the brink of an integral millennium—or at least the possibility of an integral millennium—where the sum total of extant human knowledge, wisdom, and technology is available to all. But there are several obstacles to that integral embrace, even in the most developed populations. Moreover, there is the more typical or average mode of consciousness, which is far from integral anything, and is in desperate need of its own tending. Both of those pressing issues (the integral vision as it relates to

I

the most developed and the modestly developed populations) are related directly to the contents of this volume of the *Collected Works*.

In short, what is the status of the integral vision in today's world, both in the cultural elite and in the world at large? Let us start with the leading edge, and the many obstacles to an integral vision in our cultural elite.

INTEGRAL CRITICAL THEORY

As Jack Crittenden points out in his foreword to *The Eye of Spirit*, contained in this volume, if we succeed in developing a truly holistic or integral view, then we will simultaneously develop a new type of *critical theory*, because the integral paradigm will inherently be critical of those approaches that are, by comparison, partial, narrow, shallow, less encompassing, less integral. Jack suggests that the approach set forth in several of my books (such as *Sex, Ecology, Spirituality* and *The Eye of Spirit*) is a new type of integral vision which therefore carries a new type of critical theory—that is, a theory that is critical of the present state of affairs in light of a more encompassing and desirable state, both in the individual and the culture at large.

It is certainly true that I have tried to offer both an integral vision and a critical theory; whether they succeed or not remains to be seen. It is also true that this particular integral vision especially came to fruition with *Sex, Ecology, Spirituality* (SES) and with the two books in this volume, *A Brief History of Everything* (BH) and *The Eye of Spirit* (ES). This period in my work marked the emergence of "wilber-4," or an approach that is "all-level, all-quadrant" (which I will explain in a moment), and which does indeed attempt to provide a genuinely integral or comprehensive view of the Kosmos. Not a final view or a fixed view or the only view; just a view that attempts to honor and include as much research as possible from the largest number of disciplines in a coherent fashion.

At the same time, as critics noted, these books were marked, not just by a critical tone, but by an occasionally polemical and angry tone, which was quite uncharacteristic of my work. This "angry period" in my writing, if we can call it that, lasted from *Sex, Ecology, Spirituality*, through *Brief History*, and up to the last chapter of *The Eye of Spirit*. Although the tone of anger and anguish was a small part of those books, it was noticeable. Since I am not a very angry (nor anguished) person by nature, and since of none of my books before or since displayed such a tone, theories proliferated as to its cause. Those who knew me well generally ascribed it to the aftereffects of Treya's death, which had certainly left me anguished. Those who had not met me ascribed it to my inherently nasty nature, a lack of spirituality, a refusal to engage in caring dialogue, and dozens of other equally unpleasant flaws (as well as the always popular astrology reading having something to do with Mars).

My own conscious reasons, which I outlined in the Introduction to Volume Six, were varied. There was first a genuine anger and dismay at the state of today's cultural studies, including especially "countercultural" studies. I believe this is of profound and far-reaching significance, for it bears directly on whether a truly integral vision can exist in today's climate of culture wars, identity politics, a million new and conflicting paradigms, deconstructive postmodernism, nihilism, pluralistic relativism, and the politics of self. Can an integral vision even be recognized, let alone accepted, in such a cultural state? We are talking, in other words, about the leading edge of consciousness evolution itself, and whether even the leading edge is truly ready for an integral vision. In the end we will find, I believe, that there is some very good news in all this; but first, a little bit of what I see as the bad news.

The baby boomer generation has, like any generation, its strengths and weaknesses. Its strengths include an extraordinary vitality, creativity, and idealism, plus a willingness to experiment with new ideas beyond traditional values. Some social observers have seen in the boomers an "awakening generation," evidenced by an extraordinary creativity in everything from music to computer technology, political action to lifestyles, ecological sensitivity to civil rights. I believe there is much truth and goodness in those endeavors, to the boomers' considerable credit.

Boomer weaknesses, most critics agree, include an unusual dose of self-absorption and narcissism, so much so that most people, boomers included, simply nod their heads in acknowledgment when the phrase "the Me generation" is mentioned.

Thus, it seems that my generation is an extraordinary mixture of greatness and narcissism, and that strange amalgam has infected almost everything we do. We don't seem content to simply have a fine new idea; we must have the new paradigm that will herald one of the greatest transformations in the history of the world. We don't really want to just recycle bottles and paper; we need to see ourselves dramatically saving the planet and saving Gaia and resurrecting the Goddess that previous generations had brutally repressed but we will finally liberate. We aren't able to tend our garden; we must be transfiguring the face of the planet in the most astonishing global awakening history has ever seen. We seem to need to see ourselves as the vanguard of something unprecedented in all of history: the extraordinary wonder of being us.

Well, it can be pretty funny if you think about it, and I truly don't mean any of this in a harsh way. Each generation has its foibles; this appears to be ours, at least to some degree. But I believe few of my generation escape this narcissistic mood. Many social critics have agreed, and not just in such penetrating works as Christopher Lasch's *The Culture of Narcissism*, Richard Restak's *Self Seekers*, Robert Bellah's *Habits of the Heart*, and Aaron Stern's *Me: The Narcissistic American*. Surveying the present state of cultural studies even in American universities, Professor Frank Lentricchia, writing in *lingua franca: The Review of Academic Life*, concluded: "It is impossible, this much is clear, to exaggerate the heroic self-inflation of academic literary and cultural criticism."

Well, ouch. But it's true that if you read a thousand books on cultural studies, alternative spirituality, the new paradigm, and the great transformation that will occur if the world simply listens to the author and his or her revolutionary ideas, sooner or later it starts to get to you. Any healthy soul, I believe, would get at little bit angry (or anguished) at all of this, and that anger was indeed the tone that occasionally peered out from those three books.

Toward the end of that period, I sat down and wrote a book about this strange affliction that seems to shadow my generation, this odd mixture of remarkably high cognitive capacity and wonderfully creative intelligence coupled with an unusual dose of emotional narcissism. Of course, as I said, all previous generations had their own imperfections aplenty; I am by no means picking on the boomers. It is just that "awakening generations" often have a particularly intense downside, simply because they are so intense in general; and for boomers it appears to be a bit of self-inflation, a love affair *avec soi* (along the lines of Oscar Levant's quip to Gershwin: "Tell me, George, if you had it to do all over again, would you still fall in love with yourself?").

I called the book *Boomeritis: The Pig in the Python and Other Gruesome Tales*. It chronicled dozens of areas and disciplines where an important but partial truth was blown all out of proportion by an overestimation of the power and importance of the self.[1] I have not published it yet; at this time I have less inclination to shake the tree. But in a moment I will briefly outline its general conclusions, only because, as I said, this relates directly to an integral vision and its reception in to-day's world. The idea is simple enough: the Culture of Narcissism is antithetical to an integral culture (because narcissistic, isolated selves strenuously resist communion). That topic relates directly to the present volume. After all, the subtitle of *The Eye of Spirit* was "An Integral Vision for a World Gone Slightly Mad." (Many people looked at me and said, "Only slightly?")

But the point remains: Is the world ready for integral anything? If not, what is preventing it?

THE WAVES OF EXISTENCE

One of the striking things about the present state of developmental stud-ies is how similar, in broad outline, most of its models are. Indeed, in *Integral Psychology* I assembled the conclusions of over one hundred different researchers, and, as one of them summarized the situation, "The stage sequences [of all of these theorists] can be aligned across a common *developmental space*. The harmony of alignment shown sug-gests a possible reconciliation of [these] theories. . . ."[2]

From Clare Graves to Abraham Maslow; from Deirdre Kramer to Jan Sinnott; from Jürgen Habermas to Cheryl Armon; from Kurt Fischer to Jenny Wade; from Robert Kegan to Susanne Cook-Greuter, there emerges a remarkably consistent story of the evolution of consciousness. Of course there are dozens of disagreements and hundreds of conflicting details. But they all tell a generally similar tale of the growth and devel-opment of consciousness from—to use Jean Gebser's particular ver-sion—archaic to magic to mythic to rational to integral. Most of the more sophisticated of these cartographies give around six to ten waves of development from birth to what I call the centaur level. (Beyond the centaur, into the more transpersonal waves of consciousness unfolding, agreement tapers off. I will return to this point later.)

Few of these developmental schemes are the rigid, linear, clunk-and-grind models portrayed by their critics. Development is a not a linear ladder but a fluid and flowing affair, with spirals, swirls, streams, and waves—and what appear to be an almost infinite number of multiple modalities (there appear to be as many different dimensions or modal-ities of consciousness as there are different situations in life—i.e., end-less). Most of today's sophisticated developmental theories take all of that into account, and—more important—back it with substantial research (as we will see).

I have, in numerous previous publications (especially *Integral Psychology*) given the details of many of those researchers. Here I will simply use one of them as an example. The model is called Spiral Dynamics, based on the pioneering work of Clare Graves. Graves proposed a profound and elegant system of human development, which subsequent research has refined and validated, not refuted. "Briefly, what I am proposing is that the psychology of the mature human being is an unfolding, emergent, oscillating, spiraling process marked by progressive subordination of older, lower-order behavior systems to newer, higher-order systems as an individual's existential problems change. Each successive stage, wave, or level of existence is a state through which people pass on their way to other states of being. When the human is centralized in one state of existence"—as I would put it, when the self's *center of gravity* hovers around a particular wave of consciousness—"he or she has a psychology which is particular to that state. His or her feelings, motivations, ethics and values, biochemistry, degree of neurological activation, learning system, belief systems, conception of mental health, ideas as to what mental illness is and how it should be treated, conceptions of and preferences for management, education, economics, and political theory and practice are all appropriate to that state."[3]

Graves outlined around eight major "levels or waves of human existence," ranging from autistic, magical, and animistic, through sociocentric and conventional, to individualistic and integrated. As is usually the case with Western researchers, he recognized no higher (transpersonal) levels, but the contributions he made to the prepersonal and personal realms were profound.

It should be remembered that virtually all of these stage conceptions—from Abraham Maslow to Jane Loevinger to Robert Kegan to Clare Graves—are based on extensive amounts of research and data. These are not simply conceptual ideas and pet theories, but are grounded at every point in a considerable amount of carefully checked evidence. Many of the stage theorists have had their models checked in First, Second, and Third World countries. The same is true with Graves's model; to date, it has been tested in over fifty thousand people from around the world, and there have been no major exceptions found to his general scheme.[4]

Of course, *this does not mean that any of these schemes give the whole story, or even most of it*. They are all simply partial snapshots of the great River of Life, and they are all useful when looking at the River from that particular angle. This does not prevent other pictures from being equally useful, nor does it mean that these pictures cannot be refined with further study. What it does mean is that any psychological model that does not include these pictures is not a very integral model.

Graves's work has been carried forward and refined by Don Beck and Christopher Cowan, in an approach they call Spiral Dynamics. Far from being mere armchair analysts, Beck and Cowan were participants in the discussions that led to the end of apartheid in South Africa. The principles of Spiral Dynamics have been fruitfully used to reorganize businesses, revitalize townships, overhaul education systems, and defuse inner-city tensions.

The situation in South Africa is a good example of why the idea of developmental stages (each with its own worldview, values, and needs) can actually reduce and even alleviate social tensions, not exacerbate them (as critics often charge). Spiral Dynamics (following Graves) sees human development as proceeding through eight general "value memes" or deep structures: *instinctive* (archaic-uroboric), *magical/animistic* (typhonic-magic), *power gods* (magic-mythic), *absolutist-religious* (mythic), *individualistic-achiever* (rational-egoic), *relativistic* (early vision-logic), *systematic-integrative* (middle vision-logic), and *global-holistic* (late vision-logic), each of which will be outlined in a moment. These are not rigid levels, but fluid and flowing waves, with much overlap and interweaving, resulting in a meshwork or dynamic spiral of consciousness unfolding.

The typical, well-meaning liberal approach to solving social tensions is to treat every value as equal, and then try to force a leveling or redistribution of resources (money, rights, goods, land) while leaving the values untouched. The typical conservative approach is take its particular values and try to foist them on everybody else. The developmental approach is to realize that there are many different values and worldviews; that some are more complex than others; that many of the problems at one stage of development can only be defused by evolving to a higher level; and that only by recognizing and facilitating this evolution can social justice be finally served. Moreover, by seeing that *each and every individual has all of these memes potentially available to them*, the lines of social tension are redrawn: not based on skin color, economic class, or political clout, but on the *type* of worldview from which a person, group of persons, clan, tribe, business, government, educational system, or nation is operating. As Beck puts it, "The focus is not on types *of* people, but types *in* people." This removes skin color from the game and focuses on some of the truly underlying factors (developmental values and worldviews) that generate social tensions.

We return now to Spiral Dynamics for a brief overview of one version of the many waves of consciousness unfolding. Remember that this is simply one series of photos of the great River of Life. In my own system, there are actually numerous different modules or streams proceeding relatively independently through the basic levels or waves; individuals can be at a relatively high level of development in some modules, medium in others, and low in still others—there is nothing linear about overall development! Moreover, an individual can have an *altered state* or a *peak experience* at virtually any stage of development, so the notion that spiritual experiences are available only at the higher stages is incorrect (see *Integral Psychology* for a full discussion of these topics). Spiral Dynamics does not include states of consciousness, nor does it cover the higher, transpersonal waves of consciousness.[5] But for the ground it covers, it gives one very useful and elegant model of the self and its journey through what Clare Graves called the "waves of existence."

Beck and Cowan (who have remained quite faithful to Graves's system) use various names and colors to refer to these different memes or levels of existence. The use of colors (e.g., purple for magic, blue for mythic, green for ecological sensitivity) almost always puts people off, at first.[6] But Beck and Cowan often work in racially charged areas, and they have found that it helps to take people's minds off skin color and focus on the "color of the meme" instead of the "color of the skin." Likewise in other situations: a green environmentalist might switch from "All big businesses are bad" to "Orange can be uncaring." Moreover, as much research has continued to confirm, since these are levels or memes that *everybody* has potentially available to them, the lines of tension are completely redrawn. In a particular situation it is no longer "black versus white," but perhaps blue versus purple, or orange versus green, and so on; and while skin color cannot be changed, consciousness can.

The important point is that these various waves of existence (or stages of development) are not just passing phases in the self's unfolding; they are *permanently available capacities and coping strategies* that can, once they have emerged, be activated under the appropriate life conditions (survival instincts can be activated in emergency situations; bonding capacities are activated in close human relationships, and so on). We can be red in one context, green in another, turquoise in yet another. Moreover, as Beck puts it, "The Spiral is messy, not symmetrical, with multiple admixtures rather than pure types. These are mosaics, meshes, and blends."[7]

The first six levels are "subsistence levels" marked by "first-tier thinking." Then there occurs a revolutionary shift in consciousness: the emergence of "being levels" and "second-tier thinking," of which there are two major waves. Here is a brief description of all eight waves, the percentage of the world population at each wave, and the percentage of social power held by each.[8] Remember, these are all variations on archaic to magic to mythic to rational to integral, which is the common "developmental space" revealed by most research.

1. *Beige: Archaic-Instinctual.* The level of basic survival; food, water, warmth, sex, and safety have priority. Uses habits and instincts just to survive. Distinct self is barely awakened or sustained. Forms into *survival bands* to perpetuate life.

Where seen: first human societies, newborn infants, senile elderly, late-stage Alzheimer's victims, mentally ill street people, starving masses, shell shock: 0.1% of the adult population, 0% power.

2. *Purple: Magical-Animistic.* Thinking is animistic; magical spirits, good and bad, swarm the earth leaving blessings, curses, and spells that determine events. Forms into *ethnic tribes*. The spirits exist in ancestors and bond the tribe. Kinship and lineage establish political links. Sounds "holistic" but is actually atomistic: "there is a name for each bend in the river but no name for the river."

Where seen: belief in voodoo-like curses, blood oaths, ancient grudges, good luck charms, family rituals, magical ethnic beliefs and superstitions; strong in Third World settings, gangs, athletic teams, and corporate "tribes." 10% of the population, 1% of the power.

3. *Red: Power Gods.* First emergence of a self distinct from the tribe; powerful, impulsive, egocentric, heroic. Magic-mythic spirits, dragons, beasts, and powerful people. Feudal lords protect underlings in exchange for obedience and labor. The basis of *feudal empires*—power and glory. The world is a jungle full of threats and predators. Conquers, outfoxes, and dominates; enjoys self to the fullest without regret or remorse.

Where seen: the "terrible twos," rebellious youth, frontier mentalities, feudal kingdoms, epic heroes, James Bond villains, soldiers of fortune, wild rock stars, Attila the Hun, *Lord of the Flies.* 20% of the population, 5% of the power.

4. *Blue: Mythic Order.* Life has meaning, direction, and purpose, with outcomes determined by an all-powerful Other or Order. This righteous Order enforces a code of conduct based on absolutist and unvarying principles of "right" and "wrong." Violating the code or rules has severe, perhaps everlasting repercussions. Following the code yields rewards for the faithful. Basis of *ancient nations.* Rigid social hierarchies; paternalistic; one right way and only one right way to think about everything. Law and order; impulsivity controlled through guilt; concrete-literal and fundamentalist belief; obedience to the rule of Order; strongly conventional and conformist. Often "religious" [in the mythic-membership sense; Graves and Beck refer to it as the "saintly/absolutistic" level], but can be secular or atheistic Order or Mission.

Where seen: Puritan America, Confucian China, Dickensian England, Singapore discipline, codes of chivalry and honor, charitable good deeds, religious fundamentalism (e.g., Christian and Islamic), Boy and Girl Scouts, "moral majority," patriotism. 40% of the population, 30% of the power.

5. *Orange: Scientific Achievement.* At this wave, the self "escapes" from the "herd mentality" of blue, and seeks truth and meaning in individualistic terms—hypothetico-deductive, experimental, objective, mechanistic, operational—"scientific" in the typical sense. The world is a rational and well-oiled machine with natural laws that can be learned, mastered, and manipulated for one's own purposes. Highly achievement oriented, especially (in America) toward materialistic gains. The laws of science rule politics, the economy, and human events. The world is a chessboard on which games are played as winners gain preeminence and perks over losers. Marketplace alliances; manipulate earth's resources for one's strategic gains. Basis of *corporate states.*

Where seen: the Enlightenment, Ayn Rand's *Atlas Shrugged*, Wall Street, emerging middle classes around the world, cosmetics industry, trophy hunting, colonialism, the Cold War, fashion industry, materialism, liberal self-interest. 30% of the population, 50% of the power.

6. *Green: The Sensitive Self.* Communitarian, human bonding, ecological sensitivity, networking. The human spirit must be freed from greed, dogma, and divisiveness; feelings and caring supersede cold rationality; cherishing of the earth, Gaia, life. Against hierarchy; establishes lateral bonding and linking. Permeable self, relational self, group intermeshing. Emphasis on dialogue, relationships. Basis of *value communities* (i.e., freely chosen affiliations based on shared sentiments).

Reaches decisions through reconciliation and consensus (downside: interminable "processing" and incapacity to reach decisions). Refresh spirituality, bring harmony, enrich human potential. Strongly egalitarian, antihierarchy, pluralistic values, social construction of reality, diversity, multiculturalism, relativistic value systems; this worldview is often called *pluralistic relativism*. Subjective, nonlinear thinking; shows a greater degree of affective warmth, sensitivity, and caring, for earth and all its inhabitants.

Where seen: deep ecology, postmodernism, Netherlands idealism, Rogerian counseling, Canadian health care, humanistic psychology, liberation theology, cooperative inquiry, World Council of Churches, Greenpeace, animal rights, ecofeminism, postcolonialism, Foucault/Derrida, politically correct, diversity movements, human rights issues, ecopsychology. 10% of the population, 15% of the power.

With the completion of the green meme, human consciousness is poised for a quantum jump into "second-tier thinking." Clare Graves referred to this as a "momentous leap," where "a chasm of unbelievable depth of meaning is crossed." In essence, with second-tier consciousness, one can think both vertically and horizontally, using both hierarchies and heterarchies. One can, for the first time, vividly grasp the entire spectrum of interior development, and thus see that each level, each meme, each wave is crucially important for the health of the overall spiral.

As I would word it, since each wave is "transcend and include," each wave is a fundamental ingredient of all subsequent waves, and thus each is to be cherished and embraced. Moreover, each wave can itself be activated or reactivated as life circumstances warrant.[9] In emergency situations, we can activate red power drives; in response to chaos, we might need to activate blue order; in looking for a new job, we might need orange achievement drives; in marriage and with friends, close green bonding.

But what none of those memes can do, on their own, is fully appreciate the existence of the other memes. Each of those first-tier memes thinks that its worldview is the correct or best perspective. It reacts negatively if challenged; it lashes out, using its own tools, whenever it is threatened. Blue order is very uncomfortable with both red impulsiveness and orange individualism. Orange individualism thinks blue order is for suckers and green egalitarianism is weak and woo-woo. Green egalitarianism cannot easily abide excellence and value rankings, big pictures, hierarchies, or anything that appears authoritarian, and thus green reacts strongly to blue, orange, and anything post-green.

All of that begins to change with second-tier thinking. Because second-tier consciousness is fully aware of the interior stages of development—even if it cannot articulate them in a technical fashion—it steps back and grasps the big picture, and thus second-tier thinking appreciates the necessary role that all of the various memes play. Using what we would recognize as mature vision-logic, second-tier awareness thinks in terms of the overall spiral of existence, and not merely in the terms of any one level.

Where the green meme uses early or beginning vision-logic in order to grasp the numerous different systems and pluralistic contexts that exist in different cultures (which is why it is indeed the sensitive self, i.e., sensitive to the marginalization of others), second-tier thinking goes one step further. It looks for the rich contexts that link and join these pluralistic systems, and thus it takes these separate systems and begins to embrace, include, and integrate them into holistic spirals and holarchies (Beck and Cowan themselves refer to second-tier thinking as operating with "holons"). These holarchies include both interior (consciousness) and exterior (material) waves of development, in both vertical and horizontal dimensions (i.e., hierarchical and heterarchical), resulting in a multi-leveled, multi-dimensional, multi-modal, richly holarchical view. Second-tier thinking, in other words, is instrumental in moving from *pluralistic relativism* to *universal integralism.*

The extensive research of Graves, Beck, and Cowan indicates that there are two major waves to this second-tier consciousness (corresponding to what we would recognize as middle and late vision-logic):

7. *Yellow: Integrative.* Life is a kaleidoscope of natural hierarchies [holarchies], systems, and forms. Flexibility, spontaneity, and functionality have the highest priority. Differences and pluralities can be integrated into interdependent, natural flows. Egalitarianism is complemented with natural degrees of excellence where appropriate. Knowledge and competency should supersede rank, power, status, or group. The prevailing world order is the result of the existence of different levels of reality (memes) and the inevitable patterns of movement up and down the dynamic spiral. Good governance facilitates the emergence of entities through the levels of increasing complexity (nested hierarchy).

8. *Turquoise: Holistic.* Universal holistic system, holons/waves of integrative energies; unites feeling with knowledge [centaur]; multiple lev-

els interwoven into one conscious system. Universal order, but in a living, conscious fashion, not based on external rules (blue) or group bonds (green). A "grand unification" is possible, in theory and in actuality. Sometimes involves the emergence of a new spirituality as a meshwork of all existence. Turquoise thinking uses the entire spiral; sees multiple levels of interaction; detects harmonics, the mystical forces, and the pervasive flow-states that permeate any organization.

Second-tier thinking: 1% of the population, 5% of the power.

With only 1 percent of the population at second-tier thinking (and only 0.1 percent at turquoise), second-tier consciousness is relatively rare because it is now the "leading edge" of collective human evolution. As examples, Beck and Cowan mention items ranging from Teilhard de Chardin's noosphere to the growth of transpersonal psychology, with increases in frequency definitely on the way, and even higher memes still in the offing. . . .

THE JUMP TO SECOND-TIER CONSCIOUSNESS

As Beck and Cowan have pointed out, second-tier thinking has to emerge in the face of much resistance from first-tier thinking. In fact, a version of the postmodern green meme, with its pluralism and relativism, has actively fought the emergence of more integrative and holarchical thinking. (It has also made developmental studies, which depend on second-tier thinking, virtually anathema at both conventional and alternative universities.) And yet without second-tier thinking, as Graves, Beck, and Cowan point out, humanity is destined to remain victims of a global "auto-immune disease," where various memes turn on each other in an attempt to establish supremacy.

This is why developmental studies in general indicate that many philosophical debates are not really a matter of the better *objective* argument, but of the *subjective level* of those debating. No amount of orange scientific evidence will convince blue mythic believers; no amount of green bonding will impress orange aggressiveness; no amount of turquoise holarchy will dislodge green hostility—unless the individual is ready to develop forward through the dynamic spiral of consciousness unfolding. This is why "cross-level" debates are rarely resolved, and all parties usually feel unheard and unappreciated.

As we were saying, first-tier memes generally resist the emergence of

second-tier memes. Scientific materialism (orange) is aggressively reductionistic toward second-tier constructs, attempting to reduce all interior
stages to objectivistic neuronal fireworks. Mythic fundamentalism (blue)
is often outraged at what it sees as attempts to unseat its given Order.
Egocentrism (red) ignores second-tier altogether. Magic (purple) puts a
hex on it. Green accuses second-tier consciousness of being authoritarian, rigidly hierarchical, patriarchal, marginalizing, oppressive, racist,
and sexist.

Green has been in charge of cultural studies for the past three decades.
On the one hand, the pluralistic relativism of green has nobly enlarged
the canon of cultural studies to include many previously marginalized
peoples, ideas, and narratives. It has acted with sensitivity and care in
attempting to redress social imbalances and avoid exclusionary practices. It has been responsible for basic initiatives in civil rights and environmental protection. It has developed strong and often convincing
critiques of the philosophies, metaphysics, and social practices of the
conventional religious (blue) and scientific (orange) memes, with their
often exclusionary, patriarchal, sexist, and colonialistic agendas.

On the other hand, as effective as these critiques of pre-green stages
have been, green has attempted to turn its guns on all post-green stages
as well, with the most unfortunate results. In honorably fighting many
rigid social hierarchies, green has condemned all second-tier holarchies—which has made it very difficult, and often impossible, for green
to move forward into more holistic, integral-aperspectival constructions.

Most sophisticated developmental studies describe a movement from
mythic absolutism (blue) and rational formalism (orange), through
stages of pluralism and relativism (green), to stages of integralism and
holism (yellow and turquoise).[10] The green meme, effectively challenging
the absolutisms of blue and orange, then mistook all universals and all
holarchies as being of the same order, and this often locked it into first-
tier thinking.

Nonetheless—and this is especially significant—it is *from* the healthy
green ranks that second-tier emerges, as Spiral Dynamics points out, so
most of my comments in those three books (SES, BH, ES) were directed
specifically toward green, as were the polemical nudges, in an attempt
to get green to look at its own premises more expansively. These jabs
have not, in general, endeared me to greens, but it has jolted the conversation in ways that politeness consistently failed to do.

And this is where boomeritis enters the picture.

BOOMERITIS

Because pluralistic relativism moves beyond the rigid universalisms of formal rationality into richly textured and individualistic contexts, one of its defining characteristics is its strong *subjectivism*. This means that its sanctions for truth and goodness are established most basically by individual preferences (as long as the individual is not harming others). What is true for you is not necessarily true for me; what is right is simply what individuals or cultures happen to agree on at any given moment; there are no universal claims for knowledge or truth; each person is free to find his or her own values, which are not binding on anybody else. "You do your thing, I do mine" is a popular summary of this stance.

This is why the self at this stage is indeed the "sensitive self." Precisely because it is aware of the many different contexts and numerous different types of truth (pluralism), it bends over backwards in an attempt to let each truth have its own say, without marginalizing or belittling any. As with the catchwords "antihierarchy," "pluralistic," and "egalitarian," whenever you hear the word "marginalization" and a criticism of it, you are almost always in the presence of a green meme.

This noble intent, of course, has its downside. Meetings that are run on green principles tend to follow a similar course: everybody is allowed to express his or her feelings, which often takes hours; there is an almost interminable processing of opinions, often reaching no decision or course of action, since a specific course of action would likely exclude somebody. Thus there are often calls for an inclusionary, nonmarginalizing, compassionate embrace of all views, but exactly how to do this is rarely spelled out, since in reality not all views are of equal merit. The meeting is considered a success not if a conclusion is reached, but if everybody has a chance to share his or her feelings. Since no view is supposed to be inherently better than another, no real course of action can be recommended, other than sharing all views. If any statements are made with certainty, it is how oppressive and nasty all the alternative conceptions are. (This is why one of pluralism's main activities is not advancing its own constructive conceptions, but criticizing and deconstructing everybody else's.)

In academia, this pluralistic relativism is the dominant stance. As Colin McGuinn summarizes it: "According to this conception, human reason is inherently local, culture-relative, rooted in the variable facts of human nature and history, a matter of divergent 'practices' and 'forms of life' and 'frames of reference' and 'conceptual schemes.' There are no norms of reasoning that transcend what is accepted by a society or an epoch, no objective justifications for belief that everyone must respect on pain of cognitive malfunction. To be valid is to be taken to be valid, and different people can have legitimately different patterns of taking. In the end, the only justifications for belief have the form 'justified for me.' "[11] As Clare Graves himself put it, "This system sees the world relativistically. Thinking shows an almost radical, almost compulsive emphasis on seeing everything from a relativistic, subjective frame of reference."

The point is perhaps obvious: because pluralistic relativism has such an intensely subjectivistic stance, it is especially prey to emotional narcissism. And exactly that is the crux of the problem: *pluralism becomes a supermagnet for narcissism.* Pluralism becomes an unwitting home for the Culture of Narcissism.

In green's noble attempt to move beyond conventional rules (many of which are indeed unfair and marginalizing), and in its genuine desire to deconstruct a rigid rationality (much of which can be repressive and stultifying)—in short, in green's admirable attempt to go *postconventional*, it has often inadvertently embraced *anything* nonconventional, and this includes much that is frankly *preconventional*, regressive, and narcissistic.

There is a troubling contradiction in all this. It's not just that the claims of the cultural pluralists are said to be *universally* true (the so-called performative contradiction, which means they are making claims that they insist cannot be made); the problem is deeper than that.

Pluralism, multiculturalism, and egalitarianism, in their best forms, all stem from a very high developmental stance, a *postconventional* stance (early vision-logic, postformal cognition, green meme, etc.), and from that postconventional stance of worldcentric fairness and care, the green meme attempts to treat all previous memes with equal concern and compassion, a truly noble intent. But because it embraces an intense egalitarianism, it fails to see that *its own stance*—which is the first stance that is even capable of egalitarianism—is itself a fairly rare, elite stance (somewhere between 10 and 20 percent of the population). Worse, the green meme then *actively denies* the hierarchical stages that *produced* the green meme in the first place. Pluralistic egalitarianism is the product, we have seen, of at least six major stages of hierarchical development, a hierarchy that it then turns around and aggressively denies in the name of egalitarianism!

Under the noble guise of liberal egalitarianism—and under the sanction of the intense subjectivistic stance of this pluralistic and relativistic wave—every previous wave of existence, no matter how shallow, egocentric, or narcissistic, is given encouragement to "be itself," even when "be itself" might include the most barbaric of stances. (If "pluralism" is really true, then we must invite the Nazis and the KKK to the multicultural banquet, since no stance is supposed to be better or worse than another, and so all must be treated in an egalitarian fashion—at which point the self-contradictions of undiluted pluralism come screaming to the fore.)[12]

Thus, the very high developmental stance of pluralism—the product of at least six major stages of hierarchical transformation—turns around and denies all hierarchies, *denies the very path that produced its own noble stance*, and thus it ceases to demand hierarchical transformation from anybody else, and consequently it extends an egalitarian embrace to every stance, no matter how shallow or narcissistic. The more egalitarianism is implemented, the more it destroys the very capacity for egalitarianism; the more it invites, indeed encourages, the Culture of Narcissism. And the Culture of Narcissism is the antithesis of the integral culture.

(Narcissism, at its core, is a demand that "Nobody tells me what to do!" Narcissism will therefore not acknowledge anything universal, because that places various demands and duties on narcissism that it will strenuously try to deconstruct, because "nobody tells me what to do." This egocentric stance can easily be propped up and supported with the tenets of pluralistic relativism.)

In short, the rather high cognitive development of postformal pluralism becomes a supermagnet for the rather low state of emotional narcissism. Which brings us to boomeritis.

Boomeritis is that strange mixture of very high, postconventional cognitive capacity (early vision-logic, the green meme, postformal pluralistic relativism) combined with preconventional emotional narcissism. A typical result is that the sensitive self, trying to help, excitedly exaggerates its own significance. It will possess the new paradigm, which heralds the greatest transformation in the history of the world; it will completely revolutionize spirituality as we know it; it will save the planet and save Gaia and save the Goddess; it will. . . .

Well, and off we go on some of the negative aspects of the last three decades of boomer cultural studies. This is exactly why observers on the scene have reported, as we saw with Lentricchia, that "it is impossible, this much is clear, to exaggerate the heroic self-inflation of academic literary and cultural criticism." Once again, that is not the whole story, or even the most important part of the story, of the boomers. But it appears to be an unmistakable flavor. What was so startling to me, as I gathered examples for the book, was the way boomeritis had significantly tilted and prejudiced academic studies. Virtually no topic, no matter how innocent, escaped a reworking at its hands.

The importance of *dialogue* is a prime example. An extraordinary number of brilliant philosophers, ever since Socrates, have pointed out the importance of dialogue in reaching truth and understanding. Nor is the notion lacking in modernity; in fact, it has often gained prominence: Heidegger's notions of intersubjectivity; Martin Buber's I-thou spirituality; the structuralists' and poststructuralists' absolute obsession with discourse and discursive formations; Habermas's central claim that dialogue free of domination and distortion is the means and the method of truth disclosure; my own system, whereby all subjective events occur only in the clearing created by intersubjectivity. The list of premodern, modern, and postmodern philosophers stressing the importance of dialogue is truly staggering.

Yet to hear the boomeritis version, which has appeared in literally thousands of publications, nobody seems to have really understood the importance of dialogue until just now, whereupon there follows a treatise about how important it is to listen to others, which usually runs something like this: people who, like me, engage in caring dialogue, which is free of domination and attack, have found a new way to meet each other, not on the pattern of discourse as a war to be won, but as a show of how caring and loving we really are, and you can see how caring and loving we really are by comparing us to all those people who do not follow our example (whereupon there usually ensues a list of the uncaring culprit's wicked ways, which just happens to have the advantage, not really intended, of making the lecturer's moral superiority blindingly obvious to the entire world).

I have a file in my office that contains references to over two hundred essays, books, and articles on the importance of caring dialogue, most of which tear into their opponents with a ferocity that is startling or a condescension that is measurable. At the same time, most of their opponents have *also* written articles on the importance of caring dialogue, cooperative inquiry, and sharing instead of fighting. Since everybody seems to be talking about the importance of talking, I have been trying to figure out just who it is that isn't talking, because I would like to meet that person.

In most of these calls for dialogue, there is a calculated claim of moral superiority in the very stance of condemning in others precisely what the speaker is doing himself. This pattern (claiming to be free of those features that one uses in the claim) seems to be at the heart of boomeritis—from universally damning universals to hierarchically damning hierarchies—and it is pandemic because it appears to be the central psychological mechanism that allows emotional narcissism to mask its preconventional face in postconventional pieties. If one were truly engaged in caring dialogue, one would simply do it; one would not constantly pause to point out how wonderful it is.

Well, the list is endless, and I don't mean to give a blow-by-blow of *Boomeritis*. But it was boomeritis, as it touched dozens of different disciplines, that I was angrily reacting to (in SES, BH, ES), particularly its domination of academia, conventional and especially alternative. I am not excluding myself from this criticism; as I said, I believe few of my generation escape it; but I was definitely reacting to all of that. Healthy anger, I believe, constitutes the T-cells of the psychological immune system, throwing garbage out of the system, and my T-cells went into overdrive. But there was a very important reason, I believe, for that reaction, and this is really the only point I would like to emphasize: pluralistic relativism infected with emotional narcissism is one of the major barriers to the emergence of universal integralism.

In other words, since, in normal development, pluralistic relativism eventually gives way to second-tier consciousness (and universal integralism), why did my generation become so stuck in pluralistic relativism, extreme egalitarianism, and antihierarchy flatlandism? One of the central reasons, I concluded, is that the intense subjectivism of pluralistic relativism was a prime magnet and refuge for the narcissism that, for whatever reasons, many social critics have found prevalent in the Me generation. I called that combination of pluralistic relativism and emotional narcissism "boomeritis," and it followed that boomeritis was one of the primary roadblocks to universal integralism and second-tier consciousness.

THE MANY GIFTS OF GREEN

Boomeritis is still one of the single greatest barriers to that unfolding, I believe. But with the exception of the book *Boomeritis* (which, if I publish it, would have to be counted in that "angry period"), I have no desire to keep shaking the tree in that particular fashion. In the new editions of those three books, some of the polemics have been toned down, although the critical stance—and the critical theory—definitely remains.

For the truly important point is that it is from the large fund of green memes that the second-tier emerges.[13] It is from the pluralistic perspectives freed by green that integrative and holistic networks are built. That fact is worth emphasizing. Development tends to proceed by differentiation-and-integration.[14] The green meme (which is early vision-logic, or the beginning of the postformal stages of consciousness) heroically manages to differentiate the often rigid, abstract, universal formalism of the previous rational wave (formal operational, egoic-rational, orange meme). It therefore discloses, not a rational uniformitarianism that tends to ignore and marginalize anything not of its ilk, but a beautiful tapestry of multiple contexts, richly different cultural textures, pluralistic perceptions, and individual differences, and it becomes sensitive (the sensitive self!) to all of those often unheard voices. We have seen that every meme makes an invaluable contribution to the health of the overall spiral, and this pluralistic sensitivity is one of the great gifts of green.

Once those wonderful differentiations are made, they can then be brought together into even deeper and wider contexts that disclose a truly holistic and integral world: the leap to second-tier consciousness can occur—but *only* because of the work that the green meme has accomplished. There is first differentiation, then integration. Middle and late vision-logic (yellow and turquoise) complete the task begun by early vision-logic (green), and this allows us to move from pluralistic relativism to universal integralism (e.g., Gebser's integral-aperspectival). That is what I mean when I say that the green meme frees the pluralistic perspectives that second-tier will integrate.

In short, since green is the conclusion of first-tier thinking, it prepares for the leap to second-tier. But in order to move into second-tier constructions, the fixation to pluralistic relativism and the green meme in general needs to be relaxed. Its accomplishments will be fully included and carried forward. But its attachment to its own stance needs to be eased, and it is precisely boomeritis (or a narcissistic attachment to the intense subjectivism of the relativistic stance) that makes such a letting-go quite difficult. My hope is that by highlighting our fixation to the green meme, we can begin more easily to transcend and include its wonderful accomplishments in an even more generous embrace.

BEYOND PLURALISM

Thus, as much as I have been chiding green for some of its downsides, we should never forget that it is from green that second-tier emerges, and that the many accomplishments of green are the necessary prerequisites for second-tier consciousness. All of my writing has been, in a sense, an invitation to those greens who find it appropriate to move on, not by abandoning green, but by enriching it. But when green becomes infected with boomeritis, nobody moves anywhere. . . .

But why is boomeritis one of the greatest obstacles to the emergence of an integral vision? What about the rigid conformity of mythic-membership? What about the often nasty materialism of egoic-rationality? What about the horrible economic conditions of many Third World countries? What about. . . .

Yes, all of that is true. But, as we were saying, it is only *from* the stage of pluralistic relativism (early vision-logic, green meme) that universal integralism can emerge (mature vision-logic, second-tier). Of course, *all* of the pre-green memes also "prevent" the emergence of an integral-aperspectival view. My point—and the only reason I am "picking on" boomers—is that this generation seems to be the first to significantly evolve to the green wave in large numbers, and thus this is the first major generation that has a real chance to significantly move forward into a mature vision-logic, second-tier consciousness—and to use that consciousness to organize social institutions in a truly integral fashion.

But it has not yet done so to full effect, because it has not yet gone postgreen to any significant degree (as we saw, less than 2 percent are postgreen). *But it still might do so*; and since it is only from green that it *can* do so, the boomers are still poised for a possible leap into the hyperspace of second-tier consciousness. And that is not a boomeritis grandiose claim; it is backed by substantial evidence, particularly from social and psychological developmental studies.

INTEGRAL CULTURE?

The sociologist Paul Ray has recently made the claim that a new cultural segment, whose members he calls "the cultural creatives," now make up an astonishing 24 percent of the adult American population (or around 44 million people). In order to distinguish them from the previous cultural movements of *traditionalism* and *modernism*, Ray calls this group the *integral culture.* Exactly how "integral" this group is remains to be seen, but I believe Ray's figures indeed represent a series of very real currents. The traditionalists are grounded in premodern mythic values (blue); the modernists, in rational-industrial values (orange); and the cultural creatives, in postformal/postmodern values (green). Those three movements constitute exactly what we would expect from our survey of the development and evolution of consciousness (preformal mythic to formal rational to early postformal).

But a few more points stand out. What Ray calls the integral culture is not integral as I am using the term; it is not grounded in universal integralism, mature vision-logic, or second-tier consciousness. Rather, as Ray's survey results suggest, the majority of cultural creatives are basically *activating the green meme*, as their values clearly indicate: strongly antihierarchical; concerned with dialogue; embracing a flatland holism ("holistic everything," as Ray puts it, except that all genuine holism involves holarchy, or nested hierarchy, and the cultural creatives eschew holarchy, so their holism is usually an amalgam of monological wholeness claims, such as offered by physics or systems theory); suspicious of conventional forms of most everything; admirably sensitive to the marginalization of minorities; committed to pluralistic values and subjectivistic warrants; and possessing a largely translative, not transformative, spirituality.[15] As Don Beck himself points out, using substantial research, "Ray's 'integral culture' is essentially the green meme. There are few if any indications of yellow or turquoise memes; in other words, there are few second-tier memes in most of the cultural creatives."[16]

Other empirical research strongly supports this interpretation. Ray claims that 24 percent of Americans are cultural creatives in an integral culture. I believe he has accurately measured something, but it is actually the fact that most cultural creatives are, to use Jane Loevinger and Susanne Cook-Greuter's terms, at the *individualistic* stage (green), not the *autonomous* or *integrated* stages (yellow and turquoise). Research shows that, indeed, less than 2 percent of Americans are at the autonomous or integrated stage (this also fits very closely with Beck's research—less than 2 percent at second-tier—as well as with that of most other developmentalists); the rest are at *individualistic or lower*, and that includes, by simple arithmetic, at least 92 percent of the cultural creatives.[17]

In fact, since it is the green meme that, if not let go of, is what immediately prevents the emergence of second-tier integration, what Paul Ray calls the "integral culture" is actually what is *preventing* the integral culture. Almost any way we slice the data, the "integral culture" is not that integral.

But it can be. As the cultural creatives move into the second half of life, this is exactly the time that a further transformation of consciousness, from green into mature vision-logic and second-tier awareness (and even higher), can most easily occur. As I will suggest in a moment, this transformation into second-tier integral consciousness (and higher, into genuinely transpersonal waves) can most readily be effected by *integral transformative practice*. The only reason I am talking about "boomeritis" is with the hope that, by discussing some of the obstacles to this further transformation, it might more readily occur.

These obstacles are not found exclusively in boomers or in Americans. Pluralistic relativism is a universally available wave of consciousness unfolding, and it has its own perils and stick-points, of which intense subjectivism, magnet for narcissism, is a major one. Thus "boomeritis" is by no means confined to boomers, but can afflict anybody poised for the leap into second-tier consciousness, itself the great gateway to more enduring spiritual and transpersonal awareness.

THE INTEGRAL EMBRACE

It appears, then, that approximately 1 to 2 percent of the population is at an integral, second-tier stance, but that around 20 percent are at green, poised for that possible transformation.

In order for green to go one step further and make the jump into integral-aperspectival consciousness, the following factors might be considered:

1. All systems are *context-bound*, according to green pluralism, so let us *fully* carry forward that agenda: all relativities and all pluralities are therefore *also* context-bound: they themselves have wider and deeper contexts that bind them together into even larger systems.

2. Therefore, let us acknowledge these even larger contexts, and then begin to outline the universal-integral networks binding them all together. Let us begin to move from pluralistic relativism to universal integralism.

3. The only way to arrive at such an integral stance is to include *both* hierarchies and heterarchies (and thus arrive at holarchies). Let us, then,

relax our morbid fear of all hierarchies, stages of development, levels of reality, critical judgments, qualitative distinctions, degrees, excellence, grades, and rankings. Not *all* of them are bad, and we use them anyway, never so much as when we deny them; so let us use them in a healthy, conscious, fair, and judicious fashion.

4. Once we include both hierarchies and heterarchies—both ranking and linking—we can develop a more integral vision that is "all-level, all-quadrant" (see below), a vision that includes the I and the We and the It domains—or self, culture, and nature—as they all unfold in matter, body, mind, soul, and spirit, spanning the entire spectrum of consciousness in all its radiant dimensions. This includes multiple modalities, waves, streams, states, and realms, all woven together into a global holism or universal integralism.

5. Many of the waves and streams of the spectrum of consciousness are indeed local, culturally specific, and not universal. But research has consistently confirmed that many of these patterns of richly interwoven textures are common to humanity as a whole; others are common to large areas of humanity or to various epochs; and some are merely local and idiosyncratic, varying from culture to culture and individual to individual.[18] Acknowledging and honoring the common and cross-cultural patterns in consciousness is not necessarily a marginalizing, oppressive endeavor; in its nonmarginalizing form, it is in fact the basis of universal integralism. Let us therefore attempt to include both the universally common patterns of consciousness as well as the local, specific, and pluralistic features, and thus continue to move from pluralistic relativism to universal holism.

6. This multidimensional Kosmos is therefore not just a final state, but a flow state. Not just holographic, but holodynamic. Not just given, but ceaselessly unfolding, in multiple waves and streams of existence, flowing and evolving in endless displays of Spirit's own self-blossoming. Therefore, let us honor and include these unfolding, developing, evolving currents as the Kosmos flowers in all its domains.

7. Once that happens, the important contributions of green can be taken up, embraced and included, in the ongoing unfolding of consciousness. Green is not lost or denied, but included and enriched, as a more genuinely integral vision emerges.

A FULL-SPECTRUM APPROACH

Since all of the above can sound like platitudes, clichés, and slogans unless we can actually supply details backed by reputable research, allow me to very briefly sketch the specifics of a postgreen integral map of human possibilities (a map that is presented in phase-4 books—SES, BH, ES, SS, OT, and IP). This simple overview of an integral vision will also serve to set the books in this volume into the context of my work as a whole.

Since we have already used Spiral Dynamics as one example of some of the levels or waves of consciousness unfolding, we can continue to use that model, and then plug it into an "all-level, all-quadrant" conception, as shown in figure 1. (Wyatt and Marilyne Woodsmall, well-known proponents of Graves's work, have been using a diagram similar to this ever since they read SES, as has Peter McNab; they have combined this comprehensive map with various change technologies. Don Beck has also begun using a figure similar to this, which he calls "4Q/8L" to refer to eight levels in all four quadrants. Of course, I extend the levels to include the higher, transpersonal waves, and I include numerous different altered states and developmental streams progressing through the major waves, but this simplified figure is quite adequate to make our general points.)

With reference to figure 1, we might note several items. The four quadrants—which you will find fully explained in the books in this volume—simply refer to four of the most important dimensions of the Kosmos, namely, the interior and the exterior of the individual and the collective. Here are some quick examples:

The Upper-Left quadrant (which is the interior of the individual, and which in the simplistic figure 1 only contains one stream and eight personal waves), actually contains a *full spectrum* of waves (or levels of development—stretching from matter to body to mind to soul to spirit; or again, from archaic to magic to mythic to rational to integral to transpersonal, not as rigidly discrete platforms but as interwoven nests); many different *streams* (or *lines* of development—the different modules, dimensions, or areas of development—including cognitive, moral, affective, linguistic, kinesthetic, somatic, interpersonal, etc.); different *states* of consciousness (including waking, dreaming, sleeping, altered, nonordinary, and meditative); different *types* of consciousness (or possible orientations at every level, including personality types and different

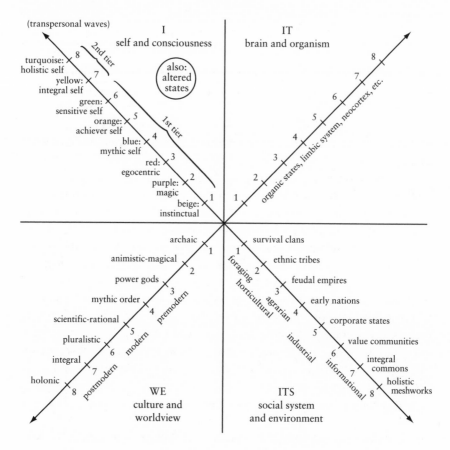

FIGURE 1. *Some Examples of the Four Quadrants in Humans*

gender styles), among numerous other factors. Taking all of these items into account allows us to utilize the important research findings from developmental studies, but also place them in a larger context that suggests their important but limited contributions, complementing them with an understanding of multiple modalities, dimensions, states, and types, to result in a richly textured, holodynamic, integral view of consciousness.

Let us focus, for a moment, on waves, streams, and types. Waves are the "levels" of development, conceived in a fluid, flowing, and intermeshing fashion, which is how most developmentalists today view them. Carol Gilligan's three major moral waves for women—selfish, care, and universal care (i.e., preconventional, conventional, and postconventional)—are typical of the holarchical levels or waves of development. Why does she maintain that these stages are (her word) "hierarchical"? Because each stage is a necessary ingredient of its successor, and thus stages cannot be skipped or reordered, as her research confirms.[19]

Through these general *waves* of development flow many different *streams* of development. We have credible evidence that these different streams, lines, or modules include cognition, morals, self-identity, psychosexuality, ideas of the good, role-taking, socioemotional capacity, creativity, altruism, several lines that can be called "spiritual" (care, openness, concern, religious faith, meditation), communicative competence, modes of space and time, affect/emotion, death-seizure, needs, worldviews, mathematical competence, musical skills, kinesthetics, gender identity, defense mechanisms, interpersonal capacity, and empathy. (You will see some of the evidence for these independent modules presented in *The Eye of Spirit*; more extensive references can be found in *Integral Psychology*).

One of the most striking items about these multiple modules or streams is that most of them develop in a relatively independent fashion. Research is still fleshing out the details of these relationships; some lines are necessary but not sufficient for others; some develop closely together. But on balance, many of the streams develop at their own rate, with their own dynamic, in their own way. A person can be at a relatively high level of development in some streams, medium in others, and low in still others.

I have indicated this, also in a very simplistic fashion, in figure 2. Here, I am using just four major waves—body, mind, soul, and spirit, each of which transcends and includes its predecessors in increasing waves of integral embrace (a true holarchy of nests within nests within nests). Through those general waves pass various developmental streams. I selected only five as examples (cognitive, moral, interpersonal, spiritual, and affective), but you can see the uneven development that is theoretically possible (and that empirical research has continued to confirm often happens).

This model sheds considerable light on the fact that, for example, some individuals—including spiritual teachers (and presidents)—may be highly evolved in certain capacities (such as meditative awareness), and yet demonstrate poor (or even pathological) development in other streams, such as the interpersonal or psychosexual.

This also allows us to spot the ways in which the spiritual traditions themselves—from shamanism to Buddhism to Christianity to indigenous

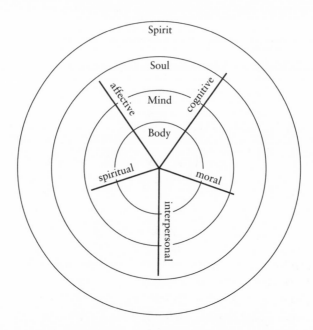

FIGURE 2. *Waves and Streams*

religions—might excel in training certain modules, but fall short in many others, or even be pathological in many others. A more integral transformative practice might therefore seek a more balanced or "all-level, all-quadrant" approach to transformation (see below).

As for *types*, see figure 3, which uses the enneagram as an example. What I have done here is take only one developmental module or stream (it can be anything—morals, cognition, defenses, etc.), and I have listed the eight or so levels or waves of development through which this particular stream will tend to unfold (using Spiral Dynamics as an example of the waves). At each level I have drawn the enneagram as an example of what might be called a *horizontal* typology, or a typology of the personality types that can exist at almost any *vertical* level of development. The point is that a person can be a particular *type* (using Jungian types, Myers-Briggs, the enneagram, etc.) at virtually any of the levels. Thus, if a person is, say, predominately enneagram type 5, then as they develop they would be purple 5, red 5, blue 5, and so on (again, not in a rigid linear fashion, but in a fluid and flowing mesh).[20]

This can occur in any of the lines. For example, in the moral line, a person might be predominately enneagram type 7 at the green wave in

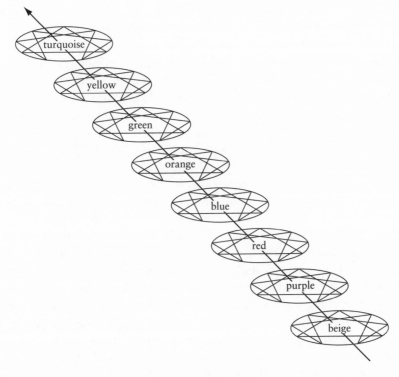

FIGURE 3. *Levels and Types*

the context of the workplace; under stress, the person might move to type 1 at the orange wave (or even blue wave); cognitively, the person might be type 4 at turquoise, and so on. Notice, however, that what the enneagram alone cannot spot is the shift in vertical levels; an orange 7 under stress might go to orange 1, but under real stress, the orange 7 will regress to blue, then purple. These are not just different types, but different levels of types. Again, by combining horizontal typologies with vertical typologies, we can make use of second-tier constructions for a more integral view.

For many radical feminists, male and female orientations also constitute a *type*. Based mostly on work by Carol Gilligan and Deborah Tannen, the idea is that the typical male orientation tends to be more agentic, autonomous, abstract, and independent, based on rights and justice; whereas the female orientation tends to be more permeable, relational, and feelingful, based on care and responsibility. Gilligan, recall, agrees that females proceed through three (or four) hierarchical stages of development, and these are essentially the same three (or four) hierarchical stages or waves through which males proceed (namely, preconventional, conventional, postconventional, and integrated).

The reason that many people, especially feminists, still incorrectly believe that Gilligan denied a female hierarchy of development is that Gilligan found that males tend to make judgments using ranking or hierarchical thinking, whereas women tend to make judgments using linking or relational thinking (what I summarize as agency and communion, respectively). But what many people overlooked is that Gilligan maintained that *the female orientation itself proceeds through three (or four) hierarchical stages*—from selfish to care to universal care to integrated. Thus, many feminists confused the idea that females tend not to think hierarchically with the idea that females do not develop hierarchically; the former is true, the latter is false, according to Gilligan herself.[21] (Why was Gilligan so widely misread and distorted in this area? Because the green meme eschews and marginalizes hierarchies in general, and thus it literally could not perceive her message accurately.)

As you will see in *The Eye of Spirit*, contained in this volume, I have summarized this research by saying that men and women *both* proceed through the same general waves of development, but men tend to do so with an emphasis on agency, women with an emphasis on communion.

This approach to gender development allows us to utilize the extensive contributions of developmental studies, but also supplement them with a keener understanding of how females evolve "in a different voice" through the great waves of existence. In the past, it was not uncommon to find orthodox psychological researchers defining females as "deficient males" (i.e., females "lack" logic, rationality, a sense of justice; they are even defined by "penis envy," or desiring that which they lack). Nowadays it is not uncommon to find, especially among feminists, the reverse prejudice: males are defined as "deficient females" (i.e., males "lack" sensitivity, care, relational capacity, embodiment, etc.).

Well, we might say, a plague on both houses. With this more integral approach, we can trace development through the great waves and streams of existence, but also recognize that males and females might navigate that great River of Life using a different style, type, or voice. This means that we can still recognize the major waves of existence—which, in fact, are gender-neutral—but we must fully honor the validity of *both* styles of navigating those waves.[22]

Finally, a person at virtually any stage of development, in virtually any line, of virtually any type, can have an *altered state* or *peak experi-*

ence, including those that are called spiritual experiences, and this can have a profound effect on their consciousness and its development. Thus, the idea that spiritual experiences can only occur at higher stages is incorrect. However, in order for altered states to become permanent traits (or structures), they need to enter the stream of enduring development.[23]

The point is that, even looking at just the Upper-Left quadrant, a more integral map of consciousness is now at least possible, one which includes waves, streams, states, and types, all of which appear to be important ingredients in this extraordinary spectrum of consciousness.

All-Quadrant

But individual or subjective consciousness does not exist in a vacuum; no subject is an island unto itself. Individual consciousness is inextricably intermeshed with the objective organism and brain (Upper-Right quadrant); with nature, social systems, and environment (Lower-Right quadrant); and with cultural settings, communal values, and worldviews (Lower-Left quadrant). Again, each of these quadrants has numerous waves, streams, types, and so on, only a pitiful few of which are indicated in figure 1. But in the following pages, you will find a wide variety of examples from each quadrant, as they relate to art and literary interpretation, feminism and gender studies, anthropology, philosophy, psychology, and religion.

The Upper-Right quadrant is the individual viewed in an objective, empirical, "scientific" fashion. In particular, this includes organic body states, biochemistry, neurobiological factors, neurotransmitters, organic brain structures (brain stem, limbic system, neocortex), and so on. Whatever we might think about the actual relation of mind-consciousness (Upper Left) and brain-body (Upper Right), we can at least agree they are intimately related. (The exact relation of mind and brain is explored in detail in *Integral Psychology*.) The point is simply that an "all-level, all-quadrant" model would certainly include the important correlations of states, waves, streams, and types of consciousness (UL) with brain states, organic substrates, neurotransmitters, and so on (UR).

There is now occurring an extraordinary amount of research into organic brain states and their relation to consciousness—so much so that most orthodox researchers tend to simply *reduce* consciousness to brain mechanisms. As you will see in the following pages, the insidiousness of this reduction of Upper Left to Upper Right is detailed in both *The Eye of Spirit* and *Brief History* (and *Integral Psychology* and SES), and it is a reductionism that is fully avoided when we take instead an all-level, all-quadrant approach, which refuses unwarrantedly to reduce any level, line, or quadrant to any other.

The Lower-Left quadrant involves all those patterns in consciousness that are shared by those who are "in" a particular culture or subculture. For you and me to understand each other at all, we need, at the very least, to share certain linguistic semantics, numerous perceptions, worldviews that overlap to some degree (so that communication is possible at all), and so on. These shared values, perceptions, meanings, semantic habitats, morals, cultural practices, ethics, and so on, I simply refer to as *culture*, or the *intersubjective* patterns in consciousness.

These cultural perceptions, all of which exist to some degree in subjective spaces in consciousness, nonetheless have *objective* correlates that can be empirically detected—physical structures and institutions, including techno-economic modes (foraging, horticultural, maritime, agrarian, industrial, informational), architectural styles, geopolitical structures, modes of information transfer (vocal signs, ideograms, movable type printing, telecommunications, microchip), social structure (survival clans, ethnic tribes, feudal orders, ancient nations, corporate states, value communes, and so on). I refer to these *interobjective* realities in general as the *social* system (the Lower-Right quadrant).

As you will see in the following pages, the integral approach that I am recommending—and which I simplistically summarize as "all-level, all-quadrant" (or even simpler: "the holonic approach")—is dedicated to including all of the nonreducible realities in all of the quadrants—which means all of the waves, streams, states, realms, and types, as disclosed by reputable, nonreductionistic researchers. All four quadrants, with all their realities, mutually interact—they "tetra-interact" and "tetra-evolve"—and a more integral approach is sensitive to those richly textured patterns of infinite interaction.

I sometimes simplify this holonic model even further by calling it a "1-2-3" approach to the Kosmos. This refers to first-person, second-person, and third-person realities. Notice that, in figure 1, the Upper-Left quadrant involves "I-language" (or first-person accounts); the Lower-Left quadrant involves "we-language" (or second-person accounts); and both Right-Hand quadrants, since they are objective patterns, involve "it-language" (or third-person accounts). Thus, the four quadrants can be simplified to the "Big Three" (I, we, and it). These important dimensions can be stated in many different ways: art, morals, and science; the Beautiful, the Good, and the True; self, culture, and nature. The point of an "all-level, all-quadrant" approach is that it would honor all of the waves of existence—from body to mind to soul to spirit—as they *all* unfold in self, culture, and nature.

A More Integral Map

Thus, what can we say about a more integral model of human possibilities? Before we can talk about *applications* of an integral vision—in education, politics, business, health care, and so on—we need to have some general notion of what it is that we are applying in the first place. When we move from pluralistic relativism to universal integralism, what kind of map might we find? We have seen that a more integral cartography might include:

- multiple *waves* of existence, spanning the entire spectrum of consciousness, subconscious to self-conscious to superconscious
- numerous different *streams*, modules, or lines of development, including cognitive, moral, spiritual, aesthetic, somatic, imaginative, interpersonal, etc.
- multiple *states* of consciousness, including waking, dreaming, sleeping, altered, nonordinary, and meditative
- numerous different *types* of consciousness, including gender types, personality types (enneagram, Myers-Briggs, Jungian), and so on
- multiple brain states and organic factors
- the extraordinarily important impact of numerous *cultural* factors, including the rich textures of diverse cultural realities, background contexts, pluralistic perceptions, linguistic semantics, and so on, none of which should be unwarrantedly marginalized, all of which should be included and integrated in a broad web of integral-aperspectival tapestries. (And, just as important, a truly "integral transformative practice" would give considerable weight to the importance of relationships, community, culture, and intersubjective factors in general, not merely as a realm of *application* of spiritual insight, but as a *mode* of spiritual transformation.)
- the massively influential forces of the *social* system, at all levels (from nature to human structures, including the all-important impact of nonhuman social systems, from Gaia to ecosystems)
- Although I have not mentioned it in this simple overview, the importance of the *self* as the navigator of the great River of Life should not be overlooked. It appears that the self is not a mono-

lithic entity but rather a society of selves with a *center of gravity*, which acts to bind the multiple waves, states, streams, and realms into something of a unified organization; the disruption of this organization, at any of its general stages, can result in pathology.[24]

Such are a few of the multiple factors that a richly holistic view of the Kosmos might wish to include. At the very least, any model that does not *coherently* include all of those items is not a very integral model.[25]

THE PRIME DIRECTIVE

The applications of the holonic model—in education, spiritual practice, politics, business, health care, and so on—will be explored in the Introduction to Volume Eight of the *Collected Works*. In the meantime, let us return to our major points—the impact of an integral vision on both the leading edge and the average mode—and note the following:

One of the main conclusions of an all-level, all-quadrant approach is that each meme—each level of consciousness and wave of existence—is, in its healthy form, *an absolutely necessary and desirable element* of the overall spiral, of the overall spectrum of consciousness. Even if every society on earth were established fully at the turquoise meme, nonetheless every infant born in that society still has to start at level 1, at beige, at sensorimotor instincts and perceptions, and then must grow and evolve through purple magic, red and blue myth, orange rationalism, green sensitivity, and into yellow and turquoise vision-logic (on the way to the transpersonal). All of those waves have important tasks and functions; all of them are taken up and included in subsequent waves; none of them can be bypassed; and none of them can be demeaned without grave consequences to self and society. *The health of the entire spiral is the prime directive, not preferential treatment for any one level.*

A MORE MEASURED GREATNESS

Because the health of the entire spectrum of consciousness is paramount, and not any particular level, this means that a genuinely universal integralism would measure more carefully its actual impact. I have long maintained that the real revolutions facing today's world involve, not a glorious collective move into transpersonal domains, but the simple, fundamental changes that can be brought to the magic, mythic, and rational waves of existence.

Human beings are born and begin their evolution through the great spiral of consciousness, moving from archaic to magic to mythic to rational to . . . perhaps integral, and perhaps from there into genuinely transpersonal domains. But for every person that moves into integral or higher, dozens are born into the archaic. The spiral of existence is a great unending flow, stretching from body to mind to soul to spirit, with millions upon millions constantly flowing through that great river from source to ocean. No society will ever simply be *at* an integral level, because the flow is unceasing (although the *center of gravity* of a culture can indeed drift upward, as it has over history—see *Up from Eden*). But the major problem remains: not how can we get everybody to the integral wave or higher, but how can we arrange *the health of the overall spiral*, as billions of humans continue to pass through it, from one end to the other, year in and year out?

In other words, most of the work that needs to done is work to make the lower (and foundational) waves more healthy in their own terms. The major reforms do not involve how to get a handful of boomers into second-tier, but how to feed the starving millions at the most basic waves; how to house the homeless millions at the simplest of levels; how to bring health care to the millions who do not possess it. An integral vision is one of the least pressing issues on the face of the planet.

THE INTEGRAL VISION IN THE WORLD AT LARGE

Let me drive this point home using calculations done by Dr. Phillip Harter of Stanford University School of Medicine. If we could shrink the earth's population to a village of only 100 people, it would look something like this:

There would be—

57 Asians
21 Europeans
14 North and South Americans
 8 Africans
30 white
70 nonwhite
 6 people would possess 59% of the world's wealth,
   and all 6 would be from the United States

80 would live in substandard housing
70 would be unable to read
50 would suffer malnutrition
 1 would have a college education
 1 would own a computer

Thus, as I suggested, an integral vision is one of the least pressing issues on the face of the planet. The health of the entire spiral, and particularly its earlier waves, screams out to us as the major ethical demand.

Nonetheless, the advantage of second-tier vision-logic awareness is that it more creatively helps with the solutions to those pressing problems. In grasping big pictures, it can help suggest more cogent solutions. It is our governing bodies, then, that stand in dire need of a more integral approach. It is our educational institutions, overcome with deconstructive postmodernism, that are desperate for a more integral vision. It is our health care facilities that could greatly benefit from the tender mercies of an integral touch. It is the leadership of the nations that might appreciate a more comprehensive vision of their own possibilities. In all these ways and more, we could indeed use "an integral vision for a world gone slightly mad"—and that is the central topic of the books in this present volume.

To Change the Mapmaker

Let us return, then, to the issue of how to more effectively implement the emergence of integral (and even transpersonal) consciousness at the leading edge. What is required, in my opinion, is not simply a new integral theory, but also a new *integral practice*. Even if we possessed the perfect integral map of the Kosmos, a map that was completely all-inclusive and unerringly holistic, that map itself would not transform people. We don't just need a map; we need ways to change the mapmaker.

Thus, although most of my books attempt to offer a genuinely integral vision, they always end with a call for some sort of integral practice—a practice that exercises body, mind, soul, and spirit in self, culture, and nature (all-level, all-quadrant). You will hear this call constantly in the following pages, along with specific suggestions for how to begin a truly integral transformative practice in your own case, if such seems desirable to you.

THE EYE OF SPIRIT

Much of my writing has been dedicated to trying to present the reader with the conclusions from researchers working with second-tier conceptions, whether from premodern, modern, or postmodern sources. Researchers, that is, who are looking at the entire spectrum of consciousness, in all its many waves, streams, states, and realms. And, beyond that, to present an all-level, all-quadrant view, which is the full spectrum in its multiple modalities—a conception that specifically attempts to accommodate the greatest amount of evidence from the greatest number of researchers.

This present volume contains two books (*A Brief History of Everything* and *The Eye of Spirit*) and a long essay ("An Integral Theory of Consciousness") that are some of the primary sources in this particular integral vision. As indicated, I have done second, revised editions of both books, included herein (just as I did a revised edition of SES [Volume Six of the CW]). *Brief History* is probably the most reworked, with many new sections and four new diagrams. *Brief History* has a reputation as being "nothing but" a simplified version of SES, which is true in some ways. But it also introduces many new concepts, such as the culture gap and industrial ontology, and thus those who enjoyed SES might still find much that is new in *Brief History*.

The Eye of Spirit contains what is still my own favorite piece of my writing, "Integral Art and Literary Theory" (chapters 4 and 5), and my favorite meditation on nondual awareness ("Always Already: The Brilliant Clarity of Ever-Present Awareness"). It also contains responses to several critics, and in general attempts to advance our understanding of universal integralism, which itself is simply a platform for more stable, transpersonal waves of consciousness unfolding. And Jack Crittenden's foreword to *The Eye of Spirit* is still probably the best single introduction to what an integral approach is trying to do.

The Eye of Spirit opens with a call to find a way to integrate Spirit and politics. This has continued to be a strong concern; I have increasingly been writing on this topic. The overview is simple enough: liberals believe primarily in objective causation of social ills (i.e., inequality is due to exterior, unfair social institutions); conservatives believe primarily in subjective causation (i.e., inequality is due to something in the character or the nature of individuals themselves). In other words, liberals emphasize the exterior quadrants but not the interior ones; conservatives emphasize interior causes more than exterior. Further, liberal political theory tends to come from both scientific materialism and pluralistic relativism (e.g., orange and green), whereas conservative political theory tends to be grounded in traditional conventional modes and mythic-membership (e.g., blue). Also, liberal and conservative both have "freedom" and "order" wings, depending upon whether they value most the "individual" (the upper quadrants) or the collective (the lower quadrants). By combining an understanding of the four quadrants with waves of development in each—that is, by adopting an all-level, all-quadrant view—one can rather seamlessly bring together the very best of liberal and conservative theory, resulting in a genuine "Third Way," as it is often being called (see the Introduction to CW 8). Several political theorists working in the field have increasingly found that an all-level, all-quadrant view is the most reliable way to effect such a synthesis, which would, if successful, perhaps move us forward through what many people perceive as the stalemate of left versus right political views.

In all of this, we see the increasing importance of finding a postliberal spirituality, a postgreen spirituality, which builds upon and honors the richness of pluralistic relativism and network sensitivity, and then transcends and includes that in an even more holistic embrace. For it is finally spirit, the eye of spirit, through which we all might see more clearly the tender role of each and all in the manifestation of our own highest possibilities. Through the eye of spirit, the Kosmos shines forth brightly, a thing of beauty and wonder in its every gesture, ornaments of one's own deepest being, testaments to one's own primordial purity. And in the eye of spirit, we all will meet, in the simple endless outflowing of this and every moment, where history as that horrible nightmare uncoils in the vast expanse of all space and the radical freedom of what is, and all waves and all streams become finally irrelevant in the radiance of just this.

Notes

1. From an overemphasis on the social construction of reality (the omnipotent cultural self creates all realities), to the relativity of knowledge (all knowledge is culturally relative, except my own omniscient knowledge that this is so), to extreme deconstruction (I have the power to explode all texts), to reader-response theory (when I view an artwork it is actually I, not the artist, who creates the artwork), to theories that will resurrect and save Gaia, Goddess, and Spirit (whereas it is usually thought that Spirit will save us, not the other way around), to the new-age notion that you create your own reality (actually, psychotics create their own reality), to UFO abductions (an extraordinarily advanced intelligence wants nothing more than to look at me), to hundreds of new paradigm

claims (I have the new paradigm which will transform the world). In an enormous number of different areas, this is an awful lot of power ascribed to the finite self, don't you think? Social critics who have perceived a considerable amount of "self-inflation" here are onto something important, it seems.

2. F. Richards and M. Commons in Alexander et al., *Higher Stages of Human Development*, p. 160, emphasis in original.

3. C. Graves, "Summary Statement: The Emergent, Cyclical, Double-Helix Model of the Adult Human Biopsychosocial Systems," Boston, May 20, 1981.

4. Don Beck, personal communication; much of this data is on computer file in the National Values Center, Denton, Texas, and is open to qualified researchers.

5. I know, from conversations with Beck, that he is very sympathetic with the existence of transpersonal states and structures. The stages outlined in Spiral Dynamics are based on research and data, and the problem, as always, is that although *altered states* are very common, higher *permanent stages* are relatively rare (greater depth, less span). If around 0.1 percent of the population is at turquoise (as will be explained in the text), you can imagine how few are stably at even higher waves of consciousness, not as a *passing state*, but as an *enduring trait* or permanent realization. For that reason, it is very hard to get much data on any sort of genuinely higher stages, which is one of the reasons that agreement as to transpersonal waves tapers off.

   In one publication, Beck and Cowan give the name "coral" to the stage beyond turquoise, and then they state: "Coral, for these authors, is still unclear." Coral, in my opinion, is the psychic wave; but you can see how difficult it is getting decent data in this regard. See *Integral Psychology* for more details.

6. There is an enormous amount of disagreement as to what colors best represent what levels of consciousness (e.g., what colors best represent the different chakras). The traditional explanation is that the colors of the rainbow represent the levels of consciousness, starting at the lowest level and progressing to the highest or most subtle—thus, the ascending order is red, orange, yellow, green, blue, indigo, and violet (representing chakras one through seven, respectively). But there is considerable variation in these color schemes, and many of the traditions that specialize in contemplative development see the colors blue and white as representing the very highest states (that is my experience as well). Spiral Dynamics, on the other hand, selected colors based on some of their common popular associations ("blue" for "true blue," the blue of many police uniforms, etc., to represent the law-and-order, mythic-membership wave; "green" for ecological sensitivity, and so on). Obviously, the use of colors is to some degree arbitrary, and this will be a confusing area for years to come, until (and if) a common usage is found.

7. Personal communication. Beck uses meme in a specific sense, which he calls a "value meme" or ᵛMEME, which is defined as "a core value system, a worldview, an organizing principle that permeates thought structures, decision-making systems, and various expressions of culture."

   The Graves/Beck system does not clearly distinguish between transitional and enduring structures, nor between basic and self-related structures. In my own system, the basic structures are enduring and remain fully active capacities available at all later stages, but most of the self-related streams (such as morals, values, and self-identity) consist of transitional stages that tend to be replaced by subsequent stages. (Subpersonalities can exist at different levels or memes, however, so that one can indeed have a purple subpersonality, a blue subpersonality, and so on. These often are context-triggered, so that one may have quite different types of moral responses, affects, needs, etc., in different situations.) But in general, for the central or proximate self, once its *center of gravity* reaches, say, green, it will not activate a pure purple meme unless it is regressing; but it can (and constantly does) activate *the corresponding basic structures of the purple meme* (namely, the emotional-phantasmic level). When a green adult "activates" a purple meme, that is not the identical meme the two-year-old child possesses. For the two-year-old, the purple meme is the basis of the infant's central identity, its proximate self (or I), whereas for a green adult, it is part of the distal self (or me). When the green adult "activates purple," he or she is actually activating the *basic capacities* (basic structures) first laid down during the "purple period" (e.g., phantasmic-emotional), but because the self's exclusive *identity* is no longer at the "purple level," the corresponding transitional structures (morals, values, worldviews) are not fully activated unless one is regressing (or unless one is activating a purple subpersonality). So, at the least, I would differentiate between "purple capacities" and "purple self"; the former are enduring, the latter is transitional. See *Integral Psychology* for a further discussion of these issues.

Still, these are technical distinctions, about which there is much room for friendly disagreement; and the Graves/Beck system, in speaking of "activating memes," offers a simple and concise way to deal with the most general and important facets of these waves of existence (such as the fact that there are indeed general waves of consciousness, but once they emerge, you can activate any of them under various circumstances, so that you can indeed be a "different person" in different situations, and so on). I also find that, especially for educational purposes, the more technical distinctions (enduring/transitional, basic/self) confuse more than edify, and a generalized discussion of memes more than suffices to help people think in terms of the entire spiral of development, the entire spectrum of consciousness. For the simple and crucial point is that all of us have all of these waves of consciousness available to us as potentials that can unfold under facilitating circumstances.

8. Much of the following descriptions consist of direct quotes or paraphrasing from various publications of Graves, Beck, and Beck and Cowan. See *Integral Psychology* for references.

9. See note 7.

10. See *Integral Psychology* for extensive references to these studies. See also the Introduction to Volume Four of the *Collected Works* for a summary.

11. See *One Taste*, November 23 entry, for references and extended discussion.

12. The healthy version of the integral-aperspectival wave (the green meme) is: all perspectives and all stances deserve to be given a fair hearing and a fully equal

opportunity; no perspective is to be unduly privileged. The pathological version is: no stance is better than another, a version which, if true, would not only undercut its own claim to moral authority (since its stance could be no better than the alternatives), it places the most shallow and most barbaric stances on the same level playing field, with Hitler and Mother Teresa staring eye to eye. The pathological version of the green meme—which is sadly the most common version in today's world—I have called *aperspectival madness* (see *Sex, Ecology, Spirituality*).

13. Jenny Wade, who has made a careful study of Graves, believes that orange (achievement) and green (affiliative) are not two different levels but two different choices offered to blue (conformist), so that both orange and green can advance directly to second-tier (authentic). Wade's book, *Changes of Mind*, is a superb overview of the spectrum of consciousness; it is discussed at length in the second edition of *The Eye of Spirit*, included in this volume.

14. See *Sex, Ecology, Spirituality*, 2nd ed. (CW6).

15. See *One Taste*, Sept. 23 entry, for a discussion of Ray's integral culture as an example of the newly emerging Person-Centered Civil Religion.

16. Don Beck, personal communication.

17. See *The Eye of Spirit* for references and discussion of this data; see also *Integral Psychology* for an overview.

18. See *Integral Psychology* for a review of cross-cultural evidence.

19. For a good summary of Gilligan's hierarchical view of male and female development, see Alexander and Langer, *Higher Stages of Human Development*, especially the editors' Introduction and Gilligan's chapter 9.

20. I first suggested using horizontal typologies, such as the enneagram, with the vertical levels of development in *A Brief History of Everything*. Other researchers have independently arrived at similar suggestions.

21. See note 19 for references.

22. Thus, using our example of Spiral Dynamics, females would develop through the great waves of existence with a more relational, permeable, or communal orientation, and an integral feminism would dedicate itself to exploring the dynamics and patterns in all of the waves, states, and streams, as they appear in this "different voice." See *The Eye of Spirit*, chap. 8, "Integral Feminism."

23. See *Integral Psychology* for a full discussion of this topic.

24. See *Integral Psychology* for a discussion of the self, the levels of pathology, and the typical treatment modalities.

25. Donald Rothberg has written a long essay, "Transpersonal Issues at the Millennium." This is a superb summary of a type of average consensus that has emerged in the last three decades or so regarding the possible directions for future theory and research. Rothberg summarizes these general conclusions and recommendations, and he calls for a more integrative stance, itself admirable. However, in my opinion the level of his analysis (and its implicit assumptions) largely reflects a green-meme approach. It does so, I believe, because the green meme is in fact the most common meme shared by alternative and countercultural consciousness, and Rothberg is brilliantly presenting and faithfully echoing this background.

Don Beck did a memetic analysis on Rothberg's article and concluded the following: "This article is approximately 90% green meme, 10% turquoise. Some of the questions asked are turquoise, but the solutions and analysis are green. There is little depth perception in the constructions; in other words, there are almost no second-tier recommendations. The article clearly allows for transpersonal realities, but the presentation is conducted through a green lens. The article does an excellent job of summarizing green's contribution to psychology and sociology."

Just that is the value of Rothberg's analysis, I believe. By outlining the green meme's general orientation to countercultural topics—from development to education to spiritual practice—Rothberg discloses many of the pluralistic modalities and heretofore marginalized areas that need to be taken up, integrated, and blended into a more holistic, second-tier approach to these issues.

Here is an example of Rothberg's central recommendations, which involve including the "excluded" and "marginalized" modes of inquiry, and one can detect the green-meme language of pluralism, communion, connection, context, diversity, multiculturalism, and so forth: "Inquiry and learning increasingly occurs in the context of a connected, collaborating, multicultural group of diverse persons, who are trained and competent in several types of somatic, emotional, rational, aesthetic, and spiritual ways of knowing. This group of individuals will be able to balance what we now call 'masculine' and 'feminine' qualities and approaches; will be interested in 'inner' and 'outer' transformation in accordance with core ethical, social, political, and spiritual values; and will be grounded in particular social, community, cultural, political, and ecological settings."

All of which is well and good, and brilliantly stated, and constitutes exactly, as I said, the nonmarginalizing sensitivity that is a hallmark of green. But let us ask a simple question: what if the "group" that we are counting on to give us a balanced education is composed of individuals who are all at Carol Gilligan's "selfish" or "preconventional" wave of development? Is a whole bunch of people at moral-stage 1 the type of group that will give us educational guidance? Obviously not. But because of green's intense antipathy to hierarchies and value gradations of any sort, including nested hierarchies and holarchies, there is in this analysis no real vertical dimension of height or depth, just a horizontal balancing of different types (not also different levels).

Rothberg clearly calls for an extended notion of *development* that includes previously marginalized modalities (he strongly endorses multiple *streams* of development). But there is no substantial discussion whatsoever about the levels or *waves* of development (reflecting, presumably, the fact that green has a great deal of difficulty with those concepts). And in the one sentence where Rothberg mentions "levels of development," he gives them as: "intrapsychic, interpersonal, group and organizational, community, social, ecological, and global." But those are not levels of *development*. Levels of development means that an entity would proceed through those levels in some sort of developmental sequence; but clearly an individual does not first develop intrapsychically, then interpersonally, then organizationally, then communally, then ecologically, and so on. In fact, most of those are still dimensions, streams, or lines of development, reflecting again, I presume, the fact that the green meme has an inordinately difficult time grasping levels or waves. This is one of the reasons that Beck's memetic analysis concluded that this article had little or no depth perception—no frank coming to terms with the holarchical unfolding of consciousness, or an explicit *depth* dimension. As such, it is a superb presentation of green concerns, but with few second-tier integral constructions, in my opinion.

(This is perhaps why the book *Ken Wilber in Dialogue*, edited by Rothberg and Kelly, is such an uneven presentation of my work—for which I assume a fair amount of the responsibility, since I half-heartedly participated in an often green-dominated dialogue. As Beck's memetic analysis harshly concluded, "This book is largely a series of typical green-meme attacks on second-tier. Several of the presentations, including Wright's and Kremer's, have little relation to Wilber's actual views. The middle section badly distorts Wilber's stance on the 'others' of body, nature, woman. This book is a model of how to treat a scholar unfairly." I think the book is a fine presentation of alternative conceptions, and I often recommend it for that. But it is not a reliable source for my own material; it often focuses on the stage-conception from wilber-2; and I was disappointed at how rarely the discussants brought in any of the wilber-4 constructions. However, writers such as John Heron and Daniel Helminiak have found the book extremely useful.)

Another transpersonally oriented theorist who writes predominately through the green meme is Jorge Ferrer. Although not as dependable as an analyst of others' works (since he tends to filter everything through the green meme), Ferrer has brought a brilliant touch to elucidating his own version of green's contribution to countercultural and spiritual issues. Since *stable* higher development rests upon green, these green articulations, if not clung to as "the" meme, are important contributions, helping to prepare a more sensitive opening to second-tier constructions.

But more integral writers have been incorporating green ideas into their holistic constructions for quite some time, and Ferrer seems here a bit behind the times, in my opinion. His critique of the perennial philosophy, like that of Heron's, is often based on tiresome green clichés and slogans, rife with the standard pluralistic performative contradictions, and bubbling with boomeritis and its suffocating claims of moral hauteur. I personally happen to like Jorge very much, and I believe he will eventually have many wonderful and important contributions to make, but his formulations to date—perhaps due to their CIIS biases (see below)—are rather disappointing, at least to me.

As we have seen, precisely because dynamic pluralism bends over backwards to avoid marginalizing viewpoints, it acts as a magnet for almost any trends, including those that are frankly regressive. This combination of high cognitive capacity (early vision-logic, postformal, green) with preformal narcissism (purple, red) is a hallmark of boomeritis.

For exactly that reason, the presence of boomeritis is particularly a problem at many of the alternative educational institutions, such as CIIS. A memetic analysis of a recent CIIS brochure found: 30% purple, 30% red, 40% green. In other words, a strongly boomeritis-driven brochure (which is fairly typical, in my opinion, of its overall agenda). This is why I cannot comfortably recommend CIIS to students. Nonetheless, there are many excellent teachers at CIIS, and it is now under new leadership, so it might begin to turn its general orientation around toward more dependable constructions. (If you end up at CIIS, be sure and check with Bert Parlee, who runs a superb study group dedicated to not marginalizing second-tier dialogue.)

One institution worth serious consideration is the Institute of Transpersonal Psychology (ITP), in Palo Alto, California, founded by James Fadiman and Robert Frager. ITP now has a fully accredited Ph.D. program, headed by Jenny Wade, whose *Changes of Mind* is an excellent summary of some of the general waves of existence. Jenny has moved to introduce second-tier and genuinely holarchical considerations into the curriculum of ITP, understandably against much resistance from green. But because of these reforms, which appear to be generally succeeding (it's still a bit early to tell), at this point ITP looks to be the alternative institution of choice.

Naropa University, in Boulder, Colorado, is another viable option, particularly if one is drawn to serious meditation practice. Naropa has a quintessentially green core (and therefore also a significant dose of boomeritis). It has also recently joined with Matthew Fox's creation college, in the Bay Area, another strongly green institution. Nonetheless, Naropa's saving grace is the genuine emphasis on meditation practice, which is a time-honored way to open oneself to the transpersonal waves of consciousness. Other alternative institutions with excellent teachers include Saybrook and JKF University in Orinda. (For a listing of alternative institutions, one might consult *The Common Boundary Education Guide*, obtainable from Common Boundary, 5272 River Rd., Suite 650, Bethesda, MD 20816; and the guide available from the Association for Transpersonal Psychology, 345 California St., Palo Alto, CA 94306.)

I would certainly not rule out the more conventional centers of learning, many of which are not only increasingly open to integral concerns, but are moving quite beyond what many of the alternative colleges are doing. Harvard's Graduate School of Education, for example, is unexcelled in developmental studies, acknowledging higher and even transpersonal waves.

Those are simply my own personal opinions of issues about which I have been recently asked. But they point up exactly what I believe is the central issue for spiritual and integral studies at the millennium: we will remain stuck in the green meme—with both its wonderful contributions (e.g., pluralistic sensitivity) and its pathologies (e.g., boomeritis). Or we will make the leap to the hyperspace of second-tier consciousness, and thus stand open to even further evolution into the transpersonal waves of Spirit's own Self-realization.

A BRIEF HISTORY
OF EVERYTHING

Foreword

SIX YEARS AGO, IN 1989, I set out across the country on my own search for wisdom. In the course of my travels, I interviewed and worked with more than two hundred psychologists, philosophers, physicians, scientists, and mystics who claimed to have the answers I was after. By the time I wrote *What Really Matters: Searching for Wisdom in America*, it was clear to me that Ken Wilber was in a category by himself. He is, I believe, far and away the most cogent and penetrating voice in the recent emergence of a uniquely American wisdom.

It has been nearly twenty years since Ken Wilber published *The Spectrum of Consciousness*. Written when he was twenty-three, it established him, almost overnight, as perhaps the most comprehensive philosophical thinker of our times. *Spectrum*, which Wilber wrote in three months after dropping out of graduate school in biochemistry, made the case that human development unfolds in waves or stages that extend beyond those ordinarily recognized by Western psychology. Only by successfully navigating each developmental wave, Wilber argued, is it possible first to develop a healthy sense of individuality, and then ultimately to experience a broader identity that transcends—and includes—the personal self. In effect, Wilber married Freud and the Buddha—until then divided by seemingly irreconcilable differences. And this was just the first of his many original contributions.

The title of this book is deceptively breezy. *A Brief History of Everything* delivers just what it promises. It covers vast historical ground, from the Big Bang right up to the desiccated postmodern present. Along the way, it seeks to make sense of the often contradictory ways that human beings have evolved—physically, emotionally, intellectually, morally, spiritually. And for all its breadth, the book is remarkably lean and compact.

Indeed, what sets *A Brief History of Everything* apart both from *Spectrum* and from Wilber's eleven subsequent books is that it not only extends the ideas advanced in those earlier works, but presents them now in a simple, accessible, conversational format. Most of Wilber's books require at least some knowledge of the major Eastern contemplative traditions and of Western developmental psychology. *A Brief History* is addressed to a much broader audience—those of us grappling to find wisdom in our everyday lives, but bewildered by the array of potential paths to truth that so often seem to contradict one another—and to fall short in fundamental ways. For those readers who want still more when they finish this book, I recommend Wilber's recent opus, *Sex, Ecology, Spirituality*, which explores many of the ideas here in more rigorous detail.

No one I've met has described the path of human development—the evolution of consciousness—more systematically or comprehensively than Wilber. In the course of my journey, I ran into countless people who made grand claims for a particular version of the truth they were promoting. Almost invariably, I discovered, they'd come to their conclusions by choosing up sides, celebrating one set of capacities and values while excluding others.

Wilber has taken a more embracing and comprehensive approach, as you will soon discover. In the pages that follow, he lays out a coherent vision that honors and incorporates the truths from a vast and disparate array of fields—physics and biology; the social and the systems sciences; art and aesthetics; developmental psychology and contemplative mysticism—as well as from opposing philosophical movements ranging from Neoplatonism to modernism, idealism to postmodernism.

What Wilber recognizes is that a given truth-claim may be valid without being complete, true but only so far as it goes, and this must be seen as part of other and equally important truths. Perhaps the most powerful new tool he brings to bear in *A Brief History* is his notion that there are four "quadrants" of development. By looking at hundreds of developmental maps that have been created by various thinkers over the years—maps of biological, psychological, cognitive, and spiritual development, to name just a few—it dawned on Wilber that they were often describing very different versions of "truth." Exterior forms of development, for example, are those that can be measured objectively and empirically. But what Wilber makes clear is that this form of truth will only take you so far. Any comprehensive development, he points out, also includes an interior dimension—one that is subjective and interpretive, and depends on consciousness and introspection. Beyond that, Wilber saw, both interior and exterior development take place not just individually, but in a social or cultural context. Hence the four quadrants.

None of these forms of truth, he argues in a series of vivid examples, can be reduced to another. A behaviorist, to take just a single case, cannot understand a person's interior experience solely by looking at his external behavior—or at its physiological correlates. The truth will indeed set you free, but only if you recognize that there are many kinds of truth.

A Brief History of Everything operates on several levels. It's the richest map I've yet found of the world we live in, and of men and women's place in it. In the dialectic of progress, Wilber suggests, each stage of evolution transcends the limits of its predecessor, but simultaneously introduces new ones. This is a view that both dignifies and celebrates the ongoing struggle of any authentic search for a more conscious and complete life. "No epoch is finally privileged," Wilber writes. "We are all tomorrow's food. The process continues, and Spirit is found in the process itself, not in any particular epoch or time or place."

At another level, Wilber serves in *A Brief History* as a demystifier and a debunker—a discerning critic of the teachers, techniques, ideas, and systems that promise routes to encompassing truth, but are more commonly incomplete, misleading, misguided, or distorted. Too often we ourselves are complicit. Fearful of any change and infinitely capable of self-deception, we are too quick to latch on to simple answers and quick fixes, which finally just narrow our perspective and abort our development.

Wilber's is a rare voice. He brings to the task both a sincere heart and a commitment to truth. He widens his lens to take in the biggest possible picture, but he refuses to see all the elements as equal. He makes qualitative distinctions. He values depth. He's unafraid to make enemies, even as he is respectful of many voices. The result is that *A Brief History of Everything* sheds a very original light, not just on the cosmic questions in our lives, but on dozens of confusing and unsettling issues of our times—the changing roles of men and women; the continuing destruction of the environment; diversity and multiculturalism; repressed memory and childhood sexual abuse; and the role of the Internet in the information age—among many others.

I cannot imagine a better way to be introduced to Ken Wilber than this book. It brings the debate about evolution, consciousness, and our capacity for transformation to an entirely new level. More practically, it will save you many missteps and wrong turns on whatever wisdom path you choose to take.

TONY SCHWARTZ

A Note to the Reader

In Douglas Adams's *Hitchhiker's Guide to the Galaxy,* a massive supercomputer is designed to give the ultimate answer, the absolute answer, the answer that would completely explain "God, life, the universe, and everything." But the computer takes seven and a half million years to do this, and by the time the computer delivers the answer, everybody has forgotten the question. Nobody remembers the ultimate question, but the ultimate answer the computer comes up with is: 42.

This is amazing! Finally, the ultimate answer. So wonderful is the answer that a contest is held to see if anybody can come up with the question. Many profound questions are offered, but the final winner is: How many roads must a man walk down?

"God, life, the universe, and everything" is pretty much what this book is about, although, of course, the answer is not quite as snappy as "42." It deals with matter, life, mind, and spirit, and the evolutionary currents that seem to unite them all in a pattern that connects.

I have written this book in a dialogue format—questions and answers. Many of these dialogues actually occurred, but most have been written specifically for this book. The questions are real enough—they are the questions I have most often been asked about my books in general and my most recent book in particular (*Sex, Ecology, Spirituality*). But there is no need whatsoever to have read that or any of my books: the following topics are interesting in themselves, I believe, and the dialogues demand no previous or specialized knowledge in these areas. (Scholars interested in references, bibliography, notes, and detailed arguments can consult *Sex, Ecology, Spirituality.*)

The first chapters deal with the material cosmos and the emergence of life. What drove chaos into order? How did matter give rise to life? What currents are afoot in this extraordinary game of evolution? Is there a "spirit" of ecology? Does it really matter?

The middle chapters explore the emergence of mind or consciousness and we will follow the evolution of this consciousness through five or six major stages in human development, from foraging to horticultura to agrarian to industrial to informational. What was the status of men and women in each of those stages? Why did some of those stages emphasize the male, and some the female, gender? Does this shed any light on today's gender wars? Are the same currents at work in human evolution as in the cosmic game at large? How does past human development relate to today's human problems? If we do not remember the past, are we condemned to repeat it?

We will then look to the Divine Domain and how it might indeed be related to the creative currents in matter and life and mind. How and why did religion historically give way to psychology? Used to be, if you were inwardly disturbed and agitated and seeking answers, you talked to a priest. Now you talk to a psychiatrist—and they rarely agree with each other. Why? What happened? Do they both perhaps have something important to tell us? Should they perhaps be not feuding but kissing cousins?

In our own lives, to whom do we turn for answers? Do we look to Adams's supercomputer for ultimate answers? Do we look to religion? politics? science? psychologists? gurus? your psychic friend? *Where* do we finally place our ultimate trust for the really important questions? Does this tell us something? Is there a way to tie these various sources together? to have them each speak their own truths in ways that balance and harmonize? Is this even possible in today's splintered world?

The last chapters deal with flatland—with the collapse of the richly textured Kosmos into a flat and faded one-dimensional world, the bleak and monochrome world of modernity and postmodernity. But we will do so not simply with an eye to condemning the modern world, but rather in an attempt to discover the radiant Spirit at work, even in our own apparently God-forsaken times. Where is God, and where the Goddess, in these shallow waters?

How many roads must we each walk down? There might be an answer to this after all, for wonder continues to bubble up, and joy rushes to the surface, with release in the recognition and liberation in the awakening. And we all know how to wonder, which speaks in the tongues of that God within, and inexplicably points home.

K.W.
Boulder, Colorado
Spring 1995

Introduction

Q: Is there any sex in *Sex, Ecology, Spirituality?*

KW: With diagrams, actually.

Q: You're kidding.

KW: I'm kidding. But yes, sexuality is one of the main themes, and especially its relation to gender.

Q: Sex and gender are different?

KW: It's common to use "sex" or sexuality to refer to the *biological* aspects of human reproduction, and "gender" to refer to the *cultural* differences between men and women that grow up around the sexual or biological differences. The sexual differences are usually referred to as *male* and *female*, and the cultural differences as *masculine* and *feminine*. And while male and female might indeed be given biologically, masculine and feminine are in large part the creation of culture.

Q: So the trick is to decide which characteristics are sex and which are gender.

KW: In a sense, yes. The sexual differences between male and female, because they are primarily biological, are universal and cross-cultural—males everywhere produce sperm, females produce ova, females give birth and lactate, and so on. But the differences between *masculine* and *feminine* are created and molded primarily by the different cultures in which the male and female are raised.

And yes, part of the turmoil between the sexes nowadays is that, while male/female differences are biological and universal—and therefore can't really be changed very much—nonetheless masculine and feminine are in many ways the product of culture, and these roles can indeed be changed in at least some significant ways. And we, as a culture, are in the difficult and tricky process of trying to change some of these gender roles.

Q: For example?

KW: Well, while it's true that, on average, the male body is more muscular and physically stronger than the female, it does not follow that masculine therefore must mean strong and assertive and feminine must mean weak and demure. And we are in a transition period where masculine and feminine roles are being redefined and re-created, which has thrown both men and women into a type of rancorous sniping at each other in various types of gender wars.

Part of the problem is that, whereas masculine and feminine roles can indeed be redefined and refashioned—a long-overdue and much-needed refurbishing—nonetheless male and female characteristics cannot be changed much, and in our attempt to level the differences between masculine and feminine, we are dangerously close to trying to erase the differences between male and female. And while the former is a fine idea, the latter is impossible. And the trick is to know the difference, I suppose.

Q: So some of the differences between men and women are here to stay, and some need to be changed?

KW: It seems so. As we continue to investigate the differences between men and women, related to both sex and gender, there are indeed certain differences, even in the cultural domain, that crop up again and again across cultures. In other words, not only certain sex differences, but certain gender differences tend to repeat themselves cross-culturally.

It's as if the biological sex differences between men and women are such a strong basic platform that these biological differences tend to invade culture as well, and thus tend to show up in gender differences also. So, even though gender is culturally molded and not biologically given, nonetheless certain constants in masculine and feminine gender tend to appear across cultures as well.

Q: Even a decade ago, that was a rather controversial stance. Now it seems more commonly accepted.

KW: Yes, even the radical feminists now champion the notion that there are, generally speaking, very strong differences between the male and female value spheres—that is, in both sex and gender. Men tend toward hyperindividuality, stressing autonomy, rights, justice, and agency, and women tend toward a more relational awareness, with emphasis on communion, care, responsibility, and relationship. Men tend to stress autonomy and fear relationship, women tend to stress relationship and fear autonomy.

Carol Gilligan's and Deborah Tannen's work has been central here, of course, but it's amazing that, in the span of just a decade or so, as you say, most orthodox researchers and most feminist researchers are now in general agreement about certain fundamental differences in the male and female value spheres. This is also central to the new field of study known as "evolutionary psychology"—the effects of biological evolution on psychological traits.

And the tricky part now is: how to acknowledge these differences without using them, once again, to disenfranchise women. Because as soon as any sort of *differences* between people are announced, the privileged will use those differences to further their advantage. You see the problem?

Q: Yes, but it seems the opposite is now occurring. It seems that these differences are being used to demonstrate that men are rather inherently insensitive slobs and testosterone mutants who "just don't get it." The message is, men should be more sensitive, more caring, more loving, more relational. What you call the male value sphere is everywhere under attack. The message is, why can't a man be more like a woman?

KW: Yes, it's a certain amount of "turnabout is fair play." Used to be that women were defined as "deficient men"—"penis envy" being the classic example. Now men are being defined as "deficient women"— defined by the feminine characteristics that they lack, not by any positive attributes that they possess. Both approaches are unfortunate, I think, not to mention demeaning to both genders.

The tricky part, as I started to suggest, is how to do two very difficult things: one, to reasonably decide just what are the major differences between the male and female value spheres (à la Gilligan), and then, two, to learn ways to value them more or less equally. Not to make them the same, but to value them equally.

Nature did not split the human race into two sexes for no reason; simply trying to make them the same seems silly. But even the most conservative theorists would acknowledge that our culture has been predominantly weighted to the male value sphere for quite some time now. And so we are in the delicate, dicey, very difficult, and often rancorous process of trying to balance the scales a bit more. Not erase the differences, but balance them.

Q: And these differences have their roots in the biological differences between male and female?

KW: In part, it seems so. Hormonal differences, in particular. Studies on testosterone—in the laboratory, cross-culturally, embryonically, and even on what happens when women are given testosterone injections for medical reasons—all point to a simple conclusion. I don't mean to be crude, but it appears that testosterone basically has two, and only two, major drives: fuck it or kill it.

And males are saddled with this biological nightmare almost from day one, a nightmare women can barely imagine (except when they are given testosterone injections for medical purposes, which drives them nuts. As one woman put it, "I can't stop thinking about sex. Please, can't you make this stop?") Worse, men sometimes fuse and confuse these two drives, with fuck it and kill it dangerously merging, which rarely has happy consequences, as women are more than willing to point out.

Q: And the female equivalent?

KW: We might point to oxytocin, a hormone that tends to flood the female even if her skin is simply stroked. Oxytocin has been described as the "relationship drug"; it induces incredibly strong feelings of attachment, relationship, nurturing, holding, touching.

And it's not hard to see that both of these, testosterone and oxytocin, might have their roots in biological evolution, the former for reproduction and survival, the latter for mothering. Most sexual intercourse in the animal kingdom occurs in a matter of seconds. During intercourse, both parties are open to being preyed upon or devoured. Brings new meaning to "dinner and sex," because you *are* the dinner. So it's slam-bam-thank-you-ma'am. None of this sharing feelings, and emoting, and cuddling—and that about sums up men. Mr. Sensitive—the man, the myth, the weenie—is a very, very recent invention, and it takes men a bit of getting used to, we might say.

But the sexual requirements of mothering are quite different. The mother has to be constantly in tune with the infant, twenty-four hours a day, especially alert to signs of hunger and pain. Oxytocin keeps her right in there, focused on the relationship, and very, very attached. The emotions are not fuck it or kill it, but continuously *relate to it*, carefully, diffusely, concernfully, tactilely.

Q: So Mr. Sensitive is a gender role that is at odds with the sex role?

KW: In some ways, yes. That doesn't mean men can't or shouldn't become more sensitive. Today, it's an imperative. But it simply means men usually have to be *educated* to do so. It's a role they have to *learn*. And there are many reasons why this role should be learned, but we have to cut men some slack as they grope toward this strange new landscape.

But likewise for women. Part of the new demands of being a woman in today's world is that she has to fight for her autonomy, and not simply and primarily define herself in terms of her relationships. This, of course, is the great call of feminism, that women begin to define themselves in terms of their own autonomy and their own intrinsic worth, and not merely in terms of relationship to an Other. Not that relationships should be devalued, but that women find ways to honor their own mature self and not merely resort to self-abnegation in the face of the Other.

Q: So both men and women are working against their biological givens?

KW: In some ways, yes. But that is the whole point of evolution: it always goes beyond what went before. It is always struggling to establish new limits, and then struggling just as hard to break them, to transcend them, to move beyond them into more encompassing and integrative and holistic modes. And where the traditional sex roles of male and female were once perfectly necessary and appropriate, they are today becoming increasingly outmoded, narrow, and cramped. And so both men and women are struggling for ways to transcend their old roles, without—and this is the tricky part—without simply erasing them. Evolution always *transcends* and *includes*, incorporates and goes beyond.

And so, males will always have a base of testosterone drivenness— fuck it or kill it—but those drives can be taken up and worked into more appropriate modes of behavior. Men will always, to some degree, be incredibly driven to break limits, push the envelope, go all out, wildly, insanely, and in the process bring new discoveries, new inventions, new modes into being.

And women, as the radical feminists insist, will always have a base of relational being, oxytocin to the core, but upon that base of relational being can be built a sturdier sense of self-esteem and autonomy, valuing the mature self even as it continues to value relationships.

So for both men and women, it's transcend and include, transcend and include. And we are at a point in evolution where the primary sex roles—hyperautonomy for men and hyperrelationship for women—are both being transcended to some degree, with men learning to embrace relational being and women learning to embrace autonomy. And in this difficult process, both sexes appear to be monsters in the eyes of the other, which is why a certain kindness on both sides is so important, I think.

Q: Now you said that our society has been male-oriented for some time, and that a certain balancing of the books seems to be in order.

KW: This is what is generally meant by the "patriarchy," a word which is always pronounced with scorn. The obvious and perhaps naive solution is to simply say that men *imposed* the patriarchy on women—a nasty and brutal state of affairs that easily could have been different—and therefore all that is now required is for men to simply say, "Oops, excuse me, didn't mean to crush and oppress you for five thousand years. What *was* I thinking? Can we just start over?"

But, alas, it is not that simple, I don't believe. It appears there were certain inescapable circumstances that made the "patriarchy" an unavoidable arrangement for an important part of human development, and we are just now reaching the point where that arrangement is no longer necessary, so that we can begin, in certain fundamental ways, to "deconstruct" the patriarchy, or more charitably balance the books between the male and female value spheres. But this is not the undoing of a brutal state of affairs that could easily have been otherwise; it is rather the outgrowing of a state of affairs no longer necessary.

Q: Which is a very different way of looking at it.

KW: Well, if we take the standard response—that the patriarchy was imposed on women by a bunch of sadistic and power-hungry men—then we are locked into two inescapable definitions of men and women. Namely, men are pigs and women are sheep. That men would intentionally want to oppress half of the human race paints a dismal picture of men altogether. Testosterone or not, men are simply not that malicious in the totality of their being.

But actually, what's so altogether unbelievable about this explanation of the patriarchy is that it paints an incredibly *flattering* picture of men. It says that men managed to collectively get together and agree to oppress half of the human race, and more amazingly, they *succeeded totally* in every known culture. Mind you, men have never been able to create a domineering government that lasted more than a few hundred years; but according to the feminists, men managed to implement this other and massive domination for five thousand—some say one hundred thousand—years. Those wacky guys, gotta love 'em.

But the real problem with the "imposition theory"—men oppressed women from day one—is that it paints a horrifyingly dismal picture of women. You simply cannot be as strong and as intelligent *and oppressed*. This picture necessarily paints women basically as sheep, as weaker and/or stupider than men. Instead of seeing that, at every stage of human evolution, men and women *co-created* the social forms of their interaction, this picture defines women primarily as molded by an Other. These feminists, in other words, are assuming and enforcing precisely the picture of women that they say they want to erase. But men are simply not that piggy, and women not that sheepy.

So one of the things I have tried to do, based on more recent feminist scholarship, is to trace out the hidden power that women have had and that influenced, co-created, the various cultural structures throughout our history, including the so-called patriarchy. Among other things, this releases men from being defined as schmucks, and releases women from being defined as duped, brainwashed, and herded.

Q: In various writings, you have traced five or six major epochs of human evolution, and you examine the status of men and women in each of those stages.

KW: Yes, one of the things we want to do, when looking at the various stages of human consciousness evolution, is also to look at the *status* of men and women *at each of those stages*. And that allows certain important conclusions to stand out, I believe.

Q: So this approach involves what, exactly? In general terms.

KW: What we want to do is *first*, isolate the biological constants that do not change much from culture to culture. These biological constants appear very simple and even trivial, such as: men on average have an advantage in physical strength and mobility, and women give birth and lactate. But those simple biological differences turn out to have an enormous influence on the types of cultural or gender differences that spring up around them.

Q: For example?

KW: For example, what if the means of subsistence in your particular culture is horse and herding? As Janet Chafetz points out, women who participate in these activities have a very high rate of miscarriage. It is to their Darwinian *advantage* not to participate in the productive sphere, which is therefore occupied almost solely by men. And indeed, over 90 percent of herding societies are "patriarchal." But *oppression* is not required to explain this patriarchal orientation. The evidence suggests, on the contrary, that women freely participated in this arrangement.

If, on the other hand, we fall into the naive and reflex action, and assume that if women in these societies weren't doing exactly what the modern feminist thinks they should have been doing, then those women *must* have been oppressed, then off we go on the men-are-pigs, women-are-sheep chase, which is horribly degrading to both sexes, don't you think?

Nobody is denying that some of these arrangements were very difficult, gruesome even. But what we find is that when the sexes are polarized or rigidly separated, then both sexes suffer horribly. The evidence suggests, in fact, that the patriarchal societies were much harder on the average male than on the average female, for reasons we can discuss if you like. But ideology and victim politics don't help very much in this particular regard. Trading female power for female victimhood is a self-defeating venture. It presupposes and reinforces that which it wishes to overcome.

Q: So you said we want to do two things, and the first was look at the universal biological differences between the sexes.

KW: Yes, and second, to look at how these constant *biological* differences played themselves out over the five or six stages of human *cultural* evolution. The general point is that, with this approach, we can isolate those factors that historically led to more "equalitarian" societies—that is, societies that gave roughly equal status to the male and female value spheres. They never *equated* male and female; they balanced them. And thus, in our present-day attempts to reach a more harmonious stance, we will have a better idea about just what needs to be changed, and what does not need to be changed.

So perhaps we can learn to value the differences between the male and female value spheres. Those differences, even according to the radical feminists, appear to be here for good—but we can learn to value them with more equal emphasis. *How* to do so is one of the things we might want to talk about.

The Scope of These Discussions

Q: The human stages of development are part of a larger project of looking at *evolution in general*. And in all sorts of domains—physical, mental, cultural, spiritual—ranging from subconscious to self-conscious to superconscious. You have done this in a dozen books, from *The Spectrum of Consciousness* to *The Atman Project* to *Up from Eden* to *Sex, Ecology, Spirituality*. What we want to do is go over these ideas—about the evolution of consciousness, spiritual development, the role of men and women, ecology and our place in the Kosmos—and see if we can discuss them in a simple and brief fashion. See if we can make them more accessible.

KW: We could start with the rather amazing fact that there seems to be a common evolutionary thread running from matter to life to mind. Certain *common patterns*, or laws, or habits keep repeating themselves in all those domains, and we could begin by looking at those extraordinary patterns, since they seem to hold the secrets of evolution.

Q: You have also looked at the higher stages of consciousness evolution itself, stages that might best be called spiritual.

KW: Yes. This takes up various themes suggested by Schelling, Hegel, Aurobindo, and other evolutionary theorists East and West. The point is that, according to these luminaries, evolution is best thought of as *Spirit-in-action*, God-in-the-making, where Spirit unfolds itself at every stage of development, thus manifesting more of itself, and realizing more of itself, at every unfolding. Spirit is not some particular stage, or some favorite ideology, or some specific god or goddess, but rather the entire process of unfolding itself, an infinite process that is completely present at every finite stage, but becomes more available to itself with every evolutionary opening.

And so yes, we can look at the higher stages of this evolutionary unfolding, according to the world's great wisdom traditions—the higher or deeper stages where Spirit becomes conscious of itself, awakens to itself, begins to recognize its own true nature.

These higher stages are often pictured as mystical or "far out," but for the most part they are very concrete, very palpable, very real stages of higher development—stages available to you and to me, stages that are our own deep potentials.

Q: You found that the world's great spiritual traditions fall into two large and very different camps.

KW: Yes, if we look at the various types of human attempts to comprehend the Divine—both East and West, North and South—what we find are two very different types of spirituality, which I call *Ascending* and *Descending*.

The Ascending path is purely transcendental and otherworldly. It is usually puritanical, ascetic, yogic, and it tends to devalue or even deny the body, the senses, sexuality, the Earth, the flesh. It seeks its salvation in a kingdom not of this world; it sees manifestation or samsara as evil or illusory; it seeks to get off the wheel entirely. And, in fact, for the Ascenders, any sort of Descent tends to be viewed as illusory or even evil. The Ascending path glorifies the One, not the Many; Emptiness, not Form; Heaven, not Earth.

The Descending path counsels just the opposite. It is this-worldly to the core, and it glorifies the Many, not the One. It celebrates the Earth, and the body, and the senses, and often sexuality. It even identifies Spirit with the sensory world, with Gaia, with manifestation, and sees in every sunrise, every moonrise, all the Spirit a person could ever want. It is purely immanent and is often suspicious of anything transcendental. In fact, for the Descenders, any form of Ascent is usually viewed as evil.

Q: One of the things we want to discuss is the history of the "war" between the Ascenders and the Descenders. They are each the devil in the other's eyes.

KW: Yes, it's at least a two-thousand-year-old war, often brutal and always rancorous. In the West, from the time roughly of Augustine to Copernicus, we have a purely Ascending ideal, otherworldly to the core. Final salvation and liberation could not be found in this body, on this Earth, in this lifetime. I mean, your present life could be okay, but things got really interesting once you died. Once you went otherworldly.

But then, with the rise of modernity and postmodernity, we see a complete and profound reversal—the Ascenders were out, the Descenders were in.

Q: You call this "the dominance of the Descenders," which is another major topic we will cover. You point out that the modern and postmodern world is governed almost entirely by a purely Descended conception, a purely Descended worldview.

KW: Yes, the idea that the sensory and empirical and material world is the only world there is. There are no higher or deeper potentials available to us—no higher transcendental stages of consciousness evolution, for example. There is merely what we can see with our senses or grasp with our hands. It is a world completely bereft of any sort of Ascending energy at all, hollow of any transcendence. And, in fact, as is usually the case with Descenders, any sort of Ascent or transcendence is looked upon as being misguided at best, evil at worst.

Q: But the point, I take it, is to integrate and include the best of both the Ascending and the Descending paths, yes?

KW: Yes. They both have some very important things to teach us, I believe.

Q: On the other hand, when they are divorced from each other, or when they try to deny each other, certain limited, partial, and oppressive schemes tend to result.

KW: I believe that is true. We all know the downsides of the merely Ascending path: it can be very puritanical and oppressive. It tends to deny and devalue and even repress the body, the senses, life, Earth, sexuality, and so forth.

The Descending path, on the other hand, reminds us that Spirit can be joyously found in body, sex, Earth, life, vitality, and diversity. But the

Descending path, in and by itself, has its own limitations. If there is no transcendence at all, then there is no way to rise above the merely sensory; no way to find a deeper, wider, higher connection between us and all sentient beings. We are merely confined to the sensory surfaces, the superficial facades, which separate us much more than join and unite us. Without some sort of transcendence or Ascent, we have *only* the Descended world, which can be shallow, alienated, and fragmented.

Q: You call the merely Descended world "flatland."

KW: Flatland, yes. We moderns and postmoderns live almost entirely within this purely Descended grid, this flat and faded world of endless sensory forms, this superficial world of drab and dreary surfaces. Whether with capitalism or Marxism, industrialism or ecopsychology, patriarchal science or ecofeminism—in most cases, our God, our Goddess, is one we can register with our senses, see with our eyes, wrap with feelings, worship with sensations, a God we can sink our teeth into, and that exhausts its form.

Whether or not we consider ourselves spiritual, we flatlanders worship at the altar of the merely Descended God, the sensory Goddess, the sensational world, the monochrome world of simple location, the world you can put your finger on. Nothing higher or deeper for us than the God that is clunking around in our visual field.

Q: You have pointed out that the great Nondual traditions, East and West, attempt instead to integrate both the Ascending and the Descending paths.

KW: Yes, to balance both transcendence and immanence, the One and the Many, Emptiness and Form, nirvana and samsara, Heaven and Earth.

Q: "Nonduality" refers to the integration of Ascending and Descending?

KW: That's right.

Q: So that is another point we want to discuss—the currents of Ascending and Descending spirituality, and how those currents can be integrated in our own daily lives.

KW: I think that is important, because, again, both paths have incredibly important things to teach us. It is in the union of the Ascending and the Descending currents that harmony is found, and not in any war between the two. It seems that only when Ascending and Descending are united can both be saved. And if we—if you and I—do not contribute to this union, then it is very possible that not only will we destroy the only Earth we have, we will forfeit the only Heaven we might otherwise embrace.

PART ONE

SPIRIT-IN-ACTION

1

The Pattern That Connects

Q: So we'll start the story with the Big Bang itself, and then trace out the course of evolution from matter to life to mind. And then, with the emergence of mind, or human consciousness, we'll look at the five or six major epochs of human evolution itself. And all of this is set in the context of spirituality—of what spirituality means, of the various forms that it has historically taken, and the forms that it might take tomorrow. Sound right?

KW: Yes, it's sort of a brief history of everything. This sounds altogether grandiose, but it's based on what I call "orienting generalizations," which simplifies the whole thing enormously.

Q: An orienting generalization is what, exactly?

KW: If we look at the various fields of human knowledge—from physics to biology to psychology, sociology, theology, and religion— certain broad, general themes emerge, about which there is actually very little disagreement.

For example, in the sphere of moral development, not everybody agrees with the details of Lawrence Kohlberg's moral stages, nor with the details of Carol Gilligan's reworking of Kohlberg's scheme. But there is general and ample agreement that human moral development goes through at least *three broad stages.*

The human at birth is not yet socialized into any sort of moral system—it is "preconventional." The human then learns a general moral scheme that represents the basic values of the society it is raised in—it becomes "conventional." And with even further growth, the individual may come to reflect on his or her society and thus gain some modest

67

distance from it, gain a capacity to criticize it or reform it—the individual is to some degree "postconventional."

Thus, although the actual details and the precise meanings of that developmental sequence are still hotly debated, everybody pretty much agrees that something like those three broad stages do indeed occur, and occur universally. These are *orienting generalizations*: they show us, with a great deal of agreement, where the important forests are located, even if we can't agree on how many trees they contain.

My point is that if we take these types of largely-agreed-upon orienting generalizations from the various branches of knowledge—from physics to biology to psychology to theology—and if we string these orienting generalizations together, we will arrive at some astonishing and often profound conclusions, conclusions that, as extraordinary as they might be, nonetheless embody nothing more than our already-agreed-upon knowledge. The beads of knowledge are already accepted: it is only necessary to string them together into a necklace.

Q: And so in these discussions we will build toward some sort of necklace.

KW: Yes, in a sense. In working with broad orienting generalizations, we can suggest a broad orienting map of the place of men and women in relation to Universe, Life, and Spirit. The details of this map we can all fill in as we like, but its broad outlines really have an awful lot of supporting evidence, culled from the orienting generalizations, simple but sturdy, from the various branches of human knowledge.

The Kosmos

Q: We'll follow the course of evolution as it unfolds through the various domains, from matter to life to mind. You call these three major domains matter or cosmos, life or the biosphere, and mind or the noosphere. And all of these domains together you call the "Kosmos."

KW: Yes, the Pythagoreans introduced the term "Kosmos," which we usually translate as cosmos. But the original meaning of Kosmos was the patterned nature or process of all domains of existence, from matter to mind to God, and not merely the *physical* universe, which is usually what both "cosmos" and "universe" mean today.

So I would like to reintroduce this term, Kosmos. And, as you point out, the Kosmos contains the cosmos (or the physiosphere), the bios (or biosphere), psyche or nous (the noosphere), and theos (the theosphere or divine domain).

So, for example, we might haggle about where exactly it is that matter becomes life—or cosmos becomes bios—but as Francisco Varela points out, autopoiesis (or self-replication) occurs only in living systems. It is found nowhere in the cosmos, but only in the bios. It's a major and profound *emergent*—something astonishingly novel—and I trace several of these types of profound transformations or emergents in the course of evolution in the Kosmos.

Q: So in these discussions we're not interested in just the cosmos, but the Kosmos.

KW: Yes. Many cosmologies have a materialistic bias and prejudice: the physical cosmos is somehow supposed to be the most real dimension, and everything else is explained with ultimate reference to this material plane. But what a brutal approach that is! It smashes the entire Kosmos against the wall of reductionism, and all the domains except the physical slowly bleed to death right in front of your eyes. Is this any way to treat a Kosmos?

No, I think what we want to do is Kosmology, not cosmology.

Twenty Tenets: The Patterns That Connect

Q: We can begin this Kosmology by reviewing the characteristics of evolution in the various realms. You have isolated *twenty patterns* that seem to be true for evolution wherever it occurs, from matter to life to mind.

KW: Based on the work of numerous researchers, yes.

Q: Let's give a few examples of these twenty tenets to show what's involved. Tenet number 1 is that reality is composed of whole/parts, or "holons." Reality is composed of holons?

KW: Is that far out? Is this already confusing? No? Well, Arthur Koestler coined the term "holon" to refer to an entity that is itself a *whole* and simultaneously a *part* of some other whole. And if you start to look closely at the things and processes that actually exist, it soon becomes obvious that they are not merely wholes, they are also parts of something else. They are whole/parts, they are holons.

For instance, a whole atom is part of a whole molecule, and the whole molecule is part of a whole cell, and the whole cell is part of a whole organism, and so on. Each of these entities is neither a whole nor a part, but a whole/part, a holon.

And the point is, everything is basically a holon of some sort or another. There is a two-thousand-year-old philosophical squabble between atomists and wholists: which is ultimately real, the whole or the part? And the answer is, neither. Or both, if you prefer. There are only whole/parts in all directions, all the way up, all the way down.

There's an old joke about a King who goes to a Wiseperson and asks how it is that the Earth doesn't fall down. The Wiseperson replies, "The Earth is resting on a lion." "On what, then, is the lion resting?" "The lion is resting on an elephant." "On what is the elephant resting?" "The elephant is resting on a turtle." "On what is the . . . ?" "You can stop right there, Your Majesty. It's turtles all the way down."

Turtles all the way down, holons all the way down. No matter how far down we go, we find holons resting on holons resting on holons. Even subatomic particles disappear into a virtual cloud of bubbles within bubbles, holons within holons, in an *infinity* of probability waves. Holons all the way down.

Q: And all the way up, as you say. We never come to an ultimate Whole.

KW: That's right. There is no whole that isn't also simultaneously a part of some other whole, indefinitely, unendingly. Time goes on, and today's wholes are tomorrow's parts. . . .

Even the "Whole" of the Kosmos is simply a *part* of the next moment's whole, *indefinitely.* At no point do we have *the* whole, because there is no whole, there are only whole/parts forever.

So the first tenet says that reality is composed neither of things nor processes, neither wholes nor parts, but whole/parts, or holons—all the way up, all the way down.

Q: So reality is not composed of, say, subatomic particles.

KW: Yikes. I know that approach is common, but it is really a profoundly reductionistic approach, because it is going to *privilege* the material, physical universe, and then everything else—from life to mind to spirit—has to be *derived* from subatomic particles, and this will never, never work.

But notice, a subatomic particle is itself a holon. And so is a cell. And so is a symbol, and an image, and a concept. What all of those entities are, before they are anything else, is a holon. So the world is not composed of atoms or symbols or cells or concepts. It is composed of holons.

Since the Kosmos is composed of holons, then if we look at what *all holons have in common,* then we can begin to see what evolution in all the various domains has in common. Holons in the cosmos, bios, psyche, theos—how they all unfold, the common patterns they all display.

Q: What all holons have in common. That is how you arrive at the twenty tenets.

KW: Yes, that's right.

Agency and Communion

Q: So tenet 1 is that the Kosmos is composed of holons. Tenet 2 is that all holons share certain characteristics.

KW: Yes. Because every holon is a whole/part, it has two "tendencies" or two "drives," we might say—it has to maintain both its *wholeness* and its *partness*.

On the one hand, it has to maintain its own wholeness, its own identity, its own autonomy, its own *agency*. If it fails to maintain and preserve its own agency, or its own identity, then it simply ceases to exist. So one of the characteristics of a holon, in any domain, is its agency, its capacity to maintain its own wholeness in the face of environmental pressures which would otherwise obliterate it. This is true for atoms, cells, organisms, ideas.

But a holon is not only a whole that has to preserve its agency, it is also a part of some other system, some other wholeness. And so, in addition to having to maintain its own autonomy as a *whole*, it simultaneously has to fit in as a *part* of something else. Its own existence depends upon its capacity to fit into its environment, and this is true from atoms to molecules to animals to humans.

So every holon has not only its own agency as a whole, it also has to fit with its *communions* as part of other wholes. If it fails at either—if it fails at agency or communion—it is simply erased. It ceases to be.

Transcendence and Dissolution

Q: And that is part of tenet number 2—each holon possesses both agency and communion. You call these the "horizontal" capacities of holons. What about the "vertical" capacities of holons, which you call "self-transcendence" and "self-dissolution"?

KW: Yes. If a holon fails to maintain its agency and its communions, then it can break down completely. When it does break down, it decomposes into its subholons: cells decompose into molecules, which break down into atoms, which can be "smashed" infinitely under intense pressure. The fascinating thing about holon decomposition is that holons tend to dissolve in the reverse direction that they were built up. And this decomposition is "self-dissolution," or simply decomposing into subholons, which themselves can decompose into their subholons, and so on.

But look at the reverse process, which is the most extraordinary: the building-up process, the process of new holons emerging. How did inert molecules come together to form living cells in the first place?

The standard neo-Darwinian explanation of chance mutation and natural selection—very few theorists believe this anymore. Evolution clearly operates in part by Darwinian natural selection, but this process simply selects those transformations that have *already* occurred by mechanisms that absolutely nobody understands.

Q: For example?

KW: Take the standard notion that wings simply evolved from forelegs. It takes perhaps a hundred mutations to produce a functional wing from a leg—a half-wing will not do. A half-wing is no good as a leg and no good as a wing—you can't run and you can't fly. It has no adaptive value whatsoever. In other words, with a half-wing you are dinner. The wing will work only if these hundred mutations *happen all at once,* in one animal—and also these *same* mutations must occur *simultaneously* in another animal of the opposite sex, and then they have to somehow find each other, have dinner, a few drinks, mate, and have offspring with real functional wings.

Talk about mind-boggling. This is infinitely, absolutely, utterly mind-boggling. Random mutations cannot even begin to explain this. The vast majority of mutations are lethal anyway; how are we going to get a hundred nonlethal mutations happening simultaneously? Or even four or five, for that matter? But once this incredible transformation has occurred, then natural selection will indeed select the better wings from the less workable wings—but the wings themselves? Nobody has a clue.

For the moment, everybody has simply agreed to call this "quantum evolution" or "punctuated evolution" or "emergent evolution"—radically novel and emergent and incredibly complex holons come into existence in a huge leap, in a quantum-like fashion—with no evidence whatsoever of intermediate forms. Dozens or hundreds of simultaneous nonlethal mutations have to happen at the same time in order to survive at all—the wing, for example, or the eyeball.

However we decide these extraordinary transformations occur, the fact is undeniable that they do. Thus, many theorists, like Erich Jantsch, simply refer to evolution as "self-realization through self-transcendence." Evolution is a wildly *self-transcending* process: it has the utterly amazing capacity to go beyond what went before. So evolution is in part a process of transcendence, which incorporates what went before and then adds incredibly novel components. The drive to self-transcendence thus appears to be built into the very fabric of the Kosmos itself.

Four Drives of All Holons

Q: And that is the fourth "drive" of all holons. So we have agency and communion, operating "horizontally" on any level, and then "vertically" we have the move to a higher level altogether, which is self-transcendence, and the move to a lower level, which is self-dissolution.

KW: Yes, that's right. Because all holons are whole/parts, they are subjected to various "pulls" in their own existence. The pull to be a whole, the pull to be a part, the pull up, the pull down: agency, communion, transcendence, dissolution. And tenet 2 simply says that all holons have these four pulls.

So that's an example of how the twenty tenets start. There is nothing magical about the number "twenty." These are just some of the common patterns I have focused on. The rest of the twenty tenets look at what happens when these various forces play themselves out. The self-transcending drive produces life out of matter, and mind out of life. And the twenty tenets simply suggest some of these types of common patterns found in the evolution of holons wherever they appear—matter to life to mind, to maybe even higher stages. Maybe even spiritual stages, yes?

Q: So there is indeed some sort of unity to evolution.

KW: Well, it certainly seems so. The *continuous* process of self-transcendence produces *discontinuities*, leaps, creative jumps. So there are both discontinuities in evolution—mind cannot be reduced to life, and life cannot be reduced to matter; and there are continuities—the common patterns that evolution takes in all these domains. And in that sense, yes, the Kosmos hangs together, unified by a single process. It is a uni-verse, one song.

Creative Emergence

Q: That one song you call Spirit-in-action, or God-in-the-making, which is a point I want to come back to later. But for now, tenet number 3 states simply: Holons emerge.

KW: Yes. As we were saying, evolution is in part a self-transcending process—it always goes beyond what went before. And in that novelty, in that emergence, in that creativity, new entities come into being, new patterns unfold, new holons issue forth. This extraordinary process builds unions out of fragments and wholes out of heaps. The Kosmos, it seems, unfolds in quantum leaps of creative emergence.

Q: Which is why one level cannot be reduced to its lower components, or why a holon cannot be reduced to its subholons.

KW: Yes. I mean, you can analyze the whole into its constituent parts, and that's a completely valid endeavor. But then you have parts, not the whole. You can take a watch apart and analyze its parts, but they won't tell you the time of day. It's the same with any holon. The wholeness of the holon is not found in any of its parts, and that puts an end to a certain reductionistic frenzy that has plagued Western science virtually from its inception. Particularly with the systems sciences, the vivid realization has dawned: we live in a universe of creative emergence.

Q: Although there are still reductionists around, the tide does seem to have turned. You hardly have to explain anymore why reductionism, in and by itself, is "bad." And nonreductionism means, in some sense, that the Kosmos is creative.

KW: Amazing, isn't it? As "ultimate categories"—which means concepts that we need in order to think about anything else at all—Whitehead listed only three: creativity, one, many. (Since every holon is actually a one/many, those categories really come down to: creativity, holons.)

But the point is, as Whitehead put it, "The ultimate metaphysical ground is the *creative advance into novelty*." New holons creatively emerge. Creativity, holons—those are some of the most basic categories that we need to think of before we can think about anything else at all!

So yes, that's tenet 3: holons emerge. And each holon has these four basic capacities—agency, communion, self-dissolution, self-transcendence—and so off we go, creating a Kosmos.

Q: This gets a little ahead of the story, so I don't want to pursue it too much right now. But you link creativity and Spirit.

KW: Well, what is creativity but another name for Spirit? If, as Whitehead said, creativity is an *ultimate*—you have to have it before you can have anything else—what is an "ultimate metaphysical ground" if not Spirit? For Spirit, I also use the Buddhist term "Emptiness," which we can talk about. But Spirit or Emptiness gives rise to form. New forms emerge, new holons emerge—and it's not out of thin air.

We already saw that many scientists *agree* that self-transcendence (or novel emergence) is built into the very fabric of the universe. By any other name, what is that self-transcending creativity? Spirit, yes? We are obviously talking in very general terms here, but so far it appears that we have: Spirit, creativity, holons.

Q: There has also been a recent warming in some scientific circles to a more spiritual or idealistic reading of creation.

KW: In a certain sense. The Big Bang has made Idealists out of almost anybody who thinks. First there was absolutely nothing, then Bang! Something. This is beyond weird. Out of sheerest Emptiness, manifestation arises.

This is a bit of a nightmare for traditional science, because it puts a time limit on the chance mutations that were supposed to explain the universe. Remember the thousand monkeys and Shakespeare—an example of how chance could give rise to the ordered universe?

Q: Given enough time, the randomly typing monkeys would manage to type out a Shakespeare play.

KW: Given enough time! One computation showed that the chance for monkey power to produce a single Shakespeare play was one in ten thousand million million million million million million. So maybe that would happen in a billion billion years. But the universe doesn't have a billion billion years. It only has twelve billion years.

Well, this changes everything. Calculations done by scientists from Fred Hoyle to F. B. Salisbury consistently show that twelve billion years isn't even enough to produce a *single enzyme* by chance.

In other words, something other than chance is pushing the universe. For traditional scientists, chance was their salvation. Chance was their god. Chance would explain all. Chance—plus unending time—would produce the universe. But they don't have unending time, and so their god fails them miserably. That god is dead. Chance is not what explains the universe; in fact, chance is what the universe is laboring mightily to overcome. Chance is exactly what the self-transcending drive of the Kosmos overcomes.

Q: Which is another way of saying that self-transcendence is built into the universe, or, as you put it, self-transcendence is one of the four drives of any holon.

KW: Yes, I think so. There is a formative drive, a telos, to the Kosmos. It has a direction. It is going somewhere. Its ground is Emptiness; its drive is the organization of Form into increasingly coherent holons. Spirit, creativity, holons.

Q: Now the "religious creationists" have made quite a big deal out of this. They say it fits with the Bible and Genesis.

KW: Well, they have seized upon the increasingly obvious truth that the traditional scientific explanation does not work very well. Creativity, not chance, builds a Kosmos. But it does not follow that you can then equate creativity with your favorite and particular God. It does not follow that into this void you can postulate a God with all the specific characteristics that make you happy—God is the God of only the Jews, or only the Hindus, or only the indigenous peoples, and God is watching over me, and is kind, and just, and merciful, and so on. We have to be very careful about these types of limited and anthropomorphic characteristics, which is one of the reasons I prefer "Emptiness" as a term for Spirit, because it means unbounded or unqualifiable.

But the fundamentalists, the "creationists," seize upon these vacancies in the scientific hotel to pack the conference with their delegates. They see the opening—creativity is an *absolute*—and they equate that absolute with their mythic god, and they stuff this god with all the characteristics that promote their own egoic inclinations, starting with the fact that if you don't believe in this particular god, you fry in hell forever, which is not exactly a generous view of Spirit.

So it is a good idea to start simple, I think, and be very careful. There is a spiritual opening in the Kosmos. Let us be careful how we fill it. The simplest is: Spirit or Emptiness is unqualifiable, but it is not inert and unyielding, for it gives rise to manifestation itself: new forms emerge, and that creativity is ultimate. Emptiness, creativity, holons.

Let's leave it there for the time being, okay? We can come back to this topic as things unfold.

Holarchy

Q: Fair enough. So we just looked at tenet number 3, "Holons emerge." Tenet number 4 is: Holons emerge holarchically. Holarchy?

KW: Koestler's term for natural hierarchy. Hierarchy today has a very bad reputation, mostly because people confuse dominator hierarchies with natural hierarchies.

A natural hierarchy is simply an order of increasing wholeness, such as: particles to atoms to cells to organisms, or letters to words to sentences to paragraphs. The whole of one level becomes a part of the whole of the next.

In other words, natural hierarchies are composed of holons. And thus, said Koestler, "hierarchy" should really be called "holarchy." He's absolutely right. Virtually all growth processes, from matter to life to mind, occur via natural holarchies, or orders of increasing holism and wholeness—wholes that become parts of new wholes—and that's natural hierarchy or holarchy.

Q: It's the dominator hierarchies that freak people out.

KW: With good reason, yes. When any holon in a natural holarchy usurps its position and attempts to dominate the whole, then you get a pathological or dominator hierarchy—a cancerous cell dominates the body, or a fascist dictator dominates the social system, or a repressive ego dominates the organism, and so on.

But the cure for these pathological holarchies is not getting rid of holarchy per se—which isn't possible anyway—but rather in arresting the arrogant holon and integrating it back into the natural holarchy, or putting it in its rightful place, so to speak. The critics of hierarchy—their names are legion—simply confuse these pathological holarchies with holarchies in general, and so they toss the baby with the bathwater.

Q: They claim in getting rid of hierarchies they are being holistic, because everything is treated equally and thus joined together.

KW: It appears to be just the opposite. The only way you get a holism is via a holarchy. When holists say "the whole is greater than the sum of its parts," that means the whole is at a *higher* or *deeper* level of organization than the parts alone—and that's a hierarchy, a holarchy. Separate molecules are drawn together into a single cell only by properties that supersede the molecules alone—the cell is holarchically arranged. And without holarchy, you simply have heaps, not wholes. You are a heapist, not a holist.

Q: But many feminists and many ecophilosophers claim that any sort of hierarchy or "ranking" is oppressive, even fascist. They say that all such value ranking is "old paradigm" or "patriarchal" or oppressive, and it ought to be replaced with a *linking*, not a *ranking*, worldview. They're very aggressive with this point; they hurl rather harsh accusations.

KW: This is a bit disingenuous, because you can't avoid hierarchy. Even the antihierarchy theorists that you mention *have their own hierarchy*, their own *ranking*. Namely, they think linking is *better* than ranking. Well, that's a hierarchy, a ranking of values. But because they don't own up to this, then their hierarchy becomes unconscious, hidden, denied. Their hierarchy denies hierarchy. They have a ranking system that says ranking is bad.

Q: You call this a "performative contradiction."

KW: Yes, the point is that the antihierarchy stance is self-contradictory. These theorists have a hierarchy; it's just hidden or concealed. With this stealth hierarchy they attack all other hierarchies, and they claim that they themselves are "free" of all that nasty ranking. So they rancorously denounce others for doing precisely what they themselves are doing. It's an altogether unpleasant affair.

Q: But hierarchy has been put to many abuses, as you yourself have explained at length.

KW: Yes, and in that regard I very much agree with these critics. But the point is not to get rid of hierarchies or holarchies altogether—that's impossible. Trying to get rid of ranking is itself a ranking. Denying hierarchy is itself a hierarchy. Precisely because the Kosmos is composed of holons, and holons exist holarchically, you can't escape these nested orders. Rather, we want to tease apart *natural* holarchies from *pathological* or *dominator* holarchies.

Q: So holarchies really are inescapable.

KW: Yes, because holons are inescapable. All evolutionary and developmental patterns proceed by holarchization, by a process of increasing orders of wholeness and inclusion, which is a type of *ranking* by *holistic* capacity. This is why the basic principle of holism is holarchy: the higher or deeper dimension provides a principle, or a "glue," or a pattern, that unites and *links* otherwise separate and conflicting and isolated parts into a coherent unity, a space in which separate parts can recognize a common wholeness and thus escape the fate of being merely a part, merely a fragment.

So linking is indeed important, but linking is itself set within ranking and holarchy, and can exist only because of holarchy, which provides the higher or deeper space in which the linking and joining can occur. Otherwise heaps, not wholes.

And when a particular holon usurps its position in any holarchy— when it wants to be only a whole, and not also a part—then that natural or normal holarchy degenerates into a pathological or dominator holarchy, which by any other name is illness, pathology, disease—whether physical, emotional, social, cultural, or spiritual. And we want to "attack" these pathological hierarchies, not in order to get rid of hierarchy per se, but in order to allow the normal or natural hierarchy to emerge in its place and continue its healthy growth and development.

The Way of All Embrace

Q: Okay, here is what we have so far. The Kosmos is composed of holons, all the way up, all the way down. All holons have four fundamental capacities—agency and communion, transcendence and dissolution. Holons emerge. Holons emerge holarchically.

KW: Yes, those are the first four tenets.

Q: So now we have tenet 5: Each emergent holon transcends but includes its predecessor(s).

KW: For example, the cell transcends—or goes beyond—its molecular components, but also includes them. Molecules transcend and include atoms, which transcend and include particles. . . .

The point is that since all holons are whole/parts, the wholeness *transcends* but the parts are *included*. In this transcendence, heaps are converted into wholes; in the inclusion, the parts are equally embraced and cherished, linked in a commonality and a shared space that relieves each of the burden of being a fragment.

And so yes, evolution is a process of transcend and include, transcend and include. And this begins to open onto the very heart of Spirit-in-action, the very secret of the evolutionary impulse.

2

The Secret Impulse

Q: The secret impulse of evolution?

KW: A molecule transcends and includes atoms. *Transcends*, in that it has certain emergent or novel or creative properties that are not merely the sum of its components. This is the whole point of systems theory and holism in general, that new levels of organization come into being, and these new levels cannot be reduced in all ways to their junior dimensions—they transcend them. But they also *include* them, because the junior holons are nonetheless components of the new holon. So, transcends and includes.

Q: So the higher has the essentials of the lower, plus something extra.

KW: Yes, that's another way of putting it, which Aristotle first pointed out—all of the lower is in the higher but not all of the higher is in the lower, which is what *invariably* establishes hierarchy or holarchy. Cells contain molecules, but not vice versa. Molecules contain atoms, but not vice versa. Sentences contain words, but not vice versa. And it is this *not vice versa* that establishes a hierarchy, a holarchy, an order of increasing wholeness.

Higher and Lower

Q: There is so much bitter argument over a level being "higher" or "lower" than another. And yet you have suggested a simple rule for establishing higher and lower in any sequence.

KW: Well, take any evolutionary development, say, atoms to molecules to cells to organisms. This is a sequence of increasing wholeness, increasing holons, each of which transcends and includes its predecessor. Now if, in a type of thought experiment, you "destroy" any particular type of holon, then all of the *higher* holons will also be destroyed, but none of the *lower* holons will be destroyed. And this simple thought experiment can help you spot what is higher, and what is lower, in any sequence.

So, for example, if you destroyed all the molecules in the universe, then all of the higher levels—cells and organisms—would also be destroyed. But none of the lower holons—atoms and subatomic particles—none of them would be destroyed.

Q: Yes, I see. So "higher" and "lower" organization is not merely a relative "value judgment."

KW: That's right. It truly is not an invention of patriarchal obnoxiousness or fascist ideology. If you destroy any particular type of holon, then all of the higher holons are also destroyed, because they depend in part on the lower holons *for their own components*. But the lower holons can get along perfectly well without the higher: atoms can exist just fine without molecules, but molecules cannot exist without atoms. A simple rule, but it helps us see what is higher, and what is lower, in terms of any holarchy.

This rule works for any developmental sequence, for any holarchy—moral development, language acquisition, biological speciation, computer programs, nucleic acid translations. It works by virtue of the simple way that wholes depend upon parts, but not vice versa. And "not vice versa," as we were saying, is holarchy, or an order of increasing wholeness.

Q: This is how you demonstrate that the biosphere is higher than the physiosphere.

KW: Yes, if you destroy the biosphere—that is, if you destroy all life forms—then the cosmos or physiosphere could and would still exist. But if you destroy the physiosphere, the biosphere is instantly destroyed as well. This happens because the biosphere transcends and includes the physiosphere, and not vice versa. And so yes, the physiosphere is a lower level of structural organization than the biosphere. That is the meaning of higher and lower organization. And the bios is *higher*, the cosmos is *lower*.

Q: In the same way, the noosphere is higher than the biosphere.

KW: In exactly the same way. The noosphere begins with the capacity to form any mental images, and this capacity begins with certain mammals, such as horses. But for this example, I'll confine the noosphere to more highly developed minds and human cultural productions, just to show what's involved—we get the same results either way.

The biosphere existed perfectly well for millions of years before human minds showed up, before the noosphere emerged. And if you destroyed that noosphere, the biosphere would and could still exist. But if you destroy the biosphere, then you destroy all human minds as well, because the biosphere is a part of the noosphere—and not vice versa. So yes, the biosphere is a lower level of structural organization than the noosphere. The noosphere transcends and includes the biosphere, it is not merely a part of the biosphere. That's reductionism.

Q: So the physiosphere is part of the higher wholeness of the biosphere, which is part of the higher wholeness of the noosphere, and not the other way around.

KW: Yes.

Depth and Span

Q: But why do so many people picture it backward?

KW: Probably because people confuse size or *span* with *depth*. And people think that great span means great depth, and this is precisely backward.

Q: So what exactly do "depth" and "span" refer to?

KW: The number of levels in any holarchy is referred to as its *depth*, and the number of holons on any given level is referred to as its *span*.

Q: So if we say atoms have a depth of one, then molecules have a depth of two, cells a depth of three.

KW: Yes, along those lines. Exactly what we want to call a "level" is somewhat arbitrary. It's like a three-story house. We can count each floor as a level, which is what we usually do, so the house would have a *depth* of *three*—three levels. But we could also count each step in the stairs as a level. Maybe there are twenty steps between floors—we would then say that the house has sixty levels, or a depth of sixty.

But the point is that, although these scales are relative or arbitrary, the relative placements are *not* arbitrary. Whether we say the house has three levels or sixty levels, the second floor is still higher than the first floor. As long as we use the same relative scale, then no problems arise, just as we can use Fahrenheit or Celsius to measure water temperature, as long as we are consistent.

So we could say quarks have a depth of one, atoms a depth of two, crystals a depth of three, molecules a depth of four, and so on. The depth is real, no matter what relative scale we decide to use.

Q: So depth and span.

KW: What confuses people is that evolution actually produces *greater depth* and *less span* on succeeding levels. And people tend to confuse collective *bigness* or *size* or *span* with *depth*, and so they get the order of significance totally backward.

Q: Evolution produces greater depth, less span. That is actually tenet number 8 (we're skipping some of them). So could you give an example of this tenet?

KW: There are fewer organisms than cells; there are fewer cells than molecules; there are fewer molecules than atoms; there are fewer atoms than quarks. Each has a *greater* depth, but *less* span.

The reason, of course, is that because the higher transcends and includes the lower, there will always be less of the higher and more of the lower, and there are no exceptions. No matter how many cells there are in the universe, there will always be more molecules. No matter how many molecules in the universe, there will always be more atoms. No matter how many atoms, there will always be more quarks.

So the greater depth always has less span than its predecessor. The *individual* holon has more and more depth, but the *collective* gets smaller and smaller. And since many people think bigger is better, they tend to confuse the direction of significance, they invert the order of being. They turn reality on its head and end up worshipping bigger as better.

Q: A holon transcends and includes its predecessors—it has *greater* depth—but the population size of the greater depth becomes *smaller*. The so-called pyramid of development.

KW: Yes. Figure 2-1 is from Ervin Laszlo's *Evolution: The Grand Synthesis*, which is generally considered to be a clear and accurate summary of the modern scientific view of evolution, such as it is. But you can see the pyramid of evolution very clearly. Where matter is favorable, life emerges; where life is favorable, mind emerges. (I would add, where mind is favorable, Spirit emerges.)

In the diagram, you can actually see that the vertical depth becomes greater, but the horizontal span becomes less. Interestingly, the perennial philosophy reached the same conclusion, in its own way.

Q: The perennial philosophy being . . . ?

KW: We might say it's the core of the world's great wisdom traditions. The perennial philosophy maintains that reality is a Great Holar-

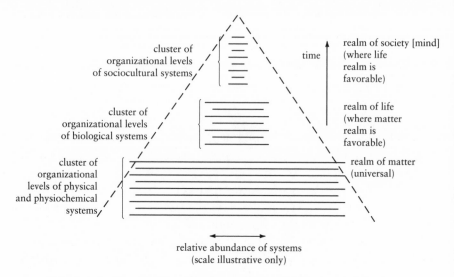

FIGURE 2-1. *The realms of evolution. From Ervin Laszlo,* Evolution:
The Grand Synthesis *(Boston: Shambhala, 1987), p. 55.*

chy of being and consciousness, reaching from matter to life to mind to
Spirit. Each dimension transcends and includes its junior dimension in a
nested holarchy, often represented by concentric circles or spheres. This
"transcend and include" is indicated in figure 2-2.

Each level includes its predecessor and then adds its own emergent
qualities, qualities that are not found in the previous dimension. So each
succeeding dimension is "bigger" in the sense of greater embrace, greater
depth. And we will see that an individual holon's *identity* actually *expands* to include more and more of the Kosmos—precisely as shown in
figure 2-2.

But since the actual *span* of the succeeding holons becomes *less* and
less—the number of holons at each higher level becomes smaller—then
this same diagram is often drawn in exactly the opposite fashion, as in
figure 2-3. Greater depth means fewer holons reach that depth—means
less span—and so the actual population size becomes smaller and
smaller, as indicated in figure 2-3, which is the perennial philosophy's
version of the pyramid of development.

Q: So we need to remember both of these progressions—greater
depth, less span.

KW: Yes. In discussing evolution, perhaps we can keep both of these
diagrams in mind. The first diagram indicates "transcend and in-

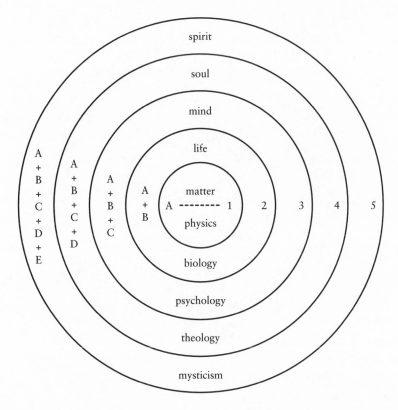

FIGURE 2-2. *Greater depth.*

clude"—an actual increase in embrace, inclusion, identity, enfolding—which gets "larger" in the sense of "deeper": it contains or *enfolds* more and more levels or dimensions of reality internal to it, as part of its very makeup, its very being, its compound individuality, and so it is more *significant*: it *signifies* or indicates that more and more of the Kosmos is *internal* to it, just as a molecule internally contains atoms, actually enfolds them in its own being.

But the second diagram reminds us that the number of holons that actually realize these deeper dimensions becomes smaller and smaller. Figure 2-2 is depth, figure 2-3 is span. The one gets bigger, the other gets smaller. Greater depth, less span.

Kosmic Consciousness

Q: But the highest level—Spirit. Isn't Spirit everywhere? It's not a level, it's everywhere.

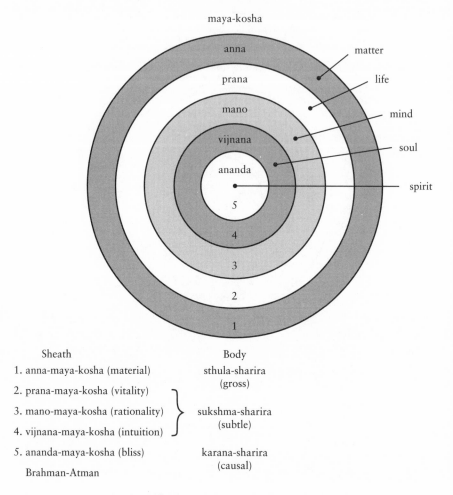

Figure 2-3. *Less span.*

KW: Each level transcends and includes its predecessor. Spirit transcends all, so it includes all. It is utterly beyond this world, but utterly embraces every single holon in this world. It permeates all of manifestation but is not merely manifestation. It is ever-present at every level or dimension, but is not merely a particular level or dimension. Transcends all, includes all, as the groundless Ground or Emptiness of all manifestation.

So Spirit is both the highest "level" in the holarchy, but it's also the paper on which the entire holarchy is written. It's the highest rung in the ladder, but it's also the wood out of which the entire ladder is made. It is both the Goal and the Ground of the entire sequence. I think this will become more obvious as we proceed.

Q: I don't want to get ahead of the story, but this also leads to an environmental ethics.

KW: Yes, the point of a genuine environmental ethics is that we are supposed to transcend and include all holons in a genuine embrace. Because human beings contain matter and life and mind, as components in their own makeup, then of course we must honor all of these holons, not only for their own *intrinsic worth*, which is the most important, but also because they are components in our own being, and destroying them is *literally* suicidal for us. It's not that harming the biosphere will eventually catch up with us and hurt us from the outside. It's that the biosphere is literally internal to us, is a part of our very being, our compound individuality—harming the biosphere is internal suicide, not just some sort of external problem.

So we can have a profoundly ecological view without being *merely* ecological, or reducing everything to the simple biosphere. We need an approach that transcends and includes ecology—precisely because the noosphere transcends and includes the biosphere, which transcends and includes the physiosphere. We don't need an approach that simply privileges ecology in a regressive flattening to one-dimensional life, to the flatland web of life.

Q: But many ecophilosophers and ecofeminists refer to mystical oneness with all nature, to what Bucke called "cosmic consciousness," where all beings are seen in an equal light, with no hierarchy at all, no higher or lower, just the great web of life.

KW: Yes, that type of mystical experience of equality is common in the higher stages of human development, and it is important to honor that.

But there are two very different issues here. Human identity can indeed expand to include the All—let's call it Kosmic consciousness, the *unio mystica*—just as in figure 2-2. Individual identity expands to Spirit and thus embraces the Kosmos—transcends all, includes all. And that is fine. But the number of humans actually realizing that supreme identity is very, very small. In other words, this very great depth has a very small span. As always, greater depth, less span.

But in that experience, the conscious identity is indeed an identity with the All, with the Kosmos. And in that identity, all beings, high or low, sacred or profane, are indeed seen to be perfect manifestations of

Spirit, precisely as they are—no lower, no higher. The *ultimate depth* is an ultimate oneness with the All, with the Kosmos.

But this *realization* is *not* given *equally* to all beings, even though all beings are equally manifestations of Spirit. This *realization* is the result of a developmental and evolutionary process of growth and transcendence.

And the web-of-life theorists usually focus on the equality of being and miss the holarchy of realization. They think that because an ant and an ape are both perfect manifestations of the Divine—which they are—then there is no difference in depth between them, which is reductionistic in the most painful fashion.

So we want our environmental ethics to honor all holons without exception as manifestations of Spirit, and also, at the same time, be able to make pragmatic distinctions in intrinsic worth, and realize that it is much better to kick a rock than an ape, much better to eat a carrot than a cow, much better to subsist on grains than on mammals.

If you agree with those statements, then you are acknowledging gradations in depth, gradations in intrinsic value—you are acknowledging a holarchy of value. Many ecophilosophers agree with those statements, but they can't say why, because they have a hierarchy that denies hierarchy—they have only the flatland web of life and bioequality, which is not only self-contradictory, it paralyzes pragmatic action and cripples intrinsic values.

The Spectrum of Consciousness

Q: Okay, I very much want to come back to all of that (in Part Three), but we need to stay on course. We were talking about the direction of evolution, the telos of the Kosmos, which is not random chance, but directionality.

KW: Evolution has a direction, yes, a principle of order out of chaos, as it is commonly phrased. In other words, a drive toward greater depth. Chance is defeated, depth emerges—the intrinsic value of the Kosmos increases with each unfolding.

Q: That's actually tenet 12, which is the last tenet I want to discuss. In that tenet, you give various indicators of directionality in evolution, which I'll just list. Evolution has a broad and general *tendency* to move in the direction of: increasing complexity, increasing differentiation/integration, increasing organization/structuration, increasing relative autonomy, increasing telos.

KW: Yes, those are some of the typically accepted—that is, scientifically accepted—directions of evolution. This doesn't mean that regression and dissolution don't occur—they do (dissolution is one of the four capacities of any holon). And it doesn't mean that every short-term development must follow those directions. As Michael Murphy says, evolution meanders more than it progresses. But over the long haul, evolution has a broad telos, a broad direction, which is particularly obvious with increasing differentiation—an atom to an amoeba to an ape!

But all of those scientific descriptions can generally be summarized as: the basic drive of evolution is to increase depth. This is the self-transcending drive of the Kosmos—to go beyond what went before, and yet include what went before, and thus increase its own depth.

Q: Now you also tie this in with consciousness. Because you add, "the greater the depth of a holon, the greater its degree of consciousness."

KW: Yes. Consciousness and depth are synonymous. All holons have some degree of depth, however minor, because there is no bottom. And with evolution, depth becomes greater and greater—consciousness becomes greater and greater. However much depth atoms have, molecules have more. And cells have more depth than molecules. And plants have more than cells. And primates more than plants.

There is a spectrum of depth, a spectrum of consciousness. And evolution unfolds that spectrum. Consciousness unfolds more and more, realizes itself more and more, comes into manifestation more and more. Spirit, consciousness, depth—so many words for the same thing.

Q: Since depth is everywhere, consciousness is everywhere.

KW: Consciousness is simply what depth looks like from the inside, from within. So yes, depth is everywhere, consciousness is everywhere, Spirit is everywhere. And as depth increases, consciousness increasingly awakens, Spirit increasingly unfolds. To say that evolution produces greater depth is simply to say that it unfolds greater consciousness.

Q: You use "unfolds and enfolds."

KW: Spirit is *unfolding* itself in each new transcendence, which it also *enfolds* into its own being at the new stage. Transcends and includes, brings forth and embraces, creates and loves, Eros and Agape, unfolds and enfolds—different ways of saying the same thing.

So we can summarize all this very simply: because evolution *goes beyond* what went before, but because it must *embrace* what went before, then its very nature is to transcend and include, and thus it has an inherent directionality, a secret impulse, toward increasing depth, increasing intrinsic value, increasing consciousness. In order for evolution to move at all, it must move in those directions—there's no place else for it to go!

Q: The general point being. . . ?

KW: Well, several. For one, because the universe has direction, we ourselves have direction. There is meaning in the movement, intrinsic value in the embrace. As Emerson put it, we lie in the lap of immense intelligence, which by any other name is Spirit. There is a theme inscribed on the original face of the Kosmos. There is a pattern written on the wall of Nothingness. There is a meaning in its every gesture, a grace in its every glance.

We—and all beings as such—are drenched in this meaning, afloat in a current of care and profound value, ultimate significance, intrinsic awareness. We are part and parcel of this immense intelligence, this Spirit-in-action, this God-in-the-making. We don't have to think of God as some mythic figure outside of the display, running the show. Nor must we picture it as some merely immanent Goddess, lost in the forms of her own production. Evolution is both God and Goddess, transcendence and immanence. It is immanent in the process itself, woven into the very fabric of the Kosmos; but it everywhere transcends its own productions, and brings forth anew in every moment.

Q: Transcends and includes.

KW: Indeed. And we are invited, I believe, to awaken as this process. The very Spirit in us is invited to become self-conscious, or even, as some would say, superconscious. Depth increases from subconscious to self-conscious to superconscious, on the way to its own shocking recognition, utterly one with the radiant All, and we awaken as that oneness.

What do you think? Is that crazy? Are the mystics and sages insane? Because they all tell variations on this same story, don't they? The story of awakening one morning and discovering that you are one with the All, in a timeless and eternal and infinite fashion.

Yes, maybe they are crazy, these divine fools. Maybe they are mumbling idiots in the face of the Abyss. Maybe they need a nice understanding therapist. Yes, I'm sure that would help.

But then, I wonder. Maybe the evolutionary sequence really is from matter to body to mind to soul to spirit, each transcending and including, each with a greater depth and greater consciousness and wider embrace. And in the highest reaches of evolution, maybe, just maybe, an individual's consciousness does indeed touch infinity—a total embrace of the entire Kosmos—a Kosmic consciousness that is Spirit awakened to its own true nature.

It's at least plausible. And tell me: is that story, sung by mystics and sages the world over, any crazier than the scientific materialism story, which is that the entire sequence is a tale told by an idiot, full of sound and fury, signifying absolutely nothing? Listen very carefully: just which of those two stories actually sounds totally insane?

I'll tell you what I think. I think the sages are the growing tip of the secret impulse of evolution. I think they are the leading edge of the self-transcending drive that always goes beyond what went before. I think they embody the very drive of the Kosmos toward greater depth and expanding consciousness. I think they are riding the edge of a light beam racing toward a rendezvous with God.

And I think they point to the same depth in you, and in me, and in all of us. I think they are plugged into the All, and the Kosmos sings through their voices, and Spirit shines through their eyes. And I think they disclose the face of tomorrow, they open us to the heart of our own destiny, which is also already right now in the timelessness of this very moment, and in that startling recognition the voice of the sage becomes your voice, the eyes of the sage become your eyes, you speak with the tongues of angels and are alight with the fire of a realization that never dawns nor ceases, you recognize your own true Face in the mirror of the Kosmos itself: your identity is indeed the All, and you are no longer *part* of that stream, you *are* that stream, with the All unfolding not around you but in you. The stars no longer shine out there, but in here. Supernovas come into being within your heart, and the sun shines inside your awareness. Because you transcend all, you embrace all. There is no final Whole here, only an endless process, and you are the opening or the clearing or the pure Emptiness in which the entire process unfolds—ceaselessly, miraculously, everlastingly, lightly.

The whole game is undone, this nightmare of evolution, and you are exactly where you were prior to the beginning of the whole show. With a sudden shock of the utterly obvious, you recognize your own Original Face, the face you had prior to the Big Bang, the face of utter Emptiness that smiles as all creation and sings as the entire Kosmos—and it is all undone in that primal glance, and all that is left is the smile, and the reflection of the moon on a quiet pond, late on a crystal clear night.

3

All Too Human

Q: The superconscious is a little ahead of our story! We have basically just covered evolution up to the emergence of human beings, the blossoming of the noosphere. You point out that each of the major stages of the evolution of human consciousness also follows the twenty tenets. So there is an overall continuity to evolution, from physiosphere to biosphere to noosphere.

KW: Which makes sense, doesn't it? And as evolution moves into the noosphere, then—based on the work of numerous researchers, such as Jean Gebser, Pitirim Sorokin, Robert Bellah, Jürgen Habermas, Michel Foucault, Peter Berger, to name a few—we can outline the predominant "worldviews" of the various epochs of human development. These stages, these worldviews, may be summarized as archaic, magic, mythic, rational, and existential.

Q: Which you also correlate with the major stages of technological/economic development.

KW: Yes, which are: foraging, horticultural, agrarian, industrial, and informational. (You can see these on figure 5-2 on page 119.)

Q: In each of those stages, you outline the types of economic production, the worldview, the modes of technology, the moral outlook, the legal codes, the types of religion . . .

KW: And here is where we also begin to look at the status of men and women in each of those stages. Because the relative status of men and women has varied tremendously across these stages, and the idea is to search for various factors that contributed to these changes.

Q: Which includes the "patriarchy."

KW: Well, yes. Based on the exciting work of recent feminist researchers, such as Kay Martin, Barbara Voorhies, Joyce Nielsen, and Janet Chafetz, we can fairly well reconstruct the relative status of men and women in each of these five or so major evolutionary stages of human development.

If we pull all of these sources together, we have: the five or six major stages of techno-economic evolution, as outlined, for example, by Gerhard Lenski; the relative status of men and women in each of those stages, as outlined by Chafetz and Nielsen and others; and the correlation with worldviews, as outlined by Gebser and Habermas.

Using these sources—and numerous others we needn't go into—we can reach some fairly sturdy conclusions about the relative status of men and women in each of these stages, and, more important, we can isolate the factors that contributed to these differences in status.

Foraging

Q: Let's give a few examples here, to see exactly what you mean.

KW: In foraging societies (also called hunting and gathering), the roles of men and women were sharply delineated and sharply separated. Men, indeed, did most of the hunting, and women most of the gathering and child rearing. An astonishing 97 percent of foraging societies follow that rather rigid pattern.

But because there were few possessions—the wheel hadn't even been invented—there was little emphasis placed on either the male or female value sphere. Men's work was men's work, and women's work was women's, and never the twain shall cross—there were very strong taboos about that, especially about menstruating women—but that didn't seem to be parlayed into any major sort of difference in status.

Because of this, these societies are eulogized by some feminists, but none of those feminists, I think, would really enjoy the rigidity of the gender roles. Um, just the opposite, I think.

Q: These societies emerged when?

KW: Foraging societies first emerged somewhere between a million and four hundred thousand years ago. As Habermas points out, what separated the first humans from apes and hominids was not an economy or even tools, but rather the invention of the role of the father—what he calls "the familialization of the male." By participating in both the productive hunt and the reproductive family, the father bridged these two value spheres, and marked off the beginning point of specifically human evolution. Since the pregnant female did not participate in the hunt, this job fell to the male, whether he wanted it or not (mostly not, I would guess).

But with the familialization of the male, we would see the beginning of the single, great, enduring, and nightmarish task of all subsequent civilization: the taming of testosterone.

Fuck it or kill it, but now in service of the family man. This is very funny, don't you think? In any event, the tribal structure has this family or kinship lineage, and different tribes, with different kinship lineages, have very, shall we say, testy relations with each other. You are on the fucking side or you are on the killing side.

The "carrying capacity" of these early foraging tribes was around forty people. The average life span, Lenski reports, was around 22.5 years. We are, of course, talking about the original tribal structure, and not about indigenous peoples today, who have been subjected to hundreds of thousands of years of further types of various development. But the basic tribal structure itself means a small group based specifically on kinship lineage, and a foraging tribe means one whose subsistence is based on pre-agriculture hunting and gathering.

The ecomasculinists (deep ecologists) are particularly fond of this period.

Q: They like these societies because they were ecologically sound.

KW: Some primal tribal societies were ecologically sound, and some definitely were not. Some tribes practiced cut and slash and burn, and some were responsible for the extinction of numerous species. As Theodore Roszak points out in The Voice of the Earth, a "sacred" outlook toward nature did not in any way guarantee an ecologically sound culture.

Men and women, everywhere and at all times, have despoiled the environment, mostly out of simple ignorance. Even the highly revered Mayan culture disappeared largely through depleting the surrounding rain forests. Modernity's ignorance about the environment is much more serious, simply because modernity has many more powerful means to destroy the environment. Tribal ignorance, on the other hand, was usually milder; but ignorance is ignorance, and is certainly nothing to emulate. The lack of means in foraging societies does not simply equate with the presence of wisdom.

So it's true that some people today eulogize the primal tribal societies because of their "ecological wisdom" or their "reverence for nature" or their "nonaggressive ways." But I don't think the evidence supports any of those views in a sweeping and general fashion. Rather, I eulogize the primal tribal societies for entirely different reasons: We are all the sons and daughters of tribes. The primal tribes are literally our roots, our foundations, the basis of all that was to follow, the structure upon which all subsequent human evolution would be built, the crucial ground floor upon which so much history would have to rest.

Today's existent tribes, and today's nations, and today's cultures, and today's accomplishments—all would trace their lineage in an unbroken fashion to the primal tribal holons upon which a human family tree was about to be built. And looking back on our ancestors in that light, I am struck with awe and admiration for the astonishing creativity—the *original* breakthrough creativity—that allowed humans to rise above a given nature and begin building a noosphere, the very process of which would bring Heaven down to Earth and exalt the Earth to Heaven, the very process of which would eventually bind all peoples of the world together in, if you will, one global tribe.

But in order for that to occur, the original, primal tribes had to find a way to transcend their *isolated* tribal kinship lineages: they had to find a way to go trans-tribal, and agriculture, not hunting, provided the means for this new transcendence.

Horticultural

Q: So foraging eventually gave way to agriculture. You point out that there are two very different types of farming cultures— horticultural and agrarian.

KW: Yes, horticultural is based on a hoe or simple digging stick. Agrarian is based on a heavy, animal-drawn plow.

Q: Sounds like a very small distinction.

KW: It is actually quite momentous. A digging stick or simple hoe can be used quite easily by a pregnant woman, and thus mothers were as capable as fathers of doing horticulture. Which they did. In fact, about 80 percent of the foodstuffs in these societies were produced by women (the men still went off and hunted, of course). Small surprise, then, that about one-third of these societies have female-only deities, and about one-third have male-and-female deities, and women's status in such societies was roughly equal with men's, although their roles were still, of course, sharply separated.

Q: These were matriarchal societies.

KW: Well, matrifocal. *Matriarchal* strictly means mother-ruled or mother-dominant, and there have never been any strictly matriarchal societies. Rather, these societies were more "equalitarian," with roughly equal status between men and women; and many such societies did indeed trace ancestry through the mother, and in other ways have a "matrifocal" arrangement. As I said, about one-third of these societies had female-only deities, particularly the Great Mother in her various guises, and conversely, *virtually every known Great Mother society is horticultural.* Almost any place you see the Great Mother religion, you know there is a horticultural background. This began roughly around 10,000 BCE in both the East and West.

Q: This is often the favorite period of the ecofeminists.

KW: Yes, these societies and a few maritime ones. Where the ecomasculinists love the foraging societies, the ecofeminists are quite fond of horticultural, Great Mother societies.

Q: Because they lived in harmony with the seasonal currents of nature, and in other ways were ecologically oriented.

KW: Yes, as long as you performed that annual ritual human sacrifice to keep the Great Mother happy and the crops growing, all was well with nature. Average life expectancy, according to Lenski's research, was about twenty-five years, which is pretty natural as well.

You see, it's the same problem as with the ecomasculinists, who eulogize the previous foraging tribes because they were supposed to be in touch with unadulterated nature. But what is "unadulterated nature"? The ecofeminists claim that these early farming societies were living with the seasonal currents of nature, in touch with the land, which was pure nature not interfered with by humans. But the ecomasculinists vociferously condemn farming of any sort as the first rape of nature, because you are no longer just gathering what nature offers; you are planting, you are artificially interfering with nature, you are digging into nature and scarring her face with farming technology, you are starting to rape the land. The heaven of the ecofeminists is the beginning of hell according to the ecomasculinists.

So yes, the ecomasculinists maintain, horticulture belongs to the Great Mother, and it was under the auspices of the Great Mother that the horrible crime of farming began, the massive crime that tore into the earth and first established human arrogance over the ways of the gentle giant of nature. And eulogizing this period is simply human arrogance at its very worst, the argument goes.

Q: You don't eulogize either foraging or horticultural, it seems.

KW: Well, evolution keeps moving, yes? Who are we to point to one period and say everything past that period was a colossal error, a heinous crime? According to whom, exactly? If we really are in the hands of the Great Spirit or the Great Mother, do we really think She doesn't know what She's doing? Tell you the truth, that seems like arrogance to me.

In any event, we're three or four major technological epochs down the line, and I doubt evolution will run backward for us.

Q: You refer often to "the dialectic of progress."

KW: Yes, the idea is that every stage of evolution eventually runs into its own inherent limitations, and these may act as triggers for the self-transcending drive. The inherent limitations create a type of turmoil, even chaos, and the system either breaks down (self-dissolution) or escapes this chaos by evolving to a higher degree of order (self-transcendence)—so-called order out of chaos. This new and higher order escapes the limitations of its predecessor, but then introduces its own limitations and problems that cannot be solved on its own level.

In other words, there is a price to be paid for every evolutionary step forward. Old problems are solved or defused, only to introduce new and sometimes more complex difficulties. But the retrogressive Romantics— whether the ecomasculinists or the ecofeminists—simply take the *problems* of the subsequent level and compare them with the *accomplishments* of the previous level, and thus claim everything has gone downhill past their favorite epoch. This is pretty perverse.

I think we all want to honor and acknowledge the many great accomplishments of past cultures the world over, and attempt to retain and incorporate as much of their wisdom as we can. But the train, for better or worse, is in motion, and has been from day one, and trying to drive by looking only in the rearview mirror is likely to cause even worse accidents.

Q: You point out that our epoch, too, will only pass.

KW: No epoch is finally privileged. We are all tomorrow's food. The process continues. And Spirit is found in the process itself, not in any particular epoch or time or place.

Agrarian

Q: I want to come back to that in a moment. We were talking about horticultural societies and the eventual shift to agrarian. Even though both are farming, this shift from hoe to plow was actually momentous.

KW: Quite extraordinary. Where a digging stick can easily be handled by a pregnant woman, an animal-drawn plow cannot. As Joyce Nielsen and Janet Chafetz have pointed out, those women who attempt to do so suffer significantly higher rates of miscarriage. In other words, it was to women's Darwinian advantage *not* to plow. And thus, with the introduction of the plow, a massive, absolutely massive shift in culture began.

First, virtually all of the foodstuffs were now produced solely by men. Men didn't want to do this, and they did not "take away" or "oppress" the female workforce in order to do so. *Both men and women decided* that heavy plowing was male work.

Women are not sheep; men are not pigs. This "patriarchy" was a conscious co-creation of men and women in the face of largely brutal circumstances. For the men, this certainly was no day at the beach, and was not nearly as much fun as, gosh, big-game hunting, which men had largely to give up. Furthermore, according to researchers such as Lenski and Chafetz, the men in these "patriarchal" societies had it considerably worse than the women, according to any number of objective "life quality" scales, starting with the fact that men alone were conscripted for defense, and men alone were asked to put life in jeopardy for the State. The idea that the patriarchy was an ole boys' club that was nothing but fun, fun, fun for men is based on rather poor research infected with much ideology, it seems.

For what we really learn from these various societies is that when the sexes are heavily *polarized*—that is, when their value spheres are sharply divided and compartmentalized—then both sexes suffer horribly.

Q: Which is what happened with the patriarchy?

KW: The polarization of the sexes, yes. Agrarian societies have the most highly sexually polarized structure of any known societal type (along with herding). This was not a male plot, nor a female plot for that matter, but was simply the best that these societies could do under the technological form of their organization at that time.

Thus, when men began to be virtually the sole producers of foodstuffs, then—no surprise—the deity figures in these cultures switched from female-oriented to almost exclusively male-oriented. Over 90 percent of agrarian societies, *wherever they appear*, have solely male primary deities.

Q: In *Sex, Ecology, Spirituality* you say, "Where females work the field with a hoe, God is a Woman; where males work the field with a plow, God is a Man."

KW: Well, that's a quick summary, yes. God and Goddess might have more profound and more transpersonal meanings—which we can talk about later—but for the *average mode* of human consciousness at that time, those mythic images usually represented much more prosaic realities. They represented, in many cases, the bedrock techno-economic realities of the given society: who put food on the table.

Q: Where God is a Man—this is one of the meanings of "patriarchy."

KW: Yes, and patriarchy, father rule, is correctly named. And here we briefly touch base with Marx: Because of the *social relations* that began to organize themselves around the *basic forces of production*—in this case, the plow—men then began to dominate the *public* sphere of government, education, religion, politics. And women dominated the *private* sphere of family, hearth, home. This division is often referred to as male production and female reproduction. Agrarian societies began to arise around 4000–2000 BCE, in both East and West, and this was the dominant mode of production until the industrial revolution.

Just as far-reaching was the fact that advanced farming created a massive surplus in foodstuffs, and this freed a great number of individuals—a great number of males—to pursue tasks other than food-gathering and food-creating, and now on a very large scale. That is, farming technology freed some men from production, but women were still largely tied to reproduction. This allowed a series of highly specialized classes to arise: men that could devote their time, not just to subsistence endeavors, but to extended cultural endeavors. Mathematics was invented, writing was invented, metallurgy—and specialized warfare.

The production of a surplus freed men, under the "kill it" part of testosterone, to begin building the first great military Empires, and across the globe, beginning around 3000 BCE, came the Alexanders and Caesars and Sargons and Khans, massive Empires that, paradoxically, began unifying disparate and contentious tribes into binding social orders. These mythic-imperial Empires would, with the rise of rationality and industrialization, give way to the modern nation-state.

And likewise, with agrarian farming a class of individuals would be freed to ponder their own existence. And thus, with these great agrarian cultures came the first sustained *contemplative* endeavors, endeavors that no longer located Spirit *merely* in the biosphere "out there" (magical, foraging to early horticultural) and not merely in the mythic Heavens "up there" (mythology, late horticultural to early agrarian), but rather located Spirit "in here," through the door of deep subjectivity, the door of interior awareness, the door of meditation and contemplation. And thus arose the great axial sages, whose . . .

Q: Axial?

KW: Karl Jaspers's term for this incredibly significant period in history, beginning around the sixth century BCE in both East and West, a period that produced the great "axial sages," Gautama Buddha, Lao Tzu, Parmenides, Socrates, Plato, Patanjali, Confucius, the sages of the Upanishads, and so forth.

Q: All men.

KW: Well, agrarian is *always* all men. And one of the great tasks of spirituality in the postmodern world is to complement and balance this male-oriented spirituality with its correlative female forms. We don't want to simply toss out everything these great wisdom traditions have to teach us, because that would be catastrophic. It would be like saying we refuse to use the wheel because a man invented it.

But indeed, virtually all of these great traditions arose in an atmosphere where men spoke to God directly and women spoke to God only through their husbands.

Industrial

Q: I want to come back to that issue of male and female spirituality, because it involves what you call "Ascending" and "Descending" spirituality, or God and Goddess spirituality, and how we might balance these two approaches.

But first, to finish with agrarian and the shift to industrial. How does this relate to "modernity"?

KW: Both "modernity" and "postmodernity" are used in a bewildering variety of ways. But "modernity" usually means the events that were set in motion with the Enlightenment, from Descartes to Locke to Kant, and the concomitant technical developments, which moved from feudal agrarian with a mythic worldview to industrialization and a rational worldview. And "postmodernity" usually means, in the broadest sense, the whole sweep of post-Enlightenment developments, which also includes postindustrial developments.

Q: So we are at the beginning of modernity, the shift from agrarian to industrialization. . . .

KW: Industrialization, for all of its horrors and all of its nightmarish secondary effects, was first and foremost a technological means to secure subsistence *not* from human muscle working on nature, but from machine power working on nature. As long as agrarian societies demanded physical human labor for subsistence (plowing), those societies *inevitably* and *unavoidably* placed a premium on *male* physical strength and mobility. No known agrarian society has anything even vaguely resembling women's rights.

But within a century of industrialization—which removed the emphasis on male physical strength and replaced it with gender-neutral engines—the women's movement emerged for the *first time in history* on any sort of large scale. Mary Wollstonecraft's *Vindication of the Rights of Women* was written in 1792; it is the first major feminist treatise anywhere in history.

It is not that all of a sudden, women became smart and strong and determined after a million years of oppression, dupedom, and sheepdom. It is that the social structures had evolved, for the first time in history, to a point that physical strength did not overwhelmingly determine power in culture. Biology was no longer destiny when it came to gender roles. Within a mere few centuries—a blink in evolutionary time—women had acted with lightning speed to secure legal rights to own property, to vote, and to "be their own persons," that is, to have a property in their own selves.

Q: The data seem to support this view, correct?

KW: The empirical evidence presented by the feminist researchers that I mentioned indicates that, as Chafetz puts it, the status of women in late industrial societies is *higher* than in any other surplus-producing society in history—including the horticultural.

Women who vocally condemn late industrial (and informational) society and glowingly eulogize Great Mother horticultural societies seem to be out of touch with a good deal of evidence, or they very selectively choose a few nice items about yesterday and ignore the rest of yesterday's nightmare, and compare that "Eden" with nothing but the very worst of modernity. This is a very suspect endeavor.

None of which means further gains aren't required in today's world, for both men and women. Remember, the polarization of the sexes is brutally hard on each. Men and women both need to be liberated from the horrendous constraints of agrarian polarization. Industrialization began this liberation, began to expand gender roles beyond biological givens—transcend and include—but we need to continue developing this freedom and transcendence.

Q: For example?

KW: For example, when men are no longer automatically expected to be the primary producers and the primary defenders, we might see the average life expectancy of men rise a little bit more toward the female level. And see women less restricted to roles involving merely reproduction, or home and hearth. The brutalities were equal and shared so the liberation will be equally shared and beneficial, I think. If anything, the men have more to gain, which is why, in the United States, polls consistently showed that a majority of men favored the Equal Rights Amendment but a majority of women opposed it, so it didn't pass, unfortunately.

Q: What about industrialization and the eco-crisis? Surely that is one of the major downsides of modernity, of the "dialectic of progress."

KW: Indeed. But it's an extremely tricky situation. The primary cause of any ecological devastation is, as we were saying, simple ignorance. It is only with scientific knowledge of the biosphere, of the precise ways in which all holons in the biosphere are interrelated, including the biological holons of the human being—it is only with that knowledge that men and women can actually attune their actions with the biosphere. A simple or sacred respect for nature will not do. A sacred outlook on nature did not prevent numerous tribes from despoiling the environment out of simple and innocent ignorance, and did not prevent the Mayans from devastating the rain forests, and it will not prevent us from doing the same thing, again out of ignorance.

Roszak points out that it is modern science, and modern science alone—the ecological sciences and systems sciences, for example—that can directly show us how and why our actions are corroding the biosphere. If the primal tribes knew that by cut and burn they would ruin their habitat and endanger their own lives—if they actually knew that with a scientific certainty—then they would at least have thought about it a little more carefully before they began their bio-destruction. If the Mayans knew that in killing the rain forests they were killing themselves, they would have stopped immediately, or at least paused considerably. But ignorance is ignorance; whether innocent or greedy, sacred or profane, ignorance destroys the biosphere.

Q: But the means have changed.

KW: That's the second point, indeed. Ignorance backed by primal or tribal technology is capable of inflicting limited damage. You can only do so much damage to the biosphere with a bow and arrow. An atomic bomb is something else. The *same* ignorance backed by industry is capable of killing the entire world. So we have to separate those two issues—the ignorance and the means of inflicting that ignorance—because with modernity and science we have, for the first time in history, a way to overcome our ignorance, at precisely the same time that we have created the means to make this ignorance absolutely genocidal on a global scale.

Q: So it's good news, bad news.

KW: The predicament of modernity, yes. Finally, we know better. At the same time, if we don't act on this knowledge, then finally, we all die. Brings new meaning to the Confucian curse, "May you live in interesting times."

4

The Great Postmodern Revolution

Q: Now we just ran through the techno-economic base of each epoch. What about the corresponding *worldviews*?

KW: The general point is fairly simple: different stages of consciousness growth present a different view of the world. The world looks different—is different—at each stage. As new cognitive capacities unfold and evolve, the Kosmos looks at itself with different eyes, and it sees quite different things.

For convenience, I generally call these worldviews archaic, magic, mythic, rational, and existential, with higher stages possible. You can see these on figure 5-2.

Q: So these are different ways that we look at the world?

KW: Yes, but we have to be very careful here. This might seem to be splitting hairs, but it really is very important: it's not that there is a single, pregiven world, and we simply look at it differently. Rather, as the Kosmos comes to know itself more fully, *different worlds* emerge.

It's like an acorn growing to an oak. An oak isn't a different picture of the same unchanging world present in the acorn. The oak has components in its own being that are quite new and different from anything found in the acorn. The oak has leaves, branches, roots, and so on, none of which are present in the acorn's actual "worldview" or "worldspace." Different worldviews create different worlds, enact different worlds, they aren't just the same world seen differently.

The Postmodern Watershed

Q: I understand the distinction, but it does seem a bit of hairsplitting. Why exactly is this distinction important?

KW: It's crucially important, because in many ways it's the great watershed separating the modern and postmodern approaches to knowledge. We want to take into account this extraordinary revolution in human understanding.

And, in fact, there is simply no way to carry these types of discussions forward unless we talk about the momentous differences between the modern and postmodern approaches to knowledge. But it's not all dull and dry. In many ways, it's even the key to locating Spirit in the postmodern world.

Q: Okay, so modern and postmodern . . .

KW: You've heard of all the "new paradigm" approaches to knowledge?

Q: Well, only that everybody seems to want the new paradigm. Or *a* new paradigm, anyway.

KW: Yes, well, the *old* paradigm that everybody *doesn't* want is the Enlightenment paradigm, which is also called the modern paradigm. It has dozens of other names, all pronounced with scorn and disgust: the Newtonian, the Cartesian, the mechanistic, the mirror of nature, the reflection paradigm.

By whatever name, that paradigm is now thought to be hopelessly outdated or at least severely limited, and everybody is in an absolute dither to get the new and therefore postmodern, or post-Enlightenment, paradigm.

But in order to understand just what a postmodern paradigm might look like, we need to understand the beast that it is desperately trying to replace.

Q: We need to understand the fundamental Enlightenment paradigm.

KW: Yes. And the fundamental Enlightenment paradigm is known as the *representation paradigm*. This is the idea that you have the self or the subject, on the one hand, and the empirical or sensory world, on the other, and all valid knowledge consists in making *maps* of the empirical world, the single and simple "pregiven" world. And if the map is accurate, if it correctly represents, or corresponds with, the empirical world, then that is "truth."

Q: Hence, the representation paradigm.

KW: Yes. The map could be an actual map, or a theory, or a hypothesis, or an idea, or a table, or a concept, or some sort of representation—in general, some sort of map of the objective world.

All of the major Enlightenment theorists, whether they were holistic or atomistic or anything in between—they all subscribed to this representation paradigm, to the belief in a single empirical world that could be patiently mapped with empirical methods.

And please remember that—whether the world was atomistic or holistic is completely beside the point. What they all agreed on was the mapping paradigm itself.

Q: But what's wrong with that representation paradigm? I mean, we do it all the time.

KW: It's not that it's wrong. It's just very narrow and very limited. But the difficulties of the representation paradigm are rather subtle, and it took a very long time—several centuries, actually—to realize what the problem was.

There are many ways to summarize the limitations of the representation paradigm, the idea that knowledge consists basically in making maps of the world. But the simplest way to state the problem with maps is: *they leave out the mapmaker.* What was being utterly ignored was the fact that the mapmaker might itself bring something to the picture!

Q: All of this reflecting and mapping left out the mapmaker.

KW: Yes. And no matter how different the various *postmodern* attacks were, *they were all united in an attack on the representation paradigm.* They all perfectly assaulted the reflection paradigm, the "mirror of nature" paradigm—the idea that there is simply a single empirical world or empirical nature, and that knowledge consists solely in mirroring or reflecting or mapping this one true world. All "post-Enlightenment" or "postmodern" parties agreed that this "mirror of nature" idea was utterly, hopelessly, massively naive.

Beginning especially with Kant, and running through Hegel, Schopenhauer, Nietzsche, Dilthey, Heidegger, Foucault, Derrida—all the great "postmodern" theorists—in all of them we find a powerful attack on the mapping paradigm, because it fails to take into account the self that is making the maps in the first place.

This self did not just parachute to earth. It has its own characteristics, its own structures, its own development, its own *history*—and all of those influence and govern what it will see, and what it *can* see, in that supposedly "single" world just lying around. The parachutist is up to its neck in contexts and backgrounds that determine just what it can see in the first place!

So the great postmodern discovery was that neither the self nor the world is simply pregiven, but rather they exist in contexts and backgrounds that have a history, a development.

Q: That evolve.

KW: That evolve, yes. The mapmaker is not a little disembodied, ahistorical, self-contained monad, antiseptic and isolated and untouched by the world it maps. The self does not have an unchanging *essence* so much as it has a *history*, and the mapmaker will make *quite different maps* at the various stages of its own history, its own growth and development.

So in this developmental process, the subject will picture the world quite differently, based not so much on what is actually "out there" in some pregiven world, but based in many ways on what the *subject itself brings to the picture.*

Q: Kant's "Copernican revolution": the mind forms the world more than the world forms the mind.

KW: Not in all ways, but in many important ways, yes. And Hegel then added the crucial point, the point that, in one way or another, defines all postmodern theories: the mind, the subject, can "*only be conceived as one that has developed.*"

Nietzsche, for example, would turn this into genealogy, the investigation of the history of a worldview that we simply took for granted, that we assumed was simply the case for people everywhere, but in fact turns out to be quite limited and historically situated. And one way or another, all postmodern roads lead to Nietzsche.

Q: So the overall point is . . .

KW: The subject is not some detached, isolated, pregiven, and fully formed little entity that simply parachutes to earth and then begins innocently "mapping" what it sees lying around out there in the "real" world, the "real" territory, the pregiven world.

Rather, the subject is *situated* in contexts and currents of its own development, its own history, its own evolution, and the "pictures" it makes of "the world" depend in large measure not so much on "the world" as on this "history."

Q: Yes, I see. And this relates to our present discussion, how?

KW: Well, one of the things we want to do is *trace the history of these worldviews.* They are part of evolution in the human domain—which means, the various forms of Spirit-in-action as it unfolds through the human mind. At each of these stages, the Kosmos looks at itself with new eyes, and thus brings forth new worlds not previously existing.

Two Paths in Postmodernity

Q: So these worldviews develop.

KW: Yes. And the overall idea that worldviews develop—that neither the world nor the self is simply pregiven—that is the great postmodern discovery.

Faced with this discovery of "not pregiven," a theorist can then take *one of two routes* through this new and confusing postmodern landscape, where nothing is foundational.

The first, and probably most common, is to go the route of extreme *constructivism*—which is the *strong version* of "not pregiven." That is, because worldviews are not pregiven, you can claim that they are all arbitrary. They are simply "constructed" by cultures based on nothing much more substantial than shifting tastes.

So we have all these books with titles like the social construction of sex, the social construction of food, the social construction of labor, the social construction of clothing, and so on. I keep expecting to see something like the social construction of the large intestine.

Everything is "socially constructed"—this is the mantra of the extremist wing of postmodernism. They think that different cultural worldviews are entirely arbitrary, anchored in nothing but power or prejudice or some "ism" or another—sexism, racism, speciesism, phallocentrism, capitalism, logocentrism, or my favorite, phallologocentrism. Wow! Does that puppy come with batteries or what?

Q: Do those approaches have any merit at all?

KW: They do. It's only that the strong constructivist approach is simply too strong, too extremist. Worldviews just aren't that arbitrary; they are actually *constrained* by the currents in the Kosmos, and those currents *limit* how much a culture can arbitrarily "construct." We won't find a consensus worldview, for example, where men give birth or where apples fall upward. So much for arbitrary worldviews. They are not "merely constructed" in the sense of totally relative and arbitrary. Even Derrida now concedes this elemental point.

A diamond will cut a piece of glass, no matter what words we use for "diamond," "cut," and "glass," and no matter what culture we find them in. It is not necessary to go overboard and deny the pre-existence of the sensorimotor world altogether! And that sensorimotor world—the cosmos and the bios—constrains the worldviews "from below," so to speak.

Further, cultural construction is limited and *constrained* by the currents in the noosphere itself. The noosphere develops, it evolves. That is, it also follows the twenty tenets, and those currents most definitely constrain and limit the construction.

So in these and many other ways, the real currents in the Kosmos constrain worldviews and prevent them from being merely collective hallucinations. Worldviews, as we'll see, are anchored in validity claims, and these claims work because the currents are real.

Q: Isn't Foucault often associated with this extreme constructivism?

KW: Yes, he started down this road, only to find that it is a dead end.

Q: In what way?

KW: If the constructivist stance is taken too far, it defeats itself. It says, all worldviews are arbitrary, all truth is relative and merely culture-bound, there are no universal truths. But that stance itself claims to be universally true. It is claiming everybody's truth is relative *except mine*, because mine is absolutely and universally true. I alone have the universal truth, and all you poor schmucks are relative and culture-bound.

This is the performative contradiction hidden in all extreme multicultural postmodern movements. And *their* absolute truth ends up being very ideological, very elitist in the worst sense, it seems. Foucault even called his own early attempts in this direction "arrogant," a point most of his American followers have ignored, unfortunately.

This extreme constructivism is really just a postmodern form of nihilism: there is no truth in the Kosmos, only those notions that men force on others. This nihilism looks into the face of the Kosmos and sees an unending hall of mirrors, which finally show it nothing but its own egoic nastiness reflected to infinity. This is a major movement in American universities.

Q: Extreme constructivism. So that is one path taken in postmodernity.

KW: Yes. That's the strong version, which is too strong, too constructivist.

The other is the more moderate approach, a more moderate constructivism, and the most common version of that is now developmental or evolutionary. In its numerous and quite varied forms—Hegel, Marx, Nietzsche, Heidegger, Gebser, Piaget, Bellah, late Foucault, Habermas.

This approach recognizes that world and worldview are not altogether pregiven, but rather develop in history. And so it simply *investigates the actual history* and unfolding of these worldviews, not as a series of merely arbitrary flailings-around, but rather as an evolutionary or developmental pattern, governed in part by the currents of evolution itself.

Q: Governed by the twenty tenets.

KW: In my particular version of developmentalism, yes, but that's my particular take.

But the important point is, in many of these developmental or evolutionary approaches, each worldview gives way to its successor because certain *inherent limitations* in the earlier worldview become apparent. This generates a great deal of disruption and chaos, so to speak, and the system, if it doesn't simply collapse, *escapes this chaos* by *evolving* to a more *highly organized* pattern. These new and higher patterns solve or defuse the earlier problems, but then introduce their own recalcitrant problems and inherent limitations that *cannot* be solved on their own level—the same process of evolution we see in the other domains as well.

Q: You mentioned these worldviews as archaic, magic, mythic, rational, and existential, with the possibility of higher stages yet to come.

KW: Yes, that's one way to summarize them, in a very general fashion. We can discuss the specifics of these worldviews later, if you like. But for now, as I said, I correlate these "mental" worldviews with the "material" modes of production at each stage of human evolution. So corresponding with those worldviews that you just mentioned, we have, respectively: foraging, horticultural, agrarian, industrial, informational. So I'll often refer to them conjointly as mythic-agrarian, or rational-industrial, and so on, understanding that there are all sorts of overlaps and hybrids (see figure 5-2).

Q: In a sentence . . .

KW: The worldview is the mind, the base is the body, of Spirit. These bodyminds evolve, and bring forth *new worlds* in the process, as Spirit unfolds its own potential, a radiant flower in Kosmic spring, not so much Big Bang as Big Bloom.

And at each stage of development the world looks different because the world *is* different—and there is the great postmodern revelation.

On the Edge of Tomorrow

Q: I have two technical questions. How exactly do the best of the postmodern approaches overcome the so-called Cartesian dualism?

KW: The representation paradigm was dualistic in this sense: the subject doing the mapping was not really a part of the world that was being mapped. Or so it was thought. The alien mapmaker simply stood back from the pregiven world and mapped it, as if the two entities had virtually nothing in common.

Most "new paradigm" approaches still fall into this dualistic trap, because it is a very, very subtle trap. Most new paradigm approaches think that simply getting a *more accurate map* will solve the problem. If we had a nice holistic and systems map, instead of a nasty atomistic and mechanistic map, that would heal the dualism.

But, as Hegel (among others) forcefully pointed out, that doesn't solve the real problem at all, but merely continues it in subtler ways. It still assumes that the thought process is so basically different from the real world that the thought process can either reflect that world accurately and holistically, or reflect it inaccurately and atomistically. But that belief *is* itself the hidden Cartesian dualism.

Rather, said Hegel, we must realize that thoughts are not merely a reflection on reality, but are also a movement of that very reality itself. Thought is a performance of that which it seeks to know, and not a simple mirror of something unrelated to itself. The mapmaker, the self, the thinking and knowing subject, is actually a product and a performance of that which it seeks to know and represent.

In short, thought is itself a movement of that which it seeks to know. It's not that there is a map on the one hand and the territory on the other—that's the nasty Cartesian dualism—but rather that the map is itself a performance of the territory it is trying to map.

This nondualistic approach doesn't deny the representation paradigm altogether; but it does say that at a much deeper level, thought itself *cannot* deviate from the currents of the Kosmos, because thought is a product and performance of those very currents. And the task of philosophy, as it were, is not simply to clarify the maps and *correct* their deviations from reality, but to *elucidate* these deeper currents from which thought couldn't deviate even if it wanted to!

Q: In simpler terms?

KW: In Zen there is a saying, "That which one can deviate from is not the true Tao." In other words, in some ways our knowledge is indeed a matter of correcting our inaccurate maps; but also, and at a much deeper level, there is a Tao, a Way, a Current of the Kosmos, from which we have not deviated and could never deviate. And part of our job is to find this deeper Current, this Tao, and express it, elucidate it, celebrate it.

And as long as we are caught in merely trying to correct our maps, then we will miss the ways in which both correct and incorrect maps are equally expressions of Spirit.

Thus, the "new paradigm" approaches, such as many of the ecophilosophers', are constantly telling us that we have deviated from nature, which is true enough. But however true that is, I believe it suggests that these theorists have not understood the true Tao, from which we do not, and could never, deviate. And it was this much deeper truth that the genuine Nondual traditions, East and West, attempted to elucidate— which is the real overcoming of the Cartesian dualism!

Might this become clearer when we talk about higher levels of development?

Q: Actually, that's my second technical question. If worldviews have evolved from archaic to magic to mythic to rational and existential, who's to say there aren't higher worldviews down the road?

KW: Yes, that's important, isn't it? To paraphrase the man, "There are more things in heaven and earth than are dreamt of in our worldview."

Magic never in its wildest dreams thought that it would be trumped by mythic. And the mythic gods and goddesses never imagined that reason could and would destroy them. And here we sit, in our rational worldview, all smug and confident that nothing higher will sweep out of the heavens and completely explode our solid perceptions, undoing our very foundations.

And yet surely, the transrational lies in wait. It is just around the corner, this new dawn. Every stage transcends and includes, and thus inescapably, unavoidably it seems, the sun will rise on a world tomorrow that in many ways transcends reason. . . .

And so, to quote another famous theorist, "Fasten your seatbelts, it's going to be a bumpy night."

Transcendence and Repression

Q: So how can you tell if there is any sort of advantage to one worldview or another?

KW: Transcends and includes. As the higher stages of consciousness emerge and develop, they themselves include the basic components of the earlier worldview, then add their own new and more differentiated perceptions. They transcend and include. Because they are more inclusive, they are more adequate.

So it's not that the earlier worldview is totally wrong and the new worldview is totally right. The earlier one was adequate, the new one is more adequate. If it's not more adequate, then it won't be selected by evolution, it won't catch the currents of the Kosmos; it will go by the wayside, flotsam and jetsam on the shores of what might have been.

Of course, this doesn't mean that a "higher" worldview is without its own problems—just the contrary. Wherever there is the possibility of *transcendence*, there is, by the very same token, the possibility of *repression*. The higher might not just transcend and include, it might transcend and repress, exclude, alienate, dissociate.

And so, in following the emergence of worldviews, we have to keep a constant watch for possible *repressions* and *dissociations* that have occurred, and are still occurring, in the historical process.

The point is that *the animal that can transcend can also repress*—at any level. The Mayans had already moved from foraging to horticulture, and that meant *not only* that they could begin to bind various contentious tribes into a larger and solidified social structure—and *not only* that they could, via farming, free a class of priests to begin developing mathematics and astronomy and a sophisticated calendar—*but also* that they, in a way foragers never could, begin to deplete the rain forests. They transcended mere foraging, only to go too far and dissociate themselves in certain crucial ways from the biosphere, which was altogether suicidal.

They didn't differentiate and integrate, they dissociated and alienated. They didn't transcend and include, they repressed and denied. Since the biosphere is an internal component of the human holon, they secured their own destruction.

So this theme—transcendence versus repression—is an altogether crucial theme of historical development, and we want to watch carefully for signs of repression at each stage of human evolution, individual and collective. And this includes, of course, the massive problems with rational-industrialization.

Q: So each new worldview faces its own grave problems.

KW: *Creates* its own grave problems. The solution of the old problem is the creation of a new one—they come into being together, although the new problems usually surface only as the worldview approaches its own demise. This is the wonder, and this the nightmare, of worldviews.

And we are at the point where the mental, rational, industrial worldview is running into the grave problems *inherent* in its own organization. We have run up against our own limitations. We have met the enemy, and of course it is us. The *modern* is struggling to give way to the *post-modern*.

The phase-specific, phase-appropriate modern worldview, having served its purposes, is now living in its own fumes. We are breathing our own exhaust. And how we handle this, how we collectively handle this, will determine whether a new and more adequate worldview emerges to defuse these problems, or whether we are buried in our own wastes.

Spirit has run up against its own limitations at this stage in its unfolding. This extraordinary modern flower blossomed in its glorious spring, and now can do nothing but watch its own leaves fall dead on the ground of a rising tomorrow. And what indeed will bloom in that new field?

5

The Four Corners of the Kosmos

Q: So is it at least fair to say that you believe we are approaching the end limit of the rational-industrial worldview?

KW: Only if we are very careful about how to interpret that. The rise of modernity—and by "modernity" I mean specifically the rational-industrial worldview, and roughly, the Enlightenment in general—served many useful and extraordinary purposes. We might mention: the rise of democracy; the banishing of slavery; the emergence of liberal feminism; the widespread emergence of empirical sciences, including the systems sciences and ecological sciences; an increase in average life span of almost three decades; the introduction of relativity and perspectivism in art and morals and science; the move from ethnocentric to worldcentric morality; and in general the undoing of dominator social hierarchies in numerous significant ways.

Those are rather extraordinary accomplishments, don't you think? The antimodernist critics who do nothing but condemn modernity, while basking in these many benefits, are being quite unfair, it seems to me.

On the other hand, the giddy promoters of modernity as nothing but a great progress report ignore the recalcitrant problems that modernity has never solved and likely can never solve.

Q: The inherent problems or limitations built into modernity.

KW: Built into the rational-industrial worldview, yes.

Q: So moving "beyond modernity"—going "postmodern"—requires what, exactly?

KW: Well, in simple terms, to transcend and include modernity—or rational-industrialization—would mean, for the *transcend* part, that we have to (1) be open to modes of consciousness that move beyond mere rationality, and (2) embed them in modes of techno-economic structures that move beyond industrialization. In other words, a change of consciousness embedded in a change of institutions. Either one alone will probably not work.

Q: So, trans-rational and trans-industrial.

KW: Yes, remembering that both rationality and industry will be *included* as well, but now as mere components in a more balanced, more inclusive, more integrated stance that will incorporate—and limit—rationality and industry. What we might call sustainable rationality, sustainable industry.

But in some ways, rationality and industry, left to their own devices, have become cancers in the body politic, runaway growths that are malignant in their effects. They overstep their limits, overrun their functions, and drift into various dominator hierarchies of one sort or another. To transcend modernity is to negate or limit these overpowering facets, while including their benign and beneficial aspects. The coming transformation will transcend and include these features of modernity, incorporating their essentials and limiting their power.

And, of course, this new and wonderful transformation, which everybody seems to be yearning for, will nevertheless bring its own recalcitrant problems and brutal limitations. It will defuse some of the problems of rational-industrialization, which is wonderful, but it will create and unleash its own severe difficulties.

And so, if this is specifically what we mean by a coming transformation—as opposed to some utopian new age—then yes, I believe this transformation is definitely under way.

The Four Quadrants

Q: So part of the coming transformation will involve both a change in consciousness and a change in institutions.

KW: I believe so, yes. It will actually involve a new worldview, set in a new techno-economic base, with a new mode of self-sense, possessing new behavioral patterns.

Q: Okay, that gets us directly into what you call *the four quadrants* (see figure 5-1). But before we talk about these four quadrants, I'm curious, how did you arrive at this concept? I haven't seen it before, and I was wondering how you came up with it.

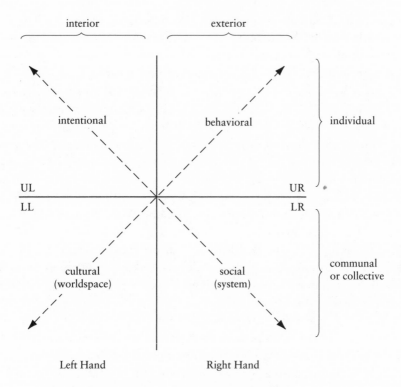

FIGURE 5-1. *The four quadrants.*

KW: You mean the mental steps I went through to arrive at the four quadrants?

Q: Yes.

KW: Well, if you look at the various "new paradigm" theorists— from holists to ecofeminists to deep ecologists to systems thinkers—you find that all of them are offering various types of holarchies, of hierarchies. Even the anti-hierarchy ecophilosophers offer their own hierarchy, which is usually something like: atoms are parts of molecules, which are parts of cells, which are parts of individual organisms, which are parts of families, which are parts of cultures, which are parts of the total biosphere. That is their defining hierarchy, their defining holarchy, and except for some confusion about what "biosphere" means, that is a fairly accurate holarchy.

And likewise, orthodox researchers offer their own hierarchies. We find hierarchies in moral development, in ego development, in cognitive development, in self needs, in defense mechanisms, and so on. And these, too, seem to be largely accurate. We also find developmental holarchies in everything from Marxism to structuralism to linguistics to computer programming—it's simply endless.

In other words, whether it's realized or not, most of the maps of the world that have been offered are in fact holarchical, for the simple reason that holarchies are impossible to avoid (because holons are impossible to avoid). We have literally hundreds and hundreds of these holarchical maps from around the world—East and West, North and South, ancient and modern—and many of these maps included the mapmaker as well.

So at one point I simply started making lists all of these holarchical maps—conventional and new age, Eastern and Western, premodern and modern and postmodern—everything from systems theory to the Great Chain of Being, from the Buddhist vijnanas to Piaget, Marx, Kohlberg, the Vedantic koshas, Loevinger, Maslow, Lenski, Kabbalah, and so on. I had literally hundreds of these things, these maps, spread out on legal pads all over the floor.

At first I thought these maps were all referring to the same territory, so to speak. I thought they were all different versions of an essentially similar holarchy. There were just too many similarities and overlaps in all of them. So by comparing and contrasting them all, I thought I might be able to find the single and basic holarchy that they were all trying to represent in their own ways.

The more I tried this, the more it became obvious that it wouldn't work. These various holarchies had some undeniable similarities, but they differed in certain profound ways, and the exact nature of these differences was not obvious at all. And most confusing of all, in some of these holarchical maps, the holons got *bigger* as development progressed, and in others, they became *smaller* (I didn't yet understand that evolution produces greater depth, less span). It was a real mess, and at several points I decided to just chuck it, forget it, because nothing was coming of this research.

But the more I looked at these various holarchies, the more it dawned on me that there were actually *four very different types* of holarchies, four very different types of holistic sequences. As you say, I don't think this had been spotted before—perhaps because it was so simple; at any event it was news to me. But once I put all of these holarchies into these four groups—and they instantly fell into place at that point—then it was very obvious that each holarchy in each group was indeed dealing with the same territory, but overall we had four different territories, so to speak.

Q: These four territories, these four different types of holistic sequences, you call the four quadrants.

KW: Yes, you can see these in figure 5-1. In figure 5-2, I've added some examples. I must emphasize that this figure only gives a very few examples from each quadrant, but you can get the general idea.

So the question then became, how did these four types of holarchies relate to each other? They couldn't just be radically different holistic sequences. They had to touch each other somehow.

Eventually it dawned on me that these four quadrants have a very simple foundation. These four types of holarchies are actually dealing

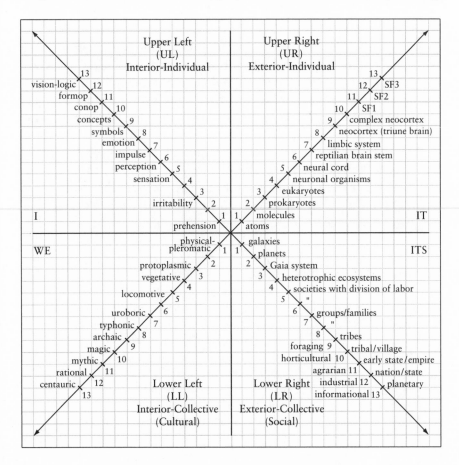

FIGURE 5-2. *Some details of the four quadrants.*

with the *inside* and the *outside* of a holon, in both its *individual* and *collective* forms—and that gives us four quadrants.

Inside and outside, singular and plural—some of the simplest distinctions we can make, and these very simple features, which are present in all holons, generate these four quadrants, or so I maintain. All four of these holarchies are dealing with real aspects of real holons—which is why these four types of holarchies keep insistently showing up on the various maps around the world.

It appears that these are some very bedrock realities, these four corners of the Kosmos.

Intentional and Behavioral

Q: Perhaps a few examples.

KW: Okay. The four quadrants are the *interior* and *exterior* of the *individual* and the *collective*, which you can see in figures 5-1 and 5-2.

We can start with the individual holon, in both its interior and exterior aspects. In other words, with the Upper-Left quadrant and the Upper-Right quadrant. Figure 5-3 is a little more detailed map of these two quadrants.

If you look at the Upper-Right column first, you can see the typical holarchy presented in any standard biology textbook. Each level transcends and includes its predecessor. Each level includes the basics of the previous level and then adds its own distinctive and defining characteristics, its own emergents. Each of these follows the twenty tenets, and so on.

prehension	atoms
irritability	cells (genetic)
rudimentary sensation	metabolic organisms (e.g., plants)
sensation	protoneuronal organisms (e.g., coelenterata)
perception	neuronal organisms (e.g., annelids)
perception/impulse	neural cord (fish/amphibians)
impulse/emotion	brain stem (reptiles)
emotion/image	limbic system (paleomammals)
symbols	neocortex (primates)
concepts	complex neocortex (humans)
UPPER LEFT	UPPER RIGHT

FIGURE 5-3. *The interior and the exterior of the individual.*

But notice that these are all *exterior* descriptions—it's what these holons look like from the outside, in an objective and empirical manner. Thus, in a scientific text, you will find the limbic system, for example, described in detail—its components, its biochemistry, when and how it evolved, how it relates to other parts of the organism, and so on. And you will probably find it mentioned that the limbic system is the home of certain very fundamental *emotions*, certain basic types of sex and aggression and fear and desire, whether that limbic system appears in horses or humans or apes.

But of those emotions, of course, you will not find much description, because emotions pertain to the *interior experience* of the limbic system. These emotions and the awareness that goes with them are what the holon with a limbic system *experiences from within*, on the *inside*, in its *interior*. And *objective* scientific descriptions are not much interested in that interior consciousness, because that interior space cannot be accessed in an objective, empirical fashion. You can only *feel* these feelings from within. When you experience a sort of primal joy, for example, even if you are a brain physiologist, you do not say to yourself, Wow, what a limbic day. Rather, you describe these feelings in intimate, personal, emotional terms, *subjective* terms: I feel wonderful, it's great to be alive, or whatnot.

So in the Upper-Left column, you can see a list of some of the basic types of *subjective* or *interior awareness* that go with these various *objective* or *exterior forms* listed in the Upper-Right column. "Irritability"—the capacity to actively respond to environmental stimuli—begins with cells. Sensations emerge with neuronal organisms, and perceptions emerge with a neural cord. Impulses emerge with a brain stem, and basic emotions with a limbic system. And so on.

This is also a holarchy, but a subjective or interior holarchy. Each level also transcends and includes it predecessor, each follows the twenty tenets, and so on. And this Left-Hand holarchy, like the Right-Hand, is based on extensive evidence already available, which we can discuss if you want.

But the main point is that this Left-Hand dimension refers to the inside, to the *interior depth* that is *consciousness* itself.

Q: You said earlier that depth is consciousness, or what depth looked like from within.

KW: Yes, exactly. The Left Hand is what the holon looks like from within; the Right Hand is what the same holon looks like from without. Interior and exterior. Consciousness and form. Subjective and objective.

Q: The Upper-Right quadrant is the one we are most familiar with, simply because it is part of the standard, objective, empirical, scientific map.

KW: Yes, and we can assume it's accurate enough, as far as it goes. It gives the typical holarchy for individual holons described in objective terms: atoms to molecules to cells (early cells, or prokaryotes, and advanced cells, or eukaryotes) to simple organisms (first with a neuronal net and then with a more advanced neural cord). Then to more complex organisms, reptiles to paleomammals to humans, the latter possessing a complex triune brain, which transcends and includes its predecessors, so that the triune brain has a *reptilian* stem and a *paleomammalian* limbic system, plus something new, a complex *neocortex* capable of abstract logic and linguistics and vision-logic (in figure 5-2, I have listed these more complex capacities as SF1, SF2, SF3, which we'll discuss later).

We don't have to agree with the exact placement of everything in figure 5-3, but most people would agree that *something* like that is occurring.

Cultural and Social

Q: So that is the upper half of the diagram, the individual. There is now the lower half, the collective.

KW: Yes. Individual holons exist only in *communities* of similar-depth holons. So we need to go through both of the columns in figure 5–3 and find the types of *communal* holons that are always associated with the *individual* holons.

Q: And this communal aspect also has an interior and an exterior, which are Lower Left and Lower Right.

KW: Yes.

Q: You call these "cultural" and "social."

KW: Yes, "cultural" refers to all of the *interior* meanings and values and identities that we share with those of similar communities, whether it is a tribal community or a national community or a world community. And "social" refers to all of the exterior, material, institutional *forms* of the community, from its techno-economic base to its architectural styles to its written codes to its population size, to name a few.

So in a very general sense, "cultural" refers to the shared collective *worldview* and "social" refers to the *material base* of that worldview. (Of course, right now I'm just talking about how these appear in human holons; we'll discuss nonhuman in a moment.) Social means any objective, concrete, material components, and especially the techno-economic base, so you see these listed as foraging, horticultural, agrarian, industrial; and the geopolitical structures of villages, states, world federation, and so on. These are all examples of the exterior forms of the collective, as you can see in figure 5-2.

Q: I think that's straightforward enough. But let's look at nonhuman holons. We usually don't think of them as having a common worldview or common worldspace—a common culture.

KW: If consciousness is depth, and depth goes all the way down, then shared depth or common depth also goes all the way down—culture goes all the way down.

Q: I'm sorry?

KW: In other words, if holons share outsides, they share insides.

Q: Their "culture," as it were.

KW: Yes. By the culture or worldspace of holons, I simply mean a shared space of what they *can* respond to: quarks do not respond to all stimuli in the environment, because they *register* a very narrow range of what will have meaning to them, what will *affect* them. Quarks (and all holons) respond only to that which *fits their worldspace*: everything else is a foreign language, and they are outsiders. The study of what holons *can* respond to is the study of shared worldspaces. It's the common world that all holons of a similar depth will respond to. That is their shared culture.

Q: Okay, perhaps an example.

KW: Nonhuman cultures can be very sophisticated. Wolves, for example, share an emotional worldspace. They possess a limbic system, the interior correlate of which is certain basic emotions. And thus a wolf orients itself and its fellow wolves to the world through the use of these basic emotional cognitions—not just reptilian and sensorimotor, but affective. They can hunt and coordinate in packs through a very sophisticated emotional signal system. They share this emotional worldspace.

Yet anything *outside* that worldspace is *not registered*. I mean, you can read *Hamlet* to them, but no luck. What you are, with that book, is basically dinner plus a few things that will have to be spat out.

The point is that a holon responds, and *can respond*, only to those stimuli that fall within its worldspace, its worldview. Everything else is nonexistent.

Q: Same with humans.

KW: Same with humans. By the time evolution reaches the neocortex, or the complex triune brain, with its interior correlates of images and symbols and concepts, these basic worldspaces have become articulated into rather sophisticated cognitive structures. These worldspaces *incorporate* the basic components of the previous worldspaces—such as cellular irritability and reptilian instincts and paleomammalian emotions—but then *add* new components that articulate or unfold new worldviews.

As we were saying earlier, the Kosmos looks different at each of these stages because the Kosmos *is* different at each of these stages. At each of these stages, the Kosmos looks at itself with new eyes, and thus brings forth new worlds not previously existing.

These cultural worldspaces are listed on the Lower Left. And you can see that they evolve from physical and vegetative and reptilian ("uroboric"—of the serpent) and limbic-emotional ("typhonic"), into more specifically hominid and then human forms: archaic, magic, mythic, rational, centauric (or existential), with possibly higher stages yet to come.

These worldviews are correlated with the *exterior* forms of the *social structures* that support each of those worldviews. For example, from the prokaryotic Gaia system to societies with a division of labor (in neural organisms) to groups/families of paleomammals to the more human forms of: *foraging* tribes to *horticultural* villages to *agrarian* empires to *industrial* states to *informational* global federation. Which is the list to date, as reconstructed from available evidence. These are all listed on the Lower Right.

Q: And these four quadrants are related to each other in exactly what fashion?

KW: I have some specific thoughts on this, but right now I don't want to push my own theory in this particular regard. I will settle for the orienting generalization that we cannot reduce these quadrants to each other without profound distortions. As usual, reductionism seems to be a bad idea. Let's just say they interrelate, or they interact, or they each have correlates in the others. When we talk about the different truths in each quadrant, I think you'll see what I mean.

An Example

Q: Why don't you take an example of a single thought, a single thought holon, and show how it has *correlates in all four quadrants*. I wonder if we could go through that example briefly.

KW: Okay. Let's say I have a thought of going to the grocery store. When I have that thought, what I actually experience is the thought itself, the interior thought and its meaning—the symbols, the images, the idea of going to the grocery store. That's Upper Left.

While I am having this thought, there are, of course, correlative changes occurring in my brain—dopamine increases, acetylcholine jumps the synapses, beta brainwaves increase, or whatnot. Those are observable behaviors in my brain. They can be empirically observed, scientifically registered. And that is Upper Right.

Now the internal thought itself only makes sense in terms of my cultural background. If I spoke a different language, the thought would be composed of different symbols and have different meanings. If I existed in a primal tribal society a million years ago, I would never even have the thought "going to the grocery store." It might be, "Time to kill the bear." The point is that my thoughts themselves arise in a *cultural background* that gives texture and meaning and context to my individual thoughts, and indeed, I would not even be able to "talk to myself" if I did not exist in a community of individuals who also talk to me.

So the cultural community serves as an *intrinsic background* to any individual thoughts I might have. My thoughts do not just pop into my head out of nowhere; they pop into my head out of a cultural background, and however much I might move beyond this background, I can never simply escape it altogether, and I could never have developed thoughts in the first place without it. The occasional cases of a "wolf boy"—humans raised in the wild—show that the human brain, left without culture, does not produce linguistic thoughts on its own. The self is far from the autonomous and self-generating monad the Enlightenment imagined.

In short, my individual thoughts only exist against a vast background of cultural practices and languages and meanings, without which I could form virtually no individual thoughts at all. And this vast background is my culture, my cultural worldview, my worldspace, which is the Lower Left.

But my culture itself is not simply disembodied, hanging in idealistic midair. It has *material components*, much as my own individual thoughts have material brain components. All *cultural* events have *social* correlates. These concrete social components include types of technology, forces of production (horticultural, agrarian, industrial, etc.), concrete institutions, written codes and patterns, geopolitical locations (towns, villages, states, etc.), and so on. And these material, social, empirically observable components—the actual *social system*—are crucial in helping to determine the types of cultural worldview.

So my supposedly "individual thought" actually has at least these four facets, these four aspects—intentional, behavioral, cultural, and social. And around the circle we go: the social system will have a strong influence on the cultural worldview, which will set limits to the individual thoughts that I can have, which will register in the brain physiology. And you can go around that circle in any direction you want. The quadrants are all interwoven. They are all mutually determining. They all cause, and are caused by, the other quadrants.

Q: Because all individual holons have these four facets.

KW: Yes, every holon has these four aspects, these four quadrants. It is not that an individual holon exists in one or another of these quadrants. It is that every individual holon has these four quadrants, these four aspects to its being. It's like a diamond with four facets, or four faces.

Of course, these four facets become very complicated and intermixed, but there are at least these four. These four seem to be the *minimum* that we need to understand any holon. And this especially holds for higher transformation, for higher states of consciousness, as I guess we'll see.

The Shape of Things to Come

Q: We started this discussion by talking about transformation in general, and any possible coming transformation in particular.

KW: This transformation is already proceeding, and if we want to consciously find these evolutionary currents operating in our own being as well—if we want to consciously join Spirit-in-action—then the four quadrants can help us orient ourselves more effectively, can help us become more conscious of the evolutionary currents already flowing around us and through us and in us.

We could say that Spirit manifests as all four quadrants. Spirit isn't just a higher Self, or just Gaia, or just awareness, or just the web of life, or just the sum total of all objective phenomena, or just transcendental consciousness. Rather, Spirit exists in and as all four quadrants, the four compass points, as it were, of the known Kosmos, all of which are needed to accurately navigate.

So what we will want to talk about, I suppose, is how this coming transformation—and the higher spiritual stages—will appear and manifest in all four quadrants. What is a higher Self? What is higher brain functioning? What is the transformation of the body as well as of the mind? What is a higher or deeper culture? How is it embedded in wider social systems? What is more highly developed consciousness? How is it anchored in new social institutions? Where is the sublime?

What would all of this look like? How can we help it along in all of these quadrants, and not just focus on Self, or just Gaia, or just the World Federation? For it appears that all of these will emerge together, or they will emerge not at all.

Q: It's a package deal.

KW: It seems to be a package deal, yes. Higher or deeper stages of consciousness development disclose deeper and wider patterns in self, in individual behavior, in culture, and in society—intentional, behavioral, cultural, and social—all four quadrants.

If we don't take all of those into account, then I think they might start the transformation without us. The transformation will occur, is occurring, but we'll be sitting in our favorite quadrant, explaining to people why we have the new paradigm, and transformation will sail on without us. We will abort our own full-quadrant participation in forces that are already in play. We will go limping into the future, all puzzles and grins, and these wider currents will not be activated in our own being. We'll be driftwood on the shore of this extraordinary stream. We will mistake our crutches for liberation, we will offer our wounds to the world, we will bleed into the future all smiles and glory.

I don't think that partial approach will ever work. It seems instead that we need an *integral* approach that will include all four quadrants, all four faces of Spirit. Perhaps the secret to higher transformation involves this more balanced, complete, and integral approach. What do you think?

6

The Two Hands of God

Q: I think that "the truth will set you free." But you started to suggest that each quadrant has a different type of truth! This does not look like we are moving toward an integral or inclusive view; it looks like we are moving into parts and fragments and lots of differences.

KW: Yes, but that's actually good news. By understanding these different truths, and acknowledging them, we can more sympathetically include them in an integral embrace. We can more expansively attune ourselves to the Kosmos. The final result might even be an attunement with the All, might even be Kosmic consciousness itself. Why not? But I think first we need to understand these various truths, so they can begin to speak to us, in us, through us—and we can begin to hear their voices and honor them, and thus invite all of them together into a rainbow coalition, an integral embrace.

These truths are behind much of the great postmodern rebellion. They are the key to the interior and transcendental dimensions; they speak eloquently in tongues of hidden gods and angels; they point to the heart of holons in general, and invite us into that interior world; they are antidote to the flat and faded world that passes for today. We might even say that these four types of truth are the four faces of Spirit as it shines in the manifest world.

Q: Tell me it's not complicated.

KW: More fun than a human should be allowed to have. But there is a very simple way to shake all of this down and summarize it; so it soon enough becomes very, very simple.

In the meantime, figure 6-1 (page 129) is a small sampling of different

	Left-Hand Paths	Right-Hand Paths
	· Interpretive	· Monological
	· Hermeneutic	· Empirical, positivistic
	· Consciousness	· Form
Individual	Freud C. G. Jung Piaget Aurobindo Plotinus Gautama Buddha	B. F. Skinner John Watson John Locke Empiricism Behaviorism Physics, biology, neurology, etc.
Collective	Thomas Kuhn Wilhelm Dilthey Jean Gebser Max Weber Hans-Georg Gadamer	Systems Theory Talcott Parsons Auguste Comte Karl Marx Gerhard Lenski

FIGURE 6-1. *Some representative theorists in each quadrant.*

theorists who have plugged in to a particular quadrant with its particular truth. It'll help if we discuss some examples of each.

Mind and Brain

Q: Okay, start with this. You have the mind—your lived experience, images, symbols, feelings, thoughts—listed on the Upper Left—and the brain on Upper Right. So you're saying that mind and brain are not the same.

KW: We can grant that they are intimately related. But for the moment, we can also grant that in many important ways they are quite different. We need to respect those differences and try to account for them.

For example, when brain physiologists study the human brain, they study all of its objective components—the neural makeup, the various synapses, the neurotransmitters such as serotonin and dopamine, the electrical brainwave patterns, and so on. All of those are *objective* or *exterior* aspects of the human being. Even though the brain is "inside" the human organism, the brain physiologist knows that brain only in an objective and exterior fashion.

But you yourself can't even see your brain as an object, unless you cut open your skull and get a mirror. That's the only way you can see your brain. But you can see and experience your *mind* directly, right now, intimately and immediately. The mind is what your awareness looks like *from within*; your brain is simply what it looks like *from without*, from the outside.

Q: And they don't look the same at all.

KW: No. Your brain looks like a big crumpled grapefruit. But your mind doesn't look like that at all. Your mind looks like your direct experience right now—images, impulses, thoughts. Perhaps we will ultimately decide that mind and brain are actually identical, or parallel, or dualist, or whatever, but we have to start with the undeniable fact they are phenomenologically quite different.

Q: But what about the idea that they really are the same thing, and we just haven't figured out how to show this?

KW: Let's look to an expert on the brain itself—say, a brain physiologist. The brain physiologist can know every single thing about my brain—he can hook me up to an EEG machine, he can use PET scans, he can use radioactive tracers, he can map the physiology, determine the levels of neurotransmitters—he can know what every atom of my brain is doing, and he still won't know a single thought in my mind.

This is really extraordinary. And if he wants to know what is going on in my *mind*, there is one and only one way that he can find out: *he must talk to me*. There is absolutely no other way that he, or anybody else, can know what my actual thoughts are without asking me, and talking to me, and communicating with me. And if I don't want to tell you, then you will never know the actual specifics of my individual thoughts. Of course, you can torture me and force me to tell—but that's the point: you force me to *talk*.

So you can know all about my brain, and that will tell you nothing about the specific contents of my mind, which you can find only by talking to me. In other words, you must engage in *dialogue*, not monologue—you must engage in *intersubjective* communication, and not simply study me as an *object* of empirical investigation—as an object of the empirical gaze—which will get you nowhere.

As we will see in greater detail as we go along, all of the Right-Hand dimensions can be accessed with this empirical gaze, this "monological" gaze, this objectifying stance, this empirical mapping—because you are only studying the exteriors, the surfaces, the aspects of holons that can be *seen* empirically—the Right-Hand aspects, such as the brain.

But the Left-Hand aspects, the *interior* dimensions, can only be accessed by communication and interpretation, by "dialogue" and "dialogical" approaches, which are not *staring* at exteriors but *sharing* of interiors. Not objective but intersubjective. Not surfaces but depths.

So I can study your brain forever, and I will never know your mind. I can know your brain by objective study, but I can only know your mind by talking to you.

The Left- and Right-Hand Paths

Q: This takes us directly to the differences between the Left- and Right-Hand paths.

KW: Yes. From virtually the inception of every major knowledge quest, East and West alike, the various approaches have fallen into one or another of these two great camps, interior versus exterior, Left versus Right. We find this in psychology (Freud vs. Watson), in sociology (Weber vs. Comte), in philosophy (Heidegger vs. Locke), in anthropology (Taylor vs. Lenski), in linguistics (hermeneutics vs. structuralism)—and even in theology (Augustine vs. Aquinas)!

Occasionally you find an approach that emphasizes both the Left- and Right-Hand dimensions, which of course would be my recommendation, but mostly you find a bitter war between these two equally important, but rarely integrated, approaches. So I think it's crucial to understand the contributions that both of these paths have made to our understanding of the human condition, because both of them are truly indispensable.

And, as we'll soon see, it seems almost impossible to understand higher and spiritual developments without taking both of these paths into account.

The Monological Gaze: The Key to the Right-Hand Paths

Q: Let's take them one at a time. The Right-Hand paths . . .

KW: Everything on the Right Hand, all the aspects on the Right half of figure 5-2, are objects or exteriors that can be seen empirically, one way or another, with the senses or their extensions—microscopes, telescopes, photographic equipment, whatnot. They are all *surfaces* that can be *seen*. They all have simple location. You don't have to *talk* to any of them. You just observe their *objective behavior*. You look at the behavior of atoms, or cells, or populations, or individuals, or societies, or ecosystems.

Q: You also call this "monological."

KW: Yes, all the Right-Hand aspects are basically monological, which means they can be seen in a monologue. You don't have to try to get at their interiors, at their consciousness. You do not need a *dialogue*, a mutual exchange of depth, because you are looking only at exteriors.

If you are getting a CAT scan of your brain, the lab technicians will talk to you only if it's unavoidable. "Would you mind moving your head over here, dearie?" The technicians couldn't care less about your interior depths, because they only want to capture your exterior surfaces, even if those exteriors are "inside" you—they're just more objects. When the lab technicians take this objective picture of your brain, do they see the real you? Do they see *you* at all?

No, you are being treated merely as an *object* of the *monological gaze*, not as a *subject* in *communication*—which is what makes empirical medicine so dehumanizing in itself. The lab technician just wants your Right Hand, not your Left Hand, not your consciousness, your feelings, your meanings, your values, your intentions, your hopes, your fears. Just the facts, ma'am. Just the exteriors. And that's fine. That's completely acceptable. That's your brain.

But you can never, and will never, see a mind that way.

Q: Feminists are always complaining about being the object of the male gaze.

KW: It's the same thing. Women often complain about being made into an object, a sexual object, in this case, of the male gaze. But it's the same general phenomenon, the same monological gaze: you are reduced from a subject in communication to an object of observation, a slab of meat, an object with no depth. "He never talks to me." And women understandably react to this. Men, on the other hand, are reduced to passive objects whenever they have to ask for directions, and of course, they'd rather die on the spot.

There is nothing wrong with these Right-Hand and empirical and scientific paths; it's just that they are not the whole story. Living life only according to the Right Hand is like living life perpetually under the gaze of a lab technician. It's all empiricism, all monological gaze, all behaviorism, all shiny surfaces and monochrome objects—no interiors, no depth, no consciousness.

I don't want to get too much ahead of the story, but we can now briefly mention that the downside of the Enlightenment paradigm was that, in its rush to be empirical, it inadvertently collapsed the Left-Hand dimensions of the Kosmos into the Right-Hand dimensions—it collapsed interior depths into observable surfaces, and it thought that a *simple mapping* of these empirical exteriors was all the knowledge that was worth knowing. This left out the mapmaker itself—the consciousness, the interiors, the Left-Hand dimensions—and, a century or two later, it awoke in horror to find itself living in a universe with no value, no meaning, no intentions, no depth, no quality—it found itself in a disqualified universe ruled by the monological gaze, the brutal world of the lab technician.

And that, of course, began the postmodern rebellion.

Interpretation: The Key to the Left-Hand Paths

Q: That's part of our next discussion (see chapter 7). We were talking about the differences between the Left- and Right-Hand paths.

KW: Yes, as we were saying, if you look at figure 5-2, every holon on the Right Hand can be empirically seen, one way or another. They all have *simple location*, because these are the physical-material correlates of all holons. And so with every Right-Hand aspect, you can physically point right at it and say, "There it is." You can put your finger right on them, so to speak. There is the brain, or there is a cell, or there is the town, or there is the ecosystem. Even subatomic particles exist as probabilities of being found in a given location at a given time!

But nothing on the Left Hand can be seen in that simple fashion, because *none of the Left-Hand aspects have simple location*. You can point to the brain, or to a rock, or to a town, but you cannot simply point to envy, or pride, or consciousness, or value, or intention, or desire. Where is desire? Point to it. You can't really, not the way you can point to a rock, because it's largely an *interior* dimension, so it doesn't have *simple location*.

This doesn't mean it isn't real! It only means it doesn't have simple location, and therefore you can't see it with a microscope or a telescope or any sensory-empirical device.

Q: So how can these interior depths be accessed or "seen"?

KW: This is where *interpretation* enters the picture. All Right-Hand paths involve perception, but all Left-Hand paths involve interpretation.

And there is a simple reason for this: surfaces can be seen, but depth must be interpreted. As you and I talk, you are not just looking at some surface, some smiling face, some empirical object. You want to know what's going on inside me. You are not just watching what I do, you want to know what I feel, what I think, what's going on within me, in my consciousness.

So you ask me some questions. "What's happening? What do you think about this? How do you feel about this?" And I will tell you some things—we will talk—and you have to figure out what I mean, you have to *interpret* what I mean. With each and every sentence, you have to interpret the meaning. What does he mean by that? Oh, I understand, you mean this. And so on.

And there is no other way to get at my interior except by interpretation. We must talk, and you must interpret. This seems unavoidable. Even if you were a great psychic and could totally read my mind, you would still have to figure out what my thoughts mean—you still have to interpret what you read.

Q: Very different from the monological gaze.

KW: Yes, this is quite different from simply staring at some surfaces with simple location and reporting what you see, whether those surfaces are rocks or cells or ecosystems or brain components. Depth does not sit on the surface waiting to be seen! Depth must be communicated, and communication must be interpreted.

Just so, everything on the Left half of figure 5-2 requires some sort of interpretation. And interpretation is absolutely *the only way* we can get at each other's depth.

So we have a very simple distinction between the Right and the Left: *surfaces can be seen, but depth must be interpreted.*

Q: That's a clear distinction!

KW: Yes. And this is why, as we'll see, the Right-Hand paths are always asking, "What does it *do*?," whereas the Left-Hand paths are always asking, "What does it *mean*?"

This is incredibly important, because it gives us two very different approaches to consciousness and how we understand consciousness. There are important contributions to be made by both of these paths, but they need to be integrated or balanced. And this in turn will determine how we approach the higher stages of consciousness development itself, in both individual and collective transformation—it will bear directly on our spiritual evolution.

We are dealing, so to speak, with the Right and Left Hands of God, of how Spirit actually manifests in the world, and to fully grasp that manifestation, we definitely need both hands!

What Does That Dream Mean?

Q: Perhaps some examples of these two paths. Start with psychology.

KW: Psychoanalysis is basically an interpretive or Left-Hand approach, and classical behaviorism is a Right-Hand or empirical approach.

In psychoanalysis, the title of Freud's first great book says it all: *The Interpretation of Dreams*. Dreams are an interior event. They are composed of symbols. The symbols can only be understood by interpretation. What does the dream *mean*? One of Freud's great discoveries was that the dream is not incoherent, but rather it possesses a meaning, a hidden meaning that can be interpreted and brought to light.

So the simplest way to summarize Freud is that the "talking cure"—the *dialogue* cure!—not monological, but dialogical—means that we must learn to interpret our own depths more adequately. We are plagued by symptoms, such as anxiety or depression, that are baffling to us. Why am I so depressed? What is the meaning of this? And thus, in the course of psychoanalysis—or really, any depth psychotherapy—I will learn to look at my dreams, or at my symptoms, or my depression, or my anxiety, in a way that makes sense of them. I will learn how to interpret them in a way that sheds light on my own interior.

Perhaps I will find that I have a hidden rage at my absent father, and this rage was disguised as symptoms of depression. I had unconsciously *misinterpreted* this anger as depression. And so in therapy, I will learn to reinterpret this depression more accurately; I will learn to translate "sad" as "mad." I will get in touch with this angry aspect of my own depth, an aspect that I had tried to hide from myself by misinterpreting it, mistranslating it, disguising it.

The more adequately I interpret my depth—the more I can see that "sad" is really "mad"—then the more my symptoms will ease, the more the depression will lift. I am more faithfully interpreting my inner depths, and so those depths stop sabotaging me in the forms of painful symptoms.

Q: So that's an example of an interpretive or Left-Hand approach for individuals. That's an Upper-Left quadrant approach.

KW: Yes. And it applies not just to psychoanalysis. All "talking therapies"—from aspects of cognitive therapy to interpersonal therapy to Jungian therapy to Gestalt therapy to transactional analysis—are all fundamentally based on this single principle, namely, the attempt to find *a more adequate interpretation for one's interior depth*. A more adequate way to find the *meaning* of my dreams, my symptoms, my depths, my life, my being.

My life is not simply a series of flatly objective events laid out in front of me like so many rocks with simple location that I am supposed to stare at until I see the surfaces more clearly. My life includes a deeply subjective component that I must come to understand and interpret to myself. It is not just surfaces; it has depths. And while surfaces can be seen, depths must be interpreted. And the more adequately I can interpret my own depths, then the more transparent my life will become to me. The more clearly I can see and understand it, the less it baffles me, perplexes me, pains me in its opaqueness.

Q: So what about the individual therapies that aim at the Upper-Right quadrant? What about the exterior approaches to the individual?

KW: The Upper-Right quadrant approaches, such as behaviorism or biological psychiatry—at their extreme, they want absolutely nothing to do with interpretation and depth and interiors and intentions. They couldn't care less about what's going on "inside," in the "black box." Many of them don't even think it exists. They are interested solely in observable, empirical, exterior behavior.

So with behaviorism, you simply find the observable response you want to increase or decrease, and you selectively reinforce or extinguish it. Your interiors are of no consequence; your consciousness is not required. With behaviorism, the therapist will engineer operant conditionings that will reinforce the desired response and extinguish the undesirable ones.

Similarly, with purely biological psychiatry, the therapist will administer a drug—Prozac, Xanax, Elavil—that will bring about a stabilization of behavioral patterns. Many psychiatrists will administer the drug within the first consultation, and then just periodically check with you, say once a month, to make sure it's having the desired effect. Of course, some medical psychiatrists will engage in a bit of the talking cure, but many don't, and we are giving "pure examples" of the Upper Right.

And with this pure biological psychiatry, as with pure behaviorism, your presence is not required. That is, there is no attempt to get at the meaning of the symptoms. There is no extensive interpretation of your predicament. There is no attempt to increase your own self-understanding. There is no attempt to explore your interior depths and come to a clearer understanding of your own being.

Q: Nonetheless, I take it that you are not condemning these exterior approaches in themselves.

KW: No, that would miss the point from the other direction. Every holon has these four aspects, these four quadrants. Empiricism and behaviorism are a superior approach to the exteriors of holons. They are basically correct as far as they go. I *fully* endorse them as far as they go.

The problem, of course, is that they don't go very far. And thus you often have to condemn them in the same breath, because they usually deny not only the importance but the very *existence* of the other quadrants. You are depressed, not because you lack values or meanings or virtues in your life, but because you lack serotonin, even though stocking your brain to the hilt with serotonin won't do a thing to develop your values.

In other words, my depression can be interiorly caused by an absent father, the exterior correlate of which might be a low level of serotonin in my brain, and Prozac can to some degree correct that serotonin imbalance. Which is fine, and sometimes extremely helpful. But Prozac will not in any way help me to understand my interior pain, to *interpret* it in a way that it takes on meaning for me and helps me to become transparent to myself. And if you are not interested in that, if you are not interested in understanding your own depth, then Prozac alone will suit your purposes.

But if you desire to see into your own depths and interpret them more adequately, then you will have to *talk* to somebody who has seen those depths before and helped others interpret them more adequately. In this intersubjective dialogue with a therapeutic helper, you will hold hands and walk the path of more adequate interpretations, you will enter a circle of intersubjective depth, and the more clearly you can interpret and articulate this depth, the less baffling you will become to yourself, the clearer you will become to yourself, the more transparent you will be.

And eventually, as we'll see, you might even become transparent to the Divine, liberated in your own infinite depth. But in any event, none of this, at any level, will open to you if you insist on hugging only the surfaces.

Social Science versus Cultural Understanding

Q: What about the collective? What about Lower-Left and Lower-Right approaches? The *cultural* and *social*? One is interpretive, the other is empirical?

KW: Yes. Like psychology, sociology has, almost from its inception, divided into two huge camps, the interpretive (Left Hand) and the naturalistic or empirical (Right Hand). The one investigates culture or cultural meanings, and attempts to get at those meanings *from within*, in a sympathetic *understanding*. The other investigates the social system or social structures and functions *from without*, in a very positivistic and empirical fashion. And so, of course, the former asks, What does it mean?; the latter, What does it do?

Q: Take them one at a time.

KW: Understanding the *cultural* meanings is an *interpretive* affair. You have to learn the language, you have to immerse yourself in the culture, you have to find out what the various practices mean. And these are the hermeneutic cultural sciences—Wilhelm Dilthey, Max Weber, Martin Heidegger, Hans-Georg Gadamer, Paul Ricoeur, Clifford Geertz, Mary Douglas, Karl-Otto Apel, Charles Taylor, Thomas Kuhn, to name a prominent few.

These approaches all involve sympathetic resonance, sharing, talking—they are dialogical, interpretive. They want to get at the interior meaning, and not just the exterior behavior. They want to get inside the black box. They want to get at the Left-Hand dimensions. And the *only* way you can get at depth is via interpretation.

But the *empirical* social sciences mostly want to study the *behavior* of societies in a detached fashion: the birthrates, the modes of production, the types of architecture, the suicide rates, the amount of money in circulation, the demographics, the population spread, the types of technology, and so on—all exterior behaviors, no interior intentions. Most of those statistics can be gathered without ever having to talk to any of the cultural natives. No nasty black boxes here.

So these approaches are mostly monological, empirical, behavioral. You are looking at the *behavior* of a "social action system," you are not inquiring into the interior meaning or depth of the culture. And to the extent that you do investigate meaning or values, you make them almost totally subservient to the social system. And these are the standard positivistic, naturalistic, empirical social sciences—August Comte, Karl Marx, Talcott Parsons, Niklas Luhmann, Gerhard Lenski, and so on.

Q: You give an example of the Hopi Rain Dance. About how the Left- and Right-Hand approaches differ.

KW: The Left-Hand approach, the interpretive approach, wants to know what is the meaning of the Rain Dance? When the native peoples engage in the Dance, what does it mean for them? Why do they value it? And as the interpretive investigator becomes a "participant observer," then he or she begins to understand that the Rain Dance is largely a way to celebrate the sacredness of nature, and a way to ask that sacredness to bless the earth with rain. And you know this is so because this is what you are told by the practitioners themselves as you continue your attempts at mutual understanding.

The Right-Hand paths want little to do with this. They look instead at what the *function* of the Dance is in the overall *behavior* of the *social system*. They are not so much interested in what the natives *say* the meaning is. Rather, they look at the behavior of the Dance in the overall observable system. And they conclude that the Dance, despite what the natives say, is actually functioning as a way to create social cohesion in the social action system. In other words, the Dance provides social integration.

Q: As I understand it, you are saying both are correct.

KW: Yes. They are the Left- and the Right-Hand approaches to the same communal holon. The Left Hand seeks to understand what the Dance means, its interior meaning and value, which can only be understood by *standing within* the culture. And the Right Hand seeks to understand what the Dance *does*, its overall *function* in the observable *behavior* of the social system, which can only be determined by *standing outside* the system in a detached and impartial fashion. Left- and Right-Hand paths.

Hermeneutics

Q: Interpretation is the meaning of "hermeneutics."

KW: Yes. Hermeneutics is the art and science of interpretation. Hermeneutics began as a way to understand interpretation itself, because when you interpret a text, there are good ways and bad ways to proceed.

In general, the Continental philosophers, particularly in Germany and France, have carried on the interpretive aspects of philosophy, and the Anglo-Saxon philosophers in Britain and North America have shunned interpretation and focused mostly on pragmatic and empiric-analytic studies. This old war between the Left- and the Right-Hand paths!

This is why Thomas Kuhn caused such an uproar with his notion of paradigms—the idea that "objective scientific theories" are actually sunk in background contexts that govern their interpretations. And why Charles Taylor caused a sensation with the publication of his seminal essay, "Interpretation and the Sciences of Man," which demonstrated that background contexts of interpretation are necessary to understand cultural movements. This could only be shocking to Anglo-Saxon philosophers, whose paradigm of knowledge is the monological gaze: I see the rock.

So even though "hermeneutics" is a fancy word, please remember it. It's the key to the entire Left-Hand dimensions. The Left Hand is composed of depth, and interpretation is the *only way* to get at depth. As Heidegger would say, interpretation goes all the way down. And mere empiricism is virtually worthless in this regard.

Q: But empiricists say interpretation is not objective and thus not "really real."

KW: It's like studying *Hamlet*. If you take a text of *Hamlet* and study it empirically, then you will find that it is made of so much ink and so much paper. That's all you can know about *Hamlet* empirically—it's composed of seven grams of ink, which is made of so many molecules, which have so many atoms—all of the things you can find in the Upper-Right quadrant.

But if you want to know the *meaning* of *Hamlet*, then you have to read it. You have to engage in intersubjective understanding. You have to *interpret* what it means.

True, this is not a merely objective affair. But neither is it subjective fantasy. This is very important, because empiric-scientific types are always claiming that if something isn't empirically true, then it isn't true at all. But interpretation is not subjective whim. There are *good* and *bad* interpretations of *Hamlet*. *Hamlet* is not about the joys of war, for example. That is a bad interpretation; it is wrong.

Q: So there are validity criteria for interpretations.

KW: Yes. The fact that the Left-Hand dimensions have this strong interpretive aspect does not mean they are merely arbitrary or ungrounded, or that they are nothing but subjective and idiosyncratic fantasies. There are good and bad interpretations, felicitous interpretations and false or distorted interpretations, interpretations that are more adequate and those that are less adequate.

And this can be determined by a community of those who have looked into the same depth. As I said, the meaning of *Hamlet* is *not*

"Have a nice day." That interpretation can be easily *rejected* by a community of those who have read and studied the text—that is, by a community of those who have entered the interior of *Hamlet*, by those who share that depth.

Even if you bring your own individual interpretations to *Hamlet*, which is fine, those interpretations are grounded in the realities and contexts of your actual lifeworld. Either way, the point is that interpretation does not mean wildly arbitrary!

This interpretive knowledge is just as important as empirical knowledge. In some ways, more important. But, of course, it's a bit trickier and requires a bit more sophistication than the head-banging obviousness of the monological gaze. But there is, alas, a type of mind that believes only those things with simple location actually exist, even though that belief itself does not have simple location. . . .

All Interpretation Is Context-Bound

Q: You point out that the crucial feature of interpretation is that it is always *context-bound*.

KW: Yes. The primary rule of interpretation is that all meaning is context-bound. For example, the meaning of the word "bark" is different in the phrases "the bark of a tree" and "the bark of a dog." The important point is that the context helps determine which interpretation is correct.

And that context itself exists in yet further contexts, and so off we go in the "hermeneutic circle." The reason, of course, is that there are only holons, and holons are nested indefinitely: holons within holons, contexts within contexts, endlessly.

So all meaning is context dependent, and contexts are boundless. We earlier mentioned that one of the prime aims of postmodernism was to emphasize the importance of interpretation. Jonathan Culler has, in fact, summarized all of deconstruction (one of the most influential of the postmodern movements, founded by Jacques Derrida) in this way: "One could therefore identify deconstruction with the twin principles of the *contextual determination of meaning* and the *infinite extendability of context*." In other words, all meaning is context dependent, and contexts are boundless. We arrived at this truth by looking at the four quadrants and the nature of holons; Derrida did so by an investigation of language, which is a vivid example of holons within holons indefinitely. (Of course, deconstruction can be taken too far, into extreme constructivism, but we needn't take that route.) The point is simply that by emphasizing the endlessly holonic nature of reality, we are in general agreement with the best of the postmodern insights.

Nested holons—contexts forever—simply means that we always need to be sensitive to background contexts in understanding meaning. And the more of these contexts we can take into account, then the richer our interpretations will be—all the way up, all the way down.

Nonhuman Interpretation

Q: So this interpretive component applies to nonhumans as well? It applies to nonhuman holons?

KW: If you want to know their *interiors*, yes, absolutely. If you want to get at the interior of any holon, what else are you going to do?

When you interact with your dog, you are not interested in just its exterior behavior. Since humans and dogs share a similar limbic system, we also share a *common emotional worldspace* ("typhonic"). You can sense when your dog is sad, or fearful, or happy, or hungry. And most people interact with those interiors. They want to share those interiors. When their dog is happy, it's easy to share that happiness. But that requires a sensitive *interpretation* of what your dog is feeling. Of course, this is not verbal or linguistic communication; but it is an *empathic resonance* with your dog's interior, with its depths, with its degree of consciousness, which might not be as great as yours, but that doesn't mean it's zero.

So you empathically interpret. And the dog does the same with you— you each *resonate* with the other's interior. In those moments, you share a common worldspace—in this case, a common emotional worldspace. You, of course, will elaborate it conceptually, which a dog can't do. But the basic emotions are similar enough, and you know it. You interpret your dog's interior feelings, and relate with those feelings. That's the whole point of getting a dog, isn't it?

Of course, the lower a holon, or the less depth it has, then the less consciousness it has, the less interior it has—and the less you can easily interpret and share. Of course, some people get on famously with their pet rocks, which I suppose shows you something.

Q: So because both you and the dog share some sort of *common background*—in this case, the emotional worldspace—then you can interpret each other to some degree.

KW: That's right. The common worldspace provides the *common context* that allows the interpretation, the sharing. As we said, all interpretation requires a context, and in this case, it is the context of the emotional worldspace, which is the common culture we share with dogs.

Of course, we also share all lower worldspaces—the physical (such as gravity), the vegetative (life), the reptilian (hunger). Since we also contain a reptilian stem, we can also share with lizards, but it becomes less fun, doesn't it? Down to pet rocks, with shared mass and gravity. Less depth, less to share. Really, all you and your pet rock can share is, you fall at the same speed.

Q: So when we reach specifically human contexts . . .

KW: Yes, when it comes specifically to humans, then *in addition* to the earlier backgrounds—cellular, reptilian-stem, mammalian-limbic—we *also* have complex cognitive and conceptual and linguistic backgrounds. And we ground our mutual interpretations in these *common cultural backgrounds* (the Lower Left). There is no other way for communication to occur.

Q: And these backgrounds evolve.

KW: Yes, all four quadrants evolve, all follow the twenty tenets. With respect to the cultural background—the Lower-Left quadrant—we saw it evolve in humans from archaic to magic to mythic to rational to existential, on the way to possibly higher worldviews. And each of these worldviews governs the *types* of ways that we *can* interpret the Kosmos.

So how indeed will you and I interpret the Kosmos? Will we interpret it magically? Will we interpret it mythically? Will we interpret it rationally? Or start to go transrational altogether?

But you can start to see why there isn't simply a pregiven world just lying around waiting to be reflected with the monological gaze.

Q: No wonder the human sciences have always divided into these two camps, Right Hand versus Left—surfaces can be seen, but depth must be interpreted.

Spiritual Interpretation

Q: But how is interpretation important in spiritual transformation or spiritual experience?

KW: Give an example.

Q: Say I have a direct experience of interior illumination—a blinding, ecstatic, mind-blowing experience of inner light.

KW: The experience itself is indeed direct and immediate. You might even become one with that light. But then you come out of that state, and you want to tell me about it. You want to talk to me about it. You want to talk to yourself about it. And here you must *interpret* what this deep experience was. What was this light? Was it Jesus Christ? Was it Buddha-mind? Was it an archetype? An angel? Was it an alien UFO? Was it just some brain state gone haywire? What was it? God? Or a piece of undigested meat? The Goddess? Or a food allergy?

You must interpret. And if you decide it was some sort of genuine spiritual experience, then of what flavor? Allah? Keter? Kundalini? Savi-kalpa-samadhi? Jungian archetype? Platonic form? This is not some unimportant or secondary issue. This is not some theoretical hair splitting. This is not some merely academic concern. Quite the contrary. How you interpret this experience will govern how you approach others with this illumination, how you share it with the world, how you fit it into your own self system, and the ways you can even speak about it to others and think about it yourself. And it will determine your future relation to this light!

And like all interpretations—whether of *Hamlet* or of the inner light—there are *good* and there are *bad* interpretations. And in this interpretation, will you do a good job or a bad job?

In other words, even if this experience of light was transmental, or beyond words altogether, still you are a compound individual. Still you are composed not only of this spiritual component—which is perhaps what the light was; you are also composed of mind and body and matter. And mentally you must orient yourself to this experience. You must interpret it, explain it, make sense of it. And if you can't *interpret it adequately*, it might very likely drive you insane. You will not be able to integrate it with the rest of your being because you cannot adequately interpret it. You don't know what it *means*. Your own extraordinary depth escapes you, confuses you, obscures you, because you cannot interpret it adequately.

Q: So interpretation is an important part of even spiritual or transmental experiences.

KW: Yes, definitely. Many people today are having just these types of spiritual or transmental experiences—experiences from the higher or deeper stages of consciousness evolution. But they *don't know how to interpret them*. They have these extraordinary intuitions, but they sometimes unpack the intuitions in an inadequate or incomplete fashion. And these inadequate interpretations tend to abort further transformation, derail it, sabotage it.

Q: So examples of "bad" interpretations would be, what? How can we tell if an interpretation is bad?

KW: Remember, one of the basic rules of interpretation is that all meaning is *context-bound*. So in any attempt to interpret these types of spiritual experiences, we want to make sure that the context against which we interpret the experience is as full and complete as possible. In other words, we want to make sure that we have checked our interpretation against *all four quadrants*. We want an "all-quadrants" view, an interpretation from the context of the Kosmos in all its dimensions.

What is happening now is that many people are trying to interpret these experiences based on the realities of just one quadrant—and sometimes just one level in one quadrant! This diminishes the other quadrants and cripples the fullness of the interpretation, cripples the fullness of the experience itself.

Q: For example?

KW: Many people interpret these spiritual experiences basically in terms of only the Upper-Left quadrant—they see the experience in terms of a higher Self, or higher consciousness, or archetypal forms, or enneagram patterns, or care of the soul, or the inner voice, or transcendental awareness, and so forth. They tend to ignore the cultural and social and behavioral components. So their insights are limited in terms of how to relate this higher Self to the other quadrants, which are then often interpreted rather narcissistically as mere extensions of their Self. The new age movement is replete with this type of Self-only interpretation.

Others see these experiences as basically a product of brain states— the Upper Right. They attempt to interpret these experiences as coming solely or predominantly from theta brain wave states, or massive endorphin release, or hemispheric synchronization, and so on. This also devastates the cultural and social components, not to mention the interior states of consciousness itself. It is hyperobjective and merely technological.

Others—especially the "new paradigm" ecological theorists— attempt to interpret these experiences mostly in terms of the Lower-Right quadrant. The "ultimate reality" for them is the empirical web of life, or Gaia, or the biosphere, or the social system, and all holons are reduced to being merely a strand in the great web. These approaches poorly understand the interior stages of consciousness development, and reduce all Left-Hand components to Right-Hand strands in the empirical web. This mistakes great span for great depth and therefore collapses vertical depth to horizontal expansion. This results in various forms of what many critics have called ecofascism.

Others attempt to interpret these experiences merely in terms of collective cultural consciousness and a coming worldview transformation—the Lower-Left quadrant. This overlooks what individual consciousness can do at any given point, and denies the importance of social structures and institutions in helping to support and embed these experiences. And so on.

Q: All of which tend to be very partial.

KW: All of these "one-quadrant" interpretations have a moment of truth to them, and an important moment at that. But because they don't adequately include the other quadrants, they cripple the original experience. They unpack this spiritual intuition very poorly, in very fragmented terms. And these fragmented interpretations do not help facilitate further spiritual intuitions. Fragmented interpretations tend to abort the spiritual process itself.

Q: So the point is. . . .

KW: Since Spirit-in-action manifests as all four quadrants, then an adequate interpretation of a spiritual experience ought to take all four quadrants into account. It's not just that we have different levels— matter, body, mind, soul, and spirit—but that each of these manifests in four facets—intentional, behavioral, cultural, and social.

Q: So a balanced or *integral* view would include all of that—all of the levels and all of the quadrants.

KW: Yes, I think so. A truly integral view would be "all-level, all-quadrant." This integral view becomes especially important as we look at the higher or deeper stages of human growth and development—at the further stages of consciousness evolution. If there is indeed a transformation in our future, it lies in these higher or deeper stages, and it looks like these can only be accessed in their richness and fullness if we honor and appreciate the different types of truth that will unfold to set us free.

Q: As for an "all-level, all-quadrant" view, many people seem to understand the "all-level" part. They realize that there is some sort of spectrum of consciousness from matter to body to mind to soul to spirit, although they might not use exactly those terms. But I'm not sure many people understand the "all-quadrant" part. The example you gave about how people tend to interpret spiritual illumination in terms of just one quadrant confirms that. I'd like to come back to the levels of consciousness evolution (see Part Two). But right now perhaps we could focus on the all-quadrant part. Because, as you say, it might be the case that the higher levels will not fully unfold without understanding all four quadrants in a balanced, integral, and inclusive fashion.

KW: These levels and quadrants are simply aspects of the Kosmos, aspects of our very own being. So the whole point, I think, is that we want to find ourselves in sympathetic attunement with all aspects of the Kosmos. We want to find ourselves at home in the Kosmos. We want to touch the truth in each of the quadrants. We begin to do so by noticing that each speaks to us with a different voice. If we listen carefully, we can hear each of these voices whispering gently their truths, and finally joining in a harmonious chorus that quietly calls us home. We can fully resonate with those liberating truths, if we know how to recognize and honor them.

From attunement to atonement to at-onement: we find ourselves in the overpowering embrace of a Kosmic sympathy on the very verge of Kosmic consciousness itself . . . if we listen very carefully.

7

Attuned to the Kosmos

Q: We must listen very carefully. You mean, to all four types of truth.

KW: Truth, in the broadest sense, means being *attuned* with the real. To be authentically in touch with the true, and the good and the beautiful. Yes?

And that implies that we can also be out of touch with the real. We can be lost, or obscured, or mistaken, or wrong in our assessments. We can be out of touch with the true, out of touch with the good, out of touch with the beautiful.

And so a collective humanity, in the course of its evolution, has discovered, through painful trial and error, the various ways that we can check our attunement with the Kosmos. Various ways to see if we are in touch with truth or lost in falsity. Whether we are honoring the good or obscuring it. Whether we are moved by the beautiful or promoting degradation.

Humanity, in other words, has painfully learned and labored hard to fashion a series of *validity claims*—tests that can help us determine if we are in touch with the real, if we are adequately attuned to the Kosmos in all of its rich diversity.

Q: So the validity claims themselves . . .

KW: The validity claims are the ways that we connect to Spirit itself, ways that we attune ourselves to the Kosmos. The validity claims force us to confront reality; they curb our egoic fantasies and self-centered ways; they demand evidence from the rest of the Kosmos; they force us outside of ourselves! They are the checks and balances in the Kosmic Constitution.

Q: As we were saying, befriending the four quadrants and their truths makes it more likely that the higher levels of consciousness will emerge in a more balanced and integral fashion. In order to get "all-level," we need first to get "all-quadrant."

KW: I believe that is very true.

Q: So perhaps we could go around the four quadrants and very briefly summarize this. The four truths, what they are, and the tests for their validity.

KW: These are listed in figure 7-1. And once we briefly review these, I promise I'll give that very, very simple way to summarize them all!

Propositional Truth

Q: Is there an easy definition of "truth"?

KW: Most people take truth to mean representational truth. Simple mapping or simple correspondence. I make a statement or a *proposition*

	INTERIOR Left-Hand Paths	EXTERIOR Right-Hand Paths
	SUBJECTIVE	OBJECTIVE
INDIVIDUAL	*truthfulness* sincerity integrity trustworthiness	*truth* correspondence representation propositional
	I	it
	we	its
COLLECTIVE	*justness* cultural fit mutual understanding rightness	*functional fit* systems theory web structural-functionalism social systems mesh
	INTERSUBJECTIVE	INTEROBJECTIVE

FIGURE 7-1. *Validity claims.*

that refers to or represents something in the concrete world. For example, I might say, "It is raining outside." Now we want to know if that is true or not. We want to know the validity or the "truth status" of that statement. So basically, we go and look outside. And if it is indeed raining, we say that the statement "It is raining outside" is a true statement.

Q: Or a true proposition.

KW: Yes. It's a simple mapping procedure. We check to see if the proposition *corresponds* with or fits the facts, if the map accurately reflects the real territory. (Usually it's more complicated, and we might try to disprove the map, and if we can never disprove it, we assume it is accurate enough.) But the essential idea is that with representational or propositional truth, my statement somehow refers to an *objective state of affairs*, and it accurately corresponds with those objects or processes or affairs.

Q: So propositional truth basically deals with just the exterior or objective or Right-Hand dimensions?

KW: Yes, that's right. Both the Upper-Right and Lower-Right quadrants contain the observable, empirical, exterior aspects of holons. We will subdivide these in a moment into the Upper and Lower versions, but the point is that all Right-Hand holons have *simple location*. These aspects can be easily seen, and thus with propositional truth, we tie our statements to these objects or processes or affairs. (This is also called the correspondence theory of truth.)

All of which is fair enough, and important enough, and I in no way deny the general importance of empirical representation. It's just not the whole story; it's not even the most interesting part of the story.

Truthfulness

Q: So an objective state of affairs—the brain, planets, organisms, ecosystems—can be represented with empirical mapping. These empirical maps are all variations on "It is raining." Objective propositions.

KW: Yes. But if we now look at the Upper Left—the actual *interior* of an individual holon—then we have an entirely different type of validity claim. The question here is not, Is it raining outside? The question here is, When I tell you it is raining outside, am I telling you the truth or am I lying?

You see, here it is not so much a question of whether the map matches the objective territory, but whether the mapmaker can be trusted.

And not just about objective truths, but especially about interior truths. I mean, you can always check and see if it is raining. You can do that yourself. But the *only* way you can know my interior, my depth, is by asking me, by *talking* to me, as we have seen. And when I report on my inner status, I might be telling you the truth, *but I might be lying*. You have no other way to get at my interior except in talk and dialogue and interpretation, and I might fundamentally distort, or conceal, or mislead—in short, I might lie.

So the way we tend to navigate in the Right Hand is by using the yardstick of propositional truth—or simply "truth" for short—but the way we navigate in the Upper Left is by using the yardstick of *truthfulness* or sincerity or honesty or trustworthiness. This is not so much a matter of *objective truth* but of *subjective truthfulness*. Two very different criteria—truth and truthfulness.

Q: So those are two different validity claims.

KW: Yes, that's right. And this is no trivial matter. Interior events are *located* in states of consciousness, not in objective states of affairs, and so you can't empirically nail them down with simple location. As we saw, they are accessed with communication and interpretation, not with the monological gaze.

And in this communication, *I might intentionally lie to you*. For various reasons, I might try to misrepresent my interior, I might try to make it appear to be something other than it really is. I might dash the entire Left-Hand dimensions against the wall of deceitfulness. I might lie to you.

Furthermore, and this is crucial, I might lie to myself. I might try to conceal aspects of my own depth from myself. I might do this intentionally, or I might do it "unconsciously." But one way or another, I might *misinterpret my own depth*, I might lie about my own interior.

And, in part, the "unconscious" is the locus of the all the ways I have lied to myself. I might have started lying to myself because of intense environmental trauma. Or maybe I learned it from my parents. Or maybe I had to do so as a defense mechanism against an even more painful truth.

But in any event, my unconscious is the locus of my insincerity, of my being less than truthful with myself, less than truthful about my subjective depth, my interior status, my deep desires and intentions. The unconscious is the locus of the lie.

Q: When we were talking about psychoanalysis and the interpretive therapies, you said their goal was to provide more truthful interpretations.

KW: Yes, that's exactly the same thing. The point of "depth psychology" and therapy is to help people *interpret* themselves more *truthfully*. The Left Hand, of course, is interpretation, and so it is no surprise that truthful or more adequate interpretation is the central therapeutic criterion.

The example we used was "sad" and "mad" about an absent father. What that means is that at some point early in my life, I started interpreting anger as depression. Perhaps I was enraged at my father for not being around. This rage, however, is very dangerous for a child. What if this rage could actually kill my father? Perhaps I had better not have this anger, because after all I love my father. So I'm angry at myself instead. I beat myself up instead. I'm rotten, no good, wretched to the core. This is very depressing. I started out mad, now I'm calling it sad.

One way or another, I have misinterpreted my interior, I have distorted my depth. I have started calling anger "sadness." And I carry this lie around with me. I cannot be truthful with myself because that would involve such great pain—to want to kill the father I love—so I would rather lie about the whole thing. And so this I do. My "shadow," my "unconscious," is now the locus of this lie, the focal point of this insincerity, the inner place that I hide from myself.

And because I lie to myself—and then forget it is a lie—then I will lie to you without even knowing it. I will probably even seem very sincere about it. In fact, if I have thoroughly lied to myself, I will honestly think I'm telling the truth. And if you give me a lie detector test, it will show that I'm telling the "truth." So much for empirical tests.

Finally, because I have misinterpreted my own depth, I will often misinterpret yours. I am cutting something off in my own depth—I am dissociating it, or repressing it, or alienating it—and so I will *distort interpretations* from that depth, both *in myself* and *in others*. My interpretations will be laced with lies, nested in insincerity. I will misinterpret myself, and I will often misinterpret you.

And you will probably notice this, notice that something is off base. I will say something so wacky, you'll have to respond, "That's not what I meant!" And you will think to yourself, "Where on earth did he get *that* one?"

Q: So these various interpretive therapies, such as psychoanalysis or Gestalt or Jungian, help you to contact and more truthfully interpret your depths.

KW: Yes, exactly. The idea is not to make some sort of more accurate map of the objective world, but to relax your resistances and sink into your interior depths, and learn to report those depths more truthfully, both to others and to yourself.

And this allows your *depth* to begin to match your *behavior*. Your words and your actions will match up. That is, your Left will match your Right. You will "walk your talk." And your left hand will know what your right hand doeth. We generally refer to this as integrity. You have the sense that the person won't lie to you, because they haven't lied to themselves.

Of course, if you live in the world of the lab technician—the empiricist, the behaviorist, the systems theorist, the cybernetic scurrying, the monological madness—you don't particularly care about interior truthfulness, because you don't particularly care about interiors, period. Not in their own terms, anyway. You just want monological truth, objective surfaces, empirical behavior, systems networks, and you don't care about interior depth and sincerity and truthfulness—in fact, there is nothing on the empirical maps that even vaguely corresponds with truthfulness!

Truthfulness, you see, doesn't have simple location, and it is not a merely empirical state of affairs, so it appears on none of the empirical maps. Not on a physicist's map, not on a biologist's map, not on a neurologist's map, not on a systems theory map, not on an ecosystem map. It is a Left-Hand, not a Right-Hand, affair!

And yet in that Left Hand exists your entire lifeworld, your actual awareness, your own depth. And if you are alive to depth at all, you will come to know that depth in yourself and in others through truthfulness and sincerity and trustworthiness.

The essential point is that the way to depth is blocked by deceit, blocked by deception. And the moment you acknowledge *interiors*, you must confront the primary roadblock to accessing those interiors: you must confront deception and deceit.

Which is precisely why we navigate in this domain by truthfulness. And yes, that is what all Left-Hand therapies work with. More truthful interpretations of your own inner depth.

Q: Different interpretive therapies do have different types of interpretations, however.

KW: Well, yes, and that's a long discussion. Perhaps I could just say that the different interpretive therapies differ primarily on *how deep* they are willing to go in their interpretations. Or how high they are willing to go. The Upper-Left quadrant is, as we were saying, a *spectrum of consciousness*—a spectrum of levels of developmental awareness.

And different therapies tend to plug into different levels of this spectrum, and use their favorite level as the basic reference point around which they will offer their interpretations.

As we saw, all interpretation is *context-bound*, and different therapies have their own favorite context within which they offer their interpretations. This doesn't mean that they are wrong, only that we have to identify their context, their favorite level. We have to situate their interpretations.

Freudians emphasize the emotional-sexual level; cognitive therapists emphasize the verbal; transpersonal therapists emphasize the spiritual. But they all primarily confront the distortions, the lies and self-deceptions with which we hide truthful aspects of these dimensions from ourselves—the lies and distortions that obscure our emotions, our self-esteem, our spiritual nature.

Q: So a full-spectrum model would be a type of composite story, including all the various levels of the spectrum of consciousness and the therapies that are most effective for each level.

KW: Yes, that is one of the tasks of a full-spectrum model, and many researchers are now hard at work on such a model (these are discussed in Part Two). An excellent introduction to this field is *Paths beyond Ego*, by Roger Walsh and Frances Vaughan.

But my basic point about these Left-Hand or interpretive therapies is that, once we strip them of their exclusiveness or their single-level partialness, then they all have something very important to teach us. They all have something to tell us about the various layers of the self—of consciousness—and about the *truthful interpretations* that can help us access these various dimensions.

Because the amazing fact is that truth alone will not set you free. Truthfulness will set you free.

Justness

Q: What about the Lower-Left quadrant?

KW: The crucial point is that the *subjective* world is *situated* in an *intersubjective* space, a cultural space, and it is this intersubjective space that *allows* the subjective space to arise in the first place. Without this cultural background, my own individual thoughts would have no meaning at all. I wouldn't even have the tools to interpret my own thoughts to myself. In fact, I wouldn't even have developed thoughts, I would be "wolf boy."

In other words, the *subjective* space is inseparable from the *intersubjective* space, and this is one of the great discoveries of the postmodern or post-Enlightenment movements.

So here, in the Lower Left, the validity claim is not so much *objective* propositional truth, and not so much *subjective* truthfulness, but *intersubjective fit*. This cultural background provides the *common context* against which my own thoughts and interpretations will have some sort of meaning. And so the validity criterion here involves the "cultural fit" with this background.

Q: So the aim of this validity claim is what, exactly? We have objective truth, we have subjective truthfulness, and we have intersubjective . . . what?

KW: The aim here is *mutual understanding*. Not that we necessarily *agree* with each other, but can we at least *understand* each other? Because if that can't happen, then we will never be able to exist in a common culture. Can you and I arrange our subjective spaces so that we see eye to eye? Can we find a common cultural background that allows communication to exist in the first place? Can we find a cultural fit, a common meaning, between ourselves? This must happen to some degree before any communication can occur at all!

Q: So the aim here is not so much the mapping of objective truth, and not simply being truthful, but reaching mutual understanding?

KW: Yes. This has many, many aspects. You and I are going to have to agree on some sort of morals and ethics if we are going to live in the same space. And we are going to have to find some sort of common law. And we are going to have to find some sort of identity that overlaps our individual selves and shows us something in common, some sort of collective identity, so that we can see something of ourselves in each other, and treat each other with care and concern.

All of that is involved in this *cultural fit*, this background of common meaning and appropriateness and justness. I have been describing this background as if it were some sort of contract that you and I consciously form, like a social contract, and sometimes it is. Sometimes we simply reach mutual agreement about, for example, the voting age or the speed limit on the highway. That is part of cultural fit, of how we agree on rules and common meanings that allow us all to fit together.

But much of cultural fit is not a conscious contract; much of it is so deeply background that we hardly know it's there. There are linguistic structures and cultural practices so deeply contextual that we are still trying to dig them up and understand them (one of Heidegger's main themes). But the point is, wherever they come from, there is no escaping these intersubjective networks that allow the subjective space to develop in the first place!

What is so remarkable about mutual understanding is not that I can take a simple word like "dog" and point to a real dog and say, "I mean that." What is so remarkable is that *you* know what *I* mean by that! Forget the simple empirical pointing! Instead, look at this intersubjective understanding. It is utterly amazing. It means you and I can inhabit each other's interior to some degree. You and I can *share* our *depth*. When we point to *truth*, and we are situated in *truthfulness*, we can reach *mutual understanding*. This is a miracle. If Spirit exists, you can begin to look for it here.

Q: So this is cultural fit or justness.

KW: Yes, justness, goodness, rightness. How do we reach the common good? What is right and appropriate for us, such that we can all inhabit the same cultural space with some sort of dignity and fairness? How do we arrange our subjective spaces so that they mesh in the common intersubjective space, the common worldspace, the common culture, upon which we have all depended for our own subjective being?

This is not a matter of arranging *objects* in the space of simple location! It is a matter of arranging *subjects* in the collective interior space of culture.

This is not simply truthfulness, and not simply the true, but the good.

Q: So, as you say, cultural fit or justness includes all sorts of items, from ethics and morals and laws, to group or collective identities, to background cultural contexts, and so on.

KW: Yes, all of which we have been summarizing as a common worldview or worldspace, which we also called "cultural," the Lower Left.

And remember, this cultural space exists for all holons, even though it might be simpler and less complex. So there is *intersubjectivity woven into the very fabric of the Kosmos at all levels*. This is not just the Spirit in "me," not just the Spirit in "it," not just the Spirit in "them"—but the Spirit in "us," in all of *us*.

And, as we will see when we return to environmental ethics, we want to arrive at a *justness* for all sentient beings: the deeper *good* for all of *us*.

Functional Fit

Q: What's the difference between Upper Right and Lower Right? You said they have a different validity claim.

KW: The Upper Right is exteriors of just *individuals*, the Lower Right is exteriors of *systems*. So the Upper Right is propositional truth in the very strictest sense: a proposition refers to a single fact. But in the Lower Right, the proposition refers to the social system, whose main validity claim is *functional fit*—how various holons fit together in the overall objective system.

Q: But doesn't the Lower Left also involve systems? You said that in cultural fit, it's how an individual fits with the whole cultural background. Isn't that also systems theory?

KW: No, it isn't, and the reason it isn't is basically the entire story of the postmodern revolt against Enlightenment modernity. In a sense, the entire post-Cartesian revolt points out dramatically why *systems theory* is just *more Cartesian dualism* in its worst aspects. Understanding why that is so is the very essence of the postmodern advance.

Q: Let's go into that, because it is certainly at odds with what the systems theorists themselves say. They say they are *overcoming* the fundamental Enlightenment paradigm.

KW: Just the opposite. The fundamental Enlightenment paradigm, as we have seen, was the representation paradigm—the mapping paradigm, the monological paradigm—and the systems theorists are just doing more of the same. They don't overcome it, they clone it.

It's true that both the Lower Right and Lower Left are dealing with "systems" in the broad sense, because the entire lower half is the communal or the collective. But the Lower Left describes that system *from within*, from the *interior*. It describes the consciousness, the values, the worldviews, the ethics, the collective identities. But the Lower Right describes the system in purely objective and exterior terms, from without. It doesn't want to know how collective values are intersubjectively shared in mutual understanding. Rather, it wants to know how their objective correlates *functionally fit* in the overall social system, which itself has simple location.

So open any good book on systems theory and you will find nothing about ethical standards, intersubjective values, moral dispositions, mutual understanding, truthfulness, sincerity, depth, integrity, aesthetics, interpretation, hermeneutics, beauty, art, the sublime. Open any systems theory text and you will find *none* of that even mentioned. All you will find are the objective and *exterior correlates* of all of that. All you will find in systems theory are information bits scurrying through processing channels, and cybernetic feedback loops, and processes within processes of dynamic networks of monological representations, and nests within nests of endless processes, all of which have *simple location*, not in an individual, but in the social system and network of objective processes.

All of which is true! And all of which *leaves out* the interiors in their own terms, the actual lived experiences and values and lifeworlds—it honors the Right Hand of the collective, but completely devastates the Left Hand.

Q: But why can't you simply say, as systems theorists do, that systems theory is the basic reality of which the subjective aspects are simply parts—all parts of the great web. That web covers everything, by definition.

KW: By exterior definition! That great web always has simple location. So with the systems approach, the split between the subjective and the objective is "healed" by *reducing* all subjects to objects in the "holistic" system. It reduces all subjective and intersubjective occasions to interobjective fit, functional fit, monological fit.

Well, that *is* the fundamental Enlightenment paradigm. This is why theorists from Taylor to Foucault to Habermas have pointed out that systems theory is just more of the same reductionistic nightmare—all of the Left Hand aspects are reduced to Right-Hand descriptions in the great system, the great web.

Q: What you call *subtle reductionism*.

KW: Yes, subtle reductionism. Gross reductionism we all know about: everything is reduced to atoms in the Upper Right. This is very gross. Subtle reductionism does not do that. In fact, it aggressively *fights* that! But it immediately gets caught in a subtle reductionism: all Left-Hand aspects are reduced to their correlates in the Right Hand. The Right Hand has extensive functional fit and a systems view, so it appears that you are being very holistic and all-inclusive, but you have just gutted the interiors of the entire Kosmos, you have just perfectly ruined the lifeworld of all holons.

Objective systems within systems within systems—atoms are parts of cells, which are parts of organisms, which are parts of ecosystems, which are parts of the biosphere, and so on. In other words, *functional fit*. The truth of the Lower Right is found in how the individual holons functionally fit into the holistic system, how each is a strand in the interrelated web, which is the primary reality. So the system theorist is always talking collective systems—Gaia, or ecosystems, or interrelated webs of interaction, or the web of life, or information flow charts as objectively mapped, or planetary federations and global networks, and so on. All in objective and monological terms.

All of which is true, but all of which totally leaves out the Left-Hand dimensions. So the systems theorists admirably fight gross reductionism, but they are totally caught in the monological madness of subtle reductionism, which is the real root of the Enlightenment nightmare, as recent scholarship has made more than clear.

Q: Systems theory does claim to be a monological science.

KW: Yes, and we don't argue with them. They are entirely correct. And that says it all.

Q: Is the difference between the Lower Left and cultural fit, versus the Lower Right and functional fit—would this be the same as the two approaches to the Rain Dance?

KW: Yes, very much. The Lower-Left approach studies the community by becoming a participant observer, and attempts to *understand* it *from within*. Remember, the validity criteria in the Lower Left is mutual understanding. And this you attempt to do by becoming a participant observer. You enter the interior meaning of the community. And you understand this meaning only by understanding its *cultural fit*—by understanding what the meaning of the Dance is, based on how it fits into the vast background of cultural and linguistic meanings and practices. And the participant observer, the hermeneutic interpreter, might find that, as we said, the Dance is part of a sacred ritual with nature. That is its interior meaning, which you *understand* by immersing yourself in this cultural background which will give you the common worldspace or *common context* against which you can now make *adequate interpretations*.

Now the standard systems scientist, or standard systems theorist, is not primarily interested in any of that, in any of the interior meaning. Rather, systems theory is interested in the *function* that the Dance performs in the overall *social system*. What the natives *say* this Dance means is not so important. What is really important is that the Dance is part of an objective social system, and this objective system in many ways determines what the individual participants are doing. The *real* function of the Dance is to provide autopoietic self-maintenance of the system. The Dance is thus part of the social system's attempt to maintain its social integration, its *functional fit*. It provides a common ritual around which social cohesion is organized. And this can be determined by observing the Dance from an *objective* stance, an "empirical" or positivistic stance—objective and monological. You can even make a monological flow chart of it, which, believe me, is not how the natives experience the Dance at all!

Q: But I suppose that, again, you do not think that one of those approaches is right and the other wrong.

KW: They are both correct, in my opinion. One approaches the sociocultural holon from within, the other from without. One is how *subjects* fit together in cultural space—how you and I reach mutual understanding or *intersubjectivity*; the other is how objects fit together in physical space, in the total objective system, in *interobjectivity*. The one uses hermeneutics, or interpretation of interior *depth*; the other uses empirical-analytic observation, or objective analysis of observable *behavior*. "What does it mean?" versus "What does it do?"

Both are entirely valid; they are each the correlates of the other. They are, in fact, the Left and Right Hands of Spirit as it manifests in the collective. But, alas, these two academic disciplines don't get along too well with each other, a cat fight we might as well avoid.

Conclusion: The Four Faces of Spirit

Q: Okay, so we have four different quadrants, each with a different type of truth, a different voice. And each has a different test for its truth—a different validity claim, as shown in figure 7-1.

KW: Yes. All of these are valid forms of knowledge, because they are *grounded* in the realities of the four facets of every holon. And therefore all four of these truth claims can be redeemed, can be confirmed or rejected by a community of the adequate. They each have a different validity claim which carefully guides us, through checks and balances, on our knowledge quest. They are all falsifiable in their *own domains*, which means false claims can be dislodged by further evidence from that domain. (So let us gently ignore the claims of any one quadrant that it alone has the only falsifiable test there is, so it alone has the only truth worth knowing!)

And over the centuries and millennia, humanity has, by very painful trial and error, learned the basic procedures for these tests for truth.

Q: Which is why they're so important.

KW: Definitely. These truths are the golden treasure of a collective humanity, hard won through blood and sweat and tears and turmoil in the face of falsity, error, deception, and deceit. Humanity has slowly and increasingly *learned*, over a million-year history, to separate truth from appearance, goodness from corruption, beauty from degradation, and sincerity from deception.

And ultimately, these four truths are simply the four faces of Spirit as it shines in the manifest world. The validity claims are the ways that we connect to Spirit itself, ways that we attune ourselves to the Kosmos. As we said at the beginning of this discussion, the validity claims force us to confront reality; they curb our egoic fantasies and self-centered ways; they demand evidence from the rest of the Kosmos; they force us outside of ourselves! They are the checks and balances in the Kosmic Constitution.

And so, following these paths to truth, we fit with the flow of the Kosmos, we are delivered into currents that take us outside of ourselves, beyond ourselves, and force us to curb our self-serving ways, as we fit into ever deeper and wider circles of truth. From attunement to atonement to at-onement: until, with a sudden and jolting shock, we recognize our own Original Face, the Face that was smiling at us in each and every truth claim, the Face that all along was whispering ever so gently but always so insistently: please remember the true, and please remember the good, and please remember the beautiful.

And so the whispering voice from every corner of the Kosmos says: let truth and truthfulness and goodness and beauty shine as the seals of a radiant Spirit that would never, and could never, abandon us.

8

The Good, the True,
and the Beautiful

Q: I want to move into the higher or transpersonal stages. But before we do that, you said there was a very simple way to summarize the four quadrants, their truths and validity claims—all of that, a simple way to summarize it!

KW: Yes. Here are the basic divisions: Everything on the Right Hand can be described in "it" language. Everything in the Upper Left is described in "I" language. And everything on the Lower Left is described in "we" language.

Q: I, we, and it. That's simple enough.

The Big Three

Q: These three languages are listed on the inside corners of figure 7-1 (page 149) and on figure 5-2 (page 119).

KW: Yes. It-language is objective, neutral, value-free surfaces. This is the standard language of the empirical, analytic, and systems sciences, from physics to biology to ecology to cybernetics to positivistic sociology to behaviorism to systems theory.

In other words, it is monological. It is a monologue with surfaces, with "its." It-language describes objective exteriors and their interrelations, observable surfaces and patterns that can be seen with the senses or their instrumental extensions—whether those empirical surfaces are "inside" you, like your brain or lungs, or "outside" you, like ecosystems. Even information scurrying through channels can be described in it-language. Information, in fact, is defined as negative entropy, which is about as it-ish as you can get. Your presence is not required.

I-language, on the other hand, *is* your presence, your consciousness, your subjective awareness. Everything on the Upper Left is basically described in I-language, in the language of interior subjectivity. The subjective component of any holon is the I-component.

Of course, this "I" or self or subjectivity becomes greater with greater depth—there is more subjectivity in an ape than in a worm—but the point is, this I-component in any case cannot be described in it-language. That would reduce the subject to a mere object, and we all instinctively resist this, and resist it aggressively. Subjects are understood, objects are manipulated.

Q: The lab technician . . .

KW: Yes, that was one example. Your "I" is treated as an "it." Whether these objects are singular, or whether they are collective strands in the great and wonderful web, people instinctively know that this reduction is dangerous.

Q: And the third language?

KW: The third language, we-language, is the Lower Left, the cultural or intersubjective dimension. The Upper Left is how "I" see the world; the Lower Left is how "we" see it. It is the collective worldview that we of a particular time and place and culture inhabit. These worldviews evolve, of course, and so we find archaic, magic, mythic, rational, which we have already briefly mentioned.

So at the very minimum, we have these three fundamental languages, and they are quite different, addressing these different domains. And the failure to differentiate these languages has caused an enormous amount of confusion.

Q: You call these "the Big Three."

KW: Yes. The Big Three—this is just a simplified version of the four quadrants, since both Right-Hand quadrants are objective exteriors ("it" or "its"). So for simplicity's sake, the four quadrants can usually be treated as three, as the Big Three—I, we, and it.

So when we say that every individual holon has four quadrants—or, in simpler form, the Big Three—we also mean that every holon has these aspects or facets that can only be described in these different languages. And the reason we can't reduce any of these languages to the others is the same reason we can't reduce any of the quadrants to the others. So we can only describe a holon adequately and fully if we *use all three languages*, so as to describe all of its quadrants, and not simply privilege one quadrant or one language, which, of course, is what usually happens.

Q: So, the Big Three. You have pointed out an enormous number of correlations with these three—such as morals, science, and art; or Plato's the Good, the True, and the Beautiful.

KW: Yes. Here are just a few of the various forms of the Big Three:

I (Upper Left):	consciousness, subjectivity, self, and self-expression (including art and aesthetics); truthfulness, sincerity.
We (Lower Left):	ethics and morals, worldviews, common context, culture; intersubjective meaning, mutual understanding, appropriateness, justness.
It (Right Hand):	science and technology, objective nature, empirical forms (including brain and social systems); propositional truth (singular and functional fit).

Science—empirical science—deals with objects, with "its," with empirical patterns. Morals and ethics concern "we" and our intersubjective world. Art concerns the beauty in the eye of the beholder, the "I." And yes, this is essentially Plato's the Good (morals, the "we"), the True (in the sense of propositional truth, objective truths or "its"), and the Beautiful (the aesthetic dimension as perceived by each "I").

The Big Three are also Sir Karl Popper's three worlds—objective (it), subjective (I), and cultural (we). And the Big Three are Habermas's three validity claims: objective truth, subjective sincerity, and intersubjective justness.

And, of enormous historical importance, the Big Three showed up in Kant's immensely influential trilogy—*The Critique of Pure Reason* (objective science), *The Critique of Practical Reason* (morals), and *The Critique of Judgment* (aesthetic judgment and art).

Dozens of examples could be given, but that's the general picture of the Big Three.

Q: Okay, I want to very briefly return to the fundamental Enlightenment paradigm—to the whole movement of "modernity" itself—and I want you to explain it in terms of the Big Three.

This is important, I think, because all of the "new paradigm" approaches claim to be overcoming the Enlightenment paradigm, and you keep saying that most of them are still thoroughly caught in it. You keep saying, for example, that systems theory is still following the Enlightenment paradigm. So, in terms of the Big Three, what was the fundamental Enlightenment paradigm?

KW: Oh, that part is fairly easy. The fundamental Enlightenment paradigm reduced all I's and all we's to mere its. The mainstream Enlightenment thought that all of reality could be captured in it-language, which alone was supposed to be "really real." So it reduced the Big Three to the big flat one of it-language. In other words, it reduced all of the Left-Hand dimensions to their Right-Hand correlates—subtle reductionism. Is this clear?

Q: It rejected art and morals in favor of science?

KW: Yes, in a sense. But the best way to get a handle on the negative aspects of modernity and the Enlightenment is to first understand their *positive* contributions. Each stage of development, remember, has a "dialectic of progress"—in plain language, every new development is good news, bad news. And we have been stressing some of the bad news, but this really doesn't make much sense without first understanding the corresponding good news. So I'd like to briefly talk about that good news of modernity, or else we get caught in merely anti-modernist rhetoric, which is unhelpful.

The Good News: Differentiation of the Big Three

Q: Okay, out of curiosity, can this "good news" of modernity also be stated in terms of the Big Three?

KW: Yes. According to theorists from Weber to Habermas, the good news of modernity was that it managed, for the first time in history, to fully *differentiate* the Big Three on a large scale. That is, to differentiate art, morals, and science; or self, culture, and nature. These domains were no longer fused with each other, no longer syncretically fused and confused.

We moderns take this differentiation so much for granted that we tend to forget what was involved in the previous mythological worldview, where art and science and religious morals were all indiscriminately fused. Not integrated, just fused! Big difference.

Here is a good example. This was a highly regarded and widely accepted "refutation" of Galileo's discovery of the moons of Jupiter: "There are seven windows given to animals in the domicile of the head, through which the air is admitted to the tabernacle of the body, to enlighten, to warm, and to nourish it. What are these parts of the *microcosm?* Two nostrils, two eyes, two ears, and a mouth. So in the heavens, as in a *macrocosmos,* there are two favorable stars, two unpropitious, two luminaries, and Mercury undecided and indifferent. From this and many other similarities in nature, such as the seven metals, etc., which it were tedious to enumerate, we gather that the number of planets is necessarily seven."

Q: Seven bodily orifices means that there *must* be seven planets.

KW: Yes. In other words, the subjective space and the objective space are so poorly differentiated that what happens in one must govern what happens in the other. Likewise, the subjective and the cultural space were still poorly differentiated, so that if you disagreed with Church religion, with the cultural background, then you were not just a *heretic,* you were also a political *criminal*—you could be tried by the Church for *heresy* and by the State for *treason,* because these had not yet been differentiated.

In other words, in all of these cases, the I and the we and the it domains were not very clearly differentiated. It is not that they were *integrated;* they simply were *not yet differentiated!* Huge difference.

Now I realize that there are certain "new paradigm" theorists who want to see this mythic indissociation as some sort of holistic heaven, but I think not one of them would actually enjoy living in that atmosphere. Most of their "new paradigm" notions would be immediately charged with both heresy and treason—a situation for which mythic-imperial cultures the world over devised numerous and unpleasant remedies. In other words, I think they are either not very informed or not very sincere about all this eulogizing of the previous mythic worldview.

Q: So the Enlightenment or modernity differentiated the Big Three for the first time.

KW: Yes, on any sort of large scale. Kant's three *Critiques* being the perfect example in this regard.

This was truly a quantum leap in human capacity. And this is why this extraordinary differentiation of the Big Three—the differentiation of art, morals, and science—has been called, by Weber and Habermas, the *dignity* of modernity, and I agree entirely. "Dignity" because the I and the we and the it domains could pursue their own knowledge without violent intrusions, or even punishments, from the other domains. You could look through Galileo's telescope without being burned at the stake. And all of that was good news indeed.

This differentiation of the Big Three would have an enormous number of beneficial gains. Here are just a few:

- The differentiation of self (I) and culture (we) contributed directly to the rise of democracy, where each self had a vote and was not simply subsumed by the dominator mythic hierarchy of the church or state. The rise of the liberal democracies on a widespread scale.
- The differentiation of mind (I) and nature (it) contributed to the liberation movements, including the liberation of women and slaves, because biological might no longer made noospheric right. The rise of liberal feminism and abolition as widespread and effective cultural movements.
- The differentiation of culture (we) and nature (it) contributed to the rise of empirical science and medicine and physics and biology, because truth was no longer subservient to state and church mythology. The rise of ecological sciences. And on and on and on . . .

Q: So liberal democracy, feminism, the ecological sciences, the abolition of slavery—all part of the good news of modernity, and all related directly to the differentiation of the Big Three. So what about the bad news?

The Bad News: Dissociation of the Big Three

KW: We have seen that one of the twenty tenets is that evolution proceeds by *differentiation* and *integration*. The good news of modernity was that it learned to *differentiate* the Big Three; the bad news was that it had not yet learned how to *integrate* them.

So the *dignity* of modernity began to slide into the *disaster* of modernity: the Big Three didn't just differentiate, they tended to *dissociate*!

Which was very bad news indeed. Because they were dissociated—that is, because the Big Three were not harmoniously balanced and integrated—they were ripe for plunder by the more aggressive approaches of the it-domain.

And thus, for various reasons that we can talk about if you want, the *rapid and explosive advances in the it-domain*—the spectacular advances in the empirical and technical sciences—began to overshadow and overrun the advances in the I and the we domains. Science began to crowd out consciousness and aesthetics and morals.

The great and undeniable advances in the empirical sciences from the

Renaissance to the Enlightenment made it appear that all of reality could be approached and described in it-language, in objective scientific terms. And conversely, if something couldn't be studied and described in an objective, empirical fashion, then it wasn't "really real." The Big Three were reduced to the "Big One" of scientific materialism, scientific exteriors and objects and systems.

And so the it-approaches began to *colonize* the I and the we domains. All knowledge had to be objective it-knowledge, and so all of reality began to look like a bunch of its, with no subjects, no consciousness, no selves, no morals, no virtues, no values, no interiors, no depths. The Left-Hand dimensions of I and we were collapsed into the Right Hand of the Big It.

Q: The Big Three collapsed into the Big One of flatland.

KW: Yes, exactly. And this project can initially seem to make a great deal of sense, precisely because every holon does indeed have an objective or Right-Hand aspect! Every component on the Left Hand has its empirical and objective and Right-Hand correlates (as you can easily see on figure 5-2). Even if I have an out-of-the-body experience, it registers some sort of changes in the empirical brain!

And since empirical and monological studies are *infinitely easier* than that messy interpretation and intersubjective hermeneutics and empathetic mutual understanding, it initially *made all the sense in the world* to restrict knowledge to the empirical domain, to the Right-Hand dimensions. This is completely understandable, and even noble in its own way.

And this is what the fundamental Enlightenment paradigm did. The basic knowledge quest was for the rational Ego to simply map or mirror the entire world in it-language. What Rorty has aptly called "the mirror of nature."

Q: The mapping paradigm, the representation paradigm.

KW: Yes, which just happened to leave out the mapmaker and the interiors altogether. Interpretation is not required; the world is simply obvious and "pregiven." And you simply map this pregiven world, the world of simple location. You map the Right-Hand world.

In this sweeping Enlightenment agenda, nature was held to be a perfectly *harmonious and interrelated system*, a great it-system, and knowledge consisted in patiently and empirically mapping this it-system in it-language.

And this great harmonious it-system, this perfectly "holistic" system, was the fundamental Enlightenment grid, the bedrock of the radical Enlightenment.

Q: But the "new paradigm" theorists strongly maintain that what was fundamental about the Enlightenment paradigm was its *atomism*. And that they are going to overcome that by replacing it with *holism*, or systems theory.

KW: Yes, they do say that, and it is deeply confused. I don't know who started that nonsense, but it is nonsense indeed.

Q: I've marked a section in *Sex, Ecology, Spirituality* where you introduce this topic, and I want to read it for the audience.

These theorists claim, for example, that the great "negative legacy" of the Enlightenment was its atomistic and divisive ontology. But atomism was *not* the dominant theme of the Enlightenment. As we will see in great detail—and as virtually every historian of the period has made abundantly clear—the dominant theme of the Enlightenment was the "harmony of an interlocking order of being," a systems harmony that was behind everything from Adam Smith's great "invisible hand" to John Locke's "great interlocking order" to the Reformers' and the Deists' "vast harmonious whole of mutually interrelated beings."

To give only a few examples now, Charles Taylor represents the virtually uncontested conclusion of scholars that "For the mainstream of the Enlightenment, nature as the whole interlocking system of objective reality, in which all beings, including man, had a natural mode of existence which dovetailed with that of all others, provided the basic model, the blueprint for happiness and hence good. The Enlightenment developed a model of nature, including human nature, as a *harmonious whole whose parts meshed perfectly*," and the "unity of the order was seen as an interlocking set calling for actions which formed a harmonious whole." As Alexander Pope would have it, speaking for an entire generation: "Such is the World's great harmony, that springs from Order, Union, full Consent of things; Where small and great, where weak and mighty, made to serve [each other], not suffer; strengthen, not invade; Parts relate to Whole; All served, all serving; nothing stands alone."

Already the *Encyclopédie*, bastion of Enlightenment thought, had announced that "everything in nature is linked together," and Lovejoy points out that "they were wont to discourse with eloquence on the perfection of the Universal System as a whole."

KW: Yes, the dominant theme of the Enlightenment was this great "web of life" conception, a great interlocking order of beings, each mutually interwoven with all others. There were indeed a few atomistic cranks, as there have been from Democritus forward. But they did not represent the dominant and central themes of the mainstream Enlightenment, as these scholars make abundantly clear.

Q: So what was the real "negative legacy" of the Enlightenment?

KW: Well, as we were saying, this Enlightenment web-of-life conception was indeed holistic and interwoven, but it acknowledged only holarchies in the Right-Hand dimensions. It did not acknowledge the holarchies in the Left Hand on *their own terms*. It *collapsed* the Big Three into the Big One—collapsed the interwoven I and we and it . . . into a flatland system of just interwoven its.

And so, of the Big Three of consciousness, culture, and nature, only sensory nature now was real, and all real knowledge must therefore be a mere *reflection* of that *only* reality. The reflection paradigm. The mirror of nature. The collapse of the Kosmos.

Systems theory isn't a cure for this negative legacy of the Enlightenment, it is an intrinsic part of that nightmare!

Q: Part of flatland.

KW: Yes, what Mumford called the disqualified universe. It-language is essentially value-free, neutral. It has *quantity*, but no *quality*. So if you describe everything in terms of quantities and objective exteriors and network processes and systems variables, then you get no qualitative distinctions whatsoever—you get the *disqualified* universe.

Recall that everything on the Right Hand has simple location, which can be *bigger* or *smaller* but not *better* or *worse*. Open-mindedness is better than narrow-minded bigotry, but a rock is not better than a planet. Because the Right Hand has some sort of physical extension, it can fairly easily be quantified and counted—1, 2, 3, 4, 5. You get amounts, not morals. And while seven might be *larger* than three, it is not *better*. And thus, if you start treating the entire world as an object—holistic or otherwise—you strip it of all value. You have disqualified the Kosmos.

And when you are done with that, and you pause to look around, you find to your utter horror that you are standing in a flat and faded universe, with no meaning, no depth, no interpretation, no beauty, no goodness, no virtue, and nothing sublime. Just a bunch of holistic its in functional fit.

Q: Whitehead's famous remark: "a dull affair, soundless, scentless, colorless; merely the hurrying of material, endlessly, meaninglessly."

KW: Yes, to which he added, "Thereby, modern philosophy has been ruined." More to the point, the modern lifeworld has been ruined. Once you go from Left to Right, from interior to exterior, from mind to brain, from compassion to serotonin, you go from value to valueless, from virtue to virtueless, from worth to worthless.

And if you think the great it-domain is the *only* reality, then you will maintain that all values and all virtues are "merely subjective." That is, they are personal choices not anchored in any sort of substantive reality. You will not see that depth is intrinsic to the Kosmos. You will not see that value is intrinsic to the Kosmos. You will not see that consciousness is intrinsic to the Kosmos.

All of that is lost, denied, erased from the shiny monochrome world that you now triumphantly inhabit. And once you have carefully scrubbed the Kosmos clean of consciousness and virtue and value, you should not be surprised if your own lifeworld starts to look completely hollow and empty. To *complain* about this state of affairs is like murdering your parents and then complaining you're an orphan.

The Task of Postmodernity: Integration of the Big Three

Q: So overcoming the negative legacy of the Enlightenment means what, exactly?

KW: Well, to begin with, to overcome the negative aspects of the Enlightenment is *not* to replace monological atomism with monological holism, with flatland systems theory. Atomism and systems holism are both Right-Hand reductionism, one gross, one subtle, but nonetheless.

Nor should we seek our solutions by *regressing* to mythic or magic indissociation of the Big Three, where self and culture and nature were *not yet* differentiated. We must preserve the dignity of modernity, even while we attempt to overcome the disaster of modernity. The dignity was differentiation; the disaster was dissociation.

So if modernity managed to differentiate the Big Three on a widespread scale, it is up to postmodernity to integrate them. The very currents of evolution—the twenty tenets—demand this differentiation and integration, and we today are on the cusp of that demand.

Q: The demand of postmodernity. The demand of an *integral* view.

KW: Yes. This does not mean that everything called "postmodern" is therefore an attempt at this integration. Much of postmodern thought is extremist, nihilistic, narcissistic. But the more authentic currents of postmodernity, as I use the term—from Hegel to Heidegger to Habermas to Foucault to Taylor—are trying to get some balance back into the picture, largely by trying to honor science and morals and aesthetics equally, and not simply reduce one to the other in an orgy of theoretical violence.

So that is exactly what we will want to watch for: ways to integrate mind and culture and nature in the postmodern world. Which is to say, ways to honor Spirit in all four quadrants, to recognize the four faces of Spirit—or simply the Big Three—and thus attune ourselves to, and situate ourselves in, and give blessings for: the Good, and the True, and the Beautiful.

The Spiritual Big Three

Q: This is where we begin to touch on spiritual themes. You have tied the Big Three in to the notions of Buddha, Dharma, and Sangha. Buddha was a great spiritual realizer, Dharma is the truth he realized, and Sangha is the community of those who are attempting this realization.

KW: Yes, those are the Big Three as consciousness evolution continues into the higher or superconscious or transpersonal domains. Of course, this is using the Buddhist terms; others will do as well.

Q: Let's briefly go over them one at a time.

KW: Figure 5-2 only lists some of the milestones in average or collective consciousness up to the present, up to modern rationality (marked "formop" and "vision-logic" in the Upper Left).

But beyond those stages there lie transrational or transpersonal or more properly spiritual developments, which I suppose we'll talk about soon enough. And my point is that these higher developments also proceed *in all four quadrants*. Or, in simplified form, in the Big Three. This higher evolution occurs in the I, and the we, and the it domains.

And the ultimate I is Buddha, the ultimate We is Sangha, and the ultimate It is Dharma.

Q: For example . . .

KW: We can put this in several different ways.

When you are ultimately *truthful* with yourself, you will eventually realize and *confess* that "I am Buddha," I am Spirit. Anything short of that is a lie, the lie of the ego, the lie of the separate-self sense, the contraction in the face of infinity. The deepest recesses of your consciousness directly intersect Spirit itself, in the supreme identity. "Not I, but Christ liveth in me"—which is to say, the ultimate I *is* Christ. This is not a state you are bringing into existence for the first time, but simply a timeless state that you are recognizing and confessing—you are being ultimately *truthful* when you state, "I am Buddha," the ultimate Beauty.

And the ultimate cultural fit or justness is, "We are all members of the Community of Spirit." *All sentient beings*—all holons in fact—contain Buddha-nature—contain depth, consciousness, intrinsic value, Spirit—and thus we are all members of the council of all beings, the mystical church, the ultimate We. Which is ultimate ethics, the ultimate Good.

And the ultimate objective truth is that all beings are perfect manifestations of Spirit or Emptiness—we are all manifestations of the ultimate It, or Dharma. Which is the ultimate Truth.

The ultimate I, the ultimate We, and the ultimate It—Buddha, Sangha, Dharma.

Q: This is why understanding the four quadrants, or just the Big Three, is so important for understanding higher or spiritual developments. This is why we need an "all-level, all-quadrant" approach.

KW: I think so, yes. Spirit manifests in all four quadrants equally, and so all four quadrants (or simply the Big Three) ought to be taken into account in order for the realization of Spirit to be full and complete and unbroken.

Q: Buddha?

KW: Well, we haven't talked about these higher stages of the Upper-Left quadrant, but the essential point is that they disclose deeper or higher stages of consciousness, to the point that the individual "I" discovers its prior identity with Spirit, however you wish to conceive that. The Buddhists would say that the individual "I" discovers its prior nature as Emptiness, so that the isolated and alienated "I" relaxes into the radically open and empty and transparent ground of all manifestation. The Sufis call it the Supreme Identity, the identity of the soul and Godhead. In Zen we have the True Self that is no-self, or no individual self at all, this primordial Emptiness that is the transparency of all Form. In Christianity, "Let this consciousness be in you which was in Christ Jesus."

The evidence is simply that the individual self discovers a primordial and unqualifiable Ground, so that its own self intersects the Ground of the Kosmos at large. The ultimate Self that is no-self: that is the Buddha-nature or Buddha-mind or Christ-consciousness in each and every sentient being. The ultimate self, the ultimate I, is Buddha. That's Upper Left.

Q: Dharma?

KW: Dharma refers to Spirit as an *objective fact*, as an objective State of Affairs. The ultimate It of the Kosmos is the Dharma, the Truth, the objective isness or suchness or thusness of all holons. The very Condition of all conditions, the very Nature of all natures, the very Itness of all holons—this is the Dharma, the objective Truth, which is that all holons, just as they are, in their Itness, are perfect manifestations of Emptiness, of Spirit. And that is the ultimate Truth!

Q: And Sangha?

KW: *Sangha* means gathering or community. It is the "we" of Spirit. In mystical Christian terms, it is the Church, the mystical communion of Christ. It is the intersubjective circle of realization, the culture of the Divine. The Lower Left.

The point is that, precisely because Spirit manifests equally in all four quadrants, or equally in the Big Three, then we can describe Spirit *subjectively* as one's own Buddha-mind—the "I" of Spirit, the Beauty. And we can describe Spirit *objectively* as Dharma—the "It" of Spirit, the ultimate Truth. And we can describe Spirit *culturally* as Sangha—the "We" of Spirit, the ultimate Good.

These four quadrants, or the Big Three, are all facets of Spirit, facets of Emptiness. When Emptiness manifests, it does so as subject and object, each of which can be singular or plural. And that gives us the four quadrants, or simply the Big Three. So Spirit can be described—and must be described—with all three languages, I and we and it.

Each of those domains evolves. Which means, each unfolds its spiritual nature more and more, and thus realizes its spiritual nature more and more. And in the uppermost reaches of that evolution, the I and the We and the It increasingly become transparent to their own true nature. They each radiate the glory of the Ground that they are.

And in that radiant awareness, every I becomes a God, and every We becomes God's sincerest worship, and every It becomes God's most gracious temple.

PART TWO

THE FURTHER REACHES OF SPIRIT-IN-ACTION

9

The Evolution of Consciousness

Q: An integral approach is all-level, all-quadrant. We've looked at all-quadrant. Now I'd like to look at all-level. I want to discuss the evolution of consciousness itself, from the lowest to the highest stages, matter to body to mind to soul to spirit.

KW: One of the simplified maps of this overall evolution is figure 9-1 (page 179). The traditional "matter, body, mind, soul, and spirit" are listed on the right, and the slightly more expanded version we will be using is given on the left.

But let me first emphasize that we are now discussing just the Upper-Left quadrant, the interior stages of consciousness evolution. So we are not discussing, for example, the correlative changes in the Upper-Right quadrant. We aren't discussing changes in the brain stem, the limbic system, the neocortex, in brain wave patterns (alpha, beta, theta, or delta states), nor hemispheric synchronization, nor neurotransmitter imbalances with pathology, and so on.

Likewise, we aren't looking specifically at the larger cultural currents (Lower Left) or social structures (Lower Right) that are inseparable from individual consciousness development, even though these other quadrants are crucially important. What good does it do to adjust and integrate the self in a culture that is itself sick? What does it mean to be a well-adjusted Nazi? Is that mental health? Or is a maladjusted person in a Nazi society the only one who is sane?

All of those are crucial considerations. A malformation—a pathology, a "sickness"—in any quadrant will reverberate through all four quadrants, because every holon has these four facets to its being. So a society with an alienating mode of production (Lower Right)—such as slave wages for dehumanizing labor—will reflect in low self-esteem for laborers (Upper Left) and an out-of-whack brain chemistry (Upper Right) that might, for example, institutionalize alcohol abuse as self-medication. Similarly, a cultural worldview that devalues women will result in a tendency to cripple individual female potential and a brain chemistry that could definitely use some Prozac.

And so on around the four-quadrant circle. Cripple one quadrant and all four tend to hemorrhage. But in this discussion we'll temporarily ignore all that—ignore family therapy, ignore brain chemistry and brain states, ignore cultural and social analysis—so we can focus on the Upper-Left quadrant itself and discuss the levels of consciousness as they appear in an individual.

But don't imagine those other quadrants are unimportant! In fact, we are fast approaching an understanding that sees individual "pathologies" as but the tip of an enormous iceberg that includes worldviews, social structures, and cultural access to depth. Individual therapy is not unimportant, but in many ways it's almost secondary. But for now, yes, we can definitely focus on the Upper Left. [Note: This chapter discusses the evolution of consciousness in abstract terms; the next two chapters give many concrete examples. So if this chapter seems abstract, please read on. . . .]

Higher Stages of Development

Q: A brief summary of the Upper Left is given in figure 9-1.

KW: Yes. If you compare this with figure 5-2, you'll see that figure 5-2 goes up to "vision-logic," which is stage 6 in figure 9-1. The reason is that figure 5-2 only lists the stages of average consciousness up to this point in collective history. It doesn't list any of the higher or deeper stages shown in figure 9-1.

Q: So the immediate question is, does this mean that somebody who lived in the past, say in the mythic-agrarian age, did not have access to these higher stages?

KW: No, not at all. In any given era, some people are above the average, some below. The Lower-Left quadrant is simply the average level at that point.

Every society has a certain *center of gravity*, we might say, around which the culture's ethics, norms, rules, and basic institutions are organized, and this center of gravity provides the basic cultural cohesion and social integration for that society.

Shambhala Publications, Inc.

Mailing List
P.O. Box 308, Back Bay Annex
Boston, Massachusetts   02117-0308

SHAMBHALA

Please print

SHAMBHALA

BOOK IN WHICH THIS CARD WAS FOUND

NAME ....

ADDRESS ....

CITY .... STATE ....

ZIP OR POSTAL CODE ....

COUNTRY (if outside U.S.A.) ....

Detach bookmark before mailing card.

If you
wish to receive
a copy of the latest
Shambhala Publications
catalogue of books and
to be placed on our
mailing list, please
send us this card
or send us an e-mail at
info@shambhala.com

SHAMBHALA

Illustration from the
Rupertsberger Kodex of
Hildegarde von Bingen

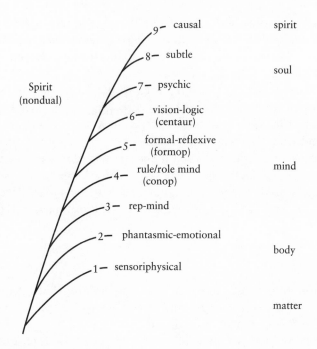

FIGURE 9-1. *The basic levels or spheres of consciousness.*

This cultural center of gravity acts like a magnet on individual development. If you are below the average level, it tends to pull you up. If you try to go above it, it tends to pull you down. The cultural center of gravity acts as a pacer of development—a magnet—pulling you up to the average expectable level of consciousness development. Beyond that, you're on your own, and lots of luck, because now the magnet will try to drag you down—in both cases, you're "outlawed."

Q: So there's a difference between average mode and most advanced mode for any culture.

KW: Yes, that's right. For example, say that five hundred years from now an anthropologist is studying America, and comes across the writings of Krishnamurti, and decides everybody in America was like Krishnamurti. This is silly, of course, but that is what many new age theorists are doing with past epochs. They take a representative of the *most advanced* mode of consciousness at the time—say, a shaman—and conclude that the *average mode* was also shamanic, that a hundred thousand years ago everybody was a shaman. Well, a hundred thousand years ago almost nobody was a shaman. A shaman—perhaps there was one per tribe—was a very rare and gifted soul, and most people did not share this shamanic awareness. In fact, most people were terrified of the power of the shaman, and they hadn't a clue as to the higher mode of awareness that the shaman accessed.

So yes, one of the things I have tried to do, in looking at these past epochs, is *first*, to define the average center of gravity—archaic, magic, mythic, rational, existential—and *second*, to look carefully at the most evolved individuals who rose above this average mode—often at great cost to themselves—and disclosed higher or deeper modes of awareness (the shaman, the yogi, the saint, the sage). These higher or deeper modes of awareness are what we are calling, in figure 9-1, the *psychic*, the *subtle*, the *causal*, and the *nondual* levels of superconscious development.

Ladder, Climber, View

Q: Those four higher stages of development are what I want to discuss. But are all of these stages really as "ladder-like" as figure 9-1 presents them? Are they really that discrete?

KW: Figure 9-1 does look like a ladder, which has confused many people, who think that developmental models are rigidly "linear." But this is a misunderstanding of what developmental models attempt to do.

The best way to think of figure 9-1 is as a series of concentric circles or nested spheres, with each higher level transcending and including its predecessor. It is an *actualization holarchy*, each stage of which *unfolds* and then *enfolds* its predecessors in a nested fashion. Figure 9-1 is simply one slice of that concentric pie. You could draw the whole figure as concentric circles, which is exactly what we did in figure 2-2, if you recall. In fact, figure 9-1 is simply a slightly expanded version of 2-2: *matter* (sensorimotor), *body* (emotional and vital), *mind* (rep-mind to vision-logic), *soul* (psychic and subtle), and *spirit* (causal and nondual). And, as we will see, this great holarchy of consciousness is the backbone of the world's great wisdom traditions, found universally and cross-culturally.

But more important, these nine levels or spheres only deal with a part of what is actually going on with consciousness development. Even if we call figure 9-1 a "ladder," there is still the *climber* of the ladder, and there are the *different views* from each rung, none of which is a simple linear step-by-step process!

Q: So ladder, climber, view. Start with the ladder—the levels or spheres.

Basic Levels: The Ladder

KW: These are depicted in figure 9-1. These nine levels or spheres are the *basic levels* of consciousness.

It's not necessary to remember any of these stages, but for reference, figure 9-1 includes: sensation and perception (sensoriphysical), impulse and image (phantasmic-emotional), symbols and concepts (rep-mind, short for representational mind), concrete rules (rule/role mind, or "conop," short for concrete operational), formal-reflexive ("formop"), and vision-logic (integrative). And then to the higher or transpersonal stages of psychic, subtle, and causal. (The paper on which the diagram is written is the "highest" stage, which is not really a stage at all but the nondual Ground of the whole display. Spirit is both the highest level—"causal"—and the Ground of all levels—"nondual.")

We can discuss all of those in a moment. They are just a few of the major milestones in consciousness development, stretching from matter to body to mind to soul to spirit. This list is by no means exhaustive, it's just a representative sample.

Q: Since these are actually nested spheres, why do you even draw them like a ladder?

KW: The ladder metaphor is useful because it indicates that the basic components of consciousness do emerge in fairly discrete stages, and if you destroy a lower rung, all the higher rungs go with it. Where the ladder metaphor fails badly is that each higher stage does not actually sit on top of the lower stage but rather *enfolds* it in its own being, much as a cell enfolds molecules which enfold atoms. As I said, it's a nested holarchy. But I myself often use the ladder metaphor because I want especially to emphasize the levels of growth involved.

For example, in development, images emerge before symbols, which emerge before concepts, which emerge before rules, and so on (as shown in figures 5-2, 5-3, and 9-1). This order is irreversible. No amount of social conditioning can alter that sequence, and we know of no societies where that order is altered. It is holarchical, it is cross-cultural, and as far as we can tell, there are no exceptions. Just as you must have words before you can have sentences, and you must have sentences before you can have paragraphs, so these basic holons build upon and incorporate their predecessors, which is why the order cannot be reversed: the higher rungs rest on the lower, and that is part of the usefulness of the ladder metaphor.

The Self: The Climber

Q: So those are the basic rungs in the ladder of awareness, or the holarchy of awareness.

KW: Yes. But that is not where the real action is, so to speak. Even if we rather crudely picture this development of basic levels as a "ladder," the real action involves the *climber* of the ladder. This climber is the *self*. Sometimes called the *self-system*. (Objectively, or in it-language, it is a self-system; subjectively, it is a person, a self, a self-sense. I use both.)

Q: So does this self or self-system have its own characteristics?

KW: Yes, the self, the climber, has specific characteristics and capacities that are *not found on the ladder itself*.

The reason is that the ladder is basically selfless—there is no inherent self-sense in any of its rungs. But the self appropriates these rungs, or *identifies* with them, and this generates various types of self-identity and various stages of self-growth, until the self falls off the ladder altogether in radical Emptiness—which is a bit ahead of the story. But the point is that the ladder and the climber of the ladder are quite different affairs!

As for the specific characteristics of the self, in *Transformations of Consciousness* I list these as identification, organization, will or attention, defense, metabolism, and navigation.

It's not necessary to go into those, but I might mention that "navigation," for example, involves the *four drives* that all holons, including the self-holon, possess—namely, agency and communion, self-transcendence and self-dissolution (regression). At each rung in the self's growth and development, it has these four basic choices about which way to go in its development. Too much or too little of any of those four drives, and the self gets into pathological trouble, and the *types* of pathology depend upon which of the nine basic rungs the trouble occurs at.

Q: So as the self negotiates or climbs these basic rungs, things can go wrong at any rung or stage.

KW: Yes, the self might be climbing the ladder of expanding consciousness, but the crucial point is that it can lose an arm or a leg at any rung!

If something goes wrong at any stage in this developmental unfolding, aspects of the self can get damaged or "left behind." This "getting left behind" is called repression, or dissociation, or alienation. The self can lose an arm or a leg at any stage, and this loss results in a pathology that is characteristic of the stage at which the loss occurred.

So we see pathology go from psychosis to borderline to neurosis to existential to spiritual, depending upon where the "accident" occurred.

I'll give some concrete examples of this in just a moment. The point for now is that not only are these basic levels growing and unfolding, but the self has to actually negotiate them, has to actually climb the developmental rungs of expanding awareness, and the self can take a bad step at any rung—and get very badly hurt.

A Fulcrum

Q: You call each of these steps a *fulcrum*.

KW: Yes, based on the very important line of research by such theorists and clinicians as Margaret Mahler, Otto Kernberg, Heinz Kohut, and Gertrude Blanck and Robert Blanck, not to mention Jung's pioneering work on individuation. A fulcrum simply describes the momentous process of differentiation and integration as it occurs in human growth and development.

One of Yogi Berra's malapropisms was: "When you come to a fork in the road, take it." Well, a fulcrum is simply a crucial fork in the developmental road, and the self has to deal with that fork. How it does so, in each case, influences its subsequent fate.

Q: So nine basic levels means there are nine corresponding fulcrums or steps for the self to negotiate.

KW: Yes, that's right. But it is really a very flowing and fluid affair. These milestones are just general markers along the way. The self must step up to each rung in the basic ladder, and that step is the fulcrum at that stage.

So every fulcrum has a 1-2-3 structure. *One*, the self evolves or develops or steps up to the new level of awareness, and it *identifies* with that level, it is "one with" that level. *Two*, it then begins to move beyond that level, or differentiate from it, or dis-identify with it, or transcend it. And *three*, it identifies with the new and higher level and centers itself there. The new rung is actually resting on the previous rungs, so they must be included and integrated in the overall expansion, and that *integration* or inclusion is the third and final subphase of the particular fulcrum. (These are summarized in fig. 9-2.)

So you can remember a fulcrum because all of them have this same 1-2-3 structure: identify, dis-identify, integrate; or fusion, differentiation, integration; or embed, transcend, include.

And if anything goes wrong with this 1-2-3 process, *at any rung*, then

LADDER	CLIMBER	VIEW
Basic rungs of aware- ness	Climber of the basic rungs	Changing view of self and other at each
Once they emerge, they remain in existence as basic building blocks or holons of con- sciousness	Each step in the climb is a fulcrum, a 1-2-3 process of: (1) fusion/identifica- tion (2) differentiation/ transcendence (3) integration/inclu- sion	stage, including a different: self-identity self-need moral sense

FIGURE 9-2. *Ladder, climber, view.*

you get a broken leg or whatnot. And the scar tissue of that disaster will depend on what the world looked like when you broke your leg. And generally, the lower the rung, the more severe the pathology.

New Worlds Emerge: Changing Views

Q: So we have the ladder and its basic rungs, and we have the self or the climber and its fulcrums—and that leaves the different views.

KW: Yes, at each rung in the developmental unfolding there is a dif- ferent view of the world—a different view of self and of others—a *differ- ent worldview*. The world looks different—is different!—at each rung in the developmental unfolding. As we have constantly seen, different worldspaces, different worlds, come into being as consciousness evolves—there is not simply a pregiven world that is monologically re- flected!

And here I would particularly emphasize that at each rung you get a different type of *self-identity*, a different type of *self-need*, and a different type of *moral stance* (see fig. 9-3). All of these are aspects of the different worlds that unfold at each rung or level or sphere of awareness.

So that's the thumbnail sketch. The ladder with its basic rungs of awareness; the climber with its fulcrums; and the different views of the world from each rung. Ladder, climber, view.

Q: So now some concrete examples.

KW: This model of consciousness development is based on the work of perhaps sixty or seventy theorists, East and West. (For a full discus-

LADDER Basic Level	CLIMBER	VIEW Maslow (self-needs)	Loevinger (self-sense)	Kohlberg (moral sense)
sensoriphysical	F-1	(physiological)	autistic / symbiotic	(premoral)
phantasmic-emotional	F-2		beginning impulsive	
rep-mind	F-3	safety	impulsive / self-protective	I. preconventional — 0. magic wish; 1. punishment/obedience; 2. naive hedonism
rule/role mind	F-4	belongingness	conformist / conscientious-conformist	II. conventional — 3. approval of others; 4. law and order
formal-reflexive	F-5	self-esteem	conscientious / individualistic	III. postconventional — 5. individual rights; 6. individual principles of conscience
vision-logic	F-6	self-actualization	autonomous / integrated	
psychic	F-7	self-transcendence		Kohlberg has suggested a higher, seventh stage: 7. universal-spiritual
subtle	F-8	self-transcendence		
causal	F-9	self-transcendence		

FIGURE 9-3. *Some examples of ladder, climber, view.*

sion of this model, see *Integral Psychology*.) Figure 9-3 gives three of them: Abraham Maslow, Jane Loevinger, and Lawrence Kohlberg. I tend to use them as examples simply because they are so well known.

Q: So ground this for me. Take the example of the rule/role mind, and run across the table for each of the columns.

KW: The rule/role mind is the capacity that begins to develop in children around age seven or so. It is the capacity to form complex mental *rules* and to take social *roles*. The child begins to understand that he or she is not just a body with impulses and desires, but also a social self among other social selves, and the child must fit into these sociocultural roles. This is a difficult and trying period.

So the example works like this. As the *basic level* of the rule/role mind emerges, the child's self will face that new rung of awareness. So it must negotiate the *fulcrum* at that level, the 1-2-3 process of stepping up to a new level of awareness. So it will first step onto that rung—it will *identify* with that rung, identify with that capacity to follow the rules and the roles. In other words, it will identify with the rule/role mind (that's phase 1 in the fulcrum).

So the self at this point is a rule/role self. That is its central identity. That is its basic *self-sense*. It has a sense of conforming with these rules and roles, and therefore, as you can see in Loevinger's column, the self-sense at this stage is *conformist*. And for the same reason, the *basic need* of the self at this stage is for *belongingness*, which you can see in Maslow's column. And the self's *moral stance* at this stage therefore centers on the conventional approval of others, which you can see in Kohlberg's column.

Q: So that's across the table—ladder, climber, view.

KW: Yes, basically. This is all terribly simplified, I hope you understand, but that's the general idea.

Q: And if development continues?

KW: If development continues, then the self will eventually grow beyond these views, and *expand its awareness* once again. In order to do so, it has to step off its present rung, or dis-identify with it, or transcend it—this differentiation or transcendence is phase 2 of the fulcrum—and then *identify* with the next-higher rung—that's phase 3, which then begins the new fulcrum, and off we go again. Until, of course, developmental arrest sets in.

Q: Now about these changing views. They are generally stage-like themselves, correct? Loevinger and Kohlberg and Maslow give stages.

KW: Yes, but in a very general sense, which again has confused many critics. All developmentalists, with virtually no exceptions, have a stage-like list, or even a ladder-like list, a holarchy of growth and development—Kohlberg, Carol Gilligan, Heinz Werner, Jean Piaget, Habermas, Robert Selman, Erik Erikson, J. M. Baldwin, Silvano Arieti, Jenny Wade, Clare Graves, Robert Kegan, Susanne Cook-Greuter, John Broughton, Deirdre Kramer, Cheryl Armon—even the contemplative traditions from Plotinus to Padmasambhava to Chih-i and Fa-tsang. And they have this ladder-like holarchy because that is what fits their data. These stages are the result of empirical, phenomenological, and interpretive evidence and massive amounts of research data. These folks are not making this stuff up because they like ladders.

But there is an important point about these holarchies. Even in their stronger versions, such as Kohlberg's, the self at any given point in its development will tend to give around 50 percent of its responses from one level, 25 percent from the level above that, and 25 percent from the level below it. No self is ever simply "at" a stage. And further, there are all sorts of regressions, spirals, temporary leaps forward, peak experiences, and so on.

Q: So it's more of an average.

KW: Yes, it's a little bit like what we were saying about cultures—they have an average *center of gravity*, with some of their members falling above, and some below, that center.

In the same way, the self-system has its own center of gravity, so to speak, which means some components of its own interior can be above, some below, its own average awareness. The climber of the ladder, in other words, is more like a blob than a discrete entity—it sort of slops along the basic spheres of expanding consciousness. Development, as I said, is really a very fluid and flowing affair.

Pathology

Q: You said the self could get hurt at any rung—lose an arm or a leg.

KW: Yes, some aspects of the climber, the blob, can get stuck at lower rungs. And these little blobs get split off from the main blob and remain stuck at those lower stages.

Q: That's repression.

KW: In the most general sense, yes. We can use the moral stages as an example.

As you can see in figure 9-3, the lower and earlier stages of moral development are egocentric, narcissistic, me-only-oriented. They tend to be very impulsive and very hedonistic. These are Kohlberg's *preconventional* stages. The middle stages are called *conventional* because, as we just saw, they tend to be very conformist—my country right or wrong. The higher stages are called *postconventional*, because they begin to transcend conventional or conformist modes and center instead on universal pluralism and individual rights. Higher than this are the "post-postconventional," or spiritual stages, which we'll get to in a moment.

Now if for various reasons there is some sort of repeated and severe trauma during the earlier stages—say, in the preconventional stages, during the first three or four years of life—then here is what tends to happen:

Since the center of gravity of the self is at this preconventional, impulsive stage, then aspects of that *impulsive self* can be split off or *dissociated*. If this dissociation is extremely severe, then self-development will come to a screeching halt. But more often than not, the self will simply limp along down the road, dissociation and all. It will continue to develop, it will continue to climb the basic rungs in expanding awareness, however haltingly or however wounded. It might bleed all over the place, but it keeps climbing.

But an aspect of the *impulsive self* has nonetheless been split off and dissociated. That split-off aspect does *not* continue the climb, does not continue to grow and develop. Rather, it sets up shop in the basement. And it has a moral worldview of stage 1, since in this example that is where the dissociation occurred. It remains at moral stage 1, even as the rest of the self continues to grow and develop. So this split-off aspect is completely narcissistic, egocentric, self-absorbed, and altogether impulsive. It continues to *interpret* the world within the categories available to it at that primitive or archaic stage.

As the main blob of the self glops on up the ladder, this little blob remains behind, sabotaging the main self with neurotic or even psychotic symptoms. The main blob is getting a higher and wider view of the world, but the little blob is committed to its self-only, narcissistic, archaic worldview, its preconventional impulses and needs.

And the *internal conflict* between the main blob, which now might be at moral stage 3 or 4 or 5 . . . well, the internal conflict between the main blob and the little blob of stage 1 can be devastating. This is not an external conflict; it is a civil war. And that, by any other name, is pathology.

And, as we'll see, one of the things we want to do in development is to help end these civil wars.

States and Stages

Q: But does this mean that a person has to negotiate all the lower levels—say, levels 1 though 6—before the higher or spiritual stages can unfold?

KW: Not at all. Individuals can have a spiritual experience—a *peak experience* or an *altered state* of consciousness—at almost any stage of their growth. The basic levels, from the lowest to the highest, are potentials in every person's being. So you can tap into the higher dimensions under various conditions—moments of elation, of sexual passion, of stress, of dream-like reverie, of drug-induced states, and even during psychotic breaks.

But look what happens. Say a person is at Kohlberg's moral stage 3. And say they have an experience, an influx, of certain subtle-realm phenomena—perhaps an intense interior illumination. This can profoundly change a person's life and open them to new worlds, new dimensions, new modes of awareness.

And perhaps it can lead to an actual transformation or evolution or development in their consciousness. So if you give this person a moral-stage test, you might find that they have indeed transformed from moral stage 3 to . . . moral stage 4. There is nowhere else for them to go! Research has consistently shown that these stages cannot be bypassed, any more than you can go from an atom to a cell and bypass molecules. So a person at moral stage 3 who has a profound spiritual experience might be motivated to move to the next stage—in this case, to stage 4. They do not, under any circumstances, go from stage 3 to stage 7.

The genuinely spiritual or transpersonal stages of development (Kohlberg's stage 7 and beyond) depend for their development upon all of the previous developments in stages 6, 5, 4, 3, and so on. Each of those stages contributes something absolutely essential for the manifestation of stage 7. And although a person can have a peak experience of a higher dimension, the person's self still has to grow and develop and evolve in order to *permanently* accommodate to those higher or deeper dimensions, in order to turn an "altered state" into a "permanent trait."

Q: You have a quote from Aurobindo: "The spiritual evolution obeys the logic of a successive unfolding; it can take a new decisive main step only when the previous main step has been sufficiently conquered: even if certain minor stages can be swallowed up or leaped over by a rapid and brusque ascension, the consciousness has to turn back to assure itself that the ground passed over is securely annexed to the new condition; a greater or concentrated speed [of development, which is indeed possible] does not eliminate the steps themselves or the necessity of their successive surmounting."

KW: Yes. One of the great problems with the field of transpersonal psychology was that, in its beginning, it tended to focus on *peak experiences*. You had the ego, which was very bad, and you had anything that was not the ego, which was very good. In fact, the view was often that anything that is not the ego, is God. So you had: ego, boooooooooo . . . not-ego, yayyyyyy.

And so you got this type of one-step transformation model: you go from the divisive and analytic and rational and nasty ego, straight to the expansive and liberated and cosmic God consciousness. Get rid of ego, you have God.

This naive notion of one-step transformation has now hooked up with a very flatland worldview, so that "cosmic consciousness" has come to mean simply that we go from the nasty Newtonian ego to the new-physics web-of-life one-with-Gaia self. We become one with flatland and we are enlightened and that saves the planet.

And, alas, it is nowhere near that simple. We don't go from an acorn to a forest in a quantum leap. There are stages in all growth, including human. These basic stages—I have listed nine of them, but that's just a summary—are based on a great deal of empirical, phenomenological, contemplative, and cross-cultural evidence. We are still refining these stages, and there are many questions that need to be answered. But this "one-step" transformation model now seems to be quite naive.

So people can have spiritual experiences and peak experiences and all sorts of altered states, but they still have to carry those experiences in their own structure. They still have to grow and develop to the point that they can actually accommodate the depth offered by the peak experiences. "States" still must be converted to "traits." You still have to go from acorn to oak if you are going to become one with the forest. So while "states" are important, "stages" are even more important.

Flatland Religion

Q: So a peak experience is kind of a "peek" experience; you get a glimpse of dimensions you might not be able to hold.

KW: Yes. And there's a related problem, which is actually more bothersome. *The ladder can develop way ahead of the self's willingness to climb it.* Technically, we say cognitive development is necessary but not sufficient for moral development.

This means, for example—and we all know cases like this—that a person can have access to level 5 rationality—they can be incredibly advanced intellectually—and still be at moral stage 1. Basically, a very bright Nazi. The ladder is much higher than the climber, who remains committed to the lower rungs. It's one thing to tap into a higher level; quite another to actually live there!

And the same thing can happen with spiritual experiences. People can temporarily access some very high rungs in the ladder or circle of awareness, but they refuse to *actually live* from those levels—they won't actually climb up there. Their center of gravity remains quite low, even debased.

And if they are to live up to their spiritual experiences, then they will have to grow and develop. They will have to start the developmental unfolding, the holarchical expansion, the actual inhabiting of the expanding spheres of consciousness. Their center of gravity has to shift—to transform—to these deeper or higher spheres of consciousness; it does no good to merely "idealize" them in theoretical chit-chat and talking religion.

So you can have a very powerful peak experience or satori. But then days, weeks, months later—where do you carry it? What happens to this experience? Where does it reside? Your actual self, your center of gravity, can only accommodate this experience according to its own structure, its own capacity, its own stage of growth. Spiritual experiences do not allow you to simply bypass the growth and development upon which enduring spiritual realization itself depends. Evolution can be accelerated, as Aurobindo said, but not fundamentally skipped over.

Q: There is such a resistance in "new paradigm" circles to this notion of stages.

KW: Yes, it's the same as the resistance to hierarchy or holarchy. Some of these objections are sincere and well-meaning, and we want to take these into account. But if you deny stages and holarchy, then you have to explain away the massive amounts of evidence that point to holarchical development, and that denial requires an aggressive ideology to explain why researchers keep finding these holarchies cross-culturally. I haven't seen any successful attempts to do this.

But some of the resistance is due to less sincere reasons. Many Americans don't like the idea of stages of anything, because we in America don't like the notion of degrees of depth. We are the living embodiment of flatland. The thought that somebody, somewhere, might be higher or deeper than me is simply intolerable.

So we prefer a "spirituality" that takes whatever level we are at and gives us a "one-step" process that will get us straight to God, instantly, like a microwave oven. We deny stages altogether and end up with a very flatland notion.

So various flatland paradigms are embraced, precisely because they do not demand actual transformation, just this "one-step" learning of the new paradigm, a sort of one-stop shopping. You just repeat that your being is one strand in the great web, and all is saved. And you aggressively *deny* there are any stages!

Q: I run into this antiholarchy prejudice all the time. It's very belligerent.

KW: The thing is, many of these "new paradigm" theorists have the same general goal: namely, the expansion of consciousness from the isolated and alienated individual to a type of global Kosmic consciousness, which includes the physiosphere and biosphere and noosphere all in one. So we can be very sympathetic with that overall goal. But these theorists are often unfamiliar with the numerous *interior transformations* that are necessary to go from an isolated bodyself to an all-inclusive Kosmic consciousness. They have a fine goal, but not much of a path. So we can agree with their goal, and help supply them with an actual path and its many important stages.

Freud and Buddha

Q: To return to the self's journey through this great spectrum of consciousness—we were talking about the fact that higher stages can be sabotaged by repressions at the lower stages—the internal civil wars.

KW: Yes, I think so. If the self represses or dissociates aspects of itself, it will have less potential left for further evolution and development. And sooner or later, this will drag development to a halt.

I don't mean to quantify this in such a simple way, but as a crude example, say the self at birth has 100 units of potential. And say that in its early growth it dissociates a small blob at moral stage 1—say it splits off 10 units of itself. It arrives at moral stage 2 with 90 units of its potential.

So the self is only 90 percent there, as it were. 10 percent of its awareness is stuck at moral stage 1, stuck in this little unconscious blob residing in the basement and using its 10 percent of awareness in an attempt to get the entire organism to act according to its archaic wishes and impulses and interpretations.

And so on, as growth and development continues. The point is that, by the time the self reaches adulthood, it might have lost 40 percent of its potential, as split-off or dissociated little selves, little blobs, little *hidden subjects*, and these little subjects tend to remain at the level of development that they had when they were split off.

So you have these little "barbarians" running around in the basement, impulsively demanding to be fed, to be catered to, to be the center of the universe, and they get very nasty if they aren't fed. They scream and yell and bite and claw, and since you don't even consciously know they are there, you *interpret* this interior commotion as depression, obsession, anxiety, or any number of neurotic symptoms that are completely baffling.

Q: So this would sabotage higher growth as well.

KW: Yes, the point is that these dissociated selves—these little hidden subjects that are clinging to lower worldviews—will take up a certain amount of your energy. Not only do they use energy themselves, your defenses against them use energy. And pretty soon, you run out of energy.

And yes, this will very likely sabotage higher or transpersonal development. Let's say it takes 65 units to get to the psychic or subtle level. If you only have 60 units left, you're not going to make it. This is why, in broad terms, we want to integrate Freud and Buddha, we want to integrate lower "depth psychology" with "height psychology."

And, in fact, we are at an extremely auspicious moment in human evolution, because, for the first time in history, we have access to both Freud and Buddha. The profound discoveries of the modern West—the whole notion of a psychodynamic unconscious, which is really found nowhere else—these discoveries can be integrated with the mystical or contemplative traditions, both East and West, for a more "full spectrum" approach.

Q: The point of uniting Freud and Buddha is that if you've got 40 units of your consciousness trapped in the basement, you're not going to make it to the higher levels, as a general rule.

KW: As a general rule. If you don't befriend Freud, it will be harder to get to Buddha.

So what we do with "depth" psychology—well, actually, that's misnamed. It's really shallow psychology, it's really dealing with the lowest and shallowest levels of the holarchy, *but for just that reason*, their narrow and narcissistic perspective can be so *crippling*.

But the point is, with "depth" psychology, we recontact these lower holons and expose them to consciousness, so that they can be released from their fixation and dissociation and rejoin the ongoing flow of consciousness evolution. They can get with the program, as it were, and cease this backward, reactionary, anti-evolutionary pull from the basement of your awareness. They can be reintegrated with your main self, so that your central self might now have 70 or 80 units of its potential available to it, and with that energy it can then continue its growth into the transpersonal.

And if that happens, and transpersonal growth is engaged with great intensity, then at some point you will climb not just up the ladder, but off it. As Zen would say, you're at the top of a hundred-foot pole, and yet you must take one more step. How do you step off a hundred-foot pole? You take that step, and where are you?

When you step off the ladder altogether, you are in free fall in Emptiness. Inside and outside, subject and object, lose all ultimate meaning. You are no longer "in here" looking at the world "out there." You are not looking at the Kosmos, you are the Kosmos. The universe of One Taste announces itself, bright and obvious, radiant and clear, with nothing outside, nothing inside, an unending gesture of great perfection, spontaneously accomplished. The very Divine sparkles in every sight and sound, and you are simply that. The sun shines not on you but within you, and galaxies are born and die, all within your heart. Time and space dance as shimmering images on the face of radiant Emptiness, and the entire universe loses its weight. You can swallow the Milky Way in a single gulp, and put Gaia in the palm of your hand and bless it, and it is all the most ordinary thing in the world, and so you think nothing of it.

10

On the Way to Global: Part 1

Q: We hear a lot about a "global perspective" or "global aware-ness"—think globally, act locally. Most of the "new paradigm" ap-proaches emphasize that we are living in a global village, a planetary network, and we need a global and systems map to reflect that global territory.

KW: A global map is one thing. A mapmaker capable of living up to it, quite another.

A global perspective is not innate; the infant is not born with it; homi-nids did not possess it. A global perspective is a rare, elite, extraordinary perspective of great depth, and there are relatively few individuals who actually make it to that depth (greater depth, less span). So it is in under-standing the evolution and emergence of global consciousness that we can actually begin to implement "new paradigms," if that is what is desired.

Q: You said that the new paradigm thinkers often have a goal of Kosmic consciousness, but not much of a path to it.

KW: Yes. There is little in the global or systems map about how this *interior development* in the mapmaker occurs. And yet that is by far the most important issue. So the global or systems map is actually of rather limited use—it's just a Right-Hand map—and yet the crucial issue is the Left-Hand development: how to get individuals to develop up to the point where they can actually inhabit a global awareness in the first place.

It is then from within and beyond this global perspective that genu-inely spiritual or transpersonal states emerge, as Spirit begins to recog-nize its own global dimensions.

Q: That's what I want to talk about. We discussed this in abstract terms—ladder, climber, view. But I would like to look at concrete examples of this development on the way to global, evolution toward the global I. Let's climb the entire ladder! Starting at the start.

The Primary Matrix

KW: For the moment, let's call birth the start. The infant at birth is basically a sensorimotor organism, a holon containing within it cells, molecules, atoms—transcending and including those subholons.

But the infant doesn't possess language, or logic, or narrative capacity; it cannot grasp historical time, or orient itself in interior psychological space. It is basically identified with the sensoriphysical dimension, or stage 1 in figure 9-1. As Piaget put it, "The self is here material, so to speak."

Of course, the self isn't actually or merely physical, but it is still predominantly oriented to the lowest and most basic dimension of all, the material and sensorimotor. In fact, the self is largely *identified* with the sensorimotor world, so much so that it can't even distinguish between inside and outside. The physical self and the physical world are *fused*— that is, they are *not yet differentiated*. The infant can't tell the difference between inside and outside—chair and thumb are the same.

This early fusion state is often called the "primary matrix," because it is the fundamental matrix that will be differentiated in subsequent development. It is also referred to as primary autism, primary narcissism, oceanic, protoplasmic, adualistic, indissociated, and so on.

We saw that every fulcrum is a 1-2-3 process: the self first *identifies* with that rung, or is in fusion with that rung; then it *differentiates* from or transcends that rung; then *integrates* and includes it.

This primary matrix is simply phase 1 of fulcrum-1. The self is in *fusion* with the sensorimotor world, both internal and external.

Q: This primary fusion is beyond the duality of subject and object?

KW: No, it's beneath it. Many Romantics like to see this primary fusion state as some sort of prefiguration of cosmic consciousness, mystical unity consciousness, nonduality, and so on. But this primary fusion state doesn't transcend subject and object; it simply can't tell the difference between them in the first place. It's primary narcissism, where the physical world is swallowed by the autistic self—the infant is all mouth, the world is all food. It's a physical affair.

There is nothing particularly spiritual about this state. It cannot take the role of other; it is locked into its own egocentric orbit; it lacks intersubjective love and compassion. Because it can't tell the difference between physical inside and physical outside, this fusion state is fairly "wide" but extremely *shallow*. There is nothing to impede it horizontally, but vertically it is stuck in the basement. And flatland theorists focus on this horizontal expanse—subject and object are one!—and thus they tend to miss the crucial factor—there is no vertical expanse at all, and thus this state is not more free, but less free, than subsequent developments. This is the shallowest and most cramped consciousness you can imagine!

And finally, this early fusion state cannot take the role of other. That is, it doesn't have the cognitive capacity to put itself in the shoes of others, and see the world through their eyes—it is stuck in only immediate impressions of the sensorimotor dimension, profoundly narcissistic. So it can't display anything resembling actual love—you can't truly love somebody until you can understand their perspective and perhaps even choose to put it above your own. So there is no compassion here, no genuine love, no tolerance and benevolence and altruism.

So in many ways, this fusion state is the complete antithesis of genuine spiritual awareness and compassion and love. Of course, we cannot rule out the fact that the infant has access to some types of spiritual states. As we said, altered states and peak experiences can occur at almost any stage of development. Nonetheless, even if the infant has a fluid access to some types of spiritual states, those states still must be converted into permanent traits if spirituality is to become a mature, stable, constant awareness, capable of taking the role of other and being reflected in genuine love and care. So once again, "states" might be important, but "stages" are even more important.

Birth Trauma

Q: What about the previous intrauterine state? Do you include that in your model?

KW: The evidence centering on the intrauterine state and the birth trauma is highly controversial. But I suspect some of it is legitimate, so I refer to these even earlier developments as fulcrum-0.

Like all fulcrums, it has that essential 1-2-3 structure: an initial fusion with the womb, then a painful process of differentiation (the actual birth trauma), then a period of consolidation and integration as a differentiated organism (post-uterine). At that point, the infant self has then begun fulcrum-1—it is now *fused* with the physical world in and around it.

Stan Grof has written extensively on these subphases of the birth process, which he calls the Basic Perinatal Matrices. Stan's research suggests that trauma at any of these subphases can result in a pathological complex. And conversely, under intense stress, or with certain types of meditation, or certain drugs, the self can regress to this fulcrum and relive its various subphases and traumas, which tends to alleviate the pathology. Stan's evidence is immensely suggestive, and if you are interested in this area, I recommend you start there.

The False Self

Q: So a trauma in the birth process could form a pathological complex that would affect subsequent development.

KW: Yes, but that is just one example of a much more general phenomenon, which is that a trauma at *any* of the fulcrums can form a pathological complex which "infects" all subsequent development. As we were saying, the self can take a bad step at any of the nine or so fulcrums, and the type of pathology that results depends upon the rung where the accident occurred.

Q: How so?

KW: As the self steps up to each new rung in expanding awareness, it faces that 1-2-3 process at each rung. And something can go wrong in any of those subphases—in the fusion subphase, the differentiation subphase, the integration subphase. The self can remain in *fusion*, or remain stuck at that stage—we have a *fixation*, a subphase 1 problem. Or the self can fail in the *differentiation* or subphase 2 of the fulcrum—it can fail to differentiate cleanly and clearly, and so it fails to establish a responsible boundary at that level. Or the self can fail in the *integration* or subphase 3 of the fulcrum—it doesn't integrate and include the previous level, but alienates and dissociates and represses it. It doesn't transcend and include, it dissociates and represses.

Once this accident occurs—once we get a "subphase malformation" at any level—then this pathology forms a *lesion in consciousness* that tends to infect and distort all subsequent development. Like a grain of sand caught in a developing pearl, the malformation "crinkles" all subsequent layers, tilts and twists and distorts them.

Q: The climber has lost an arm or a leg.

KW: Yes, there are now aspects of the self's being that it doesn't own or admit or acknowledge. It starts to hide from itself. In other words, the self begins lying to itself. A *false self system* begins to grow over the *actual self*, the self that is really there at any given moment, but is now denied or distorted or repressed. Repression, basically, is being untruthful about what is actually running around in your psyche.

And thus the *personal unconscious* begins its career. As we earlier put it, this unconscious is the locus of the self's lie. As we also put it, aspects of awareness are split off—"little blobs," little selves, little subjects, are forced into the subterranean dark. These little blobs remain at the level of development they had when they were split off and denied. They cease to grow. They remain in fusion with the level where they were repressed. They hide out in the basement, and the door to that basement is guarded by the lie.

So aspects of your potential, sealed off by the dissociation, begin eating up your energy and your awareness. They are a drain. They sabotage further growth and development. They are dead weight, the weight of a past age that should have been outgrown. But instead, protected and sheltered by the lie, they live on to terrorize.

Q: And therapy would address that lie, or untruthfulness.

KW: Interpretive therapies—Freudian to Jungian to Gestalt to cognitive—they attack the lie, yes. In all the ways that we already discussed (see chapter 7).

Q: So as we run through the stages of expanding awareness, we want to watch these fulcrums for anything that can go wrong, because that is what actually prevents the emergence of global awareness, correct?

KW: Yes, that's the central point.

Fulcrum-1: The Hatching of the Physical Self

Q: So we left off this developmental story with fulcrum-1.

KW: Yes, the self is in *fusion* with the sensorimotor world—the primary fusion state or primary narcissism. The self's identity is *physiocentric*, fused with the material dimension, with the physiosphere.

But somewhere around 4 months, the infant will begin to differentiate between physical sensations in its body and those in the environment. The infant bites a blanket and it does not hurt; bites its thumb and it does. There is a difference, it learns, between blanket and thumb. So it begins the *differentiation* phase of fulcrum-1, which is usually completed sometime in the first year, usually around 5–9 months, according to Margaret Mahler, a pioneer in this research.

She calls this the "hatching" phase—the physical self "hatches" out of this primary fusion matrix. (In other words, this hatching is phase 2 of fulcrum-1.) This hatching is the "real birth," so to speak, of the physical self.

Melanie Klein was particularly interested in this earliest of differentiations, as were Edith Jacobson, and René Spitz, not to mention Margaret Mahler. Interesting that women seem to have a particularly acute feel for these early developments, no?

Anyway, this hatching is the birth of the physical self. If the self *fails* in this differentiation—if it remains stuck or in fusion with the primary matrix—then it can't tell where its body stops and the chair begins. It is open to what is called *adualism*, which is one of the primary characteristics of *psychosis*. And that is why research consistently indicates that many of the really severe pathologies—psychosis, schizophrenia, severe affective disorders—have part of their etiology in problems with this early fulcrum, fulcrum-1. So we can start to see that a *type* of pathology is associated with the *level* at which the disruption occurs.

Q: Some of these are listed in figure 10-1 (page 201).

KW: Yes. With *psychosis*, there is severe reality distortion, marked especially by adualism, or the incapacity to establish even the physical boundaries of the self (fulcrum-1); there are often hallucinatory primary process images and thoughts; narcissistic delusions of reference; consciousness fails to seat in the physical body; thoughts of self and other are confused. There may also be an influx of subtle or transpersonal awareness, but this is fairly rare and is often badly distorted as well.

Fulcrum-2: The Birth of the Emotional Self

Q: But if all goes well with fulcrum-1?

KW: If this fulcrum is negotiated relatively well, then the infant will begin fulcrum-2, the emotional-phantasmic fulcrum. Because the infant has completed fulcrum-1, it has established the realistic boundaries of its *physical* self, but it still has not yet established the boundaries of its *emotional* self. So it can differentiate its physical self from the physical environment, but it still cannot differentiate its emotional self from the emotional environment. And this means that its emotional self is fused or identified with those around it, particularly the mother. (This is the initial fusion phase of fulcrum-2.)

And just as there was nothing "deep" or "profound" about the previous physical fusion state, there is nothing deep or profound about this

Basic Spheres of Consciousness	Corresponding Fulcrums	Characteristic Pathologies	Treatment Modalities
9 causal	F–9	causal pathology	formless mysticism
8 subtle	F–8	subtle pathology	deity mysticism
7 psychic	F–7	psychic disorders	nature mysticism
6 centauric (vision logic)	F–6	existential pathology	existential therapy
5 formal reflexive (formop)	F–5	identity neuroses	introspection
4 rule/role (conop)	F–4	script pathology	script analysis
3 rep-mind	F–3	psychoneuroses	uncovering techniques
2 phantasmic-emotional	F–2	narcissistic-borderline	structuring-building techniques
1 sensoriphysical	F–1	psychoses	physiological/pacification
0 undifferentiated or primary matrix	F–0	perinatal pathology	intense regressive therapies

FIGURE 10-1. *Spheres of consciousness correlated with fulcrums, pathologies, and treatments.*

emotional fusion state, even though it, too, sounds like a nice "holistic oneness with the world." But in fact, researchers are virtually unanimous in pointing out that this state is still extremely *egocentric* or *narcissistic*. As Mahler puts it, the self at this stage "treats the world like its oyster." Precisely because it cannot differentiate itself from the emotional and vital world around it, the infant self treats the world as an *extension of itself*—which is the technical meaning of "narcissism."

So this type of severe narcissism—which is normal, not pathological, at this stage—does not mean that the infant thinks selfishly about only itself, but on the contrary, it is incapable of thinking about itself. It is unable to differentiate itself from the world, the emotional world, and so it thinks that what it is feeling is what the world is feeling, that what it wants is what the world wants, that what it sees is what the world sees. It plays hide and seek in plain view; it thinks that if it can't see you, you can't see it; its own perspective is the only perspective in existence.

In other words, the self is here a purely ecological self, a biospheric self, a libidinal self, a natural-impulsive self. It is one with, in fusion with, the entire vital-emotional dimension of being, *both internal and external*. It is pushed and pulled by the currents of its vital life, and it does not differentiate itself from the ecological currents of existence. Its identity is *biocentric* or *ecocentric*, fused with the biosphere within and without.

And precisely because it is embedded in nature, in biology, in impulse, in the vital-emotional sphere, it cannot rise above that embeddedness and see that its perspective is not the only perspective in existence. *Biocentric* is extremely *egocentric*, as we will constantly see. It might have a certain horizontal expanse, but very little vertical depth, which is why it is so shallow and narcissistic (despite the use to which this emotional fusion has been put by Romantics in a search for any sort of "union"; I sympathize with their search, but I believe they are mistaken to look for it here [see chapter 16]).

Q: So the self at this stage has no sturdy emotional boundaries.

KW: That's right. Technically, we say self and object representations are still fused. This contributes to the general "magical" and narcissistic atmosphere that is so prevalent at this stage.

But somewhere around 15–24 months, the *emotional self* begins to differentiate itself from the *emotional environment*. Mahler actually calls this "the psychological birth of the infant." The infant is actually "born" as a separate emotional and feeling self at this stage. (The self has moved from the initial fusion phase of fulcrum-2 to the middle or differentiation phase.) The infant starts to wake up to the fact that it is a separate self existing in a separate world. It has hit the "terrible twos."

Q: Which is different from "hatching."

KW: Yes. Fulcrum-1 is hatching, or the birth of the physical self. Fulcrum-2 is the birth of the emotional self. With fulcrum-2, a truly separate-self sense awakens, with all the joy and all the terror that involves.

Q: Many theorists take this as the beginning of alienation, of really profound alienation. They have called it the basic fault, the basic default, the basic dualism, the split between subject and object, the beginning of fragmented awareness. . . .

KW: Yes, I know. An extraordinary amount has been read into this differentiation and the "loss" of the previous emotional fusion. It's supposed to be the ejection from a primal paradise, the beginning of massive alienation, the start of the human tragedy, the beginning of Paradise Lost. I think it also causes tooth decay, but I'm not sure.

The basic problem is that most of these theorists simply confuse *differentiation* with *dissociation*. Differentiation is a necessary and unavoidable part of all evolutionary growth and development, the counterpart to reaching higher integration, as when an acorn differentiates and integrates in order to become an oak. But these theorists look at any differentiation, not as prelude to higher integration, but as a brutal disruption of a prior and wonderful harmony, as if the oak were somehow a horrible violation of the acorn.

They then look back nostalgically to the days of wonderful acornness, prior to the differentiation, and wring their hands and gnash their teeth and moan the loss of paradise. They dramatically overidealize this primitive lack of differentiation. Just because the self is not aware of suffering does not mean it has a positive presence of spiritual bliss. *Lack* of awareness doesn't mean *presence* of paradise!

Q: But the Romantics assume otherwise about this early lack of differentiation. They read many positive virtues into it, so they must see the loss of this fusion as lamentable.

KW: Yes, they confuse fusion with freedom. But fusion is imprisonment; you are dominated by all that you have not transcended. But of course that transcendental growth is difficult and perilous and painful.

The manifest world is a brutal place, and as humans become aware of this, they suffer. The manifest world, the world of samsara, is an alienated and alienating place. And as the infant becomes vaguely aware of that, it suffers horribly. And yes, this is painful, but it's called waking up.

It's like frostbite disease. First there is no feeling at all; everything seems fine, you're in a paradise of no pain. You're diseased, you just don't know it. Then it thaws out, and feelings and emotions emerge, and it hurts like hell. These theorists confuse "hurts like hell" with the disease itself.

No, fulcrum-2 is simply starting to wake up to the disease of samsara. To the fact that, as a separate and sensitive emotional being, you are open to the slings and arrows of outrageous fortune. You are going to be put into a world of pain and suffering and nightmarish hell, and you have two, and only two, choices: retreat to the prior fusion, the prior frostbite, where there was no awareness of this alienation, or continue growth and transcendence until you can transcend this alienation in spiritual awakening.

But the retro-Romantic theorists simply eulogize the prior frostbitten state, and see that as a prefiguration of the Divine awakening, as being itself a type of unconscious Heaven. But the fusion state is not unconscious Heaven, it's unconscious Hell. With fulcrum-2, that hell becomes conscious, that's all. It's a big advance.

Q: Even though fulcrum-2 is a rather "unhappy" development.

KW: Bittersweet, yes. But the previous state is the state of numbness, not nonduality; ignorance, not bliss. My dog doesn't writhe in angst either, but liberation does not consist in reawakening dog consciousness. Or a "mature form" of dog consciousness.

No, when we awaken as a separate emotional self, with all the joy and all the terror that involves, we have actually *transcended* the previous fusion state. We have *awakened* to some degree. We have gained *more depth* and more consciousness, and that has its own intrinsic value, intrinsic worth. But, like all stages of growth, there is a price to be paid for every increase in consciousness. The dialectic of progress.

Q: So if everything goes relatively well at this fulcrum-2?

KW: Well, let me first say that if things go poorly at this fulcrum—that is, worse than the normal mess this fulcrum is anyway—then the self either remains in *fusion* at this emotionally narcissistic stage (the so-called narcissistic personality disorders), or the differentiation process begins but is *not resolved* and there is some sort of *dissociation* (the so-called borderline disorders). We find exactly this general classification and etiology in Kohut, Masterson, Kernberg, Mahler, Stone, and Gedo, to name a few.

In either case, there are no realistic *emotional boundaries* to the self. In the narcissistic and borderline syndromes, the individual therefore *lacks a sense of cohesive self*, and this is perhaps the central defining characteristic of these pathologies. The self either treats the world as an extension of itself (narcissistic), or is constantly invaded and tortured by the world (borderline). This level of pathology is called borderline because it is borderline between psychosis and neurosis. It's sometimes called "stably unstable." The growing self has taken a painful spill at the second big fork in the road.

Fulcrum-3: The Birth of the Conceptual Self

Q: But if all goes well at fulcrum-2?

KW: If all goes relatively well, then the self is no longer *exclusively* identified with the emotional level. It begins to transcend that level and identify with the mental or conceptual self, which is the beginning of fulcrum-3 and the representational mind.

The representational mind is similar to what Piaget called preoperational cognition. As I use it, the rep-mind consists of *images, symbols,* and *concepts.* You can see all of these listed on figure 5-3, for example.

Images begin to emerge around 7 months. A mental image looks more or less like the object it represents. If you close your eyes and picture a dog, it looks pretty much like a real dog. That's an *image.* A *symbol,* on the other hand, represents an object but does not look like the object at all, which is a much harder cognitive task. The symbol "Fido" represents my dog, but it doesn't look like my dog at all. Symbols emerge during the second year, usually with words like "ma" or "dada," and develop very rapidly. Symbols dominate awareness from 2 to 4 years, roughly.

At which point concepts begin to emerge. Where a simple symbol represents a single object, a *concept* represents an entire class of objects. The word "dog" represents all dogs, not just Fido. An even harder task. Concepts dominate awareness from 4 to 7 years. Of course, these are all basic units or holons of consciousness, so once they emerge in awareness, they will remain as basic capacities available to consciousness.

But it is when concepts emerge that a particularly *mental self*, a conceptual self, begins to emerge. When the self begins to identify with this conceptual mind, we have fulcrum-3. The self is now not just a bundle of sensations and impulses and emotions, it is also a set of symbols and concepts. It begins to enter the *linguistic* world, the noospheric world, and this, to put it mildly, changes everything. It has gone from the physiosphere of fulcrum-1 to the biosphere of fulcrum-2, and now it begins to especially enter the noosphere with fulcrum-3.

Every Neurosis Is an Ecological Crisis

Q: What would you say is the single most important thing about this new linguistic self?

KW: This new self exists in the noosphere, and the noosphere can repress the biosphere. Individually, this produces neurosis; collectively, ecological crisis.

In other words, the linguistic world is indeed a *new world*, a new worldspace. Here the self can think of the past and plan for the future (it is temporal and historical); it can begin to control its bodily functions; it can begin to picture things in its mind that are not actually present in its senses. Because it can anticipate the future, it can worry and suffer anxiety, and because it can think about the past, it can feel remorse and guilt and regret. All of these are part of its new worldspace, the linguistic world, the noosphere.

And precisely because it exists in this new and wider world, the conceptual mind can repress and dissociate its lower impulses. That is, precisely because the noosphere transcends the biosphere, it can not only transcend and include, it can repress and distort and deny. Not just differentiate, but dissociate. Both individually and at large. Individually, neurosis; at large, ecological crisis.

Q: For the moment, stick with the individual, or we'll get way off base.

KW: On an individual level, the result of the noosphere repressing the biosphere is called psychoneurosis, or simply neurosis. The mind can repress nature, both external nature (eco-crisis) and internal nature (libido).

Psychoneurosis—or just *neurosis*—in the technical sense means that a fairly stable, cohesive, mental self has emerged, and this mental-conceptual self (the ego) can repress or dissociate aspects of its bodily drives or impulses, and these repressed or distorted impulses—usually sexual or aggressive—therefore appear in disguised and painful forms known as neurotic symptoms.

In other words, every neurotic symptom is a miniature ecological crisis.

Q: So it's interesting that repression proper and the classical neuroses come into being with fulcrum-3.

KW: In a general sense, yes. You see, in the previous borderline conditions, repression proper is not so much in evidence—the self isn't strong enough to repress anything! The self can't repress its emotions, but rather, it is completely overwhelmed by them, lost in them, flooded by them. There's no "repressed unconscious" to dig up because there is no extensive repression in the first place, which is why these conditions are often referred to as "pre-neurotic."

So therapies aimed at the borderline conditions (fulcrum-2) are actually known as *structure building* therapies—they help the fragile self to differentiate and stabilize and build boundaries, as opposed to the *uncovering therapies* of the neurotic level (fulcrum-3), which aim at relaxing the repression barrier and recontacting the impulses and emotions and felt-sense that the stronger neurotic self has repressed. In fact, one of the aims of structure-building therapy is to get the borderline "up to" a capacity for repression!

Q: So neurosis is an improvement!

KW: Yes, and then you have to deal with *that*. The point is, as Vaillant demonstrated, the defense mechanisms themselves exist in a hierarchy of development. A typical fulcrum-1 defense mechanism is projective identification, where self and other are largely undifferentiated. Typical fulcrum-2 defense mechanisms include splitting and fusion (fusion of self and object representations and a splitting of all-good and all-bad objects). Repression proper is typical of fulcrum-3 defense mechanisms, and this is said to eventually give way to the "healthiest" defense of all, sublimation—which is just a psychoanalytically decontaminated word for transcendence.

Q: So defense mechanisms are holarchically arranged.

KW: In many ways, yes. Defense mechanisms, when operating naturally and normally, are like a psychological immune system. They help maintain the integrity and stability of the self boundary, and they toss out any invaders that threaten the self system.

But, as always, there can be too much of a good thing. Defense mechanisms can become an auto-immune disorder—the self starts attacking itself, eating itself up. The defending army turns into a repressive state police. The self starts defending against pain and terror by incarcerating its own citizens. It seals off its own potential. It closes its eyes. It starts to lie. No matter what the "level" of this lie—from splitting and fusion and projection to repression and reaction formation and displacement—the self hides from itself, lies to itself, becomes opaque to itself.

In place of the actual self, there grows up the false self. Beginning as

early as fulcrum-1 (some would say fulcrum-0), the fledgling and growing self can begin to distance itself from aspects of its own being, aspects
that are too threatening, too painful, or too disruptive. It does so *using
the defense mechanisms available to it at its own level of development.*
The psychotic lie, the borderline lie, the neurotic lie, and so on. The
"unconscious" in the most general sense is simply the locus of the running lie—the layers of deception, layers of insincerity, hiding the actual
self and its real potentials.

Q: So what happens to this false self?

KW: The false self—at whatever level—might simply remain in
charge for a lifetime, as the individual limps through a life of internal
insincerity. More often than not, however, the false self will at some
point collapse under its own suffocating weight—there is a "break-
down"—and the individual is then faced with several choices: rest and
recover and then resume the same false-self trajectory; drug the dilemma
out of awareness; behaviorally reinforce actions that avoid the problem;
or take up an investigation into the life of the lie, usually with a therapist
who will help you *interpret* your interior intentions more *truthfully.*

Q: The interpretive or Left-Hand therapies.

KW: Yes. In a *safe environment*, surrounded by empathy, congru-
ence, and acceptance, the individual can begin to tell the truth about his
or her interior without fear of retribution. And thus the false self—at
whatever level—tends to lose the reason for its existence. The lie—the
resistance to truthfulness—is *interpreted*, and the concealed pain and
terror and anguish disclose themselves, and the false self slowly burns in
the fire of truthful awareness. The truthful interiors are *shared* in an
intersubjective circle of care and compassion, which releases them from
their imprisonment in deception and allows them to join the ongoing
growth of consciousness—the *beauty* of the actual self shines through,
and the intrinsic joy of the new depth is its own reward.

Now we've only discussed the first three fulcrums and the pathologies
that develop up to those points—psychosis, borderline, neurosis. But the
same general phenomenon is operative throughout development, even
into the higher and transpersonal domains. At whatever level of development, we can exist as the actual self in sincerity, or the false self in
deception. And the different levels of the lie are the different levels of
pathology.

Early Worldviews: Archaic, Magic, Mythic

Q: That takes us up through fulcrum-3—the first three major spheres
or levels of consciousness growth, each of which has a different worldview.

KW: Yes. A worldview, as we were saying, is what the Kosmos looks like from a particular rung of consciousness. When you have only sensations and impulses, what does the Kosmos look like to you? We call that *archaic*. When you add images and symbols, what does the Kosmos look like then? *Magic*. When you add rules and roles, what does the Kosmos see? A *mythic* world. When formal operational emerges, what do you see? A *rational* world. And so on.

Q: Why don't you briefly summarize the early worldviews, and then we can move on to higher developments.

KW: "Archaic" is sort of a catch-all phrase. It loosely represents all the previous stages up to the hominid. Archaic is the general worldview of fulcrum-1. It's basically a sensorimotor worldview.

Q: And magic?

KW: As images and symbols begin to emerge, around the time of fulcrum-2, these early images and symbols are *not differentiated* clearly from the objects they represent. Thus, it seems that to manipulate the image is to actually change the object. If I make an image of you and stick a pin in the image, something bad will actually happen to you. The child lives in this world of magical displacement and condensation. Very "primary process." Very *magical*.

Likewise, because self and other are not well differentiated, the child populates its world with objects that have mental characteristics—the magical worldview is *animistic*. And I'm not talking about some sort of sophisticated panpsychic philosophy. It's very crude and very egocentric. The clouds move because they are following you, they want to see you. It rains because the sky wants to wash you off. It thunders because the sky is angry at you personally. Mind and world are not clearly differentiated, so their characteristics tend to get fused and confused, "magically." Inside and outside are *both* egocentric, narcissistic.

Q: What about mythic?

KW: As development moves into fulcrum-3, the child begins to understand that it cannot itself magically order the world around. It keeps hiding under the pillow, but people keep finding it! Something is not working here. Magic doesn't really work. The self can't really order the world around magically and omnipotently. But it thinks perhaps *somebody else can*, and so crashing onto the scene come a pantheon of gods and goddesses and demons and fairies and special forces, all of which can miraculously suspend the laws of nature for various, often trite and trivial, reasons. The child will ask its parents to turn the yucky spinach into candy. The child doesn't understand that the material world doesn't work like that.

But in the meantime the child develops a very complex *mythological worldview*, which is populated with all sorts of egocentric forces that are imagined to order the world around, and all of them are focused on the ego of the child. Whereas, in the previous magical phase, the infant thought that it itself could alter the world by the right word-magic, now it has to spend its time trying to appease the gods and demons and forces that can alter the world, often for the worse. Egocentric *power* gives way to egocentric *prayer* and ritual. There is a constant "bargaining" with these forces: if I eat all my dinner, the nice force will make my toothache go away.

This mythic worldview begins with the rep-mind and continues into the next major stage, the rule/role mind, and then dies down with the rational worldview, which realizes that if you want to change reality, you must work at it yourself: nobody is going to magically or mythically save you without a corresponding growth.

You can see these general correlations in figure 5-2. Worldviews are listed in the Lower Left, because they *collectively govern* individual perceptions within their horizon. (Whether magic or mythic possesses any genuinely spiritual aspects, we will discuss later. See chapter 11.)

Fulcrum-4: The Birth of the Role Self

Q: All right, so that brings us to fulcrum-4. The basic rung you have listed as the "rule/role" mind.

KW: Yes. This is roughly what Piaget called concrete operational cognition ("conop"), which emerges around age 6–7 on average, and dominates awareness until roughly age 11–14. "Concrete operational" sounds very dry and arid but is actually very rich and powerful. It involves the capacity to form mental *rules* and to take mental *roles*. And—this is crucial—the child finally learns to *take the role of other*.

There is a famous experiment, by Piaget and Inhelder, that first spotted this very clearly. I'll give a simplified version. If you take a ball colored red on one side and green on the other, and you place the ball between you and the child, and then ask the child two questions— "What color do you see?" and "What color do I see?"—preoperational children will answer both questions the same. That is, if the child is looking at the green side, he will correctly say he sees green, but he will also say *you* are seeing green. He doesn't know that you are seeing the red side. *He can't put himself in your shoes*, or see the world through your eyes. The child is still locked into his own perspective, which is still very egocentric, very preconventional, very selfcentric.

But the concrete operational child will correctly say, "I see green, you see red." The child at this stage can take the role of other. And this is a huge step *on the way to global*, on the way to being able to take a worldcentric perspective. The child is not yet fully there, but it is continuing to move in the right direction, because it is beginning to see that its view is not the only view in the world!

So its entire *moral stance* switches from a rather egocentric or *preconventional* stance to a *conventional* and often highly *conformist* stance—"my country right or wrong" and "law and order" stage. You can see this in figure 9-3.

Paradigm Shifts

Q: A change in view.

KW: It's an entire change in worldview—a paradigm shift, if you like—and as with the three previous rungs, or the three previous paradigm shifts, this involves a profound change in self-identity, in moral sense, and in self-needs, to mention a few. These changing views are all listed in figure 9-3.

Q: So each of the nine stages of consciousness evolution is actually a paradigm shift.

KW: In a broad sense, yes. Consequently, the typical adult in our culture has already undergone a half-dozen or so major paradigm shifts, worldview shifts—from archaic to magic to mythic to rational to existential, or thereabouts. You and I have *already* undergone these revolutions in consciousness, and although we might not remember any of the specifics, researchers on the scene report psychological earthquakes.

We tend to seal these earthquakes out of awareness. There are a lot of very funny stories about this. If you take children in the preoperational stage, and—right in front of their eyes—pour the water from a short glass into a tall glass, and ask them which glass has more water, they will always say the tall glass has more, even though they saw you pour the same amount from one glass to the other. They cannot "conserve volume." Certain "obvious" things that we see, they do not and *cannot* see—they live in a different worldspace. No matter how many times you pour the *same* amount of water back and forth between the two glasses, they will *insist* the tall glass has more. So much for the "pure" and "undistorted" perception of children.

If a few years later, after concrete operational awareness has emerged, you repeat this experiment, the kids will always say that both glasses have the same amount of water. They can hold volume in their mind and not be confused by its displacements. They have an internal *rule* that automatically does this (a concrete operational rule). And if you show them a videotape from the earlier period, where they were saying that the tall glass has more water, they will deny it's them! They think you've doctored the videotape. They simply cannot imagine somebody being so stupid as to think the tall glass has more water.

So they underwent this massive paradigm shift, and not a bit of it remains in awareness. The self will now *reinterpret* every single event of its previous life history from the perspective of the new worldview. It completely *rewrites its history* from within the new and higher paradigm.

So they—so all of us—will retroactively reread the earlier events in our life from this new perspective, and we tend to imagine that is the perspective we had from the start. When we think of ourselves at age 4 or 5, we think of the people around us at that time—our parents, our siblings, our friends—and we picture what they were thinking about us, or how they felt about certain things, or what was going through their minds, when in fact we could actually do none of that at the time! We could not take the role of other at that age. So we are automatically (and subconsciously) "retro-reading" our entire life from the perspective of a recently emerged worldview, and imagining all of this stuff was present from the start!

Needless to say, this considerably distorts what was actually occurring in the earlier periods. Memory is the last thing you can depend on to "report" childhood. And this leads to all sorts of problems. Romantics often imagine that childhood is a wonderful time where you see the world just like you do now, only in a marvelously "spontaneous" and "free" fashion. Archaic is nondual paradise, magic is holistically empowered wonderfulness, mythic is alive with spiritual powers, and it's all so marvelous and free. Whereas what is probably happening is that the Romantics, with access to the higher worldview of reflexive awareness, are simply reading all sorts of wonderful things back into a period which, if they could *actually* see it (on videotape, for example), they would deny any reality to at all!

Satanic Abuse and UFOs

Q: So can you recover childhood memories in any sense?

KW: The impressions of various childhood events are certainly present, sort of like bruises in the psyche. And these impressions retain the worldview of the level that was present when they were laid down—usually archaic or magical.

But when these impressions are recalled by adults, the impressions themselves are often interpreted in terms of the higher worldview now present. And then all sorts of present-day concerns can be injected back into these original impressions, and it vividly appears that these concerns were there from the start. It doesn't seem like you are reinterpreting these early impressions, because that is done subconsciously or preconsciously, and so you only see the conscious result of this extensive reworking.

In certain intense states of regression—with certain therapies, certain meditative practices, certain drugs, certain intense stresses—these original impressions can be accessed (precisely because the higher paradigm is temporarily decommissioned), but even then, a few seconds or a few minutes later, the higher worldview returns, and people begin extensive retro-reading of these impressions. And we have to be very careful about that.

Q: Satanic ritual child abuse?

KW: Well, that's one example. The FBI has found not one scrap of evidence of ritual child murder, even though thousands of people are claiming such. There ought to be corpses all over the backyards of this country. But these folks honestly and deeply believe this has happened to them. They do not feel that they are making this up. These impressions present themselves with vivid certainty. They will easily pass lie detector tests. The reworking has taken place subconsciously.

Samsara is a brutal place. Samsara, metaphorically, is a realm of ritual abuse. It is inherently a mechanism of terror. And people need to cope with this nightmare. One of the simplest ways is to imagine that this ritual abuse had a specific cause in your own personal history. So you search your childhood "memories," and eventually, with a little help from a friendly therapist, sure enough: there's mom with a butcher knife. The original impression is probably true enough: mom had a knife, she was carving the Thanksgiving turkey, and that impression is real. But it gets reworked, and now you're the turkey.

Q: Alien abduction? UFO abduction? These stories all have a very similar structure. The same events keep happening. There's the abduction, the medical experiments and anal probe and semen collection, the sending back to earth, often with a message for humanity. And it really alters these people's lives.

KW: I think the original impressions might go back to fulcrum-2 or fulcrum-1 or even fulcrum-0. But again, they get dramatically reworked. Maybe even some archetypal or Jungian material gets activated—Jung thought UFOs were actually projected archetypes. The UFO anal probe: where Freud meets Jung.

Many people are sincere in their beliefs about it. Perhaps even some higher or spiritual material gets injected into the impressions. But the impressions themselves retain a very *narcissistic* worldview. Imagine: humanity is about to enter a new phase, guided by a massive new alien intelligence. And of all the people in the entire world, you are chosen to carry this message. In fact, the aliens are collecting semen or ova from you because they are inseminating a new race, beginning a new race. And you are to be the father of this new race, the mother of this new race. The new saviors are coming, a new virgin birth is required.

You can't get much more narcissistic and egocentric than that. Some very deep fulcrum-2 (or earlier) material is being reactivated, in my opinion, and then injected with present-day adult "messages" about saving Gaia and healing the planet—which is all very nice, but it can't hide the primal scene in all of these fantasies: you are the center of the new world, the father or the mother of a new and higher race.

So it's an original and real enough impression, reworked and injected with adult material, so that it presents itself with a genuine and frightening vividness, and it retains the essential worldview of fulcrum-2 (or earlier)—namely, its intense narcissism—but then is reworked, often with the aid of a kindly and helpful therapist, into a powerful paradigm of world salvation, courtesy of you.

Q: No spiritual components at all?

KW: We haven't talked much about any of the higher stages, but it's always possible that some genuinely transpersonal or spiritual dimensions are temporarily "peek-experienced" and then translated downward into terms that will both satisfy the fulcrum-2 fixation and fit the "world-saving" paradigm fabricated by the client, often in collusion with the therapist. All of which presents itself as *vividly real* and undeniable. As we said, these individuals will, and often do, pass a lie detector test, because they are sincere in their beliefs, and their therapists are equally sincere, and neither has spotted the lie, the deep reworking that converts impressions into realities.

The therapists investigating these phenomena had a real opportunity to make pioneering observations on new forms of hysterical syndromes emerging as a sign of our troubled times, but by and large they lost that opportunity by allowing the vividness of the impressions to persuade them that they were dealing with ontological realities. They converted phenomenology into ontology. At the very worst, they were propelled by their own deep narcissism: I am therapist to the new race. At the very least, they became facilitators in the mass hysteria, and this has understandably thrown the whole profession into turmoil and bitter self-recrimination.

I suspect ritual satanic child abuse and UFO abduction are both powerful examples of what happens to spiritual realities in a culture that denies spiritual realities—casualties on the way to global, souls washed ashore on an island of cultural insincerity.

11

On the Way to Global: Part 2

Q: We were discussing the interior transformations that occur "on the way to global," and all of the problems that can prevent the emergence of this global awareness.

KW: Yes, and we had reached the point where there is a paradigm shift from preconventional to conventional modes of awareness—from fulcrum-3 to fulcrum-4, which is especially evidenced in the capacity to take the role of other. And in this shift we see a *continuing decrease in egocentrism*. In fact, the overall direction of development in humans— the telos of human development—is toward less and less egocentric states.

But this is true in general. The archbattle in the universe is always: evolution versus egocentrism. The evolutionary drive to produce greater depth is synonymous with the drive to overcome egocentrism, to find wider and deeper wholes, to unfold greater and greater unions. A molecule overcomes the egocentrism of an atom. A cell overcomes the egocentrism of a molecule. And nowhere is this trend more obvious than in human development itself.

Evolution versus Egocentrism

Q: So evolution is a continual decline of egocentrism.

KW: Yes, a continual *decentering*. Howard Gardner gives a perfect summary of the research in this area, and I want to read a short quote from him, because it pretty much says it all.

He begins by pointing out that development in general is marked by "the decline of egocentrism." He reports: "The young child is totally egocentric—meaning not that he thinks selfishly only about himself, but to the contrary, that he is incapable of thinking about himself. The egocentric child is unable to differentiate himself from the rest of the world; he has not separated himself out from others or from objects. Thus he feels that others share his pain or his pleasure, that his mumblings will inevitably be understood, that his perspective is shared by all persons, that even animals and plants partake of his consciousness. In playing hide-and-seek he will 'hide' in broad view of other persons, because his egocentrism prevents him from recognizing that others are aware of his location. The whole course of human development can be viewed as a *continuing decline in egocentrism. . . .*"

Q: So narcissism or egocentrism is *greatest* at fulcrum-1 and then steadily declines?

KW: Yes, exactly. Because differentiation is at its least, narcissism is at its worst!

This selfcentrism lessens somewhat as the infant's identity switches from physiocentric to biocentric—from fulcrum-1 to fulcrum-2. The child does not treat the physical world as an extension of itself, because physical self and physical world are now differentiated. But the emotional self and emotional world are not yet differentiated, and so the entire emotional world is an extension of the self: emotional narcissism is at its peak. The biocentric or ecological self of fulcrum-2 is thus still profoundly egocentric. What it's feeling, the world is feeling.

This narcissism is lessened, or declines once again, with the emergence of the conceptual self (fulcrum-3). The self is now a conceptual ego, but that ego still cannot yet take the role of other, so the early ego is still largely narcissistic, preconventional, egocentric.

So I sometimes summarize this declining narcissism as going from physiocentric to biocentric to egocentric, with the understanding that all three are egocentric in the general sense, but less and less so. And the whole egocentric perspective undergoes yet another radical shift with the emergence of the capacity to *take the role of other*. At which point *egocentric* shifts to *sociocentric*.

Fulcrum-4 (Continued): Life's Social Scripts

Q: In other words, fulcrum-4.

KW: Yes. At this stage, what becomes crucially important for me is not how I *fit with my biological impulses*, but how I *fit with my social roles*, my group, my peer group, or—a bit wider—how I fit with my country, my state, my people. I am now taking the role of other, and how I fit with the other is crucially important. I have *decentered* once again, differentiated once again, transcended once again—my ego is not the only ego in the universe.

So this sociocentric stance is a major transformation—or paradigm shift—from the previous and especially egocentric stances of the first three fulcrums. But notice: with fulcrum-4, care and concern are expanded from me to the group—but no further! If you are a member of the group—a member of my tribe, my mythology, my ideology—then you are "saved" as well. But if you belong to a different culture, a different group, a different mythology, a different god, then you are damned.

So this sociocentric or conventional stance tends to be very *ethnocentric*. Care and concern are expanded from me to my group, and there it stops.

So I also call this conventional or sociocentric stance by the term *mythic-membership*. The worldview of fulcrum-4 is still mythological, and so care and concern are extended to believers in the same mythology, the same ideology, the same race, the same creed, the same culture—but no further. If you are a member of the myth, you are my brother, my sister. If not, you go to hell.

In other words, I can decenter from my ego to my group, but I cannot yet decenter my group. My group is the only group in the universe. I cannot yet move from sociocentric and ethnocentric to a truly *worldcentric* or universal or global stance—a decentered, universal, pluralistic stance. But I am getting there, slowly! I am on the way to global, with each stage in this journey marked by a profound decentering, a lessening of egocentrism, a lessening of narcissism, a transcendence of the shallower and a disclosure of the deeper. Decentering, transcendence, decreasing egocentrism—so many words for the same thing, the same telos of evolution.

And, in fact, the postconventional or global or worldcentric stance is the next fulcrum, fulcrum-5.

Q: Okay, so let's finish with fulcrum-4 first. Identity switches from egocentric to sociocentric.

KW: Yes. The self is no longer relating only or primarily to its body and its immediate impulses, but is also ushered into a world of *roles* and *rules*. The self will have all sorts of *scripts*, or learned roles and rules, which it will have to play out.

Most of these scripts are useful and absolutely necessary—they are the means whereby you pull yourself out of yourself and into the circle of intersubjective culture, the circle of care and concern and relatedness and responsibility, where you begin to see in others your own expanded self, and extend care to each. You see the world through the eyes of the other, and thus find a wider consciousness that shines beyond the confines of the me and the mine.

But some of these scripts are distorted or cruel or maladaptive, and if something goes wrong with these scripts, we call this "script pathology." The person has all these false and distorted social masks and myths—"I'm a rotten person, I'm no good, I can never do anything right"—all these cruel scripts that are self-defeating and injurious.

That are, in short, lies. These false scripts are the form of the lie at this level, and the false self lives by these social lies. It is not just out of touch with its emotions; it is out of touch with the self it could be in the cultural world—out of touch with all the positive roles it could assume if it didn't keep telling itself that it can't.

Q: Which is what cognitive therapists tend to work with.

KW: Yes, and family therapy, and transactional analysis, and narrative therapy, to mention a few. It's not so much working back into the past and earlier fulcrums and trying to dig up and uncover some buried emotion or impulse, although that can definitely happen. It's more a case of directly attacking these false and distorted rules and scripts and games. These scripts are simply not true, they are not based on present evidence—they are lies, they are myths. They are anchored in a mythic disposition, which will not expose itself to rational evidence.

Aron Beck, for example, a pioneer in cognitive therapy, has found that in most cases of depression, people have a series of false scripts or beliefs, and they keep repeating these myths as if they were true. When we are depressed, we *talk* to ourselves in *untruthful* ways. "If one person doesn't like me, it means nobody will like me. If I fail at this particular task, it means I will fail at everything. If I don't get this job, my life is over. If she doesn't love me, nobody else will." And so on.

Now perhaps these false scripts got started at an earlier fulcrum, perhaps fulcrum-3 or fulcrum-2 or earlier. And a more psychoanalytically oriented therapist (or an "uncovering therapist") might try to dig back to these earlier traumas and find out why the person is generating these myths (and even magical beliefs or archaic impulses).

But the cognitive therapist tends to simply attack the myths head on. The person will be asked to monitor their interior dialogue and look for these myths, and then expose them to reason and evidence. "Okay, if I don't get this job, I guess it doesn't really mean my life is over."

Q: Most typical therapy seems to work at this level.

KW: Pretty much. Most typical therapy—your general interpretive psychotherapist—will use an amalgam of fulcrum-3 and fulcrum-4 techniques. Most therapy is simply talking about your problems, and the therapist will be on the lookout for any distorting scripts that tell you that you are a rotten person, that you're no good, that you're a failure, and so on. A false self, built on myths and deceptions, has taken charge of your life. And the therapist helps you to uproot these false scripts and replace them with a more realistic interpretation of yourself, a more *truthful interpretation* of your interior, so that the false self can give way to the actual self.

These therapists might not use terms like "scripts" and "myths" and "narrative analysis" and so on, but that is generally what is involved on the fulcrum-4 side, the script pathology side. Myths cause symptoms; expose the myths to evidence, and the symptoms go away. The idea is, *think* differently, and you will start to *feel* differently.

But if it looks like there are some strong feelings or emotions or impulses that the person *cannot* deal with or acknowledge, then the therapist often tends to switch to an "uncovering mode." What are your *feelings* about this? What is your *felt-sense?* And the therapist might notice that there are certain feelings and impulses that you are not comfortable with—you have certain "buried emotions," and therapy then tends to work at uncovering these repressed emotions, by whatever name.

So typical therapy is usually an amalgam of fulcrum-4 script analysis and fulcrum-3 uncovering analysis, although the different therapists will bring a wide variety of tools and techniques to the process.

(Fulcrum-1 pathologies are so severe they are usually handled by a medical psychiatrist, who prescribes medication. And fulcrum-2 is usually the province of therapists who specialize in structure-building techniques. These techniques have been pioneered by Kernberg, Kohut, Masterson, and Blanck and Blanck—often with reference to Margaret Mahler's groundbreaking research, which we briefly discussed earlier. Certain intense regressive therapies—e.g., Grof's holotropic breathwork and Janou's primal therapy—claim to deal with fulcrum-0, although these claims are highly controversial.)

Fulcrum-5: The Worldcentric or Mature Ego

Q: Which brings us to fulcrum-5.

KW: Around the age of 11–15 years in our culture, the capacity for formal operational awareness emerges (this is "formop" on figure 5-2). Where concrete operational awareness can operate on the concrete world, formal operational awareness can operate on thought itself. It's not just thinking about the world, it's thinking about thinking. This is not nearly as dry and abstract as it sounds!

There's also a classical experiment that Piaget used to spot this extremely important emergence or paradigm shift or worldview shift. In simplified version: the person is given three glasses of clear liquid and told that they can be mixed in a way that will produce a yellow color. The person is then asked to produce the yellow color.

Concrete operational children will simply start mixing the liquids together haphazardly. They will keep doing this until they stumble on the right combination or give up. In other words, as the name implies, they perform *concrete operations*—they have to actually do it in a concrete way.

Formal operational adolescents will first form a general picture of the fact that you have to try glass A with glass B, then A with C, then B with C, and so on. If you ask them about it, they will say something like, "Well, I need to try all the various combinations one at a time." In other words, they have a formal operation in their mind, a scheme that lets them know that you have to try *all the possible* combinations.

Q: That still sounds pretty dry and abstract to me.

KW: It's really quite the opposite. It means the person can begin to imagine different possible worlds. "What if" and "as if" can be grasped for the first time, and this ushers the person into the wild world of the true dreamer. All sorts of idealistic possibilities open up, and the person's awareness can dream of things that are not yet, and picture future worlds of ideal possibilities, and work to change the world according to those dreams. You can imagine what yet might be! Adolescence is such a wild time, not just because of sexual blossoming, but because *possible worlds* open up to the mind's eye—it's the "age of reason and revolution."

Likewise, thinking about thought means true introspection becomes possible. The interior world, for the first time, opens up before the mind's eye; psychological space becomes a new and exciting terrain.

Inward visions dance in the head, and for the first time they are not coming from external nature, nor from a mythic god, nor from a conventional other, but, in some strange and miraculous way, they come from a voice within.

And this means one other very important thing. Because you can think about thinking, you can start to *judge* the roles and the rules which, at the previous stage, you simply swallowed unreflexively. Your moral stance moves from conventional to *postconventional*. (See figure 9-3.) You can *criticize* your own conventional society. Because you can "think about thought," you can "norm the norms." You might end up agreeing with the norms, or you might disagree with them. But the point is, you can scrutinize many of them. You are no longer merely *identified* with them, and so you have some critical distance from them. To some degree, you have transcended them.

This, of course, is the 1-2-3 process as it moves from fulcrum-4 to fulcrum-5. You start out, at fulcrum-4, in *fusion* with the conventional roles and rules—you are *identified* with them, merged with them (and thus utterly at their mercy, a true conformist). Then you begin to *differentiate* or *transcend* them, gain some freedom from them, and move to the next higher stage (fulcrum-5), whereupon you will still have to *integrate* these social roles—you can still be a father without being lost in that role. But you have in general moved away from, or differentiated from, an exclusive identity with your sociocentric roles, and you particularly begin to scrutinize the rightness or appropriateness of your sociocentric and ethnocentric perspectives, which previously you would not—and could not—even question.

In short, you have gone from *sociocentric* to *worldcentric*. Another decline in narcissism. Another decentering, another transcendence. You want to know what is right and fair, not just for you and your people, but for all peoples. You take a postconventional or global or worldcentric stance. (And, just as important, you are getting very close to a genuinely spiritual or transpersonal opening.)

So, in this transformation from sociocentric to worldcentric, the self decenters once again: my group is not the only group in the universe, my tribe is not the only tribe, my god is not the only god, my ideology is not the only ideology. I went from egocentric to ethnocentric by decentering my ego into the group; now I go from ethnocentric to worldcentric by decentering my group into the world.

This is a very difficult transformation! But when it succeeds (which is fairly rare: greater depth, less span), then we have the first truly universal or global or worldcentric stance.

For the very first time in all of consciousness development and evolution, we have a worldcentric and global perspective. What a long journey!—what a rocky road!—this precious path to global.

And just as important, all further and higher developments will have this worldcentric platform as their base. It is an irreversible shift. Once you see the world in global perspectives, you cannot prevent yourself from doing so. You can never go back.

And thus Spirit has, for the first time in evolution, looked through your eyes and seen a global world, a world that is decentered from the me and the mine, a world that demands care and concern and compassion and conviction—a Spirit that is unfolding its own intrinsic value and worth, but a Spirit that announces itself only through the voice of those who have the courage to stand in the worldcentric space and defend it against lesser and shallower engagements.

Diversity and Multiculturalism

Q: Which relates directly to the moral stance. I mean, that's why it's called *post*conventional, right? Where conventional morality is sociocentric, postconventional is worldcentric, based on principles of universal pluralism, or global tolerance and fairness.

KW: Yes, that's right.

Q: Is this the same as multiculturalism?

KW: Well, we have to be very careful here. Multiculturalism does indeed emphasize cultural diversity and universal tolerance. But this fulcrum-5 stance is a very rare and very elite and very difficult accomplishment. Look at all the ground we have covered in order to get to this worldcentric stance!

Now you yourself might indeed have evolved from egocentric to ethnocentric to worldcentric perspectives, and so you will easily understand that all individuals are to be accorded equal consideration and equal opportunity, regardless of race, sex, or creed. From this stance of universal pluralism, you are genuinely multicultural and postconventional. The problem is, most individuals that you treat with universal coverage do not share your universalism. They are still egocentric or ethnocentric to the core. So you are extending universal consideration to individuals who will absolutely not extend the same courtesy to you.

So typical multiculturalists are thrown into a series of very bizarre contradictions. To begin with, they claim to be non-elitist or anti-elitist. But the capacity for postconventional and worldcentric pluralism is a very rare, very elite accomplishment. One survey found that only 10 percent of the American population actually reach this highly developed stage. So multiculturalism is a very elite stance that then claims it is not elitist. In other words, it starts to lie about its own identity, and this will lead it down some very murky roads.

Q: For instance?

KW: Multiculturalism does embrace the very noble drive to treat individuals equally and fairly, from a decentered and worldcentric perspective—everybody is equal in that sense—but it then confuses that high stance with the fact that *getting to that high stance* is a very rare accomplishment. It *ignores* the *getting there*, the developmental process that allowed it to embrace universal pluralism in the first place. So it then extends the *results* of that development to individuals who have *not* gotten to that stance themselves, and who are therefore perfectly willing to take your nice universal pluralistic stance and wipe their shoes all over it.

The multicults therefore naturally but confusedly say that we have to treat all individuals and all cultural movements as being completely equal, since no stance is better than another. They then cannot explain why Nazis and the Ku Klux Klan should be shunned. If we are really multicultural and all for diversity, how can we exclude the Nazis? Isn't everybody equal?

The answer, of course, is that no, not every stance is equal. Worldcentric is *better* than ethnocentric, which is *better* than egocentric, because each has more depth. The Nazis and the KKK are ethnocentric movements based on a particular mythology of race supremacy, and from a worldcentric perspective we judge them to be *inferior* stances.

But the typical multiculturalist cannot allow this *judgment*, because they confusedly deny distinctions between moral stances altogether—all stances are equal, no judgments allowed! (This is the typical "anti-hierarchy" stance of the extreme postmodernists.)

And so what happens, of course, is that they simply tend to become completely intolerant of those who disagree with them. They know that they have a noble stance, which in part they certainly do, but because they don't understand how they got there, they simply try to force their view down everybody's throat. Everybody is equal! No moral stance is better than another! No hierarchies here! And so off we go with vicious intolerance in the name of tolerance, with censorship in the name of compassion, with we-know-best thought police and mindless political correctness—with a bunch of elitists trying to outlaw everybody else's elitisms. It would be hilarious if it weren't so fundamentally wretched.

Q: So is this related to the pathology of this stage?

KW: This stage and the next, yes. Once you start to go worldcentric, once you begin scrutinizing your culture, and perhaps distancing yourself from its sociocentric or ethnocentric prejudice, and you strike out on your own—once you do that, then *who*, exactly, *are you*? Without all the old and comfortable roles, *who are you*? How can you fashion your own identity? What do you want from life? What do you want to be? Who are you, anyway? Erikson called this an "identity crisis," and it is perhaps the central "un-ease" or "dis-ease" of this fulcrum.

And the multiculs are in a massive identity crisis. Since their official stance is that elitism of any sort is bad, but since their actual self is in fact an elite self, then they must lie about their actual self—they must conceal, distort, deceive.

So they go from saying everybody should be judged fairly, in a non-ethnocentric way, to saying that everybody should *not be judged at all*, that all moral stances are equivalent. Except *their* stance, of course, which is superior in a world where nothing is supposed to be superior at all (oops). So they have an elite stance that denies its own elitism—they are *lying* about their actual identity. They have a false self system. And that is an identity crisis.

Q: It's very spooky. It's Orwell's newspeak and thought police. But it seems to be fairly pervasive. The universities have all but been hijacked by it.

KW: Yes, American universities today seem to specialize in it. All this is actually doing is contributing to the retribalization of America, by encouraging every egocentric and ethnocentric fragmentation and grievance politics, the politics of narcissism. All stances are equal means every preconventional and ethnocentric shallowness is given encouragement. The country is facing its own identity crisis, we might say, but I suppose that's another discussion.

Fulcrum-6: The Bodymind Integration of the Centaur

Q: Which brings us to the last major "orthodox" stage, or the highest stage most conventional researchers tend to recognize.

KW: Yes, fulcrum-6. The basic structure at this stage is vision-logic, which you can see on several figures, including 5-2 and 10-1. Vision-logic or network-logic is a type of synthesizing and integrating aware-ness. Formal operational awareness is synthesizing and integrating in many important and impressive ways, but it still tends to possess a kind of dichotomizing logic, a logic of either/or, rather like Aristotelian logic.

But vision-logic adds up the parts and sees networks of interactions. When employed in a merely objectifying or Right-Hand fashion, it pro-duces objective systems theory in general. But when it is the basis of actual interior transformation—which is not covered by systems theory! and which is very rare!—then it supports an integrated personality. When the self's center of gravity identifies with vision-logic, when the person lives from that level, then we tend to get a very highly integrated personality, a self that can actually inhabit a global perspective, and not merely talk about it.

So the highly integrative capacity of vision-logic supports an equally integrated self. Which is why I call the self of this stage the *centaur*, representing an integration of the mind and the body, the noosphere and the biosphere, in a relatively autonomous self—which doesn't mean isolated self or atomistic self or egocentric self, but rather a self inte-grated in its networks of responsibility and service.

Q: You have often used John Broughton's research on this particular stage, although he's not very well known.

KW: Well, several researchers have looked at this stage very care-fully—Loevinger, Selman, Habermas, Erikson, Graves, and Maslow, for example. But I have always liked the summary of Broughton's research: at this stage, "mind and body are both experiences of an integrated self."

That says it all in a very succinct fashion. First of all, the self at this stage is *aware of* both the mind and the body *as experiences*. That is, the *observing self* is beginning to *transcend* both the mind and the body and thus can be aware of them as objects in awareness, as experiences. It is not just the mind looking at the world; it is the observing self look-ing at both the mind and the world. This is a very powerful transcen-dence, which we will see intensify in the higher stages.

And second, precisely because the observing self is beginning to tran-scend the mind and the body, it can for just that reason begin to *integrate* the mind and body. Thus, "centaur."

So in this fulcrum, we have the same 1-2-3 process that we see in every other fulcrum, namely, initial fusion, differentiation, and integra-tion. In this case, there is the initial identification with the formal mind (of fulcrum-5). The observing self then begins to differentiate from the mind and to see it as an object. Since it is no longer exclusively identified with the mind, it can integrate the mind with the other components in awareness, with the body and its impulses. Hence, centaur—mind and body are both experiences of an integrated self.

Aperspectival Madness

Q: You also call the centaur the existential level.

KW: Well, at this stage you are really, as it were, on your own, at least at this point in evolution. You no longer have blind faith in the conventional roles and rules of society. You are no longer ethnocentric and sociocentric. You have moved deeply into a worldcentric space, where . . .

Q: This stage is also worldcentric?

KW: All stages at and beyond formal operational (fulcrum-5) are worldcentric or global—they all have a foundation of postconventional and universal perspectivism. The higher or deeper stages simply disclose more and more of this worldcentric freedom as it moves into deeper and genuinely spiritual domains.

Which is a bit ahead of the story. At the centaur level, the existential level, you are no longer egocentric or ethnocentric. You have moved deeply into a worldcentric space, where, as the multicults demonstrate, you can slip and take a very bad spill in this new freedom.

Q: You call this new freedom "aperspectival."

KW: Jean Gebser's term, yes. Vision-logic adds up all the different perspectives, and therefore it doesn't automatically privilege any one perspective over the others—it is aperspectival. But as you begin to take all the different perspectives into account, it gets very dizzifying, very aperspectival, very disorienting.

And you can get very lost in this new aperspectival awareness of vision-logic, because all perspectives start to become relative and interdependent; there is nothing absolutely foundational; no final place to rest your head and say, I've got it!

But the fact that all perspectives are *relative* does *not* mean that all perspectives are equal. That all perspectives are relative does not prevent some from being relatively better than others all the time! Worldcentric is better than ethnocentric is better than egocentric, because each has more depth than its shallower predecessors.

But forgetting that, and focusing merely on the relativity of perspectives, throws you into aperspectival madness, a dizzifying paralysis of will and judgment. "It's all relative, so there is no better and worse, and no stance is better than another." Overlooking the fact that that stance itself claims to be *better* than the alternatives—the standard performative contradiction. The multicults often rise to this level of vision-logic, with a very noble intent, but often succumb to aperspectival madness, which they sell to nice, unsuspecting students.

The aperspectival space of vision-logic simply means that Spirit is looking at the world through infinitely wondrous perspectives; it does not mean it has gone blind in the process. This is simply a further decentering, a further transcendence, another spiral in the evolution beyond egocentrism.

On the Brink of the Transpersonal

Q: So that's part of the good news of this existential or centauric stage.

KW: Yes. One of the characteristics of the *actual self* of this stage (the centaur) is precisely that it no longer buys all the conventional and numbing consolations—as Kierkegaard put it, the self can no longer tranquilize itself with the trivial. The emergence of this more authentic or existential self is the primary task of fulcrum-6.

The finite self is going to die—magic will not save it, mythic gods will not save it, rational science will not save it—and facing that cutting fact is part of becoming authentic. This was one of Heidegger's constant points. Coming to terms with one's mortality and one's finitude—this is part of finding one's own authentic being-in-the-world (authentic agency-in-communion).

The existentialists have beautifully analyzed this authentic self, the actual centauric self—its characteristics, its mode of being, its stance in the world—and most important, they have analyzed the common lies and bad faith that sabotage this authenticity. We lie about our mortality and finitude by constructing immortality symbols—vain attempts to beat time and exist everlastingly in some mythic heaven, some rational project, some great artwork, through which we project our incapacity to face death. We lie about the responsibility for our own choices, preferring to see ourselves as passive victims of some outside force. We lie about the richness of the present by projecting ourselves backward in guilt and forward in anxiety. We lie about our fundamental responsibility by hiding in the herd mentality, getting lost in the Other. In place of the authentic or actual self, we live as the inauthentic self, the false self, fashioning its projects of deception to hide itself from the shocking truth of existence.

I fully agree with all of that analysis, as far as it goes. Because, from my own point of view, not only is this type of existential authenticity important for its own sake, it is a prerequisite for entering the transpersonal not burdened with myths, or magical expectations, or egocentric and ethnocentric exaltations.

Q: But there is such a grim atmosphere in these existential writers.

KW: Yes, this is classically the home of existential dread, despair, angst, fear and trembling, sickness unto death—precisely because you have lost all the comforting consolations!

All of which is true enough, but because the existentialists recognize no sphere of consciousness higher than this, they are stuck with the existential worldview, which limits their perceptions to within its horizon.

So they make it something of a point of honor to embrace drab existential nightmares with dreadful seriousness. And if you claim there are any modes of awareness that go beyond existential angst, then you *must* be lapsing into death-denial, immortality projects, inauthenticity, bad faith. Any claim of a higher horizon is met with icy stares, and the heinous charge of "inauthentic!" comes to rest upon your head. If you *smile*, you're probably being inauthentic, because you have broken the sacred circle of the unendingly dreary.

Q: Stuck in the centaur, identified with the centaur and its existential worldview—that's the fusion phase of fulcrum-6.

KW: Yes. And that existential embeddedness becomes your point of reference for all reality. The more angst you can display, the more you can gnash your teeth as an example of cosmic insanity, then the more authentic you are. It might also help to drive a few nails into your forehead, as a sort of reminder. But in any event, never, never, never let them see you smile, or that will divulge your inauthenticity.

The whole point of the existential level is that you are not yet in the transpersonal, but you are no longer totally anchored in the personal— the whole personal domain has started to lose its flavor, has started to become profoundly meaningless. And so of course there is not much reason to smile. What good is the personal anyway—it's just going to die. Why even inhabit it?

This concern with *meaning*, and with its pervasive lack, is perhaps the central feature of fulcrum-6 pathologies, and with existential therapy.

But the interesting point is that the centaur, by all orthodox standards, ought to be happy and full and joyous. After all, it's an integrated and autonomous self, as you can see in figure 9-3. Why, by all standards, this self ought to be smiling all the time. But more often than not, it is not smiling. It is profoundly unhappy. It is integrated, and autonomous, and miserable.

It has tasted everything that the personal realm can offer, and it's not enough. The world has started to go flat in its appeal. No experience tastes good anymore. Nothing satisfies anymore. Nothing is worth pursuing anymore. Not because one has failed to get these rewards, but precisely because one has achieved them royally, tasted it all, and found it all lacking.

And so naturally this soul does not smile very much. This is a soul for whom all consolations have gone sour. The world has gone flat at exactly the moment of its greatest triumph. The magnificent banquet has come and gone; the skull grins silently over the whole affair. The feast is ephemeral, even in its grandest glories. The things on which I once could hang so much meaning and so much desire and so much fervent hope, all have melted into air, evaporated at some strange point during the long and lonely night. To whom can I sing songs of joy and exaltation? Who will hear my calls for help sent silently into that dark and hellish night? Where will I find the fortitude to withstand the swords and spears that daily pierce my side? And why even should I try? It all comes to dust, yes?, and where am I then? Fight or surrender, it matters not the least, for still my life goals bleed quietly to death, in a hemorrhage of despair.

This is a soul for whom all desires have become thin and pale and anemic. This is a soul who, in facing existence squarely, is thoroughly sick of it. This is a soul for whom the personal has gone totally flat. This is, in other words, a soul on the brink of the transpersonal.

12

Realms of the Superconscious: Part 1

Q: We can now move into the transpersonal stages, the superconscious domains. We left off development at the centaur. You described this as the observing self becoming aware of both mind and body, and thus beginning to transcend them.

KW: Yes, even orthodox research confirms this, and we gave several examples, from Broughton to Loevinger. By the time of the centaur, the observing self can witness or experience both the mind and the body, in a general sense, which means it is indeed beginning to transcend them in some important ways. As consciousness evolution continues, it discloses more and more depth—or height—to this observing self. What is this observing self? How deep, or how high, does it actually go?

And the answer given by the world's great mystics and sages is that this observing self goes straight to God, straight to Spirit, straight to the very Divine. In the ultimate depths of your own awareness, you intersect infinity.

This observing self is usually called the Self with a capital S, or the Witness, or pure Presence, or pure awareness, or consciousness as such, and this Self as transparent Witness is a direct ray of the living Divine. The ultimate I is Christ, is Buddha, is Emptiness itself: such is the startling testimony of the world's great mystics and sages.

Where the Mind Leaves Off

Q: So is this Witness an emergent?

KW: Not exactly, because pure consciousness is not an emergent.

This Self or Witness was present from the start as the basic form of awareness at whatever stage of growth a holon happened to be—it was present as prehension, as sensation, as impulse, as emotion, as symbols, as reason—but it becomes increasingly obvious as growth and transcendence matures. In other words, this Witness, this consciousness as such, is simply the depth of any holon, the interior of any holon. As we said, depth is consciousness, and depth goes all the way down. But as depth increases, consciousness shines forth more noticeably.

In humans, by the time of the centaur, this observing Witness has shed its lesser identification with both the body and the mind—it has transcended and included them—and so now it can simply witness them, which is why "both mind and body are experiences of an integrated self."

Q: It is beginning to transcend them.

KW: Yes. There is nothing occult or spooky about any of this. We have already seen identity shift from matter to body to mind, each of which involved a decentering or a dis-identifying with the lesser dimension. And by the time of the centaur, consciousness is simply continuing this process and starting to *dis-identify with the mind itself*, which is precisely why it can witness the mind, see the mind, experience the mind. The mind is no longer merely a subject; it is starting to become an object. An object of . . . the observing Self, the Witness.

And so the mystical, contemplative, and yogic traditions pick up where the mind leaves off. They pick up with the observing Self as it begins to transcend the mind, as it begins to go transmental or supramental or overmental. Or transrational, transegoic, transpersonal.

The contemplative traditions are based on a series of experiments in awareness: what if you pursue this Witness to its source? What if you inquire within, pushing deeper and deeper into the source of awareness itself? What if you push beyond or behind the mind, into a depth of consciousness that is not confined to the ego or the individual self? What do you find? As a repeatable, reproducible experiment in awareness, what do you find?

"There is a subtle essence that pervades all reality," begins one of the most famous answers to that question. "It is the reality of all that is, and the foundation of all that is. That essence is all. That essence is the real. And thou, thou art that."

In other words, this observing Self eventually discloses its own source, which is Spirit itself, Emptiness itself. And that is why the mystics maintain that this observing Self is a ray of the Sun that is the radiant Abyss and ultimate Ground upon which the entire manifest Kosmos depends. Your very Self intersects the Self of the Kosmos at large—a supreme identity that outshines the entire manifest world, a supreme identity that undoes the knot of the separate self and buries it in splendor.

So from matter to body to mind to Spirit. In each case consciousness or the observing Self sheds an exclusive identity with a lesser and shallower dimension, and opens up to deeper and higher and wider occasions, until it opens up to its own ultimate ground in Spirit itself.

And the stages of transpersonal growth and development are basically the stages of following this observing Self to its ultimate abode, which is pure Spirit or pure Emptiness, the ground, path, and fruition of the entire display.

The Transpersonal Stages

Q: So these stages . . . there are, what, several stages in this transpersonal growth?

KW: Yes, that's right, but again, in a very fluid and flowing way. In looking at these higher stages or waves of consciousness, we have a rather small pool of daring men and women—both yesterday and today—who have bucked the system, fought the average and normal, and struck out toward the new and higher spheres of awareness. In this quest, they joined with a small group or sangha of like-spirited souls, and developed *practices* or *injunctions* or *paradigms* that would disclose these higher worldspaces—injunctions or paradigms or interior *experiments* that would allow others to reproduce their results and therefore check and validate (or reject) their findings. And they left us their maps of this interior journey, with the crucial proviso that simply memorizing the map will not do, any more than studying a map of the Bahamas will replace actually going there.

So we take all these various maps and paths left by the great contemplative traditions, East and West, North and South, and we compare and contrast them (which demands that we *practice* many of them as well! This is a Left-Hand endeavor for *participant* observers, not merely a Right-Hand representation for academic study). Some paths are more complete than others; some specialize in a particular level; some leave out certain levels; some divide particular levels into literally dozens of sublevels.

From this cross-cultural comparison, grounded in practice, we attempt to create a "master template" that gives a fairly comprehensive and composite map of the various higher levels of consciousness that are available to men and women. These are higher *basic levels* present as *potentials* in all of us, but awaiting actual manifestation and growth and development.

Q: So how complicated do these higher maps get?

KW: Well, some traditions are so sophisticated they have literally hundreds of minute divisions of the various stages and components of consciousness development. But, based on the state of present research, it is fairly safe to say that there are *at least four major stages* of transpersonal development or evolution.

These four stages I call the *psychic*, the *subtle*, the *causal*, and the *nondual* (you can see these in figures 9-1 and 10-1; the nondual is the paper on which the diagram is drawn, which I'll explain in a moment). These are basic levels or spheres of consciousness, and so of course each of them has a different worldview, which I call, respectively, *nature mysticism, deity mysticism, formless mysticism*, and *nondual mysticism*.

Q: Now in what sense are these actually *stages*?

KW: The basic levels themselves are fairly discrete, identifiable structures. Their worldviews are very specific, and they differ from each other in important and easily identifiable ways—each has a different architecture with different cognitions, which support a different self-sense, different moral stances, different self-needs, and so on.

But, as always, the "ladder" is not where the real action is. The real action is the climber of the ladder—the self-system—and the fulcrums that are generated with this climb. And the self, as we said, can be all over the place. It can have a peak experience of a higher level, only to fall back into its actual and present self-stage. Conversely, a taste of the higher levels can so disrupt the self that it *regresses* to earlier fulcrums, fulcrums at which there is still some sort of fixation or repression or unfinished business. As egoic translation starts to wind down, these earlier "stick-points" jump out.

Q: So the actual growth of the self in the transpersonal stages is not linear in any sort of rigid sense.

KW: No, it's not. The fact that the higher realms are ladder-like—which means concentric spheres or nested holarchy—doesn't mean that growth through them is ladder-like. There are all sorts of ups and downs and spirals.

Q: Not to mention altered states.

KW: Yes, as we talked about earlier, the self at virtually any stage of development can have various types of peak experiences or altered states, including peak experiences of the transpersonal realms. For example, a self at the magic, mythic, rational, or existential levels can have a peak experience of the psychic, subtle, causal, or nondual realms, and in each case you would get a different type of "spiritual experience" [see *Integral Psychology*]. But, as we were also saying, these temporary states still need to be converted into enduring traits if development into these realms is to become permanent. And so even though altered states and nonordinary states get most of the attention—they're pretty exciting, after all—still, it comes back to actual development and evolution.

Q: Back to actual development through the higher levels, and not just their "peek" experience.

KW: Yes. As the self unfolds—slops and blobs—on up the spiral, the self's center of gravity will tend to organize itself around a predominant higher basic level. It will tend to *identify* its center of gravity with this level; this will be its "home base"—its major fulcrum—around which it will organize most of its perceptions, its moral responses, its motivations, its drives, and so on. Thus, its center of gravity tends to shift through these higher basic spheres of consciousness with an averagely identifiable sequence.

Q: The traditions themselves usually give various stages.

KW: Yes, the traditions themselves know this. They all have their stages of growth and development; they know the characteristics of each stage; they can spot progress and they can spot regression. And, as Aurobindo and Plotinus and Da Avabhasa have pointed out, although one can indeed speed up development through these stages, they cannot fundamentally be bypassed. You can peak-experience ahead, jump ahead, but you will have to make up the ground later, integrate and consolidate it later. Otherwise you get too "top-heavy," so to speak—you are floating upward and upward, with no grounding and no connection to the lower structures, to the mind and body and earth and senses.

Fulcrum-7: The Psychic

Q: So the first of these transpersonal stages, the psychic.

KW: As I use it, the psychic level simply means the great transition stage from ordinary, gross-oriented reality—sensorimotor and rational and existential—into the properly transpersonal domains. Paranormal events sometimes increase in frequency at the psychic level, but that is not what defines this level. The defining characteristic, the deep structure, of this psychic level is an awareness that is no longer confined exclusively to the individual ego or centaur.

Q: A few examples, perhaps.

KW: At the psychic level, a person might temporarily dissolve the separate-self sense (the ego or centaur) and find an identity with the entire gross or sensorimotor world—so-called *nature mysticism.* You're on a nice nature walk, relaxed and expansive in your awareness, and you look at a beautiful mountain, and wham!—suddenly there is no looker, just the mountain—and you are the mountain. You are not in here looking at the mountain out there. There is just the mountain, and it seems to see itself, or you seem to be seeing it from within. The mountain is closer to you than your own skin.

By any other terms, there is no separation between subject and object, between you and the entire natural world "out there." Inside and outside—they don't have any meaning anymore. You can still tell perfectly well where your body stops and the environment begins—this is *not* psychotic adualism or a "resurrection in mature form" of psychotic adualism. It is your own higher Self at this stage—fulcrum-7—which can be called the Eco-Noetic Self; some call it the Over-Soul or the World Soul. This is the fusion phase of fulcrum-7. You are a "nature mystic."

Q: But this seems like such an abrupt switch—from the individual centaur to an identity with all of nature, as it were. I don't see the smooth evolutionary progression here.

KW: Actually, it's not much of a jump at all. I think people get confused because we say identity moves from the "individual" bodymind to the "whole world," which does indeed look rather abrupt.

But that's not what happens. Look at what is actually involved. At the worldcentric centaur, one's awareness has *already* moved from an identity with the material dimension (fulcrum-1) to an identity with the biological dimension (fulcrum-2) to an identity with a mental self (fulcrum-3). That early mental self, like the previous two fulcrums, is very egocentric and narcissistic.

But with fulcrum-4, identity switches from egocentric to sociocentric. Here your awareness *already* transcends its merely *individual* aspects. Your very awareness, your very *identity*, is based upon cultural roles and collective identities and shared values. It is no longer a *body* identity, it is a *role* identity.

Thus, when you say, I am a father, I am a mother, I am a husband, I am a wife, I work at this job, I value this goal—those are already trans-body identities. Those already move beyond the individual body and its sensations, and into a circle of intersubjective roles and values and goals. Most of the items that you call your "self" are not egocentric at all, but

But once you've committed that flatland reductionism, you start to think that the way to transform the world is to simply get everybody to agree with your monological map, forgetting the six or seven interior stages the mapmaker actually had to go through in order to *get* to this point where you *can* agree in the first place.

Q: Similar to the multicults.

KW: Yes, like the multicults, you forget all the stages of transcendence that got you to this noble point, and so not only do you bizarrely condemn transcendence itself (the actual path!), you simply collapse all those stages into an incredibly simplistic "one-step" transformation: agree with my holistic Gaia map, and you will be saved. And so like many of the multicults, these folks often become rather belligerent and intolerant, claiming that all the strands in the web are equally important, but despising the strands that disagree with them.

So instead, we need to take into account the *interior* dimensions—we have to take into account the Left Hand and not just the Right Hand. We have to take into account linguistic and cultural backgrounds, methods of interpretation, the many stages of consciousness evolution, the intricate stages of moral development and decentering, the validity claims of truthfulness and sincerity and justness, holarchical degrees of depth, the hierarchy of expanding self-identity and methods of transcendence—all of those are Left-Hand dimensions, and none of those items is found on the monological and Right-Hand Gaia map!

And for just that reason, you won't find a decent discussion of the interior stages of development in any books on deep ecology, ecofeminism, or ecophilosophy. But without those factors you'll never make it to the New World, because you won't know how to get people into the boat and on their way. You have, as we said, a fine goal with no real path.

Q: So the experience of the Eco-Noetic Self might be very genuine, but it is unpacked or interpreted in an inadequate fashion.

KW: I think so. And we want to rescue this profound intuition of the Eco-Noetic Self and its Community of all beings by giving it perhaps a more adequate interpretation, based on all four quadrants of manifestation, and not based on reducing all quadrants to the Lower Right or "Gaia." Pushing that reductionistic "new paradigm" map as the central aspect of transformation simply diverts attention away from the Left-Hand dimensions where the real transformation is occurring. As such, more often than not these approaches inadvertently sabotage and derail actual transcendence and transformation, and simply encourage the various fragments to retribalize at their own level of adaptation, no matter how shallow. Any egocentric person can sell a Gaia-centric map.

Q: So the point would be, remember the Left-Hand path!

KW: Yes, very much so. We don't want to get caught in a holistic map of flatland. As we saw, that holistic flatland map *is* the fundamental Enlightenment paradigm. That *is* subtle reductionism. That collapses the Left into the Right. That reduces all "I's" and "we's" to interwoven "its"; collapses all interior depths into exterior span; collapses all values into functional fit; reduces all translogical and all dialogical to monological. That is the great holistic web of interwoven its.

Perhaps these theorists have a genuine intuition of the Eco-Noetic Self—I believe some of them do. But they tend to collapse it into flatland and monological Right-Hand terms, which does not promote global transformation but rather encourages retribalization and regressive fragmentation in consciousness. And so these often turn out to be very *preconventional* approaches that covertly encourage *egocentric* consciousness, which their maps do not let them spot because their maps contain none of this.

The Enneagram and the Basic Skeleton

Q: I want to come back to all of that when we discuss flatland and the religion of Gaia (see Part Three). But we were talking about the Eco-Noetic Self, and you said it is one of the forms of this psychic level of consciousness development. What are some others?

KW: What all of the psychic-level developments have in common is that they have one foot in the gross, ordinary, personal realm and one foot in the transpersonal realm. And so, however different these various psychic phenomena seem, they do share a specific deep structure, which involves the beginning transcendence of gross-oriented reality, the transcendence of the ordinary body and mind and culture.

Some of these transcendental phenomena include preliminary meditative states; shamanic visions and voyages; arousal of kundalini energy (and disclosure of the whole psychic anatomy of subtle channels, energies, and essences); overwhelming feelings of the numinous; spontaneous spiritual awakenings; reliving of deep past traumas, even the birth trauma; identification with aspects of nature—plant identification, animal identification—up to an identification with all of nature (cosmic consciousness, nature mysticism, and the World Soul).

Q: How do you know those phenomena actually exist?

KW: As the observing Self begins to transcend the centaur, deeper or higher dimensions of consciousness come into being, and a new world-view or worldspace comes into focus. All of the items on that list are objects that can be directly perceived in this new *psychic worldspace*. Those items are as real in the psychic worldspace as rocks are in the sensorimotor worldspace and concepts are in the mental worldspace.

If cognition awakens or develops to this psychic level, you simply perceive these new objects, as simply as you perceive rocks in the sensory world or images in the mental world. They are simply given to awareness, they simply present themselves, and you don't have to spend a lot of time trying to figure out if they're real or not.

Of course, if you haven't awakened psychic cognition, then you will see none of this, just as a rock cannot see mental images. And you will probably have unpleasant things to say about people who do see them.

Q: So the psychic level is simply a broad space, a worldspace, within which a vast array of different phenomena can occur.

KW: Yes, which is true of any worldspace. These basic spheres of consciousness that I am outlining, from the lowest to the highest, are really just the skeleton of a very rich and complex reality. And there is much important work to be done in fleshing out this skeleton—in the lower as well as higher domains.

Take, for example, the work of Howard Gardner on multiple intelligences—the idea that development involves not one capacity but many relatively independent capacities (from musical to artistic to mathematical to athletic, and so on), which I think is quite right. We can plot the depth of those developmental capacities as well. They will fall within the same basic levels of consciousness development, but they are nonetheless relatively separate talents that unfold with their own logics, as it were. None of that is denied; in fact, I very much support those approaches. In my view, there are numerous different developmental lines or streams (e.g., cognitive, moral, aesthetic, interpersonal, needs, etc.) that move relatively independently through the basic levels or waves (body to mind to soul to spirit), giving us a very rich, multidimensional tapestry of waves and streams of consciousness unfolding.

Q: Also, the basic levels or waves themselves continue to develop, right?

KW: Yes, that's right. If you look at figure 9-1 (page 179), you'll see that each of the basic levels continues outward in a curved line of ongoing development. So just because sensorimotor cognition, for example, is listed as level 1 does not mean that its development simply stops with level 2. On the contrary, as the sensorimotor dimension is taken up and enfolded in higher development, some extremely advanced sensorimotor skills can emerge. That there is a "psychic side of sports," for example, is now widely acknowledged. As Michael Murphy has documented, many great athletes and dancers enter some very profound psychic spaces, and this translates into almost unbelievable performances.

Q: How do different personality types fit in the spectrum of consciousness?

KW: Most typologies are types of character formations that can and do occur on all of the levels (except usually the end limits). The simplest and best known is probably introverted and extroverted. These are not *levels* of consciousness, they are *types* that occur on *every* level. So you can be at level 4, for example, and be an introvert or an extrovert.

Q: How about the Enneagram?

KW: The same. The Enneagram divides personality into nine basic types. These nine types are *not* levels of consciousness. They are personality types that exist on all levels of consciousness. So what you have are nine types on each of the nine or so major levels of consciousness—and you can start to see what a truly multidimensional and full-spectrum model looks like.

As the personality begins to grow and develop, during the first three fulcrums, it tends to settle into one of these nine Enneagram types, depending largely on the self's major defense mechanism as well as its major innate strength. These types persist and dominate consciousness until roughly fulcrum-7, or the beginning of the transpersonal domain, where they begin to transform into their correlative wisdom or essence.

Q: Which means what, exactly?

KW: The idea is based on the central tantric notion, found from Sufism to Buddhism, that if you enter a lower state or even a defiled state with clear awareness, then that state will transform into its corresponding wisdom. So if you enter passion with awareness, you will find compassion. If you enter anger with awareness, you will find clarity. And so on. The traditions give various accounts of these transformations, but you can see the general point, which I think is quite valid. And with higher development, the Enneagram types likewise begin to unfold their corresponding essence or wisdom.

The Enneagram does not cover subtle dimensions very well, and it does not cover the causal at all. But it does incorporate these beginning transpersonal wisdoms, and so it can be a very powerful tool in the right hands. The Enneagram itself was largely created by Oscar Ichazo. Helen

Palmer has done much work with it, and Don Riso has recently begun to use the different Enneagram types in conjunction with the spectrum of consciousness, which I would certainly support. Hameed Ali's "Diamond Approach" has its roots in the Enneagram and Sufism, but adds its own distinctive and useful tools and perspectives.

Right now the Enneagram is being popularized in America and used as a new psychological parlor game—"Want to find your Self? Take a number!"—which is a lot of fun. But it also has higher uses.

Q: So at their best, types and levels cover horizontal and vertical—both important.

KW: Yes. On the higher levels themselves, I might give the example of Roger Walsh's treatment of shamanism. Walsh accepts the basic levels of psychic/subtle, causal, and nondual, and he uses that as a type of vertical scale. He then adds a very sophisticated horizontal scale that analyzes a dozen variables on each of those levels, from ease of control to arousal to emotional affect to the ability to concentrate. He thus arrives at a multidimensional grid for the analysis of transpersonal states, and this grid has enormously advanced our knowledge of the field.

So those are all examples of how to flesh out this basic skeleton that I am presenting. And the fact that we are focusing on the evolution of just this skeleton does not mean these other aspects aren't equally important.

Fulcrum-8: The Subtle

Q: So as this general evolution continues from psychic to subtle . . . ?

KW: "Subtle" simply means processes that are subtler than gross, ordinary, waking consciousness. These include interior luminosities and sounds, archetypal forms and patterns, extremely subtle bliss currents and cognitions (shabd, nada), expansive affective states of love and compassion, as well as subtler *pathological* states of what can only be called Kosmic terror, Kosmic evil, Kosmic horror. As always, because of the dialectic of progress, this subtle development is most definitely not just a day at the beach.

But this overall type of mysticism we call *deity mysticism*, because it involves your own Archetypal Form, a union with God or Goddess, a union with saguna Brahman, a state of savikalpa samadhi, and so on. This union or fusion with Deity—union with God, by whatever name—is the beginning or fusion phase of fulcrum-8.

This is not just nature mysticism, not just a union with the gross or natural world—what the Buddhists call the Nirmanakaya—but a deeper union with the subtler dimensions of the Sambhogakaya, the interior bliss body or transformational body, which transcends and includes the gross or natural domain, but is not confined to it—nature mysticism gives way to deity mysticism.

Q: Are any of these higher levels fully present in human beings prior to their emergence? Are they lying around waiting to emerge?

KW: Fully formed, no. The *deep structures* of these higher levels are present as *potentials* in all human beings, as far as we can tell. But as these deep potentials unfold, their actual *surface structures* are created and molded *by all four quadrants*. That is, the surface structures are created and molded by intentional, behavioral, cultural, and social patterns.

The classic example is that a person has an experience of intense interior illumination, a subtle-level illumination (perhaps in a near-death experience). A Christian might see it as Christ or an angel or a saint, a Buddhist might see it as the Sambhogakaya or bliss body of Buddha, a Jungian might see it as an archetypal experience of the Self, and so on. As we said, *all depth must be interpreted,* and these interpretations are not possible without a whole set of *background contexts* which provide many of the tools with which the interpretation will proceed. One's own individual background, one's cultural background, and one's social institutions will all have a hand in interpreting this depth-experience. This is *unavoidable.*

So these higher structures are not like fully formed little treasure chests buried in your psyche, waiting to pop to the surface. The deep structures are given, but the surface structures are not, and the experience itself involves an interpretive component, which cannot proceed without various backgrounds—and those backgrounds do not exist merely in your psyche!

But if we reject that pregiven extreme, it doesn't mean we have to fall into the opposite error of extreme constructivism. The basic reality of this subtle experience of interior illumination is not simply or arbitrarily constructed by culture, because these experiences occur cross-culturally, and further, in many cases the cultural background officially denies or prohibits these experiences, and yet they still happen all the time anyway.

So just because these experiences have an interpretive component does not mean they are merely cultural creations. When you watch the sun set, you will bring interpretations to that experience as well—

perhaps romantic, perhaps rational, each with a cultural coloring, but that doesn't mean that the sun ceases to exist if your culture disappears!

No, these are ontologically real events. They actually exist. They have real referents. But these referents do not exist in the sensorimotor world-space, they do not exist in the rational worldspace, they do not exist in the existential worldspace. So you can find evidence for them in none of those worldspaces. Rather, they *exist* in the subtle worldspace, and evidence for them can be plentifully found *there*.

Jung and the Archetypes

Q: Now you mentioned this subtle level as being an archetypal level, but I know that by "archetype" you don't mean Jungian archetype.

KW: That's right. This is a very complex topic, and I don't think we have time to do it justice. But I might say that, for the most part, the Jungian archetypes are basic, collectively inherited images or forms lying in the magic and mythic dimensions of human awareness, and generally speaking these should not be confused with the developments in the psychic and subtle domains.

Q: The Jungian archetype is . . . ?

KW: The typical Jungian archetype is a basic, inherited image or form in the psyche. These basic or primordial images represent very common, very typical experiences that humans everywhere are exposed to: the experience of birth, of the mother, the father, the shadow, the wise old man, the trickster, the ego, the animus and anima (masculine and feminine), and so on.

Millions upon millions of past encounters with these *typical situations* have, so to speak, ingrained these basic images into the collective psyche of the human race. You find these basic and primordial images worldwide, and you find an especially rich fund of them in the world's great myths.

Since the rudimentary forms of these mythic images come embedded in the individual psyche, then when you have an encounter with, say, your own mother, you are not just encountering your particular mother. You also have this archetype or basic image of millions of years of mothering stamped into your psyche. So you are not just interacting with your mother, you are interacting with the world Mother, with the Great Mother, and this archetypal image can therefore have an impact on you that is way out of proportion to anything your actual mother may or may not do to you.

So in classical Jungian analysis, you have to analyze and *interpret*, not just your own individual unconscious—the specific events that happened to you in your own life, with your own mother and father, your own shadow, and so on—you also need to analyze and interpret this collective level of archetypal material.

Perhaps, for example, you have activated the Devouring Mother archetype; maybe it has nothing to do with your actual mother; maybe she is for the most part loving and attentive; and yet you are horrified of being engulfed in relationships, devoured by emotional closeness, torn apart by personal intimacy. Maybe you are in the grip, not of your actual mother, but of an archetype. And this might especially show up in dreams: maybe a big black spider is trying to eat you.

So one of the things you might want to do, as you analyze this collective archetypal level, is study the world's great mythologies, because they are repositories of the earlier and typical (and therefore archetypal) encounters, including the mothering one in general. In other words, this will give you a *background* against which to *interpret* these primordial images, and so you will be able to more sincerely and truthfully approach these images and interpret them more clearly in yourself. You will be able to *differentiate* from their choking grip on your awareness, and then *integrate* them more carefully in your life. And there is much truth to all of that, I think.

Q: So Jungian archetypes tend to be repositories of basic, collective, typical encounters of the human race in general.

KW: For the most part. And as far as it goes, I am in substantial agreement with those Jungian archetypes. I am in almost complete accord with most of that Jungian perspective, and in that specific regard I consider myself a Jungian.

But the crucial point is that *collective* is not necessarily *transpersonal*. Most of the Jungian archetypes, as I said, are simply archaic images lying in the *magic* and *mythic* structures. They exert a pull on awareness from the level of fulcrums 2, 3, and 4. There is little transrational or transpersonal about them. It is important to come to terms with these "archetypes," to differentiate them and integrate them (transcend and include), but they are not themselves the source of a transpersonal or genuinely spiritual awareness. In fact, for the most part they are regressive pulls in awareness, lead weights around higher development—precisely what has to be overcome, not simply embraced.

The point is, just because something is collective does not mean it is transpersonal. There are collective prepersonal structures (magic and mythic), collective personal structures (rational and existential), and collective transpersonal structures (psychic and subtle). Collective simply means that the structure is universally present, like the capacity for sensation, perception, impulse, emotion, and so on. This is not necessarily *transpersonal*; it is simply *collective* or common. We all collectively inherit ten toes, but if I experience my toes, I am not having a transpersonal experience.

Q: But what about the enormously popular books like Jean Bolen's *Goddesses in Everywoman* and *Gods in Everyman*? They are definitely based on mythological motifs or archetypes, and those are spiritual, aren't they?

KW: Depends on what you mean by "spiritual." If you mean "transpersonal," no, I don't think those books are particularly transpersonal. I like those books, incidentally, but there is little in them that is actually transpersonal or genuinely spiritual. In those books, there is a wonderful presentation of all the "archetypal" gods and goddesses that are collectively inherited by men and women, from the steadiness and patience of Hestia to the sexuality and sensuality of Aphrodite to the strength and independence of Artemis. But those gods and goddesses are not transpersonal modes of awareness, or genuinely mystical luminosities, but simply a collection of typical and everyday self-images and self-roles available to men and women. They are simply self-concepts (fulcrum-3) and self-roles (fulcrum-4) that represent common and typical potentials available to men and women pretty much everywhere.

And those *mythic roles* are very useful in this sense: Perhaps, as a woman, you are not aware of your own capacity for strength and independence. Perhaps you need to be more in touch with the Artemis in you. By reading the various Artemis myths and stories, you can more easily access this archetypal level in your own psyche, and thus bring forth that potential in your own life. This is terrific.

But this is not transpersonal. This is just a mythic-membership role, a persona, a type of ego relation. It is not trans-egoic. Collective typical is not transpersonal. Part of the spiritual anemia in this country is that something as prosaic as getting in touch with the strong Artemis ego in you is called transpersonal or spiritual. It's rather sad, actually.

Q: So are any of the Jungian archetypes transpersonal or transrational?

KW: Most Jungian archetypes, the mythic archetypes, are prepersonal or at least prerational (magical and mythic). A few Jungian archetypes are personal (ego, persona), and a few are vaguely transpersonal (wise old man, the Self, mandala). But those "transpersonal" archetypes are rather anemic compared to what we know about the transpersonal domains.

Take, as only one example, the eighteen stages of actual transpersonal growth outlined in the Mahamudra tradition of Tibetan Buddhism. These are extraordinarily detailed descriptions of the stages of evolution of higher and transpersonal awareness. And *none* of those stages appear in any of the world's classical myths. You will not find those stages in Zeus or Hector or Little Red Riding Hood.

The reason is, those eighteen stages of contemplative unfolding actually describe very rare, nontypical, nonordinary, transpersonal growth through the psychic and subtle and causal domains—they do not describe, nor do they spring from, typical and common and everyday experiences, and so they are not found in the archaic and magic and mythic structures, and therefore they show up in none of the world's typical mythologies. Hera and Demeter and Goldilocks, and Artemis and Persephone and Hansel and Gretel, never attempted these stages! And therefore you rarely find these higher stages in Robert Bly, James Hillman, Edward Edinger, Marie-Louise von Franz, Walter Odajnyk, or any of the great Jungian theorists.

Q: This has caused a great deal of confusion in religious studies, because for a long time Jung was the only game in town. If you were interested in both psychology and spirituality, then you were a Jungian.

KW: Pretty much. The Jungian mythic archetypes are real enough, and they are very important, as I said. But Jung consistently failed to carefully differentiate the archetypes into their prepersonal, personal, and transpersonal components, and since all three of those are collectively inherited, then there is a constant confusing of *collective* (and "archetypal") with *transpersonal* and spiritual and mystical.

And so consciousness is simply divided into two great domains: *personal* and *collective*. And the tendency is then to take *anything* collective and call it spiritual, mystical, transpersonal, whereas much of it is simply prepersonal, prerational, preconventional, and even regressive.

So we have some very popular theorists who, tired of the burdens of postconventional and worldcentric rational perspectivism, recommend a regressive slide into egocentric, vital-impulsive, polymorphous, phantasmic-emotional revival—in other words, they recommend the fulcrum-2 self. They call this fulcrum-2 self the "soul." They would like us to live from this level. But that, in my opinion, is looking for Spirit in precisely those approaches that do not transcend the ego but merely prevent its emergence in the first place.

Q: So the "real" archetypes are, what?

KW: From the Neoplatonic traditions in the West, to the Vedanta and Mahayana and Trikaya traditions in the East, the real archetypes are subtle seed-forms upon which all of manifestation depends. In deep states of contemplative awareness, one begins to understand that the entire Kosmos emerges straight out of Emptiness, out of primordial Purity, out of nirguna Brahman, out of the Dharmakaya, out of unqualifiable Godhead, radiant Ein Sof, and the first *Forms* that emerge out of this Emptiness are the basic Forms upon which all lesser forms depend for their being.

These Forms are the actual archetypes, a term which means "original pattern" or "primary mold." There is a Light of which all lesser lights are pale shadows, there is a Bliss of which all lesser joys are anemic copies, there is a Consciousness of which all lesser cognitions are mere reflections, there is a primordial Sound of which all lesser sounds are thin echoes. Those are the real archetypes.

When we find those types of statements in Plotinus or Asanga or Garab Dorje or Abhinavigupta or Shankara, they are not simply theoretical hunches or metaphysical postulates. They are direct experiential disclosures issuing directly from the subtle dimension of reality, *interpreted* according to the *backgrounds* of those individuals, but *issuing* from this profound ontological reality, this subtle worldspace.

And if you want to know what these men and women are actually talking about, then you must take up the contemplative practice or injunction or paradigm, and perform the experiment yourself. These archetypes, the true archetypes, are a meditative experience, and it is very hard to understand these archetypes without performing the experiment. They are not images existing in the mythic worldspace, they are not philosophical concepts existing in the rational worldspace; they are meditative phenomena existing in the subtle worldspace.

So this experiment will disclose these archetypal data, and then you can help interpret what they mean. And by far the most commonly accepted interpretation is, you are looking at the basic forms and foundations of the entire manifest world. You are looking directly into the Face of the Divine. As Emerson said, bid the intruders take the shoes off their feet, for here is the God within.

13

Realms of the Superconscious: Part 2

Q: You said that with the archetypes, you are looking into the Face of the Divine, the first Forms of the Divine. Most modern researchers reject all of that as "mere metaphysics" at best, none of which can be verified.

KW: Well, you yourself should perform this experiment and look at the data yourself. Then you can help interpret it. If you don't perform the experiment—the meditative injunction, the exemplar, the paradigm—then you don't have the data from which to make a good interpretation.

If you take somebody from the magic or mythic worldview, and you try to explain to them that the sum of the squares of the right sides of a right triangle is equal to the square of the hypotenuse, you won't get very far. What you are doing cannot be seen in those worlds. And yet you are correct. You are performing an experiment in the rational worldspace, and your mathematical results can be checked by all those who perform the same experiment. It's very public, very reproducible, very fallibilist, very communal knowledge *in the rational worldspace*: its results exist and can be readily checked by all who enter the rational worldspace and try the experiment.

Just so with any of the other interior experiments in awareness disclosing yet higher realms, of which meditation is one of the oldest, most tested, and most reproduced. So if you're skeptical, that's a healthy attitude, and we invite you to find out for yourself, and perform this interior experiment with us, and get the data, and help us interpret it. But if you won't perform the experiment, please don't ridicule those who do.

And by far the most common interpretation of those who have seen this data is: you are face to face with the Divine.

Fulcrum-9: The Causal

Q: You mentioned that these subtle or archetypal Forms issue directly from Emptiness, from the causal, which is the next stage, fulcrum-9.

KW: When, as a specific type of meditation, you pursue the observing Self, the Witness, to its very *source* in pure Emptiness, then no objects arise in consciousness at all. This is a discrete, identifiable state of awareness—namely, *unmanifest absorption* or *cessation*, variously known as nirvikalpa samadhi, jnana samadhi, ayin, vergezzen, nirodh, classical nirvana, the cloud of unknowing.

This is the causal state, a discrete state, which is often likened to the state of deep dreamless sleep, except that this state is not a mere blank but rather an utter fullness, and it is experienced as such—as infinitely drenched in the fullness of Being, so full that no manifestation can even begin to contain it. Because it can never be seen as an object, this pure Self is pure Emptiness.

Q: That's all very abstract. Could you be more concrete about this?

KW: You are aware of yourself in this moment, yes?

Q: I think so.

KW: So if I say, Who are you?, you will start to describe yourself—you are a father, a mother, a husband, a wife, a friend; you are a lawyer, a clerk, a teacher, a manager. You have these likes and dislikes, you prefer this type of food, you tend to have these impulses and desires, and so on.

Q: Yes, I would list all the things that I know about myself.

KW: You would list the "things you know about yourself."

Q: Yes.

KW: All of those things you know about yourself are objects in your awareness. They are images or ideas or concepts or desires or feelings that parade by in front of your awareness, yes? They are all objects in your awareness.

Q: Yes.

KW: All those objects in your awareness are precisely not the observing Self. All those things that you know about yourself are precisely not the real Self. Those are not the Seer; those are simply things that can be *seen*. All of those objects that you describe when you "describe yourself" are actually *not* your real Self at all! They are just more objects, whether internal or external, they are not the real Seer of those objects, they are not the real Self. So when you describe yourself by listing all of those objects, you are ultimately giving a list of mistaken identities, a list of lies, a list of precisely what you ultimately *are not*.

So who is this real Seer? Who or what is this observing Self?

Ramana Maharshi called this Witness the I-I, because it is aware of the individual I or self, but cannot itself be seen. So what is this I-I, this causal Witness, this pure observing Self?

This deeply inward Self is witnessing the world out there, and it is witnessing all your interior thoughts as well. This Seer sees the ego, and sees the body, and sees the natural world. All of those parade by "in front" of this Seer. But the Seer itself cannot be seen. If you see anything, those are just more objects. Those objects are precisely what the Seer is not, what the Witness is not.

So you pursue this inquiry, Who am I? Who or what is this Seer that cannot itself be seen? You simply "push back" into your awareness, and you *dis-identify* with any and every object you see or can see.

The Self or the Seer or the Witness is not any particular thought—I can see that thought as an object. The Seer is not any particular sensation—I am aware of that as an object. The observing Self is not the body, it is not the mind, it is not the ego—I can see all of those as objects. What is looking at all those objects? What in you right now is looking at all these objects—looking at nature and its sights, looking at the body and its sensations, looking at the mind and its thoughts? What is looking at all that?

Try to feel yourself right now—get a good sense of being yourself— and notice, that self is just another object in awareness. It isn't even a real subject, a real self, it's just another object in awareness. This little self and its thoughts parade by in front of you just like the clouds float by through the sky. And what is the real you that is witnessing all of that? Witnessing your little objective self? Who or what is that?

As you push back into this pure Subjectivity, this pure Seer, you won't see it as an object—you can't see it as an object, because it's not an object! It is nothing you can see. Rather, as you calmly rest in this observing awareness—watching mind and body and nature float by—you might begin to notice that what you are actually feeling is simply a sense of freedom, a sense of release, a sense of not being bound to any of the objects you are calmly witnessing. You don't see anything in particular, you simply rest in this vast freedom.

In front of you the clouds parade by, your thoughts parade by, bodily sensations parade by, and you are none of them. You are the vast expanse of freedom through which all these objects come and go. You are an opening, a clearing, an Emptiness, a vast spaciousness, in which all these objects come and go. Clouds come and go, sensations come and go, thoughts come and go—and you are none of them; you are that vast sense of freedom, that vast Emptiness, that vast opening, through which manifestation arises, stays a bit, and goes.

So you simply start to notice that the "Seer" in you that is witnessing all these objects is itself just a vast Emptiness. It is not a thing, not an object, not anything you can see or grab hold of. It is rather a sense of vast Freedom, because it is not itself anything that enters the objective world of time and objects and stress and strain. This pure Witness is a pure Emptiness in which all these individual subjects and objects arise, stay a bit, and pass.

So this pure Witness is not anything that can be seen! The attempt to see the Witness or know it as an object—that's just more grasping and seeking and clinging in time. The Witness isn't out there in the stream; it is the vast expanse of Freedom in which the stream arises. So you can't get hold of it and say, Aha, I see it! Rather, it is the Seer, not *anything* that can be seen. As you rest in this Witnessing, all that you sense is just a vast Emptiness, a vast Freedom, a vast Expanse—a transparent opening or clearing in which all these little subjects and objects arise. Those subjects and objects can definitely be seen, but the Witness of them cannot be seen. The Witness of them is an utter *release* from them, an utter Freedom not caught in their turmoils, their desires, their fears, their hopes.

Of course, we tend to *identify* ourselves with these little individual subjects and objects—and that is exactly the problem! We identify the Seer with puny little things that can be seen. And that is the beginning of bondage and unfreedom. We are actually this vast expanse of Freedom, but we identify with unfree and limited objects and subjects, all of which can be seen, all of which suffer, and none of which is what we are.

Patanjali gave the classic description of bondage as "the identification of the Seer with the instruments of seeing"—with the little subjects and objects, instead of the opening or clearing or Emptiness in which they all arise.

So when we rest in this pure Witness, we don't see this Witness as an object. Anything you can see is *not* it. Rather, it is the absence of any subjects or objects altogether, it is the *release* from all of that. Resting in the pure Witness, there is this background absence or Emptiness, and this is "experienced," *not* as an object, but as a vast expanse of Freedom and Liberation from the constrictions of identifying with these little subjects and objects that enter the stream of time and are ground up in that agonizing torrent.

So when you rest in the pure Seer, in the pure Witness, you are invisible. You cannot be seen. No part of you can be seen, because you are not an object. Your body can be seen, your mind can be seen, nature can be seen, but you are not any of those objects. You are the pure source of awareness, and not anything that arises in that awareness. So you abide as awareness.

Things arise in awareness, they stay a bit and depart, they come and they go. They arise in *space*, they move in *time*. But the pure Witness does not come and go. It does not arise in space, it does not move in time. It is as it is; it is ever-present and unvarying. It is not an object out there, so it never enters the stream of time, of space, of birth, of death. Those are all experiences, all objects—they all come, they all go. But you do not come and go; you do not enter that stream; you are aware of all that, so you are not caught in all that. The Witness is aware of space, aware of time—and is therefore itself free of space, free of time. It is timeless and spaceless—the purest Emptiness through which time and space parade.

So this pure Seer is prior to life and death, prior to time and turmoil, prior to space and movement, prior to manifestation—prior even to the Big Bang itself. This doesn't mean that the pure Self existed in a time before the Big Bang, but that it exists prior to time, period. It just never enters that stream. It is aware of time, and is thus free of time—it is utterly timeless. And because it is timeless, it is eternal—which doesn't mean everlasting time, but free of time altogether.

It was never born, it will never die. It never enters that temporal stream. This vast Freedom is the great Unborn, of which the Buddha said: "There is an unborn, an unmade, an uncreate. Were it not for this unborn, unmade, uncreate, there would be no release from the born, the made, the created." Resting in this vast expanse of Freedom is resting in this great Unborn, this vast Emptiness.

And because it is Unborn, it is Undying. It was not created with your body, it will not perish when your body perishes. It's not that it lives on beyond your body's death, but rather that it never enters the stream of time in the first place. It doesn't live on after your body, it lives prior to your body, always. It doesn't go on in time forever, it is simply prior to the stream of time itself.

Space, time, objects—all of those merely parade by. But you are the Witness, the pure Seer that is itself pure Emptiness, pure Freedom, pure Openness, the great Emptiness through which the entire parade passes, never touching you, never tempting you, never hurting you, never consoling you.

And because there is this vast Emptiness, this great Unborn, you can indeed gain liberation from the born and the created, from the suffering of space and time and objects, from the mechanism of terror inherent in those fragments, from the vale of tears called samsara.

Q: I can get a brief taste of that as you talk about it.

KW: Most people can connect fairly quickly with the Witness. Living from that Freedom is a gentle exercise, and this is where meditation is very helpful.

Q: Any specific recommendations?

KW: Well, various types of meditation often aim for different transpersonal realms. Some aim for psychic experiences, some for the deity mysticism of the subtle realm, some for the formlessness and Freedom of the causal Witness, and some for nondual Unity or One Taste, which we will discuss in a moment.

My recommendation is simply to start with the acknowledged teachers in any of the great contemplative traditions. One might start by consulting the works of Father Thomas Keating, Rabbi Zalman Schachter-Shalomi, the Dalai Lama, Sri Ramana Maharshi, Bawa Muhaiyadeen, or any of the many widely acknowledged teachers in any of the great lineages.

Perhaps later on we can talk about the importance of an *integral practice* that takes the best of these great traditions and integrates them with the best of psychotherapy, to arrive at an "all-level, all-quadrant" transformative practice.

Q: Definitely. In the meantime, we are at fulcrum-9 and the Witness. How does that Witness relate to the causal unmanifest?

KW: The Witness is itself the causal unmanifest. It is itself pure Emptiness. And if, as a yogic endeavor, you actually keep inquiring intensely into the source, into the pure Subjectivity of this Seer, then all objects and subjects will simply cease to arise at all. And that would be nirvikalpa or *cessation*—an actual yogic state, a discrete state (it is, in fact, the fusion phase of fulcrum-9). This is pure *formless mysticism*—all objects, even God as a perceived form, vanish into cessation, and so deity mysticism gives way to formless mysticism.

Because all possible objects have *not yet arisen*, this is a completely *unmanifest* state of pure Emptiness. What you actually "see" in this state is infinite nothing, which simply means that it is too Full to be contained in any object or any subject or any sight or any sound. It is pure consciousness, pure awareness, prior to any manifestation at all—prior to subjects and objects, prior to phenomena, prior to holons, prior to things, prior to anything. It is utterly timeless, spaceless, objectless. And therefore it is radically and infinitely free of the limitations and constrictions of space and time and objects—and radically free of the torture inherent in those fragments.

It is not necessary to pursue the Witness in that particularly yogic fashion, but it can be done, and it does point up the unmanifest source of the Seer itself. This is why many traditions, like Yogachara Buddhism, simply equate Emptiness and Consciousness. We needn't get involved in all the technical details and arguments about that, but you get the general point—the Witness itself, pure Consciousness itself, is not a thing, not a process, not a quality, not an entity—it is ultimately unqualifiable—it is ultimately pure Emptiness.

Q: Why is it called the "causal"?

KW: Because it is the support or cause or creative ground of all junior dimensions. Remember that we saw, as Whitehead put it, that "the ultimate metaphysical principle is the creative advance into novelty." Creativity is part of the basic ground of the universe. Somehow, some way, miraculously, new holons emerge. I say out of Emptiness, but you can call that creative ground whatever you want. Some would call it God, or Goddess, or Tao, or Brahman, or Keter, or Rigpa, or Dharmakaya, or Maat, or Li. The more scientifically oriented tend to prefer to speak simply of the "self-transcending" capacity of the universe, as does Jantsch. That's fine. It doesn't matter. The point is, stuff emerges. Amazing!

Emptiness, creativity, holons—and that is exactly where we started our account in chapter 1. These holons arise as subject and object, in both singular and plural forms—that is, the four quadrants—and they follow the twenty tenets, which is simply *the pattern that manifestation displays* as it arises, a pattern that is a potential of Emptiness, a potential of the Dharmakaya, a potential of the Godhead. And with that pattern of twenty tenets, off we go on the evolutionary drive of holons returning to their source.

That pattern embodies a creative drive to greater depth, greater consciousness, greater unfolding, and that unfolding ultimately unfolds into its own infinite ground in pure Emptiness. But that Emptiness is not itself an emergent, it is rather the creative ground, prior to time, that is present all along, but finally becomes transparent to itself in certain holons that awaken to that Emptiness, to that Spirit, to that groundless Ground.

That same Emptiness, as Consciousness, was present all along as the interior depth of every holon, a depth that increasingly shed its lesser forms until it shed forms altogether—its depth goes to infinity, its time goes to eternity, its interior space is all space, its agency is the very Divine itself: the ground, path, and fruition of Emptiness.

The Nondual

Q: So this causal unmanifest—is it the absolute end point? Is this the end of time, the end of evolution, the end of history? The final Omega point?

KW: Well, many traditions take this state of cessation to be the ultimate state, the final end point of all development and evolution, yes. And this end state is equated with full Enlightenment, ultimate release, pure nirvana.

But that is not the "final story," according to the Nondual traditions. Because at some point, as you inquire into the Witness, and rest in the Witness, the sense of being a Witness "in here" completely vanishes itself, and the Witness turns out to be everything that is witnessed. The *causal* gives way to the *Nondual*, and formless mysticism gives way to nondual mysticism. "Form is Emptiness and Emptiness is Form."

Technically, you have dis-identified with even the Witness, and then integrated it with all manifestation—in other words, the second and third phases of fulcrum-9, which leads to fulcrum-10, which is not really a separate fulcrum or level, but the reality or Suchness of all levels, all states, all conditions.

And this is the second and most profound meaning of Emptiness—it is not a *discrete* state, but the reality of *all* states, the Suchness of all states. You have moved from the causal to the Nondual.

Q: Emptiness has two meanings?

KW: Yes, which can be very confusing. On the one hand, as we just saw, it is a discrete, identifiable state of awareness—namely, unmanifest absorption or cessation (nirvikalpa samadhi, ayn, jnana samadhi, nirodh, classical nirvana). This is the causal state, a discrete state.

The second meaning is that Emptiness is not merely a particular state among other states, but rather the reality or suchness or condition of all states. Not a particular state *apart* from other states, but the reality or condition of *all* states, high or low, sacred or profane, ordinary or extraordinary. Recall that on figure 9-1 we had Spirit as both the highest level ("causal") and the ever-present Ground of all levels ("nondual").

Q: We already discussed the discrete state; now the Nondual.

KW: Yes, the "experience" of this nondual Suchness is similar to the nature unity experience we earlier discussed, except now this unity is experienced not just with gross Form out there, but also with all of the subtle Forms in here. In Buddhist terms, this is not just the Nirmanakaya—gross or nature mysticism; and not just the Sambhogakaya—subtle or deity mysticism; and not just the Dharmakaya—causal or formless mysticism. It is the Svabhavikakaya—the integration of all three of them. It is beyond nature mysticism, beyond deity mysticism, and beyond formless mysticism—it is the reality or the Suchness of each, and thus integrates each in its embrace. It embraces the entire spectrum of consciousness—transcends all, includes all.

Q: Again, rather technical. Perhaps there's a more direct way to talk about Nondual mysticism?

KW: Across the board, the sense of being any sort of Seer or Witness or Self vanishes altogether. You don't look at the sky, you are the sky. You can taste the sky. It's not out there. As Zen would say, you can drink the Pacific Ocean in a single gulp, you can swallow the Kosmos whole—precisely because awareness is no longer split into a seeing subject in here and a seen object out there. There is just pure seeing. Consciousness and its display are not-two.

Everything continues to arise moment to moment—the entire Kosmos continues to arise moment to moment—but there is nobody watching the display, there is just the display, a spontaneous and luminous gesture of great perfection. The pure *Emptiness* of the Witness turns out to be one with every *Form* that is witnessed, and that is one of the basic meanings of "nonduality."

Q: Again, could you be even more specific?

KW: Well, you might begin by getting into the state of the Witness—that is, you simply rest in pure observing awareness—you are *not* any object that can be seen—not nature, not body, not thoughts—just rest in that pure witnessing awareness. And you can get a certain "sensation" of that witnessing awareness—a sensation of freedom, of release, of great expanse.

While you are resting in that state, and "sensing" this Witness as a great expanse, if you then look at, say, a mountain, you might begin to notice that the sensation of the Witness and the sensation of the mountain are the same sensation. When you "feel" your pure Self and you "feel" the mountain, they are absolutely the same feeling.

In other words, the real world is not given to you *twice*—one out there, one in here. That "twiceness" is exactly the meaning of "duality." Rather, the real world is given to you *once*, immediately—it is one feeling, it has one taste, it is utterly full in that one taste, it is not severed into seer and seen, subject and object, fragment and fragment. It is a singular, of which the plural is unknown. You can taste the mountain; it is the same taste as your Self; it is not out there being reflected in here—that duality is not present in the immediateness of real experience. Real experience, before you slice it up, does not contain that duality—real experience, reality itself, is "nondual." You are still you, and the mountain is still the mountain, but you and the mountain are two sides of one and the same experience, which is the one and only reality at that moment.

If you relax into present experience in that fashion, the separate-self sense will uncoil; you will stop standing back from life; you will not have experience, you will suddenly become all experience; you will not be "in here" looking "out there"—in here and out there are one, so you are no longer trapped "in here."

And so suddenly, you are not in the bodymind. Suddenly, the bodymind has dropped. Suddenly, the wind doesn't blow on you, it blows through you, within you. You are not looking at the mountain, you are the mountain—the mountain is closer to you than your own skin. You *are* that, and there is *no you*—just this entire luminous display spontaneously arising moment to moment. The separate self is nowhere to be found.

The entire sensation of "weight" drops altogether, because you are not in the Kosmos, the Kosmos is in you, and you are purest Emptiness. The entire universe is a transparent shimmering of the Divine, of primordial Purity. But the Divine is not someplace else, it is just all of this shimmering. It is self-seen. It has One Taste. It is nowhere else.

Q: Subject and object are nondual?

KW: You know the Zen koan, "What is the sound of one hand clapping?" Usually, of course, we need two hands to clap—and that is the structure of typical experience. We have a sense of ourselves as a subject in here, and the world as an object out there. We have these "two hands" of experience, the subject and the object. And typical experience is a smashing of these two hands together to make a commotion, a sound. The object out there smashes into me as a subject, and I have an experience—the two hands clap together and experience emerges.

And so the typical structure of experience is like a punch in the face. The ordinary self is the battered self—it is utterly battered by the universe "out there." The ordinary self is a series of bruises, of scars, the results of these two hands of experience smashing together. This bruising is called "duhkha," suffering. As Krishnamurti used to say, in that gap between the subject and the object lies the entire misery of humankind.

But with the nondual state, suddenly there are not two hands. Suddenly, the subject and the object are one hand. Suddenly, there is nothing outside of you to smash into you, bruise you, torment you. Suddenly, you do not *have* an experience, you *are* every experience that arises, and so you are instantly released into all space: you and the entire Kosmos are one hand, one experience, one display, one gesture of great perfection. There is nothing outside of you that you can want, or desire, or seek, or grasp—your soul expands to the corners of the universe and embraces all with infinite delight. You are utterly Full, utterly Saturated, so full and saturated that the boundaries to the Kosmos completely explode and leave you without date or duration, time or location, awash in an ocean of infinite care. You are released into the All, as the All—you are the self-seen radiant Kosmos, you are the universe of One Taste, and the taste is utterly infinite.

So what is the sound of that one hand clapping? What is the taste of that One Taste? When there is *nothing outside of you* that can hit you, hurt you, push you, pull you—what is the sound of that one hand clapping?

See the sunlight on the mountains? Feel the cool breeze? What is not utterly obvious? Who is not already enlightened? As a Zen Master put it, "When I heard the sound of the bell ringing, there was no I, and no bell, just the ringing." There is no twiceness, no twoness, in immediate experience! No inside and no outside, no subject and no object—just immediate awareness itself, the sound of one hand clapping.

So you are not in here, on this side of a transparent window, looking at the Kosmos out there. The transparent window has shattered, your bodymind drops, you are free of that confinement forever, you are no longer "behind your face" looking at the Kosmos—you simply are the Kosmos. You *are* all that. Which is precisely why you can swallow the Kosmos and span the centuries, and nothing moves at all. The sound of this one hand clapping is the sound the Big Bang made. It is the sound of supernovas exploding in space. It is the sound of the robin singing. It is the sound of a waterfall on a crystal-clear day. It is the sound of the entire manifest universe—and you are that sound.

Which is why your Original Face is not *in here*. It is the sheerest Emptiness or transparency of this shimmering display. If the Kosmos is arising, you are that. If nothing arises, you are that. In either case, you are that. In either case, you are not in here. The window has shattered. The gap between the subject and object is gone. There is no twiceness, no twoness, to be found anywhere—the world is *never* given to you *twice*, but always only *once*—and you are that. You are that One Taste.

This state is not something you can *bring about*. This nondual state, this state of One Taste, is the very nature of every experience *before* you slice it up. This One Taste is not some experience you bring about through effort; rather, it is the actual condition of all experience *before* you do anything to it. This uncontrived state is *prior* to effort, prior to grasping, prior to avoiding. It is the real world *before* you do anything to it, including the effort to "see it nondually."

So you don't have to do something special to awareness or to experience in order to make it nondual. It starts out nondual, its very nature is nondual—prior to any grasping, any effort, any contrivance. If effort arises, fine; if effort doesn't arise, fine; in either case, there is only the immediacy of One Taste, prior to effort and non-effort alike.

So this is definitely not a state that is hard to get into, but rather one that is impossible to avoid. It has always been so. There has never been a moment when you did not experience One Taste—it is the only constant in the entire Kosmos, it is the only reality in all of reality. In a million billion years, there has never been a single second that you weren't aware of this Taste; there has never been a single second where it wasn't directly in your Original Face like a blast of arctic air.

Of course, we have often lied to ourselves about this, we have often been untruthful about this, the universe of One Taste, the primordial sound of one hand clapping, our own Original Face. And the nondual traditions aim, not to bring about this state, because that is impossible, but simply to *point it out* to you so that you can no longer ignore it, no longer lie to yourself about who you really are.

Q: So this nondual state—does this include the duality of mind and body, of Left and Right?

KW: Yes. The primordial state is prior to, but not other to, the entire world of dualistic Form. So in that primordial state there is no subject and object, no interior and exterior, no Left and no Right. All of those dualities *continue to arise*, but they are relative truths, not absolute or primordial truth itself. The primordial truth is the ringing; the relative truth is the "I" and the "bell," the mind and the body, the subject and the object. They have a certain relative reality, but they are not, as Eckhart would say, the final word.

And therefore the dilemmas inherent in those relative dualisms cannot be solved on the relative plane itself. Nothing you can do to the "I" or the "bell" will make them one; you can only relax into the prior ringing, the immediacy of experience itself, at which point the dilemma does not arise. It is not solved, it is dissolved—and not by reducing the subject to the object, or the object to the subject, but by recognizing the primordial ground of which each is a partial reflection.

Which is why the dilemmas *inherent* in those dualisms—between mind and body, mind and brain, consciousness and form, mind and nature, subject and object, Left and Right—cannot be solved on the relative plane—which is why that problem has *never* been solved by conventional philosophy. The problem is not solved, but rather dissolved, in the primordial state, which otherwise *leaves the dualisms just as they are*, possessing a certain conventional or relative reality, real enough in their own domains, but not absolute.

The Immediacy of Pure Presence

Q: Are there any orthodox or mainstream Western philosophers who recognize nonduality?

KW: I always found it fascinating that both William James and Bertrand Russell agreed on this crucial issue, the nonduality of subject and object in the primacy of immediate awareness. I think this is very funny, because if you can find something that these two agreed on, it might as well be coming straight from God, so I suppose we can embrace nonduality with a certain confidence.

Russell talks about this in the last chapters of his great book, *A History of Western Philosophy*, where he discusses William James's notion of "radical empiricism." We have to be very careful with these terms, because "empiricism" doesn't mean just sensory experience, it means experience itself, in any domain. It means immediate prehension, immediate experience, immediate awareness. And William James set out to demonstrate that this pure nondual immediateness is the "basic stuff" of reality, so to speak, and that both subject and object, mind and body, inside and outside, are all derivative or secondary. They come later, they come after the primacy of immediateness, which is the ultimate reality, as it were.

And Russell is quite right to credit James with being the first "mainstream" or "accepted" philosopher to advance this nondual position. Of course, virtually all of the mystical or contemplative sages had been saying this for a few millennia, but James to his eternal credit brought it crashing into the mainstream . . . and convinced Russell of its truth in the process.

James introduced this nondual notion in an essay called "Does 'Consciousness' Exist?" And he answered that consciousness does not exist, which has confused many people. But his point was simply that if you look at consciousness very carefully, it's not a thing, not an object, not an entity. If you look carefully, you'll see that consciousness is simply one with whatever is immediately arising—as we saw with the mountain, for example. You as a subject do not see the mountain as an object, but rather, you and the mountain are one in the immediacy of the actual experience. So in that sense, consciousness as a subjective entity does not exist—it's not a separate something that has an experience of a separate something else. There is just One Taste in the immediateness of experience.

So pure experience is not split into an inside and outside—there is no twiceness, no twoness, about it! As James characteristically put it, "Experience, I believe, has no such inner duplicity."

And notice that *duplicity* has the meaning of both "twoness" and "lying." The *twoness of experience is the fundamental lie*, the primordial untruthfulness, the beginning of ignorance and deception, the beginning of the battered self, the beginning of samsara, the beginning of the lie lodged in the heart of infinity. Each and every experience, just as it is, arrives as One Taste—it does not arrive fractured and split into a subject and an object. That split, that duplicity, is a lie, the fundamental lie, the original untruthfulness—and the beginning of the "small self," the battered self, the self that hides its Original Face in the forms of its own suffering.

Small wonder that D. T. Suzuki, the great Zen scholar, said that James's radical empiricism (or nondual empiricism) was as close as the West had gotten to "no-mind" or Emptiness. That's perhaps too strong, but you get the point.

Russell had a rather thin understanding of the fact that the great contemplative philosopher-sages—from Plotinus to Augustine to Eckhart to

Schelling to Schopenhauer to Emerson—had already solved or dissolved this subject/object duality. But aside from that misunderstanding, Russell introduces James's great accomplishment in a very clear fashion:

> The main purpose of this essay ["Does 'Consciousness' Exist?"] was to deny that the subject-object relation is fundamental. It had, until then, been taken for granted by philosophers that there is a kind of occurrence called "knowing," in which one entity, the knower or subject, is aware of another, the thing known or the object [the "two hands" of experience]. The knower was regarded as a mind or soul; the object known might be a material object, an eternal essence, another mind, or, in self-consciousness, identical with the knower. Almost everything in accepted philosophy was bound up with the dualism of subject and object. The distinction of mind and matter and the traditional notion of "truth," all need to be radically reconsidered if the distinction of subject and object is not accepted as fundamental.

To put it mildly. And then Russell adds, "For my part, I am convinced that James was right on this matter, and would on this ground alone, deserve a high place among philosophers."

Q: So they both caught a glimpse of nonduality.

KW: I think so, yes. It's fairly easy to catch at least a brief glimpse of nonduality. Most people can be "talked into it," as we were doing a moment ago, and at least get a little taste of it. And I think this is exactly what William James did with Bertrand Russell, in person, which is what Russell himself reports. Right after he says, "I am convinced that James was right on this matter," Russell adds, "I had thought otherwise until he persuaded me of the truth of his doctrine." I think James just pointed it right out to him! See the mountain? Where is your mind? Mind and mountain . . . nondual!

Q: So they were onto a taste of Zen? A taste of the Nondual?

KW: Well, a glimmer, a taste, a hint of the nondual—this is easy enough to catch. But for the Nondual traditions, *this is just the beginning.* As you rest in that uncontrived state of pure immediateness or pure freedom, then strange things start to happen. All of the subjective tendencies that you had previously *identified* with—all of those little selves and subjects that held open the gap between the seer and the seen—they all start burning in the freedom of nonduality. They all scream to the surface and die, and this can be a very interesting period.

As you rest in this primordial freedom of One Taste, you are no longer acting on these subjective inclinations, so they basically die of boredom, but it's still a death, and the death rattles from this liberation are very intense. You don't really have to do anything, except hold on—or let go—they're both irrelevant. It's all spontaneously accomplished by the vast expanse of primordial freedom. But you are still getting burned alive, which is just the most fun you can have without smiling.

Fundamentally, it doesn't matter what type of experience arises—the simple, natural, nondual, and uncontrived state is prior to experience, prior to duality, so it happily embraces whatever comes up. But strange things come up, and you have to stay with this "effortless effort" for quite some time, and die these little deaths constantly, and this is where real practice becomes very important.

Enlightenment

Q: You said nonduality doesn't reject dualism on its own level.

KW: No, that would miss the point. These dualisms—between subject and object, inside and outside, Left and Right—will still arise, and are *supposed* to arise. Those dualities are the very mechanism of manifestation. Spirit—the pure immediate Suchness of reality—manifests as a subject and an object, and in both singular and plural forms—in other words, Spirit manifests as all four quadrants. And we aren't supposed to simply evaporate those quadrants—they are the radiant glory of Spirit's manifestation.

But we are supposed to see through them to their Source, their Suchness. This One Taste has to permeate all levels, all quadrants, all manifestation. And precisely because this is the simplest thing in the world, it is the hardest. This effortless effort requires great perseverance, great practice, great sincerity, great truthfulness. It has to be pursued through the waking state, and the dream state, and the dreamless state. And this is where we pick up the practices of the Nondual schools.

Q: Does "Enlightenment" mean something different in these schools?

KW: Yes, in a sense. There are two rather different schools about this "Enlightened" state, corresponding to the two rather different meanings of "Emptiness" that we discussed.

The first takes as its paradigm the causal or unmanifest state of absorption (nirvikalpa, nirodh, ayn). That is a very distinct, very discrete, very identifiable state. And so if you equate Enlightenment with that state of cessation, then you can very distinctly say whether a person is "fully Enlightened" or not.

Generally, as in the Theravadin Buddhist tradition and the Samkhya yogic schools, whenever you enter this state of unmanifest absorption, it burns away certain lingering afflictions and sources of ignorance. Each time you fully enter this state, more of these afflictions are burned away. And after a certain number and type of these entrances—often four— you have burned away everything there is to burn, and so you can enter this state at will, and remain there permanently. You can enter nirvana permanently, and samsara ceases to arise in your case. The entire world of Form ceases to arise.

But the Nondual traditions do not have that as their goal. They will often use that state, and often master it. But more important, these schools—such as Vedanta Hinduism and Mahayana and Vajrayana Buddhism—are more interested in pointing out the Nondual state of Suchness, which is not a discrete state of awareness but the ground or empty condition of *all states*. So they are not so much interested in finding an Emptiness divorced from the world of Form (or samsara), but rather an Emptiness that embraces all Form even as Form continues to arise. For them, nirvana and samsara, Emptiness and Form, are not-two.

And this changes everything. In the causal traditions, you can very definitely say when a person is in that discrete state. It is obvious, unmistakable. So you have a clearly marked yardstick, so to speak, for your Enlightenment.

But in the Nondual traditions, you often get a quick introduction to the Nondual condition very early in your training. The master will simply point out that part of your awareness that is *already* nondual.

Q: How, exactly?

KW: Very similar to when we were talking about the Witness, and I sort of "talked you into" a glimpse of it; or even further with the nondual One Taste of you and the mountain. The Nondual traditions have an enormous number of these "pointing out instructions," where they simply point out what is *already* happening in your awareness anyway. Every experience you have is *already* nondual, whether you realize it or not. So it is *not* necessary for you to *change your state of consciousness* in order to discover this nonduality. Any state of consciousness you have will do just fine, because nonduality is fully present in every state.

So *change of state* is *not* the point with the Nondual traditions. Recognition is the point. Recognition of what is always already the case. Change of state is useless, a distraction.

So you will often get an initiation taste, a pointing out, of this Nondual state that is always already the case. As I said, I think this is exactly what James did with Russell, in a small way. Look at immediate awareness closely, and you will see that subject and object are actually one, are already one, and you simply need to recognize it. You don't have to engineer a special state in which to see this. One Taste is already the nature of any state, so pretty much any conscious state will do.

Q: It's simply pointed out.

KW: Yes. You've seen those newspaper puzzles, something like, "There are fifteen Presidents of the United States hidden in this picture of the ocean. Can you spot all fifteen?"

Q: The comedian Father Guido Sarducci has a joke on those—"Find the Popes in the Pizza."

KW: We'll get in trouble here! Maybe we better stick with presidents, who are used to being blankly humiliated.

The point in these games is that you are looking right at all the faces. You already have everything in consciousness that is required. You are looking right at the answer—right at the presidents' faces—but you don't recognize them. Somebody comes along and points them out, and you slap your head and say, Yes, of course, I was looking right at it.

Same with the Nondual condition of One Taste. You are looking right at it, right now. Every single bit of the Nondual condition is fully in your awareness right now. All of it. Not most of it, but absolutely all of it is in your awareness right now. You just don't recognize it. So somebody comes along and simply points it out, and you slap your head—Yes, of course, I was looking right at it all along.

Q: And this happens in the training?

KW: Yes. Sometimes right at the beginning, sometimes down the line a bit, but this transmission is crucial.

But the central point we were discussing is that, because this Nondual condition is the nature or suchness of any and all states—because this Emptiness is one with whatever Forms arise—then the world of Form will continue to arise, and you will continue to relate to Form. You will not try to get out of it, or away from it, or suspend it. You will enter it fully.

And since Forms continue to arise, then you are *never* at an *end point* where you can say, "Here, I am fully Enlightened." In these traditions, Enlightenment is an ongoing process of new Forms arising, and you relate to them as Forms of Emptiness. You are one with all these Forms as they arise. And in that sense, you are "enlightened," but in another sense, this enlightenment is *ongoing*, because new Forms are arising all the time. You are never in a *discrete* state that has no further development. You are always learning new things about the world of Form, and therefore your overall state is always evolving itself.

So you can have certain breakthrough Enlightenment experiences— satori, for example—but these are just the *beginning* of an *endless* process of riding the new waves of Form as they ceaselessly arise. So in this sense, in the Nondual sense, you are never "fully" Enlightened, any more than you could say that you are "fully educated." It has no meaning.

Q: Some of these Nondual traditions, particularly the Tantra, get pretty wild.

KW: Yes, some of them get pretty wild. They are not afraid of samsara, they ride it constantly. They don't abandon the defiled states, they enter them with enthusiasm, and play with them, and exaggerate them, and they couldn't care less whether they are higher or lower, because there is only God.

In other words, all experiences have the same One Taste. Not a single experience is closer to or further from One Taste. You cannot engineer a way to get closer to God, for there is only God—the radical secret of the Nondual schools.

At the same time, all of this occurs within some very strong ethical frameworks, and you are not simply allowed to play Dharma Bums and call that being Nondual. In most of the traditions, in fact, you have to master the first three stages of transpersonal development (psychic, subtle, and causal) before you will even be allowed to talk about the fourth or Nondual state. "Crazy wisdom" occurs in a very strict ethical atmosphere.

But the important point is that in the Nondual traditions, you take a vow, a very sacred vow, which is the foundation of all of your training, and the vow is that *you will not disappear into cessation*—you will *not* hide out in nirvana, you will not evaporate in nirodh, you will not abandon the world by tucking yourself into nirvikalpa.

Rather, you promise to ride the surf of samsara until all beings caught in that surf can see that it is just a manifestation of Emptiness. Your vow is to pass through cessation and into Nonduality as quickly as possible, so you can help all beings recognize the Unborn in the very midst of their born existence.

So these Nondual traditions do not necessarily abandon emotions, or thoughts, or desires, or inclinations. The task is simply to see the Emptiness of all Form, not to actually get rid of all Form. And so Forms continue to arise, and you learn to surf. The Enlightenment is indeed primordial, but this Enlightenment continues forever, and it forever changes its Form because new Forms always arise, and you are one with those.

So the call of the Nondual traditions is: Abide as Emptiness, embrace all Form. The liberation is in the Emptiness, never in the Form, but Emptiness embraces all forms as a mirror all its objects. So the Forms continue to arise, and, as the sound of one hand clapping, you are all those Forms. You are the display. You and the universe are One Taste. Your Original Face is the purest Emptiness, and therefore every time you look in the mirror, you see only the entire Kosmos.

PART THREE

BEYOND FLATLAND

14

Ascending and Descending

Q: In this final series of discussions, we want to bring all these pieces together into a truly integral view. We want to discuss an "all-level, all-quadrant" approach to consciousness, therapy, spirituality, and transformative practice. And we want to talk about the many obstacles in this integral view, obstacles such as flatland.

In order to do so, I wonder if you could give us the briefest possible summary of the overall discussion so far—a brief summary of the "big picture" up to this point.

KW: Okay. (But you can skip this section altogether if you hate summaries! Our narrative picks up immediately in the next section.)

A Brief Summary

KW: We started with Emptiness, creativity, holons. Or Spirit, creativity, holons. In other words, out of Emptiness, holons creatively emerge.

As they emerge, they evolve. This evolution, or Spirit-in-action, has certain features in common wherever it appears. These common features I have summarized as the twenty tenets, and we discussed a few of them. These are the patterns of manifestation.

For example, we saw that all holons have four capacities—agency and communion, self-transcendence and self-dissolution. Because of the self-transcending drive, new holons emerge. As they emerge, they emerge holarchically. They transcend and include. Cells transcend and include molecules, which transcend and include atoms, and so on.

Likewise, the self-transcending drive of the Kosmos produces holons of greater and greater depth. And we saw that the greater the depth of a holon, the greater its degree of consciousness, among other things.

But greater depth also means more things that can go wrong. Dogs get cancer, atoms don't. There is a dialectic of progress at every turn—hardly a sweetness-and-light affair!

Holons not only have an inside and outside, they also exist as individuals and as collectives. This means that every holon has four facets, which we called the four quadrants: intentional, behavioral, cultural, and social. These were indicated in figure 5-2.

So we followed the evolution of the four quadrants up to the human forms of those quadrants, at which point humans themselves begin to reflect on these quadrants, think about them, notice that they themselves are embedded in them. And in this attempt to gain knowledge about their own situation, humans generate various knowledge quests, quests for truth.

Since each of these four quadrants deals with a different aspect of holons, each of them has a different type of truth, a different validity claim. And humanity, through long and painful experimentation, slowly learned these validity tests—ways to ground knowledge in the realities of each quadrant. We saw these as truth, truthfulness, justness, and functional fit.

Since the two objective and exterior dimensions—the Right-Hand quadrants—can both be described in objective it-language, we simplified the four quadrants to the Big Three: I, we, and it. Studied, for example, in self, morals, science. Or art (self and self-expression), ethics, and objectivity. The Beautiful, the Good, and the True. In the spiritual domains: Buddha, Sangha, Dharma—the ultimate I, ultimate We, and ultimate It.

We could simplify the Big Three even further. The Left-Hand dimensions (the I and the we) can only be accessed by introspection and interpretation, whereas the Right Hand delivers itself up to perception and empiricism—and those are the Left- and Right-Hand paths. That is, the Right-Hand aspects are the exteriors of holons, and so they can be seen empirically. But the intentional and cultural—the Left-Hand quadrants—involve interior depth that can only be accessed by interpretation. Interpretation means, in the broadest sense, empathic resonance from within, as opposed to objective staring from without. *Surfaces can be seen, but depth must be interpreted.* And those are the Right- and Left-Hand paths.

But those are all just ways to talk about these four facets of any holon.

And the central point was, don't confuse these four quadrants. Simplify them, yes, but don't merely equate them, because these four quadrants, with their four different types of truth, are the basic facets of any holon, and reducing one to the others does not explain that quadrant but simply destroys it.

Therefore, as we followed the evolution of holons, we were careful to follow not only the exteriors of those holons—atoms, molecules, cells, organ systems, Gaia, etc.; we also followed their correlative interiors—sensations, images, concepts, rules, right up to subtle and causal occasions. In short, we saw this interior evolution go from prepersonal to personal to transpersonal.

And we saw that this interior evolution involves *ladder, climber,* and *view*: the ladder or basic levels or nested holarchy of consciousness; the climber or the self with a fulcrum at every stage (a 1-2-3 process of fusion/differentiation/integration); and the changing worldviews (archaic, magic, mythic, rational, etc.), each of which produces a different self-identity, needs, and moral sense.

Thus, we saw self-identity, needs, and moral response go from physiocentric to biocentric to egocentric to ethnocentric to worldcentric, the platform for all higher and truly spiritual developments. And we saw that an "accident" at any of these stages produces a pathology characteristic of the stage where the accident occurs (psychosis, borderline, neurosis, script, etc.).

And finally, we looked specifically at the four higher stages and fulcrums, the four transpersonal stages: the psychic, the subtle, the causal, and the nondual. We saw that each of these also has its own worldview and therefore its own type of mysticism, namely, nature mysticism, deity mysticism, formless mysticism, and nondual mysticism.

These higher stages are very rare, very difficult accomplishments. In the past, they were reached only by a small handful—the lone shaman, the yogi in the cave, the small sanghas and cloisters of the true seekers of wisdom. These deeper or higher states have never been anything near an average or collective mode of awareness. If we look at the evolution of the average mode, then we find something like figure 5-2, which stops at the centaur and vision-logic and a planetary federation with global or worldcentric morality—which is still an unrealized ideal for most.

If these higher or transpersonal stages emerge in our future collective evolution, then they will manifest in all four quadrants—intentional, behavioral, cultural, and social. And we are awaiting the possible forms of this future evolution, even if, individually, we pursue these higher states in our own case.

But the essential point is that at these higher or transpersonal stages, the Spirit that was present throughout the entire evolutionary process becomes increasingly conscious of its own condition. It has gone from subconscious to self-conscious to superconscious, unfolding more of itself and enfolding more of itself at every stage. Spirit slumbers in nature, begins to awaken in mind, and finally recognizes itself as Spirit in the transpersonal domains—but it is the same Spirit present throughout the entire sequence: the ground, path, and fruition of the whole display.

With Spirit's shocking Self-recognition, Forms continue to arise and evolve, but the secret is out: they are all Forms of Emptiness in the universe of One Taste, endlessly transparent and utterly Divine. There is no end limit, no foundation, no final resting place, only Emptiness and endless Grace. So the luminous Play carries on with insanely joyous regard, timeless gesture to timeless gesture, radiant in its wild release, ecstatic in its perfect abandon, endless fullness beyond endless fullness, this miraculously self-liberating Dance, and there is no one anywhere to watch it, or even sing its praises.

The Great Holarchy

Q: What you just summarized is one type of integral view, which includes all the quadrants (I, we, and it) as they evolve through all the levels (from matter to body to mind to soul to spirit). But that type of integral view tends to be denied in the West, and often in the East as well, because either some of the levels or some of the quadrants are left out.

KW: Yes, that's right. Especially in the modern West, we can't help but notice that all of the higher, transpersonal, spiritual levels of consciousness are looked upon with grave suspicion and even outright hostility. In fact, the worldview of scientific materialism, which is the "official" worldview of the modern West, aggressively denies not only the higher stages of consciousness development but the existence of consciousness itself. The only thing that is ultimately real is frisky dirt.

Q: Flatland.

KW: Yes, flatland. Either in the form of subtle reductionism, which reduces every interior or Left-Hand event to its exterior or Right-Hand correlate; or worse, gross reductionism, which reduces every Right-Hand system to Right-Hand atoms. In either case, the entire Left-Hand domains are denied irreducible reality: there is no consciousness, no mind, no soul, no spirit, no value, no depth, and no divinity found any-where in the disqualified universe, only a great web of interwoven "its" or, even worse, atomistic "its"—a truly insane worldview, wouldn't you say?

Q: We want to trace the historical rise of this flatland as carefully as we can, because otherwise a genuinely integral view will escape us. So why don't you set this up for us.

KW: Just for the moment, let's stick with the Upper-Left quadrant, with the individual *spectrum of consciousness*—these nine or so basic levels of consciousness. If you look at figure 14-1, you will see what is essentially the same basic spectrum, the Great Holarchy of conscious-ness, as it appears in both Plotinus and Aurobindo. And, of course, for both of them, this holarchy is not actually a stepladder, but a series of nested and enfolded dimensions. Figure 14-1 is just a sophisticated ver-sion of figure 2-2.

Now the really interesting point is that this Great Holarchy was, as Lovejoy put it, the dominant official philosophy of most of humankind, East and West, through the largest portion of its existence. In simplified forms we find a holarchy of earth, human, and sky (or heaven) even in the earliest foraging cultures. Chögyam Trungpa, for example, in his wonderful book *Shambhala: The Sacred Path of the Warrior*, makes this point very convincingly. This basic holarchy would later be elaborated into matter, body, mind, soul, and spirit (and in many cases that would be elaborated into even more subdivisions). But the point is that some-

Absolute One (Godhead)	Satchitananda/Supermind (Godhead)
Nous (Intuitive Mind) [subtle]	Intuitive Mind/Overmind
Soul/World-Soul [psychic]	Illumined World-Mind
Creative Reason [vision-logic]	Higher-mind/Network-mind
Logical Faculty [formop]	Logical mind
Concepts and Opinions	Concrete mind [conop]
Images	Lower mind [preop]
Pleasure/pain (emotions)	Vital-emotional; impulse
Perception	Perception
Sensation	Sensation
Vegetative life function	Vegetative
Matter	Matter (physical)
PLOTINUS	AUROBINDO

FIGURE 14-1. *The Great Holarchy according to Plotinus and Aurobindo.*

thing like this Great Holarchy has been part of the cultural background of most humans for most of our history.

That is, right up until the Enlightenment in the West. With the fundamental Enlightenment paradigm, all of reality—including the Great Holarchy—was mapped in empirical and monological terms. This was a well-intentioned but deeply confused attempt to understand consciousness and morals and values and meaning by putting them under the microscope of the monological gaze.

And do you know what happened? The interior depths completely disappeared from view. They could not be found with the monological gaze, and so they were soon pronounced nonexistent or illusory or derivative or epiphenomenal—all polite words for "not really real." All I's and all we's were reduced to mere its—atomistic or holistic, depending upon your prejudice—but all of which had only, at best, functional fit.

None of these interwoven its can be said to be better or deeper or higher or more valuable: just equally flat and endlessly faded surfaces scurrying about in objective systems, not one of which has the slightest clue as to value or depth or quality or goodness or beauty or worth.

Q: We have flatland.

KW: We have flatland. We looked at this as good news, bad news. The good news of modernity was that the Big Three were differentiated—art, science, morals. The bad news was that they had not yet been integrated, and this allowed an explosive science to colonize and dominate the I and the we domains.

Thus the downside of the Enlightenment was that it reduced all Left-Hand dimensions to their Right-Hand correlates, and it thought that a *simple mapping* of these empirical exteriors was all the knowledge that was worth knowing—the mirror of nature, the representation paradigm. This left out the mapmaker itself—the consciousness, the interiors, the Left-Hand dimensions—and resulted in nothing but the flat and faded surfaces of a brutally monochrome world.

And so, following John Locke, "the teacher of the Enlightenment," the great modern mapping game was afoot: map the entire Kosmos in empirical terms. And a century or so into this game of converting the entire Kosmos into objective its, the Enlightenment agenda awoke one morning to find to its utter horror that it was living in a thoroughly disqualified universe—a universe absolutely bereft of value, meaning, consciousness, quality, and worth. In mapping exterior correlates, it had gutted all interior depth, had eviscerated the interiors and laid them out to dry in the blazing sun of the monological gaze.

And so slowly, in an atmosphere of puzzled confusion, the bloodless corpse of the Enlightenment agenda was wheeled into the morgue—and the postmodern rebellion began. Postmodern, post-Enlightenment, post-empirical, post-whatever: something had gone profoundly, *profoundly,* wrong.

Q: The collapse of the Kosmos.

KW: Yes. The monological agenda had, in one sweeping action, completely collapsed the interior dimensions of being and consciousness and depth. It had, in other words, completely collapsed the Great Holarchy of consciousness. Whether prepersonal, personal, or transpersonal—you cannot find consciousness with the monological gaze. You cannot see it with a microscope, a telescope, a photographic plate. And so it must not exist. It must not be "really real."

And that is basically why it is *only* with the modern West that we do not have access to the Great Holarchy.

This-Worldly versus Otherworldly

Q: The history of this collapse is fascinating. And your historical research seems to challenge several longstanding myths about the Western tradition, starting with Plato.

KW: If you look at figure 14-1, it might be obvious that there are, so to speak, two major directions you can move in this Great Holarchy: you can ascend from matter to spirit, or you can descend from spirit to matter. Upward is very *transcendent,* downward is very *immanent.* Ascending is very *otherworldly,* descending is very *this-worldly.*

Q: This is where you introduce "Ascending" and "Descending" spirituality.

KW: Yes. And most people think of Plato as the Ascending or "otherworldly" philosopher, who saw this manifest world, this Earth and everything on it, as a pale shadow or copy of the eternal Forms of the other and real world.

Q: Ecophilosophers trace much of the West's "hatred" of this world to Plato.

KW: Yes, and those assumptions are quite incorrect. As Arthur Lovejoy points out, Plato actually describes two movements—what we are calling Ascent and Descent—and both of these movements are equally important in Plato.

The first movement, the Ascending movement, is a movement from the Many to the One, a movement where we see that behind the fleeting and shadowy forms of manifestation there is a single Source, a groundless Ground, the Absolute, and we rise to an understanding of this absolute Good.

Q: We "ascend" in that sense.

KW: Yes. But the other movement is equally important in Plato, namely, the movement whereby the One empties itself into all creation, gives itself to all forms, so that all of creation itself is a perfect manifestation of Spirit. So *this world*, this very Earth, Plato called "a visible, sensible God."

Q: The "descent" of the One into the Many.

KW: Yes, exactly. Now it is indeed true that Plato gave the West most of its otherworldly philosophy. But, as Lovejoy is at pains to demonstrate, Plato *also* gave the West virtually all of the terms for its thisworldly exuberance and celebration, the celebration of the visible, sensible God. The entire manifest world was seen as a manifestation or embodiment of the Good, of the Absolute, and was to be celebrated as such! The *greater the diversity* in the world, the greater the spiritual Glory and Goodness.

And indeed, most of the this-worldly philosophies of the West have their origin in Plato. Listen to Lovejoy: "The most notable—and the less noted—fact about Plato's historic influence is that he did not merely give to European otherworldliness its characteristic form and phraseology and dialectic, but that he also gave the characteristic form and phraseology and dialectic to precisely the contrary tendency—to a peculiarly *exuberant kind of this-worldliness*."

And, as Lovejoy concludes, both of these currents—Ascending and Descending, or otherworldly and this-worldly, or transcendent and immanent—were united and integrated in Plato. As Lovejoy puts it, "The two strands in Plato's thought are here fused." Ascending and Descending are united and integrated—and that is Plato's final stance, as it were.

Now what happened in subsequent history is that these two strands were brutally torn apart. There was a violent rupture between the advocates of mere Ascent and the advocates of mere Descent. These two currents, which in fact ought to be united and integrated, were catastrophically fractured into the Ascenders versus the Descenders.

Q: The point would be to integrate *both* Ascending and Descending, and that would be part of an integral view.

KW: Yes, definitely. Whitehead's famous comment—that the Western tradition is basically a series of footnotes to Plato—may be true, but the footnotes were fractured. People tended to take their favorite "half" of Plato—the otherworldly or the this-worldly—but rarely did they take the whole.

We do not have to settle for the fractured footnotes to Plato. The Ascending and Descending currents were united in Plato, and they were likewise united in Plotinus.

Q: But things begin to "fall apart" after Plotinus.

KW: In a sense, yes. It is generally agreed that Plotinus was fleshing out the essentials of Plato in a more comprehensive fashion. And in Plotinus we have the Great Holarchy of Being, as presented in figure 14-1, and we have the two basic movements in this nested holarchy, namely, Ascending and Descending, or what Plotinus calls Reflux and Efflux. Spirit constantly effluxes or empties itself into the world, so that the entire world and all its inhabitants are perfect manifestations of Spirit. And likewise the world constantly returns or refluxes to Spirit, so that this entire world is itself spiritual to the core—the visible, sensible God.

According to Plotinus, each senior dimension in the Great Holarchy transcends and includes its junior, so that each and every thing and event, without exception, is perfectly nested in Spirit, in the One, which is therefore the seamless integration and union of Ascent and Descent, Reflux and Efflux, transcendence and immanence.

Q: You point out that this becomes very clear in Plotinus's attack on the Gnostics.

KW: Yes, that's right. Most of the Gnostics were mere Ascenders. Any form of Descent was, in fact, equated with evil. So the entire manifest world—*this* world—was thought to be illusory, shadowy, corrupted, sinful. Only by ascending to the One and shunning the Many could salvation be found.

If Plotinus—carrying the Platonic torch—were really otherworldly, you would expect him to join with the Gnostics and celebrate their merely Ascending agenda and attack all this-worldly endeavors. Instead, Plotinus began an absolutely devastating attack on the Gnostics, on these mere Ascenders, precisely because they couldn't balance the Ascending current with the equally important Descending current.

In other words, the Gnostics had found the causal One, but they didn't push through to the Nondual realization that the One and the Many are not-two, that Emptiness and Form are nondual, that this-worldly and otherworldly are One Taste, that the Ascending and Descending currents need to be integrated in the nondual Heart.

And so Plotinus tears into the Gnostics with an extraordinary and altogether convincing attack, and in some of the most beautiful spiritual prose ever written, reminds the Gnostics that this entire visible world is a manifestation of Spirit and is to be loved as Spirit. And if they, the Gnostics, really loved Spirit, as they proclaim, then they would love Spirit's children, whereas they merely despise them. In effect, Plotinus accuses the Gnostics of spiritual child abuse.

Q: You quote that attack in *Sex, Ecology, Spirituality*. I wonder if you would read it for us.

KW: Plotinus is speaking:

> Do not suppose that a man becomes good by despising the world and all the beauties that are in it. They [the Gnostics] have no right to profess respect for the gods of the world above. When we love a person, we love all that belongs to him; we extend to the children the affection we feel for the parent. Now every Soul is a daughter of Spirit. How can *this world* be separated from the *spiritual* world? Those who despise what is so nearly akin to the spiritual world, prove that they know nothing of the spiritual world, except in name. . . .
>
> Let [any individual soul] make itself worthy to contemplate the Great Soul by ridding itself, through quiet recollection, of deceit [untruthfulness] and of all that bewitches vulgar souls. For it let all be quiet; let all its environment be at peace. Let the earth be quiet and the sea and air, and the heaven itself waiting. Let it observe how the Soul flows in from all sides into the resting world, pours itself into it, penetrates it and illumines it. Even as the bright beams of the sun enlighten a dark cloud and give it a golden border, so the Soul when it enters into the body of the heaven gives it life and timeless beauty and awakens it from sleep. So the world, grounded in a timeless movement by the Soul which suffuses it with intelligence, becomes a living and blessed being. . . .
>
> It [Soul/Spirit] gives itself to every point in this vast body, and vouchsafes its being to every part, great and small, though these parts are divided in space and manner of disposition, and though some are opposed to each other, others dependent on each other. But the Soul is not divided, nor does it split up in order to give life to each individual. All things live by the Soul *in its entirety* [i.e., ultimately there are no degrees, no levels, but simply pure Presence]; it is all present everywhere. The heaven, vast and various as it is, is one by the power of the Soul, and by

it is this universe of ours Divine. The sun too is Divine, and so are the stars; and we ourselves, if we are worth anything, are so on account of the Soul. Be persuaded that by it thou can attain to God. And know that thou wilt not have to go far afield. . . .

Wisdom and Compassion

Q: So that rather clearly shows the nondual orientation of Plotinus. You relate this integration of Ascent and Descent to the union of wisdom and compassion.

KW: Yes, we see this in both East and West. The Path of Ascent from the Many to the One is the *path of wisdom*. Wisdom sees that behind all the multifarious forms and phenomena there lies the One, the Good, the unqualifiable Emptiness, against which all forms are seen to be illusory, fleeting, impermanent. Wisdom is the return of the Many to the One. In the East: Prajna, or wisdom, sees that Form is Emptiness.

The Path of Descent, on the other hand, is the *path of compassion*. It sees that the One actually manifests as the Many, and so all forms are to be treated equally with kindness, compassion, mercy. Compassion or Goodness is, in fact, the very mechanism of manifestation itself. The One manifests as the Many through an infinite act of compassion and charity, and we embrace the Many with that same compassion and care. Compassion touches all manifestation with concern and gentle wonderment. In the East: Karuna, or compassion, sees that Emptiness is Form.

So we have: Wisdom sees that the Many is One, and Compassion sees that the One is the Many. Or in the East: Prajna sees that Form is Emptiness, Karuna sees that Emptiness is Form.

Q: Wisdom and Compassion—this is also Eros and Agape.

KW: Yes, ascending Eros and descending Agape, transcendence and immanence, the love that reaches up and the love that reaches down. . . .

The central historical point in all of this is that with the great Nondual systems, from Plotinus in the West to Nagarjuna in the East, we see an emphasis on *balancing and integrating these two movements*. The *Ascending* or *transcendental* current of wisdom or Eros or prajna is to be balanced with the *Descending* or *immanent* current of compassion or Agape or karuna; and the union of these two, the union of the One and the Many, of Emptiness and Form, of Wisdom and Compassion—their union in the nondual Heart of One Taste is the source and goal and ground of genuine spirituality.

God and Goddess

Q: This is also God and the Goddess—as Eros and Agape, Wisdom and Compassion, Ascent and Descent. . . .

KW: Yes, in a broad sense. If we ignore for the moment the more provincial and stage-specific notions of the horticultural Great Mother as a farming protectress, and the agrarian images of God the Father as a Big Daddy in the Sky—these mythic images are not very useful for an overall picture—and if we look instead to the broad understanding of God and Goddess, then the balanced picture that emerges is something like this:

If we wish to think in such terms, then the Masculine Face of Spirit—or God—is preeminently Eros, the Ascending and *transcendental* current of the Kosmos, ever-striving to find greater wholeness and wider unions, to break the limits and reach for the sky, to rise to unending revelations of a greater Good and Glory, always rejecting the shallower in search of the deeper, rejecting the lower in search of the higher.

And the Feminine Face of Spirit—the Goddess—is preeminently Agape, or Compassion, the Descending and *immanent* and manifesting current of the Kosmos, the principle of embodiment, and bodily incarnation, and relationship, and relational and manifest embrace, touching each and every being with perfect and equal grace, rejecting nothing, embracing all. Where Eros strives for the Good of the One in transcendental wisdom, Agape embraces the Many with Goodness and immanent care.

Q: Which you tie in with Tantra.

KW: Tantra, in the general sense, presents the ultimate Nondual reality as the sexual embrace of God and the Goddess, of Shiva and Shakti, of Emptiness and Form. Neither Ascent nor Descent is final, ultimate, or privileged, but rather, like the primordial yin and yang, they generate each other, depend upon each other, cannot exist without the other, and find their own true being by dying into the other, only to awaken together, joined in bliss, as the entire Kosmos, finding that eternity is wildly in love with the productions of time, the nondual Heart radiating as all creation, and blessing all creation, and singing this embrace for all eternity—an embrace that we are all asked to repeat in our own awareness, moment to moment, endlessly, miraculously, as the immediate presence of One Taste. This is the Nondual vision, this union of Reflux and Efflux, God and the Goddess, Emptiness and Form, Wisdom and Compassion, Eros and Agape, Ascent and Descent—perfectly and blissfully united in One Taste, the radical sound of one hand clapping.

Two Different Gods

Q: This is likewise the nondual integrative vision of Plotinus.

KW: Yes. But this union of Ascent and Descent would, in subsequent Western history, be often broken, with the otherworldly Ascenders and the this-worldly Descenders in constant and sometimes violent conflict. This subsequent war has been one of the central and defining conflicts in the Western mind.

Q: The war between the Ascenders and the Descenders.

KW: Yes. It's quite remarkable. Beginning with Augustine, and continuing right down to today, the Ascenders and the Descenders were in relentless and often brutal conflict, and this saddled the West with two *completely incompatible Gods*, as it were.

The God of the Ascenders was otherworldly to the core—my kingdom is not of this world. It was puritanical, usually monastic and ascetic, and it saw the body, the flesh, and especially sex, as archetypal sins. It sought always to flee the Many and find the One. It was purely *transcendental*, and was always pessimistic about finding happiness in this world. It shunned time in favor of eternity, and hid its face in shame from the shadows of this world.

The God of the Descenders counseled *exactly the opposite*. It fled from the One into the embrace of the Many. It was in love with the visible, sensible God, and sometimes Goddess. It was a God of pure embodiment, of pure *immanence*. It was fascinated with diversity, and found its glory in the celebration of this diversity. Not greater oneness, but greater variety was the goal of this God. It celebrated the senses, and the body, and sexuality, and earth. And delighted in a creation-centered spirituality that saw each sunrise, each moonrise, as the visible blessing of the Divine.

Q: In *Sex, Ecology, Spirituality* you trace the history of this war between the two Gods.

KW: Yes, that's right. In the West, during the millennium between Augustine and Copernicus, we see an almost exclusively *Ascending* ideal. Indeed, since this was an *agrarian* structure, there was a selection for male-biased spirituality, which consequently centered on Eros more than Agape, on Ascent more than Descent, on the One to the exclusion of, even hatred of, the Many.

And thus true salvation, true liberation, could not be found in this body, on this earth, in this lifetime. It was *otherworldly* to the core. Flesh is sin and sex is sin and earth is sin and body is sin, no matter what faint praise was given to creation itself. And so, of course, the root of sin was Eve in general—woman, body, flesh, nature, carnality: all of that becomes taboo in the deepest sense. Always, for the mere Ascenders, Descent is the Devil.

Q: In both the East and the West.

KW: Definitely. There is a constant tendency in agrarian societies, *wherever* they appear, to let the Ascending current pronounce this world evil or illusory, and to condemn earth, body, senses, sexuality (and woman). There were exceptions, of course, but this is the constant tendency in all agrarian structures: otherworldly to the core, with my kingdom not of this world, and an intense desire to find a nirvana away from the world of samsara. You find this from early Judaism to virtually all forms of Gnosticism to early Buddhism and most forms of Christianity and Islam.

And this was indeed the case in the West, especially, as I said, from the time of Augustine to the time of Copernicus. An almost exclusively Ascending ideal dominated European consciousness for a thousand years. The Way Up was the counsel that the Church gave for her perfections and her virtues, and lay not your treasures upon this earth was the one sure way to salvation—which means, find nothing in or on this earth to be treasured.

Oh, there was plenty of lip service given to the Goodness of God's creation (Goodness = Agape, Compassion, Descent), but the bottom line was that you could not gain liberation or salvation on this earth, in this life, and therein lies the entire story. Life was okay, but things got really interesting once you died. Once, that is, you got off this earth. This earth was not a place where realization could be found; this earth was simply a runway for the real take-off.

Q: All of which soon changed.

KW: Yes, all of which changed, and changed dramatically, with the Renaissance and the rise of modernity, culminating in the Enlightenment and the Age of Reason. And the simplest way to describe this entire period is that, at this point, *the Ascenders were out, the Descenders were in.*

And for mere Descenders, any form of Ascent is *always* despised. Ascent, in fact, becomes the new evil. Ascent is forever the Devil in the eyes of the Descended God.

So it is no surprise that from modernity forward, virtually any Ascent, of any variety, became the new sin. The rise of modernity, the rejection of Ascent, and the embrace of a purely Descended world—these came into being together.

And here we are on the trail of the modern West's denial of the transpersonal dimensions. Here we start to see exactly the beginning of the dismissal, or rejection, or marginalization, of the genuinely spiritual and transpersonal. Here we start to see the glorification of flatland, the embrace of the Descended grid. The eclipse of any sort of transcendental wisdom—the eclipse of any sort of Ascent—cast a shadow over the entire face of modernity, a shadow that is the signature of our times.

The Descended Grid

Q: This flatland, this Descended grid, has marked the entire modern and postmodern condition.

KW: In many ways, yes. As a general statement, yes. Salvation in the modern world—whether offered by politics, or science, or revivals of earth religion, or Marxism, or industrialization, or consumerism, or retribalism, or sexuality, or horticultural revivals, or scientific materialism, or earth goddess embrace, or ecophilosophies—salvation can be found only on this earth, only in the phenomena, only in manifestation, only in the world of Form, only in pure *immanence*, only in the Descended grid. There is no higher truth, no Ascending current, nothing *transcendental* whatsoever. In fact, anything "higher" or "transcendental" is now the Devil, is now the great enemy, is now the destroyer of the earthbound, sensory-drenched God and Goddess. And all of modernity and postmodernity moves fundamentally and almost entirely within this Descended grid, the grid of flatland.

Q: So this is not integrating Ascent and Descent . . .

KW: No, this is simply the dominance of the Descenders. And not just in "official" reality, but also in virtually every form of "counterculture" or "counterreality." The Descended grid is so entrenched, so unconscious, so background, so deeply ingrained, that even the "new paradigm" rebels often move completely within its clutches. It infects equally orthodox and avant-garde, conventional and alternative, industrialist and ecologist.

Q: That's exactly what I want to focus on next.

15

The Collapse of the Kosmos

Q: The modern and postmodern world moves within the Descended grid. So the obvious question is, why?

KW: The dialectic of progress took its first modern spill. Evolution hit a bump in the road and the whole car tilted on its side and began to skid down the road. The differentiation of the Big Three—consciousness, culture, and nature—began to career into the dissociation of the Big Three, and their subsequent collapse into the Big One of flatland.

Evolution, of course, is a self-correcting agenda, and it is in the process of slowly righting itself. As in the stock market, there is an overall and unmistakable upward trend, but this doesn't stop violent short-term fluctuations, both up and down—periods of growth and periods of depression. And starting in the eighteenth century, aspects of the cultural stock market hit a great depression, the likes of which we have rarely seen, and are just now beginning to overcome.

Q: So this collapse is not a reductionism that you find in previous cultures.

KW: That's basically correct; premodern cultures lack both the good news and the bad news of this differentiation, which sometimes confuses critics. Because earlier cultures did not differentiate the Big Three in the first place, they couldn't collapse and reduce them. The extraordinary *advance* of differentiating the Big Three allowed this extraordinary tragedy. The *dignity* of modernity began to slide into the *disaster* of modernity, and there, pretty much, is where the modern and postmodern world still rests: a fragmented lifeworld with self and culture and science at each other's throat, each struggling, not for integration, but domination, each trying to heal the fragmentation by denying reality to the other quadrants.

And so it came about that this great evolutionary leap forward brought its first great catastrophe, the dialectic of progress in its first modern form, blood all over the brand-new carpet.

The Dignity of Modernity

Q: So before we discuss this bad news, why don't you very quickly review the good news of modernity, since this seems to be where many critics get sidetracked.

KW: Yes, it's important to emphasize, because the antimodernists focus on the bad news and tend to forget the good news altogether.

Neither magic nor mythic is postconventional. But with the shift to reason and worldcentric morality, we see the rise of the modern liberation movements: liberation of slaves, of women, of the untouchables. Not what is right for me or my tribe, or my race, or my mythology, or my religion, but what is fair and right and just for all humans, regardless of race, sex, caste, or creed.

And thus, in a mere hundred-year period, stretching roughly from 1788 to 1888, slavery was outlawed and eliminated from every rational-industrial society on earth. In both the preconventional/egocentric and the conventional/ethnocentric moral stance, slavery is perfectly acceptable, because equal dignity and worth are *not* extended to all humans, but merely to those of your tribe or your race or your chosen god. But from a postconventional stance, slavery is simply wrong, it is simply intolerable.

This was the first time in history that a general societal type had eliminated slavery! Some earlier societies happened not to have slavery, but, as Gerhard Lenski's massive evidence demonstrates, no general type of society was ever free of it, until rational-industrialization.

This was true East and West, North and South—white men and black men and yellow men and red men enslaved their fellow men and women, and thought little of it. Some societies, such as early foraging, had relatively less slavery, but even foragers were not free of it altogether—in fact, they invented it.

In this regard, one of the social nightmares in America is that this country was formed right during the great transition period from agrarian slavery to industrial no-slavery. The Constitution, in fact, is still a largely agrarian document—slavery is so taken for granted it isn't even mentioned, and women are not counted as citizens (and none of that even has to be explained in the document itself!). But as the center of cultural gravity continued to switch from mythic-agrarian to rational-industrial, slavery was eliminated across the board, although its scars are still with us.

Q: Women were also "freed," so to speak.

KW: Yes, for almost identical reasons, we would see the rise of feminism and the women's movement on a culture-wide scale, generally dated, as we said, from Wollstonecraft in 1792, exactly the general beginning period of the numerous liberation movements.

This, too, was almost totally a product of rational-industrialization, and must be counted as one of modernity's many extraordinary achievements. Previously, where the Big Three weren't differentiated (where noosphere and biosphere were still indissociated), *biological* determinants, such as male physical strength, were often the dominant *cultural* determinants as well, because they weren't differentiated: male physical strength meant male cultural strength. If the mode of production did not demand much physical exertion—as in horticulture—then women lucked out, and the societies were relatively "equalitarian," although when push came to shove, women were always the shov-ee.

But with the differentiation of self and culture and nature (the differentiation of the Big Three), biological determinants became increasingly irrelevant. Biology was no longer destiny. Equal rights can *never* be achieved in the biosphere, where big fish eat little fish; but they can be achieved—or certainly aimed for—in the noosphere. And liberal feminism arose at this time in history, and not before this time, to announce this new and emergent truth—in the noosphere, women deserve equal rights—a truth centered in postconventional depth and worldcentric rationality.

Q: There was the whole movement of the democracies themselves.

KW: Yes, essentially the same phenomenon. The mythological worldview, quite contrary to the picture painted by many Romantics, was in virtually all cases shot through with dominator hierarchies. The mythic god is the god of a *particular* peoples—it is sociocentric and ethnocentric, not postconventional and worldcentric. It is the god of all peoples only if all peoples bow before that particular god. It is therefore "worldcentric" only by *forced conversion*, and, if necessary, *military conquest*, as the great mythic-imperial Empires of the Aztecs, Incas, Romans, Khans, and Ramses would make quite obvious. These dominator hierarchies generally have a single head: Pope or King or Cleopatra or Khan is on top, and stretching out beneath are various degrees of servitude. All of them conquered in the name of their mythic god or goddess, before whom all beings must bow.

The Age of Reason was therefore the Age of Revolution as well, revolution against mythic dominator hierarchies. This was a revolution not just in theory but in practice, in politics. One of the great themes of the Enlightenment was "No more myths!" because myths are precisely what divide and antagonize peoples, and set them against each other in ethnocentric ways, and inflict their cruelties on unbelievers in the name of a chosen god.

And so Voltaire's impassioned cry rang out across the continent: "Remember the cruelties!" Remember the cruelties inflicted on people in the name of the mythic god—remember the hundreds of thousands burned at the stake in order to save their souls; remember the Inquisition grotesquely inscribing its dogma on the flesh of the torture victim; remember the political inequalities inherent in mythic hierarchies; remember the brutality that in the name of compassion had crushed innumerable souls under its domineering march.

On the other hand, a postconventional moral stance extends equal opportunity to all peoples, regardless of race, sex, creed, belief, myth, or god. And again, although not everybody lives up to this postconventional or worldcentric ideal, it was indeed, beginning with modernity, firmly embedded in widespread social institutions that protected its intent. Thousands and thousands of men and women fought and died for this democratic vision of worldcentric tolerance and universal pluralism, under the slogan, "I may disagree with what you say, but I will defend to the death your right to say it."

This, too, was radically novel, on any sort of large scale. The early Greek democracies had none of this universalism. Let us remember that in the Greek "democracies," one out of three people were slaves, and women and children virtually so; the agrarian base cannot support emancipation of slaves. The city of Athens, like all city-states, had its own particular mythic god or goddess. And so the indictment handed down by the city of Athens began, "Socrates is guilty of refusing to recognize the gods of the State." It ended with, "The penalty demanded is death."

When asked, as was customary, if Socrates could suggest an alternative punishment, he suggested free meals for life.

But Socrates chose reason over myth, and drank the hemlock. Fifteen hundred years later, the world caught up with him, only this time the polis forced the gods to drink the hemlock, and from the death of those gods arose the modern democracies.

The Disaster of Modernity

Q: And we have, as good news, I suppose, the development of science itself.

KW: Yes, the differentiation of the Big Three allowed rational-empirical science to emerge unencumbered by blatant mythic dogmatisms. Empirical science—which means *rationality* tied to *empirical* observables through a hypothetico-deductive procedure—blossomed for the first time on any sort of culture-wide scale.

With empirical science there can be little quarrel, but with scientism . . . well, scientism is a different beast. And here we might as well start to look at the bad news, which was the *failure to integrate the Big Three.* Consciousness, morals, and science had indeed been freed from their magic and their mythic indissociation; each domain was set loose with its own power and its own truth and its own approach to the Kosmos, each of which had something *equally* important to say.

But by the end of the eighteenth century, the rapid, indeed extraordinary development of science began to throw the whole system off balance. The advances in the it-domain began to eclipse, and then actually *deny*, the values and truths of the I and the we domains. The Big Three began to collapse into the Big One: empirical science, and science alone, could pronounce on ultimate reality. Science, as we say, became scientism, which means it didn't just pursue its own truths, it aggressively denied that there were any other truths at all!

And thus, beginning especially, as I said, in the eighteenth century, the Left-Hand and interior dimensions were reduced to their Right-Hand empirical correlates. Only objective its with simple location were "really real"! The entire interior dimensions—in all holons, human and otherwise!—were completely gutted, and the ghost in the machine began its sad and lonely modern moan, a haunting cry made all the more plaintive in that it had not even the power to attract attention.

When only objective its with simple location are really real, then the mind itself is a *tabula* that was totally *rasa*, utterly blank until filled with *pictures* or representations of the only reality there was: objective and sensory nature. There is no real *Spirit*, there is no real *mind*, there is only empirical *nature*. No superconscious, no self-conscious, only subconscious processes scurrying endlessly, meaninglessly, in a vast system of interwoven its. The Great Holarchy utterly collapsed like a house of cards in an afternoon gust, and in its place we find only the *web of nature with its simple location.*

And thus, welcome to the modern, purely Descended world. All the truth that is fit to know is the truth of its, of mononature, of objective and empirical processes—and no Ascent of any variety is required. The Descended grid of flatland, the world of all proper troglodytes, hollow to the core.

Instrumental Rationality: A World of Its

Q: This seems to be the crux of the matter. How or why did science overrun the other domains?

KW: The extraordinary gains in empirical science—by Galileo, Kepler, Newton, Harvey, Kelvin, Clausius, Carnot—were being matched by the massive transformations wrought by industrialization. *Both of these were it-domain endeavors,* and so they fed on each other in a vicious spiral, pushing all other concerns by the wayside. In other words, the it-domain had two very powerful forces on its side—the accomplishments of empirical science and the power of industrialization.

The techno-economic base of a society (the Lower-Right quadrant) sets the *concrete forms* within which the culture moves and *can* move. The base doesn't determine the cultural superstructure in any sort of strong Marxist sense, but it does set various limits and possibilities (it's virtually impossible, for example, to outlaw slavery with an agrarian base, and equally impossible to vindicate women's rights).

Now the industrial base was a base of *instrumental productivity.* Of course, so was the bow and arrow, so was the hoe, so was the plow—but a steam engine? an internal combustion engine? In many ways the engine, the machine, was itself a simple evolution of productive capacity, stretching all the way back to the first rock used as a club or the first stick used as a spear. In that sense, there was nothing about industrialization that was a radical break with the past—men and women everywhere and at all times have tinkered with ways to secure their basic needs with instruments, with tools. But as the development of this quadrant became more and more complex, the sheer power of the machine, of the industrial base, brought instrumental productivity screaming to the fore.

Within the techno-economic base, a culture unfolds its possibilities.

And within the industrial base, an altogether productive and technical and *instrumental* mentality unfolded, a mentality that, almost of necessity, put a *premium on the it-domain*.

Now many critics—most critics, actually—tend to see a great number of problems with industrialization. It is supposed to be the cause of a mechanistic worldview; the destruction of an organic culture; the cause of an analytic and fragmented world; the displacement of social cohesion; the cause of ecological catastrophe; the ruin of religious sensibilities.

Those are important, but I don't think any of them are central. I think they are all derivative. Central is the pressure this productive base placed on consciousness to select for the it-domain. That is, the power of industrialization joined with the accomplishments of empirical science to select for a world where *its alone are real*. Everything else stems from that selection. All of those other problems stem from that problem.

The it-domain was growing like a cancer—a pathological hierarchy—invading and colonizing and dominating the I and the we domains. The *moral* decisions of the culture were rapidly being handed over to science and *technical* solutions. Science would solve *everything*. All problems in the I and the we domains were converted to technical problems in the it-domain. And thus science (theoretical and technical) would not only solve all problems, it would decide what was a problem in the first place—it would decide what was real and what was not.

Q: So the problem wasn't that the new science was analytic and divisive instead of holistic and systems-oriented.

KW: Absolutely not. The problem was that both atomistic science and holistic science were it-isms. Both contributed to the primary collapse. Atomistic its, holistic its—same basic nightmare.

Q: But we constantly hear, from the "new paradigm" folks, that we are living in a fractured world because the "old Newtonian" science was mechanistic, divisive, and atomistic, and these divisive concepts invaded society and caused its fragmentation; and that what is now required is for society to catch up with the new holistic sciences, from quantum physics to systems theory, and this will heal the divisions. And you're saying atomistic and holistic are both the culprit.

KW: Yes, that's right. When science pronounced its own mission to be the only real mission, it likewise pronounced the it-domain to be the only real domain. The empirical world of monological nature was the only real world. Humans were an inseparable part of this web of nature, and thus humans could also be known in an empirical, objective fashion.

You want consciousness? Don't *talk* to me, just cut into the brain and *look*! The monological gaze.

The idea was that the brain is part of nature, nature alone is real, so consciousness can be found in an empirical study of the brain—this is a horrible reduction to monological surfaces.

Q: But the brain *is* a part of nature!

KW: Yes, the brain is a part of nature, but the mind is not part of the brain. The mind, or consciousness, is the interior dimension, the exterior correlate of which is the objective brain. The mind is an I, the brain is an it. So, as we discussed earlier, the brain, like anything else in empirical nature, can be known by the monological gaze, by empiric-analytic investigation, but the mind can only be known by introspection, communication, and interpretation. You can look at a brain, but you must talk to a mind, and that requires not just observation but interpretation.

So when all aspects of holons were reduced to the great monological web of empirical its, then their interior dimensions were perfectly decimated. The interiors of plants and whales and wolves and chimps evaporate in the scorching blaze of the monological gaze. They are all just strands in the objective web—they have no lifeworld, they have no culture. And thus, if you reduce the Kosmos to the great web of empirical nature, you denature the interiors of nature as well. You only have empirical nature, monological nature, denatured nature, the hollow shell of the collapsed Kosmos: all I's and all we's reduced to interwoven its, reduced to the great web of simple location.

Of course, consciousness does not have simple location. Values, desires, states of consciousness, meaning, depth, peak experiences, spiritual illuminations—none of those have physical location in the exterior world of its. Consciousness exists in levels of its own interior space that are known from within, accessed by interpretation, and shared in mutual understanding guided by sincerity. And since *none* of those have simple location, then if you attempt to get at the interior beast by simply mapping its empirical-objective footprints, you will lose the very essence of the beast itself.

And then you will simply arrange your ontological holarchies based primarily on *physical* extension—*orders of magnitude* replace *orders of significance*, and so then the only "nests" you have are now based mostly on *size*: an atom is part of a bigger molecule is part of a bigger cell is part of a bigger organism is part of a bigger biosphere—and there is your holistic systems map.

At which point you have totally fallen into what Whitehead called the *fallacy of simple location*. Namely, if something can't be simply located in physical space, then it isn't "really real." You can locate Gaia, so it exists. You can locate cells, so they exist. You can locate the brain, so it exists. You can locate the biosphere, so it exists.

But you can't *simply locate* consciousness and values and meanings and morals in the same way. You can't point to them with your finger. You can't see them or find them anywhere in the great web of sensory nature. They become rambling and ridiculed ghosts in the machine, pathetic illusions in the organic system. They are merely personal tastes and subjective fantasies. The interiors *don't count* in a disqualified universe, the universe you can put your finger on.

The irony, of course, is that the universe you can put your finger on is the meaningless universe. So although consciousness and value and meaning are *intrinsic* to the *depth* of the Kosmos, they cannot be found in the cosmos. That is, they inhere in the Left-Hand dimensions of the Kosmos, not in the Right-Hand surfaces. And thus, if you are intent on only allowing the sensory surfaces, then you scrub the Kosmos clean of value and consciousness and meaning and depth, guaranteed.

And so it came about that the Great Holarchy was abandoned, essentially for the first time in history, because you couldn't put your finger on it. The ghost in the machine was indeed a ghost, because it had just committed suicide.

The Fundamental Enlightenment Paradigm

Q: So is this why theorists like Foucault have so sharply attacked the "sciences of man" that arose in the eighteenth century?

KW: Yes, very much so. Foucault beautifully summarized this monological madness with a perfect phrase: men and women, he said, became "objects of information, never subjects in communication." Foucault gave a perfect one-sentence summary of the entire nightmare of modernity. That is, human beings, like all holons, were studied only in their empirical and objective dimensions, and thus were reduced to mere its in the great interwoven web, with no depth and no intentionality and no personhood to speak of. The brutal world of the lab technician, slabs of meat each and all.

And thus, correlative with the rise of scientism, you have the rise of the "sciences of man," sciences that reduced human beings solely to objects of information. Also called "dehumanized humanism."

Q: Why did Foucault call that the "Age of Man"?

KW: Because "man" as an *object* of scientific investigation was "invented." Human beings became objects of monological rationality, something that had never happened before (because the Big Three had never been differentiated and then collapsed). In his own quirky way, Foucault would say that man had never existed before. Man was invented. And Foucault longed for "the end of man." So he concludes *The Order of Things* with the arresting metaphor, "One can certainly wager that man will be erased, like a face drawn in sand at the edge of the sea."

That's postmodernese for: the end of objectification. The end of this dehumanizing humanism, the end of "man," this *mere* objectification of the human person into monological its. To reduce all subjects to objects in the great interlocking web—this is actually power parading as knowledge, this is the tyranny of the monological gaze, this is the irony of flatland rationality, and this was one of Foucault's main targets.

So if you look at the major theorists and critics of the rise of modernity—such as Hegel, Weber, Habermas, Taylor, Foucault—a surprisingly consistent picture emerges. They all tend to agree on certain basic features of modernity: a disengaged subject surveying a holistic it-world, with knowledge being simply the empirical and objective representation or mapping of this holistic world (the representation paradigm, the mirror of nature). The subjective and intersubjective domains were thus *reduced* to empirical studies—I and we were reduced to interwoven its—and thus humans became "objects of information, never subjects in communication." This reduction of the Big Three to the Big One produced scientific materialism, dehumanized humanism, and the disqualified universe that still tends to dominate the modern and postmodern world.

No Spirit, No Mind, Only Nature

Q: So this is what you meant when you said that one broken God replaced the other.

KW: Yes, from an almost exclusively Ascending ideal, which had dominated Western consciousness for at least a thousand years, we get an almost exclusively Descended world, which has dominated modernity and postmodernity to this day. There is no translogical Spirit, and no dialogical mind; there is just monological nature. Surface nature, mononature, the world of sensory and material forms—this is the "God," this is the "Goddess," of the modern and postmodern world.

I have a handful of diagrams that might help explain this. If we go back to figure 2-2 (page 85), we will be reminded of the traditional Great Holarchy of Being, matter to body to mind to soul to spirit, with each level transcending and including its predecessors. Moving upward from the center (matter, the most fundamental) is the process of evolution (Reflux or Ascent, driven by Eros), and moving downward from spirit (the most significant) is involution (Efflux or Descent, driven by Agape). Each higher level is an emergent, marked by properties not found in its predecessors. Spirit is both the highest level (which transcends all, includes all), and the equally present Ground of each level (represented by the paper).

But what the traditional Great Nest failed to do, on any sort of significant scale, was to clearly differentiate the four quadrants. The material brain, for example, was simply placed, with all matter, on the bottom rung of existence, instead of seeing that the material brain is the exterior correlate of interior states of consciousness (so that the brain is not simply part of the lowest of all levels, but rather is the exterior correlate of some very high levels). Instead of seeing that consciousness is intimately associated with the material brain, consciousness seemed to hover above all matter, transcendental and metaphysical and completely otherworldly. (The discovery that states of consciousness have correlates in brain states—that all Left-Hand events have Right-Hand correlates—was a devastating blow to the Great Chain and all metaphysics as traditionally conceived, and rightly so, even though it went too far and contributed to the collapse of the Kosmos into nothing but scientific materialism.)

Likewise, the traditional Great Nest embodied little understanding of the profound ways that cultural contexts (Lower Left) mold all perception; of the ways that the techno-economic base (Lower Right) strongly influences individual consciousness; of the evolution of worldviews, individual consciousness, modes of production, and so on. In all these ways and more, the Great Chain was severely limited. (This did not stop individuals from using the Great Chain as a perfectly adequate map for individual spiritual development in the Upper-Left quadrant, which is what many did, including the likes of Plotinus. But it did severely limit the sensitivity of the Great Nest to those differentiated aspects of reality that we are calling the four quadrants.)

Q: But modernity did differentiate the four quadrants.

KW: Yes. All of this would change with modernity and the widespread differentiation of the Big Three. This can be represented as in figure 15-1 (and simplified as in figure 15-2), which is the Great Nest differentiated into the four quadrants (or the Big Three). This integral vision is what could have emerged, and what might yet still emerge, but what in fact did *not* emerge in any enduring way. Instead, the various levels and quadrants were all collapsed into their material (or empirical or objective) correlates, to result, soon enough, in flatland, in scientific materialism, in sensory mononature. Tracing this collapse of the Kosmos is the crux of our story at this point.

Q: You said it had to do with the fact that every Left-Hand event has a Right-Hand correlate, an "it" correlate. Coupled with industrialization and objective science, the "its" took over the world!

KW: Exactly. Every Left-Hand event does indeed have a Right-Hand or empirical correlate in the material (or objective) world—and thus it is always tempting to reduce the former (depths that require arduous interpretation) to the latter (surfaces that can be easily seen). What we called subtle reductionism.

This can be understood with reference to figure 15-3. Notice again that each level transcends and includes its predecessors. On the interior domains, we see that the theosphere (soul/spirit) transcends and includes

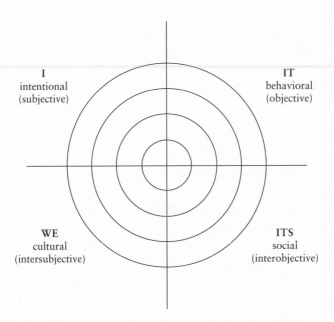

FIGURE 15-1. *The Great Nest with the Four Quadrants.*

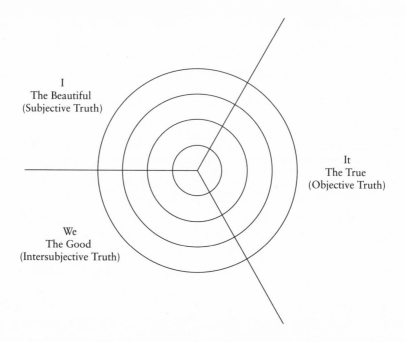

FIGURE 15-2. *The Big Three*

the noosphere (mind), which transcends and includes the biosphere (body). These are shorthand for the nine or so levels and fulcrums of interior consciousness development.

But just as important, each interior state of consciousness (from bodily consciousness to mental consciousness to spiritual consciousness) *has some sort of correlate in the material/objective brain and organism* (Upper Right). Thus, for example, even somebody who is having a spiritual experience (Upper Left) will show changes in objective brainwaves that can be measured on an EEG machine (Upper Right).

But conscious states, values, depth, and intentions cannot be reduced to material brainwaves because, although one value is better than another, one brainwave is not. You experience compassion and you know it is better than murder; while you are thinking that, your brain will be producing brainwaves that can be registered on an EEG. But, although you know that compassion is better than murder, there is nothing on the EEG machine that says, "This brainwave is more valuable; this brainwave is more moral; this brainwave is more beautiful." The EEG machine can *only* show that one brain state is *different* from another; it

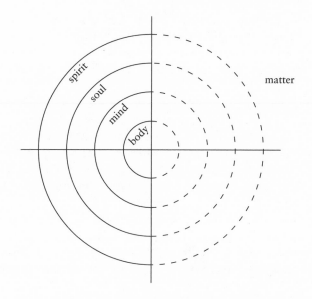

FIGURE 15-3. *Correlations of Interior (Consciousness)*
States with Exterior (Material) States

cannot say that one state is *better* than another. To make that judgment, you have to rely on interior consciousness, depth, and value recognition—holarchies of *quality*—while the EEG machine can only register holarchies of *quantity*. To reduce the Left to the Right is to reduce all quality to quantity, and thus, as we have seen, land directly in the disqualified universe, also known as flatland.

Q: Which is precisely what happened.

KW: Which is precisely what happened. As we saw, all Left-Hand and interior events were reduced to Right-Hand processes and objects and its. The rational Ego was left dangling in midair, cut off from its roots in its own body, cut off from spirit and the higher stages of its own interior development, and doing nothing but reflecting on the only reality of nature ("the mirror of nature"). Gone was spirit, and gone was mind as a real reality in itself, and all that was left was sensory nature, the empirical web of holistic its.

Q: In other words, flatland.

KW: Flatland, yes. This can be represented as in figure 15-4. The rational Ego is all that is left of the interior domains, and even its existence was challenged. The Eco—or Nature, or the Right-Hand world—is all that was believed to be ultimately real. The purely Descended world of flatland is now the ultimate reality.

Q: So you can see how the very differentiations of modernity allowed the dissociation and then the collapse into flatland. Good news, bad news.

KW: Yes, that's right. And so, once we finish our account of the historical rise of flatland, we can perhaps return to the central point: in order to have a truly *integral* view, we want to take the very best of the ancient wisdom (namely, it was "all-level," stretching from body to mind to soul to spirit) and combine that with the very best of modernity (namely, it was "all-quadrant," differentiating the Big Three), and thus arrive at an *all-level, all-quadrant* vision.

Q: Which would be something like figures 15-1, 15-2, and 15-3.

KW: Yes, that's right. For the moment, however, we are at the point that modernity embraced the "reality" of figure 15-4. Modernity fell in love with flatland, the Descended grid, the industrial ontology of a world of ITS.

The Voice of the Industrial Grid

Q: Now you were saying that the modern ecological crisis is primarily the result of the Descended grid.

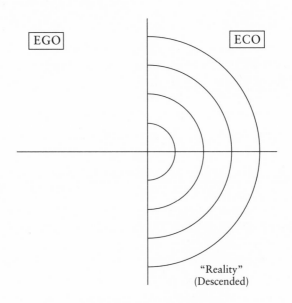

FIGURE 15-4. *Flatland*

KW: Anybody can say they are thinking "globally," but very few can actually take a worldcentric or postconventional perspective. As we saw, to *actually* live from a worldcentric or universal perspective requires five or six major interior stages of transformation and transcendence.

But if the entire Left Hand is ignored and devalued—if we ignore interiors and just rivet our eyes on a Right-Hand "global" map of Gaia or systems nature—we will ignore the actual path of getting people to that global or worldcentric stance. We will have a goal with no path. And we will have a map that denies and condemns Left-Hand transcendence, which is the actual path itself!

And all of that ignoring, all of that "ignorance," goes directly back to the subtle reductionism of the fundamental Enlightenment paradigm. We saw that rationality managed to differentiate the Big Three, but *industrialization* as much as anything collapsed them into the Big One of mononature, of empirical nature with its simple location, the world of figure 15-4.

In other words, this world of mononature is in fact a largely *industrial ontology*. The very notion that "empirical nature alone is real"—this is the modern Descended grid, and this grid is above all else the grid of industrial ontology. It is industrialization that *holds flatland in place*, that holds the objective world of simple location as the primary reality, that colonizes and dominates the interiors and reduces them to instrumental strands in the great web of sensory its. That "nature alone is real"—this is the voice of the industrial grid.

Q: Which is why you don't find this collapse in other cultures.

KW: That's right. Nature was either predifferentiated and egocentric, as in magic; or nature was devalued in favor of a mythic other world, as in mythology. Or, in the case of a Plotinus or a Padmasambhava, nature is an expression of Spirit, an embodiment of Spirit—Spirit transcends and includes nature.

But *never* in history had a differentiated nature simply been equated with the ultimate reality! Never had translogical Spirit and dialogical mind been so rudely reduced to monological nature. But with the modern industrial ontology, nature is the ultimate reality, nature alone is real.

Q: So *nature*, in that sense, is a *product* of industrialization.

KW: Yes, it appears so. As we were saying, that "nature alone is real"—this is the haunting voice of the industrial grid.

And then, with reference to Spirit, you will do one of two things: deny Spirit altogether, or claim nature is Spirit. The Enlightenment philosophers did the former, the Romantic rebellion and back-to-nature movement did the latter. *Both* thoroughly within this Descended grid of mononature, this rampant industrial ontology.

Q: Plotinus was turning in his grave?

KW: One can only imagine. Let me repeat that for Plato or Plotinus—or Emerson or Eckhart or Lady Tsogyal—nature is an *expression* of Spirit. In fact, for Plotinus, both mind and nature are expressions of Spirit, and Spirit *transcends* and *includes* both mind and nature in an integral embrace of One Taste. Or likewise with Buddhism: the Dharmakaya of Spirit gives rise to the Sambhogakaya of mind which gives rise to the Nirmanakaya of body and form and nature.

But to acknowledge *only* the Nirmanakaya? Only nature? This is the collapse of the Kosmos into empirical flatland. This is the palpable effect of the industrial ontology that began to invade and colonize and dominate the other domains—whereupon the *only* reality is nature.

Thus, only in the wake of Descended modernity could you have a Marx, a Feuerbach, a Comte. But likewise, only in the wake of modernity could you have the fully developed nature Romantics and ecophilosophers. They are all working the same side of the street, the same flatland, and finding their god, such as it is, in the Descended world of sensory nature, held secretly in place by the industrial grid. They are embracing the world depicted in figure 15-4.

Q: So this means that the Eco-Romantic movement is not a rebellion against industry but a product of industry.

KW: In many ways, yes. The belief that empirical nature is the ultimate reality—that *is* the industrial ontology. The Eco-Romantics rejected the industry but kept the ontology, and did so in the most loyal fashion. In other words, they rejected the superficial problem while embracing the deeper disaster. Like a battered kidnap victim, they fell in love with their captors.

The religion of Gaia, the worship of nature, is simply one of the main forms of industrial religion, of industrial spirituality, and it perpetuates that industrial paradigm.

Q: But the magical-foraging structure, for example, worshipped nature.

KW: No, that's not quite right. It simply wasn't differentiated from nature. That's an entirely different structure. *That* magical nature was animistically alive with egocentric impulse and undifferentiated feelings. The nature that the modern Eco-Romantics adore is necessarily a differentiated nature. Modern Romantics do not actually think that the clouds move because the clouds are following them, and they do not think the volcano exploded because it is mad at them personally (unless they're severely regressed to borderline pathology).

No, the modern nature worshipped by the Eco-Romantics is a fully differentiated nature. And that nature is the supreme reality for them. In other words, they worship the nature that was disclosed by the differentiation of the Big Three. And they think that this nature is the only reality. That is, they have made a god out of the modern collapse of the Big Three to the Big One; they have made a god of monological nature. Mononature, and mononature alone, is real. It is their God, their Goddess.

And that *collapse* of the Big Three to the Big One, we were saying, was largely the result of industrialization. The *collapse* was *held in place* by the *power* of industrialization.

In other words, the nature worshipped by the Eco-Romantics is the flatland nature of industrialization. It is the *same* mononature. The worship of Gaia is a product, and an action, of industrialization, and this worship of Gaia perpetuates the empirical-industrial paradigm. It perpetuates the primary reality of the sensorimotor world. It perpetuates the collapse of the Kosmos.

And this modern Descended grid is destroying Gaia, because it guts the interior dimensions where mutual accord and intersubjective wisdom can actually be found. The religion of Gaia is simply one of the ways the modern Descended grid reproduces itself. We might say, the cunning of the Descended grid. The modern Descended grid is destroying Gaia, and the religion of Gaia is simply one of its basic strategies.

Q: Now there's irony.

KW: Well, you know, modernity, irony.

The essential point is that the Descended grid actually destroys each of the Big Three—destroys mind and culture and nature—because it perpetuates their dissociation, their lack of integration, so that the torn fragments continue to bleed to death. Not just Gaia or nature, but also consciousness and culture are all devastated by their fragmentation and reduction.

It follows—yes?—that the ecocrisis is in large measure the result of the continued dissociation of the Big Three. We cannot align nature and culture and consciousness; we cannot align nature and morals and mind. We are altogether fragmented in this modernity gone slightly mad.

Yet it is the integration of the Big Three, and not the privileging of any one domain, that is our salvation, if such indeed exists. It is an integral vision that holds our promise. But as long as we continue to live within the Descended grid of flatland, then this integration is effectively prevented. The Eco-Romantic solution—back to nature!—is thus no solution at all, but merely the perpetuation of the Descended grid, the industrial grid.

Q: They are definitely anti-transcendence.

KW: Yes, since Descenders generally believe that transcendence or Ascent of any form is evil, they think that transcendence destroys Gaia. Those who make this claim, I believe, are confusing the mythic form of dissociative "transcendence" (which indeed is earth-denying) with transcendence in general, which is simply the form of interior development and evolution of consciousness—which is the actual path of earth-saving! But once that confusion is made, then these critics do tend to become very vocal about this, as you say. Transcendence ruins Gaia! Transcendence is the beginning of all evil!

This is the modern industrial grid speaking through their mouths. Despite the best of intentions, they are caught in the all-pervading industrial ontology of the modern and postmodern flatland. They think transcendence is destroying Gaia, whereas transcendence is the only way fragments can be joined and integrated and thereby saved. They confuse transcendence and repression; they confuse differentiation and dissociation; they confuse actualization hierarchies with dominator hierarchies. No transcendence! Just get closer to nature—closer to the Descended grid—precisely the cause of the problem, not the cure.

It is in that Descended grid that the modern and postmodern world now moves—or flounders. This Descended grid determines our goals, our desires, our consumption, our salvation. It largely governs the mainstream culture as well as the counterculture. The conformist and the avant-garde equally sing its praises. It upholds the champions of modernity and equally tucks the haters of modernity into its unsuspected fold. It is fully behind the Ego assaults and equally embraces the Eco movements. It dashes to hell any Ascent at all, and whispers in the ear of each and all: I am here for you.

Modernity smashes its head against the iron bars of this Descended grid, and calls the spilled blood knowledge. It wails with the anguish of those self-inflicted wounds, and calls that anguish authenticity. It commits itself to a deadening embrace of this flattened grid, and calls that death grip passion. And it wishes, above all else, to prove its dedication to this merciless Descent, and calls that servitude salvation. The Descended grid has sunk its unrelenting claws into everything that moves.

And—for the greatest irony in today's world—those in whom the claws are sunk most deeply are made to sing its praises most loudly.

16

The Ego and the Eco

Q: We are in search of a more integral vision, an "all-level, all-quadrant" vision. This would unite the best of ancient wisdom (all-level) with the best of modernity (all-quadrant). One of the primary roadblocks to this integral vision is the embrace of the purely Descended world, the world of flatland.

KW: Yes, I believe so. Of course, individuals can always adopt an integral view for themselves. But the hope is that one would have some sort of support for this holistic and integral vision from the culture at large.

Q: Some sort of widespread "post-flatland" view.

KW: Yes, that's right. And various sorts of "post-flatland" rebellions actually began shortly after the Enlightenment—rebellions against the flatland view of the Enlightenment. Understanding these attempts at a post-flatland view will bring us right up to the present, and to the possibility of a truly integral worldview.

Q: The post-Enlightenment or postmodern rebellions. These began sometime between the eighteenth and nineteenth centuries.

KW: Yes. The profound contradictions in the fundamental Enlightenment paradigm soon generated a series of world-shaking developments, pitting the positive gains of modernity against its ugly underbelly. The *dignities* of modernity clashed with the *disasters* of modernity, and we are all still living in the smoking ruins of that extraordinary battle. A battle we could call the Ego versus the Eco.

Ego versus Eco

Q: In the battle between the rational Enlightenment—which you simply refer to as "the Ego camps"—and nature Romanticism—which you call "the Eco camps"—for all their differences, you maintain that both of them were thoroughly caught in the modern Descended grid.

KW: Yes. Particularly under the onslaught of industrialization, the purely Descended worldview was crashing down with a vengeance. The great web of interwoven its was settling over the modern and postmodern mind like a wet blanket.

Small wonder, then, that what both the rational Enlightenment and nature Romanticism had in common was this purely industrial ontology as an ultimate reference point. Both of them were fundamentally oriented to flatland, to the Right-Hand world of empirical, sensory, objective nature, which was the "really real" world. Both of them, in other words, thoroughly accepted the world as depicted in figure 15-4. But with a difference: the Ego camps wanted to stand back from nature and map it in a disinterested, rational, calculating, scientific fashion, whereas the Eco camps wanted to get closer to nature with feelings and sympathetic communion.

So the difference is that where the Ego-Enlightenment approached the flat and Descended world with rational and industrious calculation, the Eco-Romantics approached it through feeling, sentiment, and emotion. In feelings, we could become one with flatland, one with nature, one with the world of form, and this "oneness" with the phenomenal world, with the Descended world, was thought to be salvation. The nature Romantics didn't want to control flatland, they wanted to become one with it.

The Flatland Twins

Q: Since both Ego and Eco are caught in flatland, why even bother with their squabbles?

KW: Because both of them maintained that they were overcoming the problems inherent in the dissociation of the Big Three, whereas both of them were actually contributing to the disaster.

Q: So what was the difference between them? Because they sharply disagreed on many issues.

KW: Yes. Within the purely Descended grid, they moved in two diametrically opposed directions.

The rational Ego camp—the basic Enlightenment camp, from Descartes to Locke to Fichte—generally had a desire to control, calculate, even subdue the world of nature. The life in nature was solitary, poor, nasty, brutish, and short—and at any rate, quite amoral—and so they understandably felt that the job of the rational Ego was to extricate itself from this brutish and amoral net. The job of the Ego was to *disengage* from the net of nature. Hence this rational Ego is often referred to as the disengaged self, the unencumbered self, the autonomous self, and so on (which we can see in figure 15-4: the "autonomous" Ego dangling in midair).

The Eco-Romantic rebellion found this intolerable, primarily because it introduced a massive dualism or rift between the ego and the world of nature. The founders of the broad Eco-Romantic rebellion—in various ways, Rousseau, Herder, the Schlegels, Schiller, Novalis, Coleridge, Wordsworth, Whitman—wanted above all else to introduce what they felt was some measure of wholeness, harmony, union between self and world. And especially they wanted to see the self and nature united in a broad current of cosmic Life. Not a distancing representation, but a sympathetic insertion into this great web of nature, the ultimate reality toward which all actions and all knowledge must be geared. In short, they wanted oneness with themselves by finding a oneness with nature.

But note, it's the same nature. It's the same sensorimotor nature of the Ego camps, only now approached with an entirely different intent— not to control it or calculate it or dominate it, but rather to become one with it, and thus find "wholeness" in themselves as well.

Q: They were both enthralled with the voice of sensory nature.

KW: Yes. This is why Charles Taylor is able to demonstrate (in his massive *Sources of the Self*) that the Enlightenment and Romantic versions of nature were *both* based on the same modern conception of nature, namely, nature as a great interlocking order or system of empirical processes that is itself the ultimate or foundational reality. The Ego would "reflect" on this reality (the "mirror of nature"), and the Eco would become one with it—but it was the same IT in both cases.

Q: So we have the Ego-Enlightenment on the one hand, and the Eco-Romantic rebellion on the other.

KW: In the most general sense, yes. With the collapse of the Kosmos, there emerged from the shattered debris these two crippled survivors. Whereupon there then commenced an extraordinary battle between these two camps, both despising each other, both convinced they had the solutions to modernity's dissociations, and yet both thoroughly locked within the same Descended grid that was in fact the cause of the problem—and a grid that was never once seriously questioned.

The Ego's Truth

Q: So this war. . . .

KW: The problem was that both the Ego and the Eco camps had undeniable truths that they had latched on to—scraps of truth that had managed to survive the collapse of the Kosmos—and their respective truths were so important and so crucial that neither side would let go of them, understandably.

Q: Start with the important truths of the Ego camp.

KW: The reason that the Ego camps, particularly as they began to evolve away from empiricism and toward Kant and Fichte—the reason they wanted to "get out" of nature was primarily the fact that in sensory nature, there are no conscious moral values. In the Right-Hand world of its, there are no Left-Hand morals!

In the interior or Left-Hand domains, we saw that the human being is at first biocentric and egocentric, lost in its own impulses and incapable of taking the role of other. As egocentric gives way to sociocentric, the human being starts to treat others of its group with the same courtesy it extends to itself. And then with worldcentric morality, the human being attempts to treat all humans with equal dignity or at least equal opportunity. (And with further development into the World Soul, all sentient beings are extended this courtesy, even if they can't respond.)

The rational Ego camps, at their best, represented a postconventional and worldcentric morality, a universal pluralism, and, as we saw, this was part of the dignity of the democratization movements of the Enlightenment. And they were quite right to point out that worldcentric morality exists *nowhere in the world of sensory nature.*

Of course, there is plenty of altruism in nature, but only as an unconscious display of functional fit and genetic inclusion. A consciously worldcentric moral stance is found only in humans, and, as a matter of fact, this worldcentric stance is reached only by a relatively small number of highly developed humans (greater depth, less span).

To reach this higher and relatively rare stance of universal care, I must rise above my natural *biocentric* impulses (sex and survival), my *egocentric* wishes, and my *ethnocentric* proclivities—and stand instead as a relatively *worldcentric* locus of moral awareness that insists on universal compassion. And that freedom from shallower engagements is exhilarating, because it has plugged me into a higher or deeper or truer self.

I am, of course, summarizing Immanuel Kant. And this was part of the extraordinary and exhilarating appeal of Kant. It is only by rising above my egocentric impulses, and my natural desires, and my conformist or ethnocentric perspectives—all of which Kant called "heteronomy"—it is only by rising above these shallower stances, only by taking a deeper or higher perspective, a worldcentric perspective, that I find my own highest aspirations and my own truest self. (We would say, I have evolved to at least fulcrum-5 or 6).

It is only *then* that I become capable of universal care and universal compassion, which is a freedom from the shallowness of these lesser engagements. It is only by Ascending, only by *transcending* these lower orders, that I rise above these baser instincts and find a more universal and tolerant stance. If I reduce reality to the Right-Hand world of mononature, I lose all of that!

For an entire age, Kant stood for moral freedom in worldcentric awareness, precisely by beginning to transcend the merely Descended world, the flatland world where only its and surfaces and valueless objects rule. And this indeed was the beginning of the major *modern* current of Ascent and transcendental awareness, which attempted to break out of the Descended grid of empirical nature, where conscious morals cannot be found.

Kant was outraged—or at any rate, rudely awakened from his dogmatic slumber—by Hume's perfectly mindless empiricism, and Kant responded with what many consider to be the finest and most sophisticated philosophy the West has ever produced. Whatever we decide about that, Kant's transcendental idealism was certainly impressive by any standards, and almost all modern transcendental currents, to the extent that they could be heard at all, would trace a large part of their heritage to Kant—Fichte, Schelling, Hölderlin, Hegel, Schopenhauer, Nietzsche, Bradley, Husserl, Heidegger. . . . Kant, we might say, was the first important modern to do noble and heroic battle with the trolls and troglodytes.

And so there was the Ego's enduring truth. Only in the Left-Hand currents of the Kosmos can we find a higher and wider stance that allows universal tolerance and compassion to flourish. Only with a Left-Hand path can compassion be introduced into the Right-Hand world.

The Ego's Problem

Q: But you said the Ego camps, including Kant, had some severe limitations.

KW: Well, there's a very big problem in all this. Granted that every-thing Kant said is true enough; granted that this worldcentric moral stance is found nowhere in the categories that frame sensory nature, but only in practical or ethical mind; and granted that nature in that sense is something that must be transcended. But then how do you *integrate* mind and nature? How do you not only *transcend* but also *include* na-ture? What about this split between mind and nature? The split between Left and Right? The split between Ego and Eco? Not just their differenti-ation but their dissociation? Because this split is also a split *within my own being*—my mind and my body are split as well. Mind is split from external nature and from internal nature. And what about *that*? Is the price of morality dissociation?

And Kant had no final answer to this, although he attempted to heal the split between the knowledge of morals and the knowledge of nature via aesthetics. Note that he is *trying to integrate the Big Three*—aesthetics, morals, science—which are still flying apart, and Kant cannot pull them together, try as he might.

We saw that the great *advance* of modernity was to differentiate the Big Three, and this Kant does admirably—his three great critiques deal with science, ethics, and art. But we also saw that the great *failure* of modernity was its incapacity to integrate the Big Three, and in this failure Kant was no exception, as critics (such as Hegel) would soon point out.

So in the wake of Kant—that is, in the wake of modernity—we are faced with the massive conundrum: mind and morals and nature, and how could they ever be united? Not re-united!, because they were *never* united or integrated in the first place (because they had never been differ-entiated in the first place). This differentiation was utterly new, and so was the dissociation—and *that* was the blood all over the brand-new carpet.

Here was the nightmare of the industrial wasteland, a nightmare hu-manity had never before seen, a nightmare Kant spots and brilliantly works, but a nightmare from which he cannot awaken us.

The Ego and Repression

Q: So apart from the Ego's truth, there was still this massive rift between mind and nature.

KW: Yes. And here we find the major, and I think very accurate, criticism of the Ego camps. Granted they introduced a measure of tran-scendence, but, *as always*, transcendence can simply go too far and be-come *repression*.

The rational Ego wanted to rise above nature and its own bodily impulses, so as to achieve a more universal compassion found nowhere in nature, but it often simply repressed these natural impulses instead: repressed its own biosphere; repressed its own life juices; repressed its own vital roots. The Ego tended to *repress* both external nature and internal nature (the id). And this repression, no doubt, would have something to do with the emergence of a Sigmund Freud, sent exactly at this time (and never before this time) to doctor the dissociations of modernity. (This dissociation is well represented in figure 15-4, where the Ego is dangling in midair, cut off from its own body and from the exterior world.)

All of these dualisms understandably vexed the Romantics no end. The Ego seemed to be introducing splits and dualisms and dissociations everywhere, and the Romantics wanted above all else to find instead a *wholeness* and *harmony* and *union.*

The Ego was quite happy to continue mapping the world in an objective and monological fashion, which, of course, disenchanted the world in the process. The detached and disengaged Ego would simply map this world of empirical nature with representational knowledge. If the Ego *disenchanted* nature in the process, so much the better! It is precisely by disenchanting nature that the Ego frees itself! The disenchantment of the world—fine with me, said the Ego, fine with me.

But the Eco camps were absolutely alarmed, and pointed out that this disenchantment was fast becoming disembowelment. Repression, dissociation, desiccation. There is what the rational Ego has brought us! A disenchanted world. And the Eco camps arose directly in response to this wretched disenchantment, and they took it upon themselves to re-enchant the world.

The wild, fabulous, amazing, and extraordinary attempt at re-enchantment had finally begun.

The Re-enchantment of the World

Q: So the Eco camps began with a criticism of the rational Ego.

KW: Yes, basically. Most of the Romantic criticisms could be summarized as an extreme uneasiness with the Ego's *repressive* tendencies. The rational Ego—that great autonomous master of its universe—had in fact simply sealed out and ignored its prepersonal roots as well its transpersonal illuminations. It had cut off, or pretended to cut off, its subconscious juices as well as its superconscious inspirations. And so for all of its wonderful accomplishments, the autonomous Ego had nonetheless left massive roadkill everywhere on the highway to rational heaven.

And it was especially this *repression* that the Romantic rebellion would focus on.

Q: The criticism was true.

KW: Yes, there is much truth to that criticism, and this is where the Romantic camps attacked. They found this repressive split between morals and nature, or mind and nature, or mind and body, or Ego and Eco—those are all the same split—they found this split to be intolerable. They understandably wanted *wholeness* and *unity*. So where Kant and Fichte would talk endlessly of the *autonomy* of the self from nature and nature's baser instincts, the Romantics would talk endlessly of *uniting* with nature in some sort of vital and expressive union, in some great *unitary* stream of Life and Love.

The desirability and necessity of healing this split between morals and nature—this was the great truth the Romantics came to announce, and it is a truth that is as enduring in its own way as the Kantian notion of the necessity for transcendence.

Q: But something has to give.

KW: Yes, at this historical point we reach total gridlock, complete philosophical gridlock, an utter standoff between the Ego and the Eco camps. How can you possibly reconcile these two positions? How can you reconcile the necessity to rise above nature with a necessity to become one with it?

This is still the crucial problem, isn't it? How can you reconcile Ego and Eco? This is still the critical dilemma in today's world, yes?

The Ego camp, we just saw, had no satisfactory answer. But the Eco-Romantic solution was notoriously just as unsatisfactory, by almost everybody's account, and their "solution" of the "one Life stream" was vigorously attacked by the Ego camps. How, the Ego camps sarcastically asked, can you unite with nature, become one with nature, act only on nature's impulses, and yet still preserve the worldcentric and postconventional morality that we have all fought so hard to secure?

The Romantic response was lame in the extreme, and centered mostly on defining "nature" in two very different and utterly contradictory ways, and they simply switched back and forth between these two definitions as suited their purposes.

Back to Nature

Q: The Romantics had two different definitions of nature?

KW: Yes. First they maintained, in true Descended fashion, that empirical nature is the one reality, the all-inclusive and all-embracing reality. This, of course, is the modern Descended grid, and the Romantics swallowed it hook, line, and sinker. And yet culture, they maintained, has grievously *deviated* from this nature, it has *split* from this nature, it has lost touch with the great life stream, it is ruining nature.

Q: The ecophilosophers still maintain that.

KW: Yes, but look at the two very different and contradictory definitions of nature hidden in that statement. First, nature is supposed to be the one single reality of which all organisms, including the human, are part. In this sense, nature is absolutely *all-inclusive*, nothing is outside of it. It is the ultimate and all-embracing reality, and everything that occurs is an activity of this ultimate reality.

But two, culture is supposed to have *deviated* from this nature. Culture has to some degree split itself from nature. Culture, in fact, is ruining nature. So now we have *two* natures: a nature that you can't deviate from, versus a nature that you can. And clearly they can't be the same thing. They sneaked in two natures.

So what is the relation of this Nature with a capital N that embraces *everything*, versus this nature that is *different* from culture because it is getting ruined by culture?

Q: The big Nature is supposed to include and unify culture and nature.

KW: Yes, and so again, what is the relation of Nature and nature? See, this was the whole problem.

The entire Romantic movement crashed and went up in flames over this internal contradiction. What the best of the Romantics were trying to say is that Nature with a big N is Spirit, is the entire Kosmos (both Left and Right), because Spirit does indeed *transcend* and *include* both culture and nature. And that is fine, that is true enough.

But because the Romantics were caught in the incredibly pervasive Descended grid, they simply identified Nature with nature. They identified Spirit with sensory nature. They identified Spirit with the visible, sensible, Right-Hand world, taken as a whole. They identified Spirit with the great web of nature.

And here they went up in smoke, a spectacularly narcissistic, egocentric, flamboyant explosion—because the closer you get to preconventional nature, the more egocentric you become. And in search of Nature, the Romantics headed back to nature.

The Eco and Regression

Q: So the collapse of the Kosmos is the same as the collapse of Nature to nature.

KW: Yes, that's right. Now, if you are Ego and deny any sort of spiritual reality anyway, then fine, you'll simply map this empirical nature in a disengaged fashion, no problem. You are a happy, mindless, mapping fool.

But if you are tender-hearted, and if you are open to spiritual experiences—and yet you are still inadvertently trapped in the industrial ontology—then you will simply equate Spirit with sensory nature. Your spiritual *intuition* is probably very genuine, but your *interpretation* occurs within the orbit of the industrial grid. The only reality there is— Right-Hand empirical nature—must *therefore* be the ultimate spiritual reality as well.

So even if you have a direct experience of the World Soul, or even the Nondual—pow!, it's interpreted as coming from sensory nature. The industrial grid, operating preconsciously, beats you to the interpretation, and you are secretly caught in that flatland framework.

And thus instead of *moving forward* in *evolution* to the emergence of a Nature or Spirit (or World Soul) that would indeed unify the differentiated mind and nature, you simply recommend "back to nature." Not forward to Nature, but back to nature.

Q: This regressive trend is characteristic of many Romantic movements, down to today's ecophilosophers.

KW: In many cases, yes. And here is where this regressive move becomes so historically important, becomes an incredibly influential current in the modern and postmodern world:

If nature or the biosphere is the only fundamental reality—if it is actually "spirit"—then, the Romantics announced, anything that *moves away from nature* must be *killing* spirit. Culture moves away from nature, and so culture must be killing spirit. So if sensory nature is the ultimately Real, then *culture* must be the original Crime.

And we are not simply talking about the fact that culture can go too far and repress nature; we are not talking about the fact that the mind can repress the body's impulses—granted all of that is true enough. The Romantic objection was much deeper and much stronger. Something about culture itself necessarily disrupted nature, and since nature is the sole spiritual reality, something about culture per se was antispiritual. Culture, in fact, was the original Crime against a primal Paradise of natural freedom and spiritual abundance.

This "spiritual insight" is the core of most Eco-Romantic movements, then and now. And yet this "insight" is not really spiritual in any profound sense; it is an interpretation framed largely within the secret requirements of the industrial grid. It is simply one of the numerous hidden ways that the modern Descended grid defends itself against any transcendence, defends itself against any genuine spirituality. It is a defense mechanism of a worldview that wishes to maintain the outrageous lie that finite nature alone is real. And so it must present this nature as being Spirit, and it must present anything that deviates from nature as being the devil.

And with this "insight" began the extremely influential movements of "back to nature," of "the noble savage," of a "Paradise Lost," of a primal Eden that had been disrupted and distorted by the horrible Crime of Culture.

To find a purer reality, a truer self, a more genuine feeling, and a fairer community, we must get back prior to the Crime of Culture and rediscover a historical past in which this Crime had not occurred. And once we find this Paradise Lost, we must, as a social agenda, make it the Promised Land by reverting to or incorporating the original, primal, pristine way of life into the modern world.

And here begins the retro-Romantic slide.

Paradise Lost

Q: This slide seems to appear in many different areas, from the original Romantics to many of the modern ecophilosophers.

KW: Well, it's very easy to see how it got started. Modernity had managed to differentiate the Big Three for the first time in history—and this included differentiating mind and nature. But because modernity could not yet integrate them, the Big Three tended to drift into dissociation, and this the Romantics rightly reacted to with alarm. This reaction was completely understandable; quite noble, in fact, and I believe we can all applaud the Romantics for trying to do *something* about it.

Since this dissociation was so alarming, the Romantics did the obvious but, it now appears, naive thing—they thought the problem was the differentiation itself: we simply never should have differentiated the Big Three to begin with. Failing to see that differentiation is the *necessary prelude* to *integration*, the Romantic solution was to simply head back to those days prior to the differentiation. Not prior to the *dissociation*—which would have been right—but prior to the differentiation itself!—which was the regressive slide. The only way to cure the problems of the oak is to go back to being an acorn!

And the only way to do that is to get back to the good ole days when culture and nature were undifferentiated, back to humanity's acornness, back prior to this horrible Crime that humanity had committed against nature. History was therefore depicted as a series of horrifying errors that led humanity further and further away from the original pristine state where mind and nature were "one," conveniently overlooking the fact that this original "pristine state" had none of the disasters of modernity precisely because it had none of the dignities either. For the Romantics, the oak was somehow a horrible violation of the acorn, and humanity's job was to rediscover and get back to its acornness.

Q: Whereas the real solution might be, what?

KW: We can probably all agree that typical or conventional culture is not often imbued with a great deal of genuine spirituality. But the remedy is to go post-conventional, not pre-conventional. The remedy is to go post-conventional in Spirit, not pre-conventional in nature. Spirit transcends and includes both culture and nature, and thus integrates and unifies both.

But if you recommend going back to the pre-conventional state, back to acornness, back to the original "pristine" state of nature, then you have not integrated the differentiations, you have simply obliterated them by regressing to a point before they emerged at all. You recommend magical indissociation or mythic immersion, hypocritically taking advantage of the dignities and freedoms of modernity while you endlessly complain about how rotten it all is.

This is not translogical Spirit; it is certainly not the dreaded dialogical culture; it is pure, simple, monological nature—which, by my sneaky dual definition, I have now proclaimed to be Spirit or Nature. I will get away from the Crime of Culture. I will get back to Paradise Lost. I will find the noble savage in myself. I will discover the original Eden, when none of modernity's differentiations plagued me with the burden of distinguishing my ego from reality at large. And I will then possess a damning indictment of modernity: I have found the Paradise Lost which will be the Promised Land, if only modernity will listen to me and get back to a mute and dumbfounded nature.

And in this regression from noosphere to biosphere, you are indeed released from the disasters of modernity, by releasing yourself from the dignity and the demands as well. You have cured the *repression* by *regression*.

Q: But you *can* have strong spiritual experiences in nature. This is very common. And I think that is what the nature Romantics meant by Spirit.

KW: Yes, indeed you can, but the source of these spiritual feelings is not nature itself. You might stare for hours at a sunset, and suddenly disappear into the World Soul, and feel yourself at one with all nature. This is well and good. But nature is not the source of this intuition. Worms and rats and foxes and weasels do not stare for hours at the sunset, and marvel at its beauty, and transcend themselves in that release—even though their senses are in many cases much sharper than ours, even though they see nature more clearly than we! No, nature is not the *source* of this Beauty; nature is its destination. The *source* is transcendental Spirit, of which nature is a radiant expression.

And thus when, in nature, you can relax your egoic grasping and stand as an opening or clearing in awareness—and nature is an inviting place to do so—then through that clearing might come pouring the power and the glory of the World Soul, and you are temporarily struck perfectly dead by the wonder and the beauty of it all—a beauty that takes your breath away, takes your self away, all at once—a beauty that bestows new splendor on the setting sun and renders nature insanely vivid in its display.

But if you are committed to *interpreting* this spiritual experience in a completely Descended pattern—if you are caught in the industrial grid—then you will ascribe this Spirit to simple nature itself. You will mistake the effect for the cause. You will fail to see that you got to this World Soul intuition precisely by developing from sensory-biocentric to egocentric to sociocentric to worldcentric to World Soul, each of which transcends and includes.

Thus, struck by the beauty of the World Soul that you have mistakenly reduced to sensory nature, you will recommend—not that we go from nature to culture to Spirit—but that we simply get back to nature, even though the weasel sitting next to you doesn't seem to be seeing the same thing in nature that you are—wonder why that is?

And because you now think that the World Soul or Spirit is a simple sensory impact—is nature itself—you will then start to think, not that culture is a necessary part of an evolution *on its way* to a *conscious* apprehension of Spirit as true Self, but rather that culture *hides* and *distorts* this sensory nature in which your "real self" supposedly resides. Culture is not *on the way* to the true Self, it is simply a crime against the "true self" of your biocentric feelings.

In short, you will start recommending, not that we move forward to fulcrum-7 and the Eco-Noetic Self, but that we move back to fulcrum-2 and the biocentric or ecocentric or ecological self.

Q: But when I look around me, it certainly appears that everything is a part of nature. My organism is part of nature, the landscapes, the clouds, the lakes and forests, human beings and other animals—everything is part of nature. So why couldn't an ecological approach include everything?

KW: That's just the point—when you look *around* you (the Right-Hand world). If you look *within* you (the Left-Hand world), you will find a different story, the story of the growth and evolution of consciousness itself. Those *interior* stages of growth do indeed have correlates in the world of empirical nature, just as depicted in figure 15-3. But if you reduce those interiors to their exterior correlates—reduce everything to ecology or nature or the sensorimotor world—then you land squarely in the world of interwoven its, otherwise known as flatland (just as shown in figure 15-4). A truly integral approach, on the other hand, would include both the Ego and Eco, or interiors and exteriors, or Left and Right—as we will see—but in the meantime, we are focusing on exactly those approaches that believed that "everything is part of nature," as you put it.

Q: I inadvertently bought the flatland grid.

KW: Yes, and so did the Romantics, then and now. And that tends to be regressive because it ignores the interior hierarchies and leaves us only with the sensory and material world, which pulls us into our own preconventional, egocentric levels.

Q: You said this regression was converted into a critique of modernity.

KW: Yes, the real difficulty in this approach is that it misses altogether the actual cause of modernity's problems. The real problem was the dissociation of the Big Three and their collapse to the Big One of mononature—the industrial ontology. The Romantics spotted and rejected the nastiness of industry, but not the ontology of industry. They thus attacked the superficial problem while enthusiastically promoting the deeper problem, the real nightmare.

Because the startling fact is that ecological wisdom does not consist in understanding how to live in accord with nature; it consists in understanding how to get humans to agree on how to live in accord with nature.

This wisdom is an intersubjective accord in the noosphere, not an immersion in the biosphere. No representation of the biosphere whatsoever will produce this wisdom. It can be found on none of the maps of exterior surfaces and sensory marvels; it is a path of intersubjective accord based upon mutual understanding grounded in sincerity; it has its own developmental stages, with its own logic; it can be found nowhere in empirical nature.

But if preconventional biosphere is your Goddess, then you must get back closer to sensory nature in order to be saved. And since modernity differentiated this nature, you must get back prior to that differentiation. You must in all ways go premodern.

Q: The regressive slide.

KW: Yes. And thus, where the Ego camps were perpetuating what amounted to *repression*, the Eco camps were advocating what amounted to *regression*. Repression and regression were—and are—the twin engines of the flatland game, the twin machines of industrial ontology.

The Way Back Machine

Q: The Eco-Romantics were often very specific about the lost glories of the past.

KW: Yes. Beginning in the eighteenth century, and continuing down to today, you have the Eco-Romantics basically setting their Way Back machine to the period where they felt that culture was the least differentiated from nature. The great search for Paradise Lost had begun.

Not the search for a timeless Spirit that we have alienated in this present moment by our contracting and grasping tendencies, but the search for a "spirit" that was fully present at some past time—some past historical or prehistorical period—but was then "killed" by the great Crime of Culture, or the crime of the patriarchy, or one sort of crime or another.

Q: The original Romantics were fond of Greece.

KW: Yes, for the early Romantics, such as Schiller, ancient Greece was by far the favorite stop on the Regress Express, because mind and nature were supposed to be a "unity" (they were indeed undifferentiated to any great extent). And never mind that for precisely that reason one out of three Greeks were slaves, and women and children might as well have been. There were few of the disasters of modernity, it is true—and few of the dignities either.

Ancient Greece is now quite out of favor with the Romantics, mostly because, being *agrarian*, it was patriarchal. So the Romantics set their Way Back machine one stage further back, and they arrived at *horticultural* societies. These are now by far the favorite haunt of the ecofeminists. These societies, as we saw, were often matrifocal, ruled by the Great Mother.

And let us delicately ignore the central ritual of many horticultural societies—the ritual human sacrifice, which was required, among other things, to ensure crop fertility. Let us likewise forget that, according to Lenski's massive data, an astonishing 44 percent of these societies engaged in frequent warfare and over 50 percent in intermittent warfare (which rather puts to rest the notion of the peace-loving Great Mother societies); that 61 percent had private property rights; that 14 percent had slavery; and 45 percent had bride price. These horticultural societies were anything but "pure and pristine," as the ecomasculinists themselves have pointed out.

Q: They prefer foraging.

KW: Yes, the ecomasculinists (deep ecologists) have pushed yet one stage *further back* and arrived at foraging cultures as the "pure and pristine state." And, in fact, according the ecomasculinists, the ecofeminists' beloved horticulture is not truly close to nature in a pure way, because those societies depended upon farming, which is actually a rape of the land. Hunting and gathering, now that's pure and pristine.

And let us ignore the data that show that 10 percent of these societies had slavery, 37 percent had bride price, and 58 percent engaged in frequent or intermittent warfare. This must be the pure and pristine state—because there is no further back! This *must* be it! And so I will now ignore every single unpleasant thing about any of these societies, and they will be the noble savage, period.

Although logically, of course, the thing to do is push back to apes, because they have no slavery, bride price, war, and so on. I mean, why not get serious about this retrogression and really carry it to its conclusion: everything past the Big Bang was a Big Mistake. This is the logic you get locked into if you confuse differentiation and dissociation; you think every differentiation is a mistake—you think the oak is a crime against the acorn.

And so the search for the pure and pristine state would go, pushing further and further back—scraping more and more layers of depth off the Kosmos in search of a pristine state in which the Romantic insertion into nature could occur. You cure the repression by regression. You cure the disease by getting rid of the depth. By, that is, becoming more shallow.

The Great Battle of Modernity: Fichte versus Spinoza

Q: So this historical gridlock between the Ego camps and the Eco camps. The Ego wanted to subdue the Eco, the Eco wanted to get rid of the Ego.

KW: Yes. The gridlock was, do you *transcend* nature so as to find moral freedom and autonomy, or do you become *one* with nature so as to find unity and wholeness? Are you transcendental Ego or immanent Eco?

That is, pure Ascent or pure Descent?

This fundamental problem, this recalcitrant dualism! This two-thousand-year-old battle between the Ascenders and the Descenders—the single battle that has most defined the entire Western tradition—has simply reappeared in its *modern* form as the battle between the Ego and the Eco.

And this millennia-old rivalry soon found its archetypal champions in Fichte and Spinoza.

Q: Very briefly.

KW: Very briefly: Fichte attempted to overcome the split between Ego and Eco by absolutizing the Ego, the path of Ascent. It was in the pure I, the pure transcendental Self, that liberation was to be found. And the more of the pure Ego, and the less of the Eco, then the better for everybody, said Fichte, as he bowed at the altar of the Ascending God.

The Eco-Romantics, of course, were headed in exactly the opposite direction, under the gaze of exactly the other God. They would overcome this split between Ego and Eco by absolutizing the Eco, absolutizing the path of Descent. And thus the Eco camps would find their archetypal champion in an imaginatively interpreted Spinoza (they imagined that by Nature Spinoza meant nature—but never mind, he would do just fine!). Pure freedom thus resides in a total immersion in the Great System of nature, the pure Eco. The more of the Eco, and the less of the Ego, the better for everybody, said the Romantics, as they eagerly bowed at the earth-bound altar of the purely Descending God.

Q: So we have this standoff between Ego and Eco, Fichte and Spinoza.

KW: Yes, and this wasn't a minor side issue. This was exactly the end limit of the two-thousand-year-old battle at the heart of the West's attempt to awaken. And it was an agonizing problem because everybody vaguely intuited that both camps were at least partially right. But how?

So the cry everywhere went up: We must integrate Fichte and Spinoza! Or Kant and Spinoza. Or Kant and Goethe. Variations on the same theme. This really was an obsession for an entire age, particularly toward the end of the eighteenth century.

Q: So who won?

KW: Well, it all came to the same thing: how can you transcend nature for moral freedom and yet become one with nature for wholeness? Autonomy versus wholeness. Which do you want? Freedom from nature, or freedom as nature? How can you possibly have both? How can you integrate Ascending and Descending? These fractured footnotes to Plato! Where is your salvation to be found? Where is your God to be located?

Q: In the midst of this battle came a person you are obviously quite fond of, and who perhaps solved the dilemma. In *Sex, Ecology, Spirituality*, you introduce this person by reading a letter from someone who attended the lectures. Mind if I read that letter?

KW: Go ahead.

17

The Dominance of the Descenders

Q: "Schelling is lecturing to an amazing audience, but amidst so much noise and bustle, whistling, and knocking on the windows by those who cannot get in the door, in such an overcrowded lecture hall, that one is almost tempted to give up listening to him if this is to continue. During the first lectures it was almost a matter of risking one's life to hear him. However, I have put my trust in Schelling and at the risk of my life I have the courage to hear him once more. It may very well blossom during the lectures, and if so one might gladly risk one's life—what would one not do to be able to hear Schelling?

"I am so happy to have heard Schelling's second lecture—indescribably. The embryonic child of thought leapt for joy within me when he mentioned the word 'actuality' in connection with the relation of philosophy to actuality. I remember almost every word he said after that. Here, perhaps, clarity can be achieved. This one word recalled all my philosophical pains and sufferings.—And so that she, too, might share my joy, how willingly I would return to her, how eagerly I would coax myself to believe that this is the right course—Oh, if only I could!—now I have put all my hope in Schelling. . . ."

KW: Yes, the letter is from Søren Kierkegaard, during Schelling's Berlin lectures of 1841. Attending those lectures, beside Kierkegaard, were Jakob Burkhardt, Michael Bakunin, and Friedrich Engels, collaborator of Karl Marx.

Q: So can you summarize his central point, especially about integrating mind and nature?

KW: Schelling began by saying that, if it is true that the Enlightenment had succeeded in differentiating mind and nature, it had also tended to forget the transcendental and unifying Ground of both, and thus it tended to *dissociate* mind and nature—the disaster of modernity.

This dissociation of mind and nature, Ego and Eco, with mind "mirroring" nature in scientific inquiry—what we saw as the representation paradigm—this dissociation was, of course, well under way. Representation had, Schelling pointed out, introduced a rift or cleavage between nature as external object and the reflecting self as subject—which also, he said, made humans *objects* to themselves—dehumanized humanism, as we earlier put it. And when representation is made an end in itself, it becomes "a spiritual malady," he said.

In this he was in agreement with the Romantics. In fact, Schelling was one of the principal founders of Romanticism, although he also moved quite beyond it, largely by refusing regression to nature. That is, Schelling realized that the dissociation could not be overcome by a *return* to the immediacy of feeling, "to the childhood, as it were, of the human race." There was no going back to Eco-nature, and Schelling knew it.

Rather, he maintained, we have to go forward *beyond* reason in order to discover that mind and nature are both simply different movements of one absolute Spirit, a Spirit that manifests itself in its own successive stages of unfolding. As Schelling's colleague Hegel would soon put it, Spirit is not One apart from Many, but the *very process* of the One expressing itself through the Many—it is infinite activity expressing itself in the *process of development itself*—or, as we would now say, Spirit expresses itself in the entire process of evolution.

Evolution: The Great Holarchy Unfolds in Time

Q: So this developmental or evolutionary notion was not new with Darwin.

KW: Far from it. The Great Chain theorists, beginning as early as Leibniz, began to realize that the Great Chain could best be understood as a holarchy that is not given all at once, but rather unfolds over enormous stretches of historical and geographical time—starting with matter, then the emergence of sensation in life forms, then perception, then impulse, then image, and so on.

And thus, about a century before Darwin, it was widely accepted in educated circles that the Great Chain had actually unfolded or developed over vast time. And—this was crucial—since the Great Chain contained no "gaps" or holes (because the plenitude of Spirit fills all empty spaces), the research agenda was to find any "missing links" in evolution.

Q: That's where the term actually came from?

KW: Yes, any missing links in the Chain. And so there began a massive search for the "missing links" between various species. So widespread was this understanding, so common and so taken for granted, that even the notorious circus promoter P. T. Barnum could advertise that his museum contained "the Ornithorhincus, or the connecting link between the seal and the duck; two distinct species of flying fish, which undoubtedly connect the bird and the fish; the Mud Iguana, a connecting link between reptiles and fish—with other animals forming connecting links in the Great Chain of animated Nature." That's two decades before Darwin published *Origin of Species*!

Q: That's hilarious.

KW: It's also fascinating. All of this looking for the missing links. It was behind the search for microorganisms, whose existence Leibniz had already deduced solely on the basis of the Great Chain—microorganisms simply *had* to be there to fill in certain apparent gaps in the Chain. It was behind the belief in life on other planets, which Giordano Bruno had deduced on the basis of the Great Chain. And the missing links between species—all of this was based, not initially on empirical or scientific evidence, but directly on the belief in the Great Chain.

Q: A Neoplatonic idea.

KW: Yes, all of this, in one way or another, goes back to Plotinus. Spirit is so full and complete, he said, that when it empties itself into creation, it leaves no place untouched—it leaves no holes or gaps or missing links. And Plotinus's Great Holarchy is the way these links or levels connect and include and nest each other, all the way from matter to God.

Now, if you take that Great Holarchy, exactly as presented by Plotinus (fig. 14-1), and if you realize that it unfolds in time—unfolds over vast stretches of time—then you basically have today's general understanding of the major stages of evolution. Evolution does indeed proceed from matter to sensation to perception to impulse to image to symbol, and so on.

Except, of course, we moderns, committed to a Descended grid, have no higher stages of evolution beyond reason, and we interpret the entire Great Chain in merely empirical and natural terms—which is precisely why we can't understand or explain the self-transcending drive of this evolution that has nonetheless become our modern god!

But the central point is that Plotinus temporalized equals evolution. And this was all worked out and widely accepted a century before Darwin. Schelling wrote the transcendental philosophy around 1800. We have P. T. Barnum's advertisement around 1840. Darwin published around 1860, decades after people were already going to museums to see the "missing links."

What Darwin and Wallace contributed to this already-accepted notion was the theory, not of evolution, but of evolution by natural selection—which, it turns out, can't explain macroevolution at all! Which is why Wallace always maintained that natural selection itself was not the cause but the *result* of "Spirit's manner and mode of creation," and even Darwin was most reluctant to remove Spirit from the nature of evolution.

And so, if you had to pick two of the philosophers who, after Plato, had the broadest impact on the Western mind, they very well might be Plotinus and then Schelling. For this reason alone: Plotinus gave the Great Holarchy its fullest expression, and Schelling set the Great Holarchy afloat in developmental time, in evolution. And if there is one idea that dominates the modern and postmodern mind at large, it is evolution.

And we are at the point, historically, that it is beginning to be understood that the Great Holarchy evolved over time. And standing at that crucial watershed is Schelling.

Evolution: Spirit-in-Action

Q: I take it that for Schelling, development or evolution was still a spiritual movement.

KW: It's hard to understand any other way, and Schelling knew it. Spirit is present at each and every stage of the evolutionary process, *as the very process itself*. As Hegel would soon put it, the Absolute is "the process of its own becoming; it becomes concrete or actual only by its development."

Q: Here is a quote from Hegel: "That the history of the world, with all the changing scenes which its annals present, is this process of development and the realization of Spirit—only *this* insight can reconcile Spirit with the history of the world—that what has happened, and is happening every day, is not only not 'without God', but is essentially God's work."

KW: Yes, which is why Zen would say, "That which one can deviate from is not the true Tao."

Schelling's point is that nature is not the only reality, and mind is not the only reality. *Spirit is the only reality.* But in order to create the manifest world, Spirit must go out of itself, empty itself, into manifestation. Spirit descends into manifestation, but this manifestation is nevertheless Spirit itself, a form or expression of Spirit itself.

So Spirit first goes out of itself to produce nature, which is simply *objective* Spirit. At this point in evolution Spirit is still *un-self-conscious*. Thus the whole of nature Schelling refers to as *slumbering Spirit*. Nature is not a mere inert and instrumental backdrop for mind, as the Ego camps maintained. Rather, nature is a "self-organizing dynamic system" that is "*the objective manifestation of Spirit*"—precisely Plato's "visible, sensible God," but now set developmentally afloat.

So nature is most definitely not a static or deterministic machine. For Schelling, nature is "God-in-the-making." The very processes of nature are *spiritual processes*—they are *striving* for spiritual awakening—because they are objective Spirit striving to actualize itself (Eros).

And so here Schelling is acknowledging the major contention of the Eco-Romantics—nature indeed is *not* a mechanical and doltish backdrop; *nature is spiritual to the core.* But slumbering Spirit, because Spirit has not yet become self-conscious, the Kosmos has not yet begun to consciously *reflect on itself.*

With the emergence of mind, Spirit becomes self-conscious, which, among other things, introduces conscious morals into the world, morals found nowhere in nature. And these morals represent an advance in consciousness over what can be found in slumbering nature. And here Schelling is acknowledging the rational-Ego camps and their undeniable contributions.

Spirit is starting to awaken to itself. Spirit seeks to know itself through symbols and concepts, and the result is that the universe begins to think about the universe—which produces the world of reason and, in particular, the world of conscious morals. Thus, says Schelling, where nature is *objective Spirit*, mind is *subjective Spirit.*

But unlike the Ego camps, Schelling is insisting that the Ego itself is simply one moment in the overall arc of Spirit's self-actualization. He refuses to stop with either the Eco or the Ego schools. Schelling is heading for the Nondual.

But he freely concedes that at this historical point—where mind and nature become differentiated—there does indeed appear to be a massive rift in the world, namely, between the reflecting mind and the reflected nature. But unlike the radical Ego camps, who want the mind to be supreme, and unlike the pure Eco camps, who want nature to be supreme, Schelling sees that both of them are necessary but partial moments on the way to a Spirit that will transcend and include them both, and thus awaken to its own supreme identity.

Q: So with modernity we are temporarily stuck with this battle between mind and nature, between Ego and Eco.

KW: Yes, this painful birth of modernity's acute self-consciousness is a necessary part of Spirit's awakening. We moderns must go through the fire. And no other period has had to face this fire on a collective scale. Going backward simply avoids the fire, it does not transform it.

So Schelling insists that instead of going back prior to this split, we rather must go forward beyond the Ego and beyond the Eco, both of which pretend to be "absolute." But these two "apparent absolutes," as he calls them, are *synthesized* in the third great movement of Spirit, which is the transcendence of *both* nature and mind and thus their radical union.

Q: With Fichte and Spinoza in mind.

KW: Exactly. With the pure Ego and the pure Eco in mind. This *nondual* synthesis, according to Schelling, is also the identity of subject and object in one timeless act of self-knowledge, of Spirit *directly knowing itself* as Spirit, a direct mystical intuition, says Schelling, that is *not mediated* through *any forms*, whether those forms be the *feelings* of objective nature or the *thoughts* of subjective mind.

And here we have an unmistakable and profound glimpse of the formless and nondual groundless Ground, the pure Emptiness of One Taste. Schelling would often refer to the "indifference" and the "Abyss," precisely in the lineage of Eckhart and Boehme and Dionysius. "In the ultimate dark Abyss of the divine Being, the primal ground or Urgrund, there is no differentiation but only pure identity." What we have been calling the Supreme Identity.

Thus, for Schelling (and for his friend and student Hegel), Spirit goes out of itself to produce objective nature, awakens to itself in subjective mind, and then recovers itself in pure Nondual awareness, where subject and object are one pure immediacy that unifies both nature and mind in realized Spirit.

And so: Spirit knows itself objectively as *nature*; knows itself subjectively as *mind*; and knows itself absolutely as *Spirit*—the Source, the Summit, and the Eros of the entire sequence.

Glimmers of the Nondual

Q: These three broad movements can also be referred to as subconscious, self-conscious, and superconscious.

KW: Or prepersonal, personal, and transpersonal; or prerational, rational, and transrational; or biosphere, noosphere, and theosphere, not to put too fine a point on it.

Q: So how exactly does this vision integrate the gains of both the Ego and the Eco without just forcing them together?

KW: Schelling's key insight was that the Spirit that is *realized* in a conscious fashion in the supreme identity is in fact the Spirit that was *present all along* as the *entire process* of evolution itself. All of Spirit, so to speak, is present at every stage, as the process of unfolding itself. But at each stage Spirit unfolds more of itself, realizes more of itself, and thus moves from slumber in nature to awakening in mind to final realization as Spirit itself. But the Spirit that is *realized* is the same Spirit that was present all along, as the entire process of its own awakening.

So, to answer your question specifically, Schelling could integrate Ego and Eco—Fichte and Spinoza, autonomy and wholeness—because, he pointed out, when you realize your supreme identity as Spirit, then you are *autonomous* in the fullest sense—because nothing is outside you— and therefore you are also *whole* or *unified* in the fullest sense—because nothing is outside you. Full autonomy and full wholeness are one and the same thing in the supreme identity.

So men and women don't have to sacrifice their own autonomy or will because their will ultimately aligns itself with the entire Kosmos. The entire Kosmos is something your deepest Self is doing, and you *are* that Kosmos in its entirety. Full autonomy, full wholeness.

This is a profound integration of Ego and Eco, of Ascent and Descent, of transcendence and immanence, of Spirit *descending* into even the lowest state and *ascending* back to itself, but with Spirit nonetheless fully present at each and every stage as the process of its own self-realization, a divine play of Spirit present in every single movement of the Kosmos, yet finding more and more of itself as its own Play proceeds, dancing fully and divine in every gesture of the universe, never really lost and never really found, but present from the start and all along, a wink and a nod from the radiant Abyss.

Always Already

Q: And what exactly separated this vision from the Eco-Romantic vision?

KW: The pure Romantics, then and now, would never admit that mind and Spirit transcend nature, because nothing transcends nature.

There is *only* nature, and mind and Spirit are somehow the same as this nature, or the sum total of this nature, or strands in the web of this nature.

And so most of all, the Eco-Romantics could not understand that "that which you can deviate from is not the true Tao." The ecophilosophers keep telling us what we have *deviated* from, which shows that they are aware of nature, but not Nature. They do not seem to have understood the true Tao or Spirit.

According to the Idealists—and the Nondual sages everywhere—the extraordinary and altogether paradoxical secret is that the Final Release is *always already* accomplished. The "last step" is to step off the cycle of time altogether, and find the Timeless there *from the start*, ever-present from the very beginning and at *every point* along the way, with no deviations whatsoever.

"The Good," says Hegel, "the absolutely Good, is eternally accomplishing itself in the world; and the result is that it need not wait upon us, but is *already in full actuality accomplished.*"

I have one last quote for you, from Findlay, one of Hegel's great interpreters: "It is by the capacity to understand this that the true Hegelian is marked off from his often diligent and scholarly, but still profoundly misguided misinterpreter, who still yearns after the showy spectacular climax, the Absolute coming down . . . accompanied by a flock of doves, when a simple return to utter ordinariness is in place [cf. Zen's "ordinary mind"]. Finite existence in the here and now, *with every limitation*, is, Hegel teaches, when rightly regarded and accepted, identical with the infinite existence which is everywhere and always. To live on Main Street is, if one lives in the right spirit, to inhabit the Holy City."

As Plotinus knew and Nagarjuna taught: always and always, the other world is this world rightly seen. Every Form is Emptiness *just as it is*. The radical secret of the supreme identity is that there is only God. There is only the Kosmos of One Taste, always already fully present, always already perfectly accomplished, always already the sound of one hand clapping. And the very belief that we *could* deviate from this is the arrogance of the egoic delusion, the haunting mask of divine egoism gloating over the smoking ruins of its own contracting tendencies. We can preserve nature, but Nature preserves us.

The Fading of the Vision

Q: The Idealist vision almost completely faded within a few decades.
KW: Yes. The Descended grid ate Idealism alive and spat out Gaia-

centric salvation, whether in the form of Marxism or ecocentrism or capitalism—the same grid, and the same wobbling between the only two choices available: control nature (Ego), become one with nature (Eco).

Q: So is it a matter of simply trying to bring back some form of Idealism?

KW: Not really, because evolution moves on. We have a different techno-economic base now, and Idealism as it was proposed would not now functionally fit. There will be a new type of Idealism, we might say, but the coming Buddha will speak digital. Which I suppose is another conversation.

In any event we can't simply stop with Schelling or any of the Idealists. Granted that the summary I gave of Spirit-in-action is valid—and I believe it is—nevertheless, none of the Idealists really understood the four quadrants very well, and their grasp of the actual details and stages of the transpersonal domains was rather thin. I believe we can summarize these shortcomings in two simple points.

The first was a failure to develop any truly *contemplative practices*— that is, any true paradigms, any reproducible exemplars, any actual *transpersonal practice*. Put differently: no yoga, no meditative discipline, no experimental methodology to reproduce in consciousness the transpersonal insights and intuitions of its founders.

The great Idealist systems were thus mistaken for metaphysics, or more of the same ole "mere representation" philosophy that had no actual referent, and that Kant had thoroughly demolished. And because the Idealists lacked a transpersonal practice, this harsh criticism was in many ways true, alas. Idealism tended to degenerate into monological metaphysics, and so it rightly suffered the fate of all mere metaphysics— that is, of all systems that merely *map* the world and don't sufficiently provide interior technologies to change the mapmaker.

Q: So the first failure was that they had no yoga—no transpersonal practice to reproduce their insights.

KW: That's right, no way to reproduce transpersonal awareness in a practicing community. No way to concretely disclose a deeper self (I or Buddha) in a deeper community (We or Sangha) expressing a deeper truth (It or Dharma). But yes, put simply, no yoga.

Q: And the second major failure?

KW: Although profound intuitions into the genuinely transpersonal domains were clearly some of the major, I would say *the* major, driving forces behind the Idealist movement, these intuitions and insights were often expressed almost totally in and through *vision-logic*, and this burdened Reason with a task it could never accomplish. Particularly with Hegel, the transpersonal and transrational Spirit becomes wholly *identi-*

fied with vision-logic or mature Reason, which condemns Reason to collapsing under a weight it could never carry.

"The Real is Rational and the Rational is Real"—and by "rational" Hegel means vision-logic. And this will never do. Vision-logic is simply Spirit as it appears at the centauric stage.

In 1796, Hegel wrote a poem for Hölderlin, which says in part: "For *thought cannot grasp* the soul which forgetting itself plunges out of space and time into a presentiment of infinity, and now re-awakens. Whoever wanted to speak of this to others, though he spoke with the tongues of angels, would feel the poverty of words."

Would that Hegel had remained in poverty. But Hegel decided that Reason could and should develop the tongues of angels.

This would have been fine, *if* Hegel also had more dependable practices for the developmental unfolding of the higher and transpersonal stages. Zen masters talk about Emptiness all the time! But they have a *practice* and a *methodology*—zazen, or meditation—which allows them to ground their intuitions in experiential, public, reproducible, fallibilist criteria. Zen is not metaphysics! It is not mere mapping.

The Idealists had none of this. Their insights, not easily reproducible, and thus not fallibilistic, were therefore dismissed as "mere metaphysics," and gone was a priceless opportunity that the West, no doubt, will have to attempt yet again if it is ever to be hospitable to the future descent of the World Soul.

Q: It's amazing the Idealists accomplished as much as they did.

KW: Isn't it? I keep thinking of this story: After World War II, Jean-Paul Sartre visited Stalingrad, the site of the extraordinary battle that in many ways was the turning point of the war. At that site the Russians had put up an absolutely heroic defense; over three hundred thousand German soldiers died. After surveying the site, Sartre kept saying, "They were so amazing, they were so amazing." Sartre, of course, was very sympathetic with the communist cause, so somebody finally said, "You mean the Russians were so amazing?" "No, the Germans. That they *got this far*."

I keep thinking of that phrase when I think of the Idealists. That they got this far.

The Dominance of the Descenders

Q: Yet they, too, were defeated. There is a famous phrase, that after Hegel everybody was saying "back to Kant!"

KW: Yes, which eventually meant: back to rationality and its grounding in the senses. In other words, back to mononature, back to the Right-Hand world.

The collapse of Idealism left the Descenders virtually unchallenged as the holders and molders of modernity. After some extraordinary gains for the Left-Hand dimensions in terms of consciousness and transpersonal Spirit, the Idealist current was snapped up by the industrial grid and converted, via Feuerbach and Marx, into a strongly materialistic and "naturalistic" conception. It's almost impossible to escape the modern Descended grid, and after absolutely heroic attempts by the Idealists, they were hounded out of town by the troglodytes.

And so Feuerbach, a student of Hegel, would soon announce that *any* sort of spirituality, *any* sort of Ascent, was simply a projection of men and women's human potentials onto an "other world" of wholly imaginative origin. And, according to Feuerbach, it is exactly this projection of human potential onto a "divine" sphere that cripples men and women and is the true cause of self-alienation.

He is, of course, confusing the old mythic otherworldliness with higher and interior transpersonal potentials, but it is exactly this confusion that allows him to embrace the Descended grid and maintain that nature alone is real.

Karl Marx and Friedrich Engels were paying very close attention. *"Apart from nature and human beings,"* Engels would write, "nothing exists; and the higher beings which our religious fantasy created are only the fantastic reflection of our own essence. The enthusiasm was general; we were all for the moment followers of Feuerbach."

And the entire modern and postmodern world is, in effect, the followers of Feuerbach.

The Internet

Q: But what about systems like the Internet, the computer network that now links millions and millions of people in an information exchange? Is that merely Descended? Isn't that global? And doesn't that point the way to global consciousness?

KW: What good is it if Nazis have the Net? You see the problem? The Net is simply the *exterior* social structure—the Lower-Right quadrant. But what goes through the Net—well, that involves *interior* consciousness and morals and values, which are rarely addressed by those who simply maintain the Net is a global consciousness. A horizontally extended Net is not the same as a vertically developed consciousness. Merely pushing the horizontal extension is flatland at its worst and most Descended and possibly most destructive.

The Net is simply part of the new techno-economic base (the Lower-Right quadrant), and as such, it is itself *neutral* with regard to the *consciousness* that uses it. All Right-Hand structures are neutral, value-free. What computer technology (and the Information Age) means is that the techno-base can *support* a worldcentric perspectivism, a global consciousness, *but does not in any way guarantee it.* As we have seen, cognitive advances are necessary but not sufficient for moral advances, and the cognitive means usually run way ahead of the willingness to actually climb that ladder of expanding awareness. The Net offers the possibility, but does not guarantee it.

Which is why the Net itself cannot be equated with global consciousness per se. What good is it if millions of people at moral stage 1 have the means of extending their egocentric morality? What good is it if Nazis have the Net?

All of that is overlooked when people simply focus on the holistic net of simple location. You focus on the exterior grid and ignore the interiors that are running through that grid. The flatland idea is that the Internet is global, so the consciousness using it must be global. But that's not true at all.

Most people, alas, are still at preconventional and conventional modes of awareness, egocentric and ethnocentric. And no systems map, and no Internet, will automatically change this. Neither a global holistic map, nor a global Internet, will in itself foster interior transformation, and often just the opposite, contributing to arrest or even regression. A great number of the Infobahn males are digital predators—egocentric computer warriors that couldn't care less about intersubjective cooperation and mutual recognition. So much for global consciousness. When worldcentric means are presented to less-than-worldcentric individuals, those means are simply used (and abused) to further the agenda of the less-than-worldcentric individual. The Nazis would have loved the Net. The neo-Nazis certainly do. The FBI reports that hate-group activity has dramatically skyrocketed, thanks to the Net, which allows these people to find one another.

Q: So, as usual, we need to include *development* in both Left-Hand and Right-Hand in order to achieve truly global consciousness.

KW: Yes, that's exactly the point.

The Religion of Gaia

Q: But what about such problems as overpopulation, ozone depletion, and so on? Those are immediate threats to Gaia—to us all—and the Eco-Romantics do attack those head on.

KW: Gaia's main problems are not industrialization, ozone depletion, overpopulation, or resource depletion. Gaia's main problem is *the lack of mutual understanding and mutual agreement in the noosphere* about how to proceed with those problems. We cannot rein in industry if we cannot reach mutual understanding and mutual agreement based on a worldcentric moral perspective concerning the global commons. And we reach that *worldcentric* moral perspective through a difficult and laborious process of interior growth and transcendence. In short, global problems demand global consciousness, and global consciousness is the product of five or six major interior stages of development. Simply possessing a global map won't do it. A systems map will not do it. An ecological map will not do it. Interior growth and transcendence, on the other hand, *will* do it.

But the Descended grid rejects transcendence altogether. And therefore it despises Gaia's only source of genuine salvation. This *hatred of transcendence* is the cunning of the Descended grid. This is how the Descended grid perpetuates its love affair with flatland. This is how it perpetuates the colonization of the I and the we by holistic chains of its. This is how it perpetuates the bitter fragmentation of the Good and the True and the Beautiful, and sets mind and culture and nature at fundamental odds, each not a trusted friend but a profound threat to the others, spiteful in regard, intent upon revenge.

And so of course the crude and obvious rational-Ego camps are contributing to the despoliation of Gaia, in their attempts to control and dominate nature. But it is the final irony of modernity that the religion of Gaia is also caught in the same Descended grid, and it is that grid that is the fundamental destructive force. The religion of Gaia has pledged allegiance to the grid that is killing Gaia.

And so the horrifying truth of the modern condition slowly dawns: The hatred of transcendence is the way the flatland grid reproduces itself in the consciousness of those it is destroying.

18

An Integral Vision

Q: I want to conclude these discussions by focusing on four topics: how we interpret our spiritual intuitions; environmental ethics; future world developments; and the integral vision itself.

The Writing on the Wall

Q: First, you maintain that many people are indeed having profound spiritual intuitions, but many of these people are not interpreting these intuitions very well.

KW: These spiritual intuitions are often very true and very real, I believe, but these intuitions are *interpreted*—they are *unpacked*—in less than graceful ways. We are all immersed in the modern Descended grid, to one degree or another, with its massive *dissociation* between self, culture, and nature. So spiritual intuitions often come crashing down into this dissociated grid, with less than happy results.

Q: For example?

KW: I might have an experience of Kosmic consciousness, or perhaps an intuition of the all-embracing World Soul, but I might interpret this *solely* in the terms of finding my Higher Self. I then think that if I find my Higher Self or higher consciousness, then all other problems will simply work themselves out wonderfully. I am doing the old Fichte move—the pure Self will solve everything—and I tend to ignore the *behavioral* and *social* and *cultural* components that are also necessary for transformation. I tend to get caught up in a very narcissistic orientation—find my True Self, the world will take care of itself.

Or I might take the other extreme—I have this experience of Kosmic consciousness, or maybe the World Soul, I feel one with the world, and I then decide the world that I am one with is simply sensory nature, mononature. I am indeed sensing a oneness with the mountain, with the ocean, with all life. But caught in the modern grid, I will ignore the subjective and intersubjective space that allowed me to develop to the point where I could be one with the mountain, and so I will think that this "oneness" involves nature alone.

So I will decide that if we all can just become one with Gaia, one with the pure Eco, then all our major problems will be solved. I present a nice systems map of the world, and tell everybody that they must agree that we are all strands in the Great Web, disregarding the massive interior changes in consciousness that are necessary to even be able to grasp a systems view in the first place. I am doing the old Spinoza move: insertion into the great immanent system will save us all, overlooking the fact that I can become one with the great immanent system only by a laborious process of inner transcendence (which involves six or seven fulcrums of development, at least).

This modern dissociation is so firmly entrenched in the collective psyche that when a genuine spiritual intuition descends, it descends into the *interpretive grid* of this modern fragmentation. The original spiritual intuition carries a sense of wholeness, but if I *interpret* this intuition merely in terms of my favorite quadrant, then I try to reproduce the wholeness by making my favorite fragment cover all the bases.

Q: So the intuition can be genuine, but the interpretation can get fouled up.

KW: Yes, that's the central point. As we said, surfaces can be seen, but all *depth* must be *interpreted*. And how we interpret depth is crucially important for the birth of that depth itself. Graceful and well-rounded interpretations of Spirit facilitate Spirit's further descent. Gracefully unpacking the intuition, interpreting the intuition, facilitates the emergence of that new spiritual depth.

On the other hand, ungraceful interpretations tend to prevent or abort further spiritual intuitions. Frail or shallow or fragmented interpretations derail the spiritual process. Usually this happens because the interpretations are drawn from only one quadrant—they do not equally honor and unpack all four quadrants, they do not honor and integrate the Big Three. And since Spirit manifests as all four quadrants—or simply the Big Three—then some aspect of Spirit gets denied or distorted or overemphasized, which sabotages Spirit's full expression and derails the spiritual process in its broader unfolding. We neglect the Beautiful, or the Good, or the True—we neglect the I, or the we, or the it do-mains—we neglect self, or culture, or nature—and thus send Spirit crashing into the fragments of our self-contracting ways.

The Superman Self

Q: So both the Ego and the Eco are trapped in ungraceful interpreta-tions.

KW: Very often, yes. On the Ego side, as we were saying, many indi-viduals intuit Spirit and yet unpack that intuition, interpret that intu-ition, solely or merely in terms of the Higher Self, the Inner Voice, archetypal psychology, Gnosticism, vipassana, the care of the Soul, inte-rior Witnessing, the Universal Mind, pure Awareness, Enneagram pat-terns, transcendental Consciousness, or similar such *Upper-Left quadrant terms*. And however true that aspect of the intuition is, this unpacking leaves out, or seriously diminishes, the "we" and the "it" dimensions. It fails to give a decent account of the types of community, social service, cultural activity, and *relationships* in general that are the intersubjective forms of Spirit. It ignores or neglects the changes in the techno-economic infrastructures and the social systems that are the ob-jective forms of Spirit. It centers on the intentional, but ignores the be-havioral and cultural and social—it ignores the other three quadrants, or at least relegates them to very inferior and secondary status.

The "Higher Self" camp is thus notoriously immune to social con-cerns. Everything that happens to one is said to be "one's own choice"—the hyperagentic Higher Self is responsible for *everything* that happens—this is the monological and totally disengaged Ego gone horri-bly amuck in omnipotent self-only fantasies. This simply *represses* the networks of rich social and cultural communions that are just as impor-tant as agency in constituting the manifestation of Spirit.

The idea seems to be that if I can just contact my Higher Self, then everything else will take care of itself. But this fails to see that Spirit manifests always and simultaneously *as all four quadrants of the Kos-mos*. Spirit, at any level, manifests as a self in a community with social and cultural foundations and objective correlates, and thus any *Higher Self* will inextricably involve a *wider* community existing in a *deeper* objective state of affairs. Contacting the Higher Self is not the end of all problems but the beginning of the immense and difficult new work to be done in all quadrants.

Q: But these approaches really do maintain that you create your own reality.

KW: You don't create your own reality; psychotics create their own reality. I know, the point is that a genuinely spiritual Self does manifest its own reality. So here's an old story from Vedanta Hinduism.

A man goes to an enlightened sage and asks, of course, for the meaning of life. The sage gives a brief summary of the Vedanta view, namely, that this entire world is nothing but the supreme Brahman or Godhead, and further, your own witnessing awareness is one with Brahman. Your very Self is in a supreme identity with God. Since Brahman creates all, and since your highest Self is one with Brahman, then your highest Self creates all. So far, this definitely looks like New Age city.

Off goes the gentleman, convinced that he has understood the ultimate meaning of life, which is that his own deepest Self is actually God and creates all reality. On the way home, he decides to test this amazing notion. Heading right toward him is a man riding an elephant. The gentleman stands in the middle of the road, convinced that, if he's God, the elephant can't hurt him. The fellow riding the elephant keeps yelling, "Get out of the way! Get out of the way!" But the gentleman doesn't move—and gets perfectly flattened by the elephant.

Limping back to the sage, the gentleman explains that, since Brahman or God is everything, and since his Self is one with God, then the elephant should not have hurt him. "Oh, yes, everything is indeed God," said the sage, "so why didn't you listen when God told you to get out of the way?"

It is true that Spirit creates all reality, and to the extent you identify with Spirit, you do indeed find that you are within that creative activity. But that creative activity *manifests in all four quadrants*, not *just* in or from your own particular awareness. But if you interpret spiritual awareness *merely* as a Higher Self, then you will ignore God in the other quadrants—you will ignore the elephant, or think it isn't real, or isn't important—you will ignore the cultural and social and behavioral work that desperately needs to be done in those domains in order to *fully* express the Spirit that you are.

But ignoring all of that, sooner or later you will get flattened by some sort of elephant. You will get ill, or lose a job, or fail in a relationship— some sort of elephant will run you over—and you will feel massive guilt because if you were really in touch with your true Self, the elephant wouldn't be able to hurt you. When all it really means is, you weren't listening to God in all quadrants.

Q: These approaches maintain that the more you contact higher consciousness or Higher Self, the less you worry about the world.

KW: Yes, the Real Self is Superman! And Superman never worries! And conversely, if you are "worried" or "concerned" about the poverty or injustice or anguish of the world, then this shows that you haven't found the true Self.

And in fact, it is just the opposite: the more you contact the Higher Self, the *more* you worry about the world, as a component of your very Self, the Self of each and all. Emptiness is Form. Brahman is the World. To *finally* contact Brahman is to *ultimately* engage the World. If you really contact your Higher Self, one of the first things you will want to do is not ignore the elephant but feed the elephant. That is, work in all four quadrants to help manifest this realization, and treat each and every holon as a manifestation of the Divine.

With the supreme identity, you are established in radical Freedom, it is true, but that Freedom *manifests* as compassionate activity, as agonizing concern. The Form of Freedom is sorrow, unrelenting worry for those struggling to awaken. The Bodhisattva weeps daily; the tears stain the very fabric of the Kosmos in all directions. The Heart moves into those places where Spirit remains unheralded and unheard; the work is a passion, an agony; it is always fully accomplished, and thus never ending.

But if you keep interpreting Spirit as simply a higher or sacred Self—ignoring Spirit in the other quadrants—then that is going to abort further realization. It won't just hurt others, it will profoundly sabotage your own spiritual development. It will cut off further realizations of Spirit's all-pervading presence. You will just keep retreating into your interior awareness, until that well runs dry, and you end up despising the manifest world because it "detracts" from your "real" self.

On the other hand, a more graceful unpacking facilitates further and deeper intuitions, intuitions touching the I and the We and the It domains: not just how to *realize* the higher Self, but how to see it *embraced* in culture, *embodied* in nature, and *embedded* in social institutions.

Realized, embraced, embodied, embedded: a more graceful interpretation covering all four quadrants, because Spirit itself manifests as all four quadrants. And this more graceful interpretation facilitates the birth of that Spirit which is demanding the interpretation. Graceful interpretation midwifes Spirit's birth, Spirit's descent. The more adequately I can interpret the intuition of Spirit, the more that Spirit can speak to me, the more the channels of communication are open, leading from communication to communion to union to identity—the supreme identity.

The Great-Web Gaia Self

Q: Whereas the other typical approach, the Eco approach, also tends to get caught in dissociated interpretations, but at the other extreme.

KW: Yes. There are many good souls who have a profound intuition of Spirit but unpack that intuition in merely "it" terms, describing Spirit as the sum total of all phenomena or processes interwoven together in a great unified system or net or web or implicate order or unified field— the Lower-Right quadrant.

All of which is true enough, but all of which leaves out entirely the interior dimensions of "I" and "we" as disclosed in their own terms. This less-than-adequate interpretation is unfortunately quite monological, flatland through and through.

It is the old Spinoza move, the other pole—the Eco pole—of the fundamental Enlightenment paradigm, in the form of the Romantic rebellion. It thinks that the enemy is atomism and mechanism, and that the central problem is simply to be able to prove or demonstrate once and for all that the universe is a great and unified holistic System or Order or Web. It marshals a vast amount of scientific evidence, from physics to biology to systems theory—all monological!—and offers extensive arguments, all geared to objectively proving the holistic nature of the universe. It fails to see that if we take a bunch of egos with atomistic concepts and teach them that the universe is holistic, all we will actually get is a bunch of egos with holistic concepts.

Precisely because this monological approach, with its unskillful interpretation of an otherwise genuine intuition, ignores or neglects the "I" and the "we" dimensions, it doesn't understand very well the exact nature of the inner transformations and the stages of inner transcendence that are absolutely necessary in order to be able to find an identity that embraces the All in the first place. *Talk* about the All as much as we want, nothing fundamentally changes.

And this world of empirical nature—the *biosphere*—becomes one's God, one's Goddess. Not Nature, but nature, is the great beloved.

Thus, however true the original intuition of Spirit is—and I do not doubt that it is true—it is not facilitated by these fragmented interpretations. Those interpretations, taken in and by themselves, *block* the transformative event. Those interpretations, driven originally by a true intuition of the very Divine, do not facilitate the further descent of that Divine. Those interpretations are unskillful to midwife the birth of Spirit.

Q: So they actually prevent further realizations.

KW: If I keep interpreting my Kosmic consciousness experience as a oneness with sensory nature, I sabotage Spirit in the other quadrants. I keep pushing the flatland Gaia map. And I find that people might buy the map, but nothing really fundamental is changing. They aren't really transforming. All they do is become ideologues, and try to get other people to buy the flatland map.

And I become very depressed, hollow-eyed. I say the reason I am so depressed is that Gaia is being destroyed—unaware of the hand I am playing in that downward spiral. Embracing the industrial ontology of simple location, I hug and kiss the spokes of the wheel that is grinding Gaia to her demise.

At its end limit, this approach, as we saw, fosters regression, both individual regression to biocentric and egocentric stances, and cultural regression to tribal or horticultural ideals. Reducing the Kosmos to flatland sensory nature, and then trying to become one with that nature in biocentric immersion, leads to profoundly regressive, preconventional, body-bound, narcissistic glorification. This was the entire lesson of the Romantic slide!—the closer you get to preconventional nature, the more egocentric you become. Again, profound spiritual intuitions, when interpreted ungracefully, lead to less than happy results.

Q: You were saying that ecological wisdom doesn't consist in how to live in accord with nature, but how to get subjects to agree on how to live in accord with nature. In other words, how to integrate the Big Three.

KW: Yes. People are not born wanting to take care of Gaia. That noble state of global care is the *product* of a long and laborious and difficult process of growth and transcendence (involving, as we saw, over a half-dozen interior stages or fulcrums). But, like the multicults, the typical Eco-approaches condemn the actual path of transcendence that produced the noble state.

This then completely sabotages others getting to that state, and turns everybody loose to slide to their own lowest possibilities. This has already happened with the multicults, and with many Eco-approaches as well. Indeed, the multicults and ecotheorists have often joined hands to promote the retribalization of American culture.

Q: But the basic idea of the multicults is to honor individual differences.

KW: Yes, but that can *only* be done under the *protection* of the worldcentric stance of universal pluralism, which itself does not emerge until the postconventional stages (stages 5 and 6 and higher). And thus, without demanding and fostering ways for people to develop and evolve to these higher stages, we merely encourage them to act out their shallower engagements, and thus few people actually aspire to the worldcentric stance that alone allows the protection.

Instead, every sort of retribalization, fragmentation, preconventional, egocentric, and ethnocentric shallowness—all of those "diversities" are glorified as part of the decentered worldcentric stance, whereas they are exactly what prevent and sabotage that stance, and lead it by the hand into increasingly regressive engagements and the politics of narcissism, which, if it actually succeeds, will destroy the worldcentric stance that protected the pluralism in the first place. And this in turn will open the door to actual oppression, ethnocentric wars, imperialistic nightmares—we will lose all the liberation movements secured by the good news of the Enlightenment and its worldcentric tolerance.

You simply end up fostering a lack of growth, a lack of development, a lack of transcendence, a lack of evolution. You foster a culture of regression, a politics of narcissism. And this, you will happily tell yourself, has finally freed you from that horrible oppression known as modernity.

Beyond the Postmodern Mind

Q: Speaking of which, you realize that most of the world's great wisdom traditions are, in various ways, against modernity. Modernity is viewed as the great antireligious movement, the great movement of rational secularization, which "killed" God.

KW: Killed the *mythic* God, yes. But Spirit is in the overall process, not in any favored epoch or period or time or place. Reason has more depth than mythology, and thus actually represents a further unfolding of Spirit's own potentials. The rational denial of God contains more Spirit than the mythic affirmation of God, simply because it contains more depth. The very movement of modernity is a collective increase in Spirit's freedom, evidenced, among many other things, in the great liberation movements that define the very core of modernity.

So I might eulogize, for example, the glorious mythic-agrarian Empires, which were drenched in the blessings of my favorite mythic God, and I might worship that God as being the epitome of Freedom and Benevolence and Mercy. But I can do so only by ignoring the fact that the temples and the monuments to that God, the great pyramids and stone cathedrals, were built on the broken backs of slaves, of women and children accorded the grace of animals; the great monuments to that mythic God or Goddess were inscribed on the tortured flesh of millions.

Spirit as great Freedom is one thing; Spirit actually manifested as political democracies, quite another. Reason frees the light trapped in mythology and sets it loose among the oppressed, which actually undoes their chains on earth, and not merely in some promised heaven.

All of this eulogizing of past epochs, and hatred of the present, mostly stems from confusing the average mode with the most advanced modes in those cultures. That approach simply compares the most advanced modes of past epochs with the most disastrous aspects of modernity, and so of course finds nothing but devolution.

But this is just a typical example of what you were saying, which is that most of the great religious traditions are profoundly uneasy with modernity and postmodernity. Modernity, in various ways, is viewed as the Great Satan.

And my central point is that that idea is very confused. I believe that many traditional religious thinkers simply have not clearly *understood* modernity.

Q: Haven't understood modernity, how exactly?

KW: Every great epoch of human evolution seems to have one central idea, an idea that dominates the entire epoch, and summarizes its approach to Spirit and Kosmos, and tells us something altogether profound. And each seems to build upon its predecessor. These ideas are so simple and so central, they can be put in a sentence.

Foraging: *Spirit is interwoven with earthbody.* Foraging cultures the world over sing this profound truth. The very earth is our blood and bones and marrow, and we are all sons and daughters of that earth—in which, and through which, Spirit flows freely.

Horticulture: *But Spirit demands sacrifice.* Sacrifice is the great theme running through horticultural societies, and not just in the concrete form of actual ritual sacrifice, although we certainly see it there as well. But the central and pervading notion is that certain specific human steps must be taken to come into accord with Spirit. Ordinary or typical humanity has to get out of the way, so to speak—has to be sacrificed—in order for Spirit to shine forth more clearly. In other words, there are steps on the way to a more fully realized Spiritual awareness.

Agrarian: *These spiritual steps are in fact arrayed in a Great Chain of Being.* The Great Chain is the central, dominant, inescapable theme of every mythic-agrarian society the world over, with few exceptions. And since most of "civilized history" has been agrarian history, Lovejoy was quite right in stating that the Great Chain has been the dominant idea in most of civilized culture.

Modernity: *The Great Chain unfolds in evolutionary time.* In other words, evolution. The fact that Spirit was usually left out of the equation is simply the disaster of modernity, not the dignity nor the definition of modernity. Evolution is the one great background concept that hangs over every single modern movement; it is the God of modernity. And, in fact, this is a tremendously spiritual realization, because, whether or not it consciously identifies itself as spiritual, the fact is that it plugs humans into the Kosmos in an unbroken fashion, and further, points to the inescapable but frightening fact that humans are co-creators of their own evolution, their own history, their own worldspaces, because:

Postmodernity: *Nothing is pregiven; the world is not just a perception but also an interpretation.* That this leads many postmodernists into fits of aperspectival madness is not our concern. That nothing is pregiven is the great postmodern discovery, and it plugs humans into a plastic Kosmos of their own co-creation, Spirit become self-conscious in the most acute forms, on the way to its own superconscious shock.

Q: So those are the great defining ideas of each epoch. And your point about the antimodern religious thinkers . . .

KW: Yes, is that they are all too often trapped in the agrarian worldview. They have not come to terms with the form of Spirit in either its modern or its postmodern modes. With eyes turned from the wonders and dignities of modernity, they sing the songs of yesterday's marvels. Many traditional religious thinkers don't even think evolution has occurred!

They have not grasped Spirit in its manifestation as modernity; they have not seen that evolution is, as Wallace put it, the "manner and mode of Spirit's creation." They have not grasped the essence of modernity as the differentiation of the Big Three, and so they have missed the dignities of the modern liberation movements, of the abolition of slavery, of the women's movement, of the liberal democracies, each of which sent Spirit singing through a new mode of freedom unheard of in mythic-agrarian times. They think that because modernity introduced its own disasters, evolution itself must be rejected, failing to grasp the dialectic of progress.

And they have likewise often not grasped Spirit in its manifestation as postmodernity. Nothing is pregiven. But to the agrarian mind, everything is simply and everlastingly pregiven, static, unyielding to the advances of time or the unfolding of development. The entire world is simply pregiven by the mythic God, and salvation depends upon strictly following the given commandments that are forever etched in stone. To disagree with the agrarian worldview, there is eternal sin. And never mind that that worldview is ethnocentric, racist, sexist, patriarchal, and militant, for it has been gloriously spoken by the mythic God.

And so yes, to the extent the "religious authorities" are anchored in the agrarian worldview, they of course despise modernity, despise evolution, despise the process that is in fact working to undermine their own authority.

And yet their identification of Spirit with the static and pregiven agrarian worldview is exactly what prevents the modern and postmodern world from acknowledging Spirit. Modernity will *never* accept Spirit if Spirit means merely mythic-agrarian.

On the other hand, to adopt an integral vision, and see Spirit operating in all levels in all quadrants, is to acknowledge and honor Spirit's past manifestations, *and* to recognize and honor Spirit's Presence in the accomplishments of modernity and postmodernity.

World Transformation and the Culture Gap

Q: Do you think there is a major world transformation now in progress?

KW: Haltingly, jerkily, in fits and starts. We are seeing, and have been seeing since approximately World War II, the slow shift from rational-industrial society to vision-logic informational society. This is not a spiritual New Age transformation, but it is quite profound nonetheless.

If for the moment we use the Lower-Right quadrant as an indicator, there have been six or seven major transformations in human evolution—from foraging to horticultural to early agrarian to advanced agrarian to early industrial to late industrial to early informational. So we are right on the edge of one of the half-dozen or so major, profound, worldwide transformations in the formation of the human species. These are often simplified to three major transformations—farming, industry, information—so that today is the beginning of the "third wave."

But remember, we must, in my opinion, analyze this transformation in terms of all four quadrants (at least), or we'll miss the factors actually responsible for it. This transformation is being driven by a new techno-economic base (informational), but it also brings with it a new world-view, with a new mode of self and new intentional and behavioral patterns, set in a new cultural worldspace with new social institutions as anchors. And, as usual, specific individuals may, or may not, live up to these new possibilities.

Q: So go around the quadrants.

KW: A new center of gravity is slowly emerging—the vision-logic information society, with an existential or aperspectival worldview (Lower Left), set in a techno-economic base of digital information transfer (Lower Right), and a centauric self (Upper Left) that must integrate its matter and body and mind—integrate the physiosphere and biosphere and noosphere—if its behavior (Upper Right) is to functionally fit in the new worldspace.

And this is a very tall order. Because the really crucial point is that a new transformation places a new and horrible *burden* on the world. It is hardly cause for undiluted celebration! Every new emergent and transformative development brings a new demand and a new responsibility: the higher must be integrated with the lower. Transcend and include. *And the greater the degree of development, the greater the burden of inclusion.*

Q: That's a problem.

KW: That's a big problem. And the real nightmare is this: even with a new and higher worldview available, every human being still has to *start its own development at square 1*. Everybody, without exception, starts at fulcrum-1, and has to grow and evolve through all the lower stages in order to reach the new and higher stage made available.

So even a person born into a grand and glorious and global vision-logic culture *nevertheless* begins development at the physiocentric, then biocentric, then egocentric levels, then moves to the sociocentric levels, then moves to the postconventional and worldcentric levels. There is no way to avoid or circumvent that general process. Even if you write a huge three-volume novel, you are still using the same letters of the alphabet you learned as a child, and you can't write the novel without the childhood acquisitions!

And the more vertical levels of growth there are in a culture, the more things there are that can go horribly wrong. As I was saying, the greater the depth of a society, the *greater the burden* placed on the education and transformation of its citizens. The greater the depth, the more things that can go massively, wretchedly, horribly wrong. The more levels, the more chances for lying (pathology). Our society can be sick in ways that the early foragers literally could not even imagine.

Q: So societies with greater depth face increasingly greater problems.

KW: Yes, in all four quadrants! So where many people talk of the coming transformation and get all ecstatic and giddy at the thought, I tend to see another chance for a huge nightmare coming right at us.

Q: I wonder if you could give a few examples.

KW: It is sometimes said that one of the major problems in Western societies is the gap between the rich and the poor. This is true. But that is a flatland way to look at it—merely quantified as a money gap. And as alarming as that exterior gap between individuals is, there is a more worrisome gap—an *interior* gap, a culture gap, a gap in consciousness, a gap in depth.

As a society's center of gravity puts on more and more weight—as more individuals move from egocentric to sociocentric to worldcentric (or higher)—this places a huge burden on the society's need to *vertically integrate* those individuals at different depths in their own development. And the greater the depth of a culture's center of gravity, the greater the demand and the burden of this vertical integration.

Thus, the "economic gap" between rich and poor is bad enough, but much more crucial—and much more hidden—is the *culture gap*, the "values gap," the "depth gap," which is the gap between the depth offered as a potential by the culture, and those who can actually unfold that depth in their own case.

As always, the new and higher center of gravity *makes possible*, but does *not guarantee*, the availability of the higher or deeper structures to its individual citizens. And as a society's center of gravity puts on more and more weight, there are more and more individuals who can be left behind, marginalized, excluded from their own intrinsic unfolding, disadvantaged in the cruelest way of all: in their own interior consciousness, value, and worth.

This creates an *internal tension* in the culture itself. The gap between the "haves" and the "have nots" refers not just to money but to consciousness, morals, depths. This internal tension in a culture can be devastating. And the potential for this culture gap or consciousness gap becomes *greater* with *every* new cultural transformation. Ouch!

Q: That's similar to what you were saying about individual pathology as well.

KW: Yes, the gap between the individual's main self or center of gravity and the "small selves" that remain dissociated and excluded. The internal tension, the internal civil war, drives the individual bonkers.

Just so with society and culture at large. The greater the cultural depth, then the greater the possibility of the culture gap, the gap between the average depth offered by the culture and those who can actually unfold to that depth. And this likewise creates an internal tension that can drive the culture bonkers.

Q: This is another reason cultures such as foraging had fewer internal problems.

KW: Yes.

Q: Any suggestions for solutions?

KW: Well, in a sense, the culture gap is not our real problem. The real problem is that we are not allowed to even think about the culture gap. And we are not allowed to think about the culture gap because we live in flatland. In flatland, we do not recognize degrees of consciousness and depth and value and worth. Everybody simply has the same depth, namely, zero.

And since we recognize no depth in flatland, we can't even begin to recognize the depth gap, the culture gap, the consciousness gap, which will therefore continue to wreak havoc on developed and "civilized" countries, until this most crucial of all problems is first recognized, then framed in ways that allow us to begin to work with it.

Q: So before we can discuss the solutions, we have to at least recognize the problem.

KW: Yes, and everything in flatland conspires to prevent that recognition. This culture gap—this massive problem of vertical cultural integration—cannot be solved in flatland terms, because flatland denies the existence of the vertical dimension altogether, denies interior transformation and transcendence altogether, denies the nine or so interior stages of consciousness development that is truly part of a culture's human capital, but is not even entered on the ledgers of flatland.

Q: So how does this relate to the worldwide transformation now haltingly in progress?

KW: The hypothesis, recall, is that modernity differentiated the Big Three, and postmodernity must find a way to integrate them. If that integration doesn't occur, then the twenty tenets won't mesh, evolution won't purr, and some sort of massive and altogether unpleasant readjustment will very likely result.

And the point is, you cannot integrate the Big Three in flatland. In flatland, they remain dissociated at best, collapsed at worst. And no system that we are aware of has ever gone limping into the future with these types of massive internal dissociations. If these chaotic tensions do not lead to self-transcendence, they will lead to self-dissolution. Those are the two gruesome choices evolution has always offered at each vertical emergent.

And we are very close to seeing the culture gap lead to cultural collapse, precisely because flatland will not acknowledge the problem in the first place.

Environmental Ethics: Holonic Ecology

Q: So do you think that the *culture gap* problem is more urgent than the *environmental crisis*?

KW: They're the same thing; they are exactly the same problem.

Egocentric and ethnocentric couldn't care less about the global commons—unless you scare them into seeing merely how it affects their own narcissistic existence—whereupon you have simply *reinforced* exactly the self-centric survival motives that are the cause of the problem in the first place. You just reinforce all of that with ecological scare tactics.

No, it is only at a global, postconventional, worldcentric stance (fulcrum 5, 6, and higher) that individuals can recognize the global dimensions of the environmental crisis and, more important, possess the moral vision and moral fortitude to proceed on a global basis. Obviously, then, a significant number of individuals must reach a postconventional and worldcentric level of development in order to be a significant force in global care and ecological reform.

In other words, it is only by effectively dealing with the culture gap that we can effectively deal with the ecological crisis—they're the same gap, the same problem.

Q: As you earlier put it, global problems demand global consciousness for their solution, and global consciousness is the product of at least a half-dozen interior stages of growth. Without interior growth, the problems remain.

KW: Yes, the culture gap and the environmental crisis are two of the major problems bequeathed to us by flatland. The religion of flatland denies degrees of vertical depth and interior transcendence which alone can bring humans into worldcentric and global agreement about how to proceed with protecting the biosphere and the global commons.

Q: In one of our earlier discussions, you briefly outlined an environmental ethics that would emerge if flatland were rejected. Perhaps we could go into that.

KW: Discussions of environmental ethics usually center on what is known as axiology, the theory of values. And there are four broad schools of environmental axiology.

The first is bioequality—all living holons have equal value. A worm and an ape have equal value. This is quite common with deep ecologists and some ecofeminists.

The second approach involves variations on animal rights—wherever there is any sort of rudimentary feelings in animals, we should extend certain basic rights to those animals. This school therefore attempts to draw an evolutionary line between those living forms that don't possess enough feelings to worry about—insects, for example—and those that do—such as mammals. Different theorists draw that line in different places, based on how far down one can reasonably assume that feelings or sensations exist. The lowest serious suggestion so far is shrimp and mollusks. (Of course, if you push it all the way down, this reverts to bioequality, and all living holons have equal rights.)

The third school is hierarchical or holarchical, and often based on Whitehead's philosophy (Birch and Cobb, for example). This approach sees evolution as a holarchical unfolding, with each more complex entity possessing more rights. Human beings are the most advanced and thus possess the most rights, but these rights do not include the right to instrumentally plunder other living entities, since they, too, possess certain basic but significant rights.

The fourth school involves the various stewardship approaches, where humans alone have rights, but those rights include the care and stewardship of the earth and its living inhabitants. Many conventional religious theorists take this approach as a way to anchor environmental care in a moral imperative (Max Oelschlaeger, for example).

My own particular approach to environmental ethics did not set out to synthesize those various schools, although I believe it ends up incorporating the basics of each of them.

Q: So those are four schools of value. Your approach is also based on different *types* of value.

KW: Yes. These are Ground value, intrinsic value, and extrinsic value. Briefly:

All holons have equal *Ground value*. That is, all holons, from atoms to apes, are perfect manifestations of Emptiness or Spirit, with no higher or lower, better or worse. Every holon, just as it is, is a perfect expression of Emptiness, a radiant gesture of the Divine. As a manifestation of the Absolute, all holons have equal Ground value. All Forms are equally Emptiness. And that's Ground value.

But every holon, besides being an expression of the *absolute*, is also a *relative* whole/part. It has its own relative *wholeness*, and its own relative *partness*.

As a *whole*, every holon has *intrinsic value*, or the value of its own particular wholeness, its own particular depth. And therefore the greater the wholeness—or the greater the depth—then *the greater the intrinsic value*. Intrinsic value means it has value in itself. Its very depth is valuable, because that depth *enfolds* aspects of the Kosmos into its own being. The more of the Kosmos that is enfolded into its own being—that is, the greater its depth—then the greater its intrinsic value. An ape contains cells and molecules and atoms, embraces them all in its own internal makeup—greater depth, greater wholeness, greater intrinsic value.

So even though an ape and an atom are both perfect expressions of Spirit (they both have equal Ground value), the ape has more depth, more wholeness, and therefore more intrinsic value. The atom also has intrinsic value, but relatively less. (Less value does not mean no value!) We also saw that the greater the depth of a holon, the greater its degree of consciousness, so it comes to much the same thing to say that the ape is more intrinsically valuable than the atom because it is more conscious.

But every holon is not only a whole, it is also a part. And as a *part*, it has *value for others*—it is part of a whole upon which other holons depend for their existence. So as a part, each holon has *extrinsic value*, instrumental value, value for other holons. The more it is a part, the more extrinsic value it has. An atom has more extrinsic value than an ape—destroy all apes, and not too much of the universe is affected; destroy all atoms, and everything but subatomic particles is destroyed—the atom has enormous extrinsic value, instrumental value, for other holons, because it is an instrumental part of so many other wholes.

Q: You also tie this in with rights and responsibilities.

KW: Yes. Rights and responsibilities are often used in the same breath, but without understanding why they are inseparably linked. But they are inherent aspects of the fact that every holon is a whole/part.

As a *whole*, a holon has *rights* which express its relative autonomy. These rights are simply a *description* of the conditions that are necessary to sustain its wholeness. If the rights aren't met, the wholeness dissolves into subholons. If the plant doesn't receive water, it dissolves. *Rights* express the *conditions* for the *intrinsic value* of a holon to exist, the conditions necessary to sustain its wholeness, sustain its *agency*, sustain its depth.

But further, each holon is also a part of some other whole(s), and as a *part*, it has *responsibilities* to the maintenance of that whole. Responsibilities are simply a *description* of the conditions that any holon must meet in order to be a part of the whole. If it doesn't meet those responsibilities, then it cannot sustain its functional fit with the whole, so it is ejected (or actually destroys the whole itself). If the responsibilities aren't met, then it ceases to be a part of the whole. *Responsibilities* express the *conditions* for the *extrinsic value* of a holon to exist, the conditions necessary to sustain its partness, sustain its *communion*, sustain its span. If any holon wants to be part of a whole, it has to meet certain responsibilities. Not, it would nice if it met these responsibilities; it *must* meet them or it won't sustain its communions, its cultural and functional fit.

Q: So agency and communion, intrinsic value and extrinsic value, rights and responsibilities, are twin aspects of every holon, because every holon is a whole/part.

KW: Yes, in a nested holarchy of expanding complexity and depth. Because human beings have relatively more depth than, say, an amoeba, we have more *rights*—there are more conditions necessary to sustain the wholeness of a human—but we also have many more *responsibilities*, not only to our own human societies of which we are parts, but to all of the communities of which our own subholons are parts. We exist in networks of relationships with holons in the physiosphere and the biosphere and the noosphere, and our relatively greater rights absolutely demand relatively greater responsibilities in all of these dimensions. Failure to meet these responsibilities means a failure to meet the conditions under which our holons and subholons can exist in communion—which means our own self-destruction.

Again, it's not that it would be nice if we met these responsibilities; it is a condition of existence. It is mandatory, or our communions will dissolve, and us with them. But, of course, we often seem to want to claim the rights without owning the responsibilities. We want to be a *whole* without being a *part* of anything! We want to do our own thing!

Q: The culture of narcissism, you were saying.

KW: Yes, the culture of narcissism and regression and retribalization. We are in an orgy of seeking egoic rights with no responsibilities. Everybody wants to be a separate whole and demand rights for their own agency, but nobody wants to be a part and assume the responsibilities of the corresponding communions.

But, of course, you can't have one without the other. Our feeding frenzy of rights is simply a sign of fragmentation into increasingly egocentric "wholes" that refuse also to be parts of anything other than their own demands.

Q: Does either the Ego or the Eco approach overcome these problems?

KW: I don't think so. One of the great difficulties with the modern flatland paradigm—in both Ego and Eco versions—is that the notions of rights and responsibilities were both horribly collapsed, often beyond recognition.

Q: For example.

KW: In the Ego-Enlightenment version of flatland, we have: the disengaged and autonomous Ego assigns autonomy only to itself. That is, the rational Ego alone is a self-contained wholeness, and so the rational Ego alone has *intrinsic value* and therefore *rights*. All other holons are simply *parts* of the great interlocking order, so all other holons have merely part value, *extrinsic value*, instrumental value—and no rights at all. They are all instrumental to the Ego's designs. And so the disengaged Ego can do its own thing, and push the environment around any way it wants to, because everything else is now only instrumental to the Ego.

In the Eco-Romantic version, the great interlocking web is still the only basic reality, but it, and not the reflecting Ego, is now assigned autonomy value. Since the Great Web is the ultimate reality, then the Great Web alone has wholeness value or *intrinsic value*, and all other holons (human and otherwise) are now merely *instrumental* to its autopoietic maintenance. That is, all other holons are merely parts or strands in the Web, so they have merely *extrinsic* and instrumental value. In other words, what critics have called ecofascism. The Great Web alone has *rights*, and all other holons are ultimately subservient parts. And if you are speaking for the Great Web, then you get to tell us all what to do, because you alone are speaking for intrinsic value.

This approach gets further complicated because the Eco-Romantics, unlike the Ego camps, were often in search of genuine spiritual values and harmony. But, like most movements of modernity and postmodernity, their spiritual intuitions were interpreted in purely flatland terms, unpacked in Descended terms.

So they immediately confused *Ground value* with *intrinsic value*, and arrived at the stance of "bioequality." That is, they confused Ground value (all holons have the same absolute value, which is true) with intrinsic value (all holons have the same relative value, which is false), and thus they arrived at "bioequality." In other words, no differences in intrinsic value between any holons—no difference in intrinsic value between a flea and a deer. This industrial ontology ironically runs through many of the ecological movements.

Q: So we want to honor all three values.

KW: Yes, I think so. A truly "holonic ecology" would honor all three types of value for each and every holon—Ground value, intrinsic value, and extrinsic value. We want our environmental ethics to honor all holons without exception as manifestations of Spirit—and also, at the same time, be able to make pragmatic distinctions about the differences in intrinsic worth, and realize that it is much better to kick a rock than an ape, much better to eat a carrot than a cow, much better to subsist on grains than on mammals.

Q: You said this holonic ecology ends up incorporating the essentials of the four main schools of environmental ethics. How can we do this?

KW: With the believers in bioequality, we can agree that all holons possess equal Ground value, and honor the spiritual insight that many of these theorists are attempting to express. But not all holons have equal intrinsic value, so we can agree with the animal rights activists and the Whiteheadians that there is a hierarchy or holarchy of consciousness, and the higher a sentient being is on that holarchy, the less right you have to sacrifice it for your needs. Finally, we can agree with the stewardship schools in the sense that humans, because they generally possess the greatest depth, therefore possess the greatest responsibility (or stewardship) for the biosphere's welfare.

Q: How does this work in concrete terms? What are the pragmatic implications?

KW: Our first pragmatic rule of thumb for environmental ethics is: in pursuit of our vital needs, consume or destroy as little depth as possible. Do the least amount of harm to consciousness as you possibly can. Destroy as little intrinsic worth as possible. Put in its positive form: protect and promote as much depth as possible.

But we can't stop with that imperative alone, because it covers only depth but not span; only agency and not communion; only wholes, and not parts. Rather, we want to protect and promote *the greatest depth for the greatest span*. Not just preserve the greatest depth—that's fascist and anthropocentric—and not just preserve the greatest span—that's totalitarian and ecofascist—but rather preserve the greatest depth for the greatest span.

The Basic Moral Intuition

Q: You call this the Basic Moral Intuition.

KW: Yes. The Basic Moral Intuition is "protect and promote the greatest depth for the greatest span." I believe that is the actual form of spiritual intuition, the actual structure of spiritual intuition.

In other words, when we intuit Spirit, we are actually intuiting Spirit as it appears in all four quadrants (because Spirit manifests as all four quadrants—or, in short, as I and we and it). Thus, when I am intuiting Spirit clearly, I intuit its preciousness not only in myself, but in all other beings as well, for they share Spirit with me (as their own depth). And thus I wish to protect and promote that Spirit, not just in me, but in all beings as such, and I am moved, if I intuit Spirit clearly, to *implement* this Spiritual unfolding in as many beings as possible: I intuit Spirit not only as I, and not only as We, but also as a drive to implement that realization as an Objective State of Affairs (It) in the world.

Thus, precisely because Spirit actually manifests as all four quadrants (or as I, we, and it), then Spiritual intuition, when clearly apprehended, is apprehended as a desire to extend the depth of I to the span of We as an objective state of affairs (It): Buddha, Sangha, Dharma. Thus, protect and promote the greatest depth for the greatest span.

I believe that is the Basic Moral Intuition given to all holons, human and otherwise; but the greater the depth of a holon, the more clearly it will intuit that Ground and the more fully it will unpack that Basic Moral Intuition, extending it to more and more other holons in the process.

Q: Depth across span.

KW: Yes. The idea is that in attempting to promote the greatest depth for the greatest span, we must make pragmatic judgments about differences in intrinsic worth, about the degree of depth that we destroy in an attempt to meet our own vital needs—better to kill a carrot than a cow. Alan Watts hit it right on the head when someone asked him why he was a vegetarian. "Because cows scream louder than carrots."

But that must be carried across span as well, which prevents a dominator hierarchy. To give a stark example, if it came to killing a dozen apes or killing Al Capone, I'd have to say Al. There's nothing sacrosanct about being a human holon. That in itself is meaningless. That in itself is truly anthropocentric in the worst possible sense.

I hope you can get the general picture of holarchical ethics preserving not just depth, but depth across span, all set in a prior Ground value. Resting in Emptiness, promote the greatest depth for the greatest span. Such, I believe, is the pattern of the tears shed by Bodhisattvas everywhere.

An Integral Vision

Q: So in all of these cases—the problems with the culture gap, with vertical integration, with environmental ethics—they all hinge on a rejection of flatland.

KW: Definitely. We were talking about the possibility of a coming transformation, which in many ways is already in motion. But I don't believe this new transformation can harmoniously proceed without integrating the Big Three. The dissociation of the Big Three was the gaping wound left in our awareness by the failures of modernity, and the new postmodern transformation will have to integrate those fragments or it will not meet the demands of the twenty tenets—it will not transcend and include; it will not differentiate and integrate; it will not be able to evolve further; it will be a false start; evolution might very well erase it. We cannot build tomorrow on the bruises of yesterday.

Among numerous other things, this means a new form of society will have to evolve that integrates consciousness, culture, and nature, and thus finds room for art, morals, and science—for personal values, for collective wisdom, and for technical knowhow.

And there is no way to do this without going beyond flatland. Only by rejecting flatland can the Good and the True and the Beautiful be integrated. Only by rejecting flatland can we attune ourselves with Spirit's radiant expression in all its verdant domains. Only by rejecting flatland can we arrive at an authentic environmental ethics and a council of all beings, each gladly bowing to the perfected grace in all. Only by rejecting flatland can we come to terms with the devastating culture gap, and thus set individuals free to unfold their own deepest possibilities in a culture of encouragement. Only by rejecting flatland can the grip of mononature be broken, so that nature can actually be integrated and thus genuinely honored, instead of made into a false god that ironically contributes to its own destruction. Only by rejecting flatland can we set the global commons free in communicative exchange that is decentered from egocentric and ethnocentric and nationalistic imperialism, racked with wars of race and blood and bounty. Only by rejecting flatland can we engage the real potentials of vision-logic, which aims precisely at integrating physiosphere and biosphere and noosphere in a radical display of its own intrinsic joy. Only by rejecting flatland can the technobase of the Infobahn be made servant to communion rather than master of digital anarchy, and in this way the Net might actually announce the dawn of global convergence, not global fragmentation. Only by rejecting flatland can a World Federation or Family of Nations emerge in a holarchical convergence around the World Soul itself, committed to the vigorous protection of that worldcentric space, the very form of Spirit's modern voice, glorious in its compassionate embrace.

And thus—to return to specifically spiritual and transpersonal themes—only by rejecting flatland can those who are interested in spirituality begin to integrate the Ascending and Descending currents. In flatland you can only be an Ascender or a Descender. You either deny any existence to flatland altogether (the Ascenders), or you try to make it into God (the Descenders).

Q: So we really have come full circle here, right back to the archetypal battle at the heart of the Western tradition—the Ascenders versus the Descenders.

KW: Yes. The purely Descended approaches absolutely despise the Ascending paths, and blame them for virtually all of humanity's and Gaia's problems. But not to worry, the loathing is mutual: the Ascenders maintain the Descenders are simply caught in self-dispersal and outward-bound ignorance, which is the real source of all humanity's turmoils.

The Ascenders and the Descenders, *after two thousand years*, still at each other's throat—each still claiming to be the Whole, each still accusing the other of Evil, each still perpetrating the same fractured insanity it despises in the other. The Ascenders and the Descenders—still crazy after all these years.

Q: The point is to integrate and balance the Ascending and Descending currents in the human being.

KW: Yes, the point is to bring these two currents into some sort of union and harmony, so that both wisdom and compassion can join hands in finding a Spirit that both transcends and includes this world, a Spirit eternally prior to this world and yet embracing this world and all its beings with infinite love and compassion, and care and concern, and the tenderest of mercies, and glory in the glance.

And however much the flurry of Descended religions help us to recognize and appreciate the visible, sensible God and Goddess, nonetheless, taken in and by themselves, they place an infinite burden on Gaia that poor finite Gaia cannot sustain. It might be sustainable growth, but it is unsustainable spirituality. And we desperately need both. The Ascending currents of the human being also have to be engaged, and activated, and cultivated, for it is only in being able to transcend our own limited and mortal egos that we can find that common Source and Ground of all sentient beings, a Source that bestows new splendor on the setting sun and radiates grace in each and every gesture.

Both the mere Ascenders and the mere Descenders, in tearing the Kosmos into their favorite fragments, are contributing to the brutality of this warfare, and they simply try to convert and coerce the other by sharing their diseases and waving their wounds. But it is in the union of the Ascending and the Descending that harmony is found, and not in any brutal war between the two. Only when both are united, we might say, can both be saved.

Q: Which brings us directly to the integral vision itself.

KW: Yes, to some sort of holistic and integrated view. I have concentrated on an approach that attempts to honor and include the very best of premodernity (the Great Nest of Being), the best of modernity (the differentiation of the Big Three), and the best of postmodernity (the integration of the Big Three)—to arrive at a truly "all-level, all-quadrant" approach.

Q: To arrive at an integral vision that can be summarized as in figures 15-1, 15-2, and 15-3, for example (pp. 299–301).

KW: Yes, that's right. Never before in history has this type of all-level, all-quadrant approach been possible, because never before were all the pieces of the puzzle available. Premodernity was all-level but not all-quadrant. Modernity was all-quadrant but not all-level (and that got even worse when the quadrants collapsed into flatland). Postmodernity, which set out to pick up the pieces and integrate the quadrants, instead fell into the intense gravitational field of flatland and ended up more fragmented than ever.

But the pieces are all present, and what is now required is a vision capable of weaving them together in a genuinely holistic fashion. This is what "all-level, all-quadrant" attempts to do. And if this type of integral vision succeeds, it will have immediate applications in business, education, medicine, health care, politics, cultural studies, psychology, human development—the list is truly endless, it seems.

Q: People can start to build this integral vision themselves by applying the four quadrants to whatever field they are in.

KW: That's true. In medicine, for example, you can see that any effective care would have to take into account, not just the objective medicine or physical treatment that you give the person (UR), but also the person's subjective beliefs and expectations (UL), the cultural attitudes, hopes, and fears about sickness (LL), and the social institutions, economic factors, and access to health care (LR), all of which have a causal effect on the course of a person's illness (because all four quadrants cause, and are caused by, the others). You can do the same analysis with law, education, business, politics, environmental ethics, schools of feminism, prison reform, philosophical systems, and so on.

And this will pay off in the most concrete of ways. If the four quadrants are real, then any health care system that includes all of them will be more effective (and therefore more cost efficient). Any business that takes them into account will be more efficient and thus more profitable. Any educational system will be more effective; politics will be more responsive; spirituality will be more transformative. And so on.

That is the first step of implementing a more integral vision—namely, moving from a one-quadrant approach to an *all-quadrant* approach. The second step is to move from all-quadrant to *all-level, all-quadrant*.

Q: Which would trace out the various waves and streams of development in each of the quadrants.

KW: Yes, that's right. We have especially focused on development in the Upper-Left quadrant—the nine or so fulcrums spanning the entire spectrum of consciousness, with their different needs, motivations, values, worldviews, self-identities, and so on, moving from matter to body to mind to soul to spirit. But those developments have correlates in all the other quadrants, and thus you can follow those as well. Not just, what will medicine look like if it includes all four quadrants, but what will medicine look like if it also spans the entire spectrum of consciousness in each of the quadrants? Not just, what can you do for healing if you use matter and body, but what can you do for healing if you use mind and soul and spirit as well? What would a full-spectrum medicine look like? Likewise, what would a full-spectrum education look like? Full-spectrum economy? Full-spectrum politics? Business? Marriage? Cinema? Art?

Q: Following the full spectrum in each of the quadrants. The I and the We and the It domains all evolve from body to mind to soul to spirit. Thus, all-quadrant, all-level.

KW: Yes. And we might especially want to remember, when we include soul and spirit in an integral view, that we do so in both Ascending and Descending ways. We want to include the liberating movement of wisdom that takes us from body to mind to soul to spirit, but also the incarnational movement of compassion and healing that brings soul and spirit down and into body, earth, life, and relationships—both God and Goddess equally honored.

This also opens up an enormous number of research projects—there are a thousand graduate theses on how to implement an all-level, all-quadrant approach. (For specific recommendations for following the levels and lines in each of the quadrants, see *Integral Psychology*.) But there are also all the small, daily ways that you can implement your own integral vision as well.

Q: Such as personal transformation and spiritual practice. Since an integral transformative practice would be all-level, all-quadrant, what would that actually involve?

KW: Here are some approaches where you can follow up on this if you like. Tony Schwartz, *What Really Matters: Searching for Wisdom in America*; Michael Murphy and George Leonard, *The Life We Are Given: A Long-Term Program for Realizing the Potential of Body, Mind, Heart, and Soul*; and my own *One Taste*.

The general idea is simply that we need to exercise body, mind, soul, and spirit—and to do so in self, culture, and nature.

Q: An integral vision.

KW: Yes, an integral vision. And the final result is simply to awaken to who and what you timelessly are—to awaken to the Spirit that is the actual author of this integral display.

And there, hidden in the secret cave of the Heart, where God and the Goddess finally unite, where Emptiness embraces all Form as the lost and found Beloved, where Eternity joyously sings the praises of noble Time, where Shiva uncontrollably swoons for luminescent Shakti, where Ascending and Descending erotically embrace in the sound of one hand clapping—there forever in the universe of One Taste, the Kosmos recognizes its own true nature, self-seen in a tacit recognition that leaves not even a single soul to tell the amazing tale.

And remember? There in the Heart, where the couple finally unite, the entire game is undone, this nightmare of evolution, and you are exactly where you were prior to the beginning of the whole show. With a sudden shock of the utterly obvious, you recognize your own Original Face, the face you had prior to the Big Bang, the face of utter Emptiness that smiles as all creation and sings as the entire Kosmos—and it is all undone in that primal glance, and all that is left is the smile, and the reflection of the moon on a quiet pond, late on a crystal clear night.

APPENDIX

The Twenty Tenets

The twenty tenets are simply some of the tendencies of evolutionary systems wherever we find them; they are "Kosmic patterns." There is nothing sacrosanct about the number "twenty." Some of these are simple definitions, others are real tendencies. Tenet 2 actually has four; tenet 12 has five (that's nineteen); there are three additions (twenty-two); but at least two tenets are simple definitions (e.g., seven, nine), which gives around twenty. But the interested reader can probably find more to add (or subtract). . . .

1. Reality as a whole is not composed of things or processes, but of *holons* (wholes that are parts of other wholes; e.g, whole atoms are parts of whole molecules, which are parts of whole cells, which are parts of whole organisms, and so on).
2. Holons display four fundamental capacities: (a) self-preservation (agency), (b) self-adaptation (communion), (c) self-transcendence (eros), and (d) self-dissolution (thanatos).
3. Holons emerge.
4. Holons emerge holarchically.
5. Each emergent holon transcends but includes its predecessor(s).
6. The lower sets the possibilities of the higher; the higher sets the probabilities of the lower.
7. The number of levels that a holarchy comprises determines whether it is "shallow" or "deep"; and the number of holons on any given level we shall call its "span."
8. Each successive level of evolution produces greater depth and less span.

Addition 1: The greater the depth of a holon, the greater its degree of consciousness.

9. Destroy any holon, and you will destroy all of the holons above it and none of the holons below it.
10. Holarchies co-evolve.
11. The micro is in relational exchange with the macro at all levels of its depth.
12. Evolution has directionality.
    a. increasing complexity
    b. increasing differentiation/integration
    c. increasing organization/structuration
    d. increasing relative autonomy
    e. increasing telos

Addition 2: Every holon issues an IOU to the Kosmos.

Addition 3: All IOUs are redeemed in Emptiness.

AN INTEGRAL
THEORY OF
CONSCIOUSNESS

An Integral Theory
of Consciousness

ABSTRACT: *An extensive data search among various types of developmental and evolutionary sequences yielded a "four quadrant" model of consciousness and its development (the four quadrants being intentional, behavioral, cultural, and social). Each of these dimensions was found to unfold in a sequence of at least a dozen major stages or levels. Combining the four quadrants with the dozen or so major levels in each quadrant yields an integral theory of consciousness that is quite comprehensive in its nature and scope. This model is used to indicate how a general synthesis and integration of thirteen of the most influential schools of consciousness studies can be effected, and to highlight some of the most significant areas of future research. The conclusion is that an "all-quadrant, all-level" approach is the minimum degree of sophistication that we need in order to secure anything resembling a genuinely integral theory of consciousness.* *

INTRODUCTION

There has recently been something of an explosion of interest in the development of a "science of consciousness," and yet there are at present approximately a dozen major but conflicting schools of consciousness theory and research. My own approach to consciousness studies is based on the assumption that each of these schools has something irreplace-

---

*Roger Walsh, a noted authority on brain, consciousness, and meditation research, read this article and made many valuable suggestions; he also wrote the section "Meditation: An Opportunity for Integral Research."

ably important to offer, and thus what is required is a general model sophisticated enough to incorporate the essentials of each of them. These schools include the following:

1. *Cognitive science* tends to view consciousness as anchored in functional schemas of the brain/mind, either in a simple representational fashion (such as Jackendoff's "computational mind") or in the more complex emergent/connectionist models, which view consciousness as an emergent of hierarchically integrated networks. The emergent/connectionist is perhaps the dominant model of cognitive science at this point, and is nicely summarized in Alwyn Scott's *Stairway to the Mind* (1995), the "stairway" being the hierarchy of emergents summating in consciousness.

2. *Introspectionism* maintains that consciousness is best understood in terms of intentionality, anchored in first-person accounts—the inspection and interpretation of immediate awareness and lived experience—and not merely in third-person or objectivist accounts, no matter how "scientific" they might appear. Without denying their significant differences, this broad category includes everything from philosophical intentionality to introspective psychology, existentialism, and phenomenology.

3. *Neuropsychology* views consciousness as anchored in neural systems, neurotransmitters, and organic brain mechanisms. Unlike cognitive science, which is often based on computer science and is consequently vague about how consciousness is actually related to organic brain structures, neuropsychology is a more biologically based approach. Anchored in neuroscience more than computer science, it views consciousness as intrinsically residing in organic neural systems of sufficient complexity.

4. *Individual psychotherapy* uses introspective and interpretive psychology to treat distressing symptoms and emotional problems; it thus tends to view consciousness as primarily anchored in an individual organism's adaptive capacities. Most major schools of psychotherapy embody a theory of consciousness precisely because they must account for a human being's need to create meaning and signification, the disruption of which results in painful symptoms of mental and emotional distress. In its more avant-garde forms, such as the Jungian, this approach postulates collective structures of intentionality (and thus consciousness), the fragmentation of which contributes to psychopathology.

5. *Social psychology* views consciousness as embedded in networks of cultural meaning, or, alternatively, as being largely a byproduct of the social system itself. This includes approaches as varied as ecological, Marxist, constructivist, and cultural hermeneutics, all of which maintain that the nexus of consciousness is not located merely or even principally in the individual.

6. *Clinical psychiatry* focuses on the relation of psychopathology, behavioral patterns, and psychopharmacology. For the last half century, psychiatry was largely anchored in a Freudian metapsychology, but the field increasingly tends to view consciousness in strictly neurophysiological and biological terms, verging on a clinical identity theory: consciousness is the neuronal system, so that a presenting problem in the former is actually an imbalance in the latter, correctable with medication.

7. *Developmental psychology* views consciousness not as a single static entity but as a developmentally unfolding process with a substantially different architecture at each of its stages of growth. Thus an understanding of consciousness demands an investigation of the architecture at each of its levels of unfolding. In its more avant-garde forms, this approach includes higher stages of exceptional development and well-being, and the study of gifted, extraordinary, and supranormal capacities, viewed as higher developmental potentials latent in all humans. This includes higher stages of cognitive, affective, somatic, moral, and spiritual development.

8. *Psychosomatic medicine* views consciousness as strongly and intrinsically interactive with organic bodily processes, evidenced in such fields as psychoneuroimmunology and biofeedback. In its more avant-garde forms, this approach includes consciousness and miraculous healing, the effects of prayer on remarkable recoveries, light/sound and healing, spontaneous remission, and so on. It also includes any of the approaches that investigate the effects of intentionality on healing, from art therapy to visualization to psychotherapy and meditation.

9. *Nonordinary states of consciousness,* from dreams to psychedelics, constitute a field of study that, its advocates believe, is crucial to a grasp of consciousness in general. Although some of the effects of psychedelics—to take a controversial example—are undoubtedly due to "toxic side-effects," the consensus of opinion in this area of research is that they also act as a "nonspecific amplifier of experience," and thus they can be instrumental in disclosing and amplifying aspects of consciousness that might otherwise go unstudied.

10. *Eastern and contemplative traditions* maintain that ordinary consciousness is but a narrow and restricted version of deeper or higher modes of awareness, and that specific injunctions (yoga, meditation) are necessary to evoke these higher and exceptional potentials. Moreover, they all maintain that the essentials of consciousness itself can only be grasped in these higher, postformal, and nondual states of consciousness.

11. What might be called the *quantum consciousness* approaches view consciousness as being intrinsically capable of interacting with, and altering, the physical world, generally through quantum interactions, both in the human body at the intracellular level (e.g., microtubules), and in the material world at large (psi). This approach also includes the many and various attempts to plug consciousness into the physical world according to various avant-garde physical theories (bootstrapping, hyperspace, strings).

12. *Subtle energies* research has postulated that there exist subtler types of bioenergies beyond the four recognized forces of physics (strong and weak nuclear, electromagnetic, gravitational), and that these subtler energies play an intrinsic role in consciousness and its activity. Known in the traditions by such terms as *prana, ki,* and *ch'i*—and said to be responsible for the effectiveness of acupuncture, to give only one example—these energies are often held to be the "missing link" between intentional mind and physical body. For the Great Chain theorists, both East and West, this bioenergy acts as a two-way conveyor belt, transferring the impact of matter to the mind and imposing the intentionality of the mind on matter.

13. *Evolutionary psychology* and its close relative sociobiology see behavior and consciousness in functional terms as expressions of evolutionary pressures. From this perspective, consciousness and its various forms exist because of, and are to be understood in terms of, the evolutionary advantage they confer.

The approach to consciousness described here involves a model that explicitly draws on the strengths of each of those approaches, and attempts to incorporate and integrate their essential features. But in order to understand this model, a little background information is required.

THE FOUR CORNERS OF THE KOSMOS

Figure 1 is a schematic summary of what I call the "four quadrants" of existence: intentional, behavioral, cultural, and social. These four quadrants are a summary of a data search across various developmental and evolutionary fields. I examined over two hundred developmental sequences recognized by various branches of human knowledge—ranging from stellar physics to molecular biology, anthropology to linguistics, developmental psychology to ethical orientations, cultural hermeneutics to contemplative endeavors—taken from both Eastern and Western disciplines, and including premodern, modern, and postmodern sources (Wilber, 1995b; 1996d). I noticed that these various developmental sequences all fell into one of four major classes—the four quadrants—and, further, that within those four quadrants there was substantial agreement as to the various stages or levels in each. Figure 1 is a simple summary of this data search; it thus represents an a posteriori conclusion, not an a priori assumption.

Of course, people can differ about the details of such a diagram, and figure 1 is not cast in stone. It is presented as a reasonable summary that helps carry the present discussion. Likewise, each of the quadrants might more accurately be constructed as a branching tree, and not a simple straight line, indicating the rich variation within each grade and clade (each level and line). Each quadrant includes both hierarchies (or clear gradations) and heterarchies (or pluralistic and equivalent unfoldings within a given grade). Figure 1, again, is nothing but a simple schematic summary to help further the discussion.

Upper Right

The Upper-Right quadrant is perhaps the most familiar. It is the standard hierarchy presented by modern evolutionary science: atoms to molecules to cells to organisms, each of which "transcends but includes" its predecessor in an irreversible fashion: cells contain molecules, but not vice versa; molecules contain atoms, but not vice versa, and so on—the "not vice versa" constitutes the irreversible hierarchy of time's evolutionary arrow. (SF1, SF2, and SF3 refer to higher structure-functions of the human brain, which I will explain in a moment.)

Each of these individual units, in other words, is what Arthur Koestler called a "holon," a *whole* that is simultaneously *part* of some other whole (a whole atom is part of a whole molecule, a whole molecule is part of a whole cell, etc.). The Upper-Right quadrant is simply a summary of the scientific research on the evolution of individual holons.

Lower Right

But individual holons always exist in communities of similar holons. In fact, the very existence of individual holons in many ways depends upon

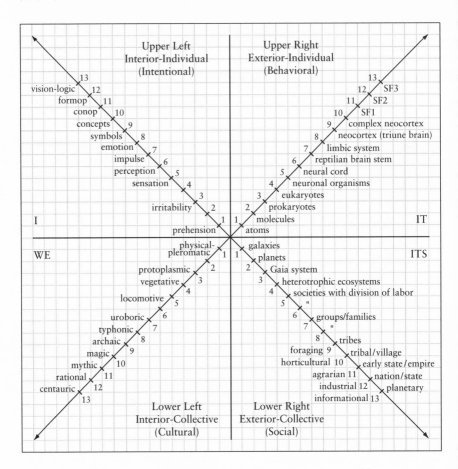

FIGURE 1. *The Four Quadrants*

communities of other holons that, if nothing else, provide the background fields in which individual holons can exist. Erich Jantsch, in his pioneering book *The Self-Organizing Universe* (1980), pointed out that every "micro" event (individual holon) exists embedded in a corresponding "macro" event (a community or collective of similarly structured holons). These communities, collectives, or societies are summarized in the Lower-Right quadrant, and they, too, simply represent the results of generally uncontested scientific research.

Thus, for example, Jantsch points out that when atoms were the most complex individual holons in existence, galaxies were the most complex collective structures; with molecules, planets; with prokaryotes, the Gaia system; with limbic systems, groups and families; and so forth.[1] Jantsch made the fascinating observation that while *individual* holons generally get *bigger* (because they transcend and include their predecessors: molecules are bigger than the atoms they contain), the *collective* usually gets *smaller* (planets are smaller than galaxies; families are smaller than planets, etc.)—the reason being that as an individual holon gets more complex (possesses more depth), the number of holons that can reach that depth become less and less, and thus the collective becomes smaller and smaller (e.g., there will always be fewer molecules than atoms, and thus the collective of molecules—planets—will always be smaller than the collective of atoms—galaxies). This entire trend I have summarized as: evolution produces greater depth, less span (Wilber, 1995b).

Those are the two "Right-Hand" quadrants. What both of those quadrants have in common is that they represent holons that all possess *simple location*—they can all be seen with the senses or their extensions; they are all empirical phenomena; they exist in the sensorimotor worldspace. They are, in other words, objective and interobjective realities; they are what individual and communal holons look like from the outside, in an exterior and objectifying fashion.

Upper Left

But various types of evidence suggest that every exterior has an interior. If we likewise do a data search among the evolutionary trends of interior apprehension, we also find a largely uncontested hierarchy of emergent properties, which I have simply summarized in the Upper-Left quadrant; prehension to irritability to sensation to perception to impulse to image to symbol to concept to rule (concrete operations, or "conop") to formal operations ("formop") and synthesizing reason ("vision-logic"; these correspond with structure-functions in the brain that I have simply labeled SF1, SF2, and SF3 in the Upper Right). The existence of most of those emergent properties is, as I said, largely uncontested by specialists in the field, and the holons listed in the Upper Left represent a simple summary of some of the major evolutionary capacities of interior apprehension. (There is still some heated discussion over the nature of "emergence," but the existence and evolutionary order of most of the various capacities themselves, from sensation to perception to image and concept, are generally uncontested.)

There is, however, rather endless debate about just how "far down" you can push prehension (or any form of rudimentary sentience). Whitehead pushes it all the way down, to the atoms of existence (actual occasions), while most scientists find this a bit much. My own sense is that, since holons are "bottomless," how much "consciousness" each of them possesses is an entirely relative affair. I don't think we need to draw a bold line in the existential sand and say, on this side of the line, consciousness; on that side, utter darkness. Indeed, the whole point of the hierarchy of evolutionary emergents of apprehension is that consciousness is almost infinitely graded, with each emergent holon possessing a little more depth and thus a bit more apprehension. However much "consciousness" or "awareness" or "sensitivity" or "responsiveness" a tree might have, a cow has more; an ape has more than that, and so on. How far down you actually push some form of prehension is up to you (and won't substantially alter my main points). I always found Teilhard de Chardin's (1964) conclusion to be the most sensible: "Refracted rearwards along the course of evolution, consciousness displays itself qualitatively as a spectrum of shifting shades whose lower terms are lost in the night."

Lower Left

That is the Upper-Left quadrant, and it represents the interior of individual holons; but, as always, every individual holon exists in a community (i.e., every agency is actually agency-in-communion). If we look at the *collective* forms of individual consciousness, we find various worldspaces or worldviews or communally shared sensitivity (from flocks of geese to human *Zeitgeist*). These various cultural or communal interiors are summarized in the Lower-Left quadrant.

Again, how far down you push a cultural background (or collective prehension) depends upon how far down you are willing to push individual prehension. I believe it shades all the way down, simply because exteriors don't make sense without interiors, and agency is always agency-in-communion. Nonetheless, my main points concern human consciousness, and we can all probably agree that humans possess not only a subjective space (the Upper Left) but also certain *intersubjective* spaces (the Lower Left). Those who have carefully investigated the *historical evolution of cultural worldviews* include researchers from Jean Gebser to Michel Foucault to Jürgen Habermas; I have outlined this research in the book *Up from Eden* (1996b) and summarized it in the Lower-Left quadrant in figure 1. "Uroboros" means reptilian (or brainstem-based); "typhonic" means emotional-sexual (limbic-system-based); archaic, magic, mythic, and rational are fairly self-explanatory (they are four of the most significant of the human cultural worldviews to evolve thus far); and "centauric" means a bodymind integration and cognitive synthesizing activity (which some researchers, including Gebser and Habermas, see starting to emerge at this time).

The Four-Quadrant Grid

Thus, the upper half of figure 1 refers to individual holons, the lower half to their collective forms. The right half refers to the exterior or objective aspects of holons, and the left half to their interior or subjective forms. This gives us a grid of exterior-individual (or behavioral), interior-individual (or intentional), exterior-collective (or social), and interior-collective (or cultural)—a grid of subjective, objective, intersubjective, and interobjective realities.

This makes a certain amount of intuitive sense; after all, some of the simplest distinctions we can make are between singular and plural, inside and outside, and it seems that evolution makes those distinctions as well, because it appears that development occurs in all four of those dimensions, and the four quadrants are a simple and very general summary of those evolutionary developments. The holons listed in each of the quadrants represent a great deal of empirical and phenomenological evidence, and, within the various disciplines addressing them, their existence is largely undisputed by serious scholars.

Unfortunately, as we will see, because many researchers specialize in one quadrant only, they tend to ignore or even deny the existence of the other quadrants. Materialist or Right-Hand theorists, for example, tend to deny substantial existence to interior, Left-Hand, and conscious intentionality. We will see many examples of this type of quadrant partiality, a reductionism that we will henceforth bracket. When I say that the holons presented in each quadrant are largely uncontested, I mean specifically by those who actually study that quadrant in its own terms.

Once we put these four quadrants together, a surprising set of further conclusions rather startlingly announce themselves. These conclusions are crucial, I believe, to grasping the overall nature of consciousness.

THE CONTOURS OF CONSCIOUSNESS

Quadrants and Their Languages

Begin with the fact that each of the quadrants is described in a different type of language. The Upper Left is described in "I" language; the Lower

Left is described in "we" language; and the two Right-Hand quadrants, since they are both objective, are described in "it" language. These are essentially Sir Karl Popper's "three worlds" (subjective, cultural, and objective); Plato's the Good (as the ground of morals, the "we" of the Lower Left), the True (objective truth or it-propositions, the Right Hand), and the Beautiful (the aesthetic beauty in the I of each beholder, the Upper Left); Habermas's three validity claims (subjective truthfulness of I, cultural justness of we, and objective truth of its). Historically of great importance, these are also the three major domains of Kant's three critiques: science or its *(Critique of Pure Reason)*, morals or we *(Critique of Practical Reason)*, and art and self-expression of the I *(Critique of Judgment)*.

In short, the Upper Left is described in *first-person*, the Lower Left in *second-person*, and the Right Hand in *third-person* language. Each of the thirteen approaches to consciousness tends to emphasize only one of those voices. The first-person, I-language, phenomenological approaches include 2, 4, 9, 10, and 12. The second-person, we-language, intersubjective accounts include 5 (which itself is a catch-all category for hermeneutics, cultural studies, and *verstehen* sociology). And third-person, it-language, objectivist accounts include 1, 3, 6, 11, and 13. One of our major conclusions is that an integral theory of consciousness would explicitly include all three types of accounts: a 1-2-3 of consciousness studies.

Quadrants and Their Validity Claims

Equally important, each of the quadrants has a different "type of truth" or *validity claim*—different types of knowledge with different types of evidence and validation procedures. Thus, propositions in the Upper Right are said to be true if they match a specific fact or objective state of affairs: a statement is true if the map matches the territory—so-called objective truth (representational truth and the correspondence theory of truth).

In the Upper-Left quadrant, on the other hand, a statement is valid not if it represents an objective state of affairs, but if it authentically expresses a subjective reality. The validity criterion here is not just truth but *truthfulness* or *sincerity*—not "Does the map match the territory?" but "Can the mapmaker be trusted?" I must trust you to report your interior status truthfully, because there is no other way for me to get to know your interior, and thus no other way for me to investigate your subjective consciousness.[2]

In the Lower-Right quadrant of interobjective realities, the validity claim is concerned with how individual holons fit together into interlocking systems; truth in this quadrant concerns the elucidating of the networks of mutually reciprocal systems within systems of complex interaction. The validity claim, in other words, is grounded in interobjective fit, or simply *functional fit.*

In the Lower-Left quadrant, on the other hand, we are concerned not simply with how objects fit together in physical space, but how subjects fit together in cultural space. The validity claim here concerns the way that my subjective consciousness fits with your subjective consciousness, and how we together decide upon those cultural practices that allow us to inhabit the same cultural space. The validity claim, in other words, concerns the *appropriateness* or *justness* of our statements and actions (ethics in the broadest sense). Not just "Is it true?" but "Is it good, right, appropriate, just?" And if you and I are to inhabit the same cultural space, we must implicitly or explicitly ask and to some degree answer those intersubjective questions. We must find ways, not simply to access objective truth or subjective truthfulness, but to reach *mutual understanding* in a shared intersubjective space. Not that we have to agree with each other, but that we can *recognize* each other, the opposite of which is, quite simply, war. (I have summarized these validity claims, and their different languages, in figure 2.)

Knowledge Acquisition

If we now look carefully at each of these four validity claims or "types of truth" and attempt to discern what all of them have in common—that is, what all authentic knowledge claims have in common—I believe we find the following (Wilber, 1996c; 1997):

Each valid mode of knowing consists of an *injunction,* an *apprehension,* and a *confirmation.* The injunction is generally of the form "If you want to know this, do this." This injunction, exemplar, or paradigm is, as Thomas Kuhn pointed out, an actual *practice,* not a mere concept. If you want to know if it is raining outside, go to the window and look. If you want to know if a cell has a nucleus, then learn to take histological sections, learn how to stain cells, put them under a microscope, and look. If you want to know the meaning of *Hamlet,* learn to read English, get the play, read it, and see for yourself.

In other words, the injunction or exemplar *brings forth a particular data domain*—a particular experience, apprehension, or evidence (the second strand of all valid knowledge).

	INTERIOR Left-Hand Paths	EXTERIOR Right-Hand Paths
	SUBJECTIVE	OBJECTIVE
INDIVIDUAL	*truthfulness* sincerity integrity trustworthiness	*truth* correspondence representation propositional
	I	it
	we	its
COLLECTIVE	*justness* cultural fit mutual understanding rightness	*functional fit* systems theory web structural-functionalism social systems mesh
	INTERSUBJECTIVE	INTEROBJECTIVE

FIGURE 2. *Validity Claims*

This apprehension, data, or evidence is then tested in the circle of those who have completed the first two strands; bad data or bad evidence is rebuffed, and this potential *falsifiability* is the third component of most genuine validity claims; it is *not* restricted to empirical or sensory claims alone: there is sensory experience, mental experience, and spiritual experience, and any specific claim in each of those domains can potentially be falsified by further data in those domains. For example, the meaning of *Hamlet* is not about the joys of war: that is a bad interpretation and can be falsified by virtually any community of adequate interpreters.

Thus, each holon seems to have at least four facets (intentional, behavioral, cultural, and social), each of which is accessed by a different type of truth or validity claim (objective truth, subjective truthfulness, intersubjective justness, and interobjective functional fit). And all of those four validity claims tend to follow the three strands of valid knowledge acquisition: injunction, apprehension, confirmation/rejection (or exemplar, evidence, falsifiability).

Notice that accessing the Left-Hand quadrants depends upon *interpretation* to some extent, whereas the Right-Hand quadrants are all, more or less, *empirical* events. Objective exteriors can be *seen,* but interior depth requires *interpretation.* My dog can see these physical words written on this page, because the signifiers exist in the sensorimotor worldspace; but you and I are trying to understand the signified meanings, which are not merely empirical and cannot be seen solely with the eye of flesh, but rather are partly intentional and thus can be seen only with the mind's interior apprehension: you must *interpret* the meaning of this sentence. "What does he *mean* by that?" You can see my behavior for yourself (with the monological gaze); but you can access my intentionality only by talking to me, and this dialogical exchange requires constant interpretation guided by mutual understanding in the hermeneutic circle.

Thus, it appears that the two Right-Hand validity claims (objective truth and functional fit) are grounded in *empirical observation* (and some sort of correspondence theory of truth); whereas the two Left-Hand validity claims (subjective truthfulness and intersubjective meaning) require extensive *interpretation or hermeneutics* (and some sort of coherence theory of truth). And perhaps we can begin to see why the human knowledge quest has almost always divided into these two broad camps: empirical vs. hermeneutic, positivistic vs. interpretive, scientific vs. intuitive, analytic vs. transcendental, Anglo-Saxon and Continental, Right Hand and Left Hand. It seems that both are indispensable, and that we should not attempt to go one-handed into that dark strange world known as ourselves.

Interdependence of the Quadrants

Most fascinating of all, perhaps, is that each quadrant seems to have correlates in all the others. That is, since very holon has these four facets (intentional, behavioral, cultural, and social), each of these facets has a very specific correlation with all the others. These can readily be seen in figure 1. For example, wherever we find a holon with a limbic system, we find that it has an interior capacity for impulse/emotion; it lives in the collective of a group, herd, or family; and it shares an emotional-sexual worldview. Apparently each quadrant causes, and is caused by, the others, in a circular and nonreducible fashion, which is likely why all four types of truth (and all four validity claims) are necessary to access the various dimensions of any holon.

The Farther Reaches of Human Nature

We need one last piece of background information. Figure 1 summarizes the four main strands of evolutionary unfolding to date. But who is to say this extraordinary unfolding has to stop with the formal or rational stage? Why not higher stages? Who can believably say that this amazing current of evolution simply came to a crashing halt once it produced you and me?

Several of the theories of consciousness summarized in the Introduction are predicated on the fact that consciousness evolution seems to show evidence of higher or postformal (or "post-postconventional") stages of growth. There appear to be, in other words, several higher stages in the Upper-Left quadrant (with correlations in the others).

The school of transpersonal psychology, in particular, has begun to investigate these higher consciousness stages. Substantial cross-cultural evidence already suggests that there are at least four broad stages of *postformal consciousness development*—that is, development that goes beyond but includes the formal operational level: the psychic, the subtle, the causal, and the nondual.* (Since each quadrant has correlates in the others, we also see different brain states associated with these postformal states, as well as different microcommunities or sanghas, the details of which are outside the scope of the present paper. See Wilber, 1995b; 1997, for further discussion.)

The precise definitions of those four postformal stages need not concern us; interested readers can consult the appropriate authorities (e.g., Walsh and Vaughan, 1993). The point is simply that there now exists a substantial amount of rather compelling evidence that interior consciousness can continue the evolutionary process of transcend and include, so that even rationality itself is transcended (but included!) in postformal stages of awareness, stages that increasingly take on characteristics that might best be described as spiritual or mystical. But this is a "mysticism" thoroughly grounded in genuine experience and verifiable by all those who have successfully followed the requisite set of conscious experiments, injunctions, and exemplars.

In Zen, for example, we have the injunction known as zazen (sitting meditation). The mastery of this exemplar or paradigm opens one to various kensho or satori experiences (direct apprehensions of the spiritual data brought forth by the injunction), experiences which are then

---

*Technically, vision-logic is the first postformal stage. [See *Integral Psychology* for an overview of standard terminology.]

thoroughly *tested* by the community of those who have completed the first two strands. Bad, partial, or inaccurate apprehensions are thoroughly rebuffed and rejected by the community of the adequate (falsifiability). Zen, in other words, follows the three strands of valid knowledge acquisition, which is probably why it has gained such a solid and "no-nonsense" reputation in spiritual studies.[3]

From these types of experimental, phenomenological, Left-Hand paths of knowledge acquisition, transpersonal researchers have concluded, as I said, that there exist at least four higher stages of postformal development available to men and women as structural potentials of their own bodymind. If, with reference to the Upper-Left quadrant, we add these four higher and postformal stages to the standard stages given in figure 1, we arrive at the *Great Chain of Being,* precisely as traditionally outlined by philosopher-sages from Plotinus to Aurobindo to Asanga to Chih-i to Lady Tsogyal. Figure 3 is a short summary of the Great Chain as given by perhaps its two most gifted exponents, Plotinus and Sri Aurobindo, showing the striking similarity of the Great Chain wherever it appeared, East or West, North or South (a truly "multicultural" map if ever there was one).

Again, the exact details need not detain us; interested readers can consult other works for a finer discussion (Smith, 1976; Lovejoy, 1964; Wilber et al., 1986). The point is simply that the interior dimensions of the human being seem to be composed of a *spectrum of consciousness,* running from sensation to perception to impulse to image to symbol to concept to rule to formal to vision-logic to psychic to subtle to causal to

Absolute One (Godhead)	Satchitananda/Supermind (Godhead)
Nous (Intuitive Mind) [subtle]	Intuitive Mind/Overmind
Soul/World-Soul [psychic]	Illumined World-Mind
Creative Reason [vision-logic]	Higher-mind/Network-mind
Logical Faculty [formop]	Logical mind
Concepts and Opinions	Concrete mind [conop]
Images	Lower mind [preop]
Pleasure/pain (emotions)	Vital-emotional; impulse
Perception	Perception
Sensation	Sensation
Vegetative life function	Vegetative
Matter	Matter (physical)
PLOTINUS	AUROBINDO

FIGURE 3. *The Great Chain of Being and Consciousness*

nondual states. In simplified form, this spectrum appears to range from subconscious to self-conscious to superconscious; from prepersonal to personal to transpersonal; from instinctual to mental to spiritual; from preformal to formal to postformal; from instinct to ego to God.

Now that is simply another way to say that *each of the quadrants consists of several different levels or dimensions,* as can be readily seen in figure 1. Moreover, these levels or dimensions have, for the most part, evolved or unfolded over time, linked by an evolutionary logic apparently pandemic in its operation (Dennett, 1995; Habermas, 1979; Wilber, 1995b).

Thus, you can perhaps start to see why I maintain that an "all-quadrant, all-level" approach is the minimum degree of sophistication that we need in order to secure anything resembling a genuinely integral theory of consciousness. And remember, all of this is suggested, not by metaphysical foundations and speculations, but by a rigorous data search on evidence already available and already largely uncontested.

That being so, let us continue drawing conclusions from this all-quadrant, all-level data base.

CONSCIOUSNESS DISTRIBUTED

If we now return to the dozen or so theories of consciousness outlined in the Introduction, we can perhaps start to see why all of them have proven to be so durable: they are each accessing one or more of the forty-plus quadrant-levels of existence, and thus each is telling us something very important (but partial) about consciousness. This is why I strongly maintain that all of those approaches are important for an integral view of consciousness. An all-level, all-quadrant approach finds important truths in each of them, and in very specific ways (which I will detail in a moment).

But it is not simply that we have a given phenomenon called "consciousness" and that these various approaches are each giving us a different view of the beast. Rather, it appears that consciousness actually exists distributed across all four quadrants with all of their various levels and dimensions. There is no one quadrant (and certainly no one level) to which we can point and say, *there* is consciousness. Consciousness does not appear to be localized in that fashion.

Thus, the first step toward a genuine theory of consciousness seems to be the realization that consciousness is not located in the organism.

Rather, consciousness is a four-quadrant affair, and it exists, if it exists at all, distributed across all four quadrants, anchored equally in each. Neither consciousness, personality, individual agency, nor psychopathology can be located simply or solely in the individual organism. The subjective domain (Upper Left) is always already embedded in intersubjective (Lower Left), objective (Upper Right), and interobjective (Lower Right) realities, all of which are partly constitutive of subjective agency and its pathologies.

It is true that the Upper-Left quadrant is the locus of consciousness as it appears in an individual, but that's the point: as it appears in an individual. Yet consciousness on the whole appears anchored in, and distributed across, all of the quadrants—intentional, behavioral, cultural, and social. If you "erase" any quadrant, they all disappear, because each seems intrinsically necessary for the existence of the others.

Thus, it is quite true that consciousness is anchored in the physical brain (as maintained by theories 1, 3, 6, 8, 13). But consciousness is also and equally anchored in interior intentionality (as maintained by theories 2, 4, 7, 10, 11), an intentionality that cannot satisfactorily be explained in physicalist or empiricist terms or disclosed by their methods or their validity claims.

By the same token, neither can consciousness be finally located in the individual (whether of the Upper Left or Upper Right or both together), because consciousness is also fully anchored in cultural meaning (the intersubjective chains of cultural signifieds), without which there is simply no individuated consciousness at all. Without this background of cultural practices and meanings (Lower Left), it appears that my individual intentions do not and even cannot develop, as the occasional cases of "wolf boy" demonstrate. In precisely the same way that there is no private language, there is no individual consciousness. You cannot generate meaning in a vacuum, nor can you generate it with a physical brain alone, but only in an intersubjective circle of mutual recognition. Physical brains raised in the wild ("wolf boy") generate neither personal autonomy nor linguistic competence, from which it certainly seems to follow that the physical brain per se is not the autonomous seat of consciousness.

Likewise, consciousness also appears to be embedded in, and distributed across, the material social systems in which it finds itself. Not just chains of cultural signifieds, but chains of social signifiers, determine the specific contours of any particular manifestation of consciousness, and without the material conditions of the social system, both individuated consciousness and personal integrity fail to emerge.

In short, it seems that consciousness is not located merely in the physical brain, nor in the physical organism, nor in the ecological system, nor in the cultural context, nor does it emerge from any of those domains. Rather, it appears anchored in, and distributed across, all of those domains with all of their available levels. The Upper-Left quadrant is simply the functional locus of a distributed phenomenon.

In particular, consciousness cannot be pinned down with "simple location" (which means, any type of location in the sensorimotor worldspace, whether that location actually be simple or dispersed or systems-oriented). Consciousness is distributed, not just in spaces of extension (Right Hand) but also in spaces of intention (Left Hand), and attempts to reduce one to the other have consistently and spectacularly failed. Consciousness is not located inside the brain, nor outside the brain either, because both of these are physical boundaries with simple location, and yet a good part of consciousness exists not merely in physical space but in emotional spaces, mental spaces, and spiritual spaces, none of which have simple location, and yet all of which are as real as (or more real than) simple physical space (they are Left-Hand, not Right-Hand, occasions).

The Right-Hand reductionists (subtle reductionists) attempt to reduce intentional spaces to extensional spaces and then "locate" consciousness in a *hierarchical network of physically extended emergents* (atoms to molecules to cells to nervous system to brain), and that, I believe, will never work. It gives us, more or less, only half the story (the Right-Hand half).

David Chalmers (1995) recently caused a sensation by having his essay "The Puzzle of Conscious Experience" published by *Scientific American*, bastion of physicalist science. Chalmers's conclusion was that subjective consciousness continues to defy all objectivist explanations. "Toward this end, I propose that conscious experience be considered a fundamental feature, irreducible to anything more basic. The idea may seem strange at first, but consistency seems to demand it" (p. 83).

Chalmers makes a series of excellent points. The first is the irreducibility of consciousness, which has to be "added" to the physical world in order to give a complete account of the universe. "Thus," he concludes, "a complete theory will have two components: physical laws, telling us about the behavior of physical systems from the infinitesimal to the cosmological, and what we might call psychophysical laws, telling us how some of those systems are associated with conscious experience. These two components will constitute a true theory of everything" (p. 83).

This attempt to reintroduce both Left- and Right-Hand domains to the Kosmos has been considered quite bold, a testament to the power of reductionism against which so obvious a statement seems radical. Chalmers moves toward a formulation: "Perhaps information has two basic aspects: a physical one and an experiential one. . . . Wherever we find conscious experience, it exists as one aspect of an information state, the other aspect of which is embedded in a physical process in the brain" (p. 85). That is, each state has an interior/intentional and exterior/physical aspect. My view, of course, is that all holons have not just those two but rather four fundamental and irreducible aspects, so that every "information state" actually and simultaneously has an intentional, behavioral, cultural, and social aspect. An all-quadrant, all-level view is much closer to a theory of everything, if such even makes any sense.

Chalmers goes on to point out that all of the physicalist and reductionist approaches to consciousness (including Daniel Dennett's and Francis Crick's) only solve what Chalmers calls "the easy problems" (such as objective integration in brain processes), leaving the central mystery of consciousness untouched. He is quite right, I believe. The funny thing is, all of the physicalist scientists who are sitting there and reading Chalmers's essay are already fully in touch with the mystery: they are already directly in touch with their lived experience, immediate awareness, and basic consciousness. But instead of directly investigating that stream (with, say, vipassana meditation [Varela et al., 1993]), they sit there, reading Chalmers's essay, and attempt to understand their own consciousness by objectifying it in terms of digital bits in neuronal networks, or connectionist pathways hierarchically summating in the joy of seeing a sunrise—and when none of those really seem to explain anything, they scratch their heads and wonder why the mystery of consciousness just refuses to be solved.

Chalmers says that "the hard problem" is "the question of how physical processes in the brain give rise to subjective experience"—that is, how physical and mental interact. This is still the Cartesian question, and it is no closer to being solved today than it was in Descartes's time.

For example, in the standard hierarchy: physical matter, sensation, perception, impulse, image, symbol, concept . . . , there is an *explanatory gap* between matter and sensation that has not yet been satisfactorily bridged—not by neuroscience nor cognitive science nor neuropsychology nor phenomenology nor systems theory. As David Joravsky (1982) put it in his review of Richard Gregory's *Mind in Science* (1982), "Seeing is broken down into component processes: *light,* which is physical; excitation in the neural network of eye and brain, which is also physical;

sensation, which is subjective and resists analysis in strictly physical terms; and *perception,* which involves cognitive inference from sensation and is thus even less susceptible to strictly physical analysis." Gregory himself poses the question "How is sensation related to neural activity?" and then summarizes the precise state-of-the-art knowledge in this area: "Unfortunately, we do not know." The reason, he says, is that there is "an irreducible gap between physics and sensation which physiology cannot bridge"—what he calls "an impassable gulf between our two realms." Between, that is, the Left and Right halves of the Kosmos.

But, of course, it is not actually an impassable gulf: you see the physical world right now, so the gulf is bridged. The question is, how? And the answer, as I suggested in *Eye to Eye,* only discloses itself to postformal awareness. The "impassable gulf" is simply another name for the subject/object dualism, which is the hallmark, not of Descartes's error, but of all manifestation, which Descartes simply happened to spot with unusual clarity. It is still with us, this gap, and it remains the mystery hidden in the heart of samsara, a mystery that absolutely refuses to yield its secrets to anything less than postformal and nondual consciousness development, or so it seems to me.

I have repeatedly had people explain to me that the Cartesian dualism can be solved by simply understanding that . . . and they then tell me their solutions, which range from Gaia-centric theories to neutral monism to first/third-person interactionism to systems theory. I always respond, "So this means that you have overcome the subject-object dualism in your own case. This means that you directly realize that you are one with the entire Kosmos, and this nondual awareness persists through waking, dream, and deep sleep states. Is that right?" "Well, no, not really."

The solution to the subject-dualism is not found in thought, because thought itself is a product of this dualism, which itself is generated in the very roots of the causal realm and cannot be undone without consciously penetrating that realm. The causal knot or primordial self-contraction—the ahamkara—can only be uprooted when it is brought into consciousness and melted in the fires of pure awareness, which almost always requires profound contemplative/meditative training. The subject-object duality is the very *form* of the manifest world of maya—the very beginning of the four quadrants (subject and object divide into singular and plural forms)—and thus one can get "behind" or "under" this dualism only by immersion in the *formless* realm (cessation, nirvikalpa, ayn, nirvana), which acts to dissolve the self-contraction and release it into pure nondual awareness—at which point, the traditions (from Zen to Eckhart) agree, you indeed realize that you are one with the entire Kosmos, a nondual awareness that persists through waking, dream, and deep sleep states: you have finally undone the Cartesian dualism.

In the meantime, one thing seems certain: the attempt to solve this dilemma by any sort of *reductionism*—attempting to reduce Left to Right or Right to Left, or any quadrant to any other, or any level to any other—is doomed to failure, simply because the four quadrants are apparently very real aspects of the human holon, aspects that aggressively resist being erased or reduced. Such reductionisms, to borrow Joravsky's phrase, "create mysteries or nonsense, or both together."

That is why I believe that an all-quadrant, all-level approach to consciousness is very likely the only viable approach to a genuinely integral theory of consciousness. We can now look briefly at what might be involved in the methodology of such an approach.

METHODOLOGY OF AN INTEGRAL APPROACH

The methodology of an integral study of consciousness would apparently require three broad wings: the first is a commitment to interdisciplinary study and thinking. In our time of information overload this is obviously no small requirement, and none of us will master it completely. However, all of us can try to seek out and be open to ideas and information outside our own base (quadrant, level).

This helps us to begin the second requirement: the simultaneous tracking of the various levels and lines in each of the quadrants, and then noting their correlations, each to all the others, and in no way trying to reduce any to the others (see below).

The third is the *interior transformation and development of the researchers themselves.* This is one reason, I suspect, that the Left-Hand dimensions of immediate consciousness have been so intensely ignored and aggressively devalued by most "scientific" researchers. Any Right-Hand path of knowledge can be engaged without a demand for interior *transformation* (or change in level of consciousness); one merely learns a new *translation* (within the same level of consciousness). More specifically, most researchers have already, in the process of growing up, transformed to rationality (formop or vision-logic), and no higher transformations are required for empiric-analytic or systems theory investigations.

But the Left-Hand paths, at the point that they begin to go postformal, *demand a transformation of consciousness in the researchers themselves.* You can master 100 percent of quantum physics without transforming consciousness; but you cannot in any fashion master Zen without doing so. You do not have to transform to understand Dennett's *Consciousness Explained;* you merely translate. But you must transform to actually understand Plotinus's *Enneads.* You are already adequate to Dennett, because you both have already transformed to rationality, and thus the *referents* of Dennett's sentences can be easily seen by you (whether or not you agree, you can at least see what he is referring to, because his referents exist in the rational worldspace, plain as day).

But if you have not transformed to (or at least strongly glimpsed) the causal and nondual realms (transpersonal and postformal), you will not be able to see the referents of most of Plotinus's sentences. They will make no sense to you. You will think Plotinus is "seeing things"—and he is, and so can you and I, if we both transform to those postformal worldspaces, whereupon the referents of Plotinus's sentences, referents that exist in the causal and nondual worldspaces, become plain as day. And that transformation seems to be an unavoidable part of the paradigm (the injunction) of an integral approach to consciousness.

So those broad wings—interdisciplinary and cross-cultural study, the nonreductionistic "simultracking" of all quadrants, and the transformation of researchers themselves—are all necessary for an integral approach to consciousness, in my opinion. Thus, I do not mean for an integral theory of consciousness to be an eclecticism of the dozen or so major approaches summarized above, but rather a tightly integrated approach that follows intrinsically from the holonic nature of the Kosmos.

The methodology of an integral approach to consciousness is obviously complex, but it follows some of the simple guidelines we have already outlined: three strands, four validity claims, ten or more levels of each. To briefly review:

- The three strands operative in valid knowledge are injunction, apprehension, confirmation (or exemplar, evidence, confirmation/rejection; or paradigm, data, fallibilism). These three strands appear to operate in the generation of valid knowledge—on any level, in any quadrant, or so I suggest.
- But each quadrant has a different architecture and thus a *different type of validity claim* through which the three strands operate: propositional truth (Upper Right), subjective truthfulness (Upper

Left), cultural meaning (Lower Left), and functional fit (Lower Right).

- Further, there are at least ten major levels or waves of development in each of those quadrants (ranging from the eye of flesh to the eye of mind to the eye of contemplation), and thus the knowledge quest takes on different forms as we move through those various waves in each quadrant. The three strands and four claims are still operating in each case, but the specific contours vary.

Meditation: An Opportunity for Integral Research

There has of late been an explosion of meditation research; a recent review listed well over one thousand publications (Murphy & Donovan, 1977). However, this research has its limitations. Most subjects have been relative beginners who have not accessed higher states and stages; many parameters have been only vaguely related to the goals of meditation (i.e., transpersonal development); many researchers have not themselves done sufficient practice to understand the significance of advanced experiences; and there has been little integration across domains. However, the opportunity for a more multileveled, multiquadrant, integrative research is available. What might such a program look like?

One place to begin would be in the Upper-Left quadrant with a careful examination of the phenomenology of meditative experiences, especially advanced ones. This could include both the content analysis of classic texts, such as Daniel Brown (1986) has begun, and with interviews of contemporary practitioners. This is essentially a *detailed phenomenology* of contemplative awareness.

These subjective data could be correlated with objective, Upper-Right-quadrant parameters, both psychometric and biological, e.g., electroencephalography, brain imaging, and biochemistry (Shapiro & Walsh, 1984; West, 1987). At the specific moment of any particular meditative experience, what are the physiological correlates?

On the systems side, it would be fascinating to see the social forms and institutions (Lower-Right quadrant) that practitioners prefer, create, and feel supported by. Considerable information is available from classical texts, which suggest settings of simplicity, quiet, service, and sangha (community of other practitioners). What are the materialities of communication, what economic factors come into play, how is the spiritual information itself disseminated? What types of social structures are created by transpersonally developed individuals, and conversely, what social structures enhance transpersonal development? How is spirituality manifest in the information age?

To complete the integral picture we will want to investigate the culture (Lower-Left quadrant) that accompanies these postformal experiences, biology, and social systems. What worldviews and ethical systems arise? What shared understandings of reality emerge, and how do they affect experience, behavior, and social institutions? What are the effects of different languages, ethical beliefs, and value systems on transpersonal development and consciousness evolution?

And, of course, we will want to examine development across time in all four quadrants, as they each influence, and are influenced by, the others: experience, behavior, culture, and society. An integral (all-quadrant, all-level) approach such as this is obviously demanding and will require cross-disciplinary skills. But the rewards might be a far richer understanding of the area than any we have had to date.

Let's now quickly run through the major schools of consciousness studies outlined in the Introduction and indicate some of the implications of an integral approach in each case.

An All-Quadrant, All-Level Approach

The *emergent/connectionist* cognitive science models (such as Alwyn Scott's *Stairway to the Mind*) apply the three strands of knowledge acquisition to the Upper-Right quadrant, the objective aspects of individual holons. Statements are thus guided by the validity claim of propositional truth tied to empirically observable events, which means that in this approach the three strands will acknowledge only those holons that register in the sensorimotor worldspace (i.e., holons with simple location, empirically observable by the senses or their extensions). Nonetheless, all holons are holarchic, or composed of hierarchical holons within holons indefinitely, and so this emergent/connectionist approach will apply the three strands to objective, exterior, hierarchical systems as they appear in the individual, objective organism (the Upper-Right quadrant).

All of this is fine, right up to the point where these approaches overstep their epistemic warrant and try to account for the other quadrants solely in terms of their own. In the case of the emergent/connectionist theories, this means that they will present a valid Upper-Right hierarchy (atoms to molecules to cells to neural pathways to reptilian stem to limbic system to neocortex), but then consciousness is somehow supposed to miraculously jump out at the top level (the Left-Hand dimensions are often treated as a monolithic and monological single entity, and then this "consciousness" is simply added on top of the Right-Hand hierarchy, instead of seeing that there are levels of consciousness which exist as the interior or Left-Hand dimension of every step in the Right-Hand hierarchy).

Thus, Scott presents a standard Upper-Right hierarchy, which he gives as atoms, molecules, biochemical structures, nerve impulses, neurons, assemblies of neurons, brain. Then, and only then, out pops "consciousness and culture," his two highest levels. But it appears that consciousness and culture are not levels in the Upper-Right quadrant, but significantly different quadrants themselves, each of which has a correlative hierarchy of its own developmental unfolding (and each of which is intimately interwoven with the Upper Right, but can in no way be reduced to or solely explained by the Upper Right).

Likewise with evolutionary psychology. The advantage of this approach, particularly in a postmodern atmosphere that attempts to reduce all biology to cultural constructs, is that it sheds significant light on the selection of specific types of neuronal networks and behavioral patterns. Evolutionary pressures (or drift) tend to drop those patterns that are not adaptive, and thus the learning mechanisms built into evolution appear to shed light on various types of human behavior. The units or holons of natural selection seem to exist in a hierarchy of inclusiveness (i.e., a holarchy), as Varela et al. (1993) point out: "A full list of units looks rather formidable: DNA short sequences, genes, whole gene families, the cell itself, the species genome, the individual, 'inclusive' groups of genes that are carried by different individuals, the social group, the actually interbreeding population, the entire species, the ecosystem of actually interacting species, and the global biosphere. Each unit [holon] harbors modes of coupling and selection constraints, has unique self-organizing qualities, and so has its own emergent status with respect to other levels . . ." (pp. 192–93).

An integral theory of consciousness would certainly include the Upper-Right hierarchy and those aspects of the emergent/connectionist and evolutionary psychology models that legitimately reflect that territory; but where those theories overstep their epistemic warrant (and are thus reduced to reductionism), we should perhaps move on.

The various schools of *introspectionism* take as their basic referent the interior intentionality of consciousness, the immediate lived experience and lifeworld of the individual (the Upper-Left quadrant). This means that, in these approaches, the three strands of valid knowledge will be applied to the data of immediate consciousness, under the auspices of the validity claim of truthfulness (because interior reporting requires sincere reports: there is no other way to get at the interiors). Introspectionism is intimately related to interpretation (hermeneutics), because most of the contents of consciousness are referential and intentional, and thus their meaning requires and demands interpretation: What is the meaning of this sentence? of last night's dream? of *War and Peace?*

As we have seen, valid interpretation generally follows the three strands (injunction, apprehension, confirmation). In this case, the three strands are being applied to symbolic/referential occasions and not merely to sensorimotor occasions (which would yield only empiric-analytic knowledge). As is commonly recognized, this interpretive and dialogical knowledge is trickier, more delicate, and more subtle than the head-banging obviousness of the monological gaze, but that doesn't mean it is less important (in fact, it means it is more significant).

The introspective/interpretative approaches thus give us the *interior contours of individual consciousness:* the three strands legitimately applied to the interior of individual holons under the auspices of truthfulness. This exploration and elucidation of the Upper-Left quadrant is an important facet of an integral approach to consciousness, and it is perhaps best exemplified in the first-person, phenomenological, and interpretive accounts of consciousness that can be found from depth psychology to phenomenology to meditation and contemplation, all of which, at their most authentic, are guided by injunction, apprehension, and confirmation, thus legitimately grounding their knowledge claims in reproducible evidence.

Developmental psychology goes one step further and inspects the actual stages of the unfolding of this individual consciousness. Since it usually aspires to a more scientific status, developmental psychology often combines an examination of the interior or Left-Hand reports of experience (the *semantics* of consciousness, guided by interpretative truthfulness and intersubjective understanding) with a Right-Hand or objective analysis of the *structures* of consciousness (the *syntax* of consciousness, guided by propositional truth and functional fit). This *developmental structuralism* traces most of its lineage to the Piagetian revolution; it seems an indispensable tool in the elucidation of consciousness and an important aspect of any integral approach. (It is rare, however, that these approaches clearly combine, via pragmatics, both the semantics and the syntax of the stages of consciousness development, which is an integration I am especially attempting to include.)

Eastern and nonordinary state models point out that there are more things in the Upper-Left quadrant than are dreamt of in our philosophy, not to mention our conventional psychologies. The three strands of valid knowledge are here applied to states that are largely nonverbal, postformal, and post-postconventional. In Zen, as we saw, we have a primary injunction or paradigm (zazen, sitting meditation), which yields experiential data (kensho, satori), which are then thrown against the community of those who have completed the first two strands and tested for validity. Bad data are soundly rejected, and all of this is open to ongoing review and revision in light of subsequent experience and further communally generated data.

Those approaches seem to be quite right: no theory of consciousness can hope to be complete that ignores the data from the higher or postformal dimensions of consciousness itself, and this exploration of the further reaches of the Upper-Left quadrant is surely a central aspect of an integral theory of consciousness. Moreover, this demands that, at some point, the researchers interested in these higher levels must transform their own consciousness in order to be adequate to the evidence. This is not a loss of objectivity but rather the prerequisite for data accumulation, just as we do not say that learning to use a microscope is the loss of one's objectivity—it is simply the learning of the injunctive strand, which is actually the precondition of a truly objective (or nonbiased) understanding of any data. In this case, the data is postformal, and so therefore is the injunction.

Advocates of *subtle energies* (prana, bioenergy) bring an important piece of the puzzle to this investigation. However, they often seem to believe that these subtle energies are the central or even sole aspect of consciousness, whereas they are merely one of the dimensions in the overall spectrum itself. For the Great Chain theorists, East and West, prana is the link between the material body and the mental domain, and in a sense I believe that is true enough. But the whole point of a four-quadrant analysis is that what the great wisdom traditions tended to represent as disembodied, transcendental, and nonmaterial modes actually have correlates in the material domain (every Left-Hand occasion has a Right-Hand correlate), and thus it is much more accurate to speak of the physical bodymind, the emotional bodymind, the mental bodymind, and so on. This simultaneously allows transcendental occasions and firmly grounds them. And in this conception, prana is simply the emotional bodymind in general, with correlates in all four quadrants (subjective: protoemotions; objective: limbic system; intersubjective: magical; interobjective: tribal). What is not helpful, however, is to claim that these energies alone hold the key to consciousness.

Psi studies (telepathy, precognition, psychokinesis, clairvoyance) are clearly some of the more controversial aspects of consciousness studies. This controversy may be beginning to resolve in light of recent advances in the field, including increasingly tight experimental designs, replicable findings across laboratories, and statistical meta-analyses, which have revealed highly significant findings. I have discussed this in *Eye to Eye* and won't repeat my observations here. I would simply like to emphasize that, once it is realized that the sensorimotor worldspace is merely one of at least ten worldspaces, we are released from the impossibility of trying to account for all phenomena on the basis of empirical occasions alone. At the same time, precisely because the sensorimotor worldspace is the anchor of the worldview of scientific materialism, as soon as some sort of proof of non-sensorimotor occasions (such as psi) is found, it can be excitedly blown all out of proportion. Psi events indeed cannot be unequivocally located in the sensorimotor worldspace, but then neither can logic, mathematics, poetry, history, meaning, value, or morals, and so what? None of the intentional and Left-Hand dimensions of consciousness follow the physical rules of simple location, and we don't need psi events to tell us that. Thus, an integral theory of consciousness would take seriously at least the *possibility* of psi phenomena, without blowing their possible existence all out of proportion; they are, at best, a slice of a very big pie.

Of the dozen or so major approaches to consciousness studies listed in the Introduction, the *quantum approaches* are the only ones that lack substantial evidence at this time, and when I say that they can be included in an integral theory of consciousness, I am holding open the possibility that they may eventually prove worthwhile. In *Eye to Eye* I review the various interpretations of quantum mechanics and its possible role in consciousness studies, and I will not repeat that discussion, except to say that to date the theoretical conclusions (such as that intentionality collapses the Schrödinger wave function) are based on speculative notions that most physicists themselves find dubious.

A central problem with these quantum approaches, as I see it, is that they are trying to solve the subject/object dualism on a level at which it cannot be solved. As suggested above, that problem is (dis)solved only in *postformal* development, and no amount of *formal* propositions will come near the solution. Nonetheless, this is still a fruitful line of research; it might help to elucidate some of the interactions between biological intentionality and matter.

All of those approaches center on the individual. But the *cultural approaches* to consciousness point out that individual consciousness does not, and cannot, arise on its own. All subjective events are always already intersubjective events. There is no private language; there is no radically autonomous consciousness. The very words we are both now sharing were not invented by you or me, were not created by you or me, do not come solely from my consciousness or from yours. Rather, you and I simply find ourselves in a vast intersubjective worldspace in which we live and move and have our being. This cultural worldspace (the Lower-Left quadrant) has a hand in the very structure, shape, feel, and tone of our consciousness, and no theory of consciousness seems complete that ignores this crucial dimension.

In these cultural hermeneutic approaches, the three strands are applied to the intersubjective circle itself, the deep semantics of the worlds of meaning in which we collectively exist. These cultural worldspaces evolve and develop (archaic to magic to mythic to mental, etc.), and the three strands applied to those worldspaces, under the auspices of mutual understanding and appropriateness, reveal those *cultural contours of consciousness*, which is exactly the course these important approaches take. This, too, seems to be a crucial component of an integral theory of consciousness.[4]

Such are some of the important (if partial) truths of cultural hermeneutics for individual consciousness. Likewise for the *social sciences,* which deal not so much with interior worldviews and interpretations, but with the exterior and objective and empirical aspects of social systems. Cultural hermeneutics (Lower Left) is a type of "interior holism" that constantly asks, "What does it *mean?*," whereas the social sciences (Lower Right) are a type of "exterior holism" that is constantly asking instead, "What does it *do?*"—in other words, mutual understanding versus functional fit. But both of these approaches tell us something very important about the collectivities in which individual consciousness is thoroughly embedded.

As for the social sciences: the materialities of communication, the techno-economic base, and the social system in the objective sense reach deep into the contours of consciousness to mold the final product. The three strands, under the auspices of propositional truth and functional fit, expose these social determinants at each of their levels, which is exactly the appropriate research agenda of the empirical social sciences.

A narrow Marxist approach, of course, has long been discredited (precisely because it oversteps its warrant, reducing all quadrants to the Lower Right); but the moment of truth in historical materialism is that the modes of material production (e.g., foraging, horticultural, agrarian, industrial, informational) have a profound and constitutive influence on the actual forms and contents of individual consciousness, and thus an understanding of these social determinants seems crucial for an integral theory of consciousness. Such an understanding would take its rightful place alongside the dozen or so other significant approaches to the study of consciousness.

Summary and Conclusion

I hope that this outline, abbreviated as it is, is nonetheless enough to indicate the broad contours of a methodology of an integral theory of consciousness, and that it sufficiently indicates the inadequacy of any less comprehensive approaches. The *integral* aspect enters in simultaneously tracking each level and quadrant in its own terms and then noting the correlations between them. This is a methodology of phenomenologically and contemporaneously tracking the various waves and streams in each of the quadrants and then correlating their overall relations, each to all the others, and in no way trying to reduce any to the others.

This "simultracking" requires a judicious and balanced use of all four validity claims (truth, truthfulness, cultural meaning, functional fit), each of which is redeemed under the warrant of the three strands of valid knowledge acquisition (injunction, apprehension, confirmation) carried out across the dozen or more waves in each of the quadrants—which means, in shorthand fashion, the investigation of sensory experience, mental experience, and spiritual experience: the eye of flesh, the eye of mind, and the eye of contemplation: all-level, all-quadrant.

And this means that, where appropriate, researchers will have to engage various injunctions that transform their own consciousness, if they are to be *adequate* to the postformal data. I cannot vote on the truth of the Pythagorean Theorem if I do not learn geometry (the injunction); likewise, I cannot vote on the truth of Buddha-nature if I do not learn meditation. All valid knowledge has injunction, apprehension, and confirmation; the injunctions are of the form "If you want to know this, you must do this"—and thus, when it comes to consciousness studies itself, the obvious but much-resisted conclusion is that certain interior injunctions will have to be followed by researchers themselves. If we do not do this, then we will not know this. We will be the Churchmen refusing Galileo's injunction: look through this telescope and tell me what you see.

Thus, an integral approach to consciousness might include the following agendas:

1. *Continue research on the various particular approaches.* That is, continue to refine our understanding of the many pieces of the puzzle of consciousness. The thirteen approaches I briefly outlined are all significant pieces to this extraordinary enigma; each is important; each deserves continued and vigorous research and development.

Why should we include all thirteen of these approaches? Aren't some of them a little "spooky" and "far out"? And perhaps shouldn't we exclude some of those? At this early stage in integral studies, I believe we need to err on the side of generosity, if only because reality itself is so consistently weird.

No human mind, I believe, is capable of producing 100 percent error. We might say, nobody is smart enough to be wrong all the time. And that means that each of the dozen or so approaches almost certainly has some sort of important truth to contribute.

2. *Confront the simple fact that, in some cases, a change in consciousness on the part of researchers themselves might be mandatory for the investigation of consciousness itself.* As numerous approaches (e.g., 7, 9, 10) have pointed out, the higher or postformal stages of consciousness development can only be adequately accessed by those who have themselves developed to a postformal level. If we are investigating postformal domains, postformal injunctions seem necessary. Failure to do so does not ensure "objectivity" in postformal studies: it ensures failure to grasp the data at the very start.

3. *Continue to grope our way toward a genuinely integral theory of consciousness itself.* Because the dozen or so approaches have tended to remain separate (and sometimes antagonistic) branches of human inquiry, it does indeed appear that they are in some ways working with different data domains, and these differences are not to be casually denied or dismissed. At the same time, I take it as plainly obvious that the universe hangs together, and thus an equally legitimate endeavor is to investigate, both theoretically and methodologically, the ways that these various holons are *intrinsically* hooked together as aspects of the unbro-

ken Kosmos. The fact that, for the most part, each approach has stayed in its own cage does not change the fact that reality itself leaps those cages all the time. To grope our way toward an integral approach means that we should attempt to follow reality and make those leaps as well.

This includes the actual *methodology* of "simultracking" the various phenomena in each level-quadrant and noting their actual interrelations and correlations (the simultracking of events in all-quadrant, all-level space). The quadrants and levels are in some sense quite different, but they are different aspects *of the Kosmos,* which means that they also *intrinsically* touch each other in profound ways. Let us note the ways in which they touch, and thus attempt to elucidate this wonderfully rich and interwoven tapestry.

Thus, each of the dozen or so approaches finds an important and indispensable place, not as an eclecticism, but as an intrinsic aspect of the holonic Kosmos. Put simply, an integral theory would attempt to seamlessly include and integrate first-, second-, and third-person accounts of consciousness. As it is now, there is a heated battle between first- and third-person approaches—between interior phenomenology and objectivist science—with second-person accounts often getting little mention by either. The analysis presented here suggests, on the contrary, that every first-person experience is embedded in second-person structures with third-person correlates, and all can, and should, be investigated simultaneously. Subjective awareness is correlated with objective forms, and both arise only in the clearing created by intersubjective structures, such that all three domains (or more specifically, all four quadrants) are mutually caused and causing: the 1-2-3 of consciousness studies.

Thus, the methodologies that purport to give us a "theory of consciousness" but which investigate only one quadrant (not to mention only one level in one quadrant) are clearly not giving us an adequate account of consciousness at all. Rather, an all-quadrant, all-level approach holds the chance of an authentic and integral theory of consciousness, if such indeed exists.

Notes

1. See Jantsch (1980) for an extended discussion of this theme. Jantsch correlates "microevolution" (of individual holons) with "macroevolution" (their collective/social forms), pointing out the coevolutionary interactions between individual and social. Thus, in the physiosphere, Jantsch traces microevolution across pho-

tons, leptons, baryons, light nuclei, light atoms, heavy atoms, and molecules; with their corresponding macroevolution (or collective/social forms) moving, respectively, across superclusters, clusters of galaxies, galaxies, stellar clusters, stars, planets, and rock formations. Likewise, in the biosphere, he traces microevolution across dissipative structures, prokaryotes, eukaryotes, multicellular organisms, and complex animals; with their corresponding macroevolution across planetary chemodynamics, Gaia system, heterotrophic ecosystems, societies with division of labor, and groups/families. All of these are simply and crudely summarized and condensed for figure 1, which is meant to be nothing more than a simple outline. I have discussed these issues in greater detail in Wilber 1995b.

2. This becomes quite significant in individual psychotherapy and depth psychology, because those disciplines have fundamentally explored the ways in which I might be *untruthful* to myself about my own interior status. "Repression" is basically a set of deceptions, concealments, or lies about the contours of my own interior space, and "therapy" is essentially learning ways to be more honest and truthful in interpreting my interior texts. Therapy is the sustained application of the validity criterion of truthfulness to one's own estate.

3. Of course, not everybody who takes up Zen—or any contemplative endeavor—ends up fully mastering the discipline, just as not everybody who takes up quantum physics ends up fully comprehending it. But those who do succeed—in both contemplation and physics, and indeed, in any legitimate knowledge quest—constitute the circle of competence against which validity claims are struck, and Zen is no exception in this regard.

4. The fact that we all exist in cultural worldspaces that are governed largely by interpretive and not merely empirical realities, and the fact that these cultural interpretations are partially constructed and relative, has been blown all out of proportion by the postmodern poststructuralists, who in effect claim this quadrant is the only quadrant in existence. They thus attempt to reduce all truth and all validity claims to nothing but arbitrary cultural constructions driven only by power or prejudice or race or gender. This cultural constructivist stance thus lands itself in a welter of performative self-contradictions: it claims that it is true that there is no such thing as truth; it claims that it is universally the case that only relativities are real; it claims that it is the unbiased truth that all truth is biased; and thus, in all ways, it exempts its own truth claims from the restrictions it places on everybody else's. As I have suggested elsewhere (Wilber, 1995a; 1997), whenever the other quadrants are denied reality, they in effect sneak back into one's system in the form of internal self-contradictions—the banished and denied validity claims reassert themselves in internal ruptures. Thus the extreme cultural constructivists implicitly claim objective and universal truth for their own stance, a stance which explicitly denies the existence of both universality and truth. Hence John Searle (1995) had to beat this approach back in his wonderful *The Construction of Social Reality*, as opposed to "the social construction of reality," the idea being that cultural realities are constructed on a base of correspondence truth which grounds the construction itself, without which no construction at all could get under way in the first place. Once again, we can

accept the partial truths of a given quadrant—many cultural meanings are indeed constructed and relative—without going overboard and attempting to reduce all other quadrants and all other truths to that partial glimpse.

References

A more complete bibliography of the various approaches can be found in Wilber 1995b [and *Integral Psychology* (Boston: Shambhala Publications, 2000)].

Chalmers, D. 1995. "The puzzle of conscious experience." *Scientific American.* December 1995.

Dennett, D. 1995. *Darwin's Dangerous Idea.* New York: Simon and Schuster.

Habermas, J. 1979. *Communication and the Evolution of Society.* Trans. T. McCarthy. Boston: Beacon Press.

Jantsch, E. 1980. *The Self-Organizing Universe.* New York: Pergamon.

Joravsky, D. 1982. "Body, mind, and machine." *New York Review of Books.* October 21, 1982.

Lovejoy, A. 1964 (1936). *The Great Chain of Being.* Cambridge: Harvard University Press.

Murphy, M., and Donovan, S. 1997. *The Physical and Psychological Effects of Meditation.* Sausalito, Calif.: Institute of Noetic Sciences.

Radin, D. 1987. *The Conscious Universe.* San Francisco: Harper SanFrancisco.

Scott, A. 1995. *Stairway to the Mind.* New York: Copernicus.

Searle, J. 1995. *The Construction of Social Reality.* New York: Free Press.

Shapiro, D., and Walsh, R. (eds.). 1984. *Meditation: Classic and Contemporary Perspectives.* New York: Aldine.

Smith, H. 1976. *Forgotten Truth.* New York: Harper.

Varela, F.; Thompson, E.; and Rosch, E. 1993. *The Embodied Mind.* Cambridge: MIT Press.

Walsh, R., and Vaughan, F. 1993. *Paths beyond Ego.* Los Angeles: Jeremy Tarcher.

West, M. 1987. *The Psychology of Meditation.* Oxford: Clarendon Press.

Wilber, K. 1995a. "An informal overview of transpersonal studies." *Journal of Transpersonal Psychology* 27, pp. 107–29.

———. 1995b. *Sex, Ecology, Spirituality: The Spirit of Evolution.* Boston and London: Shambhala Publications.

———. 1996a (1980). *The Atman Project,* 2nd ed. Wheaton, Ill.: Quest Books.

———. 1996b (1981). *Up from Eden,* 2nd ed. Wheaton, Ill.: Quest Books.

———. 1996c (1983). *Eye to Eye: The Quest for the New Paradigm.* Boston and London: Shambhala Publications.

———. 1996d. *A Brief History of Everything.* Boston and London: Shambhala Publications.

———. 1997. *The Eye of Spirit: An Integral Vision for a World Gone Slightly Mad.* Boston and London: Shambhala Publications.

Wilber, K.; Engler, J.; and Brown, D. 1986. *Transformations of Consciousness: Conventional and Contemplative Perspectives on Development.* Boston and London: Shambhala Publications.

THE EYE OF SPIRIT

*An Integral Vision for a World
Gone Slightly Mad*

What Is the Meaning of "Integral"?

JACK CRITTENDEN

T ONY SCHWARTZ, former *New York Times* reporter and author of *What Really Matters: Searching for Wisdom in America,* has called Ken Wilber "the most comprehensive philosophical thinker of our times." I think that is true. In fact, I thought that was true twenty years ago, when I founded *ReVision Journal* in large measure to provide an outlet for the integral vision that Ken was already voicing. I had just finished reading his first book, *The Spectrum of Consciousness,* which he wrote when he was twenty-three. The boy wonder was living in Lincoln, Nebraska, washing dishes, meditating, and writing a book a year. *Main Currents in Modern Thought,* which published his first essay, was just about to go out of business, and it was my desire to keep alive the integrative focus and spirit that that journal represented. This, combined with my desire to work with Ken in doing so, prompted me to drag him into the publishing business. We were both about twenty-seven at the time, and within a year or two we had *ReVision* up and running, based very much on the integral vision that we both shared and that Ken was already articulating in a powerful way.

But it is exactly the comprehensive and integral nature of Wilber's vision that is the key to the sometimes extreme reactions that his work elicits. Take, for example, his recent *Sex, Ecology, Spirituality.* The book certainly has its fans. Michael Murphy maintains that, along with Aurobindo's *Life Divine*, Heidegger's *Being and Time*, and Whitehead's *Process and Reality*, Wilber's *Sex, Ecology, Spirituality* is one of the four great books of this century. Dr. Larry Dossey proclaims it "one of the most significant books ever published," while Roger Walsh compares its scope to Hegel and Aurobindo. The most perspicuous reader of the bunch, invoking Alasdair MacIntyre's well-known choice between Aristotle and Nietzsche, claims that no, the modern world actually has three choices: Aristotle, Nietzsche, or Wilber.

The book's detractors, about some of whom you read in the following pages, are no less numerous, vocal, or determined. Feminists argue X; Jungians say Y; deconstructionists, always irritated and amazed at being outcontextualized, say Z—not to mention the generic reactions of deep ecologists, the mythopoetic movement, empiricists, behaviorists, Gnostics, neopagans, premodernists, astrologers—to name a few. Most critics have taken umbrage at Wilber's attacks on their own particular field, while they condone or concede the brilliance of his attacks on other fields. Nobody, however, has yet presented a coherent critique of Wilber's *overall* approach. The collective outrage, as it were, is astonishing, but the criticism has been little but nitpicking.

I want to focus on what is actually involved in this debate. Because, make no mistake, if Wilber's approach is more or less accurate, it does nothing less than offer a coherent integration of virtually every field of human knowledge.

Wilber's approach is the opposite of eclecticism. He has provided a coherent and consistent vision that seamlessly weaves together truth-claims from such fields as physics and biology; the ecosciences; chaos theory and the systems sciences; medicine, neurophysiology, biochemistry; art, poetry, and aesthetics in general; developmental psychology and a spectrum of psychotherapeutic endeavors, from Freud to Jung to Piaget; the Great Chain theorists from Plato and Plotinus in the West to Shankara and Nagarjuna in the East; the modernists from Descartes and Locke to Kant; the Idealists from Schelling to Hegel; the postmodernists from Foucault and Derrida to Taylor and Habermas; the major hermeneutic tradition, Dilthey to Heidegger to Gadamer; the social systems theorists from Comte and Marx to Parsons and Luhmann; the contemplative and mystical schools of the great meditative traditions, East and West, in the world's major religious traditions. All of this is just a sampling. Is it any wonder, then, that those who focus narrowly on one particular field might take offense when that field is not presented as the linchpin of the Kosmos?

In other words, to the critics the stakes are enormous, and it is not choosing sides at this point if I suggest that the critics who have focused on their pet points in Wilber's method are attacking a particular tree in the forest of his presentation. But if we look instead at the forest, and if his approach is generally valid, it honors and incorporates more truth than any other system in history.

How so? What is his actual method? In working with any field, Wilber simply backs up to a level of abstraction at which the various conflicting approaches actually agree with one another. Take, for example, the world's great religious traditions: Do they all agree that Jesus is God? No. So we must jettison that. Do they all agree that there is a God? That depends on the meaning of "God." Do they all agree on God, if by "God" we mean a Spirit that is in many ways *unqualifiable*, from the Buddhists' Emptiness to the Jewish mystery of the Divine? Yes, that works as a generalization—what Wilber calls an "orienting generalization" or "sturdy conclusion."

Wilber likewise approaches all the other fields of human knowledge: art to poetry, empiricism to hermeneutics, psychoanalysis to meditation, evolutionary theory to idealism. In every case he assembles a series of sturdy and reliable, not to say irrefutable, orienting generalizations. He is not worried, nor should his readers be, about whether *other* fields would accept the conclusions of any given field; in short, don't worry, for example, if empiricist conclusions do not match religious conclusions. Instead, simply assemble all the orienting conclusions as if each field had incredibly important truths to tell us. This is exactly Wilber's first step in his integrative method—a type of phenomenology of all human knowledge conducted at the level of orienting generalizations. In other words, assemble all of the truths that each field believes it has to offer humanity. For the moment, simply assume they are indeed true.

Wilber then arranges these truths into chains or networks of interlocking conclusions. At this point Wilber veers sharply from a method of mere eclecticism and into a systematic vision. For the second step in Wilber's method is to take all of the truths or orienting generalizations assembled in the first step and then pose this question: What coherent system would in fact *incorporate the greatest number of these truths*?

The system presented in *Sex, Ecology, Spirituality* (and clearly and simply summarized in the following pages) is, Wilber claims, the system that incorporates the greatest number of orienting generalizations from the greatest number of fields of human inquiry. Thus, if it holds up,

Wilber's vision incorporates and honors, it integrates, more truth than any other system in history.

The general idea is straightforward. It is not which theorist is right and which is wrong. His idea is that everyone is basically right, and he wants to figure out how that can be so. "I don't believe," Wilber says, "that any human mind is capable of 100 percent error. So instead of asking which approach is right and which is wrong, we assume each approach is true but partial, and then try to figure out how to fit these partial truths together, how to integrate them—not how to pick one and get rid of the others."

The third step in Wilber's overall approach is the development of a new type of *critical theory*. Once Wilber has the overall scheme that incorporates the greatest number of orienting generalizations, he then uses that scheme to criticize the partiality of narrower approaches, even though he has included the basic truths from those approaches. He criticizes not their truths, but their partial nature.

In his integral vision, therefore, is a clue to both of the extreme reactions to Wilber's work—that is, to the claims that it is some of the most significant ever published as well as to the chorus of angry indignation and attack. The angry criticisms are coming, almost without exception, from theorists who feel that their own field is the only true field, that their own method is the only valid method. Wilber has not been believably criticized for misunderstanding or misrepresenting any of the fields of knowledge that he includes; he is attacked, instead, for including fields that a particular critic does not believe are important or for goring that critic's own ox (no offense to vegetarians). Freudians have never said that Wilber fails to understand Freud; they say that he shouldn't include mysticism. Structuralists and poststructuralists have never said that Wilber fails to understand their fields; they say that he shouldn't include all those nasty other fields. And so forth. The attack always has the same form: How dare you say my field isn't the only true field!

Regardless of what is decided, the stakes, as I said, are enormous. I asked Wilber how he himself thought of his work. "I'd like to think of it as one of the first believable world philosophies, a genuine embrace of East and West, North and South." Which is interesting, inasmuch as Huston Smith (author of *The World's Religions* and subject of Bill Moyers's highly acclaimed television series *The Wisdom of Faith*) recently stated, "No one—not even Jung—has done as much as Wilber to open Western psychology to the durable insights of the world's wisdom traditions. Slowly but surely, book by book, Ken Wilber is laying the foundations for a genuine East/West integration."

At the same time, Ken adds, "People shouldn't take it too seriously. It's just orienting generalizations. It leaves all the details to be filled in any way you like." In short, Wilber is not offering a conceptual straight-jacket. Indeed, it is just the opposite: "I hope I'm showing that there is more room in the Kosmos than you might have suspected."

There isn't much room, however, for those who want to preserve their fiefdoms by narrowing the Kosmos to one particular field—to wit, their own—while ignoring the truths from other fields. "You can't honor various methods and fields," Wilber adds, "without showing how they fit together. That is how to make a genuine world philosophy." Wilber is showing exactly that "fit." Otherwise, as he says, we have heaps, not wholes, and we really aren't honoring anything.

Aristotle commented that no person could judge the value of his or her life until the end of that life, that no one could determine whether he or she had led a virtuous life except by considering that life as a whole. We, of course, know the difficulty of grasping the whole, let alone of evaluating it, especially when considering, as Wilber emphasizes, that one whole is always also a part of some greater whole. We know the ardor, and often the trauma, therefore, of trying to see how the pieces of our individual lives fit together; what they amount to; and to what, and to whom, the parts are connected.

Yet Wilber is helping us with exactly that task; he is giving us a pattern that connects all of life, of the Kosmos, of Spirit. His work amounts to a guide to the secrets of life—biological, social, cultural, and spiritual life. As you will see amply displayed in the following pages, he has drawn us a detailed map, an integral vision for the modern and post-modern world, a vision that unites the best of ancient wisdom with the best of modern knowledge. Through his truly extraordinary work he gives us encouragement to continue our own work—the life journey to wholeness that none of us can avoid but that until this integral vision few could fully comprehend.

On God and Politics

THE MOST PRESSING political issue of the day, both in America and abroad, is a way to integrate the tradition of liberalism with a genuine spirituality.

Never in history have these two strands of human striving been woven together in any sort of acceptable fashion. In fact, modern liberalism (and the general movement of the European Enlightenment) came into being in large measure precisely as a force against traditional religion. Voltaire's battle cry—"Remember the cruelties!"—rang out across the continent: remember the cruelties inflicted on men and women in the name of God, and have done with those brutalities, and that God, once and for all.

This left religion, for the most part, in the hands of the conservatives. And thus, down to today, we are saddled with two heavily armed camps, each of which profoundly distrusts the other.

In one camp we have the liberals, who champion individual rights and freedoms against the tyranny of the collective, and who therefore are deeply suspicious of any and all religious movements, precisely because the latter are always ready to impose their beliefs on others, and tell you what you must do in order to save your soul. Enlightened liberalism historically came into existence to fight such religious tyranny, and it retains deep in its heart a profound distrust—amounting at times to hatred—of all things religious and spiritual, of anything vaguely divine.

Liberals have therefore tended to replace salvation by God with salvation by economics. True liberation and freedom could be found, not in some pie-in-the-sky afterlife (or any other opiate of the masses), but rather in real gains on the real earth, starting with material and economic necessities. "Progressive" and "liberal" have often been used synonymously, precisely because progress in actual social conditions—economic, material, political freedoms—defined the very heart of liberalism.

In the place of communal tyranny, liberalism has substituted what we might call "universal individualism," the call that all individuals, regardless of race, gender, color, or creed, should be treated impartially, with fairness and equal justice. Individuals set loose from communal tyranny to pursue economic and political freedoms: one of the clarion calls of liberalism.

Granted that much good has most definitely come from such liberalism. The downside, nonetheless, was that all too often, religious tyranny was simply replaced by economic tyranny, and the God of the almighty dollar replaced the God of the Pope. Your soul could no longer be crushed by God, but it could be crushed by the factory. What was of *ultimate concern* in life ceased to be your relationship to the Divine and centered instead on your relationship to your income. And thus, even in the midst of economic plenty, your soul could slowly starve to death.

In the other camp, we have the conservatives, who are wedded more to a civic humanist tradition that sees the essence of men and women dependent upon communal standards and values, including preeminently religious values. The republican and religious strands tend to be deeply interwoven in most forms of conservatism, so much so that even when conservatives boisterously champion individual rights and "freedom from government," they do so only if those "freedoms" fit their religious tenets.

The emphasis on community and family values allows conservatives to build strong nations—but often at the expense of those who do not share their particular religious orientation. A cultural tyranny is never far from a conservative smile, and liberals recoil in horror from the "love" that conservatives profess for all God's children, because the chilling fact is that if you are not one of their God's children, unpleasant days await you.

In a very simplistic sense, then, there is a "good" and a "tyranny" in both the liberal and conservative orientations, and the ideal situation would apparently be to rescue the good of each while jettisoning their respective tyrannies.

The good of liberalism is its emphasis on individual freedom and its rejection of the herd mentality. But in its zeal to protect individual freedoms, liberalism has tended to deny any communal values—including the religious and spiritual—and replace them with a focus on material and economic measures. In itself that economic focus is not bad; but it further contributes to a liberal atmosphere that allows you to worry about anything but your soul. "Religious" talk in liberal circles is always a little embarrassing. Kant spoke perfectly for the liberal Enlightenment when he said that our relation to God is now such that if someone walked in and caught you on your knees praying, you would be profoundly embarrassed.

In the liberal atmosphere of economic and political freedoms, anything spiritual or religious still tends to be quite embarrassing. I will argue in a moment that that is because we have a mythic and impoverished view of Spirit, but the point is clear enough: liberalism historically came into existence to kill God, and on balance it has succeeded quite admirably, with the result that an "antispirit tyranny" is never far from liberalism.

Can we not find a way to keep the liberal strength (of individual freedoms) and jettison the tyranny of the anti-soul?

The good of conservatism is its realization that, for all the importance of individuals and individual liberties, we are deeply confused if we imagine that individuals are islands unto themselves. Rather, we as individuals are unavoidably set in deep contexts of family, community, and spirit, and we depend for our very existence on these profound contexts and connections. In some ways, then, even as an individual, my own deepest values are dependent, not upon my relation to myself in a self-hugging stance of autonomy, but on my relation to my family, my friends, my community, and my God, and to the extent I deny those deep connections, I not only destroy the fabric of community and set it loose in a riot of hyperindividualism, I also sever the deepest connection of all, that between a human soul and a divine Spirit.

Yes, and just whose God do you mean? the liberal responds. For as undeniably true as all of those conservative points are in the abstract, when it comes to actually practicing a particular religion with a particular moral code, the witch trials historically have never been far behind. The importance of community and spiritual context and connection all too soon degenerate into my community right or wrong, my God right or wrong, my country right or wrong: and if you do not embrace my God, then you go to hell, and I will be more than glad to help you. A cultural tyranny, thinly or thickly disguised, is never far from the conservative agenda.

Can we not find a way to take the conservative strength (particularly its embrace of spirituality) and jettison its cultural tyranny? And can we not find a way to keep the liberal strength (of individual freedoms) and jettison the tyranny of the anti-soul?

In short, can we not find a spiritual liberalism? a spiritual humanism? an orientation that sets the rights of the individual in deeper spiritual contexts that do not deny those rights but ground them? Can a new conception of God, of Spirit, find resonance with the noblest aims of liberalism? Can these two modern enemies—God and liberalism—in any way find a common ground?

I believe, as I said, that there is no more pressing question, of any variety, now facing the modern and postmodern world. Traditional/conservative spirituality alone will continue to divide and fragment the world, simply because, with that agenda, you can unify people only if they convert to your particular God—and whether that God be Jehovah or Allah or Shinto or Shiva matters not in the least: those are the names in which wars are fought.

No, the gains of the liberal Enlightenment need to be firmly retained, but set in the context of a spirituality that profoundly defuses and answers the very real and very accurate objections raised by the Enlightenment. It will be a spirituality that rests on, not denies, the Enlightenment. It will be, in other words, a postliberal Spirit, which transcends and includes both liberalism and conservatism. An *integral spirituality*, embracing the best of both and moving forward.

A postliberal God depends, first and foremost, on how we answer the question: *Where do we locate Spirit?* I will return to this topic in the last chapter and discuss it at length; and subsequent books will continue to take up this theme, in even more explicit form. But the general topic of "God and politics" itself rests, I believe, on exactly the type of theoretical issues—and the integral vision—that we will be discussing in the following pages, and this discussion must come first, before the actual political contours can be described with any persuasiveness. Thus, this book will not pursue any further the explicit theme of politics and spirituality, although that is its constant background.

Rather, and more important for the time being, an integral orientation is, in the following chapters, brought to bear on such topics as psychology, philosophy, anthropology, and art. I have chosen the word *integral* to represent this overall approach because integral means integrative, inclusive, comprehensive, balanced. The idea is to apply this integral orientation to the various fields of human knowledge and endeavors, including the integration of science and spirituality. This integral approach deeply alters our conceptions of psychology and the human mind; of anthropology and human history; of literature and human meaning; of philosophy and the quest for truth—all of those, I believe, are profoundly altered by an integral approach that seeks to bring together the best of each of these fields in a mutually enriching dialogue. This book is an introduction to just that integral vision.

Over two-thirds of the following material was written specifically for this book and appears here for the first time. Into that new material I have woven a handful of earlier essays that are directly related to the various topics. Even these are reworked, however, so I consider this, for all practical purposes, a new book. Nonetheless, each chapter can still be treated as a relatively independent essay, since each takes a particular topic—from psychology to philosophy to anthropology to art and literature—and examines it from an integral perspective.

The Introduction explains the meaning of the term *integral* and outlines the overall philosophy behind it (as does the Foreword by Jack Crittenden). In some ways, the Introduction is both the most important and most challenging of all the chapters. If you find it a "bit much," then simply read through it lightly and plunge into chapter 1, which deals with integral psychology, and in much more accessible terms. Chapter 2 covers integral anthropology, and chapter 3, integral philosophy. (If, after reading this book, you wish then to reread the Introduction, that might help complete the circle of understanding.)

Chapters 4 and 5 present an integral art and literary theory, and they are perhaps my own favorite chapters. There is probably no crazier—meaning insane—field than "lit crit," overrun as it is with political agendas parading as interpretive methods, congested as it is with constructed deconstruction, postimperial imperialism, antifemale feminists, universal anti-universalists, and other assorted self-contradictions. Art and literary theory might seem a rather narrow, esoteric, and specialized field, but I consider it the absolute litmus test for any integral theory.

ReVision Journal recently carried a three-volume series devoted to my work in general and *Sex, Ecology, Spirituality* in particular. Chapters 6, 7, 8, and 9 are based in part on my response to those essays. If you read these chapters, they need to be read in order, because otherwise they won't make much sense. But they are completely self-explanatory, and there is no need to read the original *ReVision* articles to understand any of the topics. (See note 1 to chapter 8 for my assessment of that series and the book based on it.)

In these chapters, because I was asked to respond in personal ways to specific topics, I have given what amounts to a historical summary of my own work. I discuss some of my major books and the major ideas in them, give the dates and circumstances of their origin, and compare them with other approaches circulating at the time. Ordinarily I would not write in this fashion, since it strikes me as self-involved, but I could find no other way to do it in this particular case. I therefore outline the major "phases" of my work as Wilber-I, Wilber-II, Wilber-III, and Wilber-IV, thus giving a self-serving air of importance to my ramblings.

As always, I recommend that the reader save the endnotes for, and if, a second reading. They are otherwise much too disruptive.

The last two chapters, 11 and 12, are devoted to the issue *Where exactly is Spirit to be located*? Although these chapters do not specifically touch on political issues, the topic itself, once again, is a prolegomenon to exactly that. Because the fact is, *where* we locate Spirit always translates into *political agendas*. Do we locate Spirit in the patriarchy, with the Great God? Do we locate Spirit in the matriarchy, with the Great Goddess? Do we locate Spirit in Gaia? In romantic times past? In a revelation given to a particular people? Or perhaps we locate Spirit in a great Omega point toward which we are all now rushing?

I will suggest that all of those answers are off the mark. Moreover, all of those answers, without exception, will translate into a political tyranny, because they all maintain that there are places that Spirit is, and places it is not—and once you draw that line, the gas chambers stand waiting for those who do not stand on your side of the fence.

A liberal—liberated and liberating—Spirit lies down none of those roads. *Where we locate Spirit*: this is the great question of our times, is it not? And this is the central question in the search for a post-liberal God.

In the following pages I will try to suggest the one location of Spirit that damages none, embraces all, and announces itself with the simplest of clarity, which leaves no places left untouched by care nor cuts its embrace for a chosen few; neither does it hide its face in the shadows of true believers, nor take up residence on a chosen piece of real estate, but rather looks out from the very person now reading these words, too obvious to ignore, too simple to describe, too easy to believe.

In the eye of Spirit we will all meet, and I will find you there, and you me, and the miracle is that we will find each other at all. And the fact that we do is one of the simplest proofs, no doubt, of God's insistent existence.

K.W.
Boulder, Colorado
Spring 1996

An Integral Vision

THE GOOD, THE TRUE,
AND THE BEAUTIFUL

To understand the whole, it is necessary to understand the parts. To understand the parts, it is necessary to understand the whole. Such is the circle of understanding.

We move from part to whole and back again, and in that dance of comprehension, in that amazing circle of understanding, we come alive to meaning, to value, and to vision: the very circle of understanding guides our way, weaving together the pieces, healing the fractures, mending the torn and tortured fragments, lighting the way ahead—this extraordinary movement from part to whole and back again, with healing the hallmark of each and every step, and grace the tender reward.

This introductory chapter is a short survey of the whole—the whole of this book, that is. As such, some of it might not make total sense until all the parts—the succeeding chapters—unfold. But starting in chapter 1, the parts are carefully laid out, simply and clearly, and the circle of understanding will, I believe, begin to come alive, and the integral vision clearly shine forth.

Thus, if this introductory survey is a "bit much," simply read it lightly and then jump into chapter 1. As you continue to read, I believe the integral vision will come upon you slowly but surely, carefully but fiercely, deliberately but radiantly, so that you and I will find ourselves sharing in the same circle of under-

*standing, abiding in the eye of Spirit, dancing in the freedom of
the whole, expressed in all its parts.*

THE BIG BANG has made idealists out of almost anybody who
thinks. First there was nothing, and then in less than a nanosecond
the material universe blew into existence. These early material processes
were apparently obeying mathematical laws that themselves, in some
sense, existed prior to the Big Bang, since they appear to be operative
from the very beginning. Of the two great and general philosophical
orientations that have always been available to thoughtful men and
women—namely, materialism and idealism—it appears that, whatever
else the Big Bang did, it dealt something of a lethal blow to materialism.

But this idealistic trend in modern physics goes back at least to the
twin revolutions of relativity and quantum theory. In fact, of the dozen
or so pioneers in these early revolutions—individuals such as Albert Einstein, Werner Heisenberg, Erwin Schroedinger, Louis de Broglie, Max
Planck, Wolfgang Pauli, Sir Arthur Eddington—the vast majority of
them were idealists or transcendentalists of one variety or another. And
I mean that in a rather strict sense. From de Broglie's assertion that "the
mechanism demands a mysticism" to Einstein's Spinozist pantheism,
from Schroedinger's Vedanta idealism to Heisenberg's Platonic archetypes: these pioneering physicists were united in the belief that the universe simply does not make sense—and cannot satisfactorily be
explained—without the inclusion, in some profound way, of mind or
consciousness itself. "The universe begins to look more like a great
thought than a great machine," as Sir James Jeans summarized the available evidence. And, using words that few of these pioneering physicists
would object to, Sir James pointed out that it looks more and more
certain that the only way to explain the universe is to maintain that it
exists "in the mind of some eternal spirit."[1]

It's interesting that "mental health" has always been defined as, in
some basic sense, being "in touch" with reality. But what if we look to
the very hardest of the sciences in order to determine the nature of this
bedrock reality—the reality that we are supposed to be in touch with—
and we are rudely told that reality actually exists "in the mind of some
eternal spirit"? What then? Does mental health mean being directly in
touch with the mind of some eternal spirit? And if we don't believe
these physicists as to the nature of ultimate reality, then whom are we
to believe? If sanity is the goal, then exactly what reality are we supposed
to be in touch with?

The Ghost in the Machine

One of the great problems with this "spiritual" line of reasoning is that, unless one is a mathematical physicist wrestling daily with these issues, the conclusions sound too tenuous, too speculative, too "far-out" and even spooky. Not to mention the fact that all too many theologians, Eastern as well as Western, have used the stunning loopholes in the scientific account of nature to shove their version of God into the limelight.

Which is why most modern working scientists, physicians, psychologists, and psychiatrists go on about their business without much of this strange "idealistic speculation" clouding their horizons. From cognitive behaviorism to artificial intelligence, from psychological connectionism to biological psychiatry—most researchers have simply remained very close to a materialistic explanation of mind, psyche, and consciousness. That is, the fundamental reality is assumed to be the material or physical or sensorimotor world, and mind is therefore believed to be nothing much more than the sum total of representations or reflections of that empirical world. The brain itself is said to be a biomaterial information processor, explainable in scientific and objective terms, and the information it processes consists of nothing but *representations* of the *empirical* world ("no computation without representation"). A material and objective brain simply processes a material and objective world, and the subjective domain of consciousness is, at best, an epiphenomenon generated in the wake of the physiological fireworks. The mind remains, hauntingly, the ghost in the machine. And whether that machine be computer or biomaterial processor or servomechanism matters not the least. The plaintive call of the dead and ghostly mind echoes down the imposing corridors of today's scientific research.

Typical of these objectivist approaches is Daniel Dennett's widely esteemed *Consciousness Explained*, which, others have less charitably pointed out, might better have been entitled *Consciousness Explained Away*. In all of these approaches, objective representations are sent scurrying through *connectionist networks*, and the only item that differs in most of these accounts is the exact nature of the objective network through which information bits hustle in their appointed rounds of generating the illusion of consciousness. All of these accounts—quite apart from certain undeniably important contributions—are nonetheless, in the final analysis, attempts by consciousness to deny the existence of consciousness, which is an extraordinary amount of causal activity for what after all is supposed to be an ineffectual vapor, a ghostly nothingness.

But say what we will, these empirical and objectivist accounts—analog and digital bits scurrying through information networks, or neurotransmitters hustling between dendritic pathways—are not how we *actually experience* our own interior consciousness. For when you and I introspect, we find a different world, a world not of bites and bits and digital specs, but a world of images and desires, hungers and pains, thoughts and ideas, wishes and wants, intentions and hesitations, hopes and fears. And we know these interior data in an immediate and direct fashion: they are simply given to us, they are simply there, they simply show up, and we witness them to the extent we care to. These interior data might indeed be part of extensive chains of mediated events—that is very likely true—but at the moment of introspection, that doesn't matter in the least: my interior states are simply given to awareness, immediately, whenever I take the time to look.

And thus, even if we attempt to agree with the cognitivists and functionalists and behaviorists, even if we attempt to think of consciousness as nothing but information bits hopping through neuronal networks, nonetheless that *idea itself* is known to me only in an interior and direct apprehension. I experience that idea in an interior and immediate way; at no point do I actually experience anything that even remotely looks like an information bit dashing through a connectionist pathway. That is simply a concept, and I know that concept, as I know all concepts, in an interior and conscious apprehension. The objectivist approach to experience and consciousness, in other words, cannot even account for its own experience and consciousness: cannot account for the fact that digital bits are experienced, not as digital bits, but as hopes and fears.

INTERIOR AND EXTERIOR

In short, my interior and subjective experience is given to me in terms that simply do not match the objectivistic and empirical terms of functionalism or cognitivism or neuronal connectionism. My *subjective* and interior world, known by many names—consciousness, awareness, mind, psyche, qualia, idea, idealism—definitely appears to be at odds with my *objective* and exterior description of the world, also known by many names—material, biophysical, brain, nature, empirical, materialism. Inside vs. outside, interior vs. exterior, mind vs. brain, subjective vs. objective, idealism vs. materialism, introspection vs. positivism, hermeneutics vs. empiricism. . . .

Small wonder that, almost from the inception of the human knowledge quest, theorists have generally fallen into these two rather different and apparently conflicting approaches to knowledge—interior vs. exterior. From psychology to theology, from philosophy to metaphysics, from anthropology to sociology, the human knowledge quest has almost universally consisted of these two broad paths.

(And, as we will soon see, one of the main tasks of an *integral* approach is to honor and incorporate both of these general paths, and to explain how both can be *equally* significant and important in the understanding of human consciousness and behavior.)

On the one hand are those paths that start with objective, empirical, and often quantifiable observables. These overall approaches—let us call them "exterior" or "naturalistic" or "empiric-analytic"—take the physical or empirical world as most fundamental, and all theorizing must then be carefully tied to, or anchored in, empirical observables. In *psychology*, this is classical behaviorism, and more recently, cognitive behaviorism (cognitive structures are granted reality only to the extent they manifest in observable behavior). In *sociology*, this is classical positivism (as with the founder of sociology itself, Auguste Comte); but also the extremely influential structural-functionalism and systems theory (from Talcott Parsons to Niklas Luhmann to Jeffrey Alexander), where cultural productions are taken to be significant to the extent that they are aspects of an objective social action system. And even in *theology* and *metaphysics*, this naturalistic approach starts from certain empirical and material givens, and then attempts to *deduce* the existence of spirit on the basis of empirical realities (the argument from design, for example).

Arrayed against these naturalistic and empirical approaches are those that start with the immediacy of consciousness itself—let us call them the "interior" or the "introspection and interpretation" approaches. These approaches do not deny the importance of empirical or objectivist data, but they point out, as William James did, that the definition of the word "data" is "direct experience," and the only genuinely direct experience each of us has is his or her own immediate and interior experience. The primordial data, in other words, is that of consciousness, of intentionality, of immediate lived awareness, and all else, from the existence of electrons to the existence of neuronal pathways, are deductions away from immediate lived awareness. These secondary deductions may be very true and very important, but they are, and will always remain, secondary and derivative to the primary fact of immediate experience.

Thus, in *psychology*, where the objectivist approach produces varieties of behaviorism, the subjectivist approach shows up in the various schools of depth psychology, such as psychoanalysis, Jungian, Gestalt, phenomenological-existential, and humanistic—not to mention the vast number of contemplative and meditative psychologies, East and West alike. All of these traditions take, as their starting point, immediately apprehended interior states and direct experiential realities, and they anchor their theories in those immediate data.

These schools are thus interested not so much in *behavior* as in the *meaning* and *interpretation* of psychological symbols and symptoms and signs. Freud's first great book says it all: *The Interpretation of Dreams*. Dreams are an interior and symbolic production. But all *symbols* must be *interpreted*. What is the *meaning* of *Hamlet*? of *War and Peace*? of your dreams? of your life? And the introspective and interpretive schools of psychology are attempts to help men and women interpret their interiors more accurately and more authentically, and thus to gain an understanding and a meaning for their actions, their symptoms, their distresses, their dreams, their lives.

In *sociology*, the subjectivist approach shows up in the immensely influential schools of hermeneutics and interpretive sociology (hermeneutics is the art and science of interpretation). And once again, in contrast to the objectivist approaches, which are interested in *explaining* empirical behavior, the interpretive approaches in sociology are interested in *understanding* symbolic productions. Not "How does it *work*?" but "What does it *mean*?"

Take the Hopi Rain Dance, for example. A typical objective functionalist approach attempts to explain the existence of the Dance by seeing it as a necessary aspect of the integration of the social action system. The Dance, in other words, is performing a behavioral function in the social system as a whole, and this function—which is generally unknown to the natives—is said to be the preservation of the autopoietic self-maintenance of the social action system (e.g., Parsons).

The hermeneutic approach to sociology, on the other hand, seeks instead to take the view of the cultural native and to understand the Dance *from within*, as it were, in a sympathetic stance of mutual understanding. And what the interpretive sociologist (as "participant observer") finds is that the Dance is a way to both honor Nature and sympathetically influence Nature. The interpretive sociologist thus concludes that, phenomenologically, the Dance is a pattern of connecting with a realm felt to be sacred. (Recent examples of hermeneutic sociology and anthropology include such influential theorists as Charles Taylor, Clifford Geertz, Mary Douglas; they often trace part of their lineage to Heidegger's hermeneutic ontology and Hans-Georg Gadamer's hermeneutic philosophy, and further back to such pioneers as Wilhelm Dilthey and Friedrich Schleiermacher.)

In *theology* and *metaphysics*, the exterior and interior approaches likewise tend to diverge sharply. The objectivist approach starts with certain empirical and material facts, and attempts to deduce the existence of transcendental realities from those facts. Saint Thomas Aquinas takes this approach when he gives most of his various arguments for the existence of God. He starts from certain natural facts and then attempts to show that these facts demand an Author, as it were. And right down to today, many physicists and mathematicians use the "argument from design" to conclude that there must be some sort of Designer. This approach includes the recent (and quite popular) Anthropic Principle, which maintains that, because the existence of humans is incalculably improbable, and yet they exist, then the universe simply must have been following a hidden design from the start.

The subjective and introspective approach, on the other hand, does not attempt to prove the existence of Spirit by deduction from empirical or natural events, but rather turns the light of consciousness directly onto the interior domain itself—the only domain of direct data—and looks for Spirit in the disclosures of that data. Meditation and contemplation become the paradigm, the exemplar, the actual practice upon which all theorizing must be based. The God within, not the God without, becomes the beacon call. (In the West, this is the path laid out preeminently by Plotinus and Saint Augustine, which is why the great and enduring theological tension in the West has been between Augustine and Aquinas.)

In *philosophy* itself this is, of course, the colossal divide between the modern Anglo-Saxon and Continental approaches, a difference which both camps happily announce (while just as happily denouncing each other). The typical Anglo-Saxon (British and American) approach is empiric-analytic, begun principally by John Locke and David Hume, but made most famous in that Cambridge triumvirate of G. E. Moore, Bertrand Russell, and (early) Ludwig Wittgenstein. "We make pictures of (empirical) facts" announces Wittgenstein's *Tractatus*, and the aim of all genuine philosophy is the analysis and clarification of these empirical pictures of the empirical world. No empirical pictures, no genuine philosophy.

Which always struck the great Continental philosophers as impossibly naive, shallow, and even primitive. Beginning most notably with Immanuel Kant—and running, in various ways and different guises, through Schelling, Hegel, Nietzsche, Schopenhauer, Heidegger, Derrida, and Foucault—a dramatically different theme was announced: the so-called "empirical" world is in many important ways not just a *perception* but an *interpretation*.

In other words, the allegedly simple "empirical" and "objective" world is not simply lying around "out there" waiting for all and sundry to see. Rather, the "objective" world is actually set in subjective and intersubjective contexts and backgrounds that in many ways govern what is seen, and what *can* be seen, in that "empirical" world. Thus, genuine philosophy, they would all maintain in their various ways, is not merely a matter of making pictures of the objective world, but rather of investigating the structures in the subject that allow the making of the pictures in the first place. Because, put bluntly, the mapmaker's fingerprints are all over the maps he makes. And thus the secret to the universe is not just in the objective maps but in the subjective mapmaker.

The fact that both of these approaches—the exterior and the interior, the objectivist and the subjectivist—have aggressively and persistently existed in virtually all fields of human knowledge ought to tell us something—ought to tell us, that is, that both of these approaches are profoundly significant. They both have something of incalculable importance to tell us. And the integral vision is, beginning to end, dedicated to honoring and incorporating both of these profound approaches in the human knowledge quest.

To Honor These Truths: An Integral Approach

If we look at all the examples that I just gave of the different types of approaches to the knowledge quest, we will find that they actually fall into not just two but four large camps. Because both the *interior* and the *exterior* approaches can be subdivided into *individual* and *collective*.

In other words, any phenomenon can be approached in an interior and exterior fashion, and also as an individual and as a member of a collective. And there are, already in existence, major and quite influential schools in each of those four large camps. I have included a table (see figure 1) with some well-known theorists in each of these four camps. The Upper Left is the interior of the individual (e.g., Freud). The Upper Right is the exterior of the individual (e.g., behaviorism). The Lower Left is the interior of the collective (e.g., the shared cultural values and worldviews explored by interpretive sociology). And the Lower Right is the exterior of the collective (e.g., the objective social action system studied by systems theory).

As an example covering all four of these domains, let us take a single thought, say the thought of going to the grocery store. When I have that thought, what I actually experience is the thought itself, the interior

	LEFT-HAND PATHS	RIGHT-HAND PATHS
	· Interpretive	· Monological
	· Hermeneutic	· Empirical, positivistic
	· Consciousness	· Material form
INDIVIDUAL	Freud C. G. Jung Piaget Aurobindo Plotinus Gautama Buddha	B. F. Skinner John Watson John Locke Empiricism Behaviorism Physics, biology, neurology, etc.
COLLECTIVE	Thomas Kuhn Wilhelm Dilthey Jean Gebser Max Weber Hans-Georg Gadamer	Systems Theory Talcott Parsons Auguste Comte Karl Marx Gerhard Lenski

FIGURE 1

thought and its meaning—the symbols, the images, the idea of going to the grocery store. That's the Upper Left, the interior of the individual.

While I am having this thought, there are, of course, correlative changes occurring in my brain—dopamine increases, acetylcholine jumps the synapses, beta brainwaves increase, or whatnot. Those are observable behaviors in my brain. They can be empirically observed. And that's the Upper Right.

Notice that, even though my brain is "inside" my organism, it is still not part of my actual interior awareness. In fact, I can't even see my brain without cutting open my skull and getting a mirror. My brain is an objective, physical, biomaterial organ, known in an objective and empirical manner (Upper Right). But I know my mind, my consciousness, in an immediate and direct and interior fashion (Upper Left). When I experience the thought of going to the grocery store, I do not say, "Wow, what a dopamine day"; rather, I experience the thought in its own terms, with its own contours. The brain is seen objectively, the mind is experienced subjectively. We might eventually find that they are indeed two different aspects of the same thing, or that they are parallel, or dualist, or interactionist, or whatever, but the crucial point for now is that, in any case, neither can be reduced to the other without remainder, because whatever else might be said, they each have a drastically different phenomenology.

To return to the internal thought itself (Upper Left): notice that it only makes sense in terms of my cultural background. If I spoke a different language, the thought would be composed of different symbols and have quite different meanings. If I existed in a primal tribal society a million years ago, I would never even have the thought "going to the grocery store." It might be, "Time to kill the bear." The point is that my thoughts themselves arise in a *cultural background* that gives texture and meaning and context to my individual thoughts, and indeed, I would not even be able to "talk to myself" if I did not exist in a community of individuals who also talk to me.

So the cultural community serves as an *intrinsic background* and *context* to any individual thoughts I might have. My thoughts do not just pop into my head out of nowhere; they pop into my head out of a cultural background, and however much I might move beyond this background, I can never simply escape it altogether, and I could never have developed thoughts in the first place without it. The occasional cases of a "wolf boy"—humans raised in the wild—show that the human brain, left without culture, does not produce linguistic thoughts on its own.

In short, my individual thoughts only exist against a vast background of cultural practices and languages and meanings and contexts, without which I could form virtually no individual thoughts at all. And that's the Lower Left, the interior of the collective, the intersubjective space of shared cultural contexts.

But my culture itself is not simply disembodied, hanging in idealistic midair. It has *material components,* much as my own individual thoughts have material brain components. All *cultural* events have *social* correlates. These concrete social components include types of technology, forces of production (horticultural, agrarian, industrial, etc.), concrete institutions, written codes and patterns, geopolitical locations, and so on. That's the Lower Right, the social action system. And these concrete material components—the actual *social system*—are crucial in helping to determine the types of cultural worldview, within which my own thoughts will arise.

So my supposedly "individual thought" is actually a phenomenon that intrinsically has (at least) these four aspects to it—intentional, behavioral, cultural, and social. And around the holistic circle we go: the social system will have a strong influence on the cultural worldview, which will set limits to the individual thoughts that I can have, which will register in the brain physiology. And we can go around that circle in any direction. They are all interwoven. They are all mutually determining. They all cause, and are caused by, the others, in concentric spheres of contexts within contexts indefinitely.

I am not going to make a long and drawn-out argument for this, but simply take it as plain fact that the persistent existence of these four large camps in the knowledge quest is evidence enough that none of them can be totally reduced to the others. Each approach is giving us, as it were, one corner of the Kosmos. Each is telling us something very important about various aspects of the known world. And none can be reduced to the others without aggressive and violent rupture, distortion, dismissal.

In my opinion, these four large camps of human knowledge exist precisely because these four aspects of human beings are very real, very persistent, very profound. And one of the aims of an integral approach (and what we might call *integral studies* in general) is to honor and incorporate each of these extraordinary domains—intentional, behavioral, cultural, and social.[2]

As we will continue to see, the integral approach is an "all-level, all-quadrant" approach.

THE FOUR FACES OF TRUTH

Each of these "four quadrants," in fact, has its own particular type of truth or type of "validity claim"—the ways in which it goes about accumulating and validating its data and its evidence. I have given a brief summary of these in figure 2. And to say that none of these quadrants can be reduced to the others is to say that none of their respective truths can be dismissed or reduced, either.

Here are some quick examples of the different validity claims or "types of truth," going around the four quadrants in figures 1 and 2.

Truth

The type of truth found in the Upper-Right quadrant is known variously as representational, propositional, or correspondence. In propositional truth, a statement is said to be true if it matches an objective fact. "It is

	INTERIOR Left-Hand Paths	EXTERIOR Right-Hand Paths
	SUBJECTIVE	OBJECTIVE
INDIVIDUAL	*truthfulness* sincerity integrity trustworthiness	*truth* correspondence representation propositional
	I | it	
	we | its	
COLLECTIVE	*justness* cultural fit mutual understanding rightness	*functional fit* systems theory web structural-functionalism social systems mesh
	INTERSUBJECTIVE	INTEROBJECTIVE

FIGURE 2

raining outside" is said to be a *true* statement if it actually matches the facts at that moment. Propositions are tied to single, empirical, objective observables, and if the propositions match, they are said to be true. In other words, if the *map* matches the *territory*, it is said to be a true representation or a true correspondence ("We make pictures of facts"). Most people are quite familiar with this type of truth. It guides much of empirical science, and indeed much of our everyday lives. So common is propositional truth that it is often just called "truth" for short.

Truthfulness

In the Upper-Left quadrant, on the other hand, the question is not, "Is it raining outside?" The question here is, When I tell you it is raining outside, am I telling you the truth or am I lying? Not, does the map match the territory? but can the mapmaker be trusted?

Because here, you see, we are dealing not so much with exterior and observable behavior but with interior states, and the *only* way you and I can get at each other's interiors is by dialogue and interpretation. If I want to actually know, not simply your behavior, but how you are feeling, or what you are thinking, then I must talk to you, and I must interpret what you say. And yet, when you report to me your inner status, you might be lying to me. Moreover, *you might be lying to yourself.*

And with the fact that you might be lying to yourself, we step into the whole realm of depth psychology in general. The validity claim here is not so much whether my statements match exterior facts, but whether I can *truthfully* report on my own inner status.

For, according to virtually all schools of depth psychology, "neurosis" is, in the broadest sense, a case of being out of touch with one's true feelings, or one's actual desires, or one's authentic inner state. At some point in development, most of these schools maintain, the person began to deny, repress, distort, conceal, or otherwise "lie" to himself about his own interior status; he began to *mis*-interpret his subjective condition. And these misinterpretations, these concealments, these fictions, begin to cloud awareness in the symbolic form of painful symptoms, telltale traces of the telltale lie.

And thus for these schools, therapy is first and foremost an attempt to get in touch with—and more accurately and *truthfully interpret*—one's interior states, one's symptoms, symbols, dreams, desires. A more accurate and faithful *interpretation* of the person's distresses helps the person to understand his otherwise baffling symptoms, helps him to see their *meaning*. And thus the person can become less opaque to himself, more transparent and open and undefended.

Thus, according to the schools of depth psychology, the individual's painful symptoms were generated by a misinterpretation, a concealing, a dynamic and forceful hiding, a "lying" about one's interior state; and a more truthful, faithful, and appropriate interpretation opens the depths in an individual in a more meaningful and transparent fashion, thus lessening the painful symptoms. Not so much *objective truth* as *subjective truthfulness*: and there is the validity claim of the Upper-Left quadrant.

(Incidentally, when it comes to therapy, an integral or "all-level, all-quadrant" approach would certainly not neglect the behavioral and pharmacological therapies of the Upper-Right quadrant. We are simply, at the moment, discussing each quadrant in turn, with its distinctive validity claim and type of truth.)

Notice also that, for example, the phenomenology of meditative states depends entirely upon the validity claim of subjective truthfulness, which is a totally different approach from the objective physiology of meditative states. That is, if you are interested in the neurophysiological changes that occur during meditation, you can hook me up to an EEG machine and monitor my brain states, no matter what I say about them. You simply use empirical and objective truth to map my brain physiology; you don't even have to talk to me. The machine will faithfully record what is happening in my brain.

But if you want to know what is actually going on in my awareness, in my mind, then you are going to have to ask me and talk to me—the approach is dialogical and intersubjective, not monological and merely empirical. When the needle jumps on the EEG machine, what am I experiencing? Am I seeing a brilliant interior illumination that seems to carry a compassionate depth and warmth? Or am I thinking of new ways to rob the local liquor store? The EEG machine will not, and cannot, tell you.

And in the quest for this type of interior truth, the validity claim is truthfulness, trustworthiness, sincerity (Upper Left). If I am being insincere in my reports, you will not get an accurate phenomenology of my interior states at all, but only a series of deceptions and concealments. Moreover, if I have already thoroughly *lied to myself*, I will honestly believe I'm telling the truth, and absolutely nothing on the EEG machine will be able to spot this. So much for empirical tests.

Thus, meditative physiology relies on objective data guided by the yardstick of propositional truth, whereas meditative phenomenology relies on subjective data guided by the yardstick of truthfulness; and we can see a striking example of the Upper-Right and Upper-Left approaches to consciousness, with their different but equally important validity claims.

Functional Fit

The two lower quadrants (interior-collective and exterior-collective) deal not merely with the *individual* but with the *collective* or communal. As we saw with the example of the Hopi Rain Dance, the Lower-Right camps approach the communal from an exterior and objective stance, and attempt to explain the status of the individual members in terms of their *functional fit* with the objective whole. That is, this approach attempts, with its validity claim, to situate each and every individual in an objective network that in many ways determines the function of each part. The truth, for these Lower-Right approaches, is found in the objective intermeshing of individual parts, so that the objective, empirical whole—the "total system"—is the primary reality. And it is the objective behavior of the overall social action system, considered from an empirical stance, that forms the yardstick by which truths in this domain are judged. Its validity claim, in other words, is *functional fit*, so that each proposition must be tied to the intermeshing of the total system or network.

We all know this as standard systems theory, in its many guises. And when we hear theories about Gaia (and usually the Goddess), or about global networks and systems, or about "new paradigms" that emphasize "holistic networks," or dynamic processes all interwoven into the great empirical Web of Life—these are all approaches that emphasize the Lower-Right quadrant: observable and empirical processes seamlessly intermeshed in functional fit.

Justness

Where the Lower-Right approaches attempt to explain how objects fit together in a functional whole or total web of empirical processes, the Lower-Left approaches attempt instead to understand how *subjects* fit together in acts of *mutual understanding*.

In other words, if you and I are going to live together, we have to inhabit, not just the same empirical and physical space, but also the same intersubjective space of mutual recognition. We are going to have to fit not just our bodies together in the same objective space, but our subjects together in the same cultural, moral, and ethical space. We are going to have to find ways to recognize and respect the rights of each other and of the community, and these rights cannot be found in objective matter, nor are they simply a case of my own individual sincerity, nor are they a matter of functionally fitting together empirical events: they are rather a matter of fitting our minds together in an intersubjective space that allows each of us to recognize and respect the other. Not necessarily *agree* with each other, but *recognize* each other—the opposite of which, put simply, is war.

We are interested, that is, not only in the truth, not simply in truthfulness, and not merely in functional fit: we are interested in justness, rightness, goodness, and fairness.

This *intersubjective space* (our commonly shared background contexts and worldviews) is a crucial component of the human being, without which our individual subjective identities could not even exist, and without which objective realities could not even be perceived. Moreover, this intersubjective strand develops and unfolds, just as the other quadrants do. (And thus a comprehensive theory of human consciousness and behavior will want to take all of these quadrants—and their development—into careful account. And this, I will argue, is a crucial aspect of integral studies.)

Notice that both of the collective approaches are equally *holistic*, but the social sciences tend to approach the whole from without in an objective or empirical stance, whereas cultural hermeneutics tend to approach the whole from within in an empathetic grasp. The former have a validity claim of functional fit or systems-mesh, an interobjective fit of each and every objective process with each and every other. The latter have a validity claim of cultural fit or mutual recognition, the intersubjective mesh that leads not to objective systems interlinking, but to human beings reaching mutual understanding. In other words, exterior and interior holism.

(It might be obvious that most theorists who call themselves "holistic" are ironically only exterior holists, an imbalance we need not champion. As of yet, there has historically been no "holism" that actually embraces all four quadrants in all their levels, and I will argue that this is one of the central aims of the integral approach.)

THE VALIDITY OF INTEGRAL KNOWLEDGE

The significant point is that each of these four validity claims has its own type of evidence and data, and thus particular assertions within each claim can be *adjudicated*—that is, can be confirmed or denied, justified or rebuffed, validated or rejected. Accordingly, each of these claims is open to the all-important *fallibilist criterion* of genuine knowledge.

We are all familiar with how fallibilism works in empirical sciences: maps and models and pictures that do not match empirical facts can eventually be dislodged by further facts. But the same fallibilism is at work in all of the genuine validity claims, which is precisely why *learning* can occur in all four quadrants: mistakes are dislodged by further evidence in those quadrants.

For example, *Hamlet* is an interpretive, not an empirical, phenomenon, and yet the statement *"Hamlet* is about the joys of war" is a false statement—it is a bad interpretation, it is wrong, and it can be thoroughly *rejected* by the community of those who:

1. perform the *injunction* or the *experiment* (namely, read the play called *Hamlet*);
2. gather the interpretative *data* or apprehensions (study the meaning of the play in light of the total available evidence); and
3. compare this data with others who have completed the experiment (*consensual* validation or rejection by a community of the adequate).

Those three strands of all genuine knowledge accumulation (injunction, data, confirmation) are present in all of the validity claims, which themselves are *anchored* in the very real intentional, behavioral, cultural, and social domains of human beings. In other words, these very real domains ground our quests for truthfulness, truth, justness, and functional fit, each of which proceeds by the checks and balances of injunction, data, and confirmation. (We will return to this topic in chapter 3.)

Thus, the epistemological claims of integral studies are, like any other valid knowledge claims, thoroughly grounded in experiment, data accumulation, and consensual justification.

Fortunately, there is a very easy way to simplify all of this!

I, WE, AND IT

You can see all four of these equally important validity claims or "types of truth" listed in figure 2. And you might also notice that I have written the words "I," "we," "it" (and "its") in the corners of the four quadrants. The reason is that *each of these quadrants is described in a different language.* That is, they each have a different but quite valid phenomenology, and thus each of them is natively described in a distinct language.

Thus, the events and data found in the Upper-Left quadrant are described in "I" language. The events and data of the Lower-Left quadrant are described in "we" language. And both of the Right-Hand quadrants, because they are empirical and exterior, can be described in "it" language. Thus, the four quadrants can be simplified to three basic domains: I, we, and it.

Because none of the quadrants can be reduced to the others, likewise none of these languages can be reduced to the others. Each is vitally important, and forms a crucial part of the universe on the whole—not to mention a vital part of a comprehensive understanding of the psychology and sociology of human beings. Here are just a few of the important ingredients of these three major domains of I, we, and it:

> I (Upper Left)—consciousness, subjectivity, self, and self-expression (including art and aesthetics); truthfulness, sincerity; first-person accounts
>
> We (Lower Left)—ethics and morals, worldviews, common context, culture; intersubjective meaning, mutual understanding, appropriateness, justness; second-person accounts
>
> It (Right Hand)—science and technology, objective nature, empirical forms (including brain and social systems); propositional truth (in both singular and functional fit); third-person accounts

Science—empirical science—deals with objects, with "its," with empirical patterns. Morals and ethics concern "we" and our intersubjective world of mutual understanding and justness. Art and aesthetics concern the beauty in the eye of the beholder, the "I."

And yes, this is essentially Plato's the *Good* (morals, the "we"), the *True* (in the sense of propositional truth, objective truths or "its"), and the *Beautiful* (the aesthetic dimension as perceived by each "I").

These three domains are also Sir Karl Popper's rather famous distinction of three worlds—objective (it), subjective (I), and cultural (we).

Many people, myself included, consider Jürgen Habermas the world's foremost living philosopher, and these three great domains correspond exactly with Habermas's three validity claims: objective truth, subjective sincerity, and intersubjective justness.

Of enormous historical importance, these three domains showed up in Kant's immensely influential trilogy—*The Critique of Pure Reason* (objective science), *The Critique of Practical Reason* (morals), and *The Critique of Judgment* (aesthetic judgment and art).

Even into the spiritual levels of development, these three domains show up as, to give only one example, the Three Jewels of Buddhism, namely: *Buddha, Dharma,* and *Sangha.* Buddha is the enlightened mind in each and every sentient being, the I that is no-I, the primordial awareness that shines forth from every interior. Buddha is the "I" or the "eye" of Spirit. Sangha is the community of spiritual practitioners, the "We" of Spirit. And Dharma is the spiritual truth that is realized, the "It" or "isness" or "thusness" or "suchness" of every phenomenon.

Dozens of other examples could be given, but that's the general picture of these great domains of I, we, and it. And this is obviously crucial for integral studies, because any comprehensive theory of human consciousness and behavior will want to honor and incorporate all four quadrants, or simply these three great domains, each possessing a different validity claim and a quite different language. This is simply another example of the pluralistic, multimodal, and multidimensional attitude that is a defining hallmark of an integral approach: all-level, all-quadrant.

FLATLAND

Despite the resiliency of what we might call the Left-Hand approaches of introspection and interpretation and consciousness (approaches that honor the "I" and the "we" domains), nonetheless there has been in the West, for the last three hundred years or so, a profound and aggressive attempt by modern science (and the exclusively Right-Hand approaches) to reduce the entire Kosmos to a bunch of "its." That is, the I and we domains have been almost entirely colonized by the it-domains, by scientific materialism, positivism, behaviorism, empiricism, and objectivistic-exterior approaches in general.

This entire Right-Hand imperialism, which in so many ways has been the hallmark of Western modernity, is known generally as *scientism,* which, as I would define it, is the belief that the entire world can be fully explained in it-language. It is the assumption that all subjective and intersubjective spaces can be reduced, without remainder, to the behavior of objective processes, that human and nonhuman interiors alike can be thoroughly accounted for as holistic systems of dynamically interwoven its.

Gross reductionism we all know about: it is the reduction of all complex entities to material atoms, which is gross indeed. But *subtle reductionism* is all the more widespread, insidious, and damaging. Subtle reductionism simply reduces every event in the Left Hand to its corresponding aspect in the Right Hand. That is, subtle reductionism reduces all "I"s and all "we's" to their corresponding empirical correlates, reduces them to "its." Mind is reduced to brain; praxis is reduced to techne; interiors are reduced to bits of digital its; depth is reduced to endless surfaces roaming a flat and faded system; levels of quality are reduced to levels of quantity; dialogical interpretation is reduced to monological gaze—in short, the multidimensional universe is rudely reduced to flatland.

But precisely because human beings do indeed have these four different aspects—intentional, behavioral, cultural, and social—this "scientific" approach can seem to make a great deal of sense, because every interior event does indeed have an exterior correlate. (Even if I have an out-of-the-body experience, it registers in the empirical brain!) And thus it initially makes all the sense in the world to try to simplify the knowledge quest by allowing only empirical data and objective its.

But when you have finally finished reducing all I's and all we's to mere its, when you have converted all interiors to exteriors, when you have turned all depth into shiny surfaces, then you have perfectly gutted an entire Kosmos. You have completely stripped the universe of all value, meaning, consciousness, depth, and discourse—and delivered it up dried and desiccated, laid out on the marble slab of a monological gaze.

Consciousness indeed becomes the ghost in the machine, precisely because it has just committed suicide.

And thus we end up with Whitehead's famous summary of the modern scientific worldview (of subtle reductionism): "a dull affair, soundless, scentless, colorless; merely the hurrying of material, endlessly, meaninglessly." To which, incidentally, he added: "Thereby, modern philosophy has been ruined."

It doesn't help that this subtle reductionism is often "holistic," because with subtle reductionism, the holism is always of the exterior variety alone: holistic and dynamically interwoven its! Open any textbook on holistic systems theory or the new holistic scientific paradigm, and you will find an endless discussion of chaos theory, cybernetic feedback mechanisms, dissipative structures, complexity theory, global networks, systems interactions—all described in process it-language. You will find nothing substantial on aesthetics, poetry, beauty, goodness, ethical dispositions, intersubjective development, interior illumination, transcendental intuition, ethical impulses, mutual understanding, justness, or meditative phenomenology (so much for being "holistic"). All you will find, in other words, is a monochrome world of interwoven its, without so much as an acknowledgment of the equally important and equally holistic domains of the I and the we, the subjective and intersubjective spaces that allow objective systems to be perceived in the first place.

Thus, systems theory admirably fights gross reductionism, but is itself the prime example of subtle reductionism, of the "it-ism" that has so defined modernity. "Thereby, modern philosophy has been ruined." So has modern psychology and psychiatry and cognitive science, to the extent they continue to reduce all I's and all we's to info-its running through neuronal it-pathways carried by it-neurotransmitters to it-goals. Your presence, your existence, your consciousness is not required. That these are often holistic and systems-oriented approaches is no solace at all: that's simply subtle reductionism at its worst: a flatland web of interwoven its.

But the existence of these objectivistic, empirical, systems it-approaches is not the problem. These approaches accurately and importantly report on the exteriors of various phenomena, and they are indispensable in that regard! I fully support them in that regard. The difficulty is when these approaches attempt to corner the market on truth, and to claim that the empirical it-domain is the only significant domain in existence. It is this aggressive imperialism and colonization of the I and the we domains by the monological it-approaches that we must everywhere resist, and resist in the name of other and equally honorable truths.

And remember: "In the mind of some eternal Spirit" simply gives us fair warning that a world of mere "its" is no world at all. Consciousness and form, subjective and objective, interior and exterior, Purusha and Prakriti, Dharmakaya and Rupakaya, are the warp and woof of a wondrous universe that makes precisely no sense if either is dismissed.

THE PAIN OF DENIAL

In fact, it is fast becoming quite obvious that if any system of thought (from philosophy to sociology to psychology to religion) attempts to ignore or deny any of the four validity claims, then those ignored truths actually *reappear* in the system as an internal and massive self-contradiction.

In other words, if I refuse reality to any of these truths, then that denied quadrant will in fact *sneak into my system*—I will smuggle it into my philosophy—and there it will eat away at my system from within, until it eventually gnaws its way to the surface as a jolting contradiction.

We can go around the quadrants and see what happens to our theories of knowledge if we deny any of the quadrants. This is very important, I think, because not only orthodox but "postmodern" as well as "new paradigm" approaches have often been plagued by many of these lopsided fads, which an integral approach would criticize in the name of wider and more inclusive occasions.

Scientism

As we have seen, empiricists (and positivists and scienticians in general) deny constitutive reality to virtually all Left-Hand dimensions; only the Right Hand is real. All Left-Hand occasions are at best reflections or representations of the sensorimotor world, the world of simple location, the world of its, detected by the human senses or their extensions.

But "empirical objective knowledge" arises only because of, and in the space of, an intersubjective structure that allows the differentiation of subject and object in the first place. In Thomas Kuhn's now-famous formulation, scientific facts are embedded in cultural practices or paradigms. This does *not* deny the objective component of the knowledge; it denies that the knowledge is merely objective or innocently empirical. In other words, in order to *assert* that all truth is "strictly empirical," empiricists have to stand in intersubjective structures that their own theories cannot account for. The linguistic assertion that all valid knowledge is empirical is not itself empirical, and thus in asserting their own position, they contradict themselves; the denied intersubjective quadrant retaliates with a sneak attack! (This intersubjective component of empirical knowledge is the basis of many influential critiques, not just Thomas Kuhn's attack on simple empiricism, but also Piaget's cognitive-structural revolution and Heidegger's notion of the "background"—to name a very few.)

Cultural Constructivism

More recently we have the reverse attempt: to deny any form of objective truth and dissolve it into *cultural constructivism*. (This approach is also called "social constructivism," but the technical meaning is always cultural constructivism.) That is, with the extreme versions of postmodern constructivism, there is an aggressive attempt to reduce all quadrants to the Lower-Left quadrant (i.e., an attempt to reduce all knowledge claims to intersubjective constructions). This backfires immediately and spectacularly. In fact, not even Derrida and Foucault accept this extreme constructivism (although their American followers often claim that they do). Derrida now concedes the existence of transcendental signifieds; without them, he says, we couldn't even translate between various languages. And Foucault's own archaeology is a series of universal constants in human knowing, within which culturally relative variations are constructed.

But extreme constructivists claim that there is no such thing as objective *truth* at all, because our ideas are simply *constructed* according to various *interests*—usually power, but also various "isms" and various ideologies (sexism, racism, speciesism, logocentrism, etc.).

Yet the constructivists themselves claim that their stance is *true*. And this they cannot do without asserting a theory of truth that is not itself distorted by power or ideology. In other words, they will have to acknowledge and admit the Right-Hand aspects of existence that ground correspondence claims of truth, for that is also an important aspect of all knowledge.[3] Instead, they are simply claiming that it is objectively true that there is no objective truth at all.

Aspects of knowledge are indeed intersubjectively constructed; but those constructions are set in networks of subjective, objective, and interobjective realities that *constrain* the construction. We will never, for example, find a shared cultural worldview where apples fall upward or men give birth: so much for arbitrary constructivism.

No wonder that John Searle's most recent book is an aggressive attack on mere constructivism. He calls it *The Construction of Social Reality*, as opposed to "the social construction of reality," the point being that social reality is in part constructed on a given sensorimotor world that is then reflected in correspondence, so that it itself is not socially constructed. His point is that we can't even get to the constructed aspects of reality without also having a foundation in correspondence: both are irreplaceable.

Systems Theory Reductionism

Whereas cultural constructivists attempt to reduce all reality to the Lower Left, systems theory attempts to reduce all reality to the Lower Right. That is, social reductionism attempts to reduce all truth to functional fit, to the dynamic interplay of holistic its. All I's and we's dissolve in the dynamic web of mutually interwoven its.

Of course, that dynamic web is indeed real—it is the Lower-Right quadrant of the Kosmos—but it is a partial truth that, when expanded into a complete "wholism," takes the entire Left Half of the Kosmos with it into oblivion.

In functional fit, all reality is ultimately reduced to Lower-Right terms (the social system), and so all other validity claims (from propositional truth to cultural meaning to personal integrity) are judged ultimately in terms of their capacity to *serve the holistic functioning of the social system*. All qualitative distinctions are thus reduced to terms of expediency and efficiency; nothing is "true," because all that enters the equation is usefulness (i.e., "truth" becomes anything that furthers the autopoietic regime of the self-organizing social system; such theories dissolve their own truth value in the functional fit of that which they describe).

And yet, of course, those of the social theorists, ecoholists, ecofeminists, and deep ecologists who use systems theory want to claim that their approach has a *moral superiority* to the alternatives. But this moral value cannot even be stated, let alone explained, in the terms of their own systems theory, because, in this theory, all existing things and events are equally strands in the total web of life, and so there is simply no way to say that one of them is right and one of them is wrong. Whatever happens is what the total system is actually doing, and we do not and cannot challenge the overall system because we are all equally strands in that web. What looks like evil to us is simply something the overall system is doing, and thus all ethical drives dissolve in the flatland web of dynamically interwoven its.

Of course, many systems theorists immediately attempt to sneak or smuggle moral and normative claims into their theory by saying, in effect: that which furthers the system is good, and that which harms the system is bad. But to even be able to make that claim is to actually step outside of the system in order to comment on it, and this, according to systems theory, is impossible. Thus, to the extent that systems theorists claim to offer a moral or normative direction, to just that extent they have ceased to be systems theorists. They have moved from descriptive it-language to normative I and we language, terms which systems theory does not and cannot comprehend, and terms which therefore have to be smuggled into their overall view. To just that extent, the banished I and we domains reassert themselves as formal contradictions in the flatland and exterior holism of the systems approach.

Systems theory definitely has its important (if limited) place, yet it is now, by virtue of its extensive subtle reductionism, one of the great modern enemies of the I and the we domains, of the individual lifeworld and of cultural richness—what Habermas refers to as "the colonization of the lifeworld by the imperatives of functional systems that externalize their costs on the other . . . a blind compulsion to system maintenance and system expansion."

These approaches have a wonderfully noble intent, which I believe we can all applaud, but somewhere on the way to the global wedding they took a wrong turn and found themselves deep in the flatland of subtle reductionism, which effectively perpetuates exactly the fragmentation they so nobly desire to overcome.[4] Thus, we wish to honor systems theory and its truth, but set in its own much larger context of other and equally honorable truths.

Cultural Relativity

Those theorists who focus exclusively on the Lower-Left or cultural quadrant tend to fall into various types of extreme relativism, which, in denying other quadrants, ends up self-contradictory. Cultural relativists, extreme pluralists, and multiculturalists are all caught in a similar contradiction: The claim is made that all truths are relative, that there are and can be no universal truths.

Unfortunately, that view itself is claiming to be universally true. It is making a series of *strong claims* that it insists are true for *all* cultures (the relative nature of truth, the contextuality of claims, the social relativity of all categories, the historicity of truth, and so on). This view thus claims that there are no universal truths of any sort—except for its own, which are universal and superior in a world where nothing is supposed to be universal or superior at all.

This is yet another attempt to reduce all objective truth to intersubjective agreement, and it suffers the same fate: it cannot assert its own position without contradicting itself. It is maintaining that there are several objectively true things about all cultures—and this is correct, but only if we fully acknowledge some aspect of objective truth. Otherwise, the denied quadrant once again sneaks back into the system and explodes it from within.

Some aspects of culture are most definitely constructed, and some aspects are both relative and historically bound. But many features of the human bodymind show universal commonalities across cultures. The human body everywhere has 206 bones, one heart, two kidneys. And the human mind everywhere has the capacity to produce images, symbols, concepts, and rules. The sturdy conclusion is that the human body and mind cross-culturally share certain *deep features* that, when they appear, are everywhere quite similar, but the *surface features*—the actual manifestations of these common traits—are indeed relative, culturally bound, marked by historicity, and determined contingently. The human body might indeed have 206 bones wherever it appears, but not all cultures use those bones to play baseball.

The integral approach fully acknowledges and honors the richness of cultural diversity in surface features, while also pinpointing the common deep features of the human family: neither monolithic universalism nor incoherent pluralism, but rather a genuinely universal pluralism of commonality-in-difference.

Aesthetics Only

We have recently seen a flurry of merely aesthetic theories of truth: whatever you happen to like, that is the final arbiter of truth. All objective, interobjective, and intersubjective truths are cheerfully reduced to subjective inclinations (all quadrants are reduced to the Upper Left). Personal taste alone is the arbiter of reality. I do my thing, you do yours. Nietzsche is always (incorrectly) accused of advocating this.

Integrating the aesthetic judgment (Upper Left) with truth and justness is certainly important, but a theory of knowledge that is merely aesthetic is simply inarticulate. Not only does it fail to deal with intersubjective goodness and justness, it trashes any objective aspects of any sorts of truths. And once again, as long as this aesthetic theory is totally silent and never utters its own views, it is fine. But as soon as it tries to explain why aesthetics alone works, it will smuggle in the other quadrants and end up contradicting itself. It will claim, at least implicitly, that what it is doing is true, and moreover, *better* than your view, thus sneaking in both objective and intersubjective judgments, where they explode from within, scattering the landscape with performative contradictions.

Conclusion

And so on around the four quadrants. The point is that every human being has a subjective aspect (sincerity, truthfulness), an objective aspect (truth, correspondence), an intersubjective aspect (culturally constructed meaning, justness, appropriateness), and an interobjective aspect (systems and functional fit), and our different knowledge claims are *grounded* in these very real domains. And thus, whenever we attempt to deny any of these insistent domains, we simply end up, sooner or later, smuggling them into our philosophy in a hidden and unacknowledged fashion: the empiricists use interpretation in the very act of denying its importance; the extreme constructivists and relativists use universal truth in order to universally deny its existence; extreme aestheticians use beauty alone to claim moral goodness—and on and on and on. To deny any of these domains is, as it were, to be hoist with our own petard and end up in a severe self-contradiction.

A more integral vision attempts instead to include the moment of truth in each of those approaches—from empiricism to constructivism to relativism to aestheticism—but, in stripping them of their claims to be the only type of truth in existence, releases them from their contradictions—and places them, as it were, into a genuine rainbow coalition.

THE SPECTRUM OF CONSCIOUSNESS

Integral studies in general are dedicated to an "all-level, all-quadrant" view of human consciousness and behavior. But if for the moment we focus on the Upper-Left quadrant—the interior of the individual, the site of consciousness itself—what do we find?

Biological and medical scientists are now in the midst of intensive work on the Human Genome Project, the endeavor to map all of the genes in the entire sequence of human DNA. This spectacular project promises to revolutionize our ideas of human growth, development, disease, and medical treatment, and its completion will surely mark one of the great advances in human knowledge.

Not as well known, but arguably more important, is what might be called the Human Consciousness Project, the endeavor, now well under way, to *map the entire spectrum of the various states of human consciousness* (including, as well, realms of the human unconscious). This Human Consciousness Project, involving hundreds of researchers from around the world, involves a series of multidisciplinary, multicultural, multimodal approaches that together promise an exhaustive mapping of the entire range of consciousness, the entire sequence of the "genes" of awareness, as it were.

These various attempts are rapidly converging on a "master template" of the various stages, structures, and states of consciousness available to men and women. By comparing and contrasting various multicultural approaches—from Zen Buddhism to Western psychoanalysis, from Vedanta Hinduism to existential phenomenology, from Tundra Shamanism to altered states—these approaches are rapidly piecing together a master template—*a spectrum of consciousness*—using the various approaches to fill in any gaps left by the others.

Although many of the specifics are still being intensively researched, the overall evidence for the existence of this spectrum of consciousness is already so significant as to put it largely beyond serious dispute. We will examine this spectrum in more detail in chapter 1. For the moment, we will simply note that this spectrum appears to range from instinctual to egoic to spiritual modes, from prepersonal to personal to transpersonal experiences, from subconscious to self-conscious to superconscious states, from body to mind to spirit itself.

The field that has perhaps most carefully and meticulously studied this extraordinary spectrum of consciousness is the discipline known as *transpersonal psychology*. Transpersonal psychology is sometimes called "the fourth force," after the first three of behavioristic, psychoanalytic, and humanistic schools. The word "transpersonal" itself simply means "personal plus." That is, the transpersonal orientation explicitly and carefully includes all of the facets of personal psychology and psychiatry, but then *adds* those deeper or higher aspects of human experience that transcend the ordinary and the average—experiences that are, in other words, "transpersonal," or "more than the personal," or personal plus. Thus, in the attempt to more fully and accurately reflect the entire range of human experience, transpersonal psychology and psychiatry take, as their basic starting point, the entire spectrum of consciousness.

The integral approach that I am advocating acknowledges and honors this all-inclusive spectrum of consciousness as being perhaps the best available map of the Upper-Left quadrant in general, a map that is the direct result of this extraordinary Human Consciousness Project.

But the integral approach does not stop there. The point, of course, is that *if the entire spectrum of consciousness is acknowledged and taken into account, it will dramatically alter each and every discipline it touches*—from anthropology to ecology, from philosophy to art, from ethics to sociology, from psychology to politics.

This is why we can say that integral studies in general are dedicated to an "all-level, all-quadrant" view of human consciousness and behavior—covering not just all of the quadrants, but all of the various levels and dimensions in each of those quadrants—the entire spectrum of levels in the intentional, behavioral, cultural, and social aspects of human beings.

In the following chapters, we will specifically look at examples of each of those branches of integral studies, including integral psychology (chapters 1, 9, 10), integral anthropology (chapter 2), integral philosophy (chapter 3), integral art and literary theory (chapters 4 and 5), integral feminism (chapter 8), and integral spirituality (chapters 9, 10, 11).

These are the parts that we will attempt to weave into the integral vision as a whole, thus completing, at least for this round, that extraordinary circle of understanding.

THE GREAT WISDOM TRADITIONS

Men and women, as the Christian mystics are fond of saying, have (at least) three eyes of knowing: the eye of flesh, which apprehends physical events; the eye of mind, which apprehends images and desires and concepts and ideas; and the eye of contemplation, which apprehends spiritual experiences and states. And that, of course, is a simplified version of the spectrum of consciousness, reaching from body to mind to spirit.

Indeed, the Upper-Left quadrant has historically been studied as the *Great Chain of Being*, a concept which, according to Arthur Lovejoy, "has been the dominant official philosophy of the larger part of civilized humankind through most of its history." Huston Smith, in his remarkable book *Forgotten Truth*, has demonstrated that all of the world's great wisdom traditions, from Taoism to Vedanta, Zen to Sufism, Neoplatonism to Confucianism, are based on the Great Chain—that is, based on some version of the overall spectrum of consciousness, with its levels of being and knowing.

Some postmodern critics, however, have claimed that the very notion of the Great Chain, since it is hierarchical, is somehow oppressive; it is supposed to be based on unpleasant "ranking" instead of compassionate "linking." But this is a rather unfair complaint. First, the antihierarchical and antiranking critics are themselves engaged in hierarchical judgments of ranking—namely, they claim their view is *better* than the alternatives. In other words, they themselves have a very strong ranking system—it's just hidden and inarticulate (and self-contradictory).

Second, the Great Chain is actually what Arthur Koestler called a *holarchy*: a series of concentric circles or nests, with each senior level *transcending* but *including* its juniors. This is a ranking, to be sure, but a ranking of increasing inclusiveness and embrace, with each senior level including more and more of the world and its inhabitants, so that the upper or spiritual reaches of the spectrum of consciousness are absolutely all-inclusive and all-embracing.

Of course, any hierarchy—including the feminist hierarchy that values "linking" as better than "ranking"—can be put to severe abuse, repressing or marginalizing certain values. But this condemns not hierarchies in general, but merely pathological or dominator hierarchies. As Riane Eisler has reminded us, there is a big difference between actualization hierarchies and dominator hierarchies; and the Great Nest of Being was from its inception a profound actualization holarchy, quite apart from the abuses to which it was occasionally put. (We will return to the Great Nest in chapter 1, and examine its importance more carefully.)

But apart from such abuses, the great wisdom traditions *even at their best* still neglected several crucial items, items that the early investigators of the spectrum of consciousness could not, or at any rate did not, know. Two deficiencies in the wisdom traditions especially deserve mention, because integral studies, to be genuinely integral, must directly and forthrightly address these serious inadequacies.

The first is the recognition that the very earliest stages of human development can play a decisive role in subsequent growth—Freud's pioneering work, for example. The great contemplative traditions excelled in tracing human growth from mental and egoic modes to transmental and spiritual modes, but they were extremely weak in their understanding of the stages leading up to the mental-ego itself. In Jack Engler's memorable phrase, "You have to be somebody before you can be nobody." That is, you must develop a strong and secure ego before you can transcend it; and whereas the great traditions were superb at the latter, they often failed at the former. And a truly "full spectrum" approach to psychiatry and psychology would rigorously embrace both: the move from instinct to ego, as well as from ego to spirit.

Precisely because the spectrum of consciousness develops, modern-day researchers can bring to bear the vast arsenal of developmental research techniques to help elucidate the various developmental lines of consciousness itself. That is, we can now begin to trace the developmental unfolding of such lines as cognition, affect, moral sense, object-relations, self-identity, modes of space and time, motivations, needs, and so on—and not just from pre-egoic to egoic modes, but also from egoic to transegoic modes. This gives integral studies the chance historically to be the first genuinely "full spectrum" model of human growth and development.

Likewise for integral psychotherapy. Precisely because the spectrum of consciousness develops, various "misdevelopments" can occur at any stage of this unfolding. As with any living entity, pathology can occur at any point in growth. Thus, the spectrum of consciousness is also a spectrum of different types of possible pathologies: psychotic, neurotic, cognitive, existential, spiritual. And a "full-spectrum" approach to psychology and psychiatry is devoted to a full range of treatments that address these different types of pathologies (we will return to this topic in chapters 6 and 7).

The second major weakness of the great traditions is that they did not clearly recognize that the various levels of interior consciousness *have correlates in the other quadrants.* In other words, it is not simply, as the great traditions assume, that human beings have different levels—body, mind, soul, and spirit, for example—but *also* that *each* of those levels has four aspects—intentional, behavioral, cultural, and social. This multidimensional grid—not simply "all-level" but "all-level, all-quadrant"—opens the study of human beings in a profound fashion. That, of course, is part of integral studies.

We can now, for example, begin to correlate states of meditative awareness with types of brainwave patterns (without attempting to reduce one to the other). We can monitor physiological shifts that occur with spiritual experience. We can follow the levels of neurotransmitters during psychotherapeutic interventions. We can follow the effects of psychoactive drugs on blood distribution patterns in the brain. We can trace the social modes of production and see the corresponding changes in cultural worldviews. We can follow the historical unfolding of cultural worldviews and plot the status of men and women in each period. We can trace the modes of self that correlate with different modes of techno-economic infrastructure. And so on around the quadrants: not simply "all-level," but "all-level, all-quadrant."

Thus, modern-day integral studies can do something at which the great traditions generally failed: trace the spectrum of consciousness not just in its intentional but also in its behavioral, social, and cultural manifestations, thus highlighting the importance of a multidimensional approach for a truly comprehensive overview of human consciousness and behavior.

Finally, with these broader and more sophisticated tools of behavioral, developmental, and cultural analysis, we will also be able to more clearly spot those areas where the great traditions were all-too-embedded in the social injustices of the day, from sexism to speciesism to militarism to ethnocentrism.

In short, modern-day integral studies have reconnected with the world's great wisdom traditions, honoring and incorporating many of their essential and pioneering insights, while, at the same time, adding new methodologies and techniques previously unavailable. This is multiculturalism in its best and deepest sense, cherishing cultural differences, but set in a truly universal context.

CONCLUSION

An integral approach is dedicated to an all-level, all-quadrant program, honoring the entire spectrum of consciousness, not just in the I-domain, but also in the we and the it domains, thus *integrating* art, morals, and science; self, ethics, and environment; consciousness, culture, and nature; Buddha, Sangha, and Dharma; the beautiful and the good and the true.

In the following chapters, we will see very concrete examples of each of these many facets of the Kosmos, as we attempt to weave them into a blanket of many colors.

And who knows, we might, you and I just might, in the upper reaches of the spectrum of consciousness itself, directly intuit the mind of some eternal Spirit—a Spirit that shines forth in every I and every we and every it, a Spirit that sings as the rain and dances as the wind, a Spirit of which every conversation is the sincerest worship, a Spirit that speaks with your tongue and looks out from your eyes, that touches with these hands and cries out with this voice—and a Spirit that has always whispered lovingly in our ears: Never forget the Good, and never forget the True, and never forget the Beautiful.

The integral vision is the modern and postmodern attempt to honor just that pledge.

1

The Spectrum of Consciousness

INTEGRAL PSYCHOLOGY AND
THE PERENNIAL PHILOSOPHY

Biological and medical scientists are now in the midst of intensive work on the Human Genome Project, the endeavor to map all of the genes in the entire sequence of human DNA. This spectacular project promises to revolutionize our ideas of human growth, development, disease, and medical treatment, and its completion will surely mark one of the great advances in human knowledge.

Not as well known, but arguably more important, is what might be called the Human Consciousness Project, *the endeavor, now well under way, to map the entire spectrum of human consciousness (including, as well, realms of the human unconscious). This Human Consciousness Project, involving hundreds of researchers from around the world, includes a series of multidisciplinary, multicultural, multimodal approaches that together promise an exhaustive mapping of the entire range of consciousness, the entire sequence of the "genes" of awareness, as it were.*

These various attempts are rapidly converging on a "master template" of the various stages, structures, and states of consciousness available to men and women. By comparing and contrasting various multicultural approaches—from Zen Buddhism to Western psychoanalysis, from Vedanta Hinduism to existential phenomenology, from Tundra Shamanism to altered states—these approaches are rapidly piecing together a master template—a spectrum of consciousness—*using the various approaches to fill in any gaps left by the others.*

Although many of the specifics are still being intensively researched, the overall evidence for the existence of this spectrum of consciousness is already so significant as to put it largely beyond serious dispute.

Moreover, in a rather stunning fashion, it has increasingly become obvious that this overall spectrum is quite consistent with the essential core of the world's great wisdom traditions.

The "master template" that is emerging from this modern research is therefore able to honor and connect with the essence of the world's wisdom traditions, while simultaneously attempting to update and modernize their insights where appropriate. The goal of an integral approach is thus a judicious blend of ancient wisdom and modern knowledge.

Let us start with the basics, with those items from the great traditions that seem to have withstood the test of time with flying colors, so much so that they are even making a remarkable comeback in many modern and scientific disciplines.

And they all hinge on this extraordinary spectrum of consciousness.

WHAT IS THE WORLDVIEW that, as Arthur Lovejoy pointed out, "has been the dominant official philosophy of the larger part of civilized humankind through most of its history"? The worldview that "the greater number of the subtler speculative minds and of the great religious teachers [both East and West] have, in their various fashions, been engaged in"? What is the worldview that led Alan Watts to state flatly that "we are hardly aware of the extreme peculiarity of our own position, and find it difficult to realize the plain fact that there has otherwise been a single philosophical consensus of universal extent. It has been held by [men and women] who report the same insights and teach the same essential doctrine whether living today or six thousand years ago, whether from New Mexico in the Far West or from Japan in the Far East."

And why is it of interest to anyone living in today's world?

Known as the "perennial philosophy"—"perennial" precisely because it shows up across cultures and across the ages with many similar features—this worldview has, indeed, formed the core not only of the world's great wisdom traditions, from Christianity to Buddhism to Taoism, but also of many of the greatest philosophers, scientists, and psychologists of both East and West, North and South. So overwhelmingly widespread is the perennial philosophy—the details of which I will explain in a moment—that it is either the single greatest intellectual error ever to appear in humankind's history—an error so colossally widespread as to literally stagger the mind—or it is the single most accurate reflection of reality yet to appear.

Central to the perennial philosophy is the notion of the *Great Chain of Being*. The idea itself is fairly simple. Reality, according to the perennial philosophy, is not one-dimensional; it is not a flatland of uniform substance stretching monotonously before the eye. Rather, reality is composed of several *different* but *continuous* dimensions. Manifest reality, that is, consists of different grades or levels, reaching from the lowest and most dense and least conscious to the highest and most subtle and most conscious. At one end of this continuum of being or spectrum of consciousness is what we in the West would call "matter" or the insentient and the nonconscious, and at the other end is "spirit" or "godhead" or the "superconscious" (which is also said to be the all-pervading ground of the entire sequence, as we will see). Arrayed in between are the other dimensions of being arranged according to their individual degrees of reality (Plato), actuality (Aristotle), inclusiveness (Hegel), consciousness (Aurobindo), clarity (Leibniz), embrace (Plotinus), or knowingness (Garab Dorje).

Sometimes the Great Chain is presented as having just three major levels: matter, mind, and spirit. Other versions give five levels: matter, body, mind, soul, and spirit. Still others give very exhaustive breakdowns of the Great Chain; some of the yogic systems give literally dozens of discrete yet continuous dimensions. For the time being, our simple hierarchy of matter to body to mind to soul to spirit will suffice.

The central claim of the perennial philosophy is that *men and women can grow and develop (or evolve) all the way up the hierarchy to Spirit itself*, therein to realize a "supreme identity" with Godhead—the *ens perfectissimum* toward which all growth and evolution yearns.

But before we get to that, the first thing that we can't help but notice is that the Great Chain is indeed a "hierarchy"—a word that has fallen on very hard times. Originally introduced by the great Christian mystic Saint Dionysius, it essentially meant "governing one's life by spiritual principles" (*hiero-* means sacred or holy, and *-arch* means governance or rule). But it soon became translated into a political/military power play, where "governance by spirit" came to mean "ruled by the Catholic Church"—a spiritual principle mistranslated into a despotism.

But as used by the perennial philosophy—and indeed, as used in modern psychology, evolutionary theory, and systems theory—a hierarchy is simply a ranking of orders of events *according to their holistic capacity.* In any developmental sequence, what is whole at one stage becomes merely a part of a larger whole at the next stage. A letter is part of a whole word, which is part of a whole sentence, which is part of a whole paragraph, and so on. Arthur Koestler coined the term "holon" to refer to that which, being a whole in one context, is a part of a wider whole in another. With reference to the phrase "the bark of a dog," for example, the word "bark" is a whole with reference to its individual letters, but a part with reference to the phrase itself. And the whole (or the context) can determine the meaning and function of a part—the meaning of "bark" is different in the phrases "the bark of a dog" and "the bark of a tree." The whole, in other words, is more than the sum of its parts, and that whole can influence and determine, in many cases, the function of its parts.

Hierarchy, then, is simply an order of increasing holons, representing an increase in wholeness and integrative capacity. This is why hierarchy is so central to systems theory, the theory of wholeness or holism ("wholism"). And it is absolutely central to the perennial philosophy. Each expanding link in the Great Chain of Being represents an increase in unity and wider identities, from the isolated identity of the body through the social and communal identity of the mind to the supreme identity of Spirit, an identity with literally all manifestation. This is why the great hierarchy of being is often drawn as a series of concentric circles or spheres or "nests within nests." As we will see, the Great Chain is actually the Great Nest of Being.

And finally, hierarchy *is* asymmetrical (or a "higher"-archy) because the process does not occur in the reverse. For example, there are first letters, then words, then sentences, then paragraphs, but not vice versa. And that *not vice versa* constitutes an unavoidable hierarchy or ranking or asymmetrical order of increasing wholeness.

All developmental and evolutionary sequences that we are aware of proceed in large measure by hierarchization, or by orders of increasing holism—molecules to cells to organs to organ systems to organisms to societies of organisms, for example. In cognitive development, we find awareness expanding from simple images, which represent only one thing or event, to symbols and concepts which represent whole groups or classes of things and events, to rules which organize and integrate numerous classes and groups into entire networks. In moral development (in both male and female), we find a reasoning that moves from the isolated subject to a group or tribe of related subjects, to an entire network of groups beyond any isolated element. And so on.

These hierarchical networks necessarily unfold in a sequential or stagelike fashion, because you first have to have molecules, *then* cells, *then* organs, *then* complex organisms—they don't all burst on the scene simultaneously. In other words, growth generally occurs in *stages*, and stages, of course, are *ranked* in both a logical and chronological order. The *more holistic* patterns appear *later* in development because they have to await the emergence of the parts that they will then integrate or unify, just as whole sentences emerge only *after* whole words.

And some hierarchies do involve a type of control network—the lower levels (which means, less holistic levels) can influence the upper (or more holistic) levels, through what is known as *upward causation*. But just as important, the higher levels can exert a powerful influence or control on the lower levels—so-called *downward causation*. For example, when you decide to move your arm, and you do so, all the atoms and molecules and cells in your arm move with it—an instance of downward causation.

In any developmental or growth sequence, as a more encompassing stage or holon emerges, it *includes* the capacities and patterns and functions of the previous stage (i.e., of the previous holons), and then adds its own unique (and more encompassing) capacities. In that sense, and that sense only, can the new and more encompassing holon be said to be "higher" or "wider." Whatever the important value of the previous stage, the new stage has *all* of that plus something extra (more integrative capacity, for example), and that "something extra" means "extra value" *relative* to the previous (and less encompassing) stage. This crucial definition of a "higher stage" was first introduced in the West by Aristotle and in the East by Shankara and Lieh-Tzu; it has been central to the perennial philosophy ever since.

Let me give one example. In cognitive and moral development, in both the boy and the girl, the stage of preoperational or preconventional thought is concerned largely with the individual's own point of view ("narcissistic"). The next stage, the operational or conventional stage, still takes account of the individual's own point of view, but *adds* the capacity to take the view of others into account. Nothing is lost; something is added. And so in this sense it is properly said that this stage is higher or wider, meaning more valuable and useful for a wider range of interactions. Conventional thought is *more valuable* than preconventional thought in establishing a balanced moral response (and postconventional is even more valuable, and so on). As Hegel first put it, and as developmentalists have echoed ever since, each stage is adequate and valuable, but each higher stage is more adequate, and, in that sense only, more valuable (which always means, more holistic).

It is for all these reasons that Koestler, after noting that all complex hierarchies are composed of holons, or increasing orders of wholeness, pointed out that the correct word for "hierarchy" is actually *holarchy*. He is absolutely right, and so from now on I will refer to hierarchy in general, and the Great Chain—the Great Nest—in particular, as holarchy.

So that is normal or natural holarchy, the stagelike unfolding of larger networks of increasing wholeness, with the larger or wider wholes being able to exert influence over the lower-order wholes. And as natural, desirable, and unavoidable as that is, you can already start to see how holarchies might turn *pathological*. If the higher levels can exert control over the lower levels, they can also overdominate or even repress and alienate the lower levels. That leads to a whole host of pathological difficulties, in both the individual and society at large.

It is precisely *because* the world is arranged holarchically, precisely because it contains fields within fields within fields, that things can go so profoundly wrong, that a disruption or pathology in one field can reverberate throughout an entire system. And the "cure" for this pathology, in all cases, is essentially the same: rooting out the pathological holons so the holarchy itself can return to harmony. The cure does not consist, as the reductionists maintain, in getting rid of holarchy per se, since, even if that were possible, it would simply result in a uniform, one-dimensional flatland of no value distinctions at all (which is why those critics who toss out hierarchy in general immediately replace it with a new scale of values of their own, i.e., with their own particular hierarchy).

Rather, the "cure" of any diseased system consists in rooting out any holons that have usurped their position in the overall system by abusing their power of upward or downward causation. This is exactly the "cure" we see at work in psychoanalysis (shadow holons refuse integration), democratic social revolutions (monarchical or fascist holons oppress the body politic), medical science interventions (cancerous holons invade a benign system), critical social theory (opaque ideology usurps open communication), radical feminist critiques (patriarchal holons dominate the public sphere), and so on. It is not getting rid of holarchy per se, but arresting (and integrating) its arrogant holons.

As I said, all of the world's great wisdom traditions are basically variations of the perennial philosophy, of the Great Holarchy of Being. In his wonderful book *Forgotten Truth*, Huston Smith summarizes the world's major religions in one phrase: "a hierarchy of being and knowing." Chögyam Trungpa Rinpoche pointed out, in *Shambhala: The Sacred Path of the Warrior*, that *the* essential and background idea pervading all of the philosophies of the East, from India to Tibet to China, lying behind everything from Shintoism to Taoism, is "a hierarchy of earth, human, heaven," which he also pointed out is equivalent to "body, mind, spirit." And Coomaraswamy noted that the world's great religions, bar none, "in their different degrees represent a hierarchy of types or levels of consciousness extending from animal to deity, and according to which one and the same individual may function on different occasions."

Which brings us to the most notorious paradox in the perennial philosophy. We have seen that the wisdom traditions subscribe to the notion that reality manifests in levels or dimensions, with each higher dimension being more inclusive and therefore "closer" to the absolute totality of Godhead or Spirit. In this sense, Spirit is the summit of being, the highest rung on the ladder of evolution. But it is also true that Spirit is *the wood out of which the entire ladder and all its rungs are made.* Spirit is the suchness, the isness, the essence of each and every thing that exists.

The first aspect, the highest-rung aspect, is the *transcendental* nature of Spirit—it far surpasses any "worldly" or creaturely or finite things. The entire earth (or even universe) could be destroyed, and Spirit would remain. The second aspect, the wood aspect, is the *immanent* nature of Spirit—Spirit is equally and totally present in all manifest things and events, in nature, in culture, in heaven and on earth, with no partiality. From this angle, no phenomenon whatsoever is closer to Spirit than another, for all are equally "made of" Spirit. Thus, Spirit is *both* the highest *goal* of all development and evolution, and the *ground* of the entire sequence, as present fully at the beginning as at the end. Spirit is prior to this world, but not other to this world.

Failure to take both of those paradoxical aspects of Spirit into account has historically led to some very lopsided (and politically dangerous) views of Spirit. Traditionally, the patriarchal religions have tended to overemphasize the transcendental nature of Spirit, thus condemning earth, nature, body, and woman to an inferior status. Prior to that, the matriarchal religions tended to emphasize the immanent nature of Spirit alone, and the resultant pantheistic worldview equated the finite and created Earth with the infinite and uncreated Spirit. You are free to identify with a finite and limited Earth; you are not free to call it the infinite and unlimited.

Both matriarchal and patriarchal religions, both of these lopsided views of Spirit, have had rather horrible historical consequences, from brutal and large-scale human sacrifice for the fertility of the earth Goddess to wholesale war for God the Father. But in the very midst of these outward distortions, the perennial philosophy (the esoteric or inner core of the wisdom religions) has always avoided any of those dualities—Heaven or Earth, masculine or feminine, infinite or finite, ascetic or celebratory—and centered instead on their union or integration ("nondualism"). And indeed, this union of Heaven and Earth, masculine and feminine, infinite and finite, ascending and descending, wisdom and compassion, was made explicit in the "tantric" teachings of the various wisdom traditions, from Neoplatonism in the West to Vajrayana in the East. And it is this nondual core of the wisdom traditions to which the term "perennial philosophy" most applies.

The point, then, is that if we are to try to think of Spirit in mental terms (which necessarily involves some difficulties), then at least we should remember this transcendent/immanent paradox. Paradox is simply the way nonduality looks to the mental level. Spirit itself is not paradoxical; strictly speaking, it is not characterizable at all.

This applies doubly to hierarchy (holarchy). We have said that when transcendental Spirit manifests itself, it does so in stages or levels—the Great Holarchy of Being. But I'm not saying Spirit or reality itself is hierarchical. Absolute Spirit or reality is not hierarchical. It is not qualifiable at all in mental terms (lower-holon terms)—it is *shunyata*, or *nirguna*, or *apophatic*—unqualifiable, without a trace of specific and limiting characteristics at all. But it manifests itself in steps, in layers, dimensions, sheaths, levels, or grades—whatever term one prefers—and that is holarchy. In Vedanta these are the *koshas*, the sheaths or layers covering Brahman; in Buddhism, these are the eight *vijnanas*, the eight levels of awareness, each of which is a stepped-down or more restricted version of its senior dimension; in Kabbalah these are the *sefirot*, and so on.

The whole point is that these are levels of the manifest world, of *maya*. When maya is not recognized as the play of the Divine, then it is nothing but illusion. Hierarchy is illusion. There are levels of illusion, not levels of reality. But according to the traditions, it is exactly (and only) by understanding the hierarchical nature of samsara that we can in fact climb out of it, a ladder discarded only after having served its extraordinary purpose.

We can look now at some of the actual levels or spheres of the holarchy, of the Great Nest of Being, as it appears in the three largest wisdom traditions: Judeo-Christian-Muslim, Buddhism, and Hinduism, although any mature tradition will do.

(*Let me remind you that these are the levels in the Upper-Left quadrant*, the levels in the spectrum of consciousness itself. We will, in the following chapters, see how this spectrum plays itself out in the other quadrants as well, cultural and social and behavioral—from anthropology to philosophy to art and literature. But for now we are concentrating on the spectrum of consciousness as it appears in the individual human being, the Upper-Left quadrant.)

The Christian terms are the easiest, because most of us are familiar with them: matter, body, mind, soul, and spirit. *Matter* means the physical universe as it appears in our own physical bodies (e.g., those aspects of our existence covered by the laws of physics); and whatever else we might mean by the word "matter," it means in this case the dimension with the least amount of consciousness (some would say no consciousness, and you can take your pick). *Body* in this case means the emotional body, the "animal" body, sex, hunger, vital life force, and so on (e.g., those aspects of existence studied by biology). *Mind* is the rational, reasoning, linguistic, and imaginative mind (studied by psychology). *Soul* is the higher or subtle mind, the archetypal mind, the intuitive mind, and the essence or the indestructibleness of our own being (studied by theology). And *spirit* is the transcendental summit of our being, our Godhead (studied by contemplative mysticism).

According to Vedanta Hinduism, the individual person is composed of five "sheaths" or levels or spheres of being (the koshas), often compared to an onion, so that as we peel away the outer layers we find more and more the essence. The lowest (or most outer) is called the annamayakosha, which means "the sheath made of food." This is the physical sphere. Next is the pranamayakosha, the sheath made of prana. *Prana* means vital force, bioenergy, élan vital, libido, emotional-sexual energy in general—the sphere of the emotional body (as we are using the term). Next is the manomayakosha, the sheath of manas or mind—

rational, abstract, linguistic. Beyond this is the vijnanamayakosha, the sheath of intuition, the higher mind, the subtle mind. Finally there is the anandamayakosha, the sheath made of ananda, or spiritual and transcendental bliss.

Further—and this is important—Vedanta groups these five sheaths into three major realms: gross, subtle, and causal. The gross realm is correlated with the lowest level in the holarchy, the physical body (annamayakosha). The subtle realm is correlated with the three intermediate levels: the emotional-sexual body (pranamayakosha), the mind (manomayakosha), and the higher or subtle mind (vijnanamayakosha). And the causal is correlated with the highest level, the anandamayakosha, or archetypal spirit, which is also sometimes said to be largely unmanifest, or formless. Further, Vedanta relates these three major *realms of being* with the three major *states of consciousness*: waking, dreaming, and deep dreamless sleep. Beyond all three of these states is absolute Spirit, sometimes called turiya, "the fourth," because it is beyond (and includes) the three states of manifestation; it is beyond (and thus integrates) gross, subtle, and causal.[1]

So the Vedanta version of five sheaths is almost identical to the Judeo/Christian/Muslim version of matter, body, mind, soul, and spirit, as long as we understand "soul" to mean, not just a higher self or higher identity, but higher or subtler mind and cognition. And soul also has the meaning, in *all* the higher mystical traditions, of being a "knot" or "contraction" (what the Hindus and Buddhists call the ahamkara), which has to be untied and dissolved before the soul can transcend itself, die to itself, and thus find a supreme identity with and as absolute Spirit (as Christ said, "He cannot be a true disciple who hateth not his own soul").

So "soul" is both the highest level of individual growth we can achieve, and also the final barrier, the final knot, to complete enlightenment or supreme identity, simply because as transcendental witness it stands back from everything it witnesses. Once we push through the witness position, then the soul or witness itself dissolves and there is only the play of nondual awareness, awareness that does not look at objects but is completely one with all objects (Zen says "it is like tasting the sky"). The gap between subject and object collapses, the soul is transcended or dissolved, and pure spiritual or nondual awareness—which is very simple, very obvious, very clear—arises. You realize that your intrinsic being is vast and open, empty and clear, and everything arising anywhere is arising within you, as intrinsic spirit, spontaneously.

The central psychological model of Mahayana Buddhism is the eight vijnanas, the eight levels of consciousness. The first five are the five senses. The next is the manovijnana, the mind that operates on sensory experience. Then there is manas, which means both higher mind and the center of the illusion of the separate self. It is the manas that looks at the alayavijnana (the next higher level, that of supraindividual consciousness) and mistakes it for a separate self or substantial soul, as we have defined it. And beyond these eight levels, as both their source and ground, is the pure alaya or pure empty Spirit.

I don't mean to minimize some of the very real differences between these traditions. I'm simply pointing out that they share certain deep structure similarities, which testifies eloquently to the genuinely universal nature of many of their insights.

And so we can end on a happy note: After being temporarily derailed in the nineteenth century by a variety of materialistic reductionisms (from scientific materialism to behaviorism to positivism), the Great Nest of Being, the Great Holarchy of Being, is making a stunning comeback. That temporary derailment—an attempt to reduce the holarchy of being to its lowest level, matter—was particularly galling in psychology, which first lost its spirit, then lost its soul, then lost its mind, and was reduced to studying only empirical behavior or bodily drives, a restriction that at any other time or place would be considered a precise definition of insanity.

But now evolutionary holarchy—the holistic study of the development and self-organization of fields within fields within fields—is once again a dominant theme in many scientific and behavioral disciplines (as we will see), though it goes by many names (Aristotle's "entelechy," to give only one example, is now known as "morphogenetic fields" and "self-organizing systems"). This is not to say that the modern versions of the Great Holarchy and its self-organizing principles offer no new insights, for they do, particularly when it comes to the actual evolutionary unfolding of the Great Nest itself. Each glimpse of the Great Holarchy is adequate; each advancing glimpse is more adequate. . . .

But the essentials are unmistakable. Ludwig von Bertalanffy, the founder of General System Theory, summarized it perfectly: "Reality, in the modern conception, appears as a tremendous hierarchical order of organized entities, leading, in a superposition of many levels, from physical and chemical to biological and sociological systems. Such hierarchical structure and combination into systems of ever higher order, *is characteristic of reality as a whole* and of fundamental importance especially in biology, psychology and sociology."

Thus, for example, in modern psychology, holarchy is the dominant *developmental* and *process* paradigm, cutting across the actual (and often quite different) content of the various schools. Every school of developmental psychology acknowledges some version of hierarchy, or a series of discrete (but continuous), irreversible stages of growth and unfolding. This includes the Freudians, the Jungians, the Piagetians, Lawrence Kohlberg, Carol Gilligan, and the cognitive behaviorists. Maslow, representing both humanistic and transpersonal psychology, put the "hierarchy of needs" at the center of his system—to mention only a few.

From Rupert Sheldrake and his "nested hierarchy of morphogenetic fields" to Sir Karl Popper's "hierarchy of emergent qualities" to Birch and Cobb's "ecological model of reality" based on "hierarchical value"; from Francisco Varela's groundbreaking work on autopoietic systems ("it seems to be a general reflection of the richness of natural systems to produce a hierarchy of levels") to the brain research of Roger Sperry and Sir John Eccles and Wilder Penfield ("a hierarchy of nonreducible emergents") to the social critical theory of Jürgen Habermas ("a hierarchy of communicative competence")—the Great Nest is back.

And the only reason *everybody* doesn't realize this is that it is hiding out under a variety of different names.

But no matter; realized or not, it is already well under way. And the truly wonderful thing about this homecoming is that modern theory can now reconnect with its rich roots in the perennial philosophy, reconnect with not only Plato and Aristotle and Plotinus and Maimonides and Spinoza and Hegel and Teresa in the West, but also with Shankara and Padmasambhava and Chih-i and Fa-tsang and Abinavagupta and Lady Tsogyal in the East—all made possible by the fact that many aspects of the perennial philosophy do indeed seem to be perennial—or essentially universal wherever they appear—thus cutting across times and cultures alike to point to the heart and soul and spirit of the family of humankind (indeed, all sentient beings as such).

There is, really, only one major thing left to be done, one fundamental item on the homecoming agenda. While it is true, as I said, that one of the unifying paradigms in modern thought, from physics to biology to psychology to sociology, is evolutionary holarchy (see, for example, Laszlo, Jantsch, Habermas, Lenski, Dennett), nonetheless most orthodox schools of inquiry admit the existence only of matter, body, and mind.[2] The higher dimensions of soul and spirit are not yet accorded quite the same status. We might say that the modern West has still only acknowledged three fifths of the Great Holarchy of Being. The agenda, very simply, is to reintroduce the other two fifths (soul and spirit).

Once we recognize and honor *all* the levels and dimensions of the Great Nest, we simultaneously acknowledge all the corresponding modes of knowing—not just the eye of flesh, which discloses the physical and sensory world, or just the eye of mind, which discloses the linguistic and symbolic world, but also the eye of contemplation, which discloses the soul and spirit. (We will return to this important topic in chapter 3.)

And so there is the agenda: Let us take the last step and reintroduce the eye of contemplation, which, as a sound and repeatable methodology, discloses soul and spirit. And that integral vision is, I submit, the final homecoming, the reweaving of our modern soul with the soul of humanity itself—the true meaning of multiculturalism—so that, standing on the shoulders of giants, we transcend but include, which always means honor, their ever-recurring presence. Uniting ancient wisdom with modern knowledge is thus the clarion call of the integral vision, a beacon in the postmodern wilderness.

> *An acknowledgment of the full spectrum of consciousness would alter the course of every one of the modern disciplines it touches—and that, of course, is an essential aspect of an integral approach.*
>
> *But indeed the first and most immediate impact would be on the field of psychology itself. I have explored this full-spectrum psychology in a number of books (including* The Spectrum of Consciousness, No Boundary, The Atman Project, Transformations of Consciousness, *and* A Brief History of Everything). *[See* Integral Psychology *for the most recent and most comprehensive treatment.]*
>
> *These books present a view of human development that attempts to incorporate the entire spectrum of consciousness, from instinct to ego to spirit, from prepersonal to personal to transpersonal, from subconscious to self-conscious to superconscious. If nothing animal, human, or divine is alien to me, then no state of consciousness can be dismissed from the generous embrace of a truly integral psychology. In the Preface to the new edition of* The Atman Project, *I try to suggest why such an integral and inclusive stance is so important.*

The Atman Project was, as far as we can tell, the first psychology that suggested a way of uniting East and West, conventional and contemplative, orthodox and mystical, into a single, coherent, and plausible frame-work. In so doing, it incorporated a good number of approaches, from Freud to Buddha, Gestalt to Shankara, Piaget to Yogachara, Kohlberg to Krishnamurti.

I began writing *The Atman Project* in 1976, along with its sister vol-ume, *Up from Eden*—one covering ontogeny, the other phylogeny. In the almost two decades since writing *Atman*, I have found its basic framework to be as sturdy and solid as ever, and thus I believe that its general tenets, with a little fine tuning here and there, will continue to be valid for a long and fruitful time.

A few critics complained that I had simply used various sources in a literary fashion, that my approach wasn't based on clinical or experi-mental evidence. But this is perhaps a bit disingenuous: the vast majority of theorists that I relied on were exactly those who had pioneered direct clinical and experimental evidence, from Jean Piaget's *méthode clinique* to Margaret Mahler's exhaustive videotaped observations to Lawrence Kohlberg's and Carol Gilligan's groundbreaking moral investigations—not to mention the vast phenomenological evidence presented by the contemplative traditions themselves. *The Atman Project* was directly based on the evidence of over sixty researchers from numerous ap-proaches, and hundreds of others in an informal way.

(We will return to, and carefully explore, this integral psychology in chapters 6, 9, 10, and 11.)

The Atman Project also ended my flirtation with Romanticism and its attempt to make regression into a source of salvation. I had in fact begun to write both *Atman* and *Eden* as a validation of the Romantic view: men and women start out in an unconscious union with the Di-vine—an unreflexive immersion in a type of heaven on earth, a paradisi-acal Eden, both ontogenetically and phylogenetically; then they break away from that union, through a process of alienation and dissociation (the isolated and divisive ego); then return to the Divine in a conscious and glorious union.

Human development thus proceeds, so to speak, from unconscious Heaven to conscious Hell to conscious Heaven. I started writing both books to validate that Romantic notion.

But the more I worked on those books, the more it became obvious that the Romantic view was hopelessly muddled. It combined one or two very important truths with some outrageous confusions, and the result was a theoretical nightmare. Untangling this mess was a constant preoccupation with me for several years—almost a decade, actually—

and marked one of the most turbulent theoretic times of my life. The reason that I have authored so many essays about fallacies—such as the pre/trans fallacy and the single boundary fallacy—is that the Romantics committed many of them, and I, being a good Romantic, had committed them royally; and thus understanding these fallacies from the inside, up close and very personal, I could write some very strong criticisms of them. You are never so vicious toward a theory as toward one that you yourself recently embraced.

But the crucial error of the Romantic view is fairly easy to understand. Take childhood, for example. The Romantic view, as we said, is that the infant starts out in a state of *unconscious Heaven*. That is, because the infant self isn't yet differentiated from the environment around it (or from the mother), the infant self is actually one with the dynamic Ground of Being—but in an unconscious (or "un-self-conscious") fashion. Thus, unconscious Heaven—blissful, wonderful, mystical, the paradisiacal state out of which it will soon fall, and to which it will always long to return.

And indeed, the Romantic view continues, sometime in the first few years of life, the self differentiates from the environment, the union with the dynamic Ground is lost, subject and object are separated, and the self moves from unconscious Heaven into conscious Hell—the world of egoic alienation, repression, terror, tragedy.

But, the happy account continues, the self can make a type of U-turn in development, sweep back to the prior infantile union state, reunite with the great Ground of Being, only now in a fully conscious and self-actualized way, and thus find conscious Heaven.

Hence, the overall Romantic view: one starts out in unconscious Heaven, an unconscious union with the Divine; one then *loses* this unconscious union, and thus plunges into conscious Hell; one can then regain the Divine union, but now in a higher and conscious fashion.

The only problem with that view is that the first step—the loss of the unconscious union with the Divine—is an absolute impossibility. All things are one with the Divine Ground—it is, after all, the Ground of all being! To lose oneness with that Ground is to cease to exist.

Follow it closely: there are only two general stances you can have in relation to the Divine Ground: since all things are one with Ground, you can either be aware of that oneness, or you can be unaware of that oneness. That is, you can be conscious or unconscious of your union with the Divine Ground: those are the only two choices you have.

And since the Romantic view is that you start out, as an infant, in an unconscious union with Ground, you *cannot then lose that union*! You have *already* lost consciousness of the union; you cannot then further lose the union itself or you would cease to be! So if you are unconscious of your union, it can't get any worse, ontologically speaking. That is already the pits of alienation. You are already living in Hell, as it were; you are already immersed in samsara, only you don't realize it—you haven't the awareness to recognize this burning fact. And so that is more the actual state of the infantile self: unconscious Hell. The infant self already suffers hunger, pain, rudimentary fear, and thirst—all the signs of samsara. But it registers them dimly.

What does start to happen, however, is that you begin to wake up to the alienated world in and around you. You go from unconscious Hell to *conscious* Hell, and being conscious of Hell, of samsara, of lacerating existence, is what makes growing up—and being an adult—such a nightmare of misery and alienation. The infant self is relatively peaceful, not because it is living in Heaven, but because it isn't aware enough to fully register the flames of Hell all around it. The infant is most definitely immersed in samsara, it just doesn't know it, it isn't aware enough to realize it, and enlightenment is certainly not a return to this infantile state! Or a "mature version" of this state! Neither the infant self nor my dog writhes in guilt and angst and agony, but enlightenment does not consist in recapturing dog-consciousness (or a "mature form" of dog-consciousness!).

As the infant self grows in awareness and consciousness, it slowly becomes aware of the intrinsic pain of existence, the torment inherent in samsara, the mechanism of madness coiled inherently in the manifest world: it begins to suffer. It is introduced to the first Noble Truth, a jolting initiation into the world of perception, whose sole mathematics is the torture-inducing fire of unquenched and unquenchable desire. This is not a desire-ridden world that was lacking in the infant's previous "wonderful" immersion state, but simply a world that dominated that state unconsciously, a world which the self now slowly, painfully, tragically becomes aware of.

And so, as the self grows in awareness, it moves from unconscious Hell to conscious Hell, and there it may spend its entire life, seeking above all else the numbing consolations that will blunt its raw and ragged feelings, blur its etchings of despair. Its life becomes a map of morphine, and folding itself into the anesthetic glow of all its compensations, it might even manage to convince itself, at least for an endearing blush of rose-tinted time, that the dualistic world is an altogether pretty thing.

But alternatively, the self might continue its growth and development into the genuinely spiritual domains: transcending the separate-self sense, it uncoils in the very Divine. The union with the Divine—a union or oneness that had been present but unconscious since the start—now flares forth in consciousness in a brilliant burst of illumination and a shock of the unspeakably ordinary: it realizes its Supreme Identity with Spirit itself, announced, perhaps, in nothing more than the cool breeze of a bright spring day, this outrageously obvious affair.

And thus the actual course of human ontogeny: from unconscious Hell to conscious Hell to conscious Heaven. *At no point does the self lose its union with the Ground*, or it would utterly cease to be! In other words, the Romantic agenda is right about the second and third steps (the conscious Hell and the conscious Heaven), but utterly confused about the infantile state itself, which is not unconscious Heaven but unconscious Hell.

Thus, the infantile state is not unconscious transpersonal, it is basically prepersonal. It is not transrational, it is prerational. It is not transverbal, it is preverbal. It is not transegoic, it is pre-egoic.[3] And the course of human development—*and evolution at large*—is from subconscious to self-conscious to superconscious; from prepersonal to personal to transpersonal; from under-mental to mental to over-mental; from pre-temporal to temporal to trans-temporal, by any other name: eternal.

The Romantics had simply confused pre with trans, and thus elevated the pre states to the glory of the trans (just as the reductionists would dismiss the trans states by claiming they were regression to pre states). These two confusions—the *elevationist* and the *reductionist*—are the two main forms of the pre/trans fallacy, which was first outlined and identified in the following pages. And the crucial point was that development is not regression in service of ego, but evolution in transcendence of ego.

And thus ended my Romantic fascination.

Now, there is indeed a *falling away* from Godhead, from Spirit, from the primordial Ground, and this is the truth the Romantics are trying to get at, before they slip into their pre/trans fallacies. This falling away is called *involution*, the movement whereby all things fall away from a consciousness of their union with the Divine, and thus imagine themselves to be separate and isolated monads, alienated and alienating. And once involution has occurred—and Spirit becomes unconsciously involved in the lower and lowest forms of its own manifestation—then *evolution* can occur: Spirit unfolds in a great *spectrum of consciousness*, from the Big Bang to matter to sensation to perception to impulse to image to symbol to concept to reason to psychic to subtle to causal occasions, on the way to its own shocking self-recognition, Spirit's own self-realization and self-resurrection. And in each of those stages—from matter to body to mind to soul to spirit—evolution becomes more and more conscious, more and more aware, more and more realized, more and more awake—with all the joys, and all the terrors, inherently involved in that dialectic of awakening.

At each stage of this process of Spirit's return to itself, we—you and I—nonetheless remember, perhaps vaguely, perhaps intensely, that we were once consciously one with the very Divine itself. It is there, this memory trace, in the back of our awareness, pulling and pushing us to realize, to awaken, to remember who and what we always already are.

In fact, all things, we might surmise, intuit to one degree or another that their very Ground is Spirit itself. All things are driven, urged, pushed, and pulled to manifest this realization. And yet, prior to that divine awakening, all things seek Spirit in a way that actually prevents the realization: or else we would be realized right now! We seek Spirit in ways that prevent it.

We seek for Spirit in the world of time; but Spirit is timeless, and cannot there be found. We seek for Spirit in the world of space; but Spirit is spaceless, and cannot there be found. We seek for Spirit in this or that object, shiny and alluring and full of fame or fortune; but Spirit is not an object, and it cannot be seen or grasped in the world of commodities and commotion.

In other words, we are seeking for Spirit in ways that prevent its realization, and force us to settle for substitute gratifications, which propel us through, and lock us into, the wretched world of time and terror, space and death, sin and separation, loneliness and consolation.

And that is the Atman project.

The Atman project: the attempt to find Spirit in ways that prevent it and force substitute gratifications. And, as you will see in the following pages, the entire structure of the manifest universe is driven by the Atman project, a project that continues until we—until you and I—awaken to the Spirit whose substitutes we seek in the world of space and time and grasping and despair. The nightmare of history is the nightmare of the Atman project, the fruitless search in time for that which is finally timeless, a search that inherently generates terror and torment, a self ravaged by repression, paralyzed by guilt, beset with the frost and fever of wretched alienation—a torture that is only undone in the radiant Heart when the great search itself uncoils, when the self-contraction relaxes its attempt to find God, real or substitute: the movement in time is undone by the great Unborn, the great Uncreate, the great Emptiness in the Heart of the Kosmos itself.

And so, as you read this book, try to remember: remember the great event when you breathed out and created this entire Kosmos; remember the great emptying when you threw yourself out as the entire World, just to see what would happen. Remember the forms and forces through which you have traveled thus far: from galaxies to planets, to verdant plants reaching upward for the sun, to animals stalking day and night, restless with their weary search; through primal men and women, yearning for the light, to the very person now holding this book: remember who and what you have been, what you have done, what you have seen, who you actually are in all those guises, the masks of the God and the Goddess, the masks of your own Original Face.

Let the great search wind down; let the self-contraction uncoil in the immediateness of present awareness; let the entire Kosmos rush into your being, since you are its very Ground; and then you will remember that the Atman project never occurred, and you have never moved, and it is all exactly as it should be, when the robin sings on a glorious morning, and raindrops beat on the temple roof.

2

In a Modern Light

INTEGRAL ANTHROPOLOGY AND
THE EVOLUTION OF CULTURES

An integral approach is committed to the full spectrum of consciousness as it manifests in all its extraordinary diversity. This allows an integral approach to recognize and honor the Great Holarchy of Being first elucidated by the perennial philosophy and the great wisdom traditions in general.

At the same time, Spirit moves on. Evolution continues to unfold, leaving nothing in the manifest world untouched. And the great traditions are just that—traditions—some of whose insights have stood the test of time, and some of which most definitely have not.

A truly integral approach must therefore fight on two fronts, as it were: against a modernity that is slow to recognize the full spectrum of consciousness, and against a traditionalism that refuses to recognize any substantial advances made by modernity itself.

In the previous chapter, we took the side of the great traditions against modernity, and argued for a recognition of the full spectrum of consciousness, the Great Holarchy of Being. In this chapter, we will take the side of modernity against traditionalism, and argue that, as evolution continues, new truths emerge, new insights spring forth, new realizations unfold, and therefore the great traditions are in desperate need of a modern touch as well.

The integral vision embodies an attempt to take the best of both worlds, ancient and modern. But that demands a critical stance willing to reject unflinchingly the worst of both as well.

THOUGHTFUL MEN AND WOMEN, throughout the ages, have always found the perennial philosophy a grounding and balancing influence, being, like Dr. Watson, that one constant in a changing world. It is especially appropriate, then, in these times of rapid transition and uncertain change, that we look to the ancient wisdom for some stability and guidance, since, at its core, it has always purported to represent timeless and eternal truths, beyond the ravages and turmoils of space and time. "I am come as Time, waster of peoples, ready for the hour that ripens to their ruin." And the perennial philosophy is come as antidote, balm for the wearied soul, ready for the hour that sounds its great salvation.

But, indeed, there has always been something of a problem in integrating "ancient" wisdom with "modern" times—even the terms "ancient" and "modern" sound mutually incompatible. What I therefore would like to review is exactly what we mean by the term "ancient" or "perennial," and how those "ancient" teachings can in fact be reconciled with "modern" or "progressive" society.

To begin with, when we speak of the "Ancient Wisdom" as the *philosophia perennis*, there can properly be only one correct meaning, namely, those truths—or rather, That Truth—which is radically *timeless* or *eternal*, one and whole, only and all. That Truth—using "Truth" in the broadest sense as the ultimately Real or Spirit itself—is the essence of the perennial philosophy. In other words, the perennial philosophy is not, at its core, a set of doctrines, beliefs, teachings, or ideas, for all of those are *of* the world of form, of space and time and ceaseless change, whereas very Truth is radically formless, spaceless, and timeless, encompassing all space and time but limited to none. That One—the radical Truth—is not *in* the world of space and time, except as *all* space and time, and thus it could never be enunciated in formal or doctrinal fashion. We cannot make a statement about the *whole* of Reality, because any conceivable statement is itself merely *part* of that Reality, and thus the perennial philosophy, as a direct insight-union with that Reality itself, could never be adequately captured in any set of doctrines or ideas, all of which are partial, finite, and limited. Radical Truth can be *shown* (in contemplative awareness) but never exhaustively *said* (in discursive language).

There is, in other words, an important distinction between Truth and *forms* of Truth. Radical Truth itself is formless, timeless, spaceless, changeless; its various forms, however, the various ideas, symbols, images, and thoughts we use to represent it, ceaselessly change and evolve. Radical Truth is timeless; its various forms exist in the world of time, and are subject to time's laws. Radical Truth is spaceless, whereas its various forms are space-bound, finite, and contingent. Radical Truth is not one condition among other conditions, but the very Condition of all conditions, the Nature of all natures, the suchness or thatness or isness of all phenomena and all forms, and is therefore not itself any particular phenomenon or form.

Now we can never know *all* the forms of Truth—psychological truth, sociological truth, economic truth, biological truth, and so on. These forms ceaselessly advance and evolve, alter and complexify. And although we can never know all these forms of Truth, we can know Truth itself, or the absolute reality of which all these forms are but partial and approximate reflections. In other words, although we can never know all the facts of existence, we can know the Fact of Existence which underlies and grounds all possible and relative facts, just as, once we know the ocean is wet, we know all waves are wet, even though we may never know each and every wave.

So that is one meaning of the words *ancient wisdom* or *perennial philosophy*—that absolute Truth which is timeless, formless, and spaceless, radically whole and complete, outside of which nothing exists—a Truth that can be known (via direct and formless intuition-identity), but which can never be adequately or fully captured in any form, doctrine, system, philosophy, proposition, thought or idea (all of which are merely partial, temporal, and finite reflections).

Now another meaning of the word *ancient* is "old," "archaic," "primitive." And, indeed, many individuals who speak glowingly of "ancient wisdom" mean "wisdom of past ages." And it is this "past wisdom" we are supposed to bring into the present culture as a source of meaning, stability, and salvation.

But already, you can see, there is a confusion of *past forms* of Truth with Truth itself. Once this confusion is made, then "timeless Truth" comes to mean "what the old folks said." There is a whole tendency to glorify yesterday; to see a greater "wisdom" available in the past than in the present; to eulogize ancient Egypt, China, India; to romanticize our ancestors and denigrate our contemporaries; and, on the whole, to see in the manifest realm not an *evolution* of increasing wisdom but a *devolution* of increasing ignorance. And all of this, I believe, is rather muddle-headed.

My point is that when we say "our present culture needs ancient wisdom," we must be very careful to specify exactly what we mean by "ancient wisdom." If by "ancient" we mean "timeless," then of course our culture is in desperate need of such wisdom (as have all cultures been in such need). But if by "ancient" we mean "past forms of Truth," then I believe nothing but a reactionary, antiprogressive, antiliberal, anti-evolutionary stance could ever result from such an importation.

Indeed, those who maintain that our present culture needs the "wisdom of past ages" can only mean one of two things: that the *past forms* of Truth were more adequate than the present forms; or that individuals in past ages intuited the Truth itself more clearly than we of today do or even can—and I believe both of those propositions are fundamentally incorrect.

The simplest examination of spiritual and cultural anthropology will, I believe, easily bear this out. If we believe even adequate forms of the "perennial" philosophy existed throughout all primal cultures, we are in for a rude surprise. There is, for example, precious little evidence that Paleolithic cultures had a sophisticated version of the perennial philosophy; even the central (and simplest) notion that there is one reality behind multiple phenomena was grasped, if at all, by a minuscule number of souls. And in any event, virtually all scholars agree that, as we move from Paleolithic and Mesolithic into Neolithic and Bronze Age periods, there is an unprecedented explosion of spiritual and cultural understanding, infinitely richer and more sophisticated than any of its predecessors. And then, starting around the sixth century BCE, we have the extraordinary emergence of the "axial sages"—Zoroaster, Gautama Buddha, Plato, Lao Tzu, Confucius, Moses, Socrates—whose insights clearly showed an even deeper realization of spiritual Truth and Reality.

There is a tendency among Romantics (lovers of "ancient wisdom" as "what the old folks said") to see spiritual development going straight downhill after the axial period, resulting eventually in our decadent-secular-scientific modern society. But again, I think this romantic fallacy comes precisely from confusing Truth with past forms of Truth, and that a clearer examination of the historical record shows, if anything, a continuing evolution and deepening of spiritual understanding, past the axial period and right up to (and including) modern times.

There is, first, the magnificent growth of Mahayana Buddhism in India, beginning around the second and third centuries CE; the extraordinary growth of Ch'an, T'ien T'ai, and Hua Yen Buddhism in China, especially beginning in the sixth, seventh, and eighth centuries; the exquisite Vajrayana in Tibet, which didn't even get started until the eighth century; Tantric Buddhism in India, which was developed between the eighth and eleventh centuries; and Zen in Japan, where the great Hakuin wasn't born until 1685! In Vedanta, Shankara doesn't arrive on the scene until 800 CE; Ramanuja until 1175; Ramakrishna until 1836; and the greatest of all Vedantic sages, Sri Ramana Maharshi, and the greatest of all Vedantic philosophers, Sri Aurobindo, both died only a few decades ago!

I could go on like this, building what I think is an absolutely airtight case: both the *quality* of humanity's spiritual understanding, and the *form* of its presentation, are deepening and becoming *more* adequate in modern times, not less.

There is one point in particular I would like to single out and stress, namely, the notion of evolution. It is common to assume that one of the doctrines of the perennial philosophy (i.e., one of the more common forms of radical Truth) is the idea of involution-evolution. That is, the manifest world was created as a "fall" or "breaking away" from the Absolute (involution), but that all things are now returning to the Absolute (via evolution). In fact, the doctrine of a progressive temporal return to Source (evolution) does not appear anywhere, according to such scholars as Joseph Campbell, until the axial period (i.e., a mere two thousand years ago). And even then, the idea was somewhat convoluted and backwards. The doctrine of the yugas, for example, sees the world proceeding through various stages of development, but the direction is *backward*: yesterday was the Golden Age, and time ever since has been a devolutionary slide downhill, resulting in the present-day Kali Yuga. Indeed, this notion of a *historical* fall from Eden was ubiquitous during the axial period; the idea that we are, at this moment, actually *evolving toward* Spirit was simply not conceived in any sort of influential fashion.

But sometime during the *modern* era—it's almost impossible to pinpoint exactly—the idea of history as devolution (or a fall from God) was slowly replaced by the idea of history as evolution (or a growth toward God). We see it explicitly in Schelling (1775–1854); Hegel (1770–1831) propounded the doctrine with a genius rarely equaled; Herbert Spencer (1820–1903) made evolution a universal law, and his friend Charles Darwin (1809–1882) applied it to biology. We next find it appearing in Aurobindo (1872–1950), who gave perhaps its most accurate and profound spiritual context, and Pierre Teilhard de Chardin (1881–1955), who made it famous in the West.

But here is my point: we might say that the idea of evolution as return-to-Spirit is part of the perennial philosophy, but the idea itself, in any adequate form, is no more than a few hundred years old. It might be "ancient" as timeless, but it is certainly not ancient as "old."

With this whole shift in the understanding of evolution, the form of the perennial philosophy took on an entirely new look: there is still That One, or the timeless and absolute Spirit of which the entire universe is but a manifestation, but that world of manifestation is not now devolving away from Spirit, it is evolving toward Spirit. God does not lie in our collective past, God lies in our collective future; the Garden of Eden is tomorrow, not yesterday; the Golden Age lies down the road, not up it.

This fundamental shift in the sense or form of the perennial philosophy—as represented in, say, Aurobindo, Hegel, Adi Da, Schelling, Teilhard de Chardin, Radhakrishnan, to name a few—I should like to call the "neoperennial philosophy." And it is the neoperennial philosophy—not "old wisdom"—that our present culture so desperately needs.

Thus, at the core of the neoperennial philosophy is the same Radical and Formless Truth glimpsed by the wisdom cultures of the past (and given such culture-specific and temporal names as Tao, Buddha Mind, Brahman, Goddess, Keter, etc.); but its outward *form*, its clothing cut in the relative and manifest world, has naturally changed and evolved to keep pace with the progressive evolution of the manifest world itself—and that includes, of course, the very idea of evolution. And whereas "ancient wisdom"—meaning in this case the outward doctrines, ideas, and symbols used in past ages to metaphorically represent inward and Radical Truth—is by and large outdated, outmoded, anachronistic, or simply wrong (even though they were, for their earlier time and place, perfectly phase-specific and culture-appropriate), the form of the neoperennial philosophy is much more finely tuned to present-day needs, ideas, and advances in science. There is a new koan for our age, and only the neoperennial philosophy can answer it: Does a computer have Buddha-nature?

Here is what we have: The "perennial" or "primordial" or "ancient" wisdom can have two different meanings. One, it can mean radically timeless, spaceless, formless Truth, the Ground of all Being, primordial Emptiness, pure unmanifest Spirit, the Condition of all conditions, the State of all states, the Nature of all natures, the noumenon transcendent to, but immanent in and as, all phenomena, known or realized in a timeless state of contemplative unity or identity with all manifestation. When we descend from this plane of formless, imageless, timeless union-samadhi, we naturally clothe that Realization of formless Truth in the various forms and truth-symbols available to our particular sociocultural milieu. The particular outward forms and symbols used by past wisdom cultures has led to the second widespread meaning of "ancient wisdom"—namely, the actual doctrines, words, theories, metaphors, symbols, and models used by ancient or past cultures to express and embody their own realization of that Radical Truth. And whereas radical and formless Truth, to the extent it is clearly recognized, is necessarily one and identical in all times and places, nonetheless the forms of its expression are and can only be judged according to their appropriateness for the particular sociocultural context in which they live, and from which their very metaphors and models are drawn.

Now if we use "Ancient" (with a capital A) to represent radical, timeless, and formless Truth, and if we use "ancient" (small a) for the particular past forms and expressions of radical Truth—then we can summarize our major point thus: modern culture needs Ancient truth, not ancient truth. And our corollary point: the best and most appropriate form of Ancient Truth is now the neoperennial philosophy, and not a blind allegiance to "what the old folks said." Modern culture is by and large incompatible with ancient culture, and their forced fit could never benefit more than a small percentage of the nostalgically oriented. Formless or Ancient Truth, we would all agree, is a perfect union-identity with the entire manifest world; but our *present*-day manifest world includes computers, global politics, the idea of evolution, molecular engineering, human-machine interfacing, radical medical advances, and so on. In short, the *form* of Ancient Wisdom can no longer be ancient. The neoperennial philosophy, with its adaptability to modern needs and desires, is and must now be God's witness to the new and rising wisdom culture.

We said that past forms of Truth arose in response to the needs and desires of past cultures, and that they were, for the most part, perfectly adequate during those times. Of course, some of those past forms might still find a partial and limited use in our present society (just as we still use the wheel)—but, by definition, they then become merely part of our *present* forms of Truth, adapted and fitted into a more comprehensive structure (as, for instance, Aurobindo fitted spirituality and evolution, and Vivekananda initiated the dialogue between physics and spirituality). The point is that the evolution of the *forms* of Truth clearly show a succession of *increasingly adequate* and *more comprehensive* structures for truth's expression and representation. (The notion of each developmental stage being adequate, but each successor being *more adequate*, was first elucidated by Hegel, one of the first great neoperennial philosophers.) The past had the Great Religions. The future will have the Greater Religions.

I realize that tends to yank our vision in a direction opposite to what we usually think; but what if I had made that statement in, say, 500,000 BCE? It would obviously be true. Has evolution stopped with us, giving us and not our descendants privileged status? Fact is, our so-called Great Religions will be reduced, by future spiritual evolution, to footnotes on the developmental history of Spirit, of the same status we now accord to, say, voodoo and sympathetic magic. The greater and more adequate forms of the Ancient Wisdom will appear *tomorrow*, and tomorrow and tomorrow and tomorrow again, just as they always have in the past.

Now the foregoing does not mean that any particular individuals have to wait for future evolution in order to find transcendence. Any individual, now as in the past, is perfectly free, via contemplative-meditative practices, to pursue transcendence in his or her own case. Radical Truth, being formless, does not have to await the arrival of future forms nor lament the loss of past forms. Our exclusive reliance on the future or the past simply perpetuates the confusion of Truth with its temporal forms. Radical Truth, as always, is completely and entirely available only in the timeless present. It is simply that, as consciousness on the whole continues to evolve and develop, in a now planetary fashion, then global awareness (which is a transcendence of any narrow parochialism) becomes increasingly easier, more obvious, more appealing—and therefore, I believe, more likely. We might speculate, with Sheldrake, that this is the effect of a morphic field; in any event, the evolutionary accumulation seems undeniable.

Thus, the idea that present-day rational-secular society is somehow antispiritual comes, I believe, largely from a misunderstanding of the actual nature of evolution, which, according to the neoperennial philosophers, is nothing but Spirit-in-action, or the stages of Spirit's return to Spirit as Spirit. One of those stages—according to neoperennial philosophers from Aurobindo to Hegel to Adi Da—is exactly a humanistic-scientific-rational stage, which, far from being antispiritual, is actually a necessary and intermediate form of Spirit-in-action. It is only when, failing that understanding, we make the nostalgic comparison of the present form of Spirit-in-action with its old and past forms, that we arrive at the romantically dismal conclusion that the modern era is a sorry spiritual production compared with, say, Mesopotamia (most of whose religious practices were, in fact, of the most barbaric variety imaginable).

It is time, then, to have done with our sickly yearning for yesteryear, our morbid fixation to Mother Past, our preposterous groveling at any doctrine whose only authority comes from the fact that it was uttered by a really really ancient sage, centuries or preferably millennia ago. For, ironically enough, our fixation to the past comes only from our fear of death in the present: unable to die to our egos, we latch onto the permanence and fixity of the past as a substitute immortality project. The corpse of yesteryear becomes our morbid refuge, our rancid immortality.

Let us instead appreciate the past, honor it, be thankful for its successes, upon whose base our present consciousness rests—but let us release its hold on us. When we look at the past sages, and marvel at their insight, and fall in love with some one or the other of them, what is it we really see and feel? What can it be but our own highest Self or Spirit, since Spirit is one and timeless? Our loyalty to the past is just this misplaced intuition of absolute Spirit, diverted from a present Realization onto a past idolization by the inability to fall now into timeless transcendence. So let us relax our death-grip on ancient wisdom so that Ancient Wisdom may dawn, ever new and ever renewing, pointing home ahead.

Spiritual evolution, cultural evolution, evolution itself: the past wisdom traditions rarely acknowledge any aspect of this liberal and progressive and evolutionary view. And yet, who can really blame them? How can any of us possibly subscribe to such notions as spiritual evolution when faced with the searing signs of Auschwitz, Hiroshima, Wounded Knee, Gulag, Chernobyl; where the names of Hitler, Mussolini, Stalin, Pol Pot, Amin are burned into the flesh of modernity, their scars still there for all to see?

In a book called Up from Eden: A Transpersonal View of Human Evolution, *I attempted to come to terms with these most difficult of issues. Although* Up from Eden *has increasingly gained a general acknowledgment, it originally generated an enormous controversy, for reasons I address in the Preface to the new edition, where I focus on one of the foremost problems (and central nightmares) of modern sociology and anthropology: How can we speak of cultural evolution with Auschwitz on the horizon?*

This question is crucial, because unless we can plausibly answer it, there is absolutely no way whatsoever that we can reconcile ancient and modern worldviews (since the former deny evolution while the latter embrace it). What is required, then, is a way to see evolution in a radically new light, where both the ups and downs of Spirit's journey in time can be fully honored and acknowledged.

But in order to see evolution as Spirit-in-action, certain stern objections must be answered, because, in my opinion, neither the traditionalists nor the liberal modernists have fully come to terms with the profound meaning of evolution itself. If evolution is operating throughout the universe, then it must be operating in humans as well, which means human cultures must also evolve, which means progressively advanced forms of interaction must be emerging . . . which runs smack into the contradiction known as Auschwitz.

The future of an integral vision, in other words, hinges fatefully on the precise stance we take toward evolution itself: in what domains does evolution operate, and what does it actually mean? And if we are to see evolution as Spirit-in-action, then how can we answer the Gulag?

I began work on *Up from Eden* in 1977, when it was very fashionable to believe that evolution touched all domains of the universe *except the human*. That is, the Kosmos labored mightily some twelve billion years, with every aspect of it operating under evolutionary principles, an extraordinary and all-encompassing developmental process that eventually brought forth the first human cultural productions, whereupon it promptly ceased operating.

Evolution was felt to be working in the rest of the universe, but not in humans! This rather extraordinary opinion was held by traditional religious thinkers, by retro-Romantics, and by liberal social theorists: virtually the entire pantheon of influential writers and theorists from across the spectrum of social studies.

Most religious traditionalists allowed that individual humans show development, but not a collective and cultural humanity. Traditionalists displayed this intense antipathy to cultural evolution mostly because modern history had rather thoroughly rejected traditional mythic religion, and thus if history were really being driven by evolution, then evolution had rudely passed right over them and their beliefs.

No doubt about it, modernity by and large has thoroughly rejected religion: liberal modernity does not accept traditional mythic religion in its governing and political bodies, does not accept mythic-religious explanations for scientific facts and truths, and does not accept specific mythic-religious tenets in public discourse and public morality. And thus, as well they might, traditionalists look at modernity as a largely antispiritual movement, the horrible movement of secularization and rationalization: modernity is the great Satan. And if evolution produced *this*, then please, give us less of it. More strongly: evolution is not operating in the human domain!

The retro-Romantics and neopagans fully agreed that evolution operated in the rest of the universe but not in humans; in fact, the Romantics added, in the case of humans, evolution started *running backwards*! In the general Romantic view, humans, both phylogenetically and ontogenetically, started out in a type of primal Eden, a great paradise, an original Heaven on earth, and then things promptly started going downhill from there. The massive forces operating in the Kosmos for billions and billions of years—forces that produced ants from atoms and apes from amoebas, colossal forces that propelled galaxies and quasars into planetary configurations, and from there into cells with sensations, and organisms with perceptions, and animals that could see and feel and even think—all of those forces, once humans were produced, simply came to an abrupt and crashing halt—they simply stopped working!—and for no other apparent reason than that they didn't fit with the retro-Romantics' ideas of the way the world should run. Evolution for the rest of the Kosmos; downhill for humans. What an extraordinary and vicious dualism!

This hostility to cultural evolution was also shared by liberal social theorists, and for some very understandable and even noble reasons. Social Darwinism in its most common forms was so crude and so cruel—not to mention based on the most dubious aspects of Darwinian theory—that it came to mean not much more than a colossal lack of compassion for one's fellow men and women. And thus liberal social theorists, of virtually every variety, collectively decided that instead of trying to tease apart the valid from the grotesque aspects of cultural evolution, it was better to avoid and even deny the topic altogether.

The thesis of *Eden* was thus, at the time, rather daring, certainly controversial. Various grand theorists from Teilhard de Chardin to Aurobindo and Hegel had already advanced the idea that evolution itself was actually a *spiritual unfolding*, with each stage transcending but including its predecessor. But none of them had combined that philosophical notion with an actual hard look at anthropological data, and none of them had advanced any of the specific stages of this evolution based on any sort of extensive empirical and anthropological evidence. In this regard, *Eden* was, I believe, a major advance.

At the time I was writing *Eden*, the researches of two other theorists, working in the same general area, were just becoming available to the English-speaking world: Jean Gebser and Jürgen Habermas. What I knew of Gebser was obtained from one long article published in *Main Currents* (which was then the only such article available in English), but it was enough to show me unmistakably that Gebser and I had hit upon essentially identical stages in the broad evolution of human consciousness. Out of respect and deference to the pioneering work of Gebser (he had been working on this for decades before I was even born), I immediately annexed his terminology to mine, so that the various cultural stages had names like magical-typhonic and mental-egoic.

In other words, these were *the stages of the evolution of cultural worldviews* (the stages of the evolution of the Lower-Left quadrant), stages which Gebser's pioneering studies had already identified as archaic, magic, mythic, mental, and integral-aperspectival. My research had led me to similar, almost identical, stages, which I termed uroboric, typhonic, membership, egoic, and existential. (And thus, when I annexed Gebser's terms, I would often refer to magical-typhonic, mythic-membership, and so on.)

But in my approach, beyond the integral-existential stage—Gebser's highest—there are then the further or deeper stages of spiritual and transpersonal development itself, moving from psychic to subtle to causal to nondual, stages that Gebser does not clearly recognize. But up to that point, Gebser is the unsurpassed master and one of the primary innovators in the understanding of the evolution of cultural worldviews.

(Integral studies as a discipline includes a careful investigation of the entire spectrum of cultural worldviews as they develop and evolve, because what appears in individuals as a spectrum of consciousness [the Upper Left] appears in cultures as a spectrum of worldviews [the Lower Left]. Tracing the correlations between the ontogenetic and phylogenetic formation of the human species is thus a central task of integral anthropology.)

This ties in directly with the work of Jürgen Habermas and his associates. Habermas exploded on the scene with *Knowledge and Human Interests*, a devastating attack on mere positivism and empiricism; and, by

1976, he had released *Communication and the Evolution of Society*, a succinct but altogether brilliant outline of what he saw as the universal stages of consciousness development. I came upon Habermas's work just as I was finishing *Eden*, and could only acknowledge him briefly, but it was quite obvious that Habermas, coming from a very different starting point, had also hit upon the same general stages as Gebser and myself. Habermas went on to become what many people, myself included, consider the world's greatest living philosopher, and in subsequent books I would draw heavily, and gratefully, on Habermas's unending genius.

But what Gebser and Habermas both lacked was a genuinely spiritual dimension. Gebser vigorously attempted to include the spiritual domain in his work, but it soon became obvious that he simply was not aware of—or did not deeply understand—the contemplative traditions that more readily penetrate to the core of the Divine. As I said, beyond the integral-aperspectival, which is Gebser's highest stage, there are actually several stages of transpersonal or spiritual development, which Gebser clumsily collapses into his integral stage. And Habermas, being essentially a German rationalist, did not (and still does not) understand any God higher than Reason.

What was needed, then, was something of a cross between Aurobindo, Teilhard de Chardin, Gebser, and Habermas—in other words, some sort of framework that could actually accommodate the strengths of each of their approaches. And looking back on it, I believe that is what *Up from Eden* managed to do. I have since refined the categories given in *Eden*, and I have expanded the quadrants of analysis (interested readers might consult *Sex, Ecology, Spirituality* and *A Brief History of Everything*). But the essential framework is given here, and is still as valid as ever, I believe. In fact, recent research, evidence, and theory have, if anything, substantially increased the validity of *Eden* and its central conclusions.

The crucial issue was this: In order for cultural evolution to be embraced as an explanatory principle in human history, it faces exactly those profound objections that led traditionalists, Romantics, and liberal social theorists aggressively and thoroughly to reject it. In other words, if evolution is operating in the human domain, how can we account for Auschwitz? And how dare we make judgments about some cultural productions being more evolved than others? How dare we make such value rankings? What kind of arrogance is that?

Thus, even though I started this preface by chiding the anti-evolutionary theorists, they do in fact raise several profound and significant objections, and these objections need to be taken most seriously and addressed as fairly as possible.

The traditionalists, for example, cannot believe in cultural evolution because of such modern horrors as Auschwitz, Hiroshima, Chernobyl. How can we say evolution is at work in humans when it produces such monsters? Better to deny evolution altogether than to get caught up in having to explain those obscenities.

And the Romantics are responding to what seems to be a universal human sympathy for a time prior to today's turmoils. Primal men and women, on the whole, did not suffer the disasters of modernity—no industrial pollution, little slavery, few property disputes, and so on. By any scale of quality, haven't we in fact gone downhill? Isn't it time to get back to nature, back to the noble savage, and thus find a truer self, a fairer community, a richer life?

The liberal social theorists likewise have every reason to recoil in horror from the notion of cultural evolution. Its unbelievably crude forms, such as Social Darwinism, are not just lacking in compassion; much more sinister, this type of crass "evolutionism," pressed into the hands of moral cretins, would produce exactly the type of ruinous and barbaric notions of the superman, the master race, the coming human demigods, who would chillingly goose-step their way into history, who would in fact inscribe their beliefs on the tortured flesh of millions, would press their ideology into the gas chambers and let it all be settled there. Liberal social theorists, reacting to such horrors, naturally tend to look upon any sort of "social hierarchy" as a prelude to Auschwitz.

Obviously, if consciousness evolution is to be used as any sort of explanatory principle, it faces several stern difficulties. What is therefore required is a set of tenets that can explain *both* advance and regression, good news and bad news, the ups and downs of an evolutionary thrust that is nonetheless as active in humans as it is in the rest of the Kosmos. Otherwise, we face the extremely bizarre situation of driving a virulent wedge right through the middle of the Kosmos: everything nonhuman operates by evolution; everything human does not.

What are the principles that can rehabilitate cultural evolution in a sophisticated form, and thus reunite humanity with the rest of the Kosmos, and yet also account for the ups and downs of consciousness unfolding? Here are some of the central explanatory principles that I believe we need:

1. *The dialectic of progress.* As consciousness evolves and unfolds, each stage solves or defuses certain problems of the previous stage, but then adds new and recalcitrant—and sometimes more complex and more difficult—problems of its own. Precisely because evolution in all domains (human and otherwise) operates by a process of differentiation and integration, then each new and more complex level necessarily faces problems not present in its predecessors. Dogs get cancer; atoms don't. But this doesn't damn evolution altogether! It means evolution is good news, bad news, this dialectic of progress. And the more stages of evolution there are—the greater the depth of the Kosmos—the more things that *can* go wrong!

So evolution inherently means that new potentials and new wonders and new glories are introduced with each new stage, but they are invariably accompanied by new horrors, new fears, new problems, new disasters. And *Up from Eden* is a chronicle of the new wonders and the new diseases that unfolded in the unrelenting winds of the evolution of consciousness.

2. *The distinction between differentiation and dissociation.* Precisely because evolution proceeds by differentiation and integration, something can go wrong at each and every stage—as I said, the greater the depth of the Kosmos, the more diseases there can be. And one of the most prevalent forms of evolutionary pathology occurs when *differentiation* goes too far into *dissociation*. In human evolution, for example, it is one thing to differentiate the mind and body, quite another to dissociate them. It is one thing to differentiate culture and nature, quite another to dissociate them. Differentiation is the prelude to integration; dissociation is the prelude to disaster.

As we will see in the following pages, human evolution (like evolution everywhere else) is marked by a series of important differentiations, which are absolutely normal and altogether crucial for the evolution and integration of consciousness. But at each stage, these differentiations can go too far into dissociation, which converts depth into disease, growth into cancer, culture into nightmare, consciousness into agony. And *Eden* is a chronicle not only of the necessary differentiations of consciousness evolution, but also of the pathological dissociations and distortions that all too often followed in their wake.

3. *The difference between transcendence and repression.* To say that evolution proceeds by differentiation and integration is to say that it proceeds by transcendence and inclusion. That is, each stage of evolu-

tion (human and otherwise) *transcends and includes* its predecessors. Atoms are parts of molecules, which are parts of cells, which are parts of complex organisms, and so on. Each stage thus includes its predecessor(s), and then adds its own defining and emergent qualities: it transcends and includes.

But for just that reason, with *pathology*, the senior dimension doesn't transcend and include, it transcends and represses, denies, distorts, disrupts. Each new and higher stage has exactly this choice: transcend and include, befriend, integrate, honor; or transcend and repress, deny, alienate, oppress. And *Eden* is a chronicle of the great transcendent occasions of human evolution, as well as of the grotesque repressions, oppressions, brutalities. The brighter the light, the darker the shadow, and *Eden* stares into the eyes of each.

4. *The difference between natural hierarchy and pathological hierarchy.* During the evolutionary process, that which is whole at one stage becomes a part of the whole of the next. Each and every thing in the Kosmos is thus what Arthur Koestler called a "holon," a whole that is simultaneously a part of some other whole, indefinitely. Whole atoms are parts of molecules, whole molecules are parts of cells, and so on. Each is a whole/part, a holon, existing in a *natural hierarchy*, or an order of increasing wholeness and holism.

For this reason, Koestler pointed out that normal hierarchy ought really to be called *holarchy*, and he's quite right. All processes of evolution (human and otherwise) proceed in part by hierarchization (holarchization)—each senior dimension transcends and includes its juniors: each level is a whole that is part of another whole, indefinitely, which is exactly why each unfolding stage transcends and includes its predecessor(s), and thus the Kosmos unfolds in embrace after embrace after never-ending embrace.

But that which transcends can repress. And thus normal and natural hierarchies can degenerate into pathological hierarchies, into dominator hierarchies. In these cases, an arrogant holon doesn't want to be both a whole and a part; it wants to be a whole, period. It does not want to be a mutual part of something larger than itself; it does not want to share in the communions of its fellow holons; it wants to dominate them with its own agency. Power replaces communion; domination replaces communication; oppression replaces reciprocity. And *Eden* is a chronicle of the extraordinary growth and evolution of normal hierarchies, a growth that ironically allowed a degeneration into pathological hierarchies, which left their marks burned into the tortured flesh of untold millions, a trail of terror that accompanied the animal who can not only transcend but repress.

5. *Higher structures can be hijacked by lower impulses.* Tribalism, when left to its own devices, is relatively benign, simply because its means and its technologies are relatively harmless. You can only inflict so much damage on the biosphere, and on other humans, with a bow and arrow (and this lack of means does not necessarily mean presence of wisdom). The problem is that the advanced technologies of rationalization, when hijacked by tribalism and its ethnocentric drives, can be devastating.

Auschwitz is not the result of rationality. Auschwitz is the result of the many products of rationality being used in irrational ways. Auschwitz is rationality hijacked by tribalism, by an ethnocentric mythology of blood and soil and race, rooted in the land, romantic in its dispositions, barbaric in its ethnic cleansing. You cannot seriously attempt genocide with a bow and arrow; but you can attempt it with steel and coal, combustion engines and gas chambers, machine guns and atomic bombs. These are not rational desires by any definition of rational; these are ethnocentric tribalisms commandeering the tools of an advanced consciousness and using them precisely for the lowest of the lowest motives. Auschwitz is the endgame, not of reason, but of tribalism.

Those are a handful of the distinctions that, I believe, are necessary to reconstruct the evolution of human consciousness in a much more satisfactory and compelling fashion, a fashion that can clearly account for the undeniable advances as well as the undeniable disasters of human history. And finally, this gives us a way to approach the objections of the anti-evolutionary theorists, who in many ways still dominate the theoretical discourse in this area.

To the traditionalists, we can say: You have not understood the dialectic of progress. You have included all the bad news of modernity, but you carefully leave out the good news, and so you damn the rise of modernity and its rational-secularization, failing to see that modernity is actually the form of Spirit's unfolding as the Presence of today's world. And so you worship the previous mythic-agrarian age, when the whole world bowed to the mythic God or Goddess, and religion everywhere smiled on this fair earth, and every man and woman devoutly embraced your beloved God, and all was wonderfully enchanted and alive with spiritual portent.

And let us conveniently ignore the fact that, as recent evidence has made abundantly clear, 10 percent of foraging and 54 percent of agrarian societies had slavery; 37 percent of foraging and 64 percent of agrarian societies had bride price; 58 percent of foraging and an astonishing 99 percent of horticultural societies engaged in frequent or intermittent warfare. The temples to this beloved God and Goddess were built upon the broken backs of millions of enslaved and tortured humans, who were not accorded even the simplest of human dignities, and who left their trail of blood and tears as the altar to that beloved God.

The traditionalists have reminded us of the nightmares of modernity; let them not so easily forget the nightmares of yesteryear. And as for the good news of modernity, about which the traditionalists are strangely silent, let us remind them: the great liberation movements—the freeing of slaves, of women, of the untouchables—these great emancipation movements were brought into the modern world precisely by rationality, which was—make no mistake!—the form of Spirit's unfolding in the modern world. The positive aspects of modernity—including medical advances that have single-handedly relieved more pain and suffering than any other advance in history—are exactly the Eros and the Agape of Spirit's present unfolding: the liberal democracies are Spirit's compassion manifested, not in some cruelly promised mythic heaven but right here and now on earth, in the actual lives of a vast humanity that heretofore had lived on this dear earth as slaves, as the property of another, and almost always the property of another who devoutly believed in the glories of the great and wondrous God.

And so we say to the traditionalists: You have not seen the dialectic of progress, you have not seen that the higher can be hijacked by the lower, you have not seen that the form of Spirit in the present world is precisely the good news of modernity—in these ways and more, you have lost touch with the pulse of Spirit's ongoing evolution and unfolding, the miracle of evolution as self-realization through self-transcendence.

To the retro-Romantics, we say: You have confused differentiation and dissociation, you have confused transcendence and repression. And thus, every time evolution introduces a new and necessary differentiation, you scream downfall! nightmare! horror upon horrors! devolution! the loss of Eden, the alienation of humankind, the trail of misery written on the winds of history.

The acorn has to differentiate in order to grow into an oak. But if you see every differentiation as a dissociation—if you thoroughly confuse the two—then you are forced to see the oak as a terrible violation of the acorn. And thus your solution to any problem faced by the oak is: we must get back to our wonderful acornness.

The solution, of course, is just the opposite: find those factors that prevent acorns from self-actualizing as oaks, and remove those obstacles, so that differentiation and integration can occur naturally instead of drifting into dissociation and fragmentation. We can agree with the Romantics that horrible pathologies have often crept into the ongoing march of development and evolution—there is no argument there!— but the solution is not an idealization of acornness, but a removal of the obstacles that prevent the acorn's growth to its own self-actualized oakness.

To the liberal social theorists, we say: You have not understood the difference between natural hierarchy and pathological hierarchy, and thus in your understandable zeal to erase the latter, you have destroyed the former: you have tossed the baby with the bathwater.

Value ranking—hierarchy in the broadest sense—is inescapable in human endeavors, simply because we are all holons: contexts within contexts forever, and each broader context pronounces judgment on its less encompassing contexts. And thus, even when the egalitarian social theorists assert their rejection of hierarchy, they do so using hierarchical judgments: they assert that nonranking is *better* than ranking. Well, that's a hierarchical judgment, which puts them in the embarrassing position of contradicting themselves, of secretly embracing that which they vocally condemn. They have a hierarchy that denies hierarchy, a ranking that hates ranking.

What they are trying to do, of course, is get rid of pathological hierarchies, and in this endeavor I believe we can all follow them. But the only way to get rid of pathological hierarchy is by embracing normal and natural hierarchy—that is, embracing normal holarchy, which integrates the arrogant holon back into its rightful place in a mutual reciprocity of care and communion and compassion. But without holarchy you have heaps, not wholes, and no integration is possible at all.

And thus, with this approach, and with these five or so distinctions, we can reunite humanity with the rest of the Kosmos, and not be saddled with a truly bizarre and rigid dualism: humanity over here, everything else over there.

No, we are part and parcel of a single and all-encompassing evolutionary current that is itself Spirit-in-action, the mode and manner of Spirit's creation, and thus is always going beyond what went before—

that leaps, not crawls, to new plateaus of truth, only to leap again, dying and being reborn with each new quantum lurch, often stumbling and bruising its metaphysical knees, yet always getting right back up and jumping yet again.

And do you remember the Author of this Play? As you look deeply into your own awareness, and relax the self-contraction, and dissolve into the empty ground of your own primordial experience, the simple feeling of Being—right now, right here—is it not obvious all at once? Were you not present from the start? Did you not have a hand to play in all that was to follow? Did not the dream itself begin when you got bored with being God? Was it not fun to get lost in the productions of your own wondrous imagination, and pretend it all was other? Did you not write this book, and countless others like it, simply to remind you who you are?

And so, looking back on it, *Eden* was one of the first sustained attempts, based on actual anthropological evidence, to reunite humanity with the rest of the Kosmos, to see the same currents running through our human blood that run through swirling galaxies and colossal solar systems, that crash through the great oceans and course through our own veins, that move the mightiest of mountains as well as our own glorious moral aspirations—one and the same current moves throughout the All, and drives the entire Kosmos in its every lasting gesture, and refuses to surrender until you remember who and what you are, and that you were carried to this realization by that single current of an all-pervading Love, and here "there came fulfillment in a flash of light, and vigor failed the lofty fantasy, but now my will and my desires were moved like a wheel revolving evenly, by the Love that moves the sun and other stars."

3

Eye to Eye

INTEGRAL PHILOSOPHY AND
THE QUEST FOR THE REAL

*An acknowledgment of the full spectrum of consciousness
would profoundly alter the course of every one of the modern
disciplines it touches—and that, of course, is an essential aspect
of integral studies.*

*We have seen this full-spectrum approach applied to psychol-
ogy, anthropology, and sociology. We will soon see it applied to
art and literature, feminist theory, cultural studies, and spirituality. But now we look briefly to philosophy, which traditionally
has been the queen of the mental sciences, simply because its
defining heart is the love of wisdom, in all its wondrous forms.*

*A full-spectrum approach to human consciousness and be-
havior means that men and women have available to them a
spectrum of knowing—a spectrum that includes, at the very
least, the eye of flesh, the eye of mind, and the eye of spirit.
What would happen if we took this integral vision and applied
it to philosophy?* Eye to Eye *took exactly that approach, and in
the Preface to its new edition, I outline the reasons why I believe
this integral approach is so profoundly important.*

THE VAST MAJORITY OF THE great philosophers of the West have
maintained that there does indeed exist some sort of Absolute, from

the Good to God to Geist. That has never seriously been doubted by the vast majority. The burning question, rather, has always been this: What is the relation of the absolute One to the world of the relative Many?

This crucial question has, like many of the most profound questions in Western philosophy, generated a series of utterly intractable difficulties, paradoxes, absurdities. Like the mind/body problem and the question of free will versus determinism, the absolute/relative issue has been a bloody thorn in the side of the Western tradition, a thorn that has refused to either go away or have the good sense to be solved.

And, more intriguingly, all of these central issues—mind/body, mind/brain, free will/fate, absolute/relative, noumenon/phenomena—are, we will see, precisely the same problem.

And they all have precisely the same answer.

BUT WHERE IS GOD?

Aristotle gave the classic statement of a God that has nothing substantial to do with the relative world. Aristotle's God is a God of pure Perfection, and for such a God to dirty its hands with the relative world—to be involved with relative and finite creatures—would surely indicate a lack of fullness, a lack of completeness, and thus a lack of self-contained perfection. Since God requires nothing, there is certainly no reason for God to produce or create a relative world. In fact, if God actually created the relative world, that would indicate that God lacked something in its own being, which obviously is not possible (you don't get to be God by lacking something!). Thus, God is "in" the relative world only as final cause: the Good toward which all relative creatures strive but never, never reach.

Aspects of Plato's writing could certainly be interpreted to support Aristotle's notion of an untouchable, uninvolved, totally self-contained God. This world, after all, could be seen as nothing but the fleeting and shadowy reflection of the real world, a world utterly transcendent to the relative world of sense and confused opinion.

But that is only half of Plato, so to speak. The other (and less noted) half confirms in the strongest way that the entire relative world is a production, an emanation, a mark of the Plenitude of the Good. Thus, in the *Timaeus*—arguably the most influential book of Western cosmology—an Absolute that cannot create a world is described as decidedly inferior to an Absolute that can. Contrary to Aristotle's conclusion—

that God must be totally self-contained to be perfect—the conclusion of the *Timaeus* is that a God that cannot create is no God at all. (It is even implied that a God who cannot create is envious of a God who can!) Thus, through the Absolute's *creative outflowing*, the entire manifest realm issues forth, so that all things are essentially the Plenitude of the Good. Therefore this very earth Plato describes as a "visible, sensible God."

Thus would begin this version of the West's most intractable dualism: the Absolute versus the relative, and what exactly is their relation?

The great difficulty with Aristotle's position is that it simply leaves the dualism as it finds it. Aristotle's God creates nothing; all things are driven by their desire to reach up to that God, but none of them make it. And however "clean" this might be logically, it leaves the Kosmos with a divisive wedge driven violently into its heart. God over there, us over here, and the two meet only in perpetually unrequited love.

And yet the other side of the attempted solution—God is present in the world as Plenitude—also had its own grave difficulties, at least as it was usually presented. Namely, if we intellectually picture the Absolute as substantially creating the relative world, then how do we account for the existence of evil? If God has His, Her, or Its hand in this world, then doesn't God get blamed for Auschwitz? If so, what kind of grotesque monster is that God?

This dualism between the Absolute and the relative—and their relation, if any—would split the entire tradition of Western philosophy and theology into two warring and largely irreconcilable camps: those who saw God strongly (or even totally) in this world versus those who saw God strongly (or even totally) out of this world: this-worldly versus other-worldly, the Descenders versus the Ascenders, the immanentists versus the transcendentalists, empiricists versus rationalists, one flavor or another.

The Aristotelian tradition simply stood back from the commotion of the relative world, and refused to have its God dirty its fingers. God is a self-contained and unitary perfection, and thus that God has no need to create the world or anything else. How could anything so utterly Perfect do anything further without falling away from Perfection? To create implies that something is lacking, and God lacks nothing; hence God does not create. Where the world came from, and why, is thus left literally hanging, though buried deep in the relative world's heart is the burning desire to reach the state of God-perfection, which would actually mean, for this autistic God, to simply be done with all its neighbors and disappear into its own self-contained absoluteness, basking in the wonders of its unending specialness.

But the alternative intellectual position—that the Perfect One nonetheless got itself involved with imperfect creatures—is scarcely more attractive. If the Perfect One steps down into imperfect evil, something has gone terribly wrong somewhere, and the blame for that can only rest with the One itself.

Christian theologians would, for the most part, maintain that God's Will creates the world, and since freedom is a good component of that world, God allows, but does not create, evil. The Gnostics headed in the other direction: this world is so obviously evil (as in the famous Gnostic line, "What kind of God is this?") that they maintained the entire world was created, not by the real Absolute, but by a Demiurge, an evil or at least inferior spirit. This tricky attempt to keep God out of the world! Because if we let God into the world, something has gone horribly, wretchedly wrong.

Approaching the dualism in this intellectual fashion does little to ameliorate it. If, as the Gnostics maintain, this world is phenomenal, illusory, evil, the product of the Demiurge and not of the real Godhead, then the Demiurge itself comes perilously close to absolute status, and indeed some Gnostics would simply claim that the Demiurge itself creates but is not created, and that is in fact a definition of the Absolute. So now we have two absolutes: an absolute Good, and an absolute Evil, and we have reintroduced exactly the dualism we set out to overcome.

This intractable dualism, I maintain, is the central dualism in the Western tradition, and it would appear and reappear in numerous disguises: it would show up as the dualism between noumenon and phenomena, between mind and body, between free will and determinism, morals and nature, transcendent and immanent, subject and object, ascending and descending. That these are essentially the same dualism is a theme I carefully pursued in *Sex, Ecology, Spirituality* (and its popular version, *A Brief History of Everything*), and the interested reader might consult those sources for a more detailed look.

But what I would like to emphasize here is simply that, buried in the Western tradition—and in the Eastern—is a *radical and compelling solution to these massive dualisms*, a literal solution to the West's most intractable philosophical problems, from the absolute/relative to the mind/body dilemma. But this solution—appropriately known as "nondualism"—has an unbelievably awkward characteristic: namely, its compelling answer cannot be captured in words, a type of metaphysical catch-22 that absolutely guarantees to solve all your problems as long as you don't ask it to.

And that is where *Eye to Eye* comes in.

THE EYES OF KNOWING

The premise of *Eye to Eye* is that there is a great spectrum of human consciousness; and this means that men and women have available to them a *spectrum of different modes of knowing*, each of which discloses a different type of world (a different worldspace, with different objects, different subjects, different modes of spacetime, different motivations, and so on).

Put in its simplest form, there is, at the very least, the eye of flesh, the eye of mind, and the eye of spirit (or the eye of contemplation). An exclusive or predominant reliance on one of these modes produces, for example, empiricism, rationalism, and mysticism.

The claim of *Eye to Eye* is that each of these modes of knowing has its own specific and quite valid set of referents: *sensibilia*, *intelligibilia*, and *transcendelia*. Thus, all three of these modes of knowing can be validated with similar degrees of confidence; and thus all three modes are perfectly valid types of knowledge. Accordingly, any attempt at a comprehensive and graceful understanding of the Kosmos will most definitely include all three types of knowing; and anything less comprehensive than that is gravely suspect on its own merits.

Once we allow that the Kosmos is an altogether big and wondrous thing, and once we allow that at least these three types of knowing are necessary to get a decent taste of this miracle of existence, then we very well might find that some of our most recalcitrant philosophical problems are not so recalcitrant after all. And that includes, yes, the most aggravating dualism of all—the absolute and the relative—and its dozen or so bastard offspring, from the mind/body problem to fate and free will to consciousness and brain.

THE PROBLEM OF PROOF

But is the knowledge gained by the three eyes of knowing valid knowledge? How can we confirm or justify this knowledge? How do we know we are not mistaken, confused, or even hallucinating?

Eye to Eye suggests that all valid knowledge (in any level and any quadrant) has the following strands:

1. *Instrumental injunction.* This is generally of the form, "If you want to *know* this, *do* this."
2. *Intuitive apprehension.* This is an immediate experience of the domain disclosed by the injunction; that is, a direct experience or data-apprehension. (Even if the data is mediated, at the moment of experience it is immediately apprehended.) In other words, this is the direct apprehension of the data brought forth by the particular injunction, whether that data be sensory experience, mental experience, or spiritual experience.
3. *Communal confirmation* (or rejection). This is a checking of the results—the data, the evidence—with others who have *adequately completed* the injunctive and apprehensive strands.

In order to see the moons of Jupiter, you need a telescope. In order to understand *Hamlet*, you need to learn to read. In order to see the truth of the Pythagorean Theorem, you must learn geometry. In other words, valid forms of knowledge have, as one of their significant components, an *injunction*—if you want to *know* this, you must *do* this.

The injunctive strand of valid knowledge leads to an *apprehension* or an *illumination*, a direct disclosing of the data or referents in the world-space brought forth by the injunction, and this illumination is then *checked* (confirmed or refuted) by those who have adequately performed the injunction and thus disclosed the data.

Science, of course, is often taken as *the* model of genuine knowledge; and the philosophy of science is now dominated by three major approaches, which are generally viewed as mutually exclusive: that of empiricism, Thomas Kuhn, and Sir Karl Popper.

The strength of empiricism is its demand that all genuine knowledge be grounded in experiential evidence, and I agree entirely with that demand. But not only is there sensory experience, there is mental experience and spiritual experience. In other words, there is direct data, direct experience, in the realms of sensibilia and intelligibilia and transcendelia. And thus, if we use "experience" in its proper sense as direct apprehension, then we can firmly honor the empiricist demand that *all genuine knowledge be grounded in experience*, in data, in evidence. The empiricists, in other words, are highlighting the importance of the apprehensive or *illuminative strand* in all valid knowledge.

But evidence and data are not simply lying around waiting to be perceived by all and sundry, which is where Kuhn enters the picture.

Thomas Kuhn, in one of the greatly misunderstood ideas of our time, pointed out that normal science proceeds most fundamentally by way of what he called *paradigms* or *exemplars*. A paradigm is not merely a concept, it is an *actual practice*, an injunction, a technique taken as an exemplar for generating data. And Kuhn's point is that genuine scientific knowledge is grounded in paradigms, exemplars, injunctions, which bring forth new data. New injunctions disclose new data, and this is why Kuhn maintained *both* that science is progressive and cumulative, and that it also shows certain breaks or discontinuities (new injunctions bring forth new data). Kuhn, in other words, is highlighting the importance of the *injunctive strand* in the knowledge quest, namely, that data are not simply lying around waiting for anybody to see, but rather are *brought forth* by valid injunctions.

The knowledge brought forth by valid injunctions is indeed genuine knowledge precisely because paradigms in some ways disclose data, they do not merely invent it. And the validity of this data is demonstrated by the fact that bad data can be rebuffed, which is where Popper enters the picture.

Sir Karl Popper's approach emphasizes the importance of falsifiability: genuine knowledge must be open to disproof, or else it is simply dogma in disguise. Popper, in other words, is highlighting the importance of the *confirmation/rejection strand* in all valid knowledge; and, as we will see, this falsifiability principle can be operative in every domain, sensibilia to intelligibilia to transcendelia.

Thus, this integral approach acknowledges and incorporates the moments of truth in each of these important contributions to the human knowledge quest (evidence, Kuhn, and Popper), but without the need to reduce these truths to sensibilia alone. The mistake of the empiricists is the failure to see that, in addition to sensory experience, there is mental and spiritual experience as well. The mistake of the Kuhnians is the failure to see that injunctions apply to all forms of valid knowledge, not just sensorimotor science. And the mistake of the Popperians is the attempt to restrict falsifiability to sensibilia alone and thus make "falsifiable-by-sensory-data" the criterion for mental and spiritual knowledge, whereas bad data in those domains are indeed falsifiable, but only by further data *in those domains*, not by data from lower domains! The Popperians are right about falsifiability, wrong about sensory only.

For example, a bad interpretation of *Hamlet* is falsifiable, not by any empiric-scientific data, but by further interpretations, further mental data, generated in a community of interpreters. *Hamlet* is not about the search for a sunken treasure buried in the Pacific. That is a bad interpretation, a false interpretation, and this falsifiability can easily be demonstrated by a community of researchers who have completed the first two strands (read the play, apprehend its various meanings).

As it is now, the Popperian falsifiability principle has one widespread and altogether perverted use: it is implicitly restricted *only to sensibilia*, which, in an incredibly hidden and sneaky fashion, *automatically bars all mental and spiritual experience from the status of genuine knowledge*. This unwarranted restriction of the falsifiability principle claims to separate genuine knowledge from the dogmatic, when all it is actually accomplishing, in this shrunken form, is a silent but vicious reductionism, a reductionism that cannot even be supported by its own falsifiability principle!

On the other hand, when we free the falsifiability principle from its restriction to sensibilia, and set it free to police the domains of intelligibilia and transcendelia as well, then it most definitely becomes an important aspect of the knowledge quest in all domains, sensory to mental to spiritual. And in each of those domains, it does indeed help us to separate the true from the false, the demonstrable from the dogmatic, the dependable from the bogus.

ENGAGE THE SPIRITUAL INJUNCTION

In short, all valid forms of knowledge have an *injunction*, an *illumination*, and a *confirmation*; and this is true whether we are looking at the moons of Jupiter, the Pythagorean Theorem, the meaning of *Hamlet*, or . . . the nature of the Absolute.

And where the moons of Jupiter can be disclosed by the eye of flesh (by the senses or their extensions—sensibilia), and the Pythagorean Theorem can be disclosed by the eye of mind and its inward apprehensions (intelligibilia), the nature of the Absolute can only be disclosed by the *eye of contemplation* and its directly disclosed referents—its transcendelia, its spiritual data, the brought-forth facts of the spiritual worldspace.

But in order to gain access to any of these valid modes of knowing, I must be *adequate* to the injunction—I must successfully complete the injunctive strand. This is true in the physical sciences, the mental sciences, and the spiritual sciences. If we want to *know* this, we must *do* this. And where the exemplar in physical sciences might be a telescope, and in the human sciences might be linguistic interpretation, in the spiritual sciences the exemplar, the injunction, the paradigm, the practice is: meditation or contemplation. It too has its injunctions, its illuminations, and its confirmations, all of which are generally repeatable, verifiable, or falsifiable—and all of which therefore constitute a perfectly valid mode of knowledge acquisition.

But in all cases, we must engage the injunction. We must take up the exemplary practice, and this is certainly true for the spiritual sciences as well. If we do not take up the injunctive practice, then we will not have a genuine paradigm, and therefore we will never see the data of the spiritual worldspace. We will in effect be no different from the Churchmen who refused to follow Galileo's injunction and look through the telescope itself.

And that is where the catch-22 comes in.

THE EYE OF CONTEMPLATION

As I will argue in the following pages, *we cannot solve the absolute/relative problem using the eye of flesh or the eye of mind*. This deepest of problems and mysteries directly yields its resolution only to the eye of contemplation. And, as both Kant and Nagarjuna forcefully demonstrated, if you try to state this solution in intellectual or rational terms, you will generate nothing but antinomies, paradox, contradiction.

In other words, we cannot solve the absolute/relative problem empirically, using the eye of flesh and its sensibilia; nor can we solve it rationally, using the eye of mind and its intelligibilia. The solution, rather, involves the direct apprehension of transcendelia, which are disclosed only by the eye of contemplation and are most definitely verifiable or falsifiable in that domain, using what are in fact quite *public* procedures—public, that is, to all who have completed the injunction and disclosed the illumination.

And likewise again with fate and free will, the one and the many, noumenon and phenomena, mind and brain. *Eye to Eye* argues that only with the higher stages of consciousness development—part and parcel of the meditative or contemplative unfolding—does the solution to these dilemmas become obvious. But that is not an empirical discovery nor a rational deduction; it is a contemplative apprehension.

To the question, what is the relation of mind and body—or mind and brain—typical Western answers include the *identity thesis* (they are two different aspects of the same thing), *dualism* (they are two different things), *interactionism* (they are different but mutually causal), *parallelism* (two different things that never speak to each other), *epiphenomenalism* (one is the byproduct of the other). And, despite what their adherents claim, not one of those positions has been able to carry the day, simply because they are all basically flawed in one way or another.

The reason they are inadequate, a more integral philosophy would maintain, is that the mind/body problem cannot be satisfactorily solved with the eye of flesh or the eye of mind, since those are exactly the two modes that need to be integrated, something neither of them could accomplish on its own.

Thus, the only acceptable response to the question, What is the relation of the mind and body?, is to *carefully explain the actual contemplative injunctions*—the contemplative practices or paradigms or exemplars—and invite the questioners to take up the practice and see for themselves. If you want to *know* this, you must *do* this. Although both the empiricist and the rationalist will not find this answer satisfactory—they wish only to engage their own paradigms and exemplars—nonetheless this is the only technically acceptable answer and course of action.

Both the rationalist and the empiricist press us: they want us to state our contemplative conclusions and let them check these conclusions *against their own injunctions*. That is, they want our words without our injunctions. They want to try to follow our words without the pain of having to follow our exemplars. And so we must remind them: Words without injunctions are meaningless. Words without injunctions have no means of verification whatsoever. Words without injunctions are the stuff of doggerel, dogma, and delusions. Our words and our conclusions can indeed be carefully justified—verified or rejected—but only if the injunctions are engaged.

And so when the empiricist and the rationalist demand our conclusions without the injunctions, they have guaranteed a *meaningless* answer—and they blame us for the meaninglessness! Our data cannot be generated by their particular paradigms and exemplars, and so they scratch their heads. They will *not* do this, and therefore they will *not* know this. They circle in the orbit of their self-imposed blindness, and they call this blindness reality.

SPIRITUAL TRAINING AND TRANSCENDENTAL DATA

In the East, Zen would handle the problem of the One and the Many in the following way. The question might be, as a famous Zen koan has it, "If all things return to the One, to what does the One return?" This is, of course, that intractable dilemma: what is the relation of the absolute and the relative, the One and the Many, Emptiness and Form?

But Zen, of course, will reject every intellectual response. A clever student might respond, "To the Many!" which is a perfectly good intellectual answer, yet it will earn only a sharp blow from the Master. Any intellectual response will be radically rejected, no matter what its content!

Rather, the student must take up an *injunction*, a paradigm, an exemplar, a practice, which in this case is zazen, sitting meditation. And—to make a very long and complex story brutally short—after an average of five or six years of this exemplary training, the student may begin to have a series of profound illuminations. And you will simply have to trust me that no one would go through this extended hell in order to be rewarded only with an epileptic fit or a schizophrenic hallucination.

No, this is Ph.D. training in the realm of transcendelia. And once this injunctive training begins to bear fruit, a series of illuminations—commonly called kensho or satori—begins to flash forth into direct and immediate awareness, and this data is then checked (confirmed or refuted) by the community of those who have completed the injunctive and the illuminative strands. At this point, the answer to the question "To what does the One return?" will become extremely clear and straightforward—and I will give that answer in a moment.

But the point is, the actual *answer* to the question, What is the relation of the One and the Many, the absolute and the relative, free will and fate, consciousness and form, mind and body?—the technically correct and precise answer is: satori. The technically correct answer is: take up the injunction, perform the experiment, gather the data (the experiences), and check them with a community of the similarly adequate.

We can't *state* what the answer is other than that, because if we did, we would have merely words without injunctions, and they would indeed be utterly meaningless. It's very like baking a pie: you follow the recipe (the injunctions), you bake the pie, and then actually taste it. To the question, "What does the pie taste like?" we can only give the person the recipe, and let them make it and taste it themselves. We *cannot* theoretically or verbally or philosophically or rationally describe the answer in any other satisfactory fashion: if you want to *know* this, you must *do* this.

And thus: take up the injunction or paradigm of meditation; practice and polish that cognitive tool until awareness learns to discern the incredibly subtle phenomena of transcendelia; check your observations with others who have done so, much as mathematicians will check their proofs with others who have completed the injunctions; and thus confirm or reject your results. And in the verification of that transcendelia, the relation of the One and the Many will become perfectly clear—at least as clear as rocks are to the eye of flesh and geometry is to the eye of mind—and thus will that most intractable of dualisms quite literally come unglued.

The answer to the relation of the Absolute and the relative is therefore most definitely *not*: the Absolute created the world. It most definitely is *not*: the world is illusory and the Absolute alone is real. It is *not*: we perceive only the phenomenal reflection of a noumenal reality. It is *not*: fate and free will are two aspects of one and the same process. It is *not*: all things and events are different aspects of a single interwoven web-of-life. It is *not*: the body alone is real and the mind is a reflection of that only reality. It is *not*: mind and body are two different aspects of the total organism. It is *not*: mind emerges from hierarchical brain structure. In fact, it is not even: noumenon and phenomena are not-two and nondual.

Those are all merely *intellectual symbols* that purport to give the answer, but the real answer does not lie in sensibilia or intelligibilia, it lies in transcendelia, and that domain only discloses itself after the meditative exemplar is engaged, whereupon every single one of those intellectual answers is seen to be inadequate and off the mark; each generates nothing but more insolvable and insuperable difficulties, dilemmas, and contradictions. The answer is not more talk; the answer is satori, by whatever name we wish to use to convey valid contemplative awareness.

And, much more to the point, even if this answer could be stated in words—and in fact, the answer can be stated in words, because Zen masters talk about it all the time!—nonetheless, it would make no sense to anybody who had not also performed the injunction, just as mathematical symbols can be seen by anybody but understood only by those who have completed the training.

But open the eye of contemplation, and the answer is as obvious, as perfect, as unmistakable as the play of sunlight on a crystal clear pond, early on a cool spring morning.

You see, that was the answer.

CONCLUSION

We have seen that the Western tradition has been plagued, from its inception, with a series of brutal dualisms, and that virtually all forms of Western philosophy, right up to today, have come to rest finally on one or another of these dualisms (mind/body, truth/appearance, noumenon/phenomenon, transcendental/immanent, ascending/descending, subject/object, signified/signifier, consciousness/brain).

But these dualisms, and the root issues surrounding them, cannot finally be solved by the eye of flesh and its empiricism, nor by the eye of mind and its rationalism, but only, finally, by the eye of contemplation and its radical experiential mysticism (satori by whatever name).

In the West, since Kant, metaphysics has fallen on hard times. I maintain that it has done so precisely because it attempted to do with the eye of mind that which can only be done with the eye of contemplation. Because the mind could not actually deliver the metaphysical goods, and yet kept loudly claiming that it could, somebody was bound to blow the whistle sooner or later and demand real evidence. Kant made the demand, and metaphysics collapsed—and rightly so, in its typical form.

Neither empiricism, nor pure reason, nor practical reason, nor any combination thereof can see into the realm of Spirit (and "real metaphysics"). In the smoking ruins that Kant left, the only possible conclusion is that all future metaphysics, to be genuine, must offer direct experiential evidence and data of the spiritual domain itself. And that means, in addition to sensory experience and its empiricism (scientific and pragmatic), and mental experience and its rationalism (pure and practical), there must be added spiritual experience and its mysticism (spiritual practice and its experiential data).

The possibility of the direct experience of sensibilia, intelligibilia, and transcendelia radically defuses the Kantian objections, and sets the knowledge quest firmly on the road of evidence, with each of its validity claims (truth, truthfulness, justness, functional fit) guided by the three strands of genuine knowledge accumulation (injunction, apprehension, confirmation) at every level (sensory, mental, spiritual—across the entire spectrum of consciousness, however many levels we wish to invoke).

In short, the three strands of genuine knowledge accumulation operate for all levels, in each quadrant. The application of the three strands (with their built-in demand for exemplars, evidence, and falsifiability) does indeed help us in our quest to separate the wheat from the chaff, the true from the false, the demonstrable from the dogmatic, the dependable from the bogus. Guided by the three strands, the validity claims of every quadrant can indeed be redeemed. They carry cash value. And the cash is experiential evidence, sensory to mental to spiritual.

With this approach, metaphysics regains its proper warrant, which is not sensory or mental but finally contemplative. With the eye of Spirit, God can be seen. With the eye of Spirit, the universe unfolds its innermost contours. With the eye of Spirit, noumenon announces its pure Presence. With the eye of Spirit, the Kosmos delivers its deepest secrets. And with the eye of Spirit, the intractable nightmares of the sensory and mental dilemmas yield to the radiance of Emptiness itself.

Integral philosophy cannot replace any of the other modes or functions of knowing—it cannot replace empirical science, or contemplative meditation, or even the other mental modes, from literature to poetry to history to psychoanalysis to mathematics to linguistics.

But integral philosophy is there, at the very heart of the mental world, coordinating and elucidating all of these modes of knowing, dimensions of value, levels of being. Integral philosophy itself is of the mental domain, and cannot by itself, with its mental devices alone, step beyond that sphere. But it firmly acknowledges the role of contemplation in generating data, and it takes that data into account in its own coordinating and elucidating activities. If it does not itself deliver meditative data, it firmly acknowledges the existence and importance of that data.[1] It is mandalic reason at its finest and most encompassing. It knows the difference between relative truth, which it can divulge, and absolute truth, for which it must yield to the eye of contemplation.

Integral philosophy thus mentally coordinates the Good, and the True, and the Beautiful, weaving a mandala of the many faces of Spirit, and then invites us to take up spiritual practice itself, and thus finally meet Spirit face to face.

And as for the final answer to the great Western dualism? The final answer to the mind/body problem? To the One and the Many? God and creation? Was God at Auschwitz? Are we fated or free-willed? It's all the same question, you see, so here is another perfectly complete answer:

This slowly drifting cloud is pitiful!
What dreamwalkers we all are!
Awakened, the one great truth:
Black rain on the temple roof.

Integral philosophy attempts to include and coordinate the many faces of the Good (the "we"), and the True (the "it"), and the Beautiful (the

"I"), as all of them evolve across the entire spectrum, from their sensory forms (seen with the eye of flesh) to their mental forms (seen with the eye of mind) to their spiritual forms (seen with the eye of contemplation)—a pluridimensional Kosmic mandala of unending embrace.

With science we touch the True, the "It" of Spirit. With morals we touch the Good, the "We" of Spirit. What, then, would an integral approach have to say about the Beautiful, the "I" of Spirit itself? What is the Beauty that is in the eye of the Beholder? When we are in the eye of Spirit, the I of Spirit, what do we finally see?

4

Integral Art and Literary Theory

PART I

> In the process of understanding and interpretation, part
> and whole are related in a circular way: in order to under-
> stand the whole, it is necessary to understand the parts,
> while to understand the parts it is necessary to have some
> comprehension of the whole.
> —DAVID COUZENS HOY

> Thus the movement of understanding is constantly from
> the whole to the part and back to the whole. Our task is
> to extend in concentric circles the unity of the understood
> meaning. The harmony of all the details with the whole is
> the criterion of correct understanding. The failure to
> achieve this harmony means that understanding has failed.
> —HANS-GEORG GADAMER

INTRODUCTION

WITH THE DEATH of the avant-garde and the triumph of irony,
art seems to have nothing sincere to say. Narcissism and nihilism
battle for a center stage that isn't even there; kitsch and camp crawl all
over each other in a fight for a representation that no longer matters
anyway; there seems to arise only the egoic inclination of artist and critic
alike, caught in halls of self-reflecting mirrors, admiring their image in a
world that once cared.

The aim of this essay is to step out of the narcissistic and nihilistic endgame that has so often overtaken the world of postmodern art and literature, and to introduce instead the essentials of a genuinely integral art and literary theory—what might be called *integral hermeneutics*.

I will cover both art and literature, but with an emphasis on visual art, which is actually a "trickier" and in some ways more difficult case, since it usually lacks narrative structure to help guide the interpretation. (A subsequent essay focuses specifically on an "all-level, all-quadrant" analysis of literary signification and semiotics in general.)[1]

It is no secret that the art and literary world has reached something of a cul-de-sac, a dead end. Postmodern literary theory is a stark example of the "babble of interpretations" that has overcome the art world. It used to be that "meaning" was something the author created and simply put into a text, and the reader simply pulled it out. This view is now regarded, by all parties, as hopelessly naive.

Starting with psychoanalysis, it was recognized that some meaning could be unconscious, or unconsciously generated, and this unconscious meaning would find its way into the text even though the author was unaware of it. It was therefore the job of the psychoanalyst, and not the naive reader, to pull this hidden meaning out.

The "hermeneutics of suspicion," in its many forms, thus came to view artworks as repositories of hidden meaning that could be decoded only by the knowing critic. Any repressed, oppressed, or otherwise marginalized context would show up, disguised, in the art, and the art was thus a testament to the repression, oppression, marginalization. Marginalized context was hidden subtext.

The Marxist variation was that the critics themselves existed in the context of capitalist-industrial social practices of covert domination, and these hidden contexts and meanings could be found in (and therefore pulled out of) any artwork created by a person in *that* context. Similarly, art would be interpreted in the context of racism, sexism, elitism, speciesism, jingoism, imperialism, logocentrism, phallocentrism, phallologocentrism (batteries not included).

Various forms of structuralism and hermeneutics fought vigorously to find the "real" context which would, therefore, provide the real and final *meaning*, which would undercut (or supersede) all other interpretations. Foucault, in his archaeological period, outdid them both, situating both structuralism and hermeneutics in an *episteme* that was itself the cause and context of the type of people who would even want to do hermeneutics and structuralism in the first place.

In part in reaction to some of this, the New Criticism had said, basically, let us ignore all of those interpretations. The artwork, in and by itself, is all that really matters. Ignore the personality (conscious or unconscious) of the author, ignore the historical setting, the time, the place, and look solely at the structural integrity of the artwork itself (its regime, its code, its internal pattern). "Affective stylistics" and "reader-response" theory reacted strongly to all that, and maintained that since meaning is only generated in reading (or in viewing) the artwork, then the *meaning* of the work is actually found in the *response* of the viewer. The phenomenologists (e.g., Iser, Ingarden) had tried a combination of the two: the text has gaps ("spots of indeterminacy"), and the meaning of the *gaps* can be found in the reader.

And deconstruction came along and said, basically, you're all wrong. (It's very hard to trump that.) Deconstruction maintained that all meaning is context-dependent, and contexts are boundless. There is thus no way to control, or even finally to determine, meaning—and thus both art and criticism spin endlessly out of control and into the space of unrelenting ambiguity, never to be seen or heard from again.

Postmodern deconstruction, it has finally been realized, leads more often than not to nihilism: there is no genuine meaning anywhere, only nested deceptions. And this leaves, in the place of art as sincere statement, art as anarchy, anchored only in egoic whim and narcissistic display. Into the vacuum created by the implosion that is so much of postmodernism, rushes the ego triumphant. Meaning is context-dependent, and contexts are boundless, and that leaves art and artist and critic alike lost in aperspectival space, ruled only by the purr of the selfcentric engine left driving the entire display.

The laments are loud and well known. Painter and critic Peter Fuller:

> I feel that we are living through the epilogue of the European professional Fine Art tradition—an epilogue in which the context and subject-matter of most art is art itself.[2]

And art historian Barbara Rose:

> The art currently filling the museums and galleries is of such low quality generally that no real critical intelligence could possibly feel challenged to analyze it. . . . There is an inescapable sense among artists and critics that we are at the end of our rope, culturally speaking.[3]

But who knows? Perhaps meaning is in fact context-dependent, and perhaps contexts are indeed boundless. Is there any way that this state of affairs can be viewed so as to actually restore a genuine sense of meaning to art and its interpretation? Is there any way to ground the babble of interpretations that has finally self-deconstructed? Is there any way that the nested lies announced by postmodernism could in fact be nested truths? And could this spell the endgame of the narcissism and nihilism that had so proudly announced their own ascendancy?

Could, in short, an integral orientation save art and literary theory from itself?

Contexts within Contexts Endlessly

We live in a world of holons. "Holons": the word was coined by Arthur Koestler to indicate *wholes* that are simultaneously *parts* of other wholes: a whole quark is part of a whole atom; a whole atom is part of a whole molecule; a whole molecule is part of a whole cell; a whole cell is part of a whole organism. . . . In linguistics, a whole letter is part of a whole word, which is part of a whole sentence, which is part of a whole paragraph . . . and so on.

In other words, we live in a universe that consists neither of wholes nor of parts, but of whole/parts, or holons. Wholes do not exist by themselves, nor do parts exist by themselves. Every whole simultaneously exists as a part of some other whole, and as far as we can tell, this is indeed endless. Even the whole of the universe right now is simply a part of the next moment's whole. There are no wholes, and no parts, anywhere in the universe; there are only whole/parts.

As I have tried to suggest in *A Brief History of Everything*, this is true in the physical, emotional, mental, and spiritual domains. We exist in fields within fields, patterns within patterns, contexts within contexts, endlessly. There is an old joke about a King who goes to a Wiseperson and asks, "How is it that the Earth doesn't fall down?" The Wiseperson replies, "The Earth is resting on a lion." "On what, then, is the lion resting?" "The lion is resting on an elephant." "On what is the elephant resting?" "The elephant is resting on a turtle." "On what is the. . . ?" "You can stop right there, your Majesty. It's turtles all the way down."

Holons all the way down, in a dizzyingly nested fashion, without ever hitting a foundation. The "postmodern poststructuralists"— usually associated with such names as Jacques Derrida, Michel Foucault, Jean-François Lyotard, and stretching back to Georges Bataille and Friedrich Nietzsche—have been the great foes of any sort of systematic theory or "grand narrative," and thus they might be expected to raise stern objections to any overall theory of "holons." But a close look at their own work shows that it is driven precisely by a conception of holons within holons within holons, of texts within texts within texts (or contexts within contexts within contexts), and it is this sliding play of texts within texts that forms the "foundationless" platform from which they launch their attacks.

Georges Bataille, for instance. "In the most general way"—and these are his italics—"*every isolable element of the universe always appears as a particle that can enter into composition with a whole that transcends it. Being is only found as a whole composed of particles whose relative autonomy is maintained* [a part that is also a whole]. These two principles [simultaneous wholeness and partness] dominate the uncertain presence of an *ipse* being across a distance that never ceases to put *everything* in question."[4]

Everything is put into question because everything is a context within a context forever. And *putting everything in question* is precisely what the postmodern poststructuralists are known for. And so in a language that would soon become quite typical (and by now quite comical), Bataille goes on to point out that "putting everything into question" counters the human need to arrange things violently in terms of a pat wholeness and smug universality: "With extreme dread imperatively becoming the demand for universality, carried away to vertigo by the movement that composes it, the *ipse* being that presents itself as a universal is only a challenge to the diffuse immensity that escapes its precarious violence, the tragic negation of all that is not its own bewildered phantom's chance. But, as a man, this being falls into the meanders of the knowledge of his fellowmen, which absorbs his substance in order to reduce it to a component of what goes beyond the virulent madness of his autonomy in the total night of the world."[5] Um, and so forth.

The point is *not* that Bataille himself was without any sort of system, but simply that the *system is sliding*—holons within holons forever. So the claim to simply have "no system" is a little disingenuous. Which is why André Breton, the leader of the surrealists at the time, began a counterattack on this part of Bataille, also in terms that are echoed by today's critics of postmodernists: "Bataille's misfortune is to reason: admittedly, he reasons like someone who 'has a fly on his nose,' which allies him more closely with the dead than with the living, but *he does reason.* He is trying, with the help of the tiny mechanism in him which is not completely out of order, to share his obsessions: this very fact proves that he cannot claim, no matter what he may say, to be opposed to any system, like an unthinking brute."[6]

Both sides are correct, in a sense. There is system, but the system is sliding. It is unendingly, dizzifyingly, holonic. This is why Jonathan Culler, perhaps the foremost interpreter of Jacques Derrida's deconstruction, can point out that Derrida does *not* deny truth per se, but only insists that truth and meaning are *context-bound* (each context being a whole that is also part of another whole context, which itself . . .). "One could therefore," says Culler, "identify deconstruction with the twin principles of the *contextual determination of meaning* and the *infinite extendability of context.*"[7]

Turtles all the way up, all the way down. What deconstruction puts into question is the desire to find a final resting place, in either wholeness or partness or anything in between. Every time somebody finds a final interpretation or a foundational interpretation of a text or artwork (or life or history or cosmos), deconstruction is on hand to say that the final context does not exist, because it is also unendingly a part of yet another context forever. As Culler puts it, any sort of final context is "unmasterable, both in principle and in practice. *Meaning is context bound, but context is boundless.*"[8]

Even Jürgen Habermas, who generally takes Breton's position to Derrida's Bataille, agrees with that particular point. As Habermas puts it, "These variations of context that change meaning cannot in principle be arrested or controlled, because contexts cannot be exhausted, that is, they cannot be theoretically mastered once and for all."[9]

That the system is sliding does *not* mean that meaning can't be established, that truth doesn't exist, or that contexts won't hold still long enough to make a simple point. Many postmodern poststructuralists have not simply discovered holonic space, they have become thoroughly lost in it. Georges Bataille, for example, took a good, long, hard look at holonic space and went properly insane, though which is cause, and which effect, is hard to say.

As for our main topic, we need only note that there is indeed system, but the system is sliding: The universe is composed of holons—contexts within contexts within contexts—all the way up, all the way down.

MEANING IS CONTEXT-DEPENDENT

The word "bark" means something very different in the phrases "the bark of a dog" and "the bark of a tree." Which is exactly why all meaning is context-bound; the identical word has different meanings depending upon the context in which it is found.

This context-dependency seems to pervade every aspect of the universe and our lives in it. Take, for example, a single thought, say the thought of going to the grocery store. When I have that thought, what I actually experience is the thought itself, the interior thought and its meaning—the symbols, the images, the idea of going to the grocery store. (This is the Upper-Left quadrant, the intentional.)

Now the internal thought only makes sense in terms of my cultural background. If I spoke a different language, the thought would be composed of different symbols and have quite different meanings. If I existed in a primal tribal society a million years ago, I would never even have the thought "going to the grocery store." It might be, "Time to kill the bear." The point is that my thoughts themselves arise in a *cultural background* that gives texture and meaning and context to my individual thoughts, and indeed, I would not even be able to "talk to myself" if I did not exist in a community of individuals who also talk to me. (This is the Lower-Left quadrant, the cultural.)

So the cultural community serves as an *intrinsic background* and *context* to any individual thoughts I might have. My thoughts do not just pop into my head out of nowhere; they pop into my head out of a cultural background, and however much I might move beyond this background, I can never simply escape it altogether, and I could never have developed thoughts in the first place without it. The occasional cases of a "wolf boy"—humans raised in the wild—show that the human brain, left without culture, does not produce linguistic thoughts on its own.

In short, my individual thoughts only exist against a vast background of cultural practices and languages and meanings and contexts, without which I could form virtually no individual thoughts at all. But my culture itself is not simply disembodied, hanging in idealistic midair. It has *material components*, much as my own individual thoughts have material brain components. All *cultural* events have *social* correlates. These concrete social components include types of technology, forces of production (horticultural, agrarian, industrial, etc.), concrete institutions, written codes and patterns, geopolitical locations, and so on (the Lower-Right quadrant). And these concrete material components—the actual *social system*—are crucial in helping to determine the types of cultural worldview within which my own thoughts will arise.

So my supposedly "individual thought" is actually a holon that has all these various aspects to it—intentional, behavioral, cultural, and social. And around the holonic circle we go: the social system will have a strong influence on the cultural worldview, which will set limits to the individual thoughts that I can have, which will register in the brain physiology. And we can go around that circle in any direction. They are all interwoven. They are all mutually determining. They all cause, and are caused by, the other holons, in concentric spheres of contexts within contexts indefinitely.

And this fact bears directly on the nature and meaning of art itself.

WHAT IS ART?

The simplest and perhaps earliest view of the nature and meaning of art (and thus of its interpretation as well) is that art is *imitative* or *representational*: it copies something in the real world. The painting of a landscape copies or represents the real landscape. Plato takes this view of art in the *Republic*, where he uses the example of a bed: the painting of a bed is a copy of a concrete bed (which is itself a copy of the ideal Form of a bed). Notoriously, for Plato, this puts art in a rather bad position: it is making copies of copies of the Ideal, and is thus doubly removed and doubly inferior. Later theorists would "upgrade" this Platonic conception by maintaining that the true artist is actually copying the Ideal Forms directly, seen with the mind's eye, and thus is performing a "perfectionist" artistry—as Michelangelo said, "The beauty which stirs and carries up to heaven every sound intellect."

Aristotle likewise takes the view of art as imitative or copying the real world, and in one form or another this notion of art as *mimesis* has had a long and profound influence: the *meaning* of art is that which it represents.

The grave difficulty with this view, taken in and by itself, is that it unmistakably implies that the better the imitation, the better the art, so that a perfect copy would be perfect art, which lands art squarely in the province of *trompe l'oeil* and documentary photography: a good likeness on a driver's license photo would be good art. Moreover, not all art is representative or imitative: surrealist, minimalist, expressionist, conceptual, and so forth. So while some art has representative aspects, *mimesis* alone can account for neither the nature nor the value of art.

With the rise of the Enlightenment in Europe, two other major theories of the nature and meaning of art gained prominence, and they are both still quite influential today. Not surprisingly, these theories would spring respectively from the great rational and great romantic currents that were set in motion in the seventeenth and eighteenth centuries, and which, translated into the artistic domain, came to be known generally as formalist and expressivist (rational and romantic!).

And at this point, the question became, not so much *what* is art, but *where* is art?

ART IS IN THE MAKER

If the nature, meaning, and value of art are not simply due to art's imitative capacity, perhaps the essence of art lies in its power to *express* something, and not simply to *copy* something. And indeed, in both the theory and practice of art, emphasis often began to turn from a faithful copying and representing and imitating—whether of religious icons or of a realistic nature—to an increasingly expressionistic stance, under the broad influence of the general currents of Romanticism. This view of art and its value was given strong and quite influential voice by theorists such as Benedetto Croce (*Aesthetics*), R. G. Collingwood (*Principles of Art*), and Leo Tolstoy (*What Is Art?*).

The basic conclusion of these Romantic theorists: art is, first and foremost, the *expression* of the feelings or intentions of the artist. It is not simply the imitation of an external reality, but the expression of an internal reality. We therefore can best *interpret* art by trying to understand the *original intention* of the maker of the artwork itself (whether painter, writer, composer).

Thus, for Tolstoy, art is the "contagion of feeling." That is, the artist expresses feeling in the artwork which then evokes that feeling in us, the viewers; and the quality of the art is best interpreted by the quality of the feelings it expresses and "infects" us with. For Croce—arguably the most influential aesthetician of the 1900s—art is the expression of emotion, itself a very real and primal type of knowledge, often cosmic in its power, especially when expressed and evoked by great works of art. And Collingwood made the original intention of the artist so utterly primary that the inward, psychological vision of the artist was itself said to be the actual art, whether or not that vision ever got translated into public forms.

This view of art as the expression of an original intention or feeling or vision in the artist gave rise to what is still perhaps the most widespread school of the *interpretation* of art. Modern "hermeneutics"—the art and science of interpretation—began with certain Romantically inspired philosophical trends, notably in Friedrich Schleiermacher and then Wilhelm Dilthey, and continued down to this day in such influential theorists as Emilio Betti and E. D. Hirsch. This approach, one of the oldest and in some ways the most central school of hermeneutics, maintains that the key to the correct interpretation of a text—considering "text" in the very broadest sense, as any symbol requiring interpretation, whether artistic, linguistic, poetic—the key to correct interpretation is *the recovery of the maker's original intention*, a psychological *reconstruction* of the author's (or artist's) intentions in the original historical setting.

In short, for these approaches, since the *meaning* of art is the maker's original intention, a *valid* interpretation involves the psychological reconstruction and recovery of this original intention. The hermeneutic gap between the artist and viewer is closed to the extent there is a "seeing eye to eye" with the artist's original meaning, and this occurs through the procedures of valid interpretation based on original recovery and reconstruction.

It is no accident that the *theory* of art as expression was historically paralleled by the broad trends of expressionism in the *practice* of art itself. The nineteenth-century expressionists and Postimpressionists, including Van Gogh, Gauguin, and Munch, directly opposed the Realist and Impressionist imitation of nature (Van Gogh: "Instead of trying to reproduce exactly what I have before my eyes, I use color more arbitrarily so as to express myself more forcibly"); from there to the Cubists and Fauves (Matisse: "What I am after above all is expression"); to Kandinsky and Klee and the abstract expressionism of Pollock, Kline, and de Kooning. In its various manifestations, expressionism was not just a stylistic or idealizing alteration of external representation, but an almost complete and total break with the tradition of imitation.

No sooner was this theory (and practice) of art as expression put forth than another offshoot of the broad Romantic movement—psychoanalysis—pointed out that many human *intentions* are in fact *unconscious*. And further, these intentions, even though unconscious, nonetheless can make their way in disguised forms into everyday life, perhaps as neurotic symptoms, or as symbolic dreams, or as slips of the tongue, or, in general, as compromise formations expressing the conflict between a forbidden desire and a censoring or repressing force. The psychoanalyst, trained to spot the symbolic expression of these hidden desires, could thus *interpret* these symbols and symptoms to the individual, who in turn would thus gain, it was duly hoped, some sort of understanding and amelioration of his or her distressing condition.

In the sphere of art and literature, this inevitably meant that the original maker (artist, writer, poet) would, like everybody else, have various unconscious intentions, and these intentions, in disguised forms, *would leave traces in the artwork itself.* It followed then with mathematical precision: (1) if the meaning of art is the original intention expressed in the work, and (2) if the correct interpretation of art is therefore the reconstruction of this intention, but (3) if some intentions are unconscious and leave only symbolic traces in the artwork, then (4) an important part of the correct interpretation of an artwork is the unearthing and interpreting of these unconscious drives, intentions, desires, wishes. The art critic, to be a true critic, must also be a psychoanalyst.

Art Is in the Hidden Intent: Symptomatic Theories

This soon opened a Pandora's box of "unconscious intentions." If the artwork expressed the unconscious Freudian desires of the artist, why limit it to Freudian themes? There are, after all, several different types of unconscious structures in the human being, the list of which soon exploded. The artist exists in a setting of techno-economic structures, the Marxists pointed out, and a particular artwork will inexorably reflect the "base" of economic realities, and thus the correct interpretation of a text or work of art involves highlighting the class structures in which the art is produced. Feminists soon caught the fever, and avidly tried to suggest that the fundamental and hidden structures were primarily those of gender, so that even Marxists were driven by the unconscious or thinly disguised intentions of patriarchal power. Womanists (feminists of color) very rapidly outflanked the mainstream feminists with a criticism whose opening line was, in effect, "We can't blame everything on the patriarchy, white girl. . . ." And so the list would go: racism, sexism, elitism, speciesism, anthropocentrism, androcentrism, imperialism, ecologism, logocentrism, phallocentrism.

All of those theories might best be called *symptomatic theories*: they view a particular artwork as symptomatic of larger currents, currents the artist is often unaware of—sexual, economic, cultural, ideological. They generally grant that the meaning of art is the expression of an original feeling, intention, or vision of the artist. But they immediately add that the artist might have, or exist in, structures of unconscious intention, and these unconscious structures, generally not available to the awareness of the artists themselves, would nonetheless leave symbolic traces in their works of art, and these traces could be spotted, decoded, deciphered, and interpreted by the knowing critic. A *valid* interpretation is thus one that decodes and exposes the hidden intentions, whether individual or cultural.

ART IS IN THE ARTWORK

While there may be much truth to each of those positions—and we will shortly return for an assessment—nonetheless, few critics would concede that intentions alone, conscious or unconscious, define the nature and value of art.

In part as a reaction to these originally Romantic and expressivist versions of art, there arose various more "formal" interpretations of art and literature; and this, as I suggested, was in large measure a legacy of the more *rational* side of the Enlightenment agenda.

This Enlightenment rationalism had several profound influences on art theory and practice. The general atmosphere of Enlightenment scientific realism soon translated almost directly to the realist trends in literature and painting (Zola, Balzac, Flaubert, Courbet), and from there to the Impressionists, who repudiated so much of the Romantic-expressionist trends and sought instead to capture "immediate visual impressions" rendered intensely and impersonally, the emotions of the artist being quite secondary at best (Monet, Renoir, Manet, Pissarro, Degas), as well as the objective rendering of contemporary and actual experience, sometimes verging on the documentary, and always in sympathy with a realist attitude.

But Enlightenment rationalism also entered art theory and practice in a rather strict and dry sense, namely, in the view that the nature and value of art is to be found in the *form* of the artwork itself. Much of this *formalism* had its modern origin in Kant's immensely influential *Critique of Judgment*, but it would soon be powerfully expressed in music theory by Eduard Hanslick and in the visual arts by Roger Fry and Clive Bell. Formalism would likewise find its way into literary theory, most significantly with the Russian formalists (Jakobson, Propp); the American New Critics (Wimsatt and Beardsley); the French structuralists

(Lévi-Strauss, Barthes), neo-structuralists (early Foucault), and post-structuralists (Derrida, Paul de Man, Hartman, Lyotard).

For formalism in general, the *meaning* of a text or an artwork is found in the formal relationships between elements of the work itself. A valid interpretation of the work, therefore, involves the elucidation of these formal structures. In many cases, this was (and is) coupled with an aggressive denial of the importance or significance of the maker's original intention. Indeed, the artist or the author or the subject was pronounced "dead"—totally irrelevant to the work—as in Barthes's famous "death of the author" ("amputate the art from the artist"). Language itself replaced the author as the producer of the text, and structural analysis (in its original, neo-, or post-forms) became the only sure method of artistic interpretation. The "death of the subject" meant as well the death of the subject's original intention as a source of valid interpretation, and "What comes after the subject?" became the new rallying call.

In the rather influential American New Criticism, this view was expressed most forcefully by Monroe Beardsley and William Wimsatt, Jr. In their now famous essay, "The Intentional Fallacy," they conclude bluntly that the *maker's intention* is "neither available nor desirable as a standard for judging the success of a work" of art.[10] It was to the *artwork itself* that the interpreter and critic must essentially look. After all, they maintained, how can you know the intent of the artwork if it is not expressed in the art itself? Where else could you possibly look? Intentions that don't make it into the artwork might be interesting, but they are not, by definition, part of the artwork. And thus interpretation should center first and foremost on elements intrinsic to the artwork considered as a whole in itself.

Similar formalist theories of art were put forth in music by Eduard Hanslick (*The Beautiful in Music*), who maintained that the meaning of music was in its internal forms (melody, rhythm, harmony); and in the visual arts by Roger Fry (*Vision and Design*) and Clive Bell (*Art*), who both maintained that the nature and meaning of art was to be found in its "significant form" (Cézanne, for both of them, being the great exemplar).

In all of these versions of formalism, the locus and meaning of art is *not* in the intention of the artist, nor does it lie in what the artwork might *represent*, nor what it might *express*. Rather, the nature and meaning of art lies in the formal or structural relationship of the elements manifested in the artwork itself. And thus *valid* interpretation consists primarily in the elucidating of these forms and structures.

ART IS IN THE VIEWER

As the modern world of the Enlightenment and its Romantic rebellion gave way to the postmodern world, yet another extremely influential trend in art and literary criticism emerged. Just as formalist theories killed the artist and centered solely on the artwork, this new trend further killed the artwork itself and centered solely on . . . the viewer of the art.

For these various theories of "reception and response," the meaning of art is not found in the author's original intention, nor is it found in any specific features of the artwork itself. Rather, these theories maintain, since the only way we actually get to know a work of art is by viewing it (looking, listening, reading), then the primary locus of the meaning of the artwork can only be found in the *responses* of the viewers themselves.

Thus, according to this view, the nature and meaning of art is to be found in the history of the reception and response to the artwork; and likewise, a *valid* interpretation of the artwork consists in an analysis of these responses (or the cumulative history of these responses). As Passmore summarizes it, "The proper point of reference in discussing works of art is an interpretation it sets going in an audience; that interpretation—or the class of such interpretations—is the work of art, whatever the artist had in mind in creating it. Indeed, the interpreter, not the artist, creates the work."[11]

These theories trace much of their lineage to the work of Martin Heidegger, whose hermeneutic philosophy broke with the traditional conception of truth as an unchanging and objective set of facts, and replaced it with the notion of the *historicity* of truth: human beings do not have an unchanging *nature* so much as a changing *history*, and thus what we call "truth" is, in important ways, historically situated. Moreover, we come to understand the historicity of truth not so much through scientific empiricism but rather through *interpretation* (through "hermeneutics"), just as, if you and I want to understand each other, we must interpret what we are saying to each other ("What do you mean by that? Oh, I see"). Interpretation lies at the very heart of the historicity of truth.

Heidegger's hermeneutic philosophy has had an immense influence on art and literary theory, principally through two major students of his work: Hans-Georg Gadamer and Jacques Derrida. We briefly mentioned Derrida in connection with structuralist and poststructuralist theories, which locate the meaning of a text in chains of formal signifiers (and according to "poststructuralism," the chains of signifiers are endlessly "sliding"). Gadamer's influence has been equally widespread; he is now arguably the foremost theoretician of aesthetics.

For Gadamer, even a "purely" aesthetic event, such as looking at an abstract painting, is not merely a simple sensory occasion. The moment we start to ask what the painting means, or how it affects us, or what it might be saying—the moment the mute stare gives way to meaning— then we are inexorably stepping out of the "merely sensory" and into language and history. We are stepping into the linguistic world, which itself can only be understood by *interpretation*: What does that *mean*? And all meaning exists in history; that is, all meaning is marked by historicity. What a painting means to us, today, will be different from what that painting means to, say, people a thousand years from now (if it means anything at all). In other words, for these theorists, we cannot isolate meaning from the ongoing sweep of history.

The work of art, accordingly, exists in this historical stream, which brings forth new receptions, elicits new responses, gives new interpretations, unfolds new meanings as it flows. And, according to this view, the artwork is, so to speak, the sum total of its particular historical stream. The artwork is not something that exists by itself, outside of history, isolated and self-regarding, existing only because it looks at itself; rather, the only way we know the artwork is by viewing and interpreting it, and it is those interpretations, grounded in history, that constitute the overall art.

And So *Where*, Exactly, Is Art?

We have seen that the major theories of art disagree sharply on the nature, locus, and meaning of art. Intentional theories locate art in the original intent or feeling or vision of the maker. Formalist theories locate the meaning of art in the relationships among elements of the artwork itself. Reception-and-response theories place the nature and meaning of art in the viewer. And symptomatic theories place the locus of art in larger currents operating in a mostly unconscious fashion in the artist and viewer alike.

In fact, the whole of art theory can be seen as a spirited attempt to decide exactly what the *locus* of art is, and therefore where we can find or locate the *meaning* of an artwork—and thus, finally, how we can develop valid *interpretations* of that art. In short: What and where is art?

And I am saying, the nature and meaning of art is thoroughly *holonic*. Like every other entity in the universe, art is holonic in its nature, its locus, its structure, its meaning, and its interpretation. Any specific artwork is a holon, which means that it is a whole that is simultaneously a part of numerous other wholes. The artwork exists in contexts within contexts within contexts, endlessly.

Further—and this is the crucial point—*each context will confer a different meaning on the artwork*, precisely because, as we have seen, all meaning is context-bound: change the context, you elicit a different meaning.

Thus, all of the theories that we have discussed—representational, intentional, formalist, reception-and-response, symptomatic—are basically correct; they are all true; they are all pointing to a *specific context* in which the artwork subsists, and without which the artwork could not exist, contexts that therefore are genuinely *constitutive* of the art itself—that is, part of the very being of the art.

And the only reason those theories disagree with each other is that each of them is trying to make its own context the only real or important context: paradigmatic, primal, central, privileged. Each theory is trying to make its context the only context worth serious consideration.

But the holonic nature of reality—contexts within contexts forever—means that each of these theories is part of a nested series of truths. Each is true when highlighting its own context, but false when it tries to deny reality or significance to other existing contexts. And an integral art and literary theory—covering the nature, meaning, and interpretation of art—will of necessity be a holonic theory: concentric circles of nested truths and interpretations.

The study of holons is the study of nested truths. And now we can see exactly how postmodernist deconstructionists took a wrong turn at holons and got hopelessly, helplessly lost. They looked clearly at holonic space and then, rather like Bataille, went properly insane: reality consists not of nested truths but of nested lies, deceptions within deceptions forever, precisely the features of a psychotic break. They have it exactly backwards, the photographic negative of a reality they no longer trust. And once having stepped through that inverting mirror and into Alice's Wonderland, nothing is ever what it seems, which leaves only the ego to impose its will, and nothing real to resist it—leaves the nausea of nihilism and narcissism to define a world that no longer cares.

Not nested lies, but nested truths. A comprehensive art and literary theory can more gracefully, more accurately, and more beautifully be viewed as concentric circles of enveloping truths and interpretations. We can now very briefly follow the story of art from its original impulse forward, honoring and including each of the truths in this development that is envelopment, as each whole becomes part of another whole, endlessly, miraculously, inevitably.

5

Integral Art and Literary Theory

PART 2

We can now very briefly follow the story of art from its original impulse forward, honoring and including each of the truths in this development that is envelopment, as each whole becomes part of another whole, endlessly, miraculously, inevitably. . . .

(And who knows? Proceeding thus, searching for the source of art, we might eventually find ourselves residing in the eye of Spirit, the Beauty in the eye of the Beholder, delivered unto a luminous Kosmos that, in its entirety, is the extraordinary Artwork of our own highest Self—so that the final meaning of Art will reveal its own Original Face, exquisite to infinity, obvious in the ordinary, the entire canvas of the Kosmos as its radiant vision, always and even now.)

THE PRIMAL ART HOLON

WITHOUT IN ANY WAY ignoring the other numerous contexts that will determine the artwork, in many important ways we can date its beginning with an event in the mind and being of the artist: an interior perception, feeling, impulse, concept, idea, or vision. From exactly where, nobody knows, the creative impulse bubbles up. Many contexts no doubt precede it; many more will follow. But let us start the story here, with the primal artistic perception or impulse, and let us call that the *primal holon* of art.

This primal holon may in fact represent something in the external world (the basis of imitative or representational theories). But it might also express an interior state, whether a feeling (expressionism) or an idea (conceptualism). Around that primal holon, like the layers of a pearl growing around an original grain of sand, will develop contexts within contexts of subsequent holons, as the primal holon inexorably enters the historical stream that will govern so much of its subsequent fate.

The primal artistic holon itself, even when it first bubbles up in the consciousness of the artist, nonetheless arrives into numerous contexts that *already* exist, contexts into which the primal holon is instantly subsumed: perhaps unconscious structures in the artist; perhaps structures in the artist's culture; perhaps larger currents in the universe at large, about which the artist might know little. And yet those larger holons have their fingerprints all over the primal holon from the very first instant of its existence: they indelibly stamp the primal holon with the codes of the larger currents.

But the theories that focus on the primal holon are, of course, the expressivist theories. For these theories in general, the *meaning* of art is the primal holon—the original intent of the maker—and therefore a correct *interpretation* is a matter of the accurate *reconstruction* and *recovery* of that original intent and meaning, that primal holon. Thus, we are to *understand* the artwork by trying to accurately understand the original meaning that the artwork had for the artist.

And this makes sense to most of us. After all, when we read Plato's *Republic*, we want to know, as best we can, what Plato originally meant. Most of us do not want to know what the *Republic* means to my grandmother; we want to know what it means for Plato.

In this task of recovering the original meaning, these *traditional hermeneutic theories* do indeed rely, to some extent, on other contexts. They might look at other works by the same maker (which often show a pattern that helps to explain individual works); at other works in the same genre (which might highlight originality); and at the expectations of the original audience (e.g., the fools in Shakespeare's comedies are always jousting and punning in ways that most moderns find tiresome and dull, but Elizabethans—the original audience—enjoyed and expected comedies to have this structure, and thus this expectation would be a part of the original intention of the author, which helps us to understand and interpret it). All of these other contexts will help the interpreter determine and recover the original meaning of the artwork (the text, the book, the painting, the composition). But, for these intentional theories, all of these contexts are, in a sense, secondary to—and none of them constitutive of—the primal holon.

No doubt that attempting to "reconstruct" and "recover" this original intent is a very delicate, difficult, and in some ways endless task. And it might even be that this attempt is, in the last analysis, more of an ideal than a pragmatic possibility. But this is no warrant to simply dismiss this original intent as if it did not exist at all, which is what virtually every subsequent theory of art and its interpretation has done. Art certainly cannot be limited and confined to the primal holon; but neither can it ignore it. And the idealized attempt to recover as much of the original, primal holon as is pragmatically possible: this will always be part of an integral theory of interpretation in general—including, of course, art and literary interpretation as well.

Nonetheless, the attempt to pin art down to just the primal holon and its expression is precisely where the trouble begins. All of the definitions that attempt to limit art to the original intention and its expression have failed in very significant ways. The reason, of course, is that the primal holon is a whole that is *also* a part of other wholes, and so the story unavoidably continues. . . .

For example, even if we agree that art is found first and foremost in the original intention of the artist, it is now widely acknowledged, as we were saying, that the artist can have unconscious intentions: patterns in his or her work that can be clearly spotted by others but might not be consciously known to the artists themselves.

UNCONSCIOUS INTENTIONS

No doubt, as the primal holon bubbles up, it bubbles up through structures of the artist's own being, some of which are unconscious. Freud himself was perhaps the first to dwell on these unconscious structures and their influence on the actual features of the artwork, most famously in his essay on Leonardo da Vinci (an essay which, interestingly, Freud always said was his own favorite work). As Freud points out, Leonardo da Vinci had suggestively recalled, "This writing distinctly about the vulture seems to be my destiny, because among the first recollections of my infancy it seemed to me that as I lay in my cradle a vulture came to me and opened my mouth with its tail and struck me many times with its tail inside my lips."[1]

In the psychoanalytic interpretation, this fantasy is a key to both Leonardo's infancy and the origins of his homosexuality (a fellatio fantasy), and is therefore also a key to interpreting much of his artistic endeavors. That is, whatever primal artistic holons that might well up in Leonardo's psyche, they well up through the structures of his unconscious desires. The primal holon therefore inexorably arrives on the scene already set in contexts of this unconscious wish. And thus, if the meaning of art is to be found in the original intent of the maker, then some of this meaning is unconscious because some of the intentions are unconscious. It is, therefore, the job of the psychoanalytic interpreter to discern and elucidate these deeper contexts, these background holons, within which the primal holon arises.

And that is surely true enough, and surely part of the overall story we wish to tell. Although, equally surely, it is not the entire story, nor is it the entire locus, of the artwork. To begin with, once we acknowledge that there are unconscious structures in the artist (as well as viewer and critic), we are immediately allowed to ask, What is the actual nature and extent of this unconscious? Are there no other unconscious structures besides the narrowly Freudian? When we look into the depths of the psyche of men and women, is sex and aggression really all that we will find?

The answer, of course, is no. Subsequent psychological and sociological research has demonstrated a plethora of largely unconscious structures, patterns, codes, and regimes, each of which has a hand in governing the shape of our conscious intentions. We already mentioned several of these background structures, these deeper and wider holons: linguistic, economic, cultural, historical, and so on. It is these background holons, these wider contexts, to which all of the "symptomatic theorists" look in order to discern deeper and wider meanings in the particular artwork, because, once again, context determines meaning, and thus wider contexts will disclose deeper meanings, meanings and patterns perhaps not obvious in the artist or the artwork alone.

THE SPECTRUM OF CONSCIOUSNESS

I will return to these larger symptomatic theories in a moment. Let me first point out that, even in the "individual psyche," research has unearthed, in addition to the Freudian unconscious, several important *levels* of usually unconscious contexts. In particular, the schools of existential-humanistic and transpersonal psychology—the so-called "third" and "fourth" forces of psychology (in addition to behaviorism and psychoanalysis)—have discovered and confirmed numerous "realms of the human unconscious," realms that are in many cases the very key to understanding conscious life.

The human being, like all entities in existence, is a holon, a compound individual, in this case composed of physical, emotional, mental, existential, and spiritual or transpersonal dimensions. All of those structures serve as background contexts through which our surface consciousness moves. And just as an unconscious "Freudian" structure can color and shape our conscious intentions, so any of these deeper realms can ride hidden in the Trojan horse of our everyday awareness.

We need not go into all the detailed evidence; for our simpler purposes it is enough to note that, according to transpersonal psychology, there is in fact a *spectrum of consciousness*, reaching from the isolated and individual ego, at one end, to states of "unity consciousness" and "spiritual union" at the other. This overall spectrum of consciousness consists of at least a dozen levels of awareness, each with a very recognizable structure (including instinctual, Freudian, linguistic, cognitive, existential, and spiritual levels).

The essential point is that any or all of these dimensions can contribute—consciously or unconsciously—to the artist's overall intention which eventually finds expression in the artwork. And thus a familiarity with the spectrum of consciousness would give the discerning critic a palette of interpretations quite beyond the shallower Freudian array, by elucidating deeper and wider contexts of awareness.

Thus, part of an integral or holonic theory of art interpretation and literary criticism would include all of these various realms of the human unconscious as they manifest in the intention of the primal holon and its subsequent public display (the artwork and its reception). Human intentionality is indeed "onionlike": holons within holons of intentionality in an extraordinary spectrum of consciousness. (I will later return to this spectrum of intentionality and give several examples of how it can effectively guide interpretation.)

The various schools of intentionality—covering the entire spectrum of consciousness—are most definitely on the trail of a very important aspect of the nature and meaning of art. But again, these theories— whether focusing on conscious or unconscious realms—are still, by their very nature, partial and limited. They tend to ignore the technical and formal features of the artwork itself, and thus cannot account for, say, the importance of the structure of musical harmony and melody, or plot structure and function in a narrative, or the technical applications of types of paint, or the structural conditions for various artworks, and so forth.

For all these reasons and more, many theorists began to look more closely at the actual structure and function of the artwork itself, divorced from either maker or viewer. For the fact is, when the artist attempts to express the primal holon in an actual work of art, that primal holon runs smack into the material conditions of its medium: the rock of a sculpture, the actual paint and canvas of a painting, the various instruments and their players in a musical composition, the actual grammar and syntax of a narrative: the primal holon is instantly clothed in a medium that has its own structure, follows its own rules, imposes its own limits, announces its own nature. The primal holon is now a part of another whole, the overall artwork itself.

THE ARTWORK HOLON

Art theories have historically gone back and forth in a wave of action and reaction between two extremes: trying to determine the artist's original meaning, or, tiring of that seemingly *endless* task, looking elsewhere for a way to interpret the meaning of art. The most common is to focus on the artwork itself, that is, on the *public piece of artwork* (the painting, the book, the performed play, the musical), which we will simply call the *artwork holon*.

The great strength—and great weakness—of this approach is that it intensely focuses on only one context: the public artwork as it is immediately perceived. All other contexts are bracketed or basically ignored: the maker's intentions (conscious or unconscious), the historical set and setting, the original audience expectations, the history of reception and response—all are bracketed, removed from the story, thrown out of court when it comes to judging the success or failure of the artwork.

These theorists have their reasons for these exclusions. How are we to know, they ask, what the artist's original intentions for the artwork are, except to look at the artwork itself? If the artist had intentions that didn't make it into the artwork, well then, the artist has simply failed in that regard; intentions that didn't make it into the artwork are, by definition, not part of that artwork, so they can and should be ignored (to assume otherwise is the "intentional fallacy"). And why should we even ask the artist what he or she *really* meant? Just as you and I are not always the best interpreters of our own actions (as our friends will attest), so artists are not always the best interpreters of their own works. Thus, in all cases, we must simply look to the artwork itself, and judge it on its own terms, as a whole unto itself: the artwork holon.

And that is what all artwork theories do. They judge the art as an intrinsic whole, and the meaning of the artwork is to be found in the *relationships among the elements or features of the work itself* (i.e., the relations among the "sub-holons" constituting the artwork). We already looked briefly at many variations on this theme: formalism, structuralism, neo-structuralism, post-structuralism, New Criticism—applied to music, visual arts, poetics, linguistics, and literary theory.

However limited, the merits of this approach are nonetheless obvious. There are indeed features of artworks that stand, relatively, on their own. True, the artwork is actually a whole that is *also* a part of other wholes. But the "wholeness" aspect of any holon can indeed be focused on; the wholeness aspect is very real, very genuine. Various formalist and structuralist theories have rightly gained a permanent foothold in the repertoire of legitimate interpretive tools precisely by focusing on the wholeness aspect of any holon. Doing so, such theorists have offered a list of qualities that many find valuable in the artwork: criteria such as coherence, completeness, harmony of elements within the whole; but also uniqueness, complexity, ambiguity, intensity.

All of which tell us something interesting about the artwork holon itself; none are to be excluded. Still, we cannot in the last analysis forget that every whole is also a part; it exists in contexts within contexts within contexts, each of which will confer a new and different meaning on the original whole, a meaning that is *not* obvious, and *cannot* be found, by looking at the individual holon itself.

Imagine, for example, you are watching a game of cards, perhaps poker. All of the cards are being used according to rules, but the interesting fact is that none of these rules are written on the cards themselves—none of the rules can be found anywhere on the cards. Each card is actually set in a larger context which governs its behavior and meaning, and thus only by taking a larger perspective can the actual rules and meanings of the card in that game be discovered and correctly interpreted. Focusing merely on the card itself will completely miss the rules and meanings it is obeying.

Just so, the very *content* of an artwork itself will be determined in part by the various *contexts* in which the primal holon arises and in which the artwork holon exists. Here's a quick example, which pinpoints the inadequacy of focusing on the artwork holon alone:

A Pair of Worn Shoes

In his essay entitled "The Origin of the Work of Art," Heidegger interprets a painting of a pair of shoes by Van Gogh in order to suggest that art can disclose truth. And however much we might agree with that general conclusion, Heidegger's path, in this particular case, is a prime example of what can go so horribly wrong when holonic contexts are ignored.

The painting to which Heidegger refers is simply of a pair of rather worn shoes, facing forward, laces undone, and that is pretty much all; there are no other discernible objects or items. Heidegger assumes they are a pair of peasant shoes, and he tells us that he can, with reference to the painting alone, penetrate to the essence of its message:

> There is nothing surrounding this pair of peasant shoes in or to which they might belong, only an undefined space. There are not even clods from the soil of the field or the path through it sticking to them, which might at least hint at their employment. A pair of peasant shoes and nothing more. And yet.

And yet, Heidegger will reach deeply into the form of the artwork, all by itself, and render the essence of its meaning:

> From the dark opening of the worn insides of the shoes the toilsome tread of the worker stands forth. In the stiffly solid heaviness of the shoes there is the accumulated tenacity of her slow trudge through the far-spreading and ever-uniform furrows of the field, swept by a raw wind. On the leather there lies the dampness and saturation of the soil. Under the soles there slides the loneliness of the field-path as the evening declines. In the shoes there vibrates the silent call of the earth, its quiet gift of the ripening corn and its enigmatic self-refusal in the fallow desolation of the wintry field. This equipment is pervaded by uncomplaining anxiety about the certainty of bread, the wordless joy of having once more withstood want, the trembling before the advent of birth and shivering at the surrounding menace of

> death. This equipment belongs to the *earth* and it is protected in
> the *world* of the peasant woman. From out of this protected
> belonging the equipment itself rises to its resting-in-self.[2]

That is a beautiful interpretation, beautifully expressed, lodging itself
carefully in the details of the painting, which makes it all the sadder that
virtually every statement in it is wildly inaccurate.

To begin with, these are Van Gogh's shoes, not some peasant woman's. He was by then a town and city dweller, not a toiler in the fields;
under its soles there are no corn fields, no slow trudging through uniform furrows, no dampness of the soil and no loneliness of the field-
path. Not an ounce, nary a trace, of enigmatic self-refusal in the fallow
of the desolation of the wintry field can be found. "Van Gogh's painting
is the disclosure of what the equipment, the pair of peasant shoes, *is* in
truth," exclaims Heidegger.

Perhaps, but Heidegger has not come near that truth at all. Instead—
and while not in any way ignoring the relevant features of the artwork
holon itself—we must go outside the artwork, into larger contexts, to
determine more of its meaning.

Let us go first to the maker's intent, as Van Gogh himself described
it, or rather, talked generally about the circumstances leading up to the
painting. Paul Gauguin shared a room with Van Gogh in Arles, in 1888,
and he noticed that Vincent kept a pair of badly worn shoes which
seemed to have a very important meaning for him. Gauguin begins the
story:

> In the studio was a pair of big hob-nailed shoes, all worn and
> spotted with mud; he made of it a remarkable still life painting.
> I do not know why I sensed that there was a story behind this
> old relic, and I ventured one day to ask him if he had some
> reason for preserving with respect what one ordinarily throws
> out for the rag-picker's basket.[3]

And so Vincent begins to recount the tale of these worn-out shoes.
"My father," he said, "was a pastor, and at his urging I pursued theological studies in order to prepare for my future vocation. As a young pastor
I left for Belgium one fine morning, without telling my family, to preach
the gospel in the factories, not as I had been taught but as I understood
it myself. These shoes, as you see, have bravely endured the fatigue of
that trip."

But why exactly were these shoes so important to Vincent? Why had he carried them with him for so long, beaten and worn as they were? It turns out, Gauguin continues, that "Preaching to the miners in the Borinage, Vincent undertook to nurse a victim of a fire in the mine. The man was so badly burned and mutilated that the doctor had no hope for his recovery. Only a miracle, he thought, could save him. Van Gogh tended him forty days with loving care and saved the miner's life."

It must have been an extraordinary forty days, deeply etched on Van Gogh's soul. A man so badly burned, so horribly in pain, that the doctor had abandoned him to certain and gruesome death. For more than a month, Vincent at his side. And then a vision came upon Vincent, a vision that he disclosed to his friend Gauguin, a vision that explains why this incident was so important to him.

Gauguin begins at the beginning: "When we were together in Arles, both of us mad, in continual struggle for beautiful colors, I adored red; where could one find a perfect vermilion? He, with his yellowish brush, traced on the wall which suddenly became violet:

I am whole in Spirit
I am the Holy Spirit

"In my yellow room—a small still life: violet that one. Two enormous wornout misshapen shoes. They were Vincent's shoes. Those that he took one fine morning, when they were new, for his journey on foot from Holland to Belgium. The young preacher had just finished his theological studies in order to be a minister like his father. He had gone off to the mines to those whom he called his brothers. . . .

"Contrary to the teaching of his wise Dutch professors, Vincent had believed in a Jesus who loved the poor; and his soul, deeply pervaded by charity, sought the consoling words and sacrifice for the weak, and to combat the rich. Very decidedly, Vincent was already mad."

"Vincent was already mad"—Gauguin repeats this several times, thick with irony; that we all should be graced enough to touch such madness!

Gauguin then tells of the explosion in the mine: "Chrome yellow overflowed, a terrible fiery glow. . . . The creatures who crawled at that moment . . . said 'adieu' to life that day, goodbye to their fellow-men. . . . One of them horribly mutilated, his face burnt, was picked up by Vincent. 'However,' said the company doctor, 'the man is done for, unless by a miracle. . . .'

"Vincent," Gauguin continues, "believed in miracles, in maternal care. The madman (decidedly he was mad) sat up, keeping watch forty days, at the dying man's bedside. Stubbornly he kept the air from getting into his wounds and paid for the medicines. A comforting priest (decidedly, he was mad). The patient talked. The mad effort brought a dead Christian back to life."

The scars on the man's face—this man resurrected by a miracle of care—looked to Vincent exactly like the scars from a crown of thorns. "I had," Vincent says, "in the presence of this man who bore on his brow a series of scars, a vision of the crown of thorns, a vision of the resurrected Christ."

At this point in telling Gauguin the story, Vincent picks up his brush and says, referring to the "resurrected Christ": "And I, Vincent, I painted him."

Gauguin finishes: "Tracing with his yellow brush, suddenly turned violet, Vincent cried:

I am the Holy Spirit
I am whole in Spirit

"Decidedly, this man was mad."

Psychoanalysis, no doubt, would have some therapeutic interpretations for all of this. But psychoanalytic interpretations, relatively true as they might be, do not in themselves touch any deeper "realms of the human unconscious," such as the existential or the spiritual and transpersonal. And thus, as I earlier pointed out, if we look to the school of transpersonal psychology for a finer and more comprehensive account of the deeper dimensions of human awareness, we find a compelling amount of evidence that human beings have access to higher or deeper states of consciousness quite beyond the ordinary egoic modes—a spectrum of consciousness.

And at the upper reaches of the spectrum of consciousness—in the higher states of consciousness—individuals consistently report an awareness of being one with the all, or identical with spirit, or whole in spirit, and so on. The attempt of shallower psychologies, such as psychoanalysis, to merely pathologize *all* of these higher states has simply not held up to further scrutiny and evidence. Rather, the total web of cross-cultural evidence strongly suggests that these deeper or higher states are potentials available to all of us, so that, as it were, "Christ consciousness"—spiritual awareness and union—is available to each and every one of us.

A transpersonal psychologist would thus suggest that, whatever other interpretations we wish to give to Vincent's vision, the overall evidence most clearly suggests that it was very probably a true vision of the radical potential in all of us. These higher states and visions are sometimes intermixed with personal pathologies or neuroses, but the states themselves are not pathological in their essence; quite the contrary, researchers consistently refer to them as extraordinary states of *well-being*. Thus, Vincent's central vision itself most likely was not pathological, not psychotic, not madness at all—which is why Gauguin keeps poking fun at those who would think that way: decidedly, he was mad. Which means, decidedly, he was plugged into a reality that we should all be so fortunate to see.

Thus, when Vincent said he saw the resurrected Christ, that is exactly what he meant, and that is very likely exactly what he saw. And thus he carried with him, as a dusty but dear reminder, the shoes in which this vision occurred.

And so, you see, an important part of the primal meaning of the painting of these shoes—not the only meaning, but a primal meaning—is very simple: these are the shoes in which Vincent nursed Jesus, the Jesus in all of us.

THE VIEWER HOLON

Whatever one might think of that interpretation, one thing is certainly obvious: a merely formal or artwork approach—Heidegger's, for example—would miss important meanings of Van Gogh's painting. Many moderns will stop short of my transpersonal interpretation—would it help if I pointed out that Gauguin finishes his account with this?: "And Vincent took up his palette again; silently he worked. Beside him was a white canvas. I began his portrait. I too had the vision of a Jesus preaching kindness and humility."

Are we moderns too jaded for this? Ah, well, whether we accept this transpersonal aspect of the interpretation, we can easily accept the rest of the account—the mining accident, nursing the man, and so on—as providing some very crucial contexts which confer various added meanings to the artwork holon itself (since meaning, as always, is context-bound).

Thus, the various artwork approaches (which are true but partial) suffer by overlooking the primal holon (the maker's intent in all its levels and dimensions). But they also attempt to ignore the viewer's response. These theories consequently cannot account at all for the role that interpretation itself plays in helping to *constitute* the overall nature of the art.

The artist did not parachute to earth, antiseptic and isolated and hermetically sealed. Both art and artist exist only in a stream of history, and thus the primal holon itself *never* arrives in a *tabula rasa*, a clear and blank slate formed only by the artist's isolated intention. Rather, the primal holon itself is shaped, *even as it is forming*, by a cultural background. And this cultural background is historical through and through—it is itself unfolding in history.

Thus, without in any way denying any of the other meanings of the artwork, from the primal intention of the maker to the formal elements of the artwork itself, nonetheless the fact remains: when I view the artwork, it has *meaning for me*. Each and every time a viewer sees a work and attempts to understand it, there is what Gadamer so unerringly calls a "fusion of horizons"—as I would also put it, a *new holon emerges*, which itself is a new context and thus carries new meaning.

Obviously, *the* meaning of an artwork does not reside solely in my particular response to it. Other people might have different responses. But the general point is that the meaning of an artwork cannot be divorced from the overall impact it has on viewers. And in a stronger version, "the viewer" simply means the entire cultural background, without which meaning would not and could not exist in the first place. This great intersubjective background, this cultural background, provides the ocean of contexts in which art, artist, and viewer alike necessarily float.

Even when the artist is first starting to work on a piece, he has somebody in mind; some sort of viewer looms in his awareness, however briefly or fleetingly; the *intersubjective* background is already a *context* within which his subjective intentions arise. The viewer response is thus *already* at work in shaping the art. The cultural background of interpretations is *already* a part of the very makeup of the artwork. And as the artwork goes public, it will enter a stream of further historical interpretations, each of which will form yet another layer in that temporal and historical pearl. And each new, emerging, historical context will confer a new meaning on the pearl, a new layer to the pearl which will in fact be an intrinsic part of the pearl itself, a whole that becomes part of yet other wholes and is changed in the process itself.

To give a crude example, think of the controversy today surrounding Columbus's voyage of 1492. If, as an example, we pretend that his voyage is an artwork, then what is the meaning of that art? Even a few decades ago, the meaning was something like this: Columbus was a rather brave fellow who, against some very difficult odds, made a perilous voyage that discovered the Americas—the New World—and thus brought culture and civilization to a fairly primitive and backward people.

Today, many people would give the meaning more like this: Columbus was a sexist, imperialist, lying, rather cowardly low-life, who went to the Americas on a voyage of plunder and pillage, in the process of which he brought syphilis and other scourges to the peace-loving peoples he everywhere met.

The meaning of the original artwork not only looks different, it *is* different, based on its subsequent history of reception and response. There is no way to avoid this *historicity*, this constitutive nature of interpretations. Subsequent contexts will confer new meaning on the art, because meaning is always and inevitably context-bound. And the viewer-response theories, in their various forms, focus on this history of response as constitutive of the art.

Thus, these reception-and-response theories maintain, as one critic explains it, that artistic meaning "is not a function of its genetic origin in an author's psyche [the primal holon], nor of purely intrinsic relations between the printed marks on a page [formalist theories], but of its reception in a series of readings constituting its history of influence, [which] stresses the temporality and historicity of understanding and interpretation."[4]

The partial truths of viewer response are surely part of any holonic theory of art and its interpretation. And yet, as with every other approach we have seen, the true but partial notions of viewer response, when they pretend to be the whole story, become not only distorting but outright comical.

And it is the *viewer-response theories*, coupled with the *symptomatic theories*, that have almost totally dominated the postmodern art scene—in theory and in practice—thus leading, as we earlier suggested, into increasingly narcissistic and nihilistic ramblings.

Start with viewer response.

THE WONDER OF BEING ME

Art critics have always been in a slightly awkward situation: the unkind word is "parasitic." Flaubert's view was typical: "Criticism occupies the lowest place in the literary hierarchy: as regards form, almost always; and as regards 'moral value' incontestably. It comes after rhyming games and acrostics which at least require a certain inventiveness."[5]

Couple this parasitism with another awkward fact: more than one social commentator has seen the baby boomer generation defined by a rampant narcissism, and if one item marks narcissism, it is a refusal to take a back seat to anybody.

From which it follows, art and literary theory in the hands of the boomers was going to be a wild affair. As parasitic collided with grandiose, something would have to give. The critic needed desperately to get out of the back seat and into the driver's seat.

The means for this glorious promotion were provided, as I began to suggest, by viewer-response theories coupled with symptomatic theories, together parading under the broad banner of poststructural postmodernism. If the nature and meaning of art lies solely in the viewer—"the interpreter, not the artist, creates the work"—and if only knowing interpretation is valid, then *voilà*: the critic alone creates all art.

And so it came about that the viewer response—that is to say, me—became the alpha and omega of art, which placed the critic—that is to say, me—in the very center of the creative act, not to mention at the very heart of the artworld. Thus Catherine Belsey in her *Critical Practice*: "No longer parasitic on an already given literary text, criticism constructs its object, produces the work."[6]

Which, of course, comes as news to most artists. The partial truths of viewer response became a platform from which the critic as sole creator gained (and still has) enormous currency. The embarrassing dilemma for this brand of postmodernism is that it completely and totally erases the artwork itself, and thus it ends up with a viewer-response theory that—oops!—has nothing to actually respond to.

If the artwork is not there to respond to, my ego alone remains. All of this has played precisely into the two trends, barely concealed, of extremist postmodernism—namely, nihilism and its hidden core of narcissism—as the more observant critics have recently begun to note. David Couzens Hoy points out that "freeing criticism from its object"—that is, erasing the artwork by emphasizing viewer response—"may open it up to all the possibilities of rich imaginations; yet if . . . there is now no truth of the matter, then nothing keeps it from succumbing to the sickness of the modern imagination's obsessive self-consciousness." Criticism thus becomes "only the critic's own ego-gratification." The culture of narcissism. "Then a sheer struggle for power ensues, and criticism becomes not latent but blatant aggression," part of "the emergent nihilism of recent times."[7]

These viewer-response theories, as I said, were particularly coupled with symptomatic theories—the most influential being Marxist, feminist, racist, and imperialist (postcolonial studies). The idea being, recall, that the meaning of art is found in the background social and economic contexts, contexts that are often masquerades for power and ideology, and contexts that therefore confer a specific meaning on art produced in those contexts, meanings that the knowing critic can pull out by highlighting and elucidating the particular background structures.

All true enough; and all terribly partial, lopsided, and distorted when taken in and by themselves. These views have promoted the notion, given currency by Foucault's early work, that truth itself is culturally relative and arbitrary, grounded in nothing but shifting historical tastes, or power and prejudice and ideology. Since truth is context-dependent, the argument goes, then it is completely relative to changing contexts. All truth is therefore *culturally constructed*—the social construction of gender, the social construction of the body, the social construction of pretty much everything—and because all truth is culturally constructed, there are and can be no universal truths.

Unfortunately, that view itself is claiming to be universally true. It is making a series of strong claims that it insists are true for *all* cultures (the relative nature of truth, the contextuality of claims, the social construction of all categories, the historicity of truth, and so on). This view thus claims that there is no universal truth at all—except for its own, which is universal and superior in a world where nothing is supposed to be universal or superior at all. It's not simply that this stance is hypocritical, concealing its own structures of power and domination; as an added bonus, the sheer narcissism of the stance once again rears its wonderful horrible head.

But *contextualism*, on which these symptomatic theories are all based, means neither arbitrary nor relativistic. It means determined by contexts that constrain the meaning. In other words, "context" means "constraints," not chaos. These contexts are neither arbitrary, subjective, idiosyncratic, merely constructed, nor radically relative, contrary to the abuse to which these theories have been subjected by extreme postmodernists.

Thus, even Foucault abandoned this "merely constructivist" approach to knowledge; he called it "arrogant." And even a foremost interpreter of Gadamer's very strong version of the historicity of truth could explain that "since no context is absolute, different lines of interpretation are possible. But this is not radical relativism, since not all contexts are equally appropriate or justifiable. . . . Contextualism demands justifying reasons for interpretations, and these reasons can be assumed to be as factual or 'objective' as any objectivist could produce. [Therefore] the choice of context or framework is far from arbitrary."[8]

Thus, meaning is indeed context-dependent (there are only holons!), but this means neither arbitrary nor relative, but firmly anchored in various contexts that *constrain* the meaning. And, of course, these contexts—whether in artist, artwork, viewer, or world at large—must themselves be real contexts, actually existing contexts. We are not allowed to arbitrarily dream up contexts; any ole context will not do. Rather, the context that is being used for interpretation must itself be justified according to the total web of available evidence.

And this puts many symptomatic theories at a great disadvantage, because too many of these approaches take a rather specific and often quite narrow context and make it the sole, dominating, hegemonic context within which all interpretations must be registered, whether imperialist, racist, capitalist, ecologist, feminist.

The results, as I said, have become more often than not quite comical, as minor truths are blown up to cosmic proportions. Alfred Kazin, recently called "the greatest literary critic in America" by *The New Republic*, reports on a typical scene, a session on Emily Dickinson organized by the Modern Language Association in 1989. The session was entitled "The Muse of Masturbation," and, says Kazin, "it was thronged," the point being "that the hidden strategy of Emily Dickinson's poetry is in her use of 'encoded images of clitoral masturbation to transcend sex-role limitations imposed by the nineteenth-century patriarchy.'" Kazin: "The basic idea was that Dickinson loaded her work with references to peas, crumbs, and flower buds in order to broadcast secret messages of forbidden onanistic delights to other female illuminati."[9]

It is one thing to expose a context; quite another to impose one. And too much of symptomatic theory is, alas, the imposition of the critic's pet context and ideology, bereft of confirming truth or evidence or justification (since, after all, there is no truth, only social constructions, why bother with evidence in the first place?).

And thus, from the uncontested fact that all truth is context-dependent, and that contexts are boundless, we have finally arrived, slipping and sliding, at the dizzy notion that all truths are merely subjective and relative, arbitrary and constructed. Truth is whatever you want, which leaves us nothing at all, except that shell of nihilism filled with the thickest of narcissism, a postmodern pastry from hell.

CONCLUSION

Let us realign the postmodern scene more adequately: Contexts are boundless means, not nested lies and arbitrary constructions depending only on egoic whim, but nested truths anchored in wider and deeper realities. The nihilistic and narcissistic spin is dismantled right at the beginning, and meaningless relativism gives way to richly textured contexts of value and meaning that ground sound interpretations. That all things are holons means that all things are contexts within contexts forever, and each context confers a new and genuine meaning upon the original holon itself.

Thus, to *locate* art is to situate it in its various contexts. Art includes, in its development that is envelopment:

- the primal holon or original intent of the maker, which may involve numerous levels of the psyche, both conscious and unconscious, reaching from the individual self to the transpersonal and spiritual dimensions (the spectrum of consciousness)
- the artwork holon itself, the public work materialized, in both its form and content
- the history of reception and response (the numerous viewer holons) that in important ways are constitutive of the overall work
- the wider contexts in the world at large, economic and technical and linguistic and cultural contexts, without which specific meanings could not be generated in the first place

Each of those are wholes that are parts of other wholes, and the whole confers meaning on the parts which the parts themselves do not possess. Each wider whole, each broader context, brings with it a new meaning, a new light in which to see the work, and thus constitute it anew.

Thus, any particular *meaning* of an artwork is simply the highlighting of a particular context. The *interpretation* of an artwork is the evoking and elucidating of that highlighted context. *Justifiable* interpretation means verifying that a particular context is indeed real and significant, a justification procedure that, like any other, involves a careful look at the total web of evidence.

And the *understanding* of an artwork means to hermeneutically enter, to actually enter as far as possible, the contexts determining the art, a "fusion of horizons"—the emergence of a new holon—in which the understanding of a work of art is simultaneously a process of self-understanding, liberating in its final effect. To understand the art I must to some degree enter its horizon, stretch my own boundaries, and thus grow in the process: the fusion of horizons is a broadening of self.

Thus, the validity criteria for justifiable interpretations of art and literature rest, in the last analysis, on what the critic thinks is the nature and locus of meaning in an artwork. And I am saying, it is holonic. There is no single correct interpretation because no holon has only one context. There are as many legitimate meanings as there are legitimate contexts, which does not lead to nihilism but cornucopia. This is far from arbitrary and relative, because while there is no one right interpretation, there are plenty of wrong ones (the necessary and important fallibilist criterion is most definitely part of artistic interpretation).[10]

"Interpretation is dependent upon the circumstances in which it occurs. . . . A strategy for finding a context may be essential to all interpretation as a condition for the very possibility of interpretation," points out Hoy.[11] Indeed so, but not just as a condition for the possibility of interpretation, but rather of existence itself: there are only holons.

An integral theory of art and literary interpretation is thus the multidimensional analysis of the various contexts in which—and by which—art exists and speaks to us: in the artist, the artwork, the viewer, and the world at large.[12] Privileging no single context, it invites us to be unendingly open to ever-new horizons, which broaden our own horizons in the process, liberating us from the narrow straits of our favorite ideology and the prison of our isolated selves.

CONTEMPLATING ART

Let me return to what art is finally all about. When I directly view, say, a great Van Gogh, I am reminded of what all superior art has in common: the capacity to simply take your breath away. To literally, actually, make you inwardly gasp, at least for that second or two when the art first hits you, or more accurately, first enters your being: you swoon a little bit, you are slightly stunned, you are open to perceptions that you had not seen before. Sometimes, of course, it is much quieter than that: the work seeps into your pores gently, and yet you are changed somehow, maybe just a little, maybe a lot; but you are changed.

No wonder that for the East and West alike, until just recent times, art was often associated with profound spiritual transformation. And I don't mean merely "religious" or "iconographic" art.

Some of the great modern philosophers, Schelling to Schiller to Schopenhauer, have all pinpointed a major reason for great art's power to transcend. When we look at any beautiful object (natural or artistic), we suspend all other activity, and we are simply aware, we only want to contemplate the object. While we are in this contemplative state, we do not want anything from the object; we just want to contemplate it; we want it to never end. We don't want to eat it, or own it, or run from it, or alter it: we only want to look, we want to contemplate, we never want it to end.

In that contemplative awareness, our own egoic grasping in time comes momentarily to rest. We relax into our basic awareness. We rest with the world as it is, not as we wish it to be. We are face to face with the calm, the eye in the center of the storm. We are not agitating to change things; we contemplate the object as it is. Great art has this power, this power to grab your attention and suspend it: we stare, sometimes awestruck, sometimes silent, but we cease the restless movement that otherwise characterizes our every waking moment.

It doesn't matter what the actual *content* of the art is; not for this. Great art grabs you, against your will, and then suspends your will. You are ushered into a quiet clearing, free of desire, free of grasping, free of ego, free of the self-contraction. And through that opening or clearing in your own awareness may come flashing higher truths, subtler revelations, profound connections. For a moment you might even touch eternity; who can say otherwise, when time itself is suspended in the clearing that great art creates in your awareness?

You just want to contemplate; you want it never to end; you forget past and future; you forget self and same. The noble Emerson: "These roses under my window make no reference to former roses or to better ones; they are for what they are; they exist with God today. There is no time for them. There is simply the rose; it is perfect in every moment of its existence. But man postpones or remembers; he does not live in the present, but with reverted eye laments the past, or heedless of the riches that surround him, stands on tiptoe to foresee the future. He cannot be happy and strong until he too lives with nature in the present, above time."[13]

Great art suspends the reverted eye, the lamented past, the anticipated future: we enter with it into the timeless present; we are with God today, perfect in our manner and mode, open to the riches and the glories of a realm that time forgot, but that great art reminds us of: not by its content, but by what it does in us: suspends the desire to be elsewhere. And thus it undoes the agitated grasping in the heart of the suffering self, and releases us—maybe for a second, maybe for a minute, maybe for all eternity—releases us from the coil of ourselves.

That is exactly the state that great art pulls us into, no matter what the actual content of the art itself—bugs or Buddhas, landscapes or abstractions, it doesn't matter in the least. In this particular regard—from this particular context—great art is judged by its capacity to take your breath away, take your self away, take time away, all at once.

And whatever we mean by the word "spirit"—let us just say, with Tillich, that it involves for each of us our ultimate concern—it is in that simple awestruck moment, when great art enters you and changes you, that spirit shines in this world just a little more brightly than it did the moment before.

Take it one step further: What if we could somehow manage to see *everything* in the entire universe as being exquisitely beautiful, like the finest piece of great art? What if we right now saw every single thing and event, without exception, as an object of extraordinary beauty?

Why, we would be momentarily frozen in the face of that vision; all of our grasping and avoiding would come quickly to rest; we would be released from the self-contraction and ushered into the choiceless contemplation of all that is. Just as a beautiful object or artwork momentarily suspends our will, so the contemplation of the universe as an object of beauty would open us to the choiceless awareness of that universe, not as it should be or might be or could be, but simply as it is.

Could it then be possible, just possible, that when the beauty of all things without exception is perceived, we are actually standing directly in the eye of Spirit, for which the entire Kosmos is an object of Beauty, just as it is, precisely because the entire Kosmos is in fact the radiant Art of Spirit itself?

In this extraordinary vision, the entire Kosmos is the Artwork of your own highest Self in all its shining creativity, which is exactly why every object in the universe is in truth an object of radiant Beauty when perceived with the eye of Spirit.

And conversely: if you could right here, right now, actually see every single thing and event in the entire universe as an object of sheer Beauty, then you would of necessity be undone as ego and stand instead as Spirit. You would want nothing from the Kosmos at that moment except to contemplate its unending Beauty and Perfection. You would not want to run from the universe, or grasp it, or alter it at all: in that contemplative moment you will neither fear nor hope, nor move at all. You will want nothing whatsoever, except to Witness it all, contemplate it unendingly, you want it never to end. You are radically free of will, free from grasping, free from all mean motion and commotion. You are a center of pure and clear awareness, saturated in its Being by the utter Beauty of everything it contemplates.

Not a single particle of dust is excluded from this Beauty; no object whatsoever, no matter how "ugly" or "frightening" or "painful"—not a single thing is excluded from this contemplative embrace, for each and every thing is radically, equally, unendingly the brilliant radiance of Spirit. When you behold the primordial Beauty of every single thing in the universe, then you behold the glory of the Kosmos in the eye of Spirit, the I of Spirit, the radical I-I of the entire universe. You are full to infinity, radiant with the light of a thousand suns, and all is perfect just as it is, always and eternally, as you contemplate this, your greatest Artwork, the entire Kosmos, this thing of Beauty, this object of unending joy and bliss radiant in the Heart of all that arises.

Think of the most beautiful person you have ever seen. Think of the exact moment you looked into his or her eyes, and for a fleeting second you were paralyzed: you couldn't take your eyes off that vision. You stared, frozen in time, caught in that beauty. Now imagine that *identical* beauty radiating from every single thing in the entire universe: every rock, every plant, every animal, every cloud, every person, every object, every mountain, every stream—even the garbage dumps and broken dreams—every single one of them, radiating that beauty. You are quietly frozen by the gentle beauty of everything that arises around you. You are released from grasping, released from time, released from avoidance, released altogether into the eye of Spirit, where you contemplate the unending beauty of the Art that is the entire World.

That all-pervading Beauty is not an exercise in creative imagination.

It is the actual structure of the universe. That all-pervading Beauty is in truth the very nature of the Kosmos right now. It is not something you have to imagine, because it is the actual structure of perception in all domains. If you remain in the eye of Spirit, every object is an object of radiant Beauty. If the doors of perception are cleansed, the entire Kosmos is your lost and found Beloved, the Original Face of primordial Beauty, forever, and forever, and endlessly forever. And in the face of that stunning Beauty, you will completely swoon into your own death, never to be seen or heard from again, except on those tender nights when the wind gently blows through the hills and the mountains, quietly calling your name.

6

The Recaptured God

THE RETRO-ROMANTIC
AGENDA AND ITS LIABILITIES

Transpersonal psychology is the major school in psychology today that takes spiritual experience seriously. There are perhaps five major approaches in transpersonal psychology that are particularly influential: systems theory, altered (or discrete) states of consciousness, Stan Grof's holotropic model, various forms of Jungian psychology (including Michael Washburn's "neo-Jungian" view), and my own spectrum or integral approach. I maintain not only that the integral model incorporates the essentials of the other models, but that it includes many significant areas ignored by the others—and thus it can account for considerably more research and evidence.

In this and the next chapter we will explore this claim, dialoguing with each of the major theorists of these alternative models.

A BRIEF SUMMARY OF MY CONSCIOUSNESS MODEL

W E BEGIN WITH the work of Michael Washburn and his notion of the Dynamic Ground.[1] Washburn is a very clear and careful writer, whose formulations I have always appreciated, even when we disagree. I never fail to learn something interesting from his presentations, and I have always been a staunch supporter of his publications. It is therefore rather disappointing that he tends to misrepresent my overall model. Since this misunderstanding is fairly common, I will be as careful as I can in summarizing my view.

As explained in *Transformations of Consciousness* and *Brief History* [and most recently in *Integral Psychology*], the overall consciousness system (the Upper-Left quadrant) has, I believe, at least *three main components:* the basic levels, the developmental lines, and the self.

THE BASIC LEVELS OR WAVES

The basic levels are simply the basic levels in the spectrum of consciousness—matter to body to mind to soul to spirit. The basic levels are essentially the traditional Great Holarchy of Being (as presented by, say, Plotinus or Asanga or Aurobindo), refined with numerous contributions from the modern cognitive sciences and developmental psychology. In chapter 1, I explained that this overall spectrum can be divided and subdivided in many different but valid ways. In *The Atman Project,* I give seventeen basic levels or basic structures in the overall spectrum of consciousness, including: matter, sensation, perception, impulse, image, symbol, concept, rule, formal, vision-logic, psychic, subtle, causal, and nondual. I usually simplify this to nine or ten of the most central and most important basic structures, which are, I believe, the minimum that we need to adequately characterize the overall spectrum and its development. These are: sensorimotor, vital-emotional, representational, rule/role, formal, vision-logic, psychic, subtle, causal, and nondual.

I refer to these as the basic levels, structures, or waves of consciousness. Each of those terms implies something important. *Level* means that these are qualitatively different dimensions of being and consciousness. *Structure* means that they are relatively stable patterns. And *wave* indicates that, like the colors in a rainbow, these basic dimensions shade and grade into each other. The basic levels or waves are simply the basic colors in the spectrum of consciousness. As I said, this spectrum is sometimes simplified to *matter* (sensorimotor), *body* (vital-emotional), *mind* (rep, rule, formal, vision-logic), *soul* (psychic, subtle), and *spirit* (causal, nondual). And even that is sometimes simplified to just body, mind, and spirit (or gross, subtle, and causal). But for this presentation, I will use those nine or ten basic levels as the most important colors in the overall spectrum of consciousness.

One other item about the basic levels: they are relatively permanent or *enduring structures*. Once they emerge in development, they tend to remain in existence, even though they are often subsumed or incorporated in later waves.[2] Unlike many of the stages of the developmental lines, which are temporary, the developmental levels of consciousness are permanent acquisitions. Once they emerge, matter, body, mind, soul, and spirit are all enduring patterns in consciousness, and they form the basic levels through which the many developmental lines will pass: the basic waves in the river of life through which its many streams will flow.

THE DEVELOPMENTAL LINES OR STREAMS

Through the basic levels of consciousness, numerous different developmental lines progress. Some of the more important developmental lines include cognitive, moral, aesthetic, psychosexual, self-identity, worldviews, needs, motivation (and several others we will discuss later). Thus, for example, cognition can move from body (sensorimotor cognition) to mind (concrete and formal operational cognition) to soul (subtle and archetypal consciousness) to spirit (formless and nondual). Morals can develop from body (egocentric and preconventional impulses) to mind (conventional rules and postconventional meta-rules) to soul (saintly compassion) to spirit (nondual liberation). Likewise, one's sense of self-identity unfolds from body (the narcissistic bodyego) to mind (the pluralistic ego) to soul (the pure witness) to spirit (the nondual self), not in a rigid sequence but in flowing waves of consciousness. And so on.

Of course, those examples are using just four of the basic levels of the spectrum (body, mind, soul, and spirit), but you can easily expand that to the nine or ten basic waves through which each of the developmental streams flows. For example, you can do this for *worldviews* (e.g., archaic, magic, mythic, mental, existential, psychic, subtle, causal, and nondual; cf. Gebser); *self-needs* (e.g., physiological, safety, belongingness, self-esteem, self-actualization, self-transcendence into subtle, causal, nondual; cf. Maslow); *self-identity* (e.g., pleroma, uroboros, typhon, persona, ego, centaur, soul, spirit; cf. Loevinger); and so forth.[3] The point is that through some nine or ten basic waves pass some two dozen relatively independent developmental streams, and a comprehensive or integral model would attempt to take all of those facets of consciousness into account.

"Relatively independent" means that each of the developmental lines flows through the spectrum of consciousness in a fairly independent manner. *Thus, a person can be at a relatively high level of development in some lines, a medium level of development in others, and a low level in still others.* A substantial amount of research continues to confirm that each developmental line itself (cognitive, moral, psychosexual, etc.) tends to unfold in a sequential or stage-like manner. Nonetheless, because the lines themselves develop in a relatively independent fashion—some high, some medium, some low, with no overall sequence—there is absolutely nothing "linear" about overall development. Each person's growth through the spectrum of consciousness, with its many waves and streams, will be a radically unique and individual affair.

Whereas the basic levels of development tend to be relatively permanent or enduring (once they emerge they remain in existence), the stages in the lines of development tend to be relatively temporary or transitional. For example, as a person moves from moral stage 1 to 2 to 3 to 4 to 5, each of those stages is not so much incorporated into subsequent stages as replaced by subsequent stages. With the basic levels, if you have access to a relatively high level of consciousness (say, vision-logic), you still have *full access* to all the lower basic levels (including sensorimotor, images, symbols, concepts, and so on). But when you are at, say, moral stage 5, you do not have full access to moral stages 1, 2, or 3. A person acting from postconventional moral compassion does not simultaneously act from a narcissistic self-glorifying stance.[4] Those earlier stages are not incorporated but mostly replaced, as consciousness continues its ever-expanding growth and development.

THE SELF AND ITS FULCRUMS

Navigating all the various waves and streams is the *self-system* or *self-sense* (or just the *self*), which is the third major component. The self-system is, in many ways, the most important of the three, because it is "where the action is." I have suggested that the self-system is the locus of several crucial capacities and operations, including: *identification* (the locus of self-identity), *organization* (that which gives cohesiveness to the psyche), *will* (the locus of choice within the constraints of the present developmental level), *defense* (the locus of defense mechanisms, phase-specific and phase-appropriate, hierarchically organized), *metabolism* (the "digestion" of experience), and *navigation* (developmental choices).[5]

Because the self is the locus of identification, each time the self identifies with a basic level of consciousness, that identification generates (or is the support of) a corresponding series of developmental streams. Thus, for example, when the self identifies with preoperational thought (symbols and concepts), this supports a preconventional moral stance (Kohlberg), a set of safety needs (Maslow), and a protective self-sense (Loevinger). When higher basic structures emerge (say, concrete operational rules), then the self (barring arrest) will eventually switch its central identity to this higher and wider organization, and this will help to generate a new moral stance (conventional), a new set of self-needs (belongingness), a new self-sense (conformist persona), and so forth.[6]

As the self-system negotiates each basic wave in the unfolding spectrum of consciousness, it will switch from a narrower to a wider identity, and thus it undergoes a *fulcrum* or milestone in its own development. That is, each time the self rides a new wave of consciousness (each time it identifies with a new and wider basic structure), it will go through a process of (1) merger or fusion or embeddedness, (2) differentiation or transcendence or disembedding, and (3) incorporation or integration. This 1-2-3 process is a fulcrum of self-development, and there are as many fulcrums of self-development as there are basic structures to negotiate.

Thus, at any given level of development, the self starts out identified with (or in fusion with, or embedded in) the basic structure of that level. Its locus of identification—or its *center of gravity*—circles around that basic structure: it is identified with it. But if development continues, the self will begin to disidentify, or differentiate, or "let go of," or transcend that structure, and then identify with the next higher stage while integrating the previous basic structure into the new organization. The *exclusive* identity with the lower structure is dissolved (disembedded, transcended, or negated), but the capacities and competences of that basic structure itself are incorporated and integrated (preserved and included) in the new and higher organization. The center of gravity of the self is now predominantly *identified* with a higher basic level or wave of consciousness, and this identification and embeddedness will then help to generate many of the developmental streams at *that* stage (a new moral stance, new self-needs, new self-identity, etc.). For each basic level or wave of consciousness unfolding, there is thus a corresponding fulcrum of self-development, a process of (1) fusion-merger-identification-embeddedness, (2) differentiation-disidentification-disembedding-transcendence, and (3) integration-incorporation-inclusion. Again, not in a rigid or set fashion, but in flowing waves of unfolding consciousness.

We can, of course, divide and subdivide development in numerous and virtually endless ways, but, as I said, I have found that we need at least nine or ten basic structures or levels of the spectrum of consciousness in order to account for the most pertinent facts of overall development. To each of these ten basic structures or waves there corresponds a fulcrum of self-development, that 1-2-3 process of fusion/differentiation/integration that occurs each time the self-system steps up to a new wave in the expanding spheres of consciousness.

I have also suggested that the preponderance of clinical evidence strongly suggests that each fulcrum can, if disturbed, generate a specific level of pathology—psychotic, borderline, neurotic, script, identity, existential, psychic, subtle, and causal.[7] In several publications I have given extensive examples of these developmental levels of pathology, and I have also suggested the types of therapy that seem best suited to dealing with each of them.[8] It certainly seems to make sense that a "spectrum of pathology" has a corresponding "spectrum of treatment modalities."

This model also specifically includes *states of consciousness*. States of consciousness include both *natural* states (such as waking, dreaming, and deep sleep) and *altered* or *nonordinary* states (such as religious experiences, peak experiences, meditative states, holotropic experiences, drug-induced states, etc.). An altered state (including various spiritual or peak experiences) *can occur at virtually any stage of development*. The idea that spiritual or transpersonal experiences can only occur in the higher stages of development is thus incorrect. Nevertheless, in order for these temporary states to become permanent traits, growth and development must occur (the conversion of states to structures). Focusing merely on nonordinary states tends to divert attention away from the necessary process of permanent realization. We will further explore this in later discussions.[9]

With that brief summary, we can now look at certain common misunderstandings of this model.

Wilber's model is rigidly linear, which ignores all the amorphous and nonlinear aspects of life.

This is incorrect on many counts. Overall development, as we have seen, follows no set sequence at all. The various streams flow through the waves of consciousness in a relatively independent fashion, so a person can have many different streams simultaneously all over the spectrum of consciousness.

Further, we have seen that a person can have a peak experience or an altered state of consciousness at virtually any stage of development, and there is nothing linear about that, either.

Likewise, when it comes to the self, much of its journey is radically nonlinear as well. In fact, the self can roam all over the spectrum of consciousness (or the spectrum of basic structures). This is why the self is "where the action is." It can jump ahead, regress, spiral, go sideways, or otherwise dialetically spin on its heels. As Plotinus pointed out long ago, *precisely because the basic levels themselves have no inherent self-sense, the self can identify with any of them.*[10] And, in my model, each time the self does so, it will generate a new series of developmental streams. It will see the world from its presently-identified-with basic structure (which acts as its center of gravity), and the basic limiting principles of that wave of consciousness will govern what it sees, and what it can see, from that vantage point. Growth will involve the relinquishing of a narrower and shallower level of awareness in favor of an expansion into wider and deeper and higher modes.

Nonetheless, an extraordinary amount of evidence has continued to indicate that most of the separate developmental lines *themselves* tend to unfold in a sequential or stage-like or "linear" fashion. In the cognitive line, for example, images emerge before symbols, which emerge before concepts, which emerge before rules. This is equally true in both genders; we know of no society where that sequence is bypassed; there is no amount of societal conditioning that can reverse that order; and we know of no major exceptions. In other words, research has consistently demonstrated that these important stages, when they emerge, are basically gender-neutral, cross-cultural, invariant, and holarchical ("holarchy" means "nested hierarchy"—see chapter 1).

Just as an acorn grows into an oak in a series of linear, developmental, irreversible stages, so the basic components of the human psyche unfold in a holarchical sequence of differentiation-and-integration. Letters come before words which come before sentences, because each incorporates and builds upon its predecessors, which become components in its own being (each senior holon envelops or nests its junior holons). And, of course, you cannot have sentences before you have letters. The higher and wider holons will come later in development because they will integrate and unify the earlier and more partial elements.

"Linear" is often used in a very derogatory fashion, which is contrasted with the nice holistic alternative, which is somehow supposed to be "not linear." But most organic and holistic systems actually unfold in irreversible stages of increasing inclusiveness and envelopment—acorn to oak, seed to rose—and they unavoidably do so in the linear stream of time's arrow (a point Prigogine is always emphasizing about dissipative structures).

That is the meaning of "linear" in developmental studies (irreversible nested envelopment), and some aspects of human development (including the basic structures and most developmental streams) are indeed linear, as enormous amounts of experimental and clinical evidence have made more than obvious. In fact, those theories that fail to take these linear aspects into account are severely deficient and inadequate theories.

Even so, all of the developmental stages themselves are fairly fluid in their unfolding. For example, research shows that somebody who is at, say, moral stage 3, actually only gives 50 percent of her responses from that level; 25 percent of her responses are from a *higher* level, and 25 percent are from a *lower* level. In other words, her center of gravity is at moral stage 3, but the self is still quite fluid in its growth.

Likewise, although the basic structures unfold in a holarchical fashion, with each senior wave nesting and enfolding and including its juniors, the self's journey through those expanding spheres of consciousness is nowhere near that "linear." As we said, the self can be, and usually is, all over the place—regressing, temporarily leaping forward, spiraling back and forth, immersed in all sorts of altered states from all sorts of realms (prepersonal, personal, and transpersonal). This means that, on the long view, there will be a discernible progression of the self's center of gravity from narrower to wider, from shallower to deeper—an overall expansion of identity from matter to body to mind to soul to spirit. Nonetheless, in the short view, the self's journey is altogether tumultuous, much more of a roller coaster than a linear ladder.

Thus, in terms of "linearity," we have this: the basic levels and the major streams tend to unfold in a holarchical, stage-like fashion, as research continues to confirm. But because they do so in a relatively independent fashion, there is nothing linear about overall development—a person can be highly evolved in some lines, medium in others, and low in still others. And, just as important, the self can experience altered states of consciousness at virtually any level of development, and altered states are not linear.

All of those components—basic levels, relatively independent lines, the roaming self, and nonlinear states—need to be included in any truly integral psychology, especially if we wish to honor, acknowledge, and

incorporate the substantial amounts of evidence from clinical, meditative, phenomenological, altered-states, and empirical studies, both East
and West.

Wilber doesn't give much attention to conflict in the pre-egoic stages.

Washburn makes this claim, and I find it incomprehensible. "The
main theme of the pre-egoic period, for Wilber, is the development of
lower-level basic structures."[11] Actually, as we have just seen, that is
only one-third of the story. The other two-thirds of the story concern
the developmental lines and the self-system with its fulcrums, which is
where "all the action is."

The pre-egoic period covers roughly the first four fulcrums of self-
development (fulcrum-0, or the pre- and perinatal period; fulcrum-1,
roughly the first eighteen months; fulcrum-2, generally one to three
years; and fulcrum-3, around three to six years). These fulcrums are
perhaps the most crucial in all of self development, for they set the foundation for all that is to follow. Moreover, they are the essential etiologi-
cal fulcrums for some truly severe pathologies (psychotic, borderline,
neurotic).

It is the self-system, as I earlier indicated, that is the locus of defense
mechanisms (including introjection, projection, splitting, denial, reaction formation, repression proper, etc., arrayed in a hierarchical pattern). Thus, any specific aspects of any of the structures of consciousness
can be dissociated, in one form or another, from the ongoing sweep
of consciousness unfolding, if they are sensed as a threat to the self-
system.[12]

These sealed-off (or otherwise dissociated) components act as *lesions
in awareness* that then tend to sabotage consciousness with symptomatic
expressions (i.e., various pathologies). The self cannot genuinely disembed and transcend these alienated aspects of its own being, because they
are now hidden and sealed off—they remain as pockets of unconscious
attachment, unconscious identification, unconscious embeddedness, unconscious intentionality—they are not "died to" and "let go of." They
are "little subjects" that refuse to be differentiated, transcended, and
thereby genuinely integrated, and instead carry on terrorist activities
from the basement, from the locus of their unconscious attachment and
fixation. This is self-alienation, repression, and pathology.

Because most defense mechanisms are quite common and normal
(and phase-specific), virtually nobody escapes early development totally
intact; on that point Washburn and I are in general agreement. *Our*

disagreement concerns only the nature of what exactly is being repressed or dissociated in these early stages.

For Washburn, it is nothing less than the Dynamic Ground that is being fundamentally repressed or *forced out of the consciousness* of the infant. In my opinion, what is being repressed is basically various affects, emotions, diffuse bodily feelings, sensuality, and emotional-sexual energies in general—the overall domain of prana, or life vitality.

Washburn believes that certain pre-egoic capacities and the Dynamic Ground itself are *necessarily* lost, and that the *recapture* of these lost capacities is the *prerequisite* for transpersonal development. The individual must regress to the earliest infantile stages, spiraling back to contact the lost Dynamic Ground, and then develop forward into transcendence. In virtually all cases, significant regression is necessary for transpersonal growth.

I believe that regression is common and *sometimes* necessary, not because the Dynamic Ground is lost at age one, but because repression itself tends to cripple further growth in any case. The greater the repression in the earlier stages, then the more higher growth is crippled. In my view, "regression in service of ego" is thus a return to, and a recontacting of, the alienated feelings, emotions, affects, or emotional-sexual energies that were dissociated in the early fulcrums. Once these are integrated into the self-system, then growth can more easily move forward into the higher and transegoic realms. Thus, regression in service of ego is sometimes a prerequisite for transcendence of ego, but it is not the actual mechanism of transpersonal growth itself.

The major difference, then, is whether something like a Dynamic Ground is actually forced out of the consciousness of the infant in the first year of life, as Washburn maintains. I will argue that such a stance is incoherent on its own terms (even if we include the bardo or "in between" realms, which I do, and which I will explain below). In the meantime, my own model more than accounts for the massive conflicts in the earliest years of life.

Wilber's model totally negates the self instead of including it.

Several critics have maintained that I give the self virtually no importance or even relative existence. This is difficult to maintain, in that the self-system has at least the six characteristics I listed (from identification to defense to will). That is quite a lot of activity for a nonentity. In fact, the self-system is an inherent functional capacity of the psyche. It develops and unfolds its own identity from matter to body to mind to soul to spirit, in a great holarchy of increasing inclusion and embrace.

Most of this misunderstanding stems from a colossal semantic confusion. The question is, "Does any form of the ego exist in the higher stages of development?" And the answer is, "It depends entirely on what you mean by 'ego.' " If by "ego" you mean an *exclusive* identity with the individual bodymind, then clearly that ego is largely deconstructed with the emergence of the Supreme Identity, where one's center of gravity switches from the organism to the All. The self-system no longer exclusively identifies with the basic structures of the mind (thus generating the transitional self-sense known as the ego), but instead identifies with the structures of the Kosmos at large (whose self-sense is the Supreme Identity of the Divine Self). The self-system, in other words, switches from the individual ego to the Divine Self or Spirit, which can be described as no-self or Big Self, depending on your preference. But the *exclusive* identification, the narrow "ego," is basically lost.

But if by "ego" you mean that aspect of self-awareness that develops to deal with the conventional world and its sensorimotor reality, then of course that ego remains in existence. The "ego" used in that sense means, not a transitional structure that will be replaced by higher selves until there is the only Self, but rather a functional competence that is part of the enduring structures of the psyche. In that case, the ego is obviously retained in higher development.

I have consistently maintained both of those positions from my first to my most recent book—namely, that the ego as a competency is maintained in higher development, but the ego as an exclusive sense of identity is replaced by higher and wider identities. Both are true. And I am constantly getting into arguments with people who maintain only one of those views and accuse me of maintaining only the other.

Washburn is simply the latest in a line of such critics, who in this case says that I deny that the ego remains in any form in higher development. Since he claims to be reporting the view expressed in *The Atman Project*, here is what I actually said in that book:

> The self must differentiate from the ego, dis-identify with it, transcend it, and then integrate it with the higher and newly-emergent structures. But please remember that the ego remains intact when the self dis-identifies with it—just as the body remained intact when the ego transcended it. Transcendence does not mean deformation. One still possesses an ego—it's just that one's identity is no longer exclusively bound to it. (p. 166)

Washburn summarizes five of what he believes to be the main disagreements between our models. These are particularly the features that Washburn believes my model does not take into account, and thus features that he feels recommend his approach as a better alternative. But if we actually use my overall model, and not just the truncated version that Washburn presents, we find that all of these points immediately collapse, leaving Washburn's position rather untenable.[13]

But there is still one remaining issue, namely, what is the nature of the pre-egoic potential? What is the actual nature of the "Dynamic Ground" that is supposedly "unrestrictedly present" in the infant and then lost in subsequent development? This is the only item on which Washburn's model includes something that mine does not. Thus, if Washburn's model also fails in this particular point, there is nothing left to recommend it as an alternative. It is to this topic we can now turn.

THE ROMANTIC AGENDA

I myself was once an advocate of the Romantic model. In this general view, the infant at birth (and humanity in its dawn state) is the noble savage, fully in touch with a perfectly holistic and unified Ground, "harmoniously one with the whole world." But then through the activity of the analytic and divisive ego, this Ground is historically lost, actually repressed or alienated as a past historical event (as opposed to an involutional event happening now). This historical loss—the loss of a *past actual*—is nonetheless necessary, according to the Romantic view, in order for the ego to develop its own powers of mature independence. And then, in the third great movement (after initial union and subsequent fragmentation), the ego and the Ground are *reunited* in a regenerative homecoming and spiritual marriage, so that the Ground is *recaptured*, but now "on a higher level" or "in a mature form."

Such is the general Romantic view. And, indeed, I began writing both *The Atman Project* and *Up from Eden* in an attempt to validate that view ontogenetically (*Atman Project*) and phylogenetically (*Eden*). I even fancy that I brought some new ideas to this old notion. Although this Romantic model had been eagerly embraced by Jung and the Jungians (especially Edinger and Neumann), and although I strongly agreed with their general formulations, I was also drawn to some of the more daring theorists in psychoanalytic theory (such as Roheim, Ferenczi, and Norman O. Brown), who were in fact quite in line with this Romantic model.

These psychoanalytic theorists allowed me, or so I believed, to give a very precise outline of the specific stages of this loss of primal Ground, or loss of true Self, or loss of very Atman. In ontogenetic development, for example, I postulated the following (pulling all of these various sources together): the infant begins in a state of almost pure adualism, fully in touch with the primal Ground and the true Self (Atman), so that subject and object are one; the self and the "whole world" are united. Then through what I called "primary repression," the subject and object are split, the self and the world (as the Great Mother) are fragmented and alienated from each other, and the world of duality crashes onto the scene, with all the tragedy and terror inherent in that divisive nightmare.

But the developmental damage doesn't stop there. Once the bodyego is split from the world and the Great Mother, the bodyego has two basic but contradictory desires. There is the desire to reunite with the Great Mother and thus recapture that pure oneness and paradisiacal state that it had known before subject and object were brutally split. But in order to reunite with the Great Mother, the bodyego self would have to die to its own separate existence, and this it is terrified of doing. It therefore wants reunion but is also terrified of it, and these conflicting desires drive subsequent development. I called the amalgam of these two drives "the Atman project"—the desire to attain unity (Atman) but the intense fear of it as well, which forces the self to seek substitute gratifications and substitute objects.

(The Atman project is a very real project and a very valid concept, I firmly believe, but the state of unity that is desired is not that of the infant at the mother's breast, but of the self at primordial Emptiness. As we will see, I had wildly "elevated" the nature of the early infantile and prepersonal structure to some sort of transpersonal ground and glory, and so I mistakenly believed that the drive to unity was a drive to recapture that infantile structure, but of course "in a mature form," instead of understanding that the drive to unity is an attempt to recapture something lost in the timeless moment—as I will explain below.)

Once the bodyego has split from the Great Mother or Great Surround, my early Romantic account continued, then because of this primary repression it suffers primary alienation. In the bodyego itself, I suggested, during the first three years of life, this primary alienation drives some very specific events which begin to take place in the actual distribution of emotional-sexual energy, libido, élan vital, or prana (and this is exactly where I directly incorporated the formulations of the more daring psychoanalytic thinkers). Namely, driven by the attempt to regain unity with the world (and the Great Mother), the bodyego organizes the distribution of its libido around various bodily zones where fantasies of this union take place (from the oral zone, with fantasies of uniting with the world through food, to the genital zone, with fantasies of sexually uniting with the world). All of the libidinal organizations are thus simply reduced and restricted versions of a consciousness that was once actually "one with the whole world." I therefore ended one of these early published essays with the conclusion: "God-consciousness is not sublimated sexuality; sexuality is repressed God-consciousness."[14]

That view makes a good deal of developmental sense, but only IF the infantile bodymind is actually in *full* God-consciousness or Ground-consciousness. Because the point, remember, is that this Romantic view depends upon the notion that the infant is immersed in an actual God-consciousness or a *fully present* Ground, which is then literally repressed, sometime during the first or second year of life. *But this view makes no sense whatsoever*, and has no developmental validity, if the pre-egoic structure itself is anything less than God, because it is supposed to be the actual repression of God-consciousness, by the two-year-old, that drives the subsequent developmental scheme. If the "original embedment" of the infantile self is not *fully* in touch with God-consciousness or Ground-consciousness, then this developmental view falls apart altogether.

And it is just that problem that finally undoes the Romantic position, as I quickly found out the more I tried to make that viewpoint work. Jack Crittenden and I had just founded *ReVision Journal*, and, desperate for material, I began serially publishing the early draft of *The Atman Project*, which presented the above scheme, loaded with its Romantic viewpoints and numerous pre/trans fallacies.[15]

But the more I tried to make this Romantic model work—and believe me, I tried very, very hard—the more I realized its central inadequacies and confusions, which I will outline in a moment. I thus furiously reworked the early drafts of both *The Atman Project* and *Up from Eden*—neither had yet been published in book form—to reflect this shift in my thinking, which I also explained at length in "Odyssey."[16] Incidentally, when I wrote "The Pre/Trans Fallacy,"[17] I was in effect cataloging all of the errors that I myself had made in this regard, which is why I seemed to understand them with an all-too-alarming familiarity.

Anyway, let us call my early model "Romantic/Jungian/Wilber-I," and the later model, "Wilber-II."

Now the odd thing about Wilber-I and Wilber-II is that they aren't really all that different. They both move from pre-egoic to egoic to trans-egoic. They both agree on the great domains of prepersonal to personal to transpersonal. They both see development ultimately driven by the attempt to regain Spirit. They both see involution and evolution occurring. That is why both Wilber-I and Wilber-II can handle virtually the same type and amount of available clinical and experimental evidence. The big difference—the crucial difference—is that Romantic/Wilber-I *must* see the infantile pre-egoic structure as being, in some sense, a primal Ground, a perfect wholeness, a direct God-union, a complete immersion in Self, a oneness with the whole world. Since the perfection of enlightenment is a *recontacting* of something present in the infantile structure, then that infantile structure must therefore fully possess that utter Perfection (even if unconscious). Thus, if God is not *fully* present in the infantile structure, the entire scheme collapses.

And here, of course, the Romantic/Wilber-I model runs into a series of fatal difficulties, as is probably obvious. But let's go over it a step at a time: The traditional Romantic view is that the infantile structure is one with the entire Ground or Self, but in an *unconscious* fashion. The self then divides and splits from this Ground, actually represses this Ground, alienates it and loses touch with it. Then, in the third great movement (transegoic), the self and the Ground *reunite*, the Ground is resurrected ("on a higher level," whatever that might actually mean), and a spiritual renewal and regeneration occurs.

Thus, what we might call *the traditional Romantic view* is that development moves from unconscious Heaven (pre-egoic) to conscious Hell (egoic) to conscious Heaven (transegoic). The self is totally one with the Ground in *both* the first and the third stage, but in the first the union is unconscious, in the third, conscious.

The fatal problem with that view is that the second step (the loss of unconscious union) is an absolute impossibility. As the Romantics themselves soon acknowledged, all things are one with Ground; if you actually lost your union with Ground, you would cease to exist. Rather, there are only two options you have with regard to Ground: you can be aware of your union with Ground, or you can be unaware of it. The union itself is always present, but it can be either conscious or unconscious.

Now, as we saw, according to the traditional Romantic view, the pre-egoic state is one with Ground but in an *unconscious* fashion. But if that is so, then the next step—the move from pre-egoic to egoic—*cannot* therefore be the *loss* of that unconscious union. If that happened, you would cease to exist. You can either be conscious or unconscious of the union with Ground; if you are *already* unconscious of the union, you can't get any lower! The real loss has *already* occurred. The pre-egoic structure or original embedment is *already* fallen, alienated, lost. Involution has priorly occurred. And this the Romantics, very slowly, began to realize, which, of course, undermined their entire project.

The precariousness of their position becomes even more obvious when the standard Romantic notion of "original wholeness" is carefully examined. The infantile structure is supposed to be "one with the whole world in love and bliss," as Norman O. Brown put it. But what is the neonate actually one with? Is the infantile self fully one with the world of poetry, or logic, or economics, or history, or mathematics, or morals and ethics? Of course not, for these have not yet emerged: the alleged "whole world" of the infantile self is a pitifully small slice of reality. The subject and object of the infantile structure are indeed predifferentiated to a large extent (which is simply the oceanic or fusion phase of fulcrum-1), but that fused world excludes and is ignorant of an extraordinary amount of the Kosmos. It certainly is not one with the whole world; it is one with a very small slice of the whole world.

The one-month-old self might come "trailing clouds of glory" (from the rebirth bardo, which I will explain below), but it is still actually immersed and embedded, not in nirvana, but in samsara. It has all the intense seeds of grasping, avoiding, ignoring, hunger, and thirst. The flames of samsaric hell are *already* all around the infantile self, and if this is occasionally a relatively peaceful time, it is the peace of prepersonal ignorance, not transpersonal wisdom. The infantile self is fully immersed in samsara, it just doesn't have enough awareness to register that burning fact. But as the ego develops and gains in consciousness, it will increasingly *realize* its *already* fallen state—realize the fact that it is already living in the fires of samsara.

This shocking realization, this conscious initiation into the fact that the phenomenal world is inherently marked with tears and terror, sin and suffering, trishna and duhkha, is a profound trauma to the self. This *waking-up trauma* begins, in its earliest forms, during the first or second year of life (particularly during fulcrum-2), and that is what has confused the Romantic/Wilber-I theorists: they imagine that at this point the infant is passing from nirvana into samsara, whereas the infant, born in samsara, is simply waking up to that shattering fact.

The ego, now awake to the existential nightmare of its samsaric pain, then has two basic choices in its life course: it can choose those items that favor its continuing growth and evolution of consciousness, or it can choose those items that foster regression in an attempt to blot out consciousness and numb itself to duhkha. If it chooses the former, and quickens this evolutionary growth with appropriate spiritual disciplines, it might even rediscover its own primordial and timeless nature, a primordial nature that was never actually lost in a past period of infancy, but is rather obscured in this very moment by an allegiance to the world of time itself. This is indeed a *rediscovery* and a *remembrance*, not of what was fully present at age one month, but what is fully present in the timeless now—fully present, that is, prior TO involution, not prior IN evolution.

Thus, the real course of manifest historical human development is not from unconscious Heaven to conscious Hell to conscious Heaven, but rather from unconscious Hell to conscious Hell to conscious Heaven. And such was the move from Wilber-I to Wilber-II.

ORIGINAL EMBEDMENT AND THE DYNAMIC GROUND

Washburn in many essential respects echoes a Wilber-I type of model. He uses the same general stages, with the same general terminology, and he generously acknowledges as much—as he puts it, "Wilber (1979) once held a view similar to this but later abandoned it."[18]

At the same time, Washburn has built upon this view and enormously expanded and sophisticated it. He has, after all, based two long books on it. Moreover, Washburn has at least realized some of the profound difficulties with the *traditional* Romantic version, and he has attempted to bypass some of its central and fatal difficulties. But, in my opinion, he is less than successful.

To begin with, Washburn realized early on that if the pre-egoic structure (more specifically, the "original embedment") is one with Ground, then that union with Ground must be *fully conscious in the infant*. Remember, the traditional view was that the original state was a union with the Ground but in an *unconscious* fashion, but Washburn realizes that if that is so, then that original state is *already* fallen, it is already as low as you can go (it is, in fact, not unconscious Heaven but unconscious Hell). So Washburn is forced to maintain that the one-month-old infant is fully open to, and fully conscious of, the unrestricted Dynamic

Ground. There is "the unrestricted power of the Ground within the new-born's body," evidenced in "dynamic plenitude and blissful well-being characteristic of original embedment," marked by "wholeness, fullness, and bliss . . . , undivided, boundless fullness."[19] Washburn acknowledges that the Ground itself *cannot* be lost or the ego would cease to be. So the only item that can actually be *lost* is the consciousness of Ground, and this means that the one-month-old infant must *fully possess* that consciousness of unrestricted Ground, or the entire scheme falls apart.

In short, precisely because it is the *repression* of the consciousness of Ground, starting around age one or two, that drives Washburn's developmental scheme, then if the consciousness of Ground is not fully and *unrestrictedly* present in the infantile self prior to that point, then it's not even there to be repressed, and Washburn's model abruptly collapses (or, as I found out, Wilber-I becomes Wilber-II).

Now a more coherent view of involution/evolution (as found in, say, Plotinus, Asanga, Schelling, Aurobindo, Garab Dorje, the *Lankavatara Sutra*, or, I believe, Wilber-II) would maintain something like this: Spirit manifests as the entire world in a series of increasingly holistic and holarchic spheres, stretching from matter to body to mind to soul to spirit itself. But all of these different dimensions are actually just forms of spirit, in various degrees of self-realization and self-actualization. Thus, there is really spirit-as-matter, spirit-as-prana, spirit-as-mind, spirit-as-soul, and spirit-as-spirit.

Involution (or efflux), this general view continues, is the process whereby these dimensions are manifested as forms of spirit, and *evolution* (or reflux) is the process of recollection and remembrance, moving from spirit-as-matter to a final remembrance of spirit-as-spirit: a recognition of spirit, by spirit, as spirit—the traditional realization of enlightenment.

In this scheme, the infantile self might indeed be trailing clouds of glory (which I will discuss in a moment), but it is primarily adapting to the dimensions of spirit-as-matter and spirit-as-prana (sensuality, emotional-sexual energies, élan vital, diffuse polymorphous life and vital force) as well as the very early forms of spirit-as-mind (images, symbols, protoconcepts). Developmental evolution continues with the further unfolding of the mental dimensions (spirit-as-mind) and then the beginning of the consciously spiritual dimensions (spirit-as-soul), culminating in enlightenment or the direct recognition of spirit-as-spirit, which, transcending all, embraces all.

So the infant is indeed immersed in spirit and is one with Ground—as all things are!—but it is primarily spirit-as-matter and spirit-as-prana, not spirit-as-spirit. (As we will see, not even according to the bardo view is the infantile or neonatal self in touch with spirit-as-spirit!) Thus, in all of these views, the infantile self is not conscious of spirit-as-spirit, or the pure nirvanic estate altogether free of karmic tendencies and desires and hunger and thirst.

But this general view is completely blocked to Washburn (and Wilber-I), because for Washburn the Ground *must be fully conscious and unrestrictedly present* in the one-month-old infantile structure. This forces Washburn into a series of increasingly incoherent stances in an attempt to defend this awkward assertion.

To begin with, Washburn must first separate Ground and spirit. (Since spirit is *not fully manifest* in the infantile structure, which Washburn seems to realize, then *something else* must be fully present in order to drive his scheme, and this something else will be the Dynamic Ground.) Thus, for Washburn, Ground and spirit *are not the same thing.* Ground, he says, can appear as libido, as free psychic energy, and as spirit. I myself will refer to these different organizations of Washburn's Ground with the shorthand phrases Ground-as-prana, Ground-as-psyche, and Ground-as-spirit (Washburn's terminology, for example, is "the power of the Ground as spirit"). Notice that Ground is somehow more than spirit, because it can appear in forms that apparently spirit cannot.

But there is one thing Ground is not: Ground is not the mental ego. Strangely, the Ground can appear as libido, and the Ground can appear as free psyche, and the Ground can appear as all-encompassing spirit, but the Ground is not strong enough to appear as the poor ego. In fact, the ego and the Ground are dramatically separate entities, says Washburn. But in the higher stages of development, Ground somehow appears as spirit (what I am calling Ground-as-spirit) and then Ground-as-spirit and the ego unite, according to Washburn, and thus a *super-entity* (which he never really names or specifies) then emerges: the Ground-as-spirit/one with the ego.

But, says Washburn, this is not a novel state: it is in some sense a *reunion* with the Ground that was directly repressed by the two-year-old. That, of course, is the absolutely crucial point: according to Washburn, the Ground of spiritual realization is essentially the same Ground repressed by the child's ego, which is exactly why Washburn *must* postulate that this Ground is *fully present and conscious* in the infantile structure.

This is where Washburn's very slippery definition of "Ground" becomes crucial. As we saw, Ground can appear as libido, as psyche, and as spirit. Washburn can therefore claim that the child represses the Ground *without ever claiming that the child represses spirit* (because Ground and spirit are not the same). But in order for Washburn's scheme *actually* to work, the Ground that is repressed by the young ego *must* be the Ground-as-spirit, because, Washburn makes clear, the higher union is a union *specifically with Ground-as-spirit*.

But Washburn, apparently realizing that simply will not work, therefore never *explicitly* claims the infantile self is actually in touch with Ground-as-spirit; nor does he ever claim that the young ego represses Ground-as-spirit. In fact, he consistently maintains (in the text and in his tables) that Ground-as-spirit appears *only* in the transegoic stages.

At this point, Washburn's model is starting to look suspiciously like a Wilber-II or evolutionary type of model. But Washburn wants it both ways: he wants to acknowledge that spirit actualizes *only* in the transegoic stages, but he also wants to say that the *same* reality was somehow *fully* present in the infantile structure and was then actually repressed by the ego.

The only way he can do this is to create a notion, "the Dynamic Ground," that has the power of *all three great domains at once* (the libido of the prepersonal, the psychic energy of the personal, and the spirit of the transpersonal), and then he can use the "Ground" in virtually any way he wishes. Thus, when the young ego represses Ground in its form as prana or vital bodily energy, which it certainly might, Washburn will simply claim that the *entire Ground* itself has been repressed, thus *implicitly* claiming a spiritual repression without ever *explicitly* having to say so, which he realizes will not work. Then, when the ego enters the transpersonal domain, Washburn *simply begins calling the Ground by the name "spirit,"* without ever explaining why all of a sudden the Dynamic Ground turns explicitly spiritual—and yet that is, of course, the central problem to be addressed. Instead, in the transpersonal stages Ground is now simply called "the power of the Ground as spirit," which is then *claimed* to be the *same* Ground the infant repressed, whereas in fact (and even according to the actual evidence that Washburn presents), what the infant basically repressed was Ground-as-prana, not Ground-as-spirit.

But Washburn wants it both ways, and therefore, in those rare instances when he actually attempts to define Ground, he must define it in a way that is very nebulous and thus will not challenge his reductionism. Thus, he simply defines the Ground as "physicodynamic processes" (no

further explanation is given for that term). Since Washburn loosely identifies Ground with physicodynamism, then he can hide his reductionism
and his pre/trans fallacies in this rather nebulous concept, having his
pre-egoic spiritual cake and eating it too.

There is, I believe, a fairly straightforward reason that Washburn attempts to identify the entire Dynamic Ground with "physicodynamic"
processes, and it relates directly to what I believe is his pre/trans fallacy
worldview (ptf-2). Chögyam Trungpa pointed out, in *Shambhala: The
Sacred Path of the Warrior*, and Huston Smith confirmed in *Forgotten
Truth*, that the great wisdom traditions without exception—from the
shamanic to the Vedantic, in the East as well as the West—maintain that
reality consists of at least three great realms: earth, human, and sky,
correlated with body, mind, and spirit (gross, subtle, and causal), and
these are further correlated with the three great states of human consciousness: waking (gross, body), dream (subtle, mind), and deep sleep
(causal, spirit).[20]

These are, of course, the three great domains of prepersonal, personal, and transpersonal. *But Washburn refuses to clearly acknowledge
these three domains.* Under the burden of his pre/trans collapse, he keeps
the ego-mind as one domain, but he then *fuses the gross-body with
causal-spirit*: this lump he calls the "Ground," which he then contrasts
with the ego-mind. Thus, instead of the three great domains of body,
mind, and spirit, he simply has his "two poles" of ego-mind and
Ground. And since he has collapsed causal-spirit into gross-body and its
vitality, then of course he will refer to the entire Ground as physiological
energy or "physicodynamic processes," thus completing his pre/trans
plunge. By reducing the Ground of Being to physiology, he can elevate
infancy to God.

At this point, Washburn will then accuse my model of not being as
simple and as "parsimonious" as his model, which is rather like saying
that we will have a much simpler model of the solar system if we just
leave out that annoying Jupiter.[21]

Yet it is in the highest stages that Washburn's Romantic/type-I model
faces even worse difficulties. According to Washburn, once the ego has
necessarily and rather fully repressed the Ground, then it can reunite
with the Ground. Since the Dynamic Ground "is originally lost via repression, it can be restored only via regression."[22] More than one critic
has puzzled over what that could possibly mean. Does the adult have to
regress to preverbal babbling? If not, then what?

Nonetheless, according to Washburn, the ego must regress back to the Ground which was present but repressed in the infantile period, and then these "two poles of the psyche"—namely, Ground and ego—"can be integrated to form a single, perfected, psychic whole."[23] This means, rather oddly, that Ground is now a *subset* of the whole psyche (an incoherent point I will return to below).

But what, according to Washburn, is actually *recontacted*? It is not Ground-as-spirit, since that manifests, he says, only in the transegoic. Since it can't be spirit that is recontacted, Washburn reverts to his catchall concept: the physicodynamic potentials are recontacted: "Primal repression is lifted and physicodynamic potentials are reawakened."[24] That somehow means spirit is now manifest. In any event, it is at this transegoic point that Ground can manifest as spirit.

But this means that a *completely new entity* therefore comes into being with this awakening: namely, the "single, perfected, psychic whole"—the union of ego and Ground. The real conclusion is obvious: *this whole was never repressed or lost, because it never existed before.* It is an emergent, a newly realized entity.

Thus, according to Washburn's own presentation, the infantile self is actually in touch with *neither* Ground-as-spirit *nor* the Ground-and-ego unified state, from which it follows that enlightenment or spiritual awakening is not in any essential fashion a recontacting of something fully or actually present in the infantile structure but subsequently lost. That being the case, Washburn/Wilber-I reverts to Wilber-II.

One of Washburn's central theoretical difficulties, in my opinion, is a failure to understand the difference between differentiation and dissociation. As I tried to show in *Sex, Ecology, Spirituality*, this confusion is a hallmark of the general Romantic view. Development actually proceeds by differentiation-and-integration, a failure of which involves either fusion, on one side (where differentiation fails), or dissociation, on the other (where differentiation goes too far into alienation and fragmentation).

But for Washburn, as for the Romantics, there is basically either fusion or dissociation, with no middle ground of differentiation itself. Washburn says as much. "There is no middle ground. The body ego can either yield to the Great Mother and thereby submit to continued reembedment [fusion] . . . , or it can separate itself from the Great Mother and thereby perpetuate a repression [dissociation]. . . ."[25] What he fails to see, in my opinion, is that the differentiation of self and other is neither a fusion nor a dissociation, but the necessary process of differentiation-and-integration (transcendence-and-inclusion), which is the very process of growth itself.

But once you are committed to seeing every differentiation as a dissociation, then development must be viewed as primarily a dismal downhill slide, because every normal differentiation is going to be interpreted as a horrible dissociation, fragmentation, alienation. The oak is somehow a terrible violation of the acorn.

Human development must then be viewed as doing what no other organic system ever does: in this Romanticized view, each stage grows and develops primarily by brutalizing and crippling its previous stages. (How could that even work? How would natural selection ever select for *that*? Not the occasional repression, but the actual shattering of the entire Ground of Being? Is nature that . . . confused?)

This misunderstanding of differentiation and dissociation is, I believe, exactly why Washburn must maintain that self development involves a *necessary* repression of Ground (unrestrictedly present in babies), and why he must likewise maintain that in order for spiritual awakening to occur, everybody, with virtually no exceptions, must completely regress to those potentials fully present in the one-month-old infant. Without this massive regression, in virtually all cases, there is no enlightenment and no spiritual awakening.

For Wilber-II, various types of repression (or dissociation and pathology) can occur at each of the nine or ten fulcrums of self development, and this certainly includes the first two fulcrums. As I pointed out, what is repressed or dissociated in these early fulcrums, however, is generally spirit-as-prana, not spirit-as-spirit. This repression varies in degree of severity from person to person; in harsh cases, this repression can bring development to a grinding halt. In most cases, however, individuals cope relatively well and development continues until arrest, which also varies from person to person.

Thus, for Washburn/Wilber-I, primal repression of Ground is the way development proceeds *by necessity*, and thus spiritual awakening requires the recapture of something actually and fully present in the infantile structure. Repression is part of the actual mechanism of development. For Wilber-II, repression is something that may or may not occur, but in any event it is not the mechanism of growth, and when it does occur in these early stages, it is a repression essentially of spirit-as-prana, not spirit-as-spirit. But if this repression is moderate to severe, then in the higher stages of growth, regression might have to occur in order to reintegrate these lower potentials. Whether this regression does occur will vary from person to person, and the amount of this regression will vary from person to person, but it is not a wholesale necessity for all cases, and in any event it is not a recontacting of an infantile but repressed spirit-as-spirit.

In short, for Washburn/Wilber-I, profound regression *must* occur in all spiritual development, as a recontacting of a Ground unrestrictedly present in the infantile structure. For Wilber-II, regression *might* occur, usually if necessitated by a recontacting of Ground-as-prana or some earlier-fulcrum lost potentials, dissociations, pathologies, and so on (a regression in service of ego, prior to transcendence of ego).

There are, of course, numerous cases of enlightenment occurring without wholesale infantile regression, which *prima facie* condemns the Washburn model. In the one carefully conducted investigation of the merits of Washburn versus Wilber, L. Eugene Thomas et al. conclude that, of those individuals who had reached transpersonal stages of development, "only about half gave indications of having undergone a regressive transition period. On the basis of this, and other internal evidence, support was found for Wilber's theory."[26]

7

Born Again

STAN GROF AND THE
HOLOTROPIC MIND

*Stanislav Grof is one of the world's greatest living psychologists.
He is certainly a pioneer in every sense of the word, and one
of the most comprehensive psychological thinkers of our era.
Fortunately, Stan and I are in substantial agreement about many
of the central issues in human psychology, the spectrum of consciousness, and the realms of the human unconscious.*

But we are here, of course, to discuss our differences. In Sex,
Ecology, Spirituality *I offer a sustained criticism of Grof's position, highlighting some of what I believe are major weaknesses
in his model. I'll summarize those weaknesses here, and then
generally respond to Stan's criticism of my own work.*

MONOLOGICAL SCIENCE

G ROF HAS CONSISTENTLY maintained that "Western science is approaching a paradigm shift of unprecedented proportions."[1] Perhaps so, but the new paradigm and the approaches he discusses are all
monological, which means that they reduce the world to it-language. He
points to quantum and relativity physics, cybernetics, systems theory,
M-fields, chaos and complexity theories, Young's theory of process, and
so on, all of which are unrelentingly monological. They reduce the Kos-

mos to merely Right-Hand terms; they fundamentally embody the *subtle reductionism* that is one of the unfortunate legacies of the Cartesian tradition.

Both "mechanistic" and "systems" sciences are monological. Both "causality" and "chaos" theories are monological. Both "materialism" and "organicism" are monological. Both "deterministic" and "complexity" theories are monological. Both "mechanistic" and "process theory" are monological. No matter what advantages the latter have over the former (and there are many!), they are all, in themselves, flatland approaches.

Grof and the monologically inclined theorists he cites in support of the "new paradigm" are constantly lamenting the fragmentation of the modern and postmodern world, and they emphasize the urgent need for integrative vision. I agree entirely, but this monological "new paradigm" is in fact a symptom of, not a medicine for, the primary fragmentation itself. As such, it is part of the cause, not the cure, of the modern fragmentation.

Thus, for example, when Joanna Macy criticizes *Sex, Ecology, Spirituality* by saying that it doesn't take feedback mechanisms into account and thus does not fully represent systems theory, I believe she misses the central point. Of course I take feedback into account, and explicitly say so; moreover, feedback theory is merely part of the first wave of systems sciences, which have been supplemented with chaos and complexity theories—but all of them are perfectly and equally monological, capable of being fully described in process it-language, which is the defining hallmark of subtle reductionism and the brutal stamp of the colonization of the lifeworld by monological imperialism, which actually promotes the fragmentation it wishes it to heal. To paraphrase Karl Krauss, systems theory is the disease of which it claims to be the cure.

Grof has unfortunately, in my opinion, sunk his philosophical foundations into this monological cement, and this throws his psychological model into several disadvantages.

MONOLOGICAL CONSCIOUSNESS

One of the great discoveries of the postmodern West is that what we previously took to be an unproblematic consciousness reflecting on the world at large ("the mirror of nature") is in fact anchored in a network of nonobvious *intersubjective* structures (including linguistic, ethical, cultural, aesthetic, and syntactic structures). Both subjective consciousness (Upper Left) and the objective world (Right-Hand) arise in large measure due to the differentiating powers and capacities of these intersubjective (Lower-Left) structures, structures that *do not themselves appear as objects or phenomena of immediate awareness*, but rather form the *background* context by virtue of which subjects and objects can appear in the first place (see the Introduction).

For this reason, the discovery of these intersubjective structures was not immediately available to phenomenology in any of its traditional forms, but rather awaited the developments in contextual analysis, structuralism, post-structuralism, linguistics, and semiotics: awaited, that is, the very broad movement from modernism to postmodernism in general.

The simple example I usually give is that of a card game—say, poker. In the poker game, each card follows a specific set of rules, but the actual rules of the game are not written on any of the cards. Thus, if you merely describe each card, no matter how carefully—that is, if you do a pure phenomenology—you will never discover the rules that each card is obeying, you will never discover the "inter-card patterns" (the "intersubjective" patterns) that in fact drive each and every card. Here phenomenology fails miserably, and some form of structuralism alone will disclose these patterns.

This rather extraordinary historical development was summarized by Foucault: "So the problem of language appeared and it was clear that phenomenology was no match for structural analysis in accounting for the effects of meaning that could be produced by a structure of the linguistic type. And quite naturally, with the phenomenological spouse finding herself disqualified by her inability to address language, structuralism became the new bride."[2] And this means "structuralism" in the broadest sense, which included semiology (Saussure), semiotics (Peirce), structuralism per se (Lévi-Strauss, Barthes, Lacan), developmental structuralism (Piaget, aspects of Habermas, Kohlberg, Loevinger), neo-structuralism (Foucault), and post-structuralism (Derrida, Lyotard). Despite their numerous differences, all of them share a movement from the philosophy of the subject monologically accessing a pregiven world, to a dialogical investigation of the intersubjective structures that allow subjects and objects to differentiate and appear in the first place. (In other words, postmodern theorists are united in their insistence that the Upper-Left quadrant [or individual consciousness] and the Right-Hand quadrants [or monological objects] can only be fully understood with reference to the Lower-Left or *intersubjective* domains. As I would also put it, we need an "all-quadrant" approach.)

This was further coupled with an increasing appreciation of the *historicity* of many of these intersubjective and dialogical structures (Nietzsche, Heidegger, Wittgenstein, Dewey, Rorty)—and suddenly we are out of the modern and into the postmodern mood, where, no matter how much these various theorists disagree with each other, they are all united in a firm demonstration that monological consciousness and monological methodology are severely limited models, if not outright distortions, of human experience and reality.

Now the crucial point about these developments is that most of the pioneering psychological theorists of the modern West—including Freud, Jung, Adler, Rank, James, Watson, Titchener, Wundt—were all ensconced in the pre-intersubjective era. That is, they all, without exception, were embedded in a profoundly monological framework. For each of them, a subject reports the phenomena of consciousness, and those phenomenological reports are taken as foundational, even if they eventually lead elsewhere. Thus, whether the technique is introspection (Wundt), free association (Freud), psychedelics (James), active imagination (Jung), or stream of consciousness (James), for each of them the basic adequacy of phenomenology is never profoundly questioned.[3] Each of them dramatically expanded the *content* of acceptable phenomenology, stretching it from typical rational-egoic contents into such areas as primary process, magical cognitions, collective mythic images and archetypes, religious experiences, and so forth; but none of them challenged, or were even clearly aware of, the intersubjective structures allowing this phenomenology to occur in the first place. In short, they all discovered new cards in the phenomenological game, but none spotted the nonphenomenological rules of the game itself.

Most psychological researchers to this day, including Grof, remain largely embedded in this monological consciousness framework, in my opinion, even as they continue to extend the phenomenology of consciousness into nonordinary states (NOSC). In other words, no amount of LSD, or holotropic breathing, or hypnosis, or shamanic experiences, or rituals, or intense bodywork will disclose the moral, cultural, linguistic, and syntactical structures in which and through which those subjective experiences arise. And thus, *you will find none of those crucial intersubjective patterns on any of the maps or cartographies or cosmologies in Grof's model* (nor in any of the traditions he cites in any of his works). These constitutive patterns are all invisible to Grof's mode of investigation, and, I believe, they constitute an area of neglect and inadequacy in his system.

Thus, in Grof's overall model, monological science joins with monological consciousness, and this, I believe, severely limits our understanding of human consciousness in general. It further makes it quite difficult to conceptualize how temporary *states* of consciousness can be converted into enduring *traits* (or structures) of consciousness, because these structures are, in large measure, intersubjectively constructed and will thus appear in no phenomenology of consciousness, including Grof's.

Likewise, the application of Grof's model to larger issues (historical, cultural, sociological, aesthetic) simply reproduces this inadequacy. Thus, for example, when Tarnas uses Grof's model to interpret the rise of modernity (in *The Passion of the Western Mind*), the inadequacies of the model translate themselves directly into the inadequacies in Tarnas's account, which is why, in my opinion, he seems to miss so much that is crucial to the historical emergence of modernity. Tarnas is also strongly committed to a Romantic/Washburn/Wilber-I viewpoint, which further limits his account, in my opinion.

This monological hegemony is regrettable enough, but in my view it further predisposes Grof to what I believe is the central misconception in his model, the nature and importance of the perinatal level.

PERINATAL REDUX

Grof defines the word "perinatal" as follows: "The prefix *peri-* means literally 'around' or 'near,' and *natalis* translates as 'pertaining to delivery.' It suggests events that immediately precede, are associated with, or follow biological birth."[4] In Grof's early psychedelic research, he consistently found that as a typical session unfolded, individuals would in some sense contact successively earlier stages of their own development, moving first from surface abstract or aesthetic patterns, to earlier biographical (and Freudian) material, and eventually to what appeared to be an actual reliving of biological birth. Grof named the spectrum of experiences that seemed organized around the imprints of the actual delivery process "perinatal." Once this perinatal level was contacted, it often acted as a doorway to transpersonal and spiritual experiences.

Further observations suggested that perinatal experiences in general, although not merely a reliving of biological birth, nonetheless organized themselves in four fairly distinct classes that in many important ways seemed to parallel the clinical stages of childbirth. Grof therefore postulated that "basic perinatal matrices" (BPM) were laid down during the actual biological delivery. Although not all perinatal experiences can be reduced to an actual reliving of biological birth, nonetheless these matrices, as deeply imprinted structures in the bodymind, act as formative patterns in perinatal experiences in general.

"The connection between biological birth and perinatal experiences is quite deep and specific," says Grof. "This makes it possible to use the clinical stages of delivery in constructing a conceptual model that helps us to understand the dynamics of the perinatal level of the unconscious." The general stages of clinical delivery cement the blueprints of the four basic perinatal matrices: BPM I, the oceanic or amniotic universe; BPM II, cosmic engulfment and no exit; BPM III, the death-rebirth struggle; and BPM IV, the death-rebirth experience. These blueprints, stencils, or matrices "have deep roots in the biological aspects of birth."[5]

Nonetheless, Grof points out that perinatal experiences rarely involve a simple reliving of the birth trauma. Rather, perinatal experiences tend to be *the doorway to transpersonal experiences in general*. Thus, Grof is at pains to point out that "In spite of its close connection to childbirth, the perinatal process transcends biology and has important psychological, philosophical, and spiritual dimensions. . . . Certain important characteristics of the perinatal process clearly suggest that it is a much broader phenomenon than reliving of biological birth."[6]

That very well might be true, but nonetheless, right there, I believe, Grof has begun to lose track of his definitions. He deliberately introduced the term *perinatal* because it pertained specifically to experiences surrounding the actual biological birth process. But when aspects of these experiences "clearly suggest that it is a much broader phenomenon than reliving of biological birth," he explicitly rejects the reduction of these experiences to biological birth *but keeps the term "perinatal."*

Thus, any time an intense death-rebirth struggle occurs, of any sort, at any age, under any circumstance, Grof will tend to do a dual analysis, reflecting his hidden, dual definition of perinatal. He will first claim that a reliving of the actual birth trauma is the central core of the death-rebirth phenomenon; then he will disavow reduction to that specific trauma and open his analysis to all sorts of other levels, factors, and dimensions. In doing so, he will deny reductionism to biological birth, but he will keep the term *perinatal* to describe any and all intense experiences of death-rebirth, experiences that he nevertheless continues to insist are anchored to, if not reducible to, blueprints laid down in actual childbirth.

This is typical: "On this [perinatal] level of the unconscious, the issue of death is universal and entirely dominates the picture."[7] So far, this demonstrates that all deep perinatal experiences involve intense life-and-death issues; it does not in the least demonstrate that all life-and-death issues are perinatal. So it is necessary for Grof to move from this broad and general account of perinatal as involving death, to perinatal in the specific sense of being directly related to childbirth. This he does in the next step: "The connection between biological birth and perinatal experiences is quite deep and specific."[8] "Experiential confrontation with death at this depth of self-exploration tends to be intimately interwoven with a variety of phenomena related to the birth process. . . . Subjects often experience themselves as fetuses and can relive various aspects of their biological birth . . . many of the accompanying physiological changes that take place make sense as typical concomitants of birth."[9]

Now Grof might be correct that intense life-and-death issues have at their core a biological birth stencil, but his evidence in no fashion establishes this. Rather, those particular observations stem primarily from intense LSD or holotropic sessions, where individuals might indeed regress to an actual reliving of the clinical delivery process. But on the face of it, those observations do not in any way describe, for example, the transpersonal stages of vipassana meditation as one enters nirvikalpa samadhi (the *necessity* of first experiencing oneself as a fetus is found in none of the traditional texts). Grof is referring to a specific nexus of phenomena that occur under intense LSD sessions, and, occasionally, under other intense forms of physiological stress.

I am not denying Grof's data; it very well might be quite accurate. What I am questioning is the immediate and massive generalization from this very specific and narrow situation, where intense life-and-death issues appear to coalesce around childbirth, to issues of death and rebirth in general, not all of which appear to involve a reliving of clinical delivery.

I will return to that point in a moment. But in the meantime, notice that Grof immediately makes that unwarranted and generalized leap (and he will do so using exactly his hidden, dual definition of perinatal). Thus: "The central element in the complex dynamics of the death-rebirth process seems to be reliving the biological birth trauma." He always adds that the death-rebirth is more than a mere reliving of the birth trauma, but nonetheless the core and *necessary element* is a reliving of biological birth: "Although the entire spectrum of experiences occurring on this level cannot be reduced to a reliving of biological birth, the birth trauma seems to represent an important core of the process. For this reason, I refer to this domain of the unconscious as *perinatal*."[10]

And here exactly we have the hidden dual definition. What actually is "this level of self-exploration"? It is the confrontation with death and rebirth. What is an important *core* of this confrontation—that is, a *necessary* ingredient? The reliving of biological birth, which is why it is called perinatal. But what does the *perinatal level* itself consist of? Any intense existential death-rebirth experiences. But that moves from the first definition (biological birth) to the second (any intense existential crisis in general), and does so in a fashion that is not in the least supported by Grof's evidence or arguments. There is, as he puts it, "the entire spectrum of experiences occurring on this [life-death] level," and there is the "process of biological birth," and his dual definition refers to *both* of them as perinatal.

At this point, Grof's definition of "perinatal" has slipped completely loose from its original mooring and is running indiscriminately through the existential world at large. "Deep experiential encounter with birth and death is typically associated with an existential crisis of extraordinary proportions during which the individual seriously questions the meaning of his or her life and existence in general."[11]

But all that follows from Grof's actually presented evidence is that perinatal experience can be profoundly existential; it does not follow in the least that all existential crises are perinatal. But with that elemental confusion, Grof resorts to his dual definition and anchors all *existential* death-rebirth phenomena squarely in the actual *childbirth* stencils, so much so that he begins referring to any death-rebirth experience as THE death-rebirth experience, and this monolithic death-rebirth blueprint is, of course, biological birth: "The experiences of the death-rebirth process . . . can be . . . derived from certain anatomical, physiological, and biochemical aspects of the corresponding stages of childbirth with which they are associated."[12]

When it is necessary to use his dual definition in order to expand the role of childbirth trauma beyond that warranted by his evidence, Grof will switch from biological birth to "the perinatal level," because, as we have seen, by his dual definition they are now not the same thing at all. This dual definition (childbirth/existential) allows him to implicitly keep his reductionism while explicitly denying it.

Thus, says Grof, the perinatal level of the unconscious is at the intersection between the personal and the transpersonal. But all that actually means is that *an existential death-rebirth lies between personal and transpersonal development*. Grof has not in any fashion demonstrated that a reliving of biological birth is necessary in all or even most cases in order for that development to occur. Intense LSD and holotropic sessions might indeed involve an actual reliving of childbirth; but in attempting to generalize beyond those quite specific situations to existential and transpersonal dimensions in general, Grof has stepped quite beyond the warrant of his evidence.

In fact, it is my own opinion that with this hidden, dual definition of perinatal (it means both existential and childbirth), Grof has confused chronology with ontology. With intense LSD sessions—which formed and still form the core of Grof's model—individuals might regress in a chronological sequence: from present day to early childhood (Freudian) to birth trauma (Rankian), beyond which, once the individual has dropped an exclusive identification with the gross bodymind, properly transpersonal experiences do indeed disclose themselves.

But by confusing this chronology with an actual ontology of dimensions of awareness, Grof must insert the actual biological birth process between the personal and the transpersonal domains, and that is the only fashion in which he can generalize his model beyond the specific and rather narrow conditions in which it was developed. And thus he is forced generally to postulate that a reliving of specific biological birth, in one form or another, is generally necessary for transpersonal development.

At that point Grof's model, I believe, is out of touch with the preponderance of evidence from the meditative and contemplative traditions, from Western depth psychology (including Jungian), and from most of the evidence generated in NOSC research. The issue, to state it rather crudely, is not whether an existential level exists between the personal and the transpersonal domains. Virtually all parties (including me) agree that is usually the case. Rather, the question is, does that existential level necessarily involve, in part, the actual reliving of the clinical birth delivery? Not might it occasionally, but must it as a rule, do so? Grof basically says yes, virtually everybody else says no.

You do not find the *necessity* to relive clinical birth in any of the major spiritual manuals and techniques. It is rarely if ever found in any of the ascetic practices, shamanic techniques, or contemplative yogas. You do not find it in the great classics of the perennial philosophy or in any of the major wisdom tradition texts. Nor do you find it in the vast majority of the Western depth psychologists, including James and Jung and the general Jungian tradition. (You don't even find it in Washburn, who, as a regressivist, might be expected to concur; he does not.)

Huston Smith has given what is still perhaps the definitive critique of Grof's model from the view of the great wisdom traditions. Of the many crucial points Smith makes—and I am in substantial agreement with all of them—especially relevant are the charges that (1) Grof confuses chronological regression with ontological modes of being and consciousness, thus fundamentally misunderstanding their actual origin; (2) this leads Grof to misunderstand the actual role of clinical birth in existential and spiritual domains, since they are "influenced only, not caused" by such; (3) this leads Grof to fail to appreciate that "birth and death are not physical only."[13]

On the other hand, Huston has always acknowledged that the holarchy of basic structures as I have outlined them is in substantial agreement with the perennial traditions as he summarizes them in *Forgotten Truth*. Massive amounts of meditative and phenomenological evidence from the great traditions squarely support this view, which Grof's model does not handle in its present form.

Grof tends to respond to such criticism by saying that all of those wisdom traditions do in fact recognize death-rebirth phenomena, and they all agree that such existential crises are the crucial transition from personal bondage to transpersonal liberation. This is quite true, but Grof goes further and, in the same breath, equates existential death-rebirth with perinatal/birth, which is exactly the equation that is altogether unwarranted by the preponderance of evidence, and an equation that gains currency *only* by his hidden dual definition of perinatal. Grof is assuming exactly that which he is supposed to demonstrate—namely, not that there exists an existential level lying between all personal and transpersonal development (all parties agree that is so), but that the essential core of that existential level is a stencil of clinical childbirth (which virtually nobody but Grof maintains, and for which he has presented no generalized evidence).

Thus, in my opinion, what may be typical in intense LSD and holotropic sessions has been unjustifiably made paradigmatic for all forms of transpersonal development, an extension for which there is no evidential warrant whatsoever. In doing so, this approach devalues and ignores other equally crucial components of the human psyche, most notably the constitutive nature of vast intersubjective networks of moral, cultural, linguistic, and syntactical structures, with the net result that, in my opinion, this remains an extremely important and fruitful, but quite limited, model of overall consciousness and its development.

FULCRUM-0 AND FULCRUM-6

I am not denying the existence of the basic perinatal matrices, nor the possibility that they might play a formative role in certain psychospiritual developments. I will now briefly indicate how I believe Grof's data, shorn of their hidden dual definitions, can find resonance with my own model.

Let me begin with what I call the actual *existential level*. In my model, the basic structure of this level is called "vision-logic"; the self-need is that for "self-actualization"; the moral sense is postconventional; and the self-sense or self-identity is called "centauric" or "existential" (fulcrum-6).

I have consistently, from my first book to my latest, maintained that the vast majority of evidence, culled from hundreds of sources East and West (which I have cited), clearly suggests that an existential level (by whatever name) is the great doorway to the spiritual and transpersonal dimensions. *The existential level is, as it were, the intersection between the personal and the transpersonal* (or, more technically, between the gross-oriented bodymind and the transegoic subtle and causal domains). Accordingly, in order for development to continue beyond the individual and existential level, the self (or consciousness) must break or deconstruct its exclusive identification with the gross bodymind and all its relations.[14]

This is a "death," to be sure, but in my model, as Stan acknowledges, every fulcrum possesses a signature death-rebirth struggle. Each developmental shift in the center of gravity means that the self has ceased identifying with the basic structure of that stage—has actually died to that level, disidentified with that level, transcended that level—and is reborn into the new and deeper and wider sphere of the consciousness of the next wave. Every fulcrum embodies a death to one basic level and a rebirth on the next, so that, making stepping stones of our dead selves, we are finally delivered unto the Deathless.[15]

The specific contour of each death-rebirth transformation depends upon the basic level of the given fulcrum at which it occurs: there is death to the (exclusive) pleroma, death to the uroboros, death to the typhon, death to the persona, death to the ego, death to the centaur, death to the soul (which are modes of self-sense at some of the important basic waves). *Each death is difficult in its own way*; sufficient unto the day is the death thereof.

Nonetheless, the death-rebirth struggle of the centaur/existential level is, in some ways, the most dramatic, simply because, as we noted, it is the great transition from the personal to the transpersonal domains. And, as we also noted, existential death is the deconstruction of the extensive networks of biologically oriented identifications (death to an exclusive identification with the gross-oriented bodymind in general). As such, the death-rebirth struggle of the existential level is profoundly significant and altogether intense.

Accordingly, the real question is, Does this great death-rebirth transition necessarily involve the actual reliving of the clinical delivery? I maintain, contrary to Grof, that in *some* cases this *might* indeed happen, just as Grof recounts, but it is *not necessary*, and, not being necessary, *it cannot be the actual mechanism of the great transition to the transpersonal.*

Recall that, in my own model, biological birth—the actual delivery process—is fulcrum-o. Like all fulcrums, it has that very general 1-2-3 process of fusion/differentiation/integration. These broad subphases of fulcrum-o are quite similar to Grof's BPMs.[16]

I believe that these fulcrum-o birth matrices are indeed imprinted on the gross bodymind of the human being. However, exactly how much importance they assume cannot yet be decided, given the evidence presently available. In my opinion, Grof exaggerates the evidence for these imprints and their influence; and, in any event, I believe he steps across the line of actual evidence in generalizing their importance for existential and transpersonal domains. Here is what I believe we can say on the basis of the available evidence:

A general existential level (by whatever name) lies between personal and transpersonal developments. On this, Washburn, Grof, the great traditions, and I all agree. In my model, this is fulcrum-6. This does *not* mean that transpersonal experiences cannot occur prior to fulcrum-6; they can and often do, but only as temporary states of consciousness (NOSC), or as peak experiences, or as part of the "trailing clouds of glory" (as I will explain below). But in order for such *states* to be converted to *traits* (i.e, in order for temporary and exclusive states of consciousness to be converted to enduring and incorporative structures and patterns constantly available to consciousness), the individual will have to grow and develop into them. At some point, if growth continues, he or she will confront the general existential domain, beyond which can be found more enduring transpersonal patterns.

Washburn, Grof, and I also agree that this existential transition is something of a total life/death confrontation (or series of them), often difficult and brutal, but in most cases profoundly transformative.

At that point, our accounts diverge. Both Washburn and Grof see this as (in part) a literal and necessary regression: Washburn, to fulcrum-1; Grof, further back into the intrauterine state of fulcrum-0. I myself maintain that such regression *might* occur, but it is *not* the defining or essential core and doorway to the transpersonal.

Under what circumstances, then, might an actual regression occur? In my overall model, wherever there are developmental malformations at any of the self-fulcrums, there results a "stick-point" or "lesion" in consciousness. These malformations (splitting, alienation, repression, fragmentation, fixation, dissociation, etc.) will, in various ways and degrees, sabotage subsequent development. If these dissociations are severe, higher development cannot easily proceed without recontacting and to some degree reintegrating the dissociated aspects (the "undigested experiences," since one of the self's characteristics is that it is the locus of experiential "metabolism").

Moreover, at the existential level itself, as consciousness begins to deconstruct an exclusive identity with the gross bodymind, it likewise begins to deconstruct the *repression barrier* which instituted much of the dissociation of the various aspects of that gross and vital bodymind, and consequently any particularly severe past repressions/fixations tend especially at this point to jump into awareness (or in other ways act as a regressive magnet that must be negotiated in order for further development to occur). Thus, particularly at the existential level (fulcrum-6), any significant malformations in any of the earlier fulcrums—including fulcrum-0 and fulcrum-1—might resurface to aggressively command attention.[17]

Thus, as I see it, this model can handle the evidence and data of both the Grof and Washburn models, but the reverse is not true. If, in any individual case, actual regression occurs, either to fulcrum-1 (Washburn) or fulcrum-0 (Grof), there is ample room for such phenomena in my model. But if such massive regression does *not* occur in some cases, both of their models fail. Since the total web of cross-cultural evidence indicates that regression and direct recontacting of the infantile state is not a necessary prerequisite for, say, sahaj samadhi, then these models have already failed in that regard.

Frontal and Psychic Developmental Lines

I will now suggest what I suspect is actually behind Grof's data and his perinatal orientation.

The fact that fulcrum-0 is the "beginning of the line" in terms of this life does not mean it is the beginning of the line for consciousness itself. I believe we must hold open the possibility that, prior to fulcrum-0, there are the entire bardo (and past-life) realms. I extensively outlined this possibility in *The Atman Project*—in fact, I devoted the entire last chapter to it.

As I point out in that chapter, prior to conception in the gross body-mind, consciousness has traversed the causal Dharmakaya and then the subtle Sambhogakaya, and then finally takes gross form with conception in the womb (where it then begins fulcrum-0). This is why, since *The Atman Project*, I have always used Wordsworth's "Not in entire forgetfulness . . . But trailing clouds of glory do we come" to describe this situation. This is also why I have never denied that transpersonal experiences of various sorts are available during the pre-egoic period; I have simply denied that they are due to any pre-egoic structures.

In the Tibetan Buddhist model (which I represented in *The Atman Project*), the individual psyche or consciousness is composed of two distinct essences or drops (*tigle*). That is, in the heart center of every human, there is the empty essence (*tigle*) of consciousness, divided into two layers or two drops: (1) the "lifetime indestructible drop," which develops during a particular lifetime, but perishes upon biological death, and (2), within or interior to the lifetime indestructible drop, the "eternal indestructible drop," which lasts until Buddhahood and thus transmigrates from life to life until radical Enlightenment. This interior drop is, in my terminology, the psychic/subtle being—which I also deliberately refer to as the "soul," since that, too, lasts until actual spiritual resurrection in the causal/nondual Divine Domain of pure Emptiness. (This, as we will see, is also quite similar to Aurobindo's distinction between the frontal consciousness, which develops in this lifetime, and the deeper/psychic being, which transmigrates.)[18]

In general, for this Tibetan/Aurobindo/Wilber-II model, the highest level of stable evolution reached in any given life permeates the eternal indestructible drop and thus is carried, not usually as specific memories but as a mood of adaptation, to the next life. As I explained it in *The Atman Project*, the more evolved the soul is, the less involved it is (i.e., the less it forgets its higher source and suchness), and this continues until radical Enlightenment, whereupon the soul is completely subsumed or superseded (negated and preserved) in prior Unborn Spirit or radical Emptiness, which is simply the luminous transparency of this and every moment.

In *The Atman Project*, I describe the prior bardo domains through which this soul-drop travels on its way to rebirth in the gross bodymind (i.e., the *involutionary* journey from causal to subtle to gross bodymind), where it then ends up in the prenatal state. In other words, this prenatal state is then the beginning of fulcrum-o, or the *beginning of frontal consciousness development and evolution* (the beginning of the lifetime indestructible drop), a development or evolution which occurs through the nine or ten basic structures of (frontal) consciousness and their associated self-fulcrums.

Several points might be noted in regard to this "two-source" (frontal/ soul) Tibetan/Aurobindo/Wilber-II model.

1. As frontal consciousness development gets under way, the psychic/ soul witnessing capacity is progressively forgotten. In *The Atman Project*, I specifically describe this as an *amnesis*, a forgetting, in a section called "Amnesia and the In Between" (the bardo is the "in between" state, in between death and rebirth).

2. The traditions vary on how long it takes, in infancy, for these "trailing clouds of glory" of the psychic/soul witnessing to fade. Teachers I have talked to (and various texts themselves) suggest that it seems to vary from a few weeks to a few years, depending primarily on the "strength" of the transmigrating soul-drop.

3. Any veridical memories of the prenatal and perinatal and early infancy period, should they prove valid—and I have Stan's data in mind here—would have to be carried by this psychic/soul consciousness, and *not* by any structures or consciousness in the *frontal* personality, since those structures and their neuronal supports (myelin sheaths) are very poorly developed. In my model, this is the proposed explanation for the subjective carrier of Grof's perinatal memories, should evidence continue to support their existence.[19]

4. This also means, once again, that any transpersonal occasions during the pre-egoic period are *not* due to any of the pre-egoic frontal structures themselves, but rather to the deeper psychic/soul being, which is increasingly forgotten (amnesia) as frontal development gets under way. Thus, contacting the psychic/soul level is not a recapture of any preegoic or infantile structures in the frontal line (which actually obscure that consciousness). In other words, the transpersonal psychic/soul of

the *pre-egoic period* is not in any fashion a *pre-egoic structure* laid down or developed during the pre-egoic or infantile period itself.

5. When frontal consciousness development itself passes the existential level (fulcrum-6) and reaches the actual psychic level (fulcrum-7), the psychic/soul dimension begins to enter frontal awareness.

6. For just that reason, this is precisely where a reliving of the birth trauma *might* occur, since that perinatal awareness/memory is carried, not by the ego, which did not exist at the time, but by the psychic/soul, which now emerges in frontal consciousness.

7. This reliving of the birth trauma is therefore not in any way *necessary* for spiritual growth and development; what is crucial here is simply the emergence of the psychic level into frontal awareness, and this *may or may not* involve a flashback of its entry into the gross domain.

8. In any event, this psychic/soul witness, whether trailing clouds of glory in the prenatal and perinatal state or emerging at stage 7 of frontal development, is not the ultimate or in any way the highest seat of consciousness, but is already a samsarically bound and transmigrating being. In no case, then, does it have anything to do with radical Enlightenment: it is precisely what has to be deconstructed (negated and preserved) in order for Enlightenment to shine forth.

Thus, in Wilber-I, I imagined that any transpersonal experiences of prenatal to early childhood were due to the fact that the pre-egoic structures *were themselves* transpersonal in their *actual structure*. This was the pre/trans fallacy. In Wilber-II, I maintain that any transpersonal experiences of infancy are *not* due to pre-egoic frontal structures, but (1) to these trailing clouds of glory of the psychic/soul drop; (2) to the continual cycle of waking/dream/sleep *states*, which plunges each self through the gross/subtle/causal domains every twenty-four hours (not to mention the microgenetic involutional cycle occurring every second, for which, see the last chapter in *The Atman Project*); and (3) temporary peak experiences. [See *Integral Psychology*, chapter 11, for a full discussion of this topic.]

The pre/trans fallacy results when any genuinely transegoic structure or state—including the psychic/soul consciousness, wherever it appears—is identified or confused with structures that are pre-egoic (such as emotional-vitality, polymorphous perversity, free libido distribution, infantile adualism, and so on)—which is, of course, the Romantic/Washburn/Wilber-I "mistake." In other words, the transpersonal states that appear in the pre-egoic period are not due to any pre-egoic structures.

Moreover, the pre/trans fallacy fully applies to the events in both the frontal consciousness and in the psychic/soul line. The reason, I believe, that Grof and others have sometimes found that the pre/trans fallacy is "not quite right" is that, in my opinion, they confuse these two lines of development. In other words, what is *genuinely* "trans" in one line (the psychic/soul) appears during the *pre* period of the other line (the frontal line). If we keep these two lines distinct, and realize that the pre/trans fallacy *applies to each of the lines individually*, then these confusions, I believe, will almost instantly clear up.

For example, we have already seen how the pre/trans fallacy applies to the frontal development or frontal *evolution* (i.e., pre-egoic frontal structures ought not be confused with transegoic frontal structures; to do so results either in reductionism or elevationism). *But precisely the same pre/trans principle is fully operative in the involutionary arc as well*—and the pre and the trans should not be confused in that sequence either.

In fact, the *Tibetan Book of the Dead* gives one basic and profound reason that the soul falls away from the Clear Light Emptiness and thus ends up in lower and lower states (causal to subtle to gross): namely, the soul-drop confuses the lower or pre states with the higher or trans states, and under this pre/trans confusion, the soul-drop actually *chooses the lower, thinking it is the higher*! A bad case of elevationism is exactly the mechanism that lands it in samsara! This is an excellent description of the pre/trans fallacy operating in the bardo realms and the involutionary movement, just as it operates in the evolutionary as well (although headed, of course, in the "opposite" direction).

I have always described the pre/trans fallacy as a confusing of involution per se with something that happens in evolution, and this is simply another way of saying, Don't confuse these evolutionary and involutionary lines, because the crisscrossing of those lines usually leads to a pre/trans confusion of one sort or another.

Finally, this is why I have always maintained that regressive therapies, such as rebirthing and breathwork, enter the transpersonal from the "back door." This does not mean I am somehow putting them down. I am not; I am simply describing the unarguable *chronological sequence* of certain of these experiences. When Stan describes a typical LSD session as moving from present-day concerns, to past biological events and Freudian concerns, then to Rankian childbirth trauma (which is then often the doorway to the transpersonal), there is no mistaking that chronological order: it is unarguably regressive (which is why I call that door to the transpersonal the "back door").

But what is being contacted in these regressive therapies is not *essentially* the biological birth ordeal, but the psychic/soul consciousness *present at that ordeal*. And, most important of all, that psychic/soul consciousness can *just as easily be contacted without the regression*; and in fact, in almost all forms of consciousness disciplines, it is most definitely contacted *without the regression*. After all, the psychic/soul consciousness is simply the same consciousness that emerges at stage 7, after the existential crisis (of stage 6) is negotiated. As the psychic/soul being comes to the fore, it might indeed recall its biological birth, but usually it does not, and it certainly *is not necessary* to do so for further growth, because it has already handled the crucial existential life-death crisis of fulcrum-6. And in any event, this psychic/soul being is destined itself only to pass, superseded by the unborn Spirit of the causal and nondual occasions.

Stan's dual definition of perinatal, I believe we can now see, hinges on a confusion between the psychic/soul consciousness present at fulcrum-o, and the actual stencils of that childbirth fulcrum. Fulcrum-o is the *beginning* of the pre-egoic realms, but the *end* of the bardo realms, and this intersection—the intersection toward the *beginning* of frontal *evolution* and toward the *end* of psychic/soul *involution*—generates the strange dual experiences that Stan has named perinatal.

But because he does not distinguish carefully enough between these two lines (evolution and involution), the result is that, in my opinion, he sometimes uncritically *identifies* them at their cross-section (biological birth = the gateway to the transpersonal). He then understandably denies reductionism, even though the identification itself is in fact very reductionistic (and simply not true). But if we keep these two lines separate, not only does the pre/trans fallacy still guide our path in both of them, Stan's data immediately opens itself to a more benevolent match with the world's great wisdom traditions, not to mention with my own model and the large amounts of evidence supporting it. As it is now, there are vast amounts of clinical, experimental, phenomenological, intersubjective, meditative, and psychotherapeutic evidence and data (from perennial to postmodern sources) that Grof's model, by itself, fails to take into account.[20]

Nevertheless, I would like to end on the same note with which I began: in terms of the overall "big picture" of the spectrum of consciousness and the realms of the human unconscious, there is an extraordinary amount of overlap and agreement between Washburn, Grof, and myself. I prefer to think in terms of those many similarities, even as we continue to hash out the details.

8

Integral Feminism

SEX AND GENDER ON THE
MORAL AND SPIRITUAL PATH

*Does Spirit manifest as male and female? Is there God and God-
dess? Do men and women therefore have different, if comple-
mentary, types of spirituality? At what point, if any, do we cease
to be male and female and start being human? Has feminism
outlived its usefulness? Or does it simply need a more integral
approach?*

A FEMINIST PERSPECTIVE

WHAT WOULD A TRULY integral feminism look like? An approach
to feminism that is actually "all-level, all-quadrant"? In this
chapter we will explore exactly that theme, after first addressing a few
common misconceptions that are hindering the emergence of a more
integral view.[1]

Carol Gilligan

We can start with some of the typical misunderstandings of Carol Gilligan's work and the notion of hierarchy. I believe that many feminist
writers rather badly misunderstand the nature of hierarchy, which leads
them to misconstrue both my model and Carol Gilligan's, which is a
deeply hierarchical model.

Gilligan found that men and women both move through three broad hierarchical stages of moral development, but that men tend to progress through these stages based more on judgments of rights and justice, whereas women tend to negotiate these hierarchical stages based on judgments of care and responsibility. Thus, Kohlberg's mistake was *not* the broad hierarchical stage conception itself (which Gilligan accepts),[2] but the belief that, *within* those stages, male ranking represented a higher stage than female linking, which is simply not true. (This is the confusing of permeable with prepersonal, a fallacy we most definitely want to avoid.) But notice: each successive stage of female judgment is indeed superior in its capacity to express and manifest care. Each female stage is hierarchically ranked, but within each stage, judgments occur by linking and connection. So the same vertical, hierarchical, developmental ranking of stages occurs in both men and women, but men progress through these stages while making judgments of rights and justice, women making judgments of care and responsibility.

I have summarized the large amount of research in this area by saying that both men and women exist as agency-in-communion (as do all holons), but men tend to *translate* with an emphasis on *agency*, women with an emphasis on *communion*. But both of them *transform* through the same broad, gender-neutral, holarchical stages of consciousness unfolding.

Thus, for Gilligan, women move through three general stages: selfishness to care to universal care (which she also calls selfish to conventional ethical to postconventional metaethical). These are the three broad stages of preconventional, conventional, and postconventional, which I have also termed *egocentric*, *sociocentric*, and *worldcentric* (and, in my model, the worldcentric or global stage is the platform and the gateway to higher spiritual domains). For Gilligan, each of those successive stages is *higher* and *more valuable* precisely because, as I would word it, the woman can extend the *circle of care* to more and more people (just as when men move through those same stages, they extend the *circle of justice* to more and more people, from egocentric to ethnocentric to worldcentric modes).

Gilligan has suggested that "these two distinct moral orientations . . . can be further integrated in a hierarchical moral stage beyond the formal operational level."[3]

Note also: besides being hierarchical, Gilligan's model is linear, in the sense meant by developmentalists. That is, her three (or four) major stages unfold in a linear fashion that cannot be reversed or bypassed, because each stage depends upon certain competences provided by the previous stages (you cannot get to universal care without the previous stage of care, for example). The first two things to note about Gilligan's model, then, is that it is *linear* and *hierarchical* for *both* men and women.[4]

All of this unfortunately tends to be ignored or overlooked by many feminists, who somehow imagine that Gilligan was saying women are altogether free of that nasty "ranking." I believe this is typical of a certain feminist approach that tends to ignore and deny any sort of female ranking hierarchy, under the performative contradiction of web-only models. By focusing essentially on heterarchy in women's experience, advocates of this approach ignore and devalue the important aspects of women's experience that are also hierarchical, which, I believe, badly distorts this entire approach, and makes it virtually impossible to give a coherent account of female development at all.

In other words, these linking-only models are deeply involved in what I call pathological heterarchy: not a communion but a fusion, not a linking but a meltdown, not a connecting but an indissociation—an incapacity to rank values at all, which actually devalues all values, a pathology that one feminist (observing "process queens" at work) called "the bland leading the bland."

The typical pathological form of male agency is "power over," or brutal dominance and rigid autonomy. The male does not want to be a *part* of anything else (communion), he wants only to be the *whole* himself (alienated agency): he fears relationship and values only autonomy. This is not male agency, but a pathology of male agency. Likewise, the typical pathological form of female communion is fusion: the female fears autonomy and disappears into relationship, often destroying her own identity in the process. She does not want to be a *whole* (with its own agency), but merely a *part* of something else (exaggerated communion). This is not normal female heterarchy or mutual equivalence, but pathological heterarchy or meltdown: all ranking is out, linking alone reigns.

And it is, alas, pathological heterarchy that drives too many of these "web-only" and "permeable" models of alleged female development. More accurate, I believe, is a model that acknowledges and honors both hierarchy and heterarchy in both male and female, and thus can account for both development and pathology in each sex. And one thing is certain: we do not overcome pathological masculinity with pathological femininity.[5]

The Permeable Self

Many feminists agree with the extensive research that suggests that men tend to emphasize agency (or the autonomous self) and women communion (or "connection" and the "permeable" self). However, I believe that because many feminists devalue and marginalize hierarchical integration in females, they do not often present a coherent explanation of the development of the permeable self. My approach does so, or at least attempts to do so, in the following way:

We saw that men and women both develop through the same gender-neutral basic structures or expanding spheres of consciousness, but men tend to develop through these expanding spheres with an emphasis on agency, rights, justice, and autonomy, whereas women tend to develop through the same holarchical spheres based more on communion, responsibility, relationship, care, and connection.[6]

Thus, in my model, the "permeable" self of women develops through the same general stages of egocentric, sociocentric, worldcentric, and spiritual domains as the male, but with a different emphasis ("in a different voice"), a different set of priorities, a different mood, and a rather different set of spiritual disciplines.

Accordingly, for the female, there is egocentric permeable (selfish), sociocentric permeable (care), worldcentric permeable (universal care), and spiritual permeable (universal union), precisely as the male negotiates those same general spheres with a somewhat more agentic emphasis (agentic egocentric, agentic sociocentric, and so on). The same basic stages—preconventional to conventional to postconventional to post-postconventional—are operative in both, but in a different voice.

Thus, it is absolutely not the case, as some critics have suggested, that in my model the prepersonal stages are simply equated with "permeable" boundaries, thus intrinsically devaluing the female orientation.[7] Rather, there is prepersonal permeable, personal permeable, and transpersonal permeable. Thus, in overall development, the female self becomes permeable to deeper and wider spheres of consciousness, right up to and including a permeability to Spirit or Ground—the same basic spheres through which the male develops with a more agentic orientation. Neither gender orientation is in any fashion privileged or made paradigmatic.

INTEGRAL FEMINISM: ALL-LEVEL, ALL-QUADRANT

There are today at least a dozen major schools of feminism (liberal, socialist, spiritual, eco, womanist, radical, anarchist, lesbian, Marxist, cultural, constructivist, power), and about the only thing they all agree on is that females exist (actually, at least two of the schools deny that). There simply is no consensus view on "the" voice of women, despite the claim of some feminists to be speaking for such.

Rather, I believe that what we need is a much more integral approach, an approach that, in acknowledging the truly different perspectives of a dozen or so different feminist schools, might actually find a scheme that would be more accommodating to each of them. This more integral approach is indeed part of what *Sex, Ecology, Spirituality* attempts to develop, at least in rough and outline form. SES is volume 1 of the Kosmos trilogy; in the forthcoming volume 2 (tentatively entitled *Sex, God, and Gender: The Ecology of Men and Women*), I expand and fill in the details of this general model of sex and gender.

The idea, I believe, is to bring an "all-quadrant, all-level" approach to sex and gender issues—an integral feminism. This approach, in my opinion, gives us a chance to bring together a dozen different schools of feminism, which, ironically, have heretofore resisted being linked, integrated, and connected. For example, each of the different theories of sex and gender (orthodox as well as feminist) has tended to focus on only one quadrant (and usually only one level in one quadrant), with an attempt to make it paradigmatic and exclusionary. I'll go around the four quadrants and give examples from each, and then suggest how their crucial insights, when freed of their hegemonic claims, might be honored and incorporated in a more integral embrace.

Upper Right (Behavioral)

These are the objective aspects of individual holons, which, in the case of human beings, include biological and hormonal factors, such as the effects of testosterone, oxytocin, and estrogen on individual human behavior. These factors, most researchers agree, *influence* (but do not strictly *cause*) sometimes quite different behavioral patterns in the sexes (sexual profligacy in the male being a typical example).

The *radical feminists* have particularly embraced the notion that there are dramatic, biologically based differences between the sexes, as have their strange bedfellows, the sociobiologists. For radical feminists, this is sometimes portrayed as: estrogen is the Goddess, testosterone is the Devil. (There is more than a grain of truth to that, alas; but on balance, both hormonal dispositions have their own appropriate and equally important work to do.) Both the radical feminists and the sociobiologists are onto some important (if limited) aspects of the biological basis of some very significant differences in the sexes. This approach also forms an important part of the increasingly influential school of evolutionary psychology.

These Upper-Right factors also include the macrobiological constants that researchers also agree are present universally and cross-culturally. For example, women give birth and lactate, while men have an average advantage in physical strength and mobility. Both second- and third-wave feminists, as well as orthodox researchers, agree on the existence and importance of most of these factors (they are crucial, for example, in explaining the statistically different roles of men and women in the productive and private spheres, once oppression fails as a causal category).

As I would summarize all of their conclusions, there is a *biological basis* for males to tend toward agency, women toward communion, and these tendencies are the product of perhaps several million years of natural selection, which is why we find them *cross-culturally*—there is nothing "androcentric" about these sex differences, as many radical feminists have made quite clear. However, the actual value attached to these sex differences does indeed *vary from culture to culture* (on this, see the next section.)

Lower Left (Cultural)

The reason that these biological factors are *tendencies*, not *causes*, is that whatever biological factors are present, they nonetheless are taken up and reworked by powerful cultural factors, which can in many cases increase, neutralize, or reverse the biological tendencies.

Most researchers refer to these *biological* differences as *sex*, and the *cultural* differences as *gender*. Likewise, researchers usually refer to the biological sexes as *male* and *female*, and the cultural differences as *masculine* and *feminine*.

There are, in my opinion, two errors that are constantly being made in the study of sex and gender. The first (common with conservatives) is to assume that all gender issues are totally determined by sex differences (so that biology is destiny). The second (common with liberals) is that all sexual differences are merely culturally constructed (so that biology can be ignored). Both of these stances are distorted, I believe, and almost always seem driven by ideology.

What we want to do instead, it seems to me, is to acknowledge and honor the moments of truth in both those positions: biologically constant sex differences (such as the fact that women give birth and lactate, males have an average advantage in physical strength) are taken up and reworked, often in dramatic ways, by cultural factors and influences.

In this regard, I have particularly focused on the role of *worldviews* in the formation of gender. These worldviews (archaic, magic, mythic, mental, existential, etc.) are, recall, part of the intersubjective cultural patterns *within which* individual subjects and objects arise. As such, they play a decisive role in helping to *select which factors from the male and female value spheres will in fact be honored in any given society.*[8] The point is that women and men co-create (sometimes intentionally, sometimes unintentionally) the intersubjective patterns within which their own subjects and objects will be manifest and recognized, and these cultural patterns are sometimes decisive in sex and gender issues as well.

The *constructivist feminists* and the *cultural feminists* have furthered to a great degree our understanding of the important role of this Lower-Left quadrant, and their voices are very much needed in the choir. Unfortunately, they sometimes go beyond the warrant of their own evidence and claim that this quadrant is the only important quadrant in existence, which not only lands them in performative self-contradictions, but also distorts the equally important voices of the other quadrants (and the other schools of feminism). What then happens is that the *influence* of those other quadrants, since they are not fully acknowledged on their own terms, must be ascribed to *oppression*, because the constructivists can figure out no other way that they got there. Thus, for example, biological differences in function must be ascribed to male imposition of ideology. Giving birth and lactating are somehow a male plot of the patriarchy, since all differences are culturally constructed.

That approach, of course, *defines* women as primarily molded by an Other (precisely the definition these feminists say they wish to overcome). And it defines males as essentially oppressors of one sort or another—"All men are rapists" being the most typical example, which is simply outrageous. All men are not rapists; as everybody knows, all men are horse thieves.

But we can ignore those differences of emphasis for the moment, and simply note that all of these important Lower-Left approaches are united in the affirmation of the strong and crucial role played by intersubjective cultural factors in the unfolding of sex and gender.

Lower Right (Social)

Nonetheless, worldviews are not disembodied structures, hanging in idealistic midair. That is, all worldviews—indeed, all cultural factors in general—are strongly anchored in the material components of the society—such as the forces of production, modes of technology, architectural structures, economic base, geopolitical locations, and so forth, all of which I refer to as "social." In other words, all cultural factors have social correlates (all four quadrants have correlates in all the others, and this applies to the cultural and social as well). The social system and cultural worldviews are intimately interwoven, and this, of course, directly relates to gender issues.

In particular, there is now almost overwhelming evidence that, as I would put it, *worldviews follow the base*, not in any strong Marxist or deterministic fashion, but in the general sense that the techno-economic base sets certain broad limits within which worldviews tend to unfold. For example, agrarian (plow) societies place the means of production (the heavy animal-drawn plow) almost exclusively in male hands, and the accompanying worldviews are thus intensely androcentric. There are other factors involved, of course; I am simply pointing out that the techno-economic base is one of the crucial factors.

Thus, with regard to sex and gender issues, the discussion at this point turns to an analysis of *the types of gender roles available to men and women at each of the five or six major stages of techno-economic development in the formation of the human species*. These stages include foraging (scavenging, hunting, gathering), early and late horticultural, early and late agrarian, early and late industrial, and early informational.

These stages, of course, like all evolutionary stages, are asymmetrical and irreversible: steam engines never precede plows. Time's arrow, as always, sinks its claws into the thermodynamics of the material domain, and any theories of social and techno-economic development that ignore these irreversible and "linear" processes are severely deficient, as Prigogine and Jantsch and Laszlo keep reminding us. These social systems are, as I said, interactive with corresponding cultural worldviews, precisely because all four quadrants are mutually interactive. (The five broad technological stages correlate respectively with archaic, magic, mythic, mental, and existential worldviews.)

What we find, with this more integral approach, is that the techno-economic base has a profound influence in *selecting those factors from the male and female value spheres that will be evolutionarily advantageous for a given society.*

For example, horse and herding societies place a premium on physical strength and mobility, which selects for the male value sphere in the public and productive domain (indeed, 97 percent of such societies are strongly patriarchal, with oppression playing no explanatory *causal* role). Likewise, horticultural societies, whose primary force of production is the digging stick or hoe, place a premium on the female work force, because pregnant women can easily handle a hoe with no serious side effects (indeed, 80 percent of the foodstuffs in all horticultural societies are produced by women). Not surprisingly, one-third of these societies have female-only deities (so that wherever you find the Great Mother religions, you find a horticultural base, with only one or two maritime exceptions).[9]

The *Marxist feminists* and the *social feminists* have contributed much to our understanding of the importance of this Lower-Right quadrant for an overall view. Likewise, one of my favorite writers, Janet Chafetz, has contributed a social systems–oriented analysis that is brilliant and thorough. And the *ecofeminists* have emphasized the role of Gaia as the ultimate social system.[10]

All of those factors—behavioral, cultural, and social (at each of their developmental waves)—will have a strong hand in determining how individual men and women experience their own embodiment, engenderment, and gender status. Which brings us to the Upper-Left quadrant.

Upper Left (Intentional)

The Upper-Left quadrant is, recall, the interior of the individual, the site of consciousness itself, which is composed of (at least) the self-system and the developmental streams as they all unfold through preconventional, conventional, postconventional, and post-postconventional waves of the overall spectrum.

Within this spectrum of consciousness, it is important to examine both the horizontal dimension—that of *translation*—and the vertical dimension—that of *transformation*. Translation is a process of agency-in-communion, or the relational exchange between any holon and its interwoven environs. Transformation is the shift to a higher or deeper domain altogether (a different level of agency-in-communion).

Where agency and communion operate horizontally on every level, Eros and Agape operate between levels, as it were. Eros is ascending or evolving transformation, Agape is descending or involving transformation (which I will explain in a moment). The important point is simply that both the horizontal or translative dimension and the vertical or transformative dimension need to be taken into account.

If we do so, with regard to sex and gender differences, I believe we will find the following: Men *translate* with an emphasis on agency, women with an emphasis on communion. And men *transform* with an emphasis on Eros, women with an emphasis on Agape.

This is where the Gilligan/Tannen approach becomes an important (if limited) part of the overall picture, and where the extensive research on male agency and female communion needs to be taken into account. But it is not enough simply to contrast male and female in the *translative* dimension (agency/separation versus communion/relationship), because men and women tend to *transform* with a different emphasis as well—namely, Eros/ascending versus Agape/descending.

This tends to confuse people, because they imagine it means that men only ascend and women only descend, which is not the case at all. Rather, it means that, in any stage of vertical growth and development, men and women tend to face in different directions when they negotiate these stages, and these directions are not explainable merely in terms of agency and communion, but of ascending and descending *orientations in the nested holarchy of their own being.* Eros tends to reach up, as it were, and assault the heavens, whereas Agape tends to reach down and embrace the earth. Eros is more transcendental, Agape more immanent (and each has its own agency and communion, which refer to horizontal, not vertical, orientations).

These are not airy abstractions but a rather good summary of much of the cross-cultural research on modes of transformative (or developmental) orientation in men and women. Thus, to give only one brief example, Phil Zimbardo, in his widely acclaimed psychology series on public television, summarizes the cross-cultural differences in the behavioral patterns already demonstrated in young boys and girls—differences that show up in everything from eating habits to types of friendships to styles of play: "Girls have roots, boys have wings."

Roots and wings. Agape and Eros. It is this vertical dimension of depth that needs to be added to the horizontal dimension of agency and communion in order to take into account the multidimensional differences in the native styles of men and women.

Thus, in my view, men and women develop through the same gender-neutral basic structures (the same basic waves in the spectrum of consciousness), but they tend to do so with somewhat different values and styles in both the translative and transformative domains: men tend toward agency and Eros, women toward communion and Agape. (Of course, any specific individual will show a unique proportion of those four factors, and all four factors are decisively present in men and women alike. These are simple tendencies and average probabilities, not causal determinants!)

Nonetheless, and most significantly, these simple sex-class probabilities allow us immediately to stop interpreting females as being deficient males, or the more recent trend of trying to interpret males as being deficient females. Neither the male nor female disposition is itself higher or lower, or deeper or wider, on the nested holarchy of basic waves of consciousness unfolding.

Moreover, this approach prevents the more recent attempts, by various spiritual feminists, to remove female spirituality from any sort of transformational requirements at all. This attempt simply paints women as the "permeable" (communion) self, which is fine, but it then rather straightforwardly equates this permeable self with a spiritual self and an ecological self, thus effectively denying the demand for any hierarchical transformation in women. This unfortunately ignores not only Gilligan's female hierarchy but all others as well, which effectively aborts any sort of transformation in women at all.

What that flatland approach fails to take into account is that the permeable self (or the self-in-connection) itself undergoes growth, development, and transformation. The permeable self holarchically unfolds and transforms through the same expanding spheres of consciousness that the male agentic self must also negotiate in its own fashion (thus, for the female: egocentric permeable, sociocentric permeable, worldcentric permeable, spiritual permeable). The permeable self is not, in itself, a spiritual self at all—only its highest or deepest reaches are. In fact, the lower stages of the permeable self (the prepersonal stages) are just as egocentric, narcissistic, and altogether unpleasant as the shallower stages of the male agentic self. Both of them are equally locked into the orbit of their own endless self-regard, which is, by any definition, the antithesis of all things spiritual.

And as for the permeable self and its alleged regard for ecological connections, it is often quite the opposite. The lower stages of the permeable self (like the lower stages of the agentic self) are altogether prepersonal, preconventional, and egocentric in their stance—which is precisely the stance that is the prime contributor to ecological despoliation in general. Simple communion or permeability will, in itself, do nothing to alleviate this: it simply extends its own narcissism, spreads its own egocentricity, permeably shares its own disease.

Communion is the interwoven, weblike relationship of all of the elements in a given domain, but Agape is the capacity to embrace deeper domains altogether. When we understand that communion and Agape are not simply the same thing, then it becomes obvious that merely possessing a permeable self is not, as these feminists imagine, enough to bring moral light and salvation into the wretched world of male agency. Rather, the shallower and egocentric stages of the permeable self, along with the shallower and egocentric stages of the agentic self, are the twin faces of evil in this world, and one of those smiling faces has female written all over it.

FEMALE SPIRITUALITY

It is precisely the two basic native differences in the male and female value spheres (males tending toward agency and Eros, females toward communion and Agape) that, when they unfold through the basic waves of consciousness, under the influence of different worldviews and different stages of techno-economic development, generate the various modes of gender that have historically been observed in men and women.

This "all-quadrant, all-level" approach gives us a chance, I believe, to bring together an enormous number of very important, indeed crucial, factors in the discussion of sex and gender. Thus, the gender-neutral basic waves play themselves out differently for men and women, dependent on factors in all four quadrants, from hormonal differences to worldviews to modes of production to translative/transformative differences. Since all four quadrants intimately interact, none of those factors can be overlooked in a genuinely comprehensive theory of sex and gender.

And this relates directly, I believe, to spiritual development as well. Volume 2 of the Kosmos trilogy is a sustained look at the different types of spiritual development—in many cases, decisively different from male patterns—that certain highly original women saints, shamans, and yogis have pioneered over the centuries. These female practices generally involve an intense mode, not merely of *translative* communion and permeability, but of *transformative* Agape (incarnational, body-centered, immanent, descended, involutional, and profoundly *embodied mysticism*). They offer a stunning contrast to the more traditionally ascending, transcendental, agentic, and Eros-driven modes of spirituality typical of males.

But these more female-oriented spiritual practices are still practices in profound *transformation*, not mere translation. As such, these women mystics offer a stinging criticism of the merely "permeable" self theories that find permeability in itself to be spiritual (as if communion and Agape were simply the same).

In other words, in order to manifest a genuine spiritual consciousness, women have just as much hard work to do as the men. As we noted, "permeable" and "spiritual" are not even remotely the same thing. Rather, only the deepest stages of the permeable self are genuinely spiritual ("spirit-as-spirit"), and these deeper developments require intense and sustained spiritual practice. But where the men need to transform their agentic selves, the women need to transform their permeable selves (from selfish to care to universal care to spiritual recognition). These are the same expanding waves of consciousness (egocentric to sociocentric to worldcentric to authentic spiritual), but negotiated with different styles.

What too many "permeable self" theorists actually mean is, "I am a woman, and by virtue of my permeable self, I am already more spiritual than men." What the genuine female mystics demonstrate, on the contrary, is that for women actually to transform their permeable selves, and not merely translate differently, requires an enormous amount of intense and profound work (just as it does in the men). These extraordinary women mystics say to their sisters, in effect: "Fine, you have a relational, embodied, permeable self. But within those givens, here is what you still must do—with intensity and fire and unrelenting dedication—in order to actually transform that self and render it fully transparent to the Depths of the Divine."

Indeed, some of the transformative practices of these remarkable women—which almost always involve wrenching bodily ordeals as they bring Spirit down and into the bodily being via descending or incarnational Agape and its unrelenting compassion—are so intense that they even make for difficult reading; in any event, they are not for the fainthearted, and they put to shame the "wonderful permeable self" assumptions of merely translative female spirituality. These extraordinary women practitioners are blazing beacons of what a woman actually has to do if she is genuinely to transform in depth, and not merely claim a superiority based on translative permeability.

At the same time, we simply cannot forget that both men and women have decisive access to both agency and communion, as well as to Eros and Agape. That they might inherently tend to emphasize one or the other does not mean that they are different species altogether. This is why, I believe, we need constantly to keep our eye on both the profound similarities as well as the intricate differences between men and women, and resist the urge to sink our discussion in an ideological fervor to promote one at the expense of the other.

MALE AND FEMALE MORAL DEPTH

Which brings us to our last and somewhat delicate area, that of actual moral development itself. Many radical feminists and ecofeminists constantly claim, explicitly or implicitly, that the general female mode is in some profound sense more moral or ethical than the male mode. But actual feminist research itself demonstrates something quite different— and much more fascinating.

Radical feminists and ecofeminists emphasize, quite correctly it seems to me, that women do indeed tend to stress embodied personal relationship (the "connected self"). And this very fact, it seems, makes it rather difficult for women to develop to Gilligan's third and highest stage of female moral development—that is, from the stage Gilligan calls "conventional ethical" to what she calls "postconventional metaethical" (she also calls this moving from care to universal care).

In other words, precisely because women tend to remain attached to personal and conventional relationships, they find it harder to reach the postconventional and universal stages *in their own female development* (based on their own relational terms, not on male agentic terms). Thus, even if we use the Jane Loevinger test originally developed using solely women, more men reach the higher stages. Men, being less personally attached to sociocentric relationships, find it easier to take a universal and postconventional "big picture" view, and thus more men make it into the universal, postconventional moral stages than do women (even when the women are judged by their own scales and values).

On balance, male and female moral development tend to display an interesting split. Just as, in IQ tests, more males score both lower and higher than females (most of the really dumb, and really brilliant, are male), so men score both lower and higher than women in most scales of generalized moral development. Again, women seem to gravitate to personal, embedded, conventional relationships, and thus they have a harder time moving from *conventional communion* (care) to *postconventional communion* (universal care, Gilligan's "postconventional metaethical").

Men, on the other hand, due to their predominantly agentic outlook, tend to gravitate *to either side of that conventional divide*: more of them reach the postconventional worldcentric stage of universal embrace, but more of them also remain at the preconventional and egocentric mode. For every Abraham Lincoln and Mahatma Gandhi, there is a Charles Manson and Son of Sam. Historically, this has made men both truly stunning moral and spiritual beacons, as well as the most viciously evil animals, without exception, to walk the face of the earth.

But the point, once again, is that simply possessing female communion, as opposed to male agency, is not enough to make you spiritual or moral. In fact, it might slow your growth into universal and global domains (spiritual as well as moral), and it might actually cripple anything resembling a genuine global ecological stance (which calls into question one of the central tenets of ecofeminism, namely, the native superiority of the female when it comes to the global biosphere).

But the central conclusion, in all cases, is that the communion self needs just as much work as the agentic self, sometimes more, in order to move from egocentric selfish, to sociocentric care, to worldcentric universal care, there to stand open to the radiance of the Divine. Women, just like men, face years, and often decades, of blood, sweat, tears, and toil, in order to claim their birthright.

9

How Straight Is the Spiritual Path?

THE RELATION OF PSYCHOLOGICAL
AND SPIRITUAL GROWTH

Does psychological growth have to be completed before genuine spiritual growth can occur? What is the relation of psychotherapy and meditation? Are there actually stages of spiritual development? If there are stages of spiritual growth, are they the same for everybody? How can these stages be ascertained? Is there a direction to Spirit's unfolding? Does it really matter?

DAVID BOHM, JENNY WADE, AND THE HOLONOMIC PARADIGM

JENNY WADE'S *Changes of Mind: A Holonomic Theory of the Evolution of Consciousness* is an account of the evolution of consciousness according to what she calls a "holonomic paradigm." This is an enormously competent book with much to recommend it. It gives a fine overview of transpersonal developmental psychology, drawing on sources both ancient and modern, and it is grounded in much data and information from numerous researchers. The core of the book is a transpersonal developmental stage model of consciousness, consisting of nine basic stages (quite compatible with the nine basic waves and fulcrums of development). Around this stage model Wade adds a "two-source" theory of consciousness (also quite compatible with a frontal/soul model), and

David Bohm's implicate/explicate notions. My only reservations about the book are that it doesn't clearly distinguish between levels and lines (which is easily remedied), and it attempts to use David Bohm's purely monological notion of an implicate order to explain the richness of dialogical and translogical realms. But the central message of the book is quite clear: consciousness evolution is at the core of any truly integral psychology.

Transpersonal Developmental Psychology

In chapter 6 I mentioned that, in my own theoretical work, I had moved from a Romantic/Wilber-I to a Wilber-II model because of what I believe are certain recalcitrant difficulties in the Jungian and retro-Romantic orientations. And, as I indicated, Wilber-II was first presented in *The Atman Project*—a model with seventeen general stages, from birth to enlightenment (stages that are variations on matter, body, mind, soul, and spirit); it also specifically included the bardo stages of preconception, prenatal, and postlife states (the frontal/soul or evolution/involution lines).[1] In that and subsequent books, I usually simplified these seventeen waves to nine or so (although the seventeen are still necessary for the overall model, and even those can be further subdivided). But these simplified nine waves (and the corresponding self-fulcrums) are the ones that I emphasize, for example, in *Transformations of Consciousness* and *A Brief History of Everything*.

These nine stages are quite similar to the nine stages that Wade presents in her model, and her rigorous defense of these basic waves points up the truly imposing amount of evidence in support of such a model.[2] What I especially appreciate about her treatment of the first six or seven stages (the conventional stages, from prepersonal to personal) is the wealth of data she brings to the model.[3] This is exactly the type of detailed work that needs to be done, and for the most part, I found this part of the book thorough, accurate, and compelling. Wade has an exceptional gift for assembling innumerable details into a coherent presentation, and this is especially obvious in these sections of the book.

Among other things, this part of Wade's presentation highlights once again the central importance of the stage model in transpersonal studies, and points up why a developmental model is so crucial to the field. It also, by implication, demonstrates how impoverished the alternatives are. This is a superb contribution on Wade's part, and it will have, I believe, a lasting impact on the field. As we will see in a moment, a developmental model needs to be supplemented in several important areas, but it certainly seems that its basic features will be central to any truly comprehensive model of consciousness.

Wade also adopts the "two-source" thesis (a deeper psychic being and the frontal development). Although this is essentially the Aurobindo/Vajrayana concept, she brings a wealth of research data to the task, and this, too, is a very useful part of the book. I particularly liked the phenomenological approach to prenatal and neonatal experiences, and her graphs of the psychic awareness "behind" or "alongside" the frontal. This is another fine contribution, and adds yet further support to the frontal/soul model.

Levels and Lines

In addition to these superb contributions, there are a few minor weaknesses in the book, I believe. In keeping with the reflections on the history of my own work, I might introduce these "mistakes"—or what I believe are mistakes, anyway—by saying that I understand them fairly well because, once again, I made most of them myself.

Almost as soon as I had published the Atman Project/Wilber-II model, I realized that it needed to be refined in a very specific direction. The seventeen basic waves (or basic colors in the spectrum of consciousness) were still generally valid, but that model did not fully *differentiate the various lines of development through each of those waves* (nor did that model carefully distinguish between, for example, enduring structures and transitional structures).

Thus, less than one year after I published Wilber-II, I published its refinement, which we might as well call Wilber-III. Wilber-II and Wilber-III still share the same basic stages, but Wilber-III explicitly distinguishes *the different developmental streams that unfold through those basic waves.* These different developmental lines include affective, cognitive, moral, interpersonal, object-relations, self-identity, and so on, *each of which develops in a relatively independent fashion through the general levels or basic waves of consciousness.* There is no single, monolithic line that governs all of these developments (as I will further explain below).

I also distinguished between the enduring and the transitional features of each of those developmental sequences; outlined six major characteristics of the self-system navigating the basic waves in its own development (resulting in the corresponding "self-fulcrums"); and emphasized even more the importance of temporary *altered states* and *peak experiences* in addition to the more directional and structural frontal unfolding (although, as usual, in order for these temporary states to become enduring traits, they must be converted to permanent structures via development).

That is the model (Wilber-III) that I have consistently presented since its first publication (1981), and that I generally summarize as "self, waves, streams, and states."[4] It was becoming fairly obvious by that time that a monolithic "one line" developmental spectrum would not do justice to the evidence. On the other hand, using waves, streams, and states, one could follow both the "linear" or purely developmental and hierarchical aspects of consciousness unfolding *and* the many nonlinear, amorphous, holographically interwoven aspects as well.

Thus, it was somewhat disappointing to see Wade follow mostly a "levels" model and not enough of a "levels and lines" model. Among other things, the Wade/Wilber-II model does tend toward a unilinear development, which is why I abandoned it (or rather, refined it into Wilber-III).[5]

Let me give a specific example. Wade observes the following: "An individual's noetic [consciousness] growth is not uniform across all social domains. Thus a person may operate at one stage in one social milieu and at a higher or lower one in another setting." I believe that is quite true, and a Wade/Wilber-II model can easily handle that fact; individuals simply fluctuate up or down the basic levels of consciousness in different settings, depending on, for example, social triggers.

But what the Wade/Wilber-II model cannot handle is the fact that a person in the *same* setting has components of his or her consciousness each existing at a different level. In the *same* social domain, and in a *single* transaction, a person can, for example, be at a very high cognitive level of development (e.g., formop), while *simultaneously* being at a low level of moral development (e.g., stage 2), with an unconscious fixation at an even earlier affective stage (some facet of the self dissociated at, say, stage 1).

The Wade/Wilber-II model fails in accounting for those facts—because it fails, in general, to distinguish carefully enough between levels and lines (and further, to account for just what is preserved, and what is negated, in evolution).[6] These distinctions are just the minimum, I believe, that we need to account for development in general and nonlinear developments in particular. [Subsequent discussions with Jenny indicate that she is comfortable with a "waves, streams, and states" type of model, and she hopes to bring out a second edition of *Changes of Mind* that will reflect her specific thoughts on these issues.]

The Implicate Order

Wade's use of David Bohm's notions of an implicate/explicate order is the least satisfactory part of the book, in my opinion. The central difficulty with Bohm's theory is that, based on physics, it is purely monological. (Physics only adequately covers the lowest levels in the Upper-Right quadrant, and trying to make it "foundational" for all other quadrants is the essence of reductionism.) But Bohm makes the attempt to extend this purely monological conception into dialogical and translogical realms, at which point the monological approach, appropriate in its own domain, becomes distortingly reductionistic.

The results are unfortunate. Reality is forced into a two-level hierarchy, the explicate and the implicate. Models based on this explicate/implicate notion then tend to identify the explicate order with the world of separate things and events, Newtonian physics, ordinary time and space, separate selves, and so on, and the implicate order is identified with unity, wholeness, a holographic reality, a spiritual unity, a timeless ground of being, and so forth. This is a simple two-tier monological model, which allows only physics and spirit. A more acceptable holarchy might include, as we have seen: matter, body, mind, soul, and spirit. But the explicate/implicate notion forces any theorist who adopts it to basically acknowledge only matter and spirit, with nothing much in between. Poor biology, psychology, and theology are all therefore going to feel the monological hammer come crashing down to crack their skulls—they are all forced into the monological scheme.

Bohm himself tended to realize the inadequate nature of his position, and for a while he went through an awkward period of adding implicate levels. There was the implicate level, and then along with that there was a super-implicate level, then at one point, a super-super-implicate level. And all of this was claiming to be based on empirical findings in physics!

I published (1982b) a strong criticism of Bohm's position, which has never been answered by him or any of his followers. It was a heady time, and Marilyn Ferguson's *Brain/Mind Bulletin* had just awarded its fourth Annual Greatest Breakthrough of the Century Award to Bohm and Pribram for the holographic paradigm. I was editor-in-chief of *ReVision* at the time, and we pulled together dozens of essays on this new paradigm, which we published, appropriately enough, as *The Holographic Paradigm*. It was the editor of the book, yet in the awkward position of being the only strongly dissenting voice. Nobody wanted to hear criticisms of the new paradigm; everybody thought me an altogether rude fellow.

In my critique, I pointed out that, according to the Great Holarchy theorists, what is explicate at one level is implicate at the next (that is, what is explicitly whole at one level is an enfolded and implicit part of the next), and thus you can construct an explicate/implicate relation *at each of the levels in the Great Holarchy,* which preserves the moment of Bohm's truth but without the necessity to engage in reductionism. I also pointed out what seemed to be the many self-contradictions that resulted from Bohm's constant attempt to qualify that which he maintained was unqualifiable.[7] Until this critique is answered, I believe we must consider Bohm's theory to be suspect. And, anyway, over the last decade and a half it has generally fallen into disrepute (and it has little support from most physicists).

I was therefore surprised to see Wade attempt to inject transpersonal theory into this monological model. But it is indeed this implicate/explicate notion—the "holonomic paradigm"—with which Wade wishes to ground her transpersonal developmental model, and unfortunately this infects it with Bohm's reductionism and monological flatland approach, or so it seems to me.

I realize that Wade is in some ways simply using Bohm's ideas as a metaphor for the interconnectedness of all events. But I believe that whatever usefulness might be gained by claiming support from physics for a "mystically interwoven world" is actually outweighed by the fact that the "support" is purely monological and thus profoundly reductionistic. (Not to mention based on interpretations of physics that most physicists reject; but even if they didn't, the "support" is still monological, claiming that the holons in the Upper-Right quadrant are the "really real" holons upon which all theory must be grounded: and there is the monological nightmare.)

But why even worry about this? So what if physics is monological? So what if systems sciences, complexity theory, chaos theory, autopoiesis, and so on are all monological, Right-Hand theories? Can't they be a welcomed part of any integral approach? Absolutely. The problem is, as they are usually presented, they are not used *in addition* to Left-Hand interior transformations of consciousness but *instead of* those interior transformations—at which point they hurt, not help, the actual evolution of consciousness.

Let us assume that the nine or ten basic waves of consciousness development exist, just as outlined by Jenny. Any truly new and integral paradigm would then say something like this: The world is a unified whole, a great interwoven system of mutually interpenetrating events. Even modern physics and systems theories agree. But in order to fully realize this great Unity, individuals must grow and evolve their own consciousness to the degree that they can actually embrace this Unity in their own being—where they can fully realize it as an awakened reality and not merely as a concept or idea. Research has consistently suggested that this growth and evolution occurs through at least nine basic waves of consciousness unfolding. What is therefore required, by the new paradigm, is not a new monological description of the Right-Hand world, but the understanding that individuals need to actually grow and develop through all nine waves of their own interior potentials. We do not need merely a more accurate map of the unified Kosmos; we need ways for the mapmaker to grow and evolve through at least nine major waves of his or her own consciousness, thereupon to stand open to a direct and authentic Unity with the Kosmos. We do not need more maps; we need ways to change the mapmaker. We need new forms of *practice,* not just new forms of *theory.* And simply *thinking* about the world in holistic terms does little to transform and move the thinker through those nine waves toward a genuine Unity. *Theoria* just isn't enough; *praxis* is required.

As it is now, most "new paradigm" approaches are completely silent about the *interior stages* of growth and practice required for any genuinely integral paradigm. They simply present a unified systems theory of the Right-Hand world, a theory that itself can be learned and memorized without the slightest interior growth and Left-Hand development. *Right-Hand theories can be learned without Left-Hand transformation*—and there, in a nutshell, is the problem with most of the "new paradigms" based merely on "holistic thinking" instead of interior stages of growth.

Of course, an integral paradigm would include all of the above—it would be all-level, all quadrant. And I know that Jenny Wade is generally of the same opinion. But the danger of attempting to ground an integral theory in monological, Right-Hand models (from physics to ecological sciences to systems theory to chaos and complexity theory) is that it downplays, and in many cases even neglects, the necessity for Left-Hand growth. It is not just about finding a new objective model of the world, it is about how to transform subjects, that constitutes a truly integral approach.

Jenny Wade is a natural-born developmentalist, with a keen eye and a sure grasp of many developmental issues, and I believe she can be a very important voice in the field of transpersonal developmental theory. But I urge her to be careful about the use of Bohm's monological notions. A theorist of such talent is rare in any field, and I believe Wade will have many further contributions to make.

ARE THERE STAGES OF SPIRITUAL DEVELOPMENT?

Are there really universal and invariant stages of spiritual development for everybody? What is the relation of spiritual and psychological development? Does a person have to complete psychological development before genuine spiritual development can occur?

My overall view on "stages" is exactly as Rothberg summarizes it: "Development doesn't somehow proceed in some simple way through a series of a few comprehensive stages which unify all aspects of growth. . . . The [different] developmental lines may be in tension with each other at times, and some of them do not show evidence, Wilber believes, of coherent stages. . . . There might be a high level of development cognitively, a medium level interpersonally or morally, and a low level emotionally. These disparities of development seem especially conditioned by general cultural values and styles."[8]

As we have briefly seen, in my overall model (Wilber-III), there are the basic waves of consciousness (the spectrum of consciousness), as a type of central skeletal frame, but through those basic waves there move at least a dozen different developmental streams. These developmental lines include affective, moral, interpersonal, spatiotemporal, death-seizure, object-relations, cognition, self-identity, self-needs, worldview, psychosexual, conative, aesthetic, intimacy, creativity, altruism, various specific talents (musical, sports, dance, artistic), and so forth. These are relatively independent ("quasi-independent") lines of development, loosely held together by, of course, the self-system.[9]

The immediate question then becomes: Is spirituality itself a separate developmental line? Or is spirituality simply the highest level(s)—the deepest or highest reaches—of the other lines?

In other words, the meaning of the word "spiritual" becomes crucial in this discussion, because all of the arguments in this area tend to reduce to two different definitions of that word. There are those who define "spiritual" as a *separate developmental line* (in which case spiritual development is alongside or parallel to psychological and emotional and interpersonal development). And there are those who define "spiritual" as the *highest reaches* of all of those lines (in which case spiritual development can only occur *after* psychological development is mostly completed).

I believe that both of those stances are correct, but in each case we must indicate exactly what we mean by "spiritual." If, for example, we define "spiritual" specifically as transmental, then clearly the transmental cannot stably emerge until the mental has in some rudimentary sense been solidified. Likewise, if we define "spiritual" as transverbal, or as transegoic, or as specifically transpersonal, then the spiritual domain cannot stably emerge until there is a verbal, mental, egoic self to transcend in the first place.

On the other hand, if we define spirituality as a separate developmental line, then clearly it can develop alongside, or behind, or parallel with developments in the other lines, affective, interpersonal, moral, and so on.

Take several examples: in the affective line, we have preconventional affect (e.g., narcissistic rage), conventional affect (feelings of belongingness), postconventional affect (global concern, universal love), and post-postconventional affect (ananda, transcendental love-bliss). In the moral line, we have preconventional morals (what I wish is what is right), conventional morals (my country right or wrong), postconventional morals (universal social contract), and post-postconventional morals (bodhisattvic vows). In the cognitive line, we have preconventional cognition (sensorimotor, preoperational), conventional cognition (concrete schemas, rule/role), postconventional cognition (formal rational to postformal vision-logic), and post-postconventional cognition (prajna, gnosis, savikalpa, nirvikalpa, post-postformal).

Now, in the first definition, spirituality is the highest or post-postconventional level of each of those lines. In the second definition, spirituality would be a separate line alongside those, most likely with its own unfolding forms. Since this topic is obviously crucial to this particular discussion, it bears looking at a little more closely. Let's set aside the meaning of "spirituality" for the moment, and focus on "levels and lines" in general. We will then return to the definition of "spiritual" and attempt closure. (At that point, I will also discuss altered states and peak experiences and their relation to spirituality.)

Streams and Waves

My general thesis is this: an overall spectrum of consciousness through which more than a dozen different developmental lines proceed, each of which may have a different architecture, dynamic, structure, and function—"quasi-independent" of each other—but all loosely held together by the self-system. This thesis was implicit in *The Atman Project* (1980) but then made very explicit, as I said, a year later, with the full-fledged emergence of what we are calling Wilber-III.

But at that time, there was very little evidence for such a conjecture. The term "developmental line" had been suggested by Anna Freud (which is where I got it), but her use was very narrow and restricted. Indeed, the dominant developmental paradigm was Piagetian, which saw virtually all developmental lines subsumed in one dominant domain, that of logico-mathematical cognitive development.

In the intervening fifteen years, several types of theory and research have made a general Wilber-III ("levels and lines") thesis much more plausible, and I will here simply mention a few of the more significant and influential.

Howard Gardner's *Frames of Mind*, published in 1983, was instrumental in highlighting the need to "loosen" the Piagetian scheme without abandoning its enduring strengths. Piaget himself had already opened the door: "Piaget conceded that formal thought did not necessarily obtain across all domains [logico-cognitive development was not the sole axis of development], but in fact might be found only in those lines of practice where an individual worked steadily. Here was a tacit recognition of a plurality of domains [plurality of developmental lines] in which humans can be competent, as well as acknowledgment of the possibility that the processes or products involved in one domain might not be identical to those that figure in others."[10]

Gardner points out that today "There is increasing evidence to suggest that [development] is better thought of as composed of a variety of domains [developmental lines], including not only logical-mathematical thought [the Piagetian line, and the line that is still typically but narrowly called "cognitive"] and linguistic knowledge [e.g., Chomsky], but also . . . visual-spatial thinking, bodily-kinesthetic activity, musical knowledge, and even various forms of social understanding [including moral and interpersonal competence]."[11]

Gardner and his colleagues have intensively investigated early development in several of these quasi-independent lines (what he calls "domains"), including language, symbolic play, music, number, drawing, block building, and bodily expression or dance. "Our effort has been to provide a portrait of . . . development in each of these several domains, but even more, to *establish what commonalities might obtain across different [domains]*."[12]

The crucial point, in other words, besides tracing the different development *lines*, is to see if they share any similar *levels* of development (or commonalities across domains). The conclusion of their empirical research, a conclusion I strongly share, is this: "Much of what happens within each symbol system [developmental line] proves peculiar to that symbol system. . . . Part of the story of symbol development is an account of the ordinal scales in each of these particular domains—what we have elsewhere labeled the 'streams' of symbolization [the developmental lines]. Yet there are *definite parallels across development in particular domains*."[13]

What Gardner and his associates found was that the different developmental lines each progressed through what Gardner calls "waves," to indicate the flowing and fluid nature of these stages. He and his associates found four invariant waves in each of the domains (narrative, music, dance, drawing, symbolic play, etc.), and another two or three waves that appear invariant but require further research. Gardner summarizes all of these waves as being *preconventional, conventional*, and *postconventional*. (Add post-postconventional, and we are in full accord!)

According to Gardner's research, these waves are universal, invariant, and based on deep biological (and probably psychological/cultural) constants. "The waves of symbolization are obligatory. The child has no choice but to use them, and to do so in the order in which they emerge."[14]

In other words, both the *streams* (different developmental lines) and the *waves* (the stage-like sequence common to all the streams) show features that are largely universal, even though their specifics often vary. "We have been equipped by our biological heritage with mechanisms— here termed streams and waves of symbolization—for making preliminary sense of these symbol systems. It is our speculation that those streams and waves arise in rather similar ways in human beings around the world. . . ."[15]

At the same time, different cultures would emphasize different lines or streams, although all of those would still navigate the same stage-like waves. Thus, "Symbolic development does not consist of a single strand. Rather, it comes in multiple lines that reflect the particular domains that cultures may stress at various phases of development. The waves [preconventional, conventional, postconventional—and, we add, post-postconventional] *are brought to bear in each domain*, but the importance of each wave, and the time at which it makes its maximum impact, will depend upon the particular symbolic domain in question."[16]

Finally, and this deserves emphasis, Gardner points out that this approach (combining both lines and levels, or streams and waves) "may offer hope for reconciling an increasingly severe split in developmental psychology. We have come to think of Piaget, on the one hand, as focusing on the most general aspects of development and presupposing that there is one pivotal domain, that of logical-rational thought. Chomsky (and others influenced by the 'modularity hypothesis') have been cast as embracing the contrasting view that development occurs differently in each of a number of domains (if development occurs at all). Our waves suggest that certain general wavelike psychological processes may occur across domains but that the particular way in which they are realized may well reflect the nature and the structure of particular domains. Were this theory to help reconcile two seemingly conflicting structuralist approaches, it would be a desirable theoretical outcome indeed."[17]

A Spiritual Line?

Thus, in my view, the common axis (of which precon, con, postcon, and post-postcon are all measures) is simply *consciousness* as such—the basic waves themselves, the Great Holarchy of Being, the spectrum of consciousness (which I usually present as nine or ten basic levels of consciousness, which can also be simply summarized as precon to con to postcon to post-postcon). These are the universal waves through which the dozen or so developmental lines quasi-independently proceed. The levels of the spectrum constitute the waves of developmental unfolding; the various lines are the different streams that move through those waves; and the self-system is that which attempts to juggle and balance those quasi-independent streams with their cascading waves of development.

To return to "spirituality." In the first definition, spirituality is simply the post-postconventional levels of any of the lines. In the second definition, spirituality is itself a separate line with its own unfolding. I believe both of those are completely acceptable usages, as long as we specify exactly what we mean, because they obviously are referring to rather different phenomena.

Let us start with spirituality as a separate line. I believe we can do this, but nonetheless we are immediately faced with several difficulties. To begin with, how can we define "spiritual" in a way that does *not* use only the terms of higher, transpersonal, transmental levels? You see, if we define "spiritual" using any of those "trans" or "post" terms—transverbal, transmental, transconventional, postformal, transegoic—then we revert to the other model (where spirituality exists only in the higher domains, and thus can develop only *after* the lower domains). Nor can we define "spirituality" using only the terms of *other* developmental lines (affective, moral, interpersonal, cognitive, etc.). In order to make spirituality a separate line of development, we cannot define spirituality as emotional openness, or as love, or as moral compassion, or as affective bliss, or as cognitive intuition and insight, and so on (for all of those already have their own developmental lines).

Defining the "spiritual line," you see, becomes extremely tricky, and most people who maintain that spiritual development is parallel to psychological and other lines do so only by not defining "spiritual" in any specific sense at all.

Those difficulties are the main reasons that, in the past, I have sometimes (but by no means always)[18] kept a studied silence about a separate "spiritual line" alongside the others. I have instead usually confined my discussion specifically to more definable lines such as cognition, affect, motivation, self-sense, moral response, self-needs, worldviews, and so on. This has led to the understandable (but incorrect) view that I think spirituality only exists in the "higher" levels. Although I often refer to those higher domains as "spiritual" (or "authentically spiritual"), I have never maintained that spirituality is simply absent in the lower levels (since, in fact, all levels are levels of Spirit!). Not only are altered states or spiritual peak experiences available at virtually any stage of development (see below), but we can also look to a spiritual line itself.

Thus, I have often referred to magical religion, mythic religion, rational religion, psychic religion (shamans/yogis), subtle religion (saints), causal religion (sages), and nondual religion (siddhas), each of which is a level or wave of the spiritual line or stream—in other words, the developmental line of spirituality as it spans the entire spectrum of consciousness.

The real difficulty, as I see it, is not in identifying or characterizing a developmental line that we might call "spiritual." It is getting almost anybody else to agree with what we call "spiritual." The term is virtually useless for any sort of coherent discussion, let alone model. (And remember, to define a spiritual line of development, we must use terms neither from the higher transpersonal levels, nor from other developmental lines, or else we are dealing with an amalgam of other lines and levels, not a genuinely separate spiritual line itself.)

So I will simply state my own preference. I will follow Paul Tillich in defining the spiritual line as that line of development in which the subject holds its *ultimate concern*. That is, the spiritual line of development is the developmental line of ultimate concern, regardless of its content. And, like almost all other developmental lines, the line of ultimate concern will itself unfold through the same general expanding spheres of consciousness, from preconventional concern (egocentric), to conventional concern (sociocentric), to postconventional concern (worldcentric), to post-postconventional concern (bodhisattvic). Or again, in more detail, using the terms of the associated worldviews: archaic concern to magic concern to mythic concern to mental concern to psychic concern to subtle concern to causal concern.[19]

Fowler's work in this area is a beginning, of course, and I have gratefully made use of his pioneering efforts. Fowler's six stages do not reach much beyond vision-logic/psychic, but up to that point they are an almost perfect match.[20] Moreover, Fowler deserves much credit for the truly pioneering nature of his research and his sophisticated evidence for the early to intermediate levels of the stages of the spiritual line of development.

Spiritual Level and Spiritual Line

Thus, so far we have two very different uses of the term "spiritual," both of which I believe are acceptable, as long as we carefully specify which we mean. In the first, it is a level; in the second, a line.

In the first, "spiritual" generally means *the post-postconventional waves of any of the developmental lines*. Thus, post-postconventional cognition (e.g., savikalpa and nirvikalpa samadhi, gnosis, jnana) is spoken of as "spiritual cognition," whereas concrete schemas and conventional rules generally are not. Likewise, post-postconventional affect (e.g., transcendental love-bliss) is spoken of as spiritual, whereas preconventional narcissistic rage is not. The post-postconventional modes of self-identity (soul, Self) are spoken of as spiritual, whereas the conventional ego is not, and so on.

In that usage, the "further reaches" of human nature—the post-post-conventional stages of any of the developmental lines, including cognition, affect, morals, and self-sense—are generally referred to as "spiritual" or "authentically spiritual" or similar terms. And in each of those lines, research to date strongly indicates that the developmental sequence is generally from precon to con to postcon to post-postcon, either in a "strong" or "soft" sense, but present nonetheless. Thus, in this sense, spiritual developments (post-postconventional developments) cannot stably emerge until the precon, con, and postcon waves have been, at least to a significant degree, secured.

In the second major use, "spiritual" means a *separate developmental line itself*, and thus spiritual developments can occur alongside (or parallel to) developments in the other lines, cognitive, affective, moral, interpersonal, psychological, and so on. But it is incumbent on those who use this meaning to specify *exactly what characteristics* they mean by the "spiritual line," because they can use neither the characteristics that define other lines (love, awareness, morality, etc.), nor can they use simply the highest reaches of the other lines (that is the first usage).

Fowler, for example, has on occasion been criticized because his working definition of "faith" is sometimes indistinguishable from "morality" (which is why the Kohlberg test and the Fowler test show an extremely high correlation of results, so much so that some researchers claim they are measuring the same thing). But whatever we decide, you can see the delicate and tricky nature of defining a separate spiritual line.

When I use spiritual as a separate line, I have defined it as the line of ultimate concern. This clearly differentiates it from morality (one's ultimate concern might be for food), from interpersonal development (ultimate concern is sometimes nonpersonal), and from self-development (ultimate concern is not necessarily subject-oriented). But this is simply my own working specification, and it by no means rules out any other legitimate definitions.[21]

So those are the two usages (a separate stream and the highest waves of any stream), and as I said, I believe both of those uses are acceptable, but we must be extremely careful to specify exactly what we mean. Most of the arguments about the relation of "psychology" and "spirituality"—or psychotherapy and meditation—arise only because those terms are not clearly specified.

We will return to this general topic in the next chapter, and give several more examples (at that point, I will also discuss altered states or peak experiences). In the meantime, let us simply keep these two different uses of "spiritual" firmly in mind.

Spiritual Stages

We can now return to our original question: Are there actually stages of spiritual unfolding?

According to the first usage, the spiritual is simply the higher reaches of any of the lines, and so with that usage spirituality is definitely a stage-like phenomenon. The post-postconventional stages of any line emerge only after the earlier stages are generally consolidated.

The question then becomes, if we view spirituality as a separate line, are there also stages there?

I believe that almost any separate spiritual line that might be postulated will be, in some respects, a developmental holarchy. I believe it will show important stage-like aspects because each wave will unavoidably build upon previous competences, while adding new and defining features that replace the narrower and shallower orientations.

Thus, for example, in order to move from preconventional spirituality (archaic, magic, egocentric) to conventional spirituality (mythic-membership), it is *necessary* to learn to take the role of other. Care and concern simply cannot expand from the self to the group without that growth, and there is no corresponding unfolding of a deeper spiritual concern without it. (Cf. "The waves of symbolization are obligatory. The child has no choice but to use them, and to do so in the order in which they emerge.")

That is an example of why the general stage conception is so important, and why I believe it is crucial in the spiritual line as well. It does not tell the whole story by any means (we still have to discuss altered states), but it seems to be a very important part of the story. Moreover, no alternative account that completely leaves out the stage aspect has yet been credibly advanced (I keep hearing alternative metaphors like a flower unfolding, but flowers unfold in stages).

Thus, although many details need to be refined, the stage conception itself continues to match the great preponderance of available evidence. In Alexander and Langer's thoughtful book, *Higher Stages of Human Development*, the editors present a rather comprehensive overview of the models of development that acknowledge higher or deeper domains than the typical egoic state, and of the twelve major models that are presented, the editors point out that most of them acknowledge hierarchical stages (including Carol Gilligan, Daniel Levinson, Robert Kegan, Michael Commons, and Charles Alexander). This is the baby that we must not toss with the bathwater. And given the American climate of hostility to "stages" (and anything "higher" than the ego), it is a baby whose life we must carefully defend.

Greater Depth, Less Span

This brings us to a rather delicate issue. One study showed that only 1–2 percent of the population reach the autonomous stage on Loevinger's scale, which is her next-to-highest stage, and less than 0.5 percent reach the highest or integrated stage (those two stages correspond to middle and late centauric). Similar studies have shown that less than 4 percent reach Kohlberg's stage 6; Fowler found less than 1 percent reached his highest stage; and so on. Let us simply accept, for argument's sake, that those are generally true statistics.

The question then becomes: Does this mean that people have to pass through those stages (autonomous, integrated, centauric, postconventional) *in order to make genuine spiritual progress?*

Once again, you see, it depends upon the meaning of "spiritual." If we define spirituality as postformal and post-postconventional, the answer is yes, definitely. But if we define spiritual as being a separate line of development, the answer is no, definitely not. In that case, spiritual development is occurring alongside or behind or parallel to those other lines of development, and thus it may race ahead of, or lag behind, those other lines.

But that simply pushes the question back: If we view spirituality as a separate line, does stable postconventional spiritual development then depend upon passing from its own preconventional wave to its conventional wave to its postconventional wave? And I believe the answer, backed by the preponderance of evidence, is most definitely yes.

Either way, then, we arrive at a similar conclusion: Whether spirituality is the highest wave or a separate stream, the same general waves still have eventually to be negotiated—precon to con to postcon to post-postcon (or, generally, gross to subtle to causal).

To say the same thing using other terms, the spiritual line itself moves from a *prepersonal* wave (archaic, food, safety, preconventional concern) to a *personal* wave (from belongingness and conventional concern to postconventional/global concern) to a *transpersonal* wave (post-postconventional, subtle, causal, bodhisattvic concern). In short, the spiritual stream runs through subconscious to conscious to superconscious waves, by whatever name.

Nonetheless, this is not a rigid clunk and grind view. There are, as always, regressions, spirals, and temporary leaps forward, in all sorts of fluid and flowing ways. And the self, as usual, can be "all over the place." Moreover—and this is perhaps the most important item—an individual at virtually any stage of development can have an *altered state* or *peak experience* of psychic, subtle, causal, or nondual realms. Many people define "genuine spirituality" in terms of such peak experiences (in fact, that is probably the third most common meaning of "spirituality"). I fully acknowledge that meaning; the only reason I am not stressing it here is that in order for temporary altered states to become stable traits, they must be converted into permanent realizations (or permanently available structures in consciousness), and that demands development. Thus, the altered-states view of spirituality eventually connects to one of the two developmental definitions (level or line), although all three are important components of an integral view, I believe. [See *Integral Psychology* for a comprehensive statement of this model and its relation to levels, lines, and states of spirituality, as well as childhood spirituality.]

But the developmental aspects of spirituality are truly significant, for example, because you simply *cannot* get from preconventional concern to conventional concern without learning to take the role of other. And you *cannot* get from conventional concern to postconventional or global concern without learning to establish perspectivism. In that sense, spiritual development most definitely progresses through these broad and general waves in a stage-like fashion. The spiritual stream runs through the same general waves as any other skill acquisition, if it is to be a stable adaptation and not merely a peak experience or a temporary state.

At the same time, those developments are occurring quasi-independently from the other developmental lines, so that one's spiritual development (as a separate stream) may forge ahead of, or it may lag behind, one's development in psychological, affective, interpersonal, artistic, object-relations, defense mechanisms, and other lines.

If we focus now specifically on the spiritual stream—and given the fact that late postconventional *anything* is very rare (1–2 percent or so)—does that mean that even less than 1 percent of the general population will actually develop to the *post-postconventional* or transpersonal wave of spirituality (psychic, subtle, causal)? In my opinion, yes. (This is no real surprise, in that evolution produces greater depth, less span.)

In fact, I would even say that not much more than 1 percent of the *meditating* population develops stably to the post-postconventional levels of the spiritual line (or any other line, for that matter). But this, of course, is a matter for empirical research (see below).

Discriminating Wisdom

This is a particularly delicate issue for spiritual teachers of any persuasion. A large number of individuals who come to, say, a meditation retreat, might be at a preconventional level of moral, self, and interpersonal development. They might make strides in the spiritual line of concern or in the cognitive line of insight, only to see those insights gobbled up by the low center of gravity operating in the rest of the psyche. Spiritual teachers constantly find themselves having to cater to these lowest common denominator trends, where, no matter how much development one might accomplish in the spiritual line, it is not enough to pull the other lines along with it, and might itself be merely dragged down.

At the same time, we all know of spiritual teachers who have glimpsed very high stages of spiritual and/or cognitive development, while their moral, affective, defense, object-relations, and interpersonal lines are very poorly developed—often with disastrous consequences. Moreover, the great traditions themselves often emphasize the spiritual line alone (particularly in its ascending mode), and thus they sorely neglect the interpersonal, affective, and psychological lines, so that they remain, as it were, the last place to look for help in these areas.

My suggestion for an "all-level, all-quadrant" approach is a suggestion for a more integral orientation, drawing on the strengths of the various approaches (psychological to interpersonal to spiritual to social) in an attempt to fill in the gaps left by each alone. I am by no means alone in this call; but it is disappointing to see the widespread resistance to a more integral and balanced approach.

Another difficulty for spiritual teachers in America is that, as Jack Engler noted, a disproportionately large number of people who are drawn to transpersonal spirituality are often at a preconventional level of self development. This means that much of what American teachers have to do is actually engage in supportive psychotherapy, not transformative and transpersonal spirituality. Needless to say, these teachers will rarely see stages of development of anything.

As I earlier suggested, for the post-postconventional stages of spiritual awareness, I would say that, in any given meditation retreat—and speaking very generally—less than 1 percent will actually reach a profound satori or rigpa cognition (stable causal or nondual access). I have been in retreats of several hundred dedicated and long-term practitioners where only two people strongly accessed rigpa and had it fully confirmed. Two people is not exactly a huge pool from which to draw data, and yet it is only from such a pool that the full dimensions of the stage conception will stand forth. (We will return to this research and its implications in the next chapter.)

The Poor Self

It might be appropriate to mention why I have consistently placed the self-system (or the self) at the center of all of the various streams and waves, levels and lines, structures and stages and states. Namely, the self is the balancing act of the psyche. It has to balance—as best it can—virtually every other aspect of the psychic system (indeed, balance the four quadrants in general as they impinge on the individual).

Some critics have implied that I conceptualize transpersonal development around cognitive structures, and this is not quite right. The basic structures are, as I said, simply the Great Holarchy of Being, and that certainly has a cognitive aspect. *But the self is where the action is.* And if we are to speak generally of "overall development" or "development on the whole," it would be driven, in my view, not by a Piagetian cognitive motor (which is a type of cognitive dissonance that attempts to overcome discord by developing toward formal equilibration, where it can come to rest), but rather by something like "self-dissonance," in which the self juggles the various developmental lines, and is pushed (by Eros) and pulled (by Agape) until it comes to rest in Emptiness. That is not the end of the story, but the beginning of post-Enlightenment unfolding, as the sage enters the marketplace with open hands.

To take it a step at a time. The self has to juggle (and navigate) whatever basic levels of consciousness are present, and whatever developmental lines are present, and all the various states of consciousness, heterarchic competences, and discrete talents: all of those, juggled by the self. And development "on the whole" is driven by the tension within (and beyond) that juggling act. Some developmental lines have omega points, and thus are pulled; some are more causal, and thus are pushed; some are spiral, and run in circles; some are mandalic, and unfold from within. But the self—the poor lonely self—has to juggle them all, to the degree it can. And it is a calculus of those pushes and pulls and spirals and swirls that constitutes the overall developmental unfolding. The stage conception is an important part—but just a part—of the overall story.

Does this *overall self* follow an invariant sequence of stages? Not at all, precisely because it is an amalgam, a juggling act, a mixture, of whatever developmental levels and lines are occurring. There are specific aspects of self-identity in a narrow sense (such as ego development) that research has shown follow a stagelike unfolding, which I will explain in an endnote.[22] But those are simply aspects of the overall self—they constitute one line among many, not one line that dominates all—and thus, once again, the self-system is all over the place. And its sole job, so to speak, is to get over itself.

Is This Trip Really Necessary?

Some people, I believe, are put off by the notion that rationality (and vision-logic) might somehow be a *necessary* prerequisite for higher or transpersonal development. And these folks especially do not trust this notion when it comes from egghead theorists. Does the transpersonal really "integrate" the rational, and if so, what about nontechnological cultures that do not seem to access rationality? Do we deny them spirituality?[23]

Developmental psychologists (such as Kegan) and philosophers (such as Habermas) tend to use "rational" in a very broad and general fashion, which sometimes confuses people. The simple capacity to *take the perspective of another person*, for example, is a rational capacity. You must be able mentally to step out of your own perspective, cognitively picture the way the world looks to the other person, and then place yourself in the other's shoes, as it were—all extremely complicated cognitive capacities, and all referred to as "rational" in the very general sense.

Thus, as I explain in SES, rational in this broad sense means, among other things, the capacity for perspectivism, for sustained introspection, and for imagining "as-if" and "what-if" possibilities. Rationality, to put it simply, is the sustained capacity for cognitive *pluralism* and *perspectivism*.

Some theorists have claimed that "rationality" (as used by Piaget or Habermas) might actually be, in effect, Eurocentric, and that its "lack" in other cultures might reflect Western biases. But, as Alexander et al. point out, several researchers "have convincingly argued that formal operational capacities are evident within nontechnological societies when tasks appropriate to the culture are employed."[24] Rationality doesn't mean you have to be Aristotle; it means you can take perspectives. This is why Habermas maintains that even in foraging societies, formal operations were available to a significant number of men and women. You are operating within reason when you operate within perspective. You don't have to be doing calculus.

Likewise, vision-logic does not mean that you have to be Hegel or Whitehead. Rationality means perspective; vision-logic means integrating or coordinating different perspectives. Even in the earliest foraging tribes, it is quite likely that a chieftain would have to take multiple perspectives in order to coordinate them: vision-logic. The Western forms of reason and vision-logic are just that: Western forms, but the deep capacities themselves are not.

But you can't coordinate perspectives if you can't take perspective in the first place; and you can't take perspective if you can't take the role of other. And there, once again, is the limited but crucial role of the stage conception.

And yes, I most definitely believe that *postconventional* spirituality depends upon the capacity to coordinate different perspectives. I do not believe, for example, that the bodhisattva vow can operate fully without it—without, that is, vision-logic. I believe it is the gateway through which stable psychic, subtle, causal, and nondual stages of spirituality must pass, and upon which they rest. Indeed, by definition, the bodhisattva vow rests upon vision-logic, because if you have ever vowed to liberate all perspectives, you have operated with vision-logic.

Nevertheless, you certainly can have spiritual development without perspectival reason and without integral-aperspectival vision-logic, for the simple reason that the spiritual line is a quasi-independent line of development (not to mention temporary states). The spiritual line goes right down to the archaic, sensorimotor level, where one's religion—one's ultimate concern—is food. And the spiritual line will continue through the early prerational realms (magical, egocentric). With the capacity to take the role of other, the spiritual line will begin to expand its ultimate concern from the self to the group and its beliefs (mythic-membership). From there it will learn to take a more universal perspective (mythic-rational, rational), where its ultimate concern will begin to include the welfare of a global humanity, regardless of race, gender, creed. That awareness will flower into a global vision-logic, with its concern for *all sentient beings as such*, and that will be the platform of the transpersonal spiritual stages themselves, which take as their foundation the liberation of the consciousness of all sentient beings without exception.

Thus, you can have all sorts of spirituality without "integrating reason." But you cannot have a global spirituality, a bodhisattvic spirituality, a post-postconventional spirituality, an authentically transpersonal spirituality, unless the perspectives of all sentient beings are taken into account and fully honored. Unless, that is, you integrate the deep capacities of reason and vision-logic, and then proceed from there.

Anybody can say they are being "spiritual"—and they are, because everybody has some type and level of concern. Let us therefore see their actual conception, in thought and action, and see how many perspectives it is in fact concerned with, and how many perspectives it actually takes into account, and how many perspectives it attempts to integrate, and thus let us see how deep and how wide runs that bodhisattva vow to refuse rest until all perspectives whatsoever are liberated into their own primordial nature.

10

The Effects of Meditation

SPEEDING UP THE ASCENT TO GOD
AND THE DESCENT OF THE GODDESS

What is the relation of meditation and psychotherapy? Does meditation alter the course of psychological development? If there are stages of spiritual growth, can they be accelerated? What exactly does meditation do, anyway?

VEDIC PSYCHOLOGY AND TRANSCENDENTAL MEDITATION

CHARLES ALEXANDER has been an important voice in transpersonal developmental psychology for many years, beginning with his doctoral dissertation at Harvard (1982) on ego development and personality changes in prison inmates practicing Transcendental Meditation (TM).* I have always appreciated his work, and I especially appreciate the wealth of research and empirical findings he always brings to the task. Instead of merely talking about a "new paradigm," he and his colleagues have been actually gathering data, collecting evidence, and proposing injunctions (such as meditation) to engage the higher levels of development, without which mere talk about the new paradigm is rather useless.

---

*With great sadness I must report that Skip Alexander recently died. He was one of those few "beloved by all"; his loss is truly tragic.

Moreover, unlike most of the meditation teachers in this country, Alexander and his colleagues have been taking standard tests of the various developmental lines (including Loevinger's ego development, Kohlberg's moral development, tests of capacity for intimacy, altruism, and so on) and applying them to populations of meditators, with extremely significant and telling results. The importance of this line of research is simply incalculable.[1]

In "Growth of Higher Stages of Consciousness: Maharishi's Vedic Psychology of Human Development," Alexander et al. present their model for the overall stages of consciousness development. They note that "Although independently drawn from a wide range of Eastern and Western traditions, Wilber's model, in particular, bears certain similarities to our own."[2]

It is within that broad range of agreement that I would like to proceed, but focusing mostly on some of the details of disagreement. But I will end, as usual, with a reaffirmation of our many commonalities.

STATES, STAGES, AND STRUCTURES

One of the central difficulties in their overall model, I believe, is a confusion of temporary states, enduring structures, and transitional stages.

Their model is explicitly based on the Vedic (more properly, the Vedantic) notion of the five koshas or five sheaths: matter, prana/desire, lower or concrete mind, higher mind or intellect, and transcendental intuition, beyond which is the ahamkara (root of the separate-self sense, the ultimate contraction in awareness), and then the pure Self (the causal), and finally, the ultimate Nondual (Brahman-Atman). That is, of course, yet another version of the traditional Great Holarchy of Being and Consciousness—the spectrum of basic structures of consciousness—and obviously I am in substantial agreement with that basic spectrum.[3] They maintain that these basic levels are universal and invariant, and that, as they emerge, they remain in existence and are hierarchically integrated in subsequent development.

In fact, the overall thesis of Alexander et al. is exactly that suggested in *The Atman Project*, namely, that development moves hierarchically from physical and sensorimotor to cosmic and ultimate consciousness, with each stage differentiating-and-integrating its predecessors: "According to our life-span model, during growth from the sensorimotor period to cosmic consciousness, progressively deeper levels of [consciousness] are differentiated, but each continues to operate at its own characteristic level of refinement, while being hierarchically reorganized within an increasingly integrated whole."[4]

But then they make what I believe are two unfortunate theoretical moves: they attempt to turn those *levels* of consciousness into the major developmental *lines* as well (they try to derive all of their important streams from their waves), and then, following on that, they further confuse various *transitional* states and stages with those *enduring* hierarchical levels.

The first difficulty is that they take their developmental levels (level 1: sensorimotor; level 2: prana-desire; level 3: representational mind; level 4: abstract mind; level 5: transcendental intuition; level 6: self or ego; level 7: pure Self) and attempt to turn them into the important developmental *lines* as well, so that anything not found in their levels does not show up as a line. Obviously, music is not a particular level of consciousness; neither is ethics, nor aesthetics, nor dance, nor object relations, nor needs, nor worldviews, and so on. Those are all lines, not levels, and therefore, if you try to make your levels serve also as the major lines, then you will be forced to ignore all of those real lines—which is exactly what Alexander et al. do.[5]

I quite agree with Alexander et al. when they state that "all knowledge in the domains of cognitive, social, and moral development is a function of the depth of unfoldment of consciousness awareness," but in fact their model actually has no domains that are moral and social (or musical, or dance, or artistic, etc.), because their domains are nothing but a horizontal unfolding of their vertical basic levels. This is why their diagram, which summarizes their model, has nothing listed on it that corresponds to moral, interpersonal, artistic, worldview, musical, dance, and so forth.

Moreover, this confusion extends then into a confusion between the *enduring* basic structures or levels of consciousness—which indeed are hierarchically integrated as the authors indicate—and the various *transitional* structures that develop around those basic levels, and which are not so much integrated as replaced. In other words, Alexander et al. confuse transitional with enduring, and this renders their account of development occasionally incoherent.

For example, when the authors state, "Thus, even in cosmic consciousness, sensory perception may remain, though witnessed from the level of the Self," that is certainly true—basic structures essentially remain (though subsumed). But you do not, and cannot, at the level of the

Self, have equal access to the moral structures of stage 1: those are long gone, so thoroughly differentiated and integrated that they are basically lost in any sort of original form. You absolutely do not have access to those at the level of cosmic consciousness! And since the authors' model is predicated on hierarchic inclusion alone, it fails in these particular areas.

In short, I believe that, apart from the many profound and important aspects of the model presented by Alexander et al., they unfortunately attempt to make their levels of consciousness serve also as the major lines of development, and this redundancy distorts both, forcing them as well to confuse enduring and transitional structures.[6]

Subject Permanence

Let us look now to the self that is navigating the basic levels of consciousness.

"[We] propose that the primary mechanism of development is the spontaneous shifting of the locus of conscious awareness to progressively deeper inherent levels of mind."[7] This "locus of conscious awareness" that shifts from level to level is, in my view, the self (or self-system), the locus of proximate self-identity. This is the pure Self (or consciousness as such) *identified with a particular and limited level of its own manifestation.* As the authors put it, and I concur: "The unbounded Self, in projecting itself through the currently available structure of the mind [level of consciousness], becomes embedded in or restricted by the limits of that structure and hence assumes the status of a 'bounded I,' or self."[8]

They also call this bounded self the "the stationing of awareness," a phrase that is particularly appropriate. In my model, this is the stationing of proximate self-identity, the actual stations of the self-sense, the stages of the I on its way to the I-I or pure Witness. In that developmental unfolding, the pure Witness is stably reached at the causal level, and the authors refer to the *stable attainment* of this pure Witnessing as "subject permanence." In their view (and I agree), just as the acquisition of *object permanence* (the ability to uninterruptedly follow objects) marks the great transition from the prerepresentational realm (sensorimotor/gross) to the representational realm (mental/subtle), so the acquisition of stable Witnessing or *subject permanence* marks the great transition from the representational to the postrepresentational (causal) realm. (And please, no Buddhist bickering: this Self permanence is simply unbroken mindfulness, which discloses all objects to be selfless—Self permanence is no-self awareness.)

This "subject permanence" is a constant state of witnessing carried unbroken through waking, dream, and deep sleep states, a constancy which, I entirely agree, is prerequisite and mandatory to full realization of nondual Suchness (and a constancy which is unmistakable, self-referential, postrepresentational, nondual, self-validating, self-existing, and self-liberating). [See *One Taste* for examples of this.]

To return to the "bounded I" or the proximate self-sense, the authors also refer to it as "the dominant locus of functional awareness." The central dynamic of their model is the identifying of the unbounded Self with a particular level of consciousness (which generates a "bounded self"), followed by the subsequent disidentifying with that level (and identifying with the next deeper/higher level), until the pure Self reawakens as Itself. As they put it, "In this view, the ultimate status of the knower is always pure consciousness. However, in the process of experience, awareness becomes localized as the individual [self] and identified with (i.e., unable to distance or distinguish itself clearly from) the processes of the current dominant level of [consciousness]."[9]

Now that is quite similar to the dynamic set forth in detail in *The Atman Project*, and before proceeding any further, it might help to briefly review that dynamic.

THE FORM OF DEVELOPMENT

Chapter 10 of *The Atman Project* begins, "This chapter—the most important in the book—will be short and succinct, because I would like its major points, simple in themselves, to stand alone. For what has so amazed me, as I surveyed the overall stages of development, is that although the content of each developmental growth is quite different, the *form* is essentially similar. The form of development, the form of transformation—this is constant, as far as I can tell, from the womb to God."

I outlined this form in a few paragraphs, which I will reprint for convenience. Here is the rest of the chapter:

At each stage, a higher-order structure—more complex and *therefore* more unified—*emerges* through a differentiation of the preceding, lower-order level. This higher-order structure is introduced to consciousness, and eventually (it can occur almost instantaneously or it can take a fairly prolonged time), the self *identifies* with that emergent structure. For example, when the body emerged from its pleromatic fusion with the material world, consciousness became, for the first time, a bodyself: which means, *identified with the body*. The self was then no longer *bound* to the pleromatic fusion, but it *was* bound to the body. As language emerged in consciousness, the self began to shift from a solely biological bodyself to a syntaxical ego—the self eventually identified itself with language, and operated *as* a syntaxical self. It was then no longer bound exclusively to the body, but it *was* bound to the mental-ego. Likewise, in advanced evolution, the deity-Archetype emerges, is introduced to consciousness (in the subtle realm), the self then identifies with and as that Deity, and operates from that identification. The self is then no longer exclusively bound to the ego, but it *is* bound to its own Archetype. The point is that as each higher-order structure emerges, the self eventually identifies with that structure—which is normal, natural, appropriate.

As evolution proceeds, however, each level in turn is differentiated *from* the self, or "peeled off," so to speak. The self, that is, eventually *dis-identifies* with its present structure so as to *identify* with the next higher-order emergent structure. More precisely (and this is a very important technical point), we say that the self detaches itself from its *exclusive* identification with that lower structure. It doesn't throw that structure away, it simply no longer exclusively identifies with it [i.e., basic/enduring vs. transitional/exclusivity]. The point is that because the self is differentiated from the lower structure, it *transcends* that structure (without obliterating it), and can thus *operate* on that lower structure using the tools of the newly emergent structure.

Thus, when the bodyego was differentiated from the material environment, it could operate on the environment using the tools of the body itself (such as the muscles). As the ego-mind was then differentiated from the body, it could operate on the body and world with *its* tools (concepts, syntax, etc.). As the subtle self was differentiated from the ego-mind, it could operate on the mind, body, and world using its structures (psi, siddhi), and so on.

Thus, at each point in growth or development, we find: (1) a higher-order structure emerges in consciousness; (2) the self identifies its being with that higher structure; (3) the next higher-order structure eventually emerges; (4) the self dis-identifies with the lower structure and shifts its essential identity [proximate identity] to the higher structure; (5) consciousness thereby transcends the lower structure; (6) and becomes capable of operating on that lower structure from the higher-order level; (7) such that all preceding levels can then be integrated in consciousness, and ultimately as Consciousness. We noted that each successively higher-order structure is more complex, more organized, and more unified—and evolution continues until there is only Unity, ultimate in all directions, whereupon the force of evolution is exhausted, and there is perfect release in Radiance as the entire World Flux.

Every time one remembers a higher-order deep structure, the lower-order structure is subsumed within it. That is, at each point in evolution, what is the *whole* of one level becomes merely a *part* of the higher-order whole of the next level [i.e., holon]. We saw, for example, that the body is, during the earlier stages of growth, the *whole* of the self sense—that is the bodyego. As the mind emerges and develops, however, the sense of identity shifts to the mind, and the body becomes merely one aspect, one part, of the total self. Similarly, as the subtle level emerges, the mind and body—which together *had* constituted the whole of the self-system—become merely aspects or parts of the new and more encompassing self [i.e., in each shift, the proximate self becomes distal, merely part of the new overall self].

In precisely the same way, we can say that at each point in evolution or remembrance [anamnesis], a *mode* of self becomes merely a *component* of a higher-order self (e.g., the body was *the* mode of the self before the mind emerged, whereupon it becomes merely a component of self). This can be put in several different ways, each of which tells us something important about development, evolution, and transcendence: (1) what is *whole* becomes *part*; (2) what is *identification* becomes *detachment*; (3) what is *context* becomes *content* (i.e., the context of cognition/experience of one level becomes simply a content of experience of the next); (4) what is *ground* becomes *figure* (which releases higher-order ground); (5) what is *subjective* becomes *objective* (until both of these terms become meaningless); (6) what is *condition* becomes *element* (e.g., the mind, which is the a priori condition of conventional experience, becomes merely an a posteriori element of experience in the higher-order realms; as it was put in *The Spectrum of Consciousness*, one is then looking at these structures, and therefore is not using them as something with which to look at, and thus distort, the world).

Each of those points is, in effect, a definition of *transcendence*. Yet each is also a definition of a stage of *development*. It follows that the two are essentially identical, and evolution, as has been said, is actually "self-realization through self-transcendence."

The point is that development and transcendence are two different words for the very same process. "Transcendence" has often been thought of as something odd, strange, occult, or even psychotic—whereas in fact there is nothing special about it all. The infant learning to differentiate his body from the environment is simply *transcending* the pleromatic world; the child learning mental language is simply *transcending* the world AND the simple body; the person in subtle meditation is simply transcending the world AND the body AND the mind. The soul in causal meditation is transcending the world AND the body AND the mind AND the subtle realm. The form of each growth is essentially the same, and it is the form of transcendence, the form of development: it traces a gentle curve from subconsciousness through self-consciousness to superconsciousness, remembering more and more, transcending more and more, integrating more and more, unifying more and more, until there is only that Unity which was always already the case the from start, and which remained both the alpha and omega of the soul's journey through time.

The Embedded Self

After presenting that summary of the form of development, I then outlined five different types of unconscious processes that occur in the wake of development itself. I called these the ground-unconscious, the archaic-unconscious, the submergent-unconscious, the embedded-unconscious, and the emergent-unconscious. I personally believe this is one of the most important contributions of that book, but here I will focus on only one: the embedded-unconscious, because it bears directly on the present discussion.

The essential point is that, as the self identifies with each basic level or wave of consciousness, the self is thoroughly *embedded* in those structures, fused with those structures, so much so that they cannot be seen or experienced as an object. The actual subjective structures of the self, at that stage, are unconscious: they are the embedded-unconscious. They are part of the seer, and thus cannot themselves be seen—not at that level, anyway. At the next stage, the self will *dis-embed* from those structures (disidentify with them, detach, differentiate, transcend), and then identify with the next higher level, which will then constitute the embedded-self, whose structures the self cannot see as an object, and thus whose structures constitute the embedded-unconscious at that stage.[10] Development is a constant process of embedding and disembedding, identifying with and then transcending. And we are controlled by everything we have not transcended.

Shortly after *The Atman Project* was published, Robert Kegan, now senior lecturer at the Harvard Graduate School of Education and the Massachusetts School of Professional Psychology, published a truly wonderful book, *The Evolving Self.* In it, he outlined five major stages of the evolving self—incorporative (pleromatic), impulsive (typhonic), imperial (magical), interpersonal (mythic-membership), institutional/ formal (mental-egoic), and interindividual/postformal (relational, vision-logic, centauric). Although he recognized no post-postconventional or transpersonal stages, the match up to that point was almost perfect.

But what I appreciated most about *The Evolving Self* was the way that Kegan took the concept of embeddedness (a concept that he developed independently, based on the work of Schachtel and Piaget, who also influenced me) and made it a central pillar of development. As he brilliantly summarizes it, "We have begun to see not only how the subject-object balance can be spoken of as the deep structure in meaning-evolution, but also that there is something regular about the process of evolution itself. Growth always involves a process of differentiation, of emergence from embeddedness, thus creating out of the former subject a new object to be taken by the new subjectivity. This movement involves what Piaget calls 'decentration,' the loss of an old center, and what we might call 'recentration,' the recovery of a new center."[11]

Thus, in Kegan's overall model, "The subject is always embedded within and identified with the organizing principles (the cognitive structures) [for me, the more general basic structures], whereas the object is that which gets organized. A new stage arises when the subjective pole undergoes differentiation through the de-embedding of the self from the organizing structures. Standing outside of these structures, the self can systematically organize them and render them as objects. However, it can do so only through a higher level of organizing structures within which it in turn becomes embedded."[12]

The similarities are striking, almost identical (at least in this regard). *The Atman Project* was published in 1980, *The Evolving Self* in 1982, and thus we arrived at these conceptions independently, which I take as my great good fortune, in that disagreeing with Kegan is not a good sign for your model. We have each been asked about the other's model, and I regret that I did not have access to Kegan's extensive formulations when I was doing *The Atman Project.* For Kegan's part, he reports that people are always pointing out the similarities of his general model with

Eastern models and with mine. Thus, in his latest book, *In Over Our Heads* (which I highly recommend),[13] Kegan points out that "What we take as subject and object are not necessarily fixed for us. They are not permanent. They can change. In fact, transforming our epistemologies, making what was subject into object so that we can 'have it' rather than 'be had' by it—this is the most powerful way I know to conceptualize the growth of the mind. [Indeed!] It is a way of conceptualizing the growth of the mind that is as faithful to the self-psychology of the West as to the 'wisdom literature' of the East."[14] With Kegan, you become a ditto-head. He graciously adds that "For those interested in an integration of Eastern philosophy with [this] perspective more generally, see the work of Ken Wilber: *The Atman Project, Up from Eden*, and especially, 'The Spectrum of Development' in *Transformations of Consciousness*."[15] Thus, Kegan and I have been theoretically crossing paths for fifteen years, and it is a pleasure to finally have the chance to acknowledge how important his work has been and continues to be.

My major disagreement, of course, is that Kegan might wish to consider even more seriously the genuinely post-postconventional or transpersonal waves of growth. *The same principles apply, the same form of development is operative*, and his entire scheme can easily be continued from self-consciousness into superconsciousness, at which point one's entire bodymind becomes object—as Dogen Zenji summarized Enlightenment, "Bodymind dropped!" That is, exclusive identity with the bodymind drops; the entire bodymind becomes object of the True Self; you relate to your entire bodymind in exactly the same way you relate to clouds floating through a clear autumn sky. The entire bodymind floats in transparent Emptiness, in the radical I-I that is one's Original Face: all subjects have been transcended, all deaths have been died, all selves disembedded, and there stands instead the radiant Self that is the Kosmos at large, released into its own true nature, self-liberated in its own condition, self-seen in its own recognition—the Self of all that was, and all that is, and all that ever will be.

The Self-System

We can return now to Alexander et al. and pick up their story of consciousness development. For Alexander et al., "We suggest that [development] occurs through the very process of spontaneously shifting the dominant locus of awareness [proximate self-identity] to progressively deeper levels of mind [levels of consciousness]. . . . In our view, the shifting of awareness to function actively from each deeper level under-lies the differentiation of this new mental structure from the prior levels of mind. Further, when awareness shifts from the cognitive structure in which it was previously 'embedded,' it becomes capable of hierarchically integrating and controlling all cognitive processes occurring at the prior level. . . . Thus, the deep motive of development may be seen as the progressive rediscovery ["remembrance" or anamnesis] by the Self of its own inner nature as the basis for increasing perspective on and mastery over the subjective and objective world."[16] At each of these stages of recollection, what is whole becomes part of a larger whole, so that, as they put it, each "takes on the status of a subsystem within, rather than executor of, mental life."

All of that is virtually identical to *The Atman Project*, and as far as it goes, I am obviously in complete agreement. But again, the full useful-ness of this view is blocked to Alexander et al. because of what I believe is their confusion of level and line, as well as of enduring and transi-tional. (In other words, I believe that they have a certain amount of difficulty refining what amounts to a Wilber-II type of model into a Wilber-III type of conception.)

This becomes especially obvious, I believe, if we look at what they call the four higher stages of growth (which they term transcendental consciousness, cosmic consciousness, refined cosmic consciousness, and unity consciousness), because two of those are actually enduring basic structures that remain in subsequent development, and two are merely transitional stages, lost in subsequent development. The enduring struc-tures are the causal Self and the nondual Brahman-Atman. The *tempo-rary state* of tasting the causal is transcendental consciousness, usually evoked in meditation. As this transcendental consciousness becomes *constant* and *unbroken* through the waking, dreaming, and deep sleep state, the authors call that cosmic consciousness: it is the permanent realization of the Self, the Witness (subject permanence). Thus transcen-dental consciousness—the *temporary* taste of the Self—is lost as such (it is negated; it is transitional); but the causal Self disclosed in cosmic consciousness is the enduring Atman (the causal realm).

With refined cosmic consciousness, the Self begins to break down the final and subtle dualism between the subject and object. This *transitional* stage (of refined cosmic consciousness) is completed when the Self is subsumed (negated and preserved, differentiated and integrated) in pure Nonduality as Such (Brahman-Atman), a permanent and unbroken realization that persists in the midst of all manifestation, now recognized as forms of its own involvement.[17]

Thus, more carefully distinguishing enduring and transitional, as well as level and line, would allow Alexander et al. to move to a more balanced and comprehensive model, a model that includes waves, streams, and states (which I have called Wilber-III), but a model that, by whatever name, attempts to come to terms with these more subtle and interesting facets of transpersonal development.

MEDITATION AND DEVELOPMENT

The role of meditation in human development is an extremely large and complicated topic, consisting of at least the following issues, about which I will make a few quick and general comments:

The effect of meditation on the psychological unconscious

In *The Atman Project*, I pointed out that the effect of meditation on the unconscious depends on what you mean by "the unconscious." I then outlined the five types of the unconscious that I mentioned above (ground, archaic, submergent, embedded, emergent), and I gave examples of how meditation affects each of those differently. Interested readers can consult that discussion, but in general, we might note the following:

Meditation sooner or later begins to *dislodge the embedded-self* and the embedded-unconscious. By assuming a witnessing stance of mindfulness, one's subjective structures start to become objective, and thus one begins to disidentify or detach from one's present level of development (the embedded-self is loosened and dislodged from its given subjective attachment; the embedded-unconscious is de-embedded).[18] Precisely because this embedded-unconscious houses the *repressing* structures of the psyche, then when this repressing structure is deconstructed (or profoundly relaxed and loosened), two different things tend to happen, sometimes simultaneously: the lower or submergent unconscious (the "shadow") comes rushing up, and the higher or emergent consciousness (the superconscient and supramental) comes rushing down.

Not only does this confuse meditators, it has completely confused many theorists, who cannot decide whether meditation is the door to the Devil or to God—that is, whether meditation is catatonic withdrawal (Dr. Franz Alexander's characterization of Zen), or perhaps regression to oceanic adualism (Freud's response to Romain Rolland), or, in general, a deautomatization or move down the mental hierarchy to lower and less differentiated (and more infantile and primitive) states. Or is it rather a contacting of our deeper Self, our true Nature, the God within, the angels and the archetypes of our highest possibilities?

I am saying it is both. But this depends on a precise understanding of the nature of the submergent-unconscious, the emergent-unconscious, and the embedded-unconscious which lies between them. By seeing that the embedded-self is the filtering screen that hides both the lower/submergent and the higher/emergent, we can see that the disembedding that generally occurs with intense meditation sets both of those realms free to roam. Which leads directly to the next issue.

The effect of meditation on human development

What is the effect of meditation on the overall growth and development of the human being? Aurobindo gave a pioneering and now classic formulation: "The spiritual evolution obeys the logic of a successive unfolding; it can take a new decisive main step only when the previous main step has been sufficiently conquered: even if certain minor stages can be swallowed up or leaped over by a rapid and brusque ascension, the consciousness has to turn back to assure itself that the ground passed over is securely annexed to the new condition; a greater or concentrated speed [which is indeed possible] does not eliminate the steps themselves or the necessity of their successive surmounting." Aurobindo's point is that meditation (or spiritual practice in general) can accelerate—but not alter the form or sequence—of this developmental unfolding.

As profound as Aurobindo's point is, let us refine it. That is, let us move from that type-II model to a type-III model, and ask instead: given that there are at least a dozen different lines of development, then (1) how does the development in one line affect the development in the others, and (2) what is the effect of meditation on each of those lines?

The relation of the various lines of development

The various quasi-independent lines of development include the following: moral development, self-identity or proximate-self development (generally called "ego development"), visual-spatial thinking, logico-mathematical thought, linguistic-narrative knowledge, cognitive development, worldviews, interpersonal capacity, psychosexual, conative and motivational drives, intimacy, spiritual development (ultimate concern), self-needs, altruism, creativity, affective development, level of typical defense mechanisms, mode of spacetime (spatiotemporal architecture), form of death-seizure, epistemic mode, various specific talents (musical, artistic, bodily-kinesthetic, sports, dance), and object relations—among others.

Based on research to date, it appears that these various developmental lines often stand in a relation of *"necessary but not sufficient."* From what we can tell so far, physiological development is necessary but not sufficient for cognitive development, which is necessary but not sufficient for interpersonal (and self) development, which is necessary but not sufficient for moral development. Research to date has repeatedly confirmed those relationships.

But all of those lines reach right down to the archaic level, so none of them are stacked rigidly on top of each other. They are not sitting on top of each other like so many bricks, but rather occur alongside each other like columns in a building. But there is one proviso: due to the specific nature of their interrelations, *some of the columns can never be taller than others*, a fact we have determined to be so empirically, and that we understand theoretically as a "necessary but not sufficient" relation (some lines are serving as necessary contexts for others).

Thus, even though these lines are occurring alongside each other, the "necessary but not sufficient" nature of their relationship means that ethical development cannot race ahead of interpersonal development, which cannot race ahead of cognitive development, which itself rests on certain physiological maturational schedules (all juggled, of course, by the self).

Conversely, the "necessary" part *can* race ahead of the "sufficient" part. For example, a person can be at very high level of cognition and yet still be at stage 1 moral development. We all know people who are very smart and yet quite immoral; but highly moral people are also highly cognitively developed: cognitive is necessary but not sufficient for moral.

The reason for this seems to be that, although the basic ladder of awareness can develop quite rapidly, the self's willingness to actually climb that ladder might not. You can *think* from a higher level (that's fairly easy) without actually *living from* that level (which requires moral courage). You can talk the talk but not walk the walk.

Thus, the ladder of basic structures can develop quite ahead of the self's willingness to actually climb those rungs. The self and its "center of gravity"—which is always where the action is—can remain quite low, even debased, while talking a mighty fine talk. (This applies as well, of course, to "spiritual development"—a "peak experience" is one thing; a stable adaptation, quite another.)[19]

The self will have to undergo a disembedding from the lower level—a death to the lower level—and a rebirth on the next higher level, in order to actually live from that higher and wider wave of awareness, an authentic living which will then be directly reflected in its actual moral stance, interpersonal relations, affective mode, and so forth. In order to live from a higher level, the self has to actually die to its embeddedness in a lower level, and it is much easier to chat about the higher level than to actually die to the lower. . . .

The specific details of these "necessary but not sufficient" relationships between the quasi-independent developmental lines will, for the most part, yield to direct empirical and phenomenological investigation. There are several hundred graduate-level research projects waiting to be undertaken.

The effect of meditation on any given line of development

We have seen that the various lines of development often stand in a necessary but not sufficient relation. Let us now ask, what might be the effect of meditation on each of the two dozen or so developmental lines?

That is a question that will also yield to direct empirical and phenomenological investigation—a hundred more graduate theses await, and it is a field that is virtually wide open. So far, much of the work in this area has been done by Alexander and his associates, yet another reason that I find their contributions so significant; and Daniel P. Brown, a coauthor of *Transformations of Consciousness.*

The protocol is relatively simple: administer the various tests (Loevinger scale of ego development, Kohlberg test of moral development, standard tests of altruism, defense mechanisms, empathy, interpersonal competence, creativity, physical coordination, T-scope, etc.) to groups of individuals at various stages of meditative competence. Graph the results (or otherwise analyze).

On the basis of research to date, I believe we already have enough data to answer: *Meditation can profoundly accelerate the unfolding of a given line of development, but it does not significantly alter the sequence or the form of the basic stages in that developmental line.* Streams flow faster, but through the same waves.

Meditation, for example, can accelerate moral development (gauged by the Kohlberg test), but under no circumstances has it been shown to bypass any of those stages. Meditation might help you move from stage

1 to stage 2 to stage 3 more quickly, but it will not allow you to skip stage 2. (Likewise, LSD might rattle your world, open you to higher possibilities, reintegrate past actuals, revive various traumas, heal various fractures; but it will not allow you to permanently bypass stage 2 in your moral development.)

Theoretically, of course, this makes perfect sense: stage 3, even though it basically replaces stage 2, is nonetheless built upon certain competences and skills developed in stage 2. An acorn cannot get to an oak by skipping the seedling stage.

Alexander's work has been instrumental in gathering a great deal of research data that rather unequivocally supports this conclusion, and I urge those interested to consult his published accounts. In the meantime, his overall research conclusion is that meditation will "accelerate development of consciousness markedly without altering its basic form or sequence."[20]

Conclusions

Whatever else meditation does, and it does many things, it eventually begins to loosen the embedded-unconscious; it begins to deconstruct the embedded-self (the nexus of identifications that constitute the proximate self-sense at any given wave of its development). As the embedded-unconscious begins to loosen, the self's hold on *all* of the various developmental lines begins to loosen; *all of the developmental lines are put into play.*

The self-system, recall, is that which juggles and balances all of the different developmental lines, and attempts to give some sort of coherence to the psyche. As the self's present level of identity begins to loosen—as the embedded-unconscious shakes loose—the self begins to disembed from that level, disidentify with that level, and this sets everything in play; the various development lines are all set loose to some degree.

For example, in the developmental line of defense mechanisms, there might be a (usually temporary) regression to earlier, more primitive, less differentiated defenses; but if these are negotiated, and meditation progresses, there is often a substantial growth in the level of defenses employed, moving along the developmental hierarchy which itself runs from: psychotic defenses (delusional projection, distortion, hallucinatory wish fulfillment, projective identification), to borderline defenses (projection, splitting, selfobject fusion), to neurotic defenses (displacement, isolation/intellectualization, repression, reaction formation), to mature-ego defenses (suppression, sublimation)—and from there into the transpersonal defense mechanisms characteristic of the psychic, subtle, and causal realms (which I outlined in *Transformations of Consciousness*). This, too, is open to a variety of direct empirical and phenomenological investigations.

Thus, as the self disembeds and disidentifies with a given level, and the various lines are all put into play, there might indeed be temporary regression in any of the lines (including defenses, moral response, visual-spatial perceptions, and so on), but the net effect, on the long haul, is that the natural tendency of the psyche to grow (that is, Eros), and the natural tendency of the higher levels to emerge and descend (that is, Agape), are all more intensely engaged.

Empirical and phenomenological tests of each of the developmental lines, administered longitudinally to various groups of meditators, will yield significant empirical data on precisely these crucial issues. What we will likely find, as we have thus far, is that meditation *accelerates but does not alter the sequence or form of these various lines.* Temporary regression in any of the lines is quite possible at any point due to the *continual disembedding that is the essence of meditation.* But the overall net effect is an intensification of Eros (the Ascent to God) and Agape (the descent of the Goddess). The self finds its own higher and deeper engagements accelerated by the meditative stance, which is most profoundly nothing but an opening to one's own deepest possibilities.

PSYCHOTHERAPY AND MEDITATION:
AN INTEGRAL THERAPY

The relation of meditation and psychotherapy is obviously an intricate and complicated topic, with dozens of difficult and obscure factors all entering into a series of complex equations we have not yet begun to decipher.

Nonetheless, the transpersonal field has moved beyond its initial and introductory statements in this area—such as, "Meditation increases capacity for witnessing and equanimity, and thus can facilitate the 'evenly hovering attention' requisite for analysis." Or "Meditation relaxes the repression barrier and thus can facilitate regression in service of the ego." Or "Meditation allows deep reparation of narcissistic wounds, thus speeding the formation of a cohesive self." Or "Meditation encourages a mental spaciousness that lessens the defensive stance." All of those might be true enough in a general and introductory fashion, but we now have enough data, evidence, and advanced theoretical models to start to decipher those equations with a little more precision.

I believe that, as research and theory continue to become more sophisticated, we will very soon be able to proceed in something like this fashion:

A DSM-IV diagnosis would be accompanied by a "psychograph" of the levels of each of the major developmental lines in the client, including the vertical level (not just horizontal type)[21] of self development (i.e., the level of "ego development"), level of basic pathology,[22] level of object relations, level of major defense mechanism(s), predominant self-needs, moral stage, spiritual development, and so on. Of course, once again, these are fluid waves of development and not rigidly discrete levels, but they are very useful for a general orientation on the evolution of consciousness through its many domains.

Based on that psychograph, an *integral therapy* could then be suggested. This integral therapy will itself depend on continued research into *the effects of various transformative practices on each of the major developmental lines.*

Thus, for example, what is the effect of, say, hatha yoga on the developmental line of object relations? What is the effect of vipassana meditation on proximate self-sense (or "ego development")? What is the effect of concentrative-type meditation on defense mechanisms?

The various transformative practices include (moving up the spectrum): physical or gross body practices (hatha yoga, diet, nutritional supplements, weight training, aerobic exercise; "physical" also includes the effects of pharmacological agents, no matter what level they actually elicit); affective psychotherapy (emotional catharsis therapy); bioenergetics ("prana" therapy); psychoanalytic and various uncovering therapies; hypnotherapy; script, role, and cognitive therapy; existential therapy; kundalini yoga; deity yoga; nada and shabd yoga; tsogyal and spontaneous luminosity; vipassana, causal inquiry, witnessing meditation; shikantaza, trekchod; sahaj and bhava samadhi. (That is simply a very brief sampling of some of the transformative practices addressing the various levels of the spectrum of consciousness; the list is by no means complete.)

The research agenda is then very simple to state: clinically determine the effect of each of those transformative practices on each of the major developmental lines.

Then, based on the psychograph of the client, and the knowledge of the effect of various transformative practices on each developmental line, an integral therapy could be prescribed that would be the most likely to (1) renormalize the bodymind of the individual seeking help; (2) engage postformal development if desired.

To give a few crude examples:

- A client with borderline pathology, impulsive ego, preconventional morality, and splitting defense mechanism might be offered: structure building therapy, bibliotherapy, weight training, nutritional supplements, pharmacological agents (as required), verbalization and narrative training, and short sessions of a concentration-type meditation (not awareness-training meditation, which tends to dismantle subjective structure, which the borderline does not yet adequately possess).
- A client with anxiety neurosis, phobic elements, conventional morality, repression and displacement defense mechanisms, belongingness needs, and persona self-sense might be offered: uncovering psychotherapy, bioenergetics, script analysis, jogging or biking (or some other individual sport), desensitization, dream analysis/therapy, and vipassana meditation.
- A client with existential depression, postconventional morality, suppression and sublimation defense mechanisms, self-actualization needs, and a centauric self-sense might be offered: existential analysis, dream therapy, a team sport (e.g., volleyball, basketball), bibliotherapy, t'ai chi chuan (or prana circulating therapy), community service, and kundalini yoga.
- A client who has been practicing Zen meditation for several years, but suffers life-goal apathy and depression, deadening of affect, postconventional morality, postformal cognition, self-transcendence needs, and psychic self-sense might be offered: uncovering therapy, combination weight training and jogging, tantric deity-yoga (visualization meditation), tonglen (compassion training), and community service.

Those are obviously simplistic examples, but I think the point of an integral therapy is clear enough.[23] I would simply like to repeat that those types of integral recommendations will rest on actual clinical evidence and research into the effects of various transformative practices on the major developmental streams. We are simply following the evolution of consciousness through its pluridimensional domains, looking for ways to help facilitate that evolution, and for ways to help unblock it whenever it gets "stuck." This will allow us to determine, not only which practices are indicated for specific occasions, but just as important, which are contraindicated (I gave the example of intense awareness training being contraindicated with borderline syndromes; I believe we will find numerous and very specific indications and contraindications as the research data accumulates).

As it is now, each transpersonal therapist in effect follows that protocol in an intuitive, hit-and-miss fashion. I believe the field is now ready and capable of moving to an entirely new level in this regard.

PSYCHOLOGY AND SPIRITUALITY

We are now in a position to address the issue at the crux of the "psychology and spirituality" debate: Is psychological development necessary for spiritual development?

We begin by unpacking those terms. What we loosely call "psychological" development is actually an amalgam of several different developmental lines, including the line of self-identity or proximate-self development (generally called "ego development"), the line of defense mechanisms (which usually follow the line of self development, but may be split off and operate at earlier and more primitive levels), the line of interpersonal development (the capacity for role taking and self-other interaction), and the line of affect (disposition, feeling-awareness). All of those are quasi-independent lines, and although they generally develop as a "bundle" (held together by the self-sense), nonetheless disjunctures and tensions between them can and often do occur. (And, as we saw, meditation in general can be expected to accelerate but not alter the sequence or form of each of those lines.)

"Spirituality" is likewise a loose and vague term. As we have seen, some people use it to refer mostly to the higher stages of any of the developmental lines, and some people use it to refer to a separate spiritual line itself. Let us start with the former. In this sense, "spiritual" means the specifically post-postconventional, transpersonal, supramental stages of any of the developmental lines: transpersonal affect (bliss), transpersonal consciousness (the superconscient), transpersonal self (both the psychic/subtle soul and the causal Self or Witness), transpersonal interpersonal (compassion), transpersonal cognition (prajna, jnana, gnosis), and transpersonal states (nirvikalpa, nirvana, nirodh).

In that common usage, "psychological" tends to mean "mental and personal," and "spiritual" tends to mean "supramental and transpersonal." Or, to say essentially the same thing, in that quite common usage, "psychological" means the precon, con, and postcon levels of any of the lines, and "spiritual" means the post-postcon levels in any of the lines. Thus, for example, the conventional ego is generally considered to be in the realm of the personal/psychological, and the transpersonal soul is in the realm of the spiritual. The preconventional affect of rage is in the realm of psychology, the post-postconventional affect of transcendental love is in the realm of the spiritual, and so on. I am not saying those are the only definitions of "psychological" and "spiritual," simply that they are two of the most common, and since they do refer to legitimate realities (precon, con, postcon, and post-postcon waves), let us use those to start the discussion.

Using those specific definitions, then *in any particular developmental stream,* psychological development must generally be completed before spiritual development can begin. As much research has confirmed, for actual developmental lines there exists something like precon, then con, then postcon, then post-postcon waves, because each successive wave builds upon certain necessary competences provided by its predecessors (just as you must have letters, then words, then sentences, then paragraphs). And to the extent that we define psychology as letters/words/sentences, and we define spirituality as the all-encompassing paragraphs, then we must complete psychology before spirituality can begin.

This has given rise to the commonly accepted view that personal development must be generally completed before transpersonal development can begin in any stable fashion. This is the general "you have to be somebody before you can be nobody" view, the general Aurobindo view ("a logic of successive unfolding"), and the view of the Wilber-II type of models, all of which have been (derogatorily) summarized as the "linear" or "ladder" view.[24]

As far as it goes, I believe that view is quite correct. But, as we will see, the problem is that it leaves out several other, equally important facets of spirituality and development. Thus, opponents of that ladder view have pointed out that spirituality is nowhere near that linear. These opponents generally have one of two alternative models in mind: spirituality involves altered states (which can happen at any time), or spirituality is a separate line *alongside* the others (not something occurring *after* the others). In these alternative conceptions, psychology and spirituality occur together, not one after the other.

But what both the proponents and the opponents of the ladder view tend to miss, in my opinion, is a third option, which I have been calling Wilber-III, and which, I believe, effectively includes both of those views.

Thus, even if, for the moment, we use the common meaning of psychology and spirituality—namely, as the personal waves and the post-personal (or transpersonal) waves in any of the lines, respectively—the fact is that these lines develop in a relatively independent fashion, and thus a person can be at a very high (or "spiritual") level in some lines and a low or medium (or "psychological") level in others. Thus, although in any one line, psychological development must be generally completed before spiritual development can begin, *overall development shows no such requirements at all,* so that numerous psychological and spiritual developments are occurring simultaneously at almost every point.

Say there are ten developmental lines (affective, cognitive, moral, interpersonal, and so on). Say that a person is at a preconventional wave in lines 1 and 5; a conventional wave in lines 3 and 8; a postconventional wave in lines 4 and 9; and a post-postconventional wave in lines 2, 6, and 10. Using the common definitions, this person is at a psychological (or personal) level in six lines and a spiritual (or transpersonal) level in four lines. Obviously, psychological development does *not* have to be completed before spiritual development can begin. And yet, in each of the lines, that *does* have to happen. By adopting a type-III model, we can easily understand, or so it seems to me, exactly why both of those views are correct (the ladder view of spirituality after psychology, *and* the simultaneous view of spirituality concurrent with psychology). Both of those views are correct, and both have substantial evidence supporting them, and only a type-III model, I believe, can integrate those findings.

Let us also look at the other two common meanings of "spiritual" (altered states and separate line); they, too, can be accommodated in a III-type model. As for spirituality being a separate line itself, which unfolds *alongside* the other lines (beginning as early as fulcrum-0 or fulcrum-1, like many other developmental lines), then it is quite true that, in this case, psychological development does not have to be completed before spiritual development (since they are occurring alongside each other). But note: the spiritual line itself—to the extent it is a genuine line—unfolds in its own waves of precon, con, postcon, and post-postcon, and thus the early stages in that line need to be completed before the higher stages can stably unfold (as, e.g., Fowler's research demonstrated).[25]

In that sense, the early personal/psychological stages of the spiritual line need to be completed before the higher/transpersonal stages of the spiritual line can unfold—and thus proponents of this view are right back to a ladder model of spiritual development, which, as we saw, is completely valid *as far as it goes*. It just leaves out altered states (see below) and it leaves out all the other developmental streams, each of which can be at a "psychological" or "spiritual" wave in their own unfolding, so that overall development itself follows no ladder sequence at all.

As for altered states, we have seen that a spiritual peak experience (of the psychic, subtle, causal, or nondual realms) can occur at virtually any level or stage of development. As such, a "spiritual" influx can occur at any psychological stage. Thus, there is no "ladder" sequence here, either. But, as we also noted, for altered states to become permanent traits, they must enter the stream of stable development, at which point altered states become a developmental stream themselves, and accordingly "spirituality" reverts to one of the previous two definitions (highest levels in any stream, a separate stream itself).

Summary

We have seen that the relation of "spirituality" and "psychology" depends in large part upon how we define those terms. Using some of the most common definitions—where psychology means personal (precon, con, and postcon) and spirituality means transpersonal (post-postcon)—then in any single developmental line, the psychological must be generally completed before spiritual development can stably begin. Likewise, if spirituality is considered its own developmental line, the personal stages in that line (precon, con, and postcon) need to be generally completed before the transpersonal (or post-postcon) stages can stably unfold. Thus, even if we define spirituality as its own separate line, that line or stream still unfolds through the same basic waves as the other streams (from precon to con to postcon to post-postcon), so that it is still quite true that, in any given stream, "You have to be con before you can be postcon." And it is still as true as ever that, in any given stream, we do not want to confuse preconventional and postconventional simply because both are nonconventional.

From the evidence we have seen thus far, we might expect that meditation would accelerate—but not alter—that sequence of spiritual unfolding, in both male and female modes.[26] Thus, whether we use "spiritual" to mean the highest waves of any of the streams, or whether we use it to mean a separate stream itself, it appears that meditation helps to accelerate, but not otherwise alter, the unfolding of those streams.

Altered states can occur at any stage, but in order for them to become permanent realizations, they will have to enter the stream of development and thus follow its currents as well, and thus altered states eventually fall into one of the two previous definitions.

Nonetheless, even though in any given line the psychological generally has to be completed before the spiritual can begin, because the lines themselves develop in a relatively independent manner, a person can be at numerous psychological waves in some lines and numerous spiritual waves in others—*psychological development most definitely does not have to be completed before spiritual development can occur.* Sometimes psychological issues will predominate, sometimes spiritual issues will come to the fore, and always they will interpenetrate and mutually influence each other, from the earliest to the highest stages. (Even if someone is stably at the "spiritual" or post-postcon waves in all streams, much of the conventional or "psychological" waves still remain as basic waves and functional capacities in awareness, mutually interacting with the spiritual realms.) As usual, overall development follows no set sequence at all, and each individual's journey through the spectrum of consciousness is a multifaceted, flowing, fluid affair of waves, streams, states, and realms.

Thus, all three common uses of "spiritual" find room in a type-III model. Spirituality as the highest levels, spirituality as a separate line, and spirituality as an altered state or religious experience all fit comfortably in an integral view, or so it seems to me. And all three of those uses of "spiritual" are valid, in my opinion, but it is important to specify which is meant before suggestions on the relation of psychology and spirituality are offered.

ON THE PHYSIOLOGY OF MEDITATION

Since the physiological and cognitive lines are the two earliest strands in the "necessary but not sufficient" sequence (which I gave above), this means that they are the most fundamental lines, the foundational lines, upon which all the others tend to rest, at least according to most research to date. (They are, it seems, the Right- and Left-Hand foundations of the entire sequence; the physiological is the foundation of the Upper-Right quadrant; the cognitive, of the Upper-Left).

This, too, is an important area of empirical investigation to which the TM researchers (particularly Wallace, Orme-Johnson, and Dillbeck) have significantly contributed; namely, the physiological correlates of meditative states and stages.

Recall that it was Wallace's 1970 landmark publication in *Science* ("The Physiological Effects of Transcendental Meditation") that shocked the scientific world into recognizing that *something real* was happening in meditation. Of course, empirical scientists recognize *only* the Right-Hand (or empirical) aspects of any holon anyway, but since all holons do indeed possess those aspects, then meditation ought to clearly register in that empirical and physiological domain. It does, Wallace proved it, and that dramatically exploded the dogma that meditation was ineffectual fantasy. This opened an enormous number of doors for further scientific-empirical research, of which the TM movement has remained in the forefront.

As we will see in the next chapter, an integral approach to consciousness would attempt to simultaneously track events in an all-level, all-quadrant fashion, and that would certainly include the physiological correlates of consciousness states. But such an all-level, all-quadrant approach also bears directly on *spiritual practice* itself. As I suggested in chapter 9, what we especially need at this point is not just an integral *theory* of the Kosmos, but an *integral practice* that can help us effectively actualize that integral potential in all of us.

INTEGRAL PRACTICE

The fact that the physiological (or "material") and the cognitive (or "mental") are two of the most fundamental lines in the human being ("matter" and "consciousness," Right and Left) means that a truly integral spiritual practice would, at the very least, put an equal emphasis on both body and mind at each and every stage of general evolution, gross bodymind to subtle bodymind to causal bodymind.

As straightforward as that conclusion might sound now, it is historically a rather radical idea, as Michael Murphy knows. Drawing on the pioneering insights of Aurobindo, but extending them in many profound and significant ways, Murphy has been arguing for many years that what is sorely needed is a truly *integral practice*. His masterwork, *The Future of the Body*, is devoted to just that topic. Charles Tart noted that "The only way to adequately describe this book is to state that it is the most important work on the relationship between mind and body ever written."

But by "mind" and "body" Murphy does not mean the standard and rather narrow notions of material flesh and immaterial soul. He rather means the entire sweep of the Upper-Left quadrant ("mind" or consciousness in the broadest sense) and the entire sweep of the Upper-Right quadrant ("body" in the broadest sense). And his point is: you cannot actually have one without the other at any level of human development, and therefore we ought to *consciously engage both*, equally, intensely, fully. This integral engagement then acts as an accelerator of evolution from the gross bodymind to the subtle bodymind to the causal bodymind, each stage of which embraces and radiantly transfigures its predecessors, uniting the ascending current of evolution with the descending current of involution, transforming the self, the body, and the world in the process.

Murphy is also fully aware of the importance, in overall practice, of integrating not just the Upper Left and Upper Right, but also the Lower Left and Lower Right—intentional, behavioral, cultural, and social—that is, an "all-level, all-quadrant" approach to integral practice. Thus, in his latest book, *The Life We Are Given*, coauthored with his friend George Leonard, the authors develop a program of balanced practice set in the context of family and community and service, which they call Integral Transformative Practice.

Mike and I have often discussed the "three waves" that the human potential movement itself has gone through in the last several decades. The first wave was the introduction, in the '60s, of the initial human potential movement. Although a varied beast, it tended to focus on the quick fix, the peak experience, the weekend workshop, the satori-in-seven-days seminar. It was a wild explosion, marvelous and frightening, wonderful and warped, glorious and grotesque. It was centered at Esalen Institute, cofounded by Mike and his friend Richard Price.

Within a decade or so, the goal of a "peak experience" started to give way to the goal of a "plateau experience," and the second wave of the human potential movement began. The limitations of the quick fix started to become all too apparent; useful as it was for an initial wakeup, the results tended to fade rapidly, sometimes leaving the individual in even worse shape than before. In any event, it soon became obvious that to engage in genuine transformation requires time, effort, work, and sustained intentionality—in a word, practice. People began to take up actual transformative practices: perhaps Zen, or yoga, or sustained psychotherapy, or prolonged body work, or extended dream work, or physical/sports/body training, and so on. The five-day fix gave way to the five-year engagement.

But even those forms of commendable practice had a limitation: they usually exercised only one faculty of the human organism—perhaps awareness, or dreams, or physical skill, or insight training, or emotional openness—while neglecting the others. That is, these approaches generally emphasized one line of development and followed it through its various levels—they grabbed one stream and surfed its waves—only to find, at the conclusion of that otherwise commendable practice, that the other lines of development were still rather immature, undeveloped, poorly evolved, or even withered, but now with the added difficulty: the person was burdened with a very unbalanced constitution. The poor self, which has to juggle all the various developmental lines, often found itself saddled with one giant and a dozen pygmies. And the more its particular practice genuinely *advanced*, the *worse* the situation got, which totally confused everybody.

Thus, the second wave of specific practice gave way to the third wave of integral practice. Once again the field transcended and included, negated and preserved, as it went through its own three waves of learning.

In other words, the field itself evolved from its initial sensory-dominated explosiveness ("lose your mind and come to your senses!") to its second wave of concrete practice, all of which were necessary for its third wave, just now starting, of universal/integral practice—its own precon, con, and postcon waves.

And, it might be noted, Michael Murphy was instrumental in all three waves. It has been Murphy who, working quietly and often behind the scenes, has prepared much of the ground in which each of those three waves could unfold. Michael Murphy very well might be the most significant spiritual pioneer of our generation, if for no other reason than the extraordinary spaces that he created in which others could transform as well.

The third wave of integral practice is in its infancy, but, like all infants, growing at a dizzying speed. Indicative of the trend is the book *What Really Matters: Searching for Wisdom in America*, by former *New*

York Times reporter Tony Schwartz. I think if Tony had the book to do over, there are a few small points he might change, but the book remains a fine compendium of the best of the transformative technologies now available. And the overall conclusion of the book is unmistakable: integral practice is now the most viable mode of human transformation.

To catch the crest of the third wave: has there ever been a more exciting surfing adventure in consciousness?

11

Heading toward Omega?

WHERE EXACTLY IS THE
GROUND OF BEING?

Where are we to locate Spirit? What are we actually allowed to acknowledge as Sacred? Where exactly is the Ground of Being? In infancy? In the matriarchy? In enlightenment? In Gaia? At some far-off but perhaps rapidly approaching Omega Point? Where is this ultimate Divine?

In this and the next chapter we address this most crucial of all questions.

WHERE IS THE SACRED ACTUALLY LOCATED?

MAX PLANCK IS CREDITED with first pointing out that old paradigms die only when the believers in old paradigms die. Because paradigms are self-confirming, there is no type of data that can dislodge the paradigm from within, and so new evidence or better arguments rarely dissuade believers. And thus, as I have often paraphrased Planck, the knowledge quest proceeds funeral by funeral.

On this, everybody agrees, and it is simply a matter of being honest about whose funeral you await.

Gus diZerega and Richard Smoley published a review of *Sex, Ecology, Spirituality* that is most interesting, and in many ways strikes me as something of a "paradigm clash," irresolvable with evidence. They begin by questioning my interpretation of Aristotle as being one of the West's archetypal Ascenders. They point out that Aristotle spent so much time categorizing the Many that he couldn't have been much of an Ascender. True, Aristotle spent most of his time in this-worldly study, and much of the West's science, for example, finds roots in Aristotle. I don't contest that. But in that section of the book I am discussing where various theorists located *ultimate reality*. And Arthur Lovejoy's extremely perceptive point was that, for Aristotle, ultimate reality (God) was not to be found anywhere in this world. Aristotle's God, rather, is entirely otherworldly; his God neither creates nor is substantially immanent in any manifest domain (things strive to reach God as final cause, but they never succeed).

Thus, to the utterly fundamental question, *Where is the real and final and ultimate reality?*, Aristotle would say: Not anywhere on this earth. And thus, when you look to the extraordinarily important notion of where final reality lies—and therefore, what is to be viewed as *profoundly sacred*—Aristotle is, in every way, otherworldly and ascending. Lovejoy makes that fascinating point—a point which had profound historical ramifications—and that is what I was reporting.

Lovejoy's concomitant point is that if we then look at Plato (who also in the conventional mentality is viewed as the real "otherworldly" philosopher, as opposed to the "this-worldly" orientation of Aristotle), we again find that things are actually reversed on this deepest of levels. Of course Plato had an enormously powerful otherworldly component to his philosophy; but as Lovejoy points out (and I quote this directly in the book): "But the most notable—and the less noted—fact about [Plato's] historic influence is that he did *not* merely give to European otherworldliness its characteristic form and phraseology and dialectic, but that he also gave the characteristic form and phraseology and dialectic to precisely the contrary tendency—to a peculiarly *exuberant kind of this-worldliness*." For example, Plato in the *Timaeus* describes the actual manifestation of this world from the ultimate reality, so that this very earth he calls "a visible, sensible God." This is the strand that would give rise to the Neoplatonic emphasis on sacred manifestation, which would easily see this earth and this world as sacred to the core, something for which Aristotle—and his immense influence—had no room at all.

Now *that's* fascinating, it seems to me, and quite true, and it much more clearly sets the record straight on just where *ultimate reality* could be found in these two most influential thinkers—and thus, just what could, or could not, *be viewed as sacred*. This, of course, upsets a common ecophilosopher and neopagan prejudice, which views a strawman Plato as being nothing but a fountain of Western hatred of this world. And it further goes to show why Plato, not Aristotle, could *actually* be (and was in fact historically) the father of so much of the West's this-worldly pantheism, neopaganism, and naturalism. All of this seems to be ignored by diZerega and Smoley, unfortunately.

They then attempt a similar questioning of my treatment of Emerson, although they do not in any fashion demonstrate that I misunderstood or misrepresented Emerson.[1] My interpretation of Emerson is so mainstream, so widely accepted, so uncontroversial, that you can even find it in standard college texts.[2] I stayed right down the middle of the interpretive road on such giants as Emerson and Plotinus, simply because, in claiming to integrate their views, I could not afford to be charged with integrating a "far-out" or contested interpretation, and thus I intentionally adopted a very safe, widely-accepted stance.[3] This balanced interpretation upset what I believe are the rather narrow, neopagan interpretations of diZerega and Smoley, and "paradigm clash" circled hauntingly in the background. Smoley's most recent book (with Kinney) continues to misrepresent my work as phase-II only (ignoring phases III and IV); but Gus diZerega's work on ecology and economic theory is really quite impressive, and I find myself in much agreement with his recent work (we are planning a few joint ventures).

POINTS OF LIGHT

1. I have often described Roger Walsh as one of the guiding lights of transpersonal studies, and I am always glad to have the opportunity to repeat my deep appreciation for his work (and our friendship). I have a similar estimate of his partner, Frances Vaughan, and their combined voices are a strong beacon for the entire field.

Roger wrote a superb summary of some of the central themes of *Sex, Ecology, Spirituality*, which has been published in several journals.[4] Given that his essay, in its various forms, has now been read by approximately three times the number of people who have read SES itself, you will understand that I am altogether relieved that it is fair, accurate, and informative.

2. Another superb summary of SES is by Kaisa Puhakka, "Restoring Connectedness in the Kosmos: A Healing Tale of a Deeper Order,"

which appeared in *The Humanistic Psychologist* (Fall 1996). It was truly gratifying to see the summaries by Walsh and Puhakka. You don't look for reviewers to necessarily agree with you, but simply to show that they have to some degree understood you. And I must say, these are two pieces that especially seemed to genuinely understand *Sex, Ecology, Spirituality*, and I can recommend them very highly on that count alone.

3. A sign that the transpersonal orientation is starting to have a major impact on conventional and mainstream psychology is the recent publication, by Basic Books, of the *Textbook of Transpersonal Psychiatry and Psychology*, edited by Bruce Scotton, M.D., Allan B. Chinen, M.D., and John Battista, M.D. This is an excellent collection of articles and essays touching on almost every aspect of the transpersonal orientation, and it deserves the widest possible readership.

At the same time, this is simply the most recent in a line of superb anthologies on adult and postformal development, beginning perhaps with *Beyond Formal Operations*, edited by Michael L. Commons, Francis A. Richards, and Cheryl Armon. This was (and still is) a pioneering work, appearing in 1984, and excellent in every respect. I will mention several other important anthologies in an endnote.[5]

All of these works are a clear indication that the fields of psychiatry and psychology are increasingly ready to move beyond their postconventional to their own post-postconventional wave of awareness, a healthy sign by any standard.

4. Bryan Wittine's review of *Sex, Ecology, Spirituality* in *The Journal of Transpersonal Psychology* (1995, 27[2]) is thoughtful, balanced, and perceptive. But within a broad range of agreement, he had several criticisms. One was that I presented a rigidly stratified view of development with clear-cut levels. This, of course, is not the case (see chapters 9 and 10), but I understand how a reviewer could get that impression from my short summary in SES.

Wittine's second criticism concerned my treatment of Jung and the archetypes. Again, I can understand how Bryan might get some of his impressions from the short summary I gave in SES. The problem is that Jung (and his followers) had at least three different uses of "archetype," and I believe that there are insuperable difficulties with all of them.

The first and most common use is *archaic image*. This was Jung's earliest formulation, and it is still the most prevalent and most widely used (for example, by the mythopoetic movement, the men's movement, and folk psychology). These collectively inherited archaic images, Jung believed, were a phylogenetic heritage, "the instinct's perception of itself." Jung believed that a particularly rich fund of these archetypes could be found in the world's mythologies (which led Jung's early critics to accuse him of "mythomania"). These archaic mythic images were nonrational, and because of this, Jung felt they were a direct source of spiritual awareness, which is exactly what he had in mind when he stated that "mysticism is experience of the archetypes."

In that usage, Jung is most definitely guilty of the pre/trans fallacy. He simply does not differentiate with sufficient clarity between prerational and transrational occasions, and thus he tends to elevate prerational infantilisms to spiritual glory, for no other reason than that they are not rational. This use of "archetype," because it is still the most common and most widely associated with Jung's name, is the use I have criticized the most. In this usage, the archetypes are found in the earlier stages of evolution, phylogenetic and ontogenetic. I have pointed out that those archaic image "archetypes" should therefore really be called "prototypes," because they are prerational, magic, and mythic forms, not subtle, transrational, and post-postconventional forms (which is the way they are used in the perennial philosophy, from Plotinus to Garab Dorje to Asanga and Vasubandhu).[6]

Jung's second use of archetype was much broader; it simply referred to archetypes as collectively inherited "forms devoid of content." In *The Atman Project* I quote him saying exactly that, and I point out that if that is our definition of archetype, then all of the deep structures of each level of the spectrum of consciousness (except the formless) can be called *archetypal*, and that is fine with me. But then that has absolutely nothing to do with archaic images, does it?

That use of archetype (as deep structures devoid of content) is one of the uses that Wittine wishes to rehabilitate. "My understanding is that archetypes are innate structural predispositions that are definable only in terms of ordering principles, never in terms of specific content." Wittine says I ignore this use, which, as we just saw, is not the case. I simply point out that that definition is massively at variance with Jung's first and most common usage. If Wittine wishes to follow that definition, that is completely acceptable, but a great deal of clarity is required in order to differentiate it from the first use and avoid pre/trans fallacies. I myself have not found the Jungian literature useful in this regard.

The third use of archetype by Jung and his followers is more in line with the perennial philosophy, which sees archetypes as *the first forms in involution*. The entire manifest world arises out of the Formless (or causal Abyss), and the first forms to do so are the forms upon which all others will rest—they are "arche-forms" or archetypes. Thus, in this use, the archetypes are the highest Forms of our own possibilities, the deepest Forms of our own potentials—but also the last barriers to the Formless and Nondual.

As the first (and earliest) forms in involution or manifestation (or movement away from causal Source), the archetypes are the last (and highest) forms in evolution or return to Source. As the Forms right on the edge of the Formless, they are the first forms the soul embraces as it contracts in the face of infinity and hides its own true nature; but they are also, for just that reason, the highest beacons on the way back to the Formless, and the final barrier to be deconstructed on the edge of a radiant infinity.[7]

(And note: because these archetypes are the first forms in *early involution*, they are almost the exact opposite of archaic images, which are some of the first forms that arise in *early evolution*—yet another reason that confusing them has caused such theoretical problems.)[8]

Jung and the Jungians *occasionally* use archetype in this high fashion, but even then it tends to be a rather anemic discussion. I believe Hameed Ali has brutally but accurately summarized the situation: "Jung got very close to [high archetypal] essence and its various manifestations but stayed on the level of imagination. So he fell short of realizing [archetypal] essence and living it, and his psychology remained a mental construct not directly connected with the presence of essence."[9]

Thus, we have three different uses of "archetype" by Jung and the Jungians, and all of them, I believe, are problematic. The archaic images exist, but they have little if anything to do with post-postconventional development. Archetypes as deep structures devoid of content is an acceptable usage, but it is almost totally at variance with the first use (e.g., formal operational has a deep structure and is "archetypal" in that sense, but you do not find formop in archaic images), and the Jungian development of this use I have found rather limited. Finally, archetype as "high archetype" or forms of the subtle (the first forms in involution, the last forms in evolution) is also acceptable, but here I find the Jungian use, as does Hameed Ali, to be anemic (see below).

And in all three of those uses, the Jungian archetype is still profoundly monological (see note 3 to chapter 7). For all of these reasons, I have increasingly found the Jungian approach, pioneering as it was, to be less than fruitful for third-wave transpersonal studies. Of course, any individual can make exemplary exercise of the Jungian path, using its strengths to transcend its limitations. Bryan Wittine is such a one, and there are many others. But the Jungian light is one we must use with much caution, I now believe.

5. In the late seventies, the system known as Psychosynthesis, developed by Roberto Assagioli, became a fairly popular and widespread spiritual psychology and therapy. Assagioli was an extraordinary pioneer in the transpersonal field, weaving the best of many important psychological and spiritual traditions together into a powerful approach to inner growth. Among many other contributions, he was one of the first to call for an integration of "depth psychology" with what he called "height psychology," and to combine "psychoanalysis" with "psychosynthesis."

Nonetheless, for various reasons, Psychosynthesis as a major force declined in influence.[10] I had always wondered if there would arise another fairly popular yet well-rounded approach to psychology and therapy, uniting both depth and height psychology, and in the past several years, it appears that there has: the Diamond Approach, originated by Hameed Ali.

I will reserve a long discussion of this approach for an endnote.[11] Here I will simply say that, in my opinion, the Diamond Approach is a superb combination of some of the best of modern Western psychology with ancient (and spiritual) wisdom. It is one type of a more integral approach, uniting Ascending and Descending, spiritual and psychological, into an effective form of inner work.

As is always the case with these more public and popular movements, much hinges on the actual personalities of those drawn to the approach. Psychosynthesis floundered in part because, although it was a fairly well-rounded theory, its emphasis on disidentification meant that in practice it attracted a large number of dissociative types, inmates who in some cases took over the hospital. The Diamond Approach thus far seems to be running smoothly, and it has earned recognition from many quarters, including my hard-to-impress friends Larry Spiro and Tony Schwartz. We will simply have to wait and see what forces surface as this generally well-rounded approach grows into a large organization with much influence: whom it will attract, what fate awaits it, what forces are unleashed as it moves into the culture at large.

In the meantime, the fact that such a therapeutic/growth system can

gain a strong and respected foothold in the culture—this, too, a sign of
the post-postconventional waves that are very slowly but very surely
washing upon our collective shores.

THE IDEALIST DREAM

A few reviewers categorized *Sex, Ecology, Spirituality* as being primarily
an Idealist treatise. I can understand why that might seem to be the case
(especially for reviewers, who don't often have a great deal of time to
spend with a book, not to mention an 800-page book). Nonetheless,
although I have some profound sympathies with the Idealist project, I
am not a member of that camp in any strict sense. In SES I express great
appreciation for the Idealists—especially Schelling—because they were
some of the first to attempt to articulate a modern form of spirituality—
that is, a transpersonal philosophy that would take into account the
worldview of modernity, including development and evolution, which is
basically something that no spiritual view had done prior to that time
(and which traditional spiritual approaches still often neglect). Evolution as "Spirit-in-action" is simply one of many Idealist tenets that I
have happily adopted.

But I outline two severe inadequacies that prevent the typical Idealist
approach from finally working: it has no injunctions or paradigms or
yoga; and it tends to equate vision-logic with spirit. These are crucial
points, because they indicate what I believe to be the only viable way
out of the Idealist impasse.

Lacking injunctions means lacking a genuine methodology to reproduce transpersonal knowledge. The great Idealist philosophers—indeed,
many great "spiritual" philosophers, including Spinoza, Schelling,
Fichte, Hegel, Nietzsche, Schopenhauer, Whitehead, James—almost certainly had a variety of profound "peak experiences" or glimpses into the
transpersonal (or post-postconventional) waves of awareness.

But a peak experience is not a reproducible mode of knowledge acquisition. The peak experience must give way to the plateau experience,
which must give way to permanent adaptation, before the knowledge of
that level of development becomes verifiable (confirmable/rejectable)
and thus can actually enter the stream of valid knowledge.

In other words, to have any genuine cognitive status, these temporary
states of consciousness must be converted into stable and enduring *traits*
or structures of consciousness. And this, by any other name, is the role

and function of yoga—a sustained practice, injunction, exemplar, or paradigm which acts as the foundation of all genuine transpersonal knowledge. None of the philosophers that I just listed had a stable transpersonal practice, exemplar, or paradigm, and thus all of their views soon degenerated into metaphysics (where "metaphysics" means a system of thought without experiential proof).

But if a genuine yoga (transpersonal injunction and practice) is fully engaged, and if consciousness grows and evolves and gains in strength—precisely through the ongoing flow of developmental structuration—it will increasingly remain "awake" under all possible states. In the advanced waves of spiritual practice, the self will remain fully conscious in waking, dream, and deep sleep ("subject permanence"), and thus it will eventually recognize *that which remains the same under all possible changes of state.* In other words, it will recognize the changeless, the timeless, the spaceless—it will recognize, or re-cognize, its own Original Face, its own primordial nature, the ever-present Emptiness in which and through which all states arise, remain a bit, and pass. God-consciousness has become, not a changing state, but an enduring trait. Moreover, this is not merely a philosophical thought, but a direct and reproducible cognition. [See *One Taste* for further discussion of this theme.]

Thus, as sympathetic as I am with all of those philosophers, I cannot finally be counted among their ranks. What the postmodern West is struggling to evolve, I believe, is a postempirical, postidealist yoga. Since Kant, we have been forced to acknowledge, not that metaphysics is meaningless, but that metaphysics without direct experience is meaningless. And direct *transpersonal experience* relies on genuine transpersonal practices, paradigms, injunctions, and exemplars, which disclose the domains of post-postconventional experience that alone can ground a verifiable spiritual knowledge, thus fulfilling the Idealist promise precisely by transcending its limited agenda.

AN INTEGRAL THEORY OF CONSCIOUSNESS

The first step toward a genuine theory of consciousness, I believe, is the realization that consciousness is not located in the organism. Rather, consciousness is a four-quadrant affair, and it exists, if it exists at all, distributed across all four quadrants, anchored equally in each.[12]

There has recently been something of an explosion of interest in the development of a "science of consciousness." The major approaches in this recent surge of interest include the following:

1. *Cognitive science,* which tends to view consciousness as anchored in functional schemas of the brain/mind, either in a simple representational fashion (such as Jackendoff's "computational mind") or in the more complex emergent/connectionist models, which view consciousness as an emergent of hierarchically integrated networks. The emergent/connectionist is perhaps the dominant model of cognitive science at this point, and is nicely summarized in Alwyn Scott's *Stairway to the Mind,* the "stairway" being the hierarchy of emergents summating in consciousness.

2. *Introspectionism* maintains that consciousness is best understood in first-person accounts—the inspection and interpretation of immediate awareness and lived experience—and not in third-person or objectivist accounts, no matter how "scientific" they might appear. This includes introspective psychology, existentialism, phenomenology.

3. *Neuropsychology* views consciousness as anchored in neural systems, neurotransmitters, and organic brain mechanisms. Unlike cognitive science, which is often based on computer science and is consequently vague about how consciousness is actually related to organic brain structures, neuropsychology is a more biologically based approach. Anchored in neuroscience more than computer science, it views consciousness as intrinsically residing in organic neural systems of sufficient complexity.

4. *Individual psychotherapy* uses introspective and interpretive psychology to treat distressing symptoms and emotional problems; it thus tends to view consciousness as primarily anchored in an individual organism's adaptive capacities.

5. *Social psychology* views consciousness as embedded in networks of cultural meaning, or, alternatively, as being largely a byproduct of the social system itself. This includes approaches as varied as ecological, Marxist, constructivist, and cultural hermeneutic.

6. *Clinical psychiatry* focuses on the relation of psychopathology, behavioral patterns, and psychopharmacology; it increasingly views consciousness in neurophysiological terms: consciousness resides in the neuronal system.

7. *Developmental psychology* views consciousness not as a single entity but as a developmentally unfolding process with a substantially different architecture at each of its stages of growth.

In its more avant-garde forms, this approach includes higher stages of exceptional development and well-being, and the study of gifted, extraordinary, and supranormal capacities, viewed as higher developmental potentials latent in all humans. This includes higher stages of cognitive, affective, somatic, moral, and spiritual development.

8. *Psychosomatic medicine* views consciousness as strongly and intrinsically interactive with organic bodily processes, evidenced in such fields as psychoneuroimmunology and biofeedback. In its more avant-garde forms, this approach includes consciousness and miraculous healing, the effects of prayer on remarkable recoveries, light/sound and healing, spontaneous remission, and so on. It also includes any of the approaches that investigate the effects of intentionality on healing, from art therapy to visualization to psychotherapy and meditation.

9. *Nonordinary states of consciousness,* from dreams to psychedelics, constitute a field of study that, its advocates believe, is crucial to a grasp of consciousness in general. Although some of the effects of psychedelics—to take a controversial example—are undoubtedly due to "toxic side-effects," the consensus of opinion in this area of research is that they also act as a "nonspecific amplifier of experience," and thus they can be instrumental in disclosing and amplifying aspects of consciousness that might otherwise go unstudied.

10. *Eastern and contemplative traditions* maintain that ordinary consciousness is but a narrow and restricted version of deeper or higher modes of awareness, and that specific injunctions (yoga, meditation) are necessary to evoke these higher and exceptional potentials.

11. What might be called the *quantum consciousness* approaches view consciousness as being intrinsically capable of interacting with, and altering, the physical world, generally through quantum interactions, both in the human body at the intracellular level (e.g., microtubules), and in the material world at large (psi). This approach also includes the many and various attempts to plug consciousness into the physical world according to various avant-garde physical theories (bootstrapping, hyperspace, strings).

12. *Subtle energies* research has postulated, and in some cases apparently confirmed, that there exist subtler types of bioenergies

beyond the four recognized forces of physics (strong and weak nuclear, electromagnetic, gravitational), and that these subtler energies play an intrinsic role in consciousness and its activity. Known in the traditions by such terms as prana, ki, and chi—and held to be responsible for the effectiveness of acupuncture, to give only one example—these energies are often held to be the "missing link" between intentional mind and physical body. For the Great Chain theorists, both East and West, this bioenergy acts as a two-way conveyor belt, transferring the impact of matter to the mind and imposing the intentionality of the mind on matter.

13. *Evolutionary psychology* and its close relative sociobiology see behavior and consciousness in functional terms as expressions of evolutionary pressures. From this perspective, consciousness and its various forms arise because of, and are to be understood in terms of, the evolutionary advantage they confer.

You might guess that I will maintain that all of those approaches are equally important for an integral view of consciousness, and that is true enough. An "all-level, all-quadrant" approach finds important truths in each of them, and in very specific ways. But it is not simply that we have a given phenomenon called "consciousness" and that these various approaches are each giving us a different view of the beast. Rather, consciousness actually exists distributed across all four quadrants with all of their various levels and dimensions. There is no one quadrant (and certainly no one level) to which we can point and say, There is consciousness. Consciousness is in no way localized in that fashion, in my opinion.

It is true that the Upper-Left quadrant is the locus of consciousness as it appears in an individual, but that's the point: as it appears in an individual. Yet consciousness on the whole is anchored in, and distributed across, all of the quadrants—intentional, behavioral, cultural, and social. If you "erase" any quadrant, they all disappear, because each is intrinsically necessary for the existence of the others.

Thus, it is quite true that consciousness is anchored in the physical brain (as maintained by theories 1, 3, 6, 8). But consciousness is also and equally anchored in interior intentionality (as maintained by theories 2, 4, 7, 10, 11), an intentionality that cannot be explained in physicalist or empiricist terms nor disclosed by their methods.

By the same token, neither can consciousness be finally located in the individual (whether of the Upper Left or Upper Right or both together), because consciousness is also fully anchored in cultural meaning (the intersubjective chains of cultural signifieds), without which there is simply no individuated consciousness at all. Without this background of cultural practices and meanings, my individual intentions do not and cannot even develop, as the occasional cases of "wolf boy" demonstrate. In precisely the same way that there is no private language, there is no strictly individual consciousness. You cannot generate meaning in a vacuum, nor can you generate it with a physical brain alone, but only in an intersubjective circle of mutual recognition. Physical brains raised in the wild ("wolf boy") generate neither personal autonomy nor linguistic competence, from which it plainly follows, the physical brain per se is not the autonomous seat of consciousness.

Likewise, consciousness is also embedded in, and distributed across, the material social systems in which it finds itself. Not just chains of cultural signifieds, but chains of social signifiers, determine the specific contours of any particular manifestation of consciousness, and without the material conditions of the social system, both individuated consciousness and personal integrity fail to emerge.

In short, if you take away any of those quadrants—intentional, behavioral, cultural, or social—you will destroy any manifest consciousness. And that means, very simply, that consciousness is located solely in none of those domains. Consciousness is not located merely in the physical brain, nor in the physical organism, nor in the ecological system, nor in the cultural context, nor does it emerge from any of those domains. Rather, it is anchored in, and distributed across, all of those domains with all of their available levels.[13]

Thus, the methodologies that purport to give us a "theory of consciousness," but which investigate only one quadrant (not to mention only one level in one quadrant) are clearly not giving us an adequate account of consciousness at all. Rather, I believe that an "all-quadrant, all-level" approach holds the only chance of an authentic theory of consciousness, if such indeed exists.

HOLONIC ECOLOGY

Michael Zimmerman's essay, "A Transpersonal Diagnosis of the Ecological Crisis," is a thoughtful review of *Sex, Ecology, Spirituality*. As usual, I am in substantial and widespread agreement with much of Zimmerman's presentation, and I am glad to again have the opportunity to publicly express appreciation for the clarity, care, and brilliance he always brings to the task at hand. I cannot speak too highly of his expositions of Heidegger (*Eclipse of the Self* and *Heidegger's Confrontation with Modernity*), as well as his own *Contesting Earth's Future*.

Zimmerman's main point is that, whether one agrees with all the minor details in SES, it constitutes a genuinely transpersonal approach to ecophilosophy, an approach that simultaneously challenges most of the standard ecophilosophies (including deep ecology and ecofeminism). Zimmerman particularly focuses on one of the central tenets in SES—namely, that the biosphere is a part of the noosphere, and not vice versa—and points out that such a tenet strongly undercuts most ecophilosophies while simultaneously offering a genuinely transpersonal alternative (which SES refers to as *holonic ecology*).

Within that broad agreement, Zimmerman raises a handful of criticisms. He particularly believes that my treatment in SES of the actual schools of ecophilosophy is short and sometimes overgeneralized. This is true; but volume 2 is devoted to a full discussion, with all the appropriate differences and distinctions, of the major schools of this broad and varied movement (including the work of W. Fox, Naess, Swimme, Berry, Warren, Eckersley, Merchant, Spretnak, Bookchin, et al.). Zimmerman knows, from personal correspondence, that I have relied on his wonderful *Contesting Earth's Future* as a superb source, and that in many ways I am in substantial and widespread agreement with the important views he advances therein.

Zimmerman nonetheless maintains that my treatment of the ecophilosophers in SES is occasionally distorted and that I have not been fair to the deeper aspects of ecophilosophy. I disagree, and I think volume 2 will bear this out amply.

Zimmerman gives as an example of my alleged misrepresentation the work of Arne Naess, whose philosophy Zimmerman maintains is compatible with the great Nondual traditions of Mahayana Buddhism and Advaita Vedanta (which Naess also claims). But this "similarity" or "compatibility," I believe, is true in only the most superficial sense. In volume 2 I present an in-depth analysis of Naess's Ecosophy T, and find it lacking in many respects when compared with the great Nondual traditions. Even Naess himself, when attempting to present the similarities, fails to account for even the simplest and most crucial issues—for example, the notion of unity-in-multiplicity, a hallmark of Nondual realization. Naess fumbles in the worst of ways: "The widening and deepening of the individual selves *somehow* never makes them into one 'mass'. . . . How to work this out in a fairly precise way I do not know" (his italics).[14] I point out the same problems for representatives of each of the major ecophilosophies, and thus their "compatibility" with the Nondual traditions likewise is exposed as largely superficial. Not one of them, for example, even mentions "subject permanence," which the Nondual traditions recommend as an important prerequisite of nondual awareness (see chap. 10).

Thus, the generalizations I make in SES about ecofeminism, deep ecology, and the general ecophilosophies, far from being "distorted" or "lumped together," are based on a deep level of analysis which reveals that most of them are caught in flatland orientations, and the detailed analysis of volume 2 supports that conclusion. These are not wild generalizations, but the summary of a series of very specific and detailed analyses. Holonic ecology is presented as an alternative that embraces the spirit of the ecological movements but in a more full-spectrum fashion.

Zimmerman, in what seems to be a rare nod to political correctness for its own sake, implies that all "big pictures" command totalizing agendas that inherently marginalize social differences. Since SES is a big picture, couldn't it be marginalizing?

Some "totalizing" schemes are indeed marginalizing; others offer dramatically different incentives. My "big picture" explicitly does the following: it simply says, here are some areas of research and theory and evidence that perhaps you should look at. I am not trying to cram all differences into monological uniformitarianism. I thoroughly condemn that approach. Rather, my "big picture" is simply an explicit offer to take a larger view of things, a view that invites researchers to stop any marginalization that they might otherwise be involved with. It's open-ended; it is not a "foregone conclusion" nor a conceptual straightjacket.

There is nothing inherently alienating in open-ended big pictures. And, in fact, it is increasingly becoming obvious that those critics, such as Lyotard or Rorty, who rail against metanarratives and big pictures, do so only under severe performative contradictions. Ask them why big pictures are not desirable or even possible, and they will give you a very big picture of why big pictures don't work. This performative contradiction has been pointed out by theorists from Charles Taylor to Quentin Skinner to Gellner to Habermas. Karl-Otto Apel is simply the most recent theorist to point out that "Rorty himself confirms this structure by the validity claims raised by each one of his own verdicts against all universal validity claims of philosophy. He thus ends up with the novel rhetorical figure of constantly committing a *performative self-contradiction*."[15]

Human beings, it seems, are bound to create big pictures of one sort or another. Therefore, choose your big pictures with care. I simply think an all-level, all-quadrant approach is one of the better alternatives.

SHAKING THE SPIRITUAL TREE

Robert McDermott, in his essay "The Need for Dialogue in the Wake of Ken Wilber's *Sex, Ecology, Spirituality*," raises the issue of whether polemical discourse is ever appropriate for academic and especially spiritual dialogue. He ends up rather strongly condemning polemic, his major point being that it isn't "spiritual." But I believe that this reflects an impoverished and narrow view of spirit—what it is, and where it is located.

McDermott asks if we would ever hear polemic from the great spiritual philosophers, such as Aurobindo or James or Plotinus. The answer, of course, is yes. In fact, the vast majority of spiritual philosophers have engaged at one time or another in intense polemical discourse—Plato, Hegel, Kierkegaard, Nietzsche, Fichte, Schopenhauer, Schelling, Augustine, Origen, Plotinus, to name a very few. They do so, I believe, precisely because they understand the difference between what Chögyam Trungpa Rinpoche called "compassion" and "idiot compassion." This is perhaps the hardest lesson to learn in politically correct America, where idiot compassion—the abdication of discriminating wisdom and the loss of the moral fiber to voice it—is too often equated with "spirituality."

I think, on the contrary, that we admire these spiritual philosophers because idiot compassion was foreign to them, because they all had the moral courage to speak out in the most acerbic of terms when necessary, to make the hard calls and make them loud and clear. People too often imagine that "choiceless awareness" means making no judgments at all. But that itself is a judging activity. Rather, "choiceless awareness" means that both judging and no judging are allowed to arise, appropriate to circumstances. I think this is why so many great spiritual philosophers engaged in such incredibly *intense* polemic, Plotinus being a quite typical example. Plotinus so aggressively attacked the astrologers that Dante felt it necessary to consign the entire lot of them to the eighth ring of hell, and Plotinus unrelentingly tore into the Gnostics as having "no right to even speak of the Divine."

I used to think that if somebody engaged in that type of forceful polemic, they couldn't be very enlightened. I see now it is exactly the opposite. We tend to believe genuine spirituality should avoid all that,
whereas in fact it quite often engages it passionately as a manifestation
of its capacity to judge depth (i.e., its capacity for discriminating wisdom). Plotinus's acerbic and occasionally sarcastic attack on the astrologers and gnostics is paradigmatic: they were a politically powerful and
unpleasant lot, and it took courage to claim they had no right to even
speak of the Divine. If McDermott is sincere about his pronouncements,
then he would have been there to publicly condemn Plotinus, no doubt;
but the point is that right or wrong Plotinus stood up to be counted, and
it is a service to us that he did so in no uncertain terms. Moreover,
Plotinus is not saying one thing in public and another in private; you
know exactly where he stands.

The question is thus not whether these great spiritual philosophers
engaged in polemic, for they did; the question is why. When such sages
engage in intense polemic, I suppose we sometimes get nothing but their
lingering neurosis; but we often get the full force of the overall judgment
of their entire being, a shout from the heart in a sharp scream. It takes
no effort at all to act out the former; it takes courage to stand up and
voice the latter, and this is what I have come to admire in all the sages
and philosophers I mentioned who have left us the full force of their
summary judgments.

Contrary to McDermott's misplaced pronouncements, such polemic
comes not from this, but from the other, side of equanimity. One Taste
is the ground of intense judgments, not their abdication. These are not
lunatics blathering prejudices; more like what the Tibetans would call
the wrathful aspect of enlightened awareness.

McDermott tells us that he used to publicly and passionately voice
his own judgments of qualitative distinctions and discriminating wisdom, but that he quit doing so in order to become a better administrator.
I accept his choice. But I think it would be unfortunate for everybody in
the spiritual field to adopt that same stance and abdicate the public voicing of their discriminating wisdom.[16]

There are many who see all too clearly the sad shape our field is in.
They talk about it often in private. They tell me about it all the time.
They are truly alarmed by the reactionary, prerational, and regressive
fog thickly creeping over the entire field. Yet most of them are not willing to stand up and be counted, precisely because the countercultural
police await, poised and ready to sanctimoniously damn them. A little

less administrative juggling, and a little more discriminating wisdom backed with occasional polemic, is exactly what the entire field could use, in my opinion. I, at any rate, can no longer sit by and smile numbly as depth takes a vacation. And in a more honest process, where our public pronouncements actually match our private statements, we just might find that spiritual awareness includes, not excludes, the fiercest of judgments.

OMEGA POINT

A few reviewers assumed that I believed we were heading for an ultimate Omega point, a final point in manifest time where spirit realizes itself as spirit and we all go up in light. It is true that, in individuals, spirit can awaken as spirit ("spirit-as-spirit," traditional enlightenment). And it is true that this is in some important ways a *developmental* or *evolutionary* process. That is, certain developments clear the way for this timeless realization: both humans and rocks are equally spirit, but only humans can consciously realize that fact, and between the rock and the human lies evolution.

This is behind the Buddhist prayer of thanks "for this precious human body"—only in a human body can enlightenment be attained. Not gods, not animals, not demons, not angels: only with this human body can I awaken to the empty Ground that is equally present in all other sentient beings. This, too, is Aurobindo's and Murphy's emphasis on *The Future of the Body*, the precious human body. And that human body is, among many other things, the product of evolution.

And *that* means that Spirit has evolved the vehicle for its own self-realization. Because Spirit is involved with and as this world, this world evolves with and as Spirit, to the point that Spirit superconsciously realizes its own Original Face. The possibility of that realization is a product of Spirit's own evolutionary unfolding, and in that sense, this realization has a very strong developmental aspect.

But it is not the whole story. Evolution occurs in the world of time and space and form, whereas Spirit's primordial nature is finally timeless and Formless, prior to the world of evolution but not other to it. We do not find Spirit or Emptiness by reaching some evolutionary Omega point in time, but rather by stepping off the cycle of time and evolution altogether (or ceasing to contract into it).

In other words, a certain amount of evolution is required before you can step off of evolution, out of time, and into the timeless itself—into that shocking re-cognition of your own True Self, the Self that was prior to the Big Bang, prior to the temporal world altogether, eternally shining in this and every moment, untouched by the ravages of time and the motion sickness of space: your own primordial awareness is not the Omega point of the show but the Emptiness of the show, radiant in all directions, full beyond what time or space could ever do for it, yet embracing all time and all space for no other reason than that Eternity is in love with the productions of time and Infinity those of space.

Once you learn to count, you don't have to count to a million to get the point. Once you profoundly recognize Emptiness, you don't have to watch its endless displays in order to awaken. Emptiness is fully present at every point of evolution; it is not merely the end point of evolution. The game is undone in that primal Glance, and all that remains is the radiance itself, perfectly obvious in the singing of a robin, early on a bright spring dawn.

In the next chapter, we will follow the great Nondual traditions into this timeless, ever-present awareness, which is said to be nothing less than the actual location of Spirit itself.

12

Always Already

THE BRILLIANT CLARITY OF EVER-PRESENT AWARENESS

Where are we to locate Spirit? What are we actually allowed to acknowledge as Sacred? Where exactly is the Ground of Being? Where is this ultimate Divine?

THE GREAT SEARCH

THE REALIZATION OF the Nondual traditions is uncompromising: there is only Spirit, there is only God, there is only Emptiness in all its radiant wonder. All the good and all the evil, the very best and the very worst, the upright and the degenerate—each and all are radically perfect manifestations of Spirit precisely as they are. There is nothing but God, nothing but the Goddess, nothing but Spirit in all directions, and not a grain of sand, not a speck of dust, is more or less Spirit than any other.

This realization undoes the Great Search that is the heart of the separate-self sense. The separate-self is, at bottom, simply a sensation of seeking. When you feel yourself right now, you will basically feel a tiny interior tension or contraction—a sensation of grasping, desiring, wishing, wanting, avoiding, resisting—it is a sensation of effort, a sensation of seeking.

In its highest form, this sensation of seeking takes on the form of the

Great Search for Spirit. We wish to get from our unenlightened state (of sin or delusion or duality) to an enlightened or more spiritual state. We wish to get from where Spirit is not, to where Spirit is.

But there is no place where Spirit is not. Every single location in the entire Kosmos is equally and fully Spirit. Seeking of any sort, movement of any sort, attainment of any sort: all profoundly useless. The Great Search simply reinforces the mistaken assumption that there is some place that Spirit is not, and that I need to get from a space that is lacking to a space that is full. But there is no space lacking, and there is no space more full. There is only Spirit.

The Great Search for Spirit is simply that impulse, the final impulse, which prevents the present realization of Spirit, and it does so for a simple reason: the Great Search presumes the loss of God. The Great Search reinforces the mistaken belief that God is not present, and thus totally obscures the reality of God's ever-present Presence. The Great Search, which pretends to love God, is in fact the very mechanism of pushing God away; the mechanism of promising to find tomorrow that which exists only in the timeless now; the mechanism of watching the future so fervently that the present always passes it by—very quickly— and God's smiling face with it.

The Great Search is the loveless contraction hidden in the heart of the separate-self sense, a contraction that drives the intense yearning for a tomorrow in which salvation will finally arrive, but during which time, thank God, I can continue to be myself. The greater the Great Search, the more I can deny God. The greater the Great Search, the more I can feel my own sensation of seeking, which defines the contours of my self. The Great Search is the great enemy of what is.

Should we then simply cease the Great Search? Definitely, if we could. But the effort to stop the Great Search is itself more of the Great Search. The very first step presumes and reinforces the seeking sensation. There is actually nothing the self-contraction can do to stop the Great Search, because the self-contraction and the Great Search are two names for the same thing.

If Spirit cannot be found as a future product of the Great Search, then there is only one alternative: Spirit must be fully, totally, completely present right now—AND you must be fully, totally, completely aware of it right now. It will not do to say that Spirit is present but I don't realize it. That would require the Great Search; that would demand that I seek a tomorrow in which I could realize that Spirit is fully present, but such seeking misses the present in the very first step. To keep seeking would be to keep missing. No, the realization itself, the awareness itself: this, too, must somehow be fully and completely present right now. If it is not, then all we have left is the Great Search, doomed to presume that which it wishes to overcome.

There must be something about our *present* awareness that contains the entire truth. Somehow, no matter what your state, you are immersed fully in everything you need for perfect enlightenment. You are somehow looking right at the answer. One hundred percent of Spirit is in your perception right now. Not 20 percent, not 50 percent, not 99 percent, but literally 100 percent of Spirit is in your awareness right now—and the trick, as it were, is to recognize this ever-present state of affairs, and not to engineer a future state in which Spirit will announce itself.

And this simple recognition of an *already present* Spirit is the task, as it were, of the great Nondual traditions.

TO MEET THE KOSMOS

Many people have stern objections to "mysticism" or "transcendentalism" of any sort, because they think it somehow denies this world, or hates this earth, or despises the body and the senses and its vital life, and so on. While that may be true of certain dissociated (or merely Ascending) approaches, it is certainly not the core understanding of the great Nondual mystics, from Plotinus and Eckhart in the West to Nagarjuna and Lady Tsogyal in the East.

Rather, these sages universally maintain that absolute reality and the relative world are "not-two" (which is the meaning of "nondual"), much as a mirror and its reflections are not separate, or an ocean is one with its many waves. So the "other world" of Spirit and "this world" of separate phenomena are deeply and profoundly "not-two," and this nonduality is a direct and immediate realization which occurs in certain meditative states—in other words, seen with the eye of contemplation— although it then becomes a very simple, very ordinary perception, whether you are meditating or not. Every single thing you perceive is the radiance of Spirit itself, so much so that Spirit is not seen apart from that thing: the robin sings, and just that is it, nothing else. This becomes your constant realization, through all changes of state, very naturally, just so. And this releases you from the basic insanity of hiding from the Real.

But why is it, then, that we ordinarily don't have that perception?

All the great Nondual wisdom traditions have given a fairly similar answer to that question. We don't see that Spirit is fully and completely present right here, right now, because our awareness is clouded with some form of *avoidance*. We do not want to be choicelessly aware of the present; rather, we want to run away from it, or run after it, or we want to change it, alter it, hate it, love it, loathe it, or in some way agitate to get ourselves into, or out of, it. We will do anything except come to rest in the pure Presence of the present. We will not rest with pure Presence; we want to be elsewhere, quickly. The Great Search is the game, in its endless forms.

In nondual meditation or contemplation, the agitation of the separate-self sense profoundly relaxes, and the self uncoils in the vast expanse of all space. At that point, it becomes obvious that you are not "in here" looking at the world "out there," because that duality has simply collapsed into pure Presence and spontaneous luminosity.

This realization may take many forms. A simple one is something like this: You might be looking at a mountain, and you have relaxed into the effortlessness of your own present awareness, and then suddenly the mountain is all, you are nothing. Your separate-self sense is suddenly and totally gone, and there is simply everything that is arising moment to moment. You are perfectly aware, perfectly conscious, everything seems completely normal, except you are nowhere to be found. You are not on this side of your face looking at the mountain out there; you simply are the mountain, you are the sky, you are the clouds, you are everything that is arising moment to moment, very simply, very clearly, just so.

We know all the fancy names for this state, from unity consciousness to sahaj samadhi. But it really is the simplest and most obvious state you will ever realize. Moreover, once you glimpse that state—what the Buddhists call One Taste (because you and the entire universe are one taste or one experience)—it becomes obvious that you are not entering this state, but rather, it is a state that, in some profound and mysterious way, has been your primordial condition from time immemorial. You have, in fact, never left this state for a second.

This is why Zen calls it the Gateless Gate: on this side of that realization, it looks like you have to do something to enter that state—it looks like you need to pass through a gate. But when you do so, and you turn around and look back, there is no gate whatsoever, and never has been. You have never left this state in the first place, so obviously you can't enter it. The gateless gate! "Every form is Emptiness just as it is," means that all things, including you and me, are always already on the other side of the gateless gate.

But if that is so, then why even do spiritual practice? Isn't that just another form of the Great Search? Yes, actually, spiritual practice is a form of the Great Search, and as such, it is destined to fail. But that is exactly the point. You and I are already convinced that there are things that we need to do in order to realize Spirit. We feel that there are places that Spirit is not (namely, in me), and we are going to correct this state of affairs. Thus, we are already committed to the Great Search, and so nondual meditation makes use of that fact and engages us in the Great Search in a particular and somewhat sneaky fashion (which Zen calls "selling water by the river").

William Blake said that "a fool who persists in his folly will become wise." So nondual meditation simply speeds up the folly. If you really think you lack Spirit, then try this folly: try to become Spirit, try to discover Spirit, try to contact Spirit, try to reach Spirit: meditate and meditate and meditate in order to get Spirit!

But of course, you see, you cannot really do this. You cannot reach Spirit any more than you can reach your feet. You always already are Spirit, you are not going to reach it in any sort of temporal thrashing around. But if this is not obvious, then try it. Nondual meditation is a serious effort to do the impossible, until you become utterly exhausted of the Great Search, sit down completely worn out, and notice your feet.

It's not that these nondual traditions deny higher states; they don't. They have many, many practices that help individuals reach specific states of postformal consciousness. These include states of transcendental bliss, love, and compassion; of heightened cognition and extrasensory perception; of Deity consciousness and contemplative prayer. But they maintain that those altered states—which have a beginning and an end in time—ultimately have nothing to do with the timeless. The real aim is the stateless, not a perpetual fascination with changes of state. And that stateless condition is the true nature of this and every conceivable state of consciousness, so any state you have will do just fine. Change of state is not the ultimate point; recognizing the Changeless is the point, recognizing primordial Emptiness is the point, recognizing unqualifiable Godhead is the point, recognizing pure Spirit is the point, and if you are breathing and vaguely awake, that state of consciousness will do just fine.

Nonetheless, traditionally, in order to demonstrate your sincerity, you must complete a good number of preliminary practices, including a mastery of various states of meditative consciousness, summating in a stable post-postconventional adaptation, all of which is well and good. But none of those states of consciousness are held to be final or ultimate or privileged. And changing states is not the goal at all. Rather, it is precisely by entering and leaving these various meditative states that you begin to understand that *none* of them constitute enlightenment. All of them have a beginning in time, and thus none of them are the timeless. The point is to realize that change of state is *not* the point, and *that* realization can occur in *any* state of consciousness whatsoever.

EVER-PRESENT AWARENESS

This primordial recognition of One Taste—not the creation but the recognition of the fact that you and the Kosmos are One Spirit, One Taste, One Gesture—is the great gift of the Nondual traditions. And in simplified form, this recognition goes like this:

(What follows are various "pointing out" instructions, direct pointers to mind's essential nature or intrinsic Spirit. Traditionally this involves a great deal of intentional repetition. If you read this material in the normal manner, you might find the repetitions tedious and perhaps irritating. If you would like the rest of this particular section to work for you, please read it in a slow and leisurely manner, letting the words and the repetitions sink in. You can also use these sections as material for meditation, using no more than one or two paragraphs—or even one or two sentences—for each session.)

We begin with the realization that the pure Self or transpersonal Witness is an *ever-present* consciousness, even when we doubt its existence. You are right now aware of, say, this book, the room, a window, the sky, the clouds. . . . You can sit back and simply notice that you are aware of all those objects floating by. Clouds float through the sky, thoughts float through the mind, and when you notice them, you are effortlessly aware of them. There is a simple, effortless, spontaneous witnessing of whatever happens to be present.

In that simple witnessing awareness, you might notice: I am aware of my body, and therefore I am not just my body. I am aware of my mind, and therefore I am not just my mind. I am aware of my self, and therefore I am not just that self. Rather, I seem somehow to be the Witness of my body, my mind, my self.

This is truly fascinating. I can see my thoughts, so I am not those thoughts. I am aware of bodily sensations, so I am not those sensations. I am aware of my emotions, so I am not merely those emotions. I am somehow the Witness of all of that!

But what is this Witness itself? Who or What is it that witnesses all of these objects, that watches the clouds float by, and thoughts float by, and objects float by? Who or What is this true Seer, this pure Witness, which is at the very core of what I am?

That simple witnessing awareness, the traditions maintain, is Spirit itself, is the enlightened mind itself, is Buddha-nature itself, is God itself, *in its entirety*.

Thus, according to the traditions, getting in touch with Spirit or God or the enlightened mind is not something difficult to achieve. It is your own simple witnessing awareness in exactly this moment. If you see this book, you already have that awareness—all of it—right now.

A very famous text from Dzogchen or Maha-Ati Buddhism (one of the very greatest of the Nondual traditions) puts it like this: "At times it happens that some meditators say that it is difficult to recognize the nature of the mind"—in Dzogchen, "the nature of the mind" means primordial Purity or radical Emptiness—it means nondual Spirit by whatever name. The point is that this "nature of the mind" is *ever-present witnessing awareness*, and some meditators, the text says, find this hard to believe. They imagine it is difficult or even impossible to recognize this ever-present awareness, and that they have to work very hard and meditate very long in order to attain this enlightened mind— whereas it is simply their own ever-present witnessing awareness, fully functioning right now.

The text continues: "Some male or female practitioners believe it to be impossible to recognize the nature of mind. They become depressed with tears streaming down their cheeks. There is no reason at all to become sad. It is not at all impossible to recognize. Rest directly in that which thinks that it is impossible to recognize the nature of the mind, and that is exactly it."

As for this ever-present witnessing awareness being hard to contact: "There are some meditators who don't let their mind rest in itself [simple present awareness], as they should. Instead they let it watch outwardly or search inwardly. You will neither see nor find [Spirit] by watching outwardly or searching inwardly. There is no reason whatsoever to watch outwardly or search inwardly. Let go directly into this mind that is watching outwardly or searching inwardly, and that is exactly it."[1]

We are aware of this room; just that is it, just that awareness is ever-present Spirit. We are aware of the clouds floating by in the sky; just that is it, just that awareness is ever-present Spirit. We are aware of thoughts floating by in the mind; just that is it, just that awareness is ever-present Spirit. We are aware of pain, turmoil, terror, fear; just that is it.

In other words, the ultimate reality is not something seen, but rather the ever-present Seer. Things that are seen come and go, are happy or sad, pleasant or painful—but the Seer is none of those things, and it does not come and go. The Witness does not waver, does not wobble, does not enter that stream of time. The Witness is not an object, not a thing seen, but the ever-present Seer of all things, the simple Witness that is the I of Spirit, the center of the cyclone, the opening that is God, the clearing that is pure Emptiness.

There is never a time that you do not have access to this Witnessing awareness. At every single moment, there is a spontaneous awareness of whatever happens to be present—and that simple, spontaneous, effortless awareness is ever-present Spirit itself. Even if you think you don't see it, that very awareness is it. And thus, the ultimate state of consciousness—intrinsic Spirit itself—*is not hard to reach but impossible to avoid.*

And just that is the great and guarded secret of the Nondual schools.

It does not matter what objects or contents are present; whatever arises is fine. People sometimes have a hard time understanding Spirit because they try to see it as an object of awareness or an object of comprehension. But the ultimate reality is not anything seen, it is the Seer. Spirit is not an object; it is radical, ever-present Subject, and thus it is not something that is going to jump out in front of you like a rock, an image, an idea, a light, a feeling, an insight, a luminous cloud, an intense vision, or a sensation of great bliss. Those are all nice, but they are all objects, which is what Spirit is not.

Thus, as you rest in the Witness, you won't see anything in particular. The true Seer is nothing that can be seen, so you simply begin by disidentifying with any and all objects:

I am aware of sensations in my body; those are objects, I am not those. I am aware of thoughts in my mind; those are objects, I am not those. I am aware of my self in this moment, but that is just another object, and I am not that.

Sights float by in nature, thoughts float by in the mind, feelings float by in the body, and I am none of those. I am not an object. I am the pure Witness of all those objects. I am Consciousness as such.

And so, as you rest in the pure Witness, you won't see anything in particular—whatever you see is fine. Rather, as you rest in the radical subject or Witness, as you stop identifying with objects, you will simply begin to notice a sense of vast Freedom. This Freedom is not something you will see; it is something you are. When you are the Witness of thoughts, you are not bound by thoughts. When you are the Witness of feelings, you are not bound by feelings. In place of your contracted self there is simply a vast sense of Openness and Release. As an object, you are bound; as the Witness, you are Free.

We will not see this Freedom, we will rest in it. A vast ocean of infinite ease.

And so we rest in this state of the pure and simple Witness, the true Seer, which is vast Emptiness and pure Freedom, and we allow whatever is seen to arise as it wishes. Spirit is in the Free and Empty Seer, not in the limited, bound, mortal, and finite objects that parade by in the world of time. And so we rest in this vast Emptiness and Freedom, in which all things arise.

We do not reach or contact this pure Witnessing awareness. It is not possible to contact that which we have never lost. Rather, we rest in this easy, clear, ever-present awareness by simply noticing what is *already* happening. We already see the sky. We already hear the birds singing. We already feel the cool breeze. The simple Witness is already present, already functioning, already the case. That is why we do not contact or bring this Witness into being, but simply notice that it is always already present, as the simple and spontaneous awareness of whatever is happening in this moment.

We also notice that this simple, ever-present Witness is completely effortless. It takes no effort whatsoever to hear sounds, to see sights, to feel the cool breeze: it is already happening, and we easily rest in that effortless witnessing. We do not follow those objects, nor avoid them. Precisely because Spirit is the ever-present Seer, and not any limited thing that is seen, we can allow all seen things to come and go exactly as they please. "The perfect person employs the mind as a mirror," says Chuang Tzu. "It neither grasps nor rejects; it receives, but does not keep." The mirror effortlessly receives its reflections, just as you effortlessly see the sky right now, and just as the Witness effortlessly allows all objects whatsoever to arise. All things come and go in the effortless mirror-mind that is the simple Witness.

When I rest as the pure and simple Witness, I notice that I am not caught in the world of time. The Witness exists only in the timeless present. Yet again, this is not a state that is difficult to achieve but impossible to avoid. The Witness sees only the timeless present because only the timeless present is actually real. When I think of the past, those past thoughts exist right now, in this present. When I think of the future, those future thoughts exist right now, in this present. Past and future thoughts both arise right now, in simple ever-present awareness.

And when the past actually occurred, it occurred right now. When the future actually occurs, it will occur right now. There is only right now, there is only this ever-present present: that is all I ever directly know. Thus, the timeless present is not hard to contact but impossible to avoid, and this becomes obvious when I rest as the pure and simple Witness, and watch the past and future float by in simple ever-present awareness.

That is why when we rest as the ever-present Witness, we are not in time. Resting in simple witnessing awareness, I notice that time floats by in front of me, or through me, like clouds float through the sky. And that is exactly why I can be aware of time; in my simple Presentness, in my I AMness as pure and simple Witness of the Kosmos, I am timeless.

Thus, as I right now rest in this simple, ever-present Witness, I am face to face with Spirit. I am with God today, and always, in this simple, ever-present, witnessing state. Eckhart said that "God is closer to me than I am to myself," because both God and I are one in the ever-present Witness, which is the nature of intrinsic Spirit itself, which is exactly what I am in the state of my I AMness. I am not this, I am not that; I rest as pure open Spirit. When I am not an object, I am God. (And every I in the entire Kosmos can say that truthfully.)

I am not entering this state of the ever-present Witness, which is Spirit itself. I cannot *enter* this state, precisely because it is ever-present. I cannot *start* Witnessing; I can only notice that this simple Witnessing is *already* occurring. This state never has a beginning in time precisely because it is indeed ever-present. You can neither run from it nor toward it; you *are* it, always. This is exactly why Buddhas have *never* entered this state, and sentient beings have *never* left it.

When I rest in the simple, clear, ever-present Witness, I am resting in the great Unborn, I am resting in intrinsic Spirit, I am resting in primordial Emptiness, I am resting in infinite Freedom. I cannot be seen, I have no qualities at all. I am not this, I am not that. I am not an object. I am neither light nor dark; neither large nor small; neither here nor there; I have no color, no location, no space and no time; I am an utter Emptiness, another word for infinite Freedom, unbounded to infinity. I am the opening or clearing in which the entire manifest world arises right now, but I do not arise in it—it arises in me, in this vast Emptiness and Freedom that I am.

Things that are seen are pleasant or painful, happy or sad, joyous or fearful, healthy or sick—but the Seer of those things is neither happy nor sad, neither joyous nor fearful, neither healthy nor sick, but simply Free. As pure and simple Witness I am free of all objects, free of all subjects, free of all time and free of all space; free of birth and free of death, and free of all things in between. I am simply Free.

When I rest as the timeless Witness, the Great Search is undone. The Great Search is the enemy of the ever-present Spirit, a brutal lie in the face of a gentle infinity. The Great Search is the search for an ultimate experience, a fabulous vision, a paradise of pleasure, an unendingly good time, a powerful insight—a search for God, a search for Goddess, a search for Spirit—but Spirit is not an object. Spirit cannot be grasped or reached or sought or seen: it is the ever-present Seer. To search for the Seer is to miss the point. To search forever is to miss the point forever. How could you possibly search for that which is right now aware of this page? YOU ARE THAT! You cannot go out looking for that which is the Looker.

When I am not an object, I am God. When I seek an object, I cease to be God, and that catastrophe can never be corrected by more searching for more objects.

Rather, I can only rest as the Witness, which is already free of objects, free of time, free of suffering, and free of searching. When I am not an object, I am Spirit. When I rest as the free and formless Witness, I am with God right now, in this timeless and endless moment. I taste infinity and am drenched with fullness, precisely because I no longer seek, but simply rest as what I am.

Before Abraham was, I am. Before the Big Bang was, I am. After the universe dissolves, I am. In all things great and small, I am. And yet I can never be heard, felt, known, or seen; I AM is the ever-present Seer.

Precisely because the ultimate reality is not anything seen but rather the Seer, it doesn't matter in the least what is seen in any moment. Whether you see peace or turmoil, whether you see equanimity or agitation, whether you see bliss or terror, whether you see happiness or sadness, matters not at all: it is not those states but the Seer of those states that is *already* Free.

Changing states is thus beside the point; acknowledging the ever-present Seer is the point. Even in the midst of the Great Search and even in the worst of my self-contracting ways, I have immediate and direct access to the ever-present Witness. I do not have to try to bring this simple awareness into existence. I do not have to enter this state. It involves no effort at all. I simply notice that there is already an awareness of the sky. I simply notice that there is already an awareness of the clouds. I simply notice that the ever-present Witness is already fully functioning: it is not hard to reach but impossible to avoid. I am always already in the lap of this ever-present awareness, the radical Emptiness in which all manifestation is presently arising.

When I rest in the pure and simple Witness, I notice that this awareness is not an experience. It is aware of experiences, it is not itself an experience. Experiences come and go. They have a beginning in time, they stay a bit, and they pass. But they all arise in the simple opening or clearing that is the vast expanse of what I am. The clouds float by in this vast expanse, and thoughts float by in this vast expanse, and experiences float by in this vast expanse. They all come, and they all go. But the vast expanse itself, this Free and Empty Seer, this spacious opening or clearing in which all things arise, does not itself come and go, or even move at all.

Thus, when I rest in the pure and simple Witness, I am no longer caught up in the search for experiences, whether of the flesh or of the mind or of the spirit. Experiences—whether high or low, sacred or profane, joyous or nightmarish—simply come and go like endless waves on the ocean of what I am. As I rest in the pure and simple Witness, I am no longer moved to follow the bliss and the torture of experiential displays. Experiences float across my Original Face like clouds floating across the clear autumn sky, and there is room in me for all.

When I rest in the pure and simple Witness, I will even begin to notice that the Witness itself is not a separate thing or entity, set apart from what it witnesses. All things arise within the Witness, so much so that the Witness itself disappears into all things.

And thus, resting in simple, clear, ever-present awareness, I notice that there is no inside and no outside. There is no subject and no object. Things and events are still fully present and clearly arising—the clouds float by, the birds still sing, the cool breeze still blows—but there is no separate self recoiling from them. Events simply arise as they are, without the constant and agitated reference to a contracted self or subject. Events arise as they are, and they arise in the great freedom of not being defined by a little I looking at them. They arise with Spirit, as Spirit, in the opening or clearing that I am; they do not arise to be seen and perceptually tortured by an ego.

In my contracted mode, I am "in here," on this side of my face, looking at the world "out there," on the "objective" side. I exist on this side of my face, and my entire life is an attempt to save face, to save this self-contraction, to save this sensation of grasping and seeking, a sensation that sets me apart from the world out there, a world I will then desire or loathe, move toward or recoil from, grasp or avoid, love or hate. The inside and the outside are in perpetual struggle, all varieties of hope or fear: the drama of saving face.

We say, "To lose face is to die of embarrassment," and that is deeply true: we do not want to lose face! We do not want to die! We do not want to cease the sensation of the separate-self! But that primal fear of losing face is actually the root of our deepest agony, because saving face—saving an identity with the bodymind—is the very mechanism of suffering, the very mechanism of tearing the Kosmos into an inside versus an outside, a brutal fracture that I experience as pain.

But when I rest in simple, clear, ever-present awareness, I lose face. Inside and outside completely disappear. It happens just like this:

As I drop all objects—I am not this, not that—and I rest in the pure and simple Witness, all objects arise easily in my visual field, all objects arise in the space of the Witness. I am simply an opening or clearing in which all things arise. I notice that all things arise in me, arise in this opening or clearing that I am. The clouds are floating by in this vast opening that I am. The sun is shining in this vast opening that I am. The sky exists in this vast opening that I am; the sky is in me. I can taste the sky, it's closer to me than my own skin. The clouds are on the inside of me; I am seeing them from within. When all things arise in me, I am simply all things. The universe is One Taste, and I am That.

And so, when I rest as the Witness, all things arise in me, so much so that I am all things. There is no subject and object because I do not see the clouds, I am the clouds. There is no subject and object because I do not feel the cool breeze, I am the cool breeze. There is no subject and object because I do not hear the thunder clapping, I am the thunder clapping.

I am no longer on this side of my face looking at the world out there; I simply am the world. I am not in here. I have lost face—and discovered my Original Face, the Kosmos itself. The bird sings, and I am that. The sun rises, and I am that. The moon shines, and I am that, in simple, ever-present awareness.

When I rest in simple, clear, ever-present awareness, every object is its own subject. Every event "sees itself," as it were, because I am now that event seeing itself. I am not looking at the rainbow; I am the rainbow, which sees itself. I am not staring at the tree; I am the tree, which sees itself. The entire manifest world continues to arise, just as it is, except that all subjects and all objects have disappeared. The mountain is still the mountain, but it is not an *object* being looked at, and I am not a separate *subject* staring at it. Both I and the mountain arise in simple, ever-present awareness, and we are both set free in that clearing, we are both liberated in that nondual space, we are both enlightened in the opening that is ever-present awareness. That opening is free of the set-apart violence called subject and object, in here versus out there, self against other, me against the world. I have utterly lost face, and discovered God, in simple ever-present awareness.

When you are the Witness of all objects, and all objects arise in you, then you stand in utter Freedom, in the vast expanse of all space. In this simple One Taste, the wind does not blow on you, it blows within you. The sun does not shine on you, it radiates from deep within your very being. When it rains, you are weeping. You can drink the Pacific Ocean in a single gulp, and swallow the universe whole. Supernovas are born and die all within your heart, and galaxies swirl endlessly where you thought your head was, and it is all as simple as the sound of a robin singing on a crystal clear dawn.

Every time I *recognize* or *acknowledge* the ever-present Witness, I have broken the Great Search and undone the separate self. And that is the ultimate, secret, nondual practice, the practice of no-practice, the practice of *simple acknowledgment*, the practice of remembrance and recognition, founded timelessly and eternally on the fact that there is only Spirit, a Spirit that is not hard to find but impossible to avoid.

Spirit is the only thing that has *never* been absent. It is the *only* constant in your changing experience. You have known this for a billion years, literally. And you might as well acknowledge it. "If you understand this, then rest in that which understands, and just that is Spirit. If you do not understand this, then rest in that which does not understand, and just that is Spirit." For eternally and eternally and always eternally, there is only Spirit, the Witness of this and every moment, even unto the ends of the world.

THE EYE OF SPIRIT

When I rest in simple, clear, ever-present awareness, I am resting in intrinsic Spirit; I am in fact nothing other than witnessing Spirit itself. I do not become Spirit; I simply recognize the Spirit that I always already am. When I rest in simple, clear, ever-present awareness, I am the Witness of the World. I am the eye of Spirit. I see the world as God sees it. I see the world as the Goddess sees it. I see the world as Spirit sees it: every object an object of Beauty, every thing and event a gesture of the Great Perfection, every process a ripple in the pond of my own eternal Being, so much so that I do not stand apart as a separate witness, but find the witness is one taste with all that arises within it. The entire Kosmos arises in the eye of Spirit, in the I of Spirit, in my own intrinsic awareness, this simple ever-present state, and I am simply that.

From the ground of simple, ever-present awareness, one's entire bodymind will resurrect. When you rest in primordial awareness, that awareness begins to saturate your being, and from the stream of consciousness a new destiny is resurrected. When the Great Search is undone, and the separate-self sense has been crucified; when the continuity of witnessing has stabilized in your own case; when ever-present awareness is your constant ground—then your entire bodymind will regenerate, resurrect, and reorganize itself around intrinsic Spirit, and you will arise, as from the dead, to a new destiny and a new duty in consciousness.

You will cease to exist as separate self (with all the damage that does to the bodymind), and you will exist instead as vehicle of Spirit (with the bodymind now free to function in its highest potential, undistorted and untortured by the brutalities of the self-contraction). From the ground of ever-present awareness, you will arise embodying any of the enlightened qualities of the Buddhas and Bodhisattvas—"one whose being (sattva) is ever-present awareness (bodhi)."

The Buddhist names are not important; the enlightened qualities they represent are. The point is simply that, once you have stably recognized simple, ever-present awareness—once the Great Search and the self-contraction have been robbed of separative life and returned to God, returned to their ground in ever-present awareness—then you will arise, from the ground of ever-present awareness, and you will embody any of the highest possibilities of that ground. You will be vehicle of the Spirit that you are. That ever-present ground will live through you, as you, in a variety of superordinary forms.

Perhaps you will arise as Samantabhadra, whose ever-present awareness takes the form of a vast equality consciousness: you will realize that the ever-present awareness that is fully present in you is the *same awareness* that is fully present in all sentient beings without exception—one and the same, single and only—one heart, one mind, one soul that breathes and beats and pulses through all sentient beings as such—and your very countenance will remind all beings of that simple fact, remind them that there is only Spirit, remind them that nothing is closer to God than anything else, for there is only God, there is only Goddess.

Perhaps you will arise as Avalokiteshvara, whose ever-present awareness takes the form of gentle compassion. In the brilliant clarity of ever-present awareness, all sentient beings arise as equal forms of intrinsic Spirit or pure Emptiness, and thus all beings are treated as the sons and daughters of the Spirit that they are. You will have no choice but to live this compassion with a delicate dedication, so that your very smile will warm the hearts of those who suffer, and they will look to you for a promise that they, too, can be liberated into the vast expanse of their own primordial awareness, and you will never turn away.

Perhaps you will arise as Prajnaparamita, the mother of the Buddhas, whose ever-present awareness takes the form of a vast spaciousness, the womb of the great Unborn, in which the entire Kosmos exists. For in deepest truth, it is exactly from the ground of your own simple, clear, ever-present awareness that all beings are born; and it is to the ground of your simple, clear, ever-present awareness that all beings will return. Resting in the brilliant clarity of ever-present awareness, you watch the worlds arise, and all the Buddhas arise, and all sentient beings as such arise. And to you they will all return. And you will smile, and receive, in this vast expanse of everlasting wisdom, and it will all begin again, and yet again, and always yet again, in the womb of your ever-present state.

Perhaps you will arise as Manjushri, whose ever-present awareness takes the form of luminous intelligence. Although all beings are equally intrinsic Spirit, some beings do not easily acknowledge this ever-present Suchness, and thus discriminating wisdom will brilliantly arise from the ground of equality consciousness. You will instinctively see what is true and what is false, and thus you will bring clarity to everything you touch. And if the self-contraction does not listen to your gentler voice, your ever-present awareness will manifest in its wrathful form, which is said to be none other than the dreaded Yamantaka, Subduer of the Lord of Death.

And so perhaps you will arise as Yamantaka, fierce protector of ever-present awareness and samurai warrior of intrinsic Spirit. Precisely those items that pretend to block ever-present awareness must be quickly cut through, which is why ever-present awareness arises in its many wrathful forms. You will simply be moved, from the ground of equality consciousness, to expose the false and the shallow and the less-than-ever-present. It is time for the sword, not the smile, but always the sword of discriminating wisdom, which ruthlessly cuts all obstacles in the ground of the all-encompassing.

Perhaps you will arise as Bhaishajyaguru, whose ever-present awareness takes the form of a healing radiance. From the brilliant clarity of ever-present awareness, you will be moved to remind the sick and the sad and those in pain that although the pain is real, it is not what they are. With a simple touch or smile, contracted souls will relax into the vast expanse of intrinsic awareness, and disease will lose all meaning in the radiance of that release. And you will never tire, for ever-present awareness is effortless in its functioning, and so you will constantly remind all beings of who and what they really are, on the other side of fear, in the radical love and unflinching acceptance that is the mirror-mind of ever-present awareness.

Perhaps you will arise as Maitreya, whose ever-present awareness takes the form of a promise that, even into the endless future, ever-present awareness will still be simply present. From the brilliant clarity of primordial awareness, you will vow to be with all beings, even unto an eternity of futures, because even those futures will arise in simple present awareness, the same present awareness that now sees just exactly this.

Those are simply a few of the potentials of ever-present awareness. The Buddhist names don't matter; any will do. They are simply a few of the forms of your own resurrection. They are a few of the possibilities that might animate you after the death of the Great Search. They are a few of the ways the world looks to the ever-present eye of Spirit, the ever-present I of Spirit. They are what you see, right now, when you see the world as God sees it, from the groundless ground of simple ever-present awareness.

AND IT IS ALL UNDONE

Perhaps you will arise as any or all of those forms of ever-present awareness. But then, it doesn't really matter. When you rest in the brilliant clarity of ever-present awareness, you are not Buddha or Bodhisattva, you are not this or that, you are not here or there. When you rest in simple, ever-present awareness, you are the great Unborn, free of all qualities whatsoever. Aware of color, you are colorless. Aware of time, you are timeless. Aware of form, you are formless. In the vast expanse of primordial Emptiness, you are forever invisible to this world.

It is simply that, as embodied being, you also arise in the world of form that is your own manifestation. And the intrinsic potentials of the enlightened mind (the intrinsic potentials of your ever-present awareness)—such as equanimity, discriminating wisdom, mirrorlike wisdom, ground consciousness, and all-accomplishing awareness—various of these potentials combine with the native dispositions and particular talents of your own individual bodymind. And thus, when the separate self dies into the vast expanse of its own ever-present awareness, you will arise animated by any or all of those various enlightened potentials. You are then motivated, not by the Great Search, but by the Great Compassion of these potentials, some of which are gentle, some of which are truly wrathful, but all of which are simply the possibilities of your own ever-present state.

And thus, resting in simple, clear, ever-present awareness, you will arise with the qualities and virtues of your own highest potentials—perhaps compassion, perhaps discriminating wisdom, perhaps cognitive insight, perhaps healing presence, perhaps wrathful reminder, perhaps artistic accomplishment, perhaps athletic skill, perhaps great educator, or perhaps something utterly simple, maybe being the best flower gardener on the block. (In other words, any of the developmental lines released into their own primordial state, released into their own post-postconventional condition.)[2] When the bodymind is released from the brutalities inflicted by the self-contraction, it naturally gravitates to its own highest estate, manifested in the great potentials of the enlightened mind, the great potentials of simple, ever-present awareness.

Thus, as you rest in simple, ever-present awareness, you are the great Unborn; but as you are born—as you arise from ever-present awareness—you will manifest certain qualities, qualities inherent in intrinsic Spirit, and qualities colored by the dispositions of your own bodymind and its particular talents.

And whatever the form of your own resurrection, you will arise, driven not by the Great Search, but by your own Great Duty, your limitless Dharma, the manifestation of your own highest potentials, and the world will begin to change, because of you. And you will never flinch, and you will never fail in that great Duty, and you will never turn away, because simple, ever-present awareness will be with you now and forever, even unto the ends of the worlds, because now and forever and endlessly forever, there is only Spirit, only intrinsic awareness, only the simple awareness of just this, and nothing more.

But that entire journey to what is begins at the beginningless beginning: we begin by simply recognizing that which is always already the case. ("If you understand this, then rest in that which understands, and just that is exactly Spirit. If you do not understand this, then rest in that which does not understand, and just that is exactly Spirit.") We allow this recognition of ever-present awareness to arise—gently, randomly, spontaneously, through the day and into the night. This simple, ever-present awareness is not hard to attain but impossible to avoid, and we simply notice that.

We do this gently, randomly, and spontaneously, through the day and into the night. Soon enough, through all three states of waking, dreaming, and sleeping, this recognition will grow of its own accord and by its own intrinsic power, outshining the obstacles that pretend to hide its nature, until this simple, ever-present awareness announces itself in an unbroken continuity through all changes of state, through all changes of space and time, whereupon space and time lose all meaning whatsoever, exposed for what they are, the shining veils of the radiant Emptiness that you alone now are—and you will swoon into that Beauty, and die into that Truth, and dissolve into that Goodness, and there will be no one left to testify to terror, no one left to take tears seriously, no one left to engineer unease, no one left to deny the Divine, which only alone is, and only alone ever was, and only alone will ever be.

And somewhere on a cold crystal night the moon will shine on a silently waiting Earth, just to remind those left behind that it is all a game. The lunar light will set dreams afire in their sleeping hearts, and a yearning to awaken will stir in the depths of that restless night, and you will be pulled, yet again, to respond to those most plaintive prayers, and you will find yourself right here, right now, wondering what it all really means—until that flash of recognition runs across your face and it is all undone. You then will arise as the moon itself, and sing those dreams in your very own heart; and you will arise as the Earth itself, and glorify all of its blessed inhabitants; and you will arise as the Sun itself, radiant to infinity and much too obvious to see; and in that One Taste of primordial purity, with no beginning and no end, with no entrance and no exit, with no birth and no death, it all comes radically to be; and the sound of a singing waterfall, somewhere in the distance, is all that is left to tell this tale, late on that crystal cold night, bathed so beautifully in that lunar light, just so, and again, just so.

When the great Zen master Fa-ch'ang was dying, a squirrel screeched out on the roof. "It's just this," he said, "and nothing more."

Notes

Introduction

1. See K. Wilber, *Quantum Questions: Mystical Writings of the World's Great Physicists* (Boston: Shambhala Publications, 1985).
2. "Integral" and "integral studies" have sometimes been associated with Sri Aurobindo, his student Haridas Chaudhuri, and the California Institute of Integral Studies (founded by Chaudhuri and others), so perhaps a few words on each of those is in order.

   As the following pages will make clear, Aurobindo has been and continues to be an influence on my work. In fact, in chapter 6 we will see that he was instrumental in my moving from what I call a "Romantic/wilber-1" model to an "Aurobindo/wilber-2" model. Nonetheless, I eventually refined that model into "wilber-3" and "wilber-4," as I will explain in chapters 9, 10, and 11. Those chapters therefore constitute my critique of Aurobindo (and Chaudhuri).

   The essence of the critique is that both Aurobindo and Chaudhuri were pioneers in individual integral yoga and practice. This yoga especially focused on integrating the Ascending and Descending currents in the human being, thus embracing the entire spectrum of consciousness in both a transcendental/ascending and immanent/descending fashion. "Ascent and descent are then two inseparable aspects of the movement of integral yoga; they are the systole and diastole of integral self-discipline" (Chaudhuri, 1965, p. 41).

   I fully agree. But that approach is really just the beginning of a much more integral view (which I will explain in later chapters as wilber-3 and wilber-4). A truly integral yoga needs to take a much fuller account of the Western contributions to psychology, psychotherapy, and personal transformation (wilber-3), and it needs most especially to be set in the context of the four quadrants and their historical unfolding (wilber-4). Thus, my criticism of Aurobindo and Chaudhuri is a refinement, not a repudiation; but it is a refinement without which their systems are, I believe, limited and partial. This will become clear, I trust, in the succeeding chapters. [See *Integral Psychology* for a full elaboration of these themes.]

   The California Institute of Integral Studies is one of the few institutions of higher learning that will allow students to pursue a more integral orientation, including East/West studies. Nonetheless, it has also recently become, in my opinion, a source of much teaching that is quite anti-evolutionary, anti-Aurobindo, anti-Chaudhuri, and frankly regressive. I can no longer without qualifications recommend this institution to students. At the same time, it is the home of some gifted teachers, and students simply need to be cautious and selective in their courses. The same caution is due, I believe, the Naropa University in Boulder, Colorado. But with that proviso, these are two institutions where, with a little help from a sympathetic advisor, a student might be able to put together an integral program, even though the general atmosphere might resist it. Other noteworthy institutions include the Institute for Transpersonal Psychology, in Palo Alto, and JFK University, in Orinda, California. (For a complete listing of schools offering transpersonal courses and programs, see *The Common Boundary Education Guide*, obtainable from Common Boundary, 5272 River Rd., Suite 650, Bethesda, MD 20816. Also the guide from the Association for Transpersonal Psychology, 345 California St., Palo Alto, CA 94306. Those interested in meditation research might contact the Meditation Research Network, Institute of Noetic Sciences, 475 Gate 5 Road, Sausalito, CA 94965.)

At the same time, as the following chapters will make clear, the integral approach is now widely recognized (if not widely pursued) in many of the nation's higher centers of learning, from Harvard to West Georgia State, from Berkeley to the University of Connecticut, from Stanford to Norwich, from Vermont to Arizona State. A sympathetic advisor at almost any university nowadays can make a course in integral studies a genuine possibility.

3. With extreme constructivism, the individual subject (the I) is dissolved into intersubjective linguistic signifiers, loudly announced in the celebrated death of the subject, the death of the author, the death of man. Language itself replaces the individual self as the real subject of discourse (i.e., you are not talking, language alone is talking through you), and thus you and I are simply along for the irrelevant ride: the I is deconstructed into nothing but the linguistic We, and the death of the subject haunts the halls of the postmodern vacuum.

Not only are all I's (with their truthfulness) dissolved into a linguistic We, all its (with their objective truths) are likewise evaporated in the game of arbitrary construction. Gone is truth and gone is truthfulness, and in their place reigns a cultural construction driven only by power, by ideology, by gender, by this centrism or that centrism, by ugly motives of ugly people all lined up in a row.

And yet by the very fact of setting forth their theories they are actually doing something that their theories categorically state is impossible (namely, present what they feel is a power-free and ideology-free theory). The I and the it, which are both denied real existence in the face of the almighty constructing We, in fact reassert themselves as internal contradictions. And only by admitting the rejected domains can the partial truths of constructivism be taken up and worked into a larger, more open, more integral view.

4. It is very illuminating to contrast the cultural constructivists—who reduce everything to a dynamic collective We (Lower Left)—with the systems theorists, who reduce everything to a dynamic collective It (Lower Right). This is, in other words, another version of *interior* holism versus *exterior* holism.

Thus, for cultural constructivism (or interior holism), truth is primarily a *co-*

herence theory of truth, or intersubjective mesh and cultural meaning, because there are no objective its to anchor any correspondence theories of truth. The cultural alone is real, the We alone is real, and thus all truth and truthfulness are reduced to cultural interests and arbitrary constructions, which themselves exist only because they have a measure of coherence: the cultural alone is real, and all other "truths" are derivative to the great constructing We. No "I's" and no "its" need apply for membership in this culture club—they are barred from entry at the door.

For systems theory (or external holism), truth is found in functional fit, or interobjective mesh: the social alone is the primary reality. What both interior and exterior holism have in common is that they anchor their truth claims in the collective—one cultural (Lower Left), the other social (Lower Right). Since they are both "holistic," you might think they would be happy partners in the cause, but in fact they fairly despise each other, because the former is the epitome of subjectivism, the latter, of objectivism—the big system We versus the big system It.

Thus, you will never hear a systems theorist say that all systems are merely constructed, or arbitrary, or exist only as an ideology of gender, power, racism, and so on. No, systems theorists are by and large dedicated scientists, monological to a great degree, and they believe their systems are actually there, actually existing, largely independent of the terms used to describe them: real scientists study real systems in the real world! None of this "arbitrary constructivism," thank you very much. Exterior holists are realists in almost every sense.

But, of course, the interior holists—the cultural constructivists—don't believe in any independent or realistic "its" at all—whether dynamic, process, interwoven, systems or otherwise—because all "its" and all "I's" are culturally constructed products of the linguistic We. They therefore believe that the "systems" of the systems scientists are just arbitrary fabrications of a Eurocentric rationality driven by its attempt to gain power, a power that finds its ultimate expression in grand narratives and totalizing agendas such as systems theory, agendas that are driven by the worst sort of marginalizing, hegemonic, oppressive, and brutalizing aggression, all dressed up in the name of a knowledge that is in fact nothing but thinly disguised power.

Interior and exterior holism: both of them, ironically, partially true but thus ultimately quite nonholistic—and therefore constantly at each other's throats. And in each case the denied and oppressed quadrants wonderfully reassert themselves, upsetting the imperialists from within as massive self-contradictions, exploding their narrowness in a wider and more open vision, calling to us all in the name of a more integral embrace.

Chapter 1: The Spectrum of Consciousness

1. The Vedanta system (and its distant cousin, the Vajrayana) contains an exquisite overall model of the structures and states of consciousness, which I would explain more technically as follows:

The five sheaths are sheaths of consciousness or "mind" in the very broadest sense—physical consciousness, emotional consciousness, conceptual consciousness, intuitive consciousness, bliss consciousness. These are what I refer to as the *basic structures* of consciousness, the (upper) Left-Hand dimensions and levels of the human psyche.

But Vedanta realized that there is no mind without body, no consciousness without its support. Thus, each mind is supported by a body—the gross body (supporting the lowest mind), the subtle body (supporting the three "middle" minds), and the causal body (supporting the highest or unmanifest mind). These bodies are simply the "material" support of the "conscious" process—they are, in other words, the Right-Hand dimensions of the human psyche. (In Vajrayana, and Tantra in general, the three minds are supported by three "winds" or energy currents, also referred to as gross, subtle, and very subtle.)

Thus, we can quite accurately represent the Vedanta/Vajrayana view by speaking of the gross bodymind, the subtle bodymind, and the causal bodymind, covering the spectrum in both the Left- and Right-Hand domains, with the important proviso: God is always two-handed (i.e., these domains are inseparable, gross mind always occurring with gross body, subtle mind with subtle body, and so on).

Further, according to Vedanta/Vajrayana, these *basic structures*—the levels of the bodymind, gross to subtle to causal, which are permanent sheaths or levels available to human beings—are correlated with temporary consciousness (not permanent *structures*, but temporary *states*) in this fashion: the gross bodymind is experienced most typically in the waking state, the subtle bodymind in the dream state, and the causal bodymind in the deep dreamless state (the unmanifest). What is important here is that structures and states are not simply the same thing (a failure to grasp this elemental distinction has hobbled many transpersonal theories).

In various meditative *states*, the higher levels of the bodymind are brought into awareness, first as temporary states, and then eventually as permanent structures. The final result of this converting of states into traits is moksha, or radical liberation—a radical freedom from all manifestation, as all manifestation. In other words, the radical recognition of that Spirit which is both the goal and the ground of all states and all structures (turiya, the "fourth" beyond the gross, subtle, and causal bodyminds—in other words, the Emptiness and Suchness of the entire display, which is not a change of state but the stateless condition of all states).

This is an extraordinary model of human consciousness, easily the most comprehensive in all of the traditions (incorporating structures, states, and levels of both body/Right and mind/Left). What it lacks, in my opinion, are the developmental details (an approach specialized in by the modern West). With a more Western/developmental sensitivity, we can add an understanding of the developmental *lines* associated with each of those basic *levels*. The result of that synthesis would be a genuinely East-West overview. I present such a model in chapters 6 through 10, and discuss why I believe these additions are necessary to fill out the Vedanta/Vajrayana model.

Finally, what the Vedanta/Vajrayana model lacks—indeed, what the perennial philosophy in general lacks—is an understanding of how the Lower Left (cultural) and Lower Right (social) profoundly influence, and often govern, the individual consciousness and behavior which they otherwise understand so well (Upper Left and Upper Right). The Great Chain, for example, looks different—*is* different—in the magical, mythical, and mental worldspaces. This is yet another way of saying that integral studies must be not just "all-level" but "all-level, all-quadrant." The studies of Gebser (LL) and Marx (LR), for example, make no sense to a traditional Great Chain theorist, and, indeed, find no room in the traditional view, a view that, to just that extent, is woefully inadequate.

2. Stephen Jay Gould is the one theorist that almost everybody quotes when they wish to deny that hierarchy exists in nature. Gould is a staple of antihierarchical, flatland, heterarchical theorists, even though Gould himself has thoroughly abandoned the antihierarchical stance. In fact, Gould now quite avidly embraces hierarchy, both in nature and in our explanatory principles.

In a recent issue of *Sciences* (July/August 1995), Gould states that "Our stories about sequential stages seem to follow one of two modes: either as increments of progress (simple to complex) or as steps in refinement (inchoate to differentiated). The model for the first is addition; for the second, differentiation.

"I had always viewed the primal stories of addition and differentiation as our literary biases imposed upon nature's greater richness. But here nature . . . seems to be telling us that she acquiesces in these alternative readings of her fundamental sequences" (p. 36).

Hierarchical stages, in other words, are quite real, and not simply our anthropocentric creations. Gould is very explicit: "I freely confess my own strong preference . . . for a model that views selection as operating at several levels of a genealogical hierarchy including genes, organisms, local populations, and species. . . . Nature is organized as a hierarchy. . . . Entities at each level of the hierarchy can act as biological 'individuals,' and Darwin's process of selection can therefore occur at all levels . . ." (*New York Review of Books*, Nov. 19, 1992, p. 47).

I totally agree. In fact, in SES (note 49 for chapter 2) I outline the view that the "unit of selection" is in fact any holon in the overall holarchy, which is essentially Gould's view (as he says, "Selection can therefore occur at all levels"). Moreover, according to Gould, each level is ranked according to its *inclusiveness*: "Entities [exist] in a sequence of levels with unique explanatory principles emerging at each more inclusive plateau. This hierarchical perspective must take seriously the principle that phenomena of one level cannot automatically be extrapolated to work in the same way as others" (NYRB, Mar. 3, 1983). This is why, he adds, that emergent properties are real properties of organisms: "Organisms clearly have emergent properties, since their features . . . are products of complex and nonadditive interactions" (NYRB, Nov. 19, 1992, p. 47).

Thus, for Gould—as for virtually all of the great biological theoreticians, from Francisco Varela to Ernst Mayr—nature is hierarchically ordered; the units of Darwinian evolution are hierarchically ordered; and biology's explanatory principles are hierarchically ordered. Isn't it time the antihierarchy folks stopped using Gould to support their untenable position?

3. This is not to say that infancy and childhood can have no types of spiritual experiences. I have never maintained that view. Rather, as I pointed out in *Up from Eden*, even the infant experiences waking (gross), dreaming (subtle), and deep sleep (causal) states, and goes through this entire cycle every twenty-four hours. Further, as I suggested in *The Atman Project*, the infant might indeed come "trailing clouds of glory" from the intermediate bardo realms (via the psychic or deeper being). All of these are indeed temporary transpersonal states, but they are *not* enduring transpersonal structures, which only unfold in the course of ontogenetic (frontal) development. Thus, any of the transpersonal states in infancy are not due to *pre-egoic structures*. All of these points are elaborated in detail in chapters 7, 9, and 10.

Chapter 3: Eye to Eye

1. When philosophy, or intellectual awareness in general, is highly focused on its own source (i.e., witnessing subjectivity, the pure self), then such philosophy can indeed begin to shade into jnana yoga, the yoga of using the mind to transcend the mind. By deeply, profoundly, uninterruptedly inquiring into the Witness of all knowledge, this specific type of philosophical inquiry opens onto contemplative awareness: the mind itself subsides in the vast expanse of primordial awareness, and philosophia gives way to contemplatio.

Rare is the philosopher who uses the mind to transcend the mind. Jnana yoga is quite common in the East, but it only occasionally makes its appearance in the West, although when it does, it is sometimes quite profound (if sporadic). In SES I identified this as "Western Vedanta," and pointed out a few of its practitioners, including Augustine, Descartes, Fichte, Schelling, Hegel, Husserl, Sartre.

Thus, the heart of integral philosophy, as I conceive it, is primarily a *mental activity* of coordinating, elucidating, and conceptually integrating all of the various modes of knowing and being, so that, even if integral philosophy itself does not *deliver* the higher modes, it fully *acknowledges* them, and then allows and invites philosophia to open itself to the practices and modes of contemplatio. Integral philosophy is also, by virtue of its comprehensiveness, a powerful *critical theory*, critical of all less encompassing approaches—in philosophy, psychology, religion, social theory, and politics.

And, finally, it is a *theoria* that is inseparable from *praxis*, on all levels, in all quadrants.

Chapter 4: Integral Art and Literary Theory: Part 1

1. For an outline of integral semiotics, see chapter 5, note 12.
2. Quoted in Passmore, *Serious art*, p. 16.

3. Quoted ibid.
4. G. Bataille, *Visions of Excess*, p. 174.
5. Ibid., p. 174.
6. Quoted in ibid., p. xi.
7. J. Culler, *On Deconstruction*, p. 215. My italics.
8. Ibid., p. 123. My italics.
9. J. Habermas, *The Philosophical Discourse of Modernity*, p. 197.
10. Wimsatt and Beardsley, The Intentional Fallacy, in W. K. Wimsatt, 1966.
11. Passmore, *Serious Art*, p. 34.

Chapter 5: Integral Art and Literary Theory: Part 2

1. Quoted in M. Schapiro, *Theory and Philosophy of Art*, p. 154.
2. Quoted ibid., pp. 135–36.
3. Quoted ibid., chaps 5 and 6. Schapiro deals with the question: to which of the several paintings of shoes Heidegger and Gauguin are referring; since Heidegger says his point can be made with any of the various paintings, my general conclusion is unaffected by the final outcome of this issue. Gauguin has given two extremely moving accounts of this story; I have combined them for fullness of detail.

Meyer Schapiro's many books are a wonderful source of material (including *Late Antique, Early Christian and Mediaeval Art*; *Romanesque Art*; *Modern Art*; and *Theory and Philosophy of Art: Style, Artist, and Society*), and I highly recommend them.

Incidentally, when I claim that all four quadrants evolve, this includes the claim that *art itself evolves*. I am constantly challenged on this point. A few people understandably feel that if, for example, Picasso was doing primitivist themes, how could this be *development* with any sort of *directionality*? Or if this is directional, isn't it going backwards? How could art be following the twenty tenets that SES claimed to be operative in all domains? Further, you might like modern, I might like African, she might like postmodern, and so on; what kind of arrogance says one of these is "more evolved"? (The standard postmodern horror of qualitative distinctions—which, of course, is itself a massive qualitative distinction: its stance is *better* than the alternatives!)

As usual with evolutionary themes, the topic only comes into focus if we back up a sufficiently far distance, so as to let truly long-range trends come into clear focus. Centering on particular artistic styles and contents, although useful and interesting itself, is usually worthless in spotting Eros.

So let's look to the few art historians who have actually investigated the historical unfolding of artistic fundamentals at a sufficiently deep level (the deep structures of the aesthetic dimension). Meyer Schapiro's book *Theory and Philosophy of Art* is such an approach. Schapiro is a very rare bird: a famous artist himself, he is also a first-rate philosopher and a gifted writer. Richard Wollheim (Mill Professor of Philosophy at Berkeley) summarizes one of the central conclusions of Schapiro's research, which, says Wollheim, "is surely among the fundamental writings of art history":

In the beginning, our ancestors made figurative images of the animals they hunted. In doing so, they paid no attention to the surface on which the images were inscribed. Then they did, and, when they did, found uses for the ground, either representational or to enhance the image. But they paid no attention to the fact that, as surfaces do in nature, the ground had its bounds. Then they did, and, when they did, distinguished between the horizontal and vertical edges, and found distinctive uses for each, but they paid no attention to the fact that the ground with its edges could be looked at various ways up. Then they did, and, when they did, settled for the one way as the right way up, and started to find uses for orientation. And so on [including the further emergence of perspective within the orientation . . .].

Step by step, and not without regression, intentional or accidental, a medium was developed out of the natural materials as each aspect was explicitly recognized. . . . (*London Review of Books*, June 22, 1995)

In other words, we are looking at the unfolding or emergence of worldspaces, each of which transcends and includes the fundamental and learned elements of the previous worldspace (or else it would not and could not itself emerge: the more significant rests on the more fundamental, because it actually incorporates it internally).

And, as Wollheim and Schapiro both make quite clear, the same is true in the artistic and aesthetic dimension itself on a broad scale. "They paid no attention" means "they did not see," precisely because "what they did not see" simply was not in their worldspace: it had not yet emerged, it literally did not yet exist. "And when they did" means, "And then they could" or "and then they could see it," precisely because it had now emerged, it now existed in the new worldspace, it had now come into being: it had now developed or emerged or evolved, building upon its predecessors precisely by incorporating and then transcending them.

As Habermas is fond of saying, learning cannot not occur. And learning occurred in the aesthetic dimension just as it does everywhere else. Schapiro gives a superb summary of the extremely fundamental elements of aesthetic perception as they were historically learned, selected, and passed on (i.e., evolution). And all of this development is missed if you focus on the surface style, content, theme, and so on.

Thus, even when Picasso "regresses" to primitivism, he is using techniques and perspectives that were not present in the original primitives; he has transcended and included those fundamentals even as he tries to hide his own advanced techniques in the crudeness of his simple lines. This is enough to confuse most art critics (who don't see the evolution), but not Schapiro. Perhaps because he himself is a gifted painter and knows all the tricks, he can see ever so clearly the profound developmental progression even in Picasso's wonderful wanderings.

And thus, put bluntly, the aesthetic dimension develops and unfolds/enfolds, just like holons everywhere else in the Kosmos. I would simply add that each of these aesthetic unfoldings has correlates in the other quadrants. A new aesthetic perception will go with a new mode of production, a new sense of self (with new motivations), a new cultural worldview (with new intersubjective values), a new set of behavioral patterns, and so on.

But the aesthetic dimension I have a particular fondness for; it reminds us of the Beauty of each and every stage of Spirit's self-actualization; it leaves a clearly marked trail of beauty to beauty to beauty, shining from the radiant void, inviting each of us to fall in love all over again with the entire majesty of the radiant display, and reminds us always that Beauty is not just a pretty surface but a profoundly deep manner and mode of knowing: Beauty is the direct apprehension of the Depth of the Divine, and as that Depth unfolds, so does that wondrous Beauty.

The history of that unfolding is the history of art and the aesthetic in its many dimensions. And that history ends for any individual when the depth goes to infinity, the beauty goes to Godhead, the I itself dissolves in I-I, agency issues in purest Emptiness—which is the ultimate Depth of the Divine and the ultimate Beauty of Spirit, this vast and infinite Freedom whose It is Dharma, whose We is Sangha, and whose I is Buddha: the True, and the Good, and the Beautiful.

4. D. Hoy, *The Critical Circle*, p. 9.
5. Quoted in Passmore, p. 27.
6. Quoted ibid.
7. Hoy, pp. 164–65.
8. Ibid., p. 69.
9. Quoted in C. Benfey, Native American, *The New Republic*, Oct. 9, 1995, p. 38.
10. In other words, the three strands of all valid knowledge accumulation (injunction, apprehension, confirmation; or exemplar, evidence, justification; or paradigm, data, fallibilism) are most definitely at work in the hermeneutic endeavor, just as they are at work in empirical science and contemplative endeavors.

Incidentally, the interpretation of art symbols has much in common with the interpretation of dreams, and I definitely intend this integral hermeneutics to cover both (as part of an integral semiotics in general).

In chapter 5 of *Transformations of Consciousness*, I outline a theory of dream interpretation that suggests that any given dream symbol might in fact be a carrier of meaning from virtually any level of the spectrum of consciousness, and often the same symbol can *simultaneously* carry numerous multilevel meanings. I suggested that the easiest way to interpret such dreams is to start at the lower levels and work one's way up (physical meaning to emotional meaning to mental meaning to existential meaning to spiritual meaning), using each expanding context to shed new light and new meaning on the dream symbol (each meaning is particularly valid if it "clicks" or elicits the "aha" response, or is otherwise charged and vivid).

The same, of course, is true of art (and symbols in general). The spectrum of consciousness is at work in both the maker (as part of the conscious or unconscious intentionality of the primal holon) and the viewer (any level of the spectrum might be elicited in a particular viewer response). The identical art symbol (e.g., the pair of shoes) can be read on any number of levels of the spectrum—in both artist and viewer alike—and all of those multilevel interpretations might be valid (just as with the dream symbol—or any symbol, for that matter).

Part of integral hermeneutics is the actual determination, as far as possible, of *those levels that can legitimately be invoked for a justifiable interpretation in any given case.* For example, which levels of the spectrum of consciousness are actually operative in the making of any particular piece of art (consciously or unconsciously)? Which levels are most commonly invoked in most viewers (consciously or unconsciously)? Is this evocation intentional or not on the part of the maker? And so on.

The example of Van Gogh's shoes indicated how important the higher levels of the spectrum can be in valid interpretation. As I have been maintaining throughout this volume, the admission of the entire spectrum of consciousness would alter every discipline it touches, and art is no exception.

11. Hoy, pp. 69, 76.

12. We can now do a quick four-quadrant summary of the various theories of art interpretation, which is also a summary of the four facets present in every holon, including the art holon.

The actual material artwork itself (the material painting, book, public display, performed music) is the Upper-Right quadrant. The theories that focus on this artwork holon are particularly the formalist theories: the relation between the elements in the material, signifying artwork—the actual *form* of the artwork holon as it exists in public space.

That artwork is, in part, the expression of the original intention of the artist or maker, and that original intention—the primal holon—is the Upper-Left quadrant. This quadrant is the site of the spectrum of consciousness as it manifests in any individual, which means that there is actually a spectrum of intentionality available to all of us (including, of course, the artist or maker). Any or all of these levels of consciousness and intentionality might have a hand in the formation of the primal holon (the original intent of the artist that eventually finds expression in the public, material artwork). Theories of interpretation that focus on the primal holon include the expressivist and intentionality theories, which seek to reconstruct and recover the original intent of the maker (the primal holon); and also certain symptomatic theories, when they seek to disclose, decode, and interpret any individual unconscious intentionality. (And, we add, *the entire spectrum of consciousness* provides the most complete context against which to discern these overall intentionalities, conscious or unconscious, in artist and viewer alike.)

But neither the primal holon nor the artwork holon exists as an isolated and self-regarding element. They are both set in wider and deeper cultural and social contexts. The intersubjective cultural background in which the primal holon arises is the Lower-Left quadrant. This is the vast pool of collective signifieds and worldviews, within which, and upon which, individual meaning floats like a cork on water, governing which interpretations are and can be made. Theories that focus on this historically embedded cultural background include the theories of reception and response and viewer response, as well as those symptomatic theories that focus on the cultural construction of meaning.

In addition to this intersubjective cultural background, the primal and artwork holons exist in a vast interobjective social system, the Lower-Right quadrant. This is the sum total of the material, structural, institutional, and techno-economic systems—and the vast pool of collective signifiers—that govern the materialities of communication and the social action system in general. It includes everything from forces of production to geopolitical locations, from modes of information transfer to social class distinctions, from income distribution to structures of linguistic signifiers—all of which considerably impact the artist and artwork. Theories of interpretation that focus on the Lower-Right quadrant include Marxist, social feminist, imperialist, ecologist—in short, the symptomatic theories insofar as they focus on the wider currents in the social system.

The point, of course, is that *integral hermeneutics*—integral art and literary theory, and integral semiotics in general—explicitly includes all of those quadrants, *and all of the levels in each of them*: all-quadrant, all-level. And it does so, not as an eclecticism, but as a coherent explication of the very structures of holons.

Finally, a brief word about an *integral theory of semiotics* in general. Some of the pieces of the puzzle here include Ferdinand de Saussure's *semiology*, which maintains that all signs indicating referents are composed of a material (or exterior) *signifier* and a mental (or interior) *signified*; Charles Peirce's *semiotics*, which maintains that signs are not just dyadic (signifier and signified) but rather triadic (as he put it, "an action, or influence, which is, or involves, an operation of *three* subjects, such as a sign, its object, and its interpretant, this trirelative influence not being in any way resolvable into an action between pairs"); *speech-act theory* of J. L. Austin and John Searle; *communicative action theory* of Habermas; *developmental structuralism* (e.g., Piaget); and traditional *hermeneutics*—to mention a prominent few. Although "semiotics" in the narrow sense refers to Peirce's approach to the topic, it is common to use that term to refer to the entire field of signs and symbols.

Given the failure of the empiricist, positivist, behaviorist, and representational paradigms to account for the generation of the many varieties of linguistic meaning, the central issue of semiotics (and knowledge in general) has become where exactly to *locate the referents of utterances*. To give a simple example, when I say, "I see the dog," we can all look and point to the real dog, assuming it's there. The real dog has simple location in empirical space, and thus locating that referent is fairly easy. But when I say, "George is green with envy because John has already shown that he has more courage," then where exactly are we to locate "envy" and "courage"? They don't have simple location in physical space, and thus we can't point to them empirically. We can't "put our finger" on them.

Just so, we can't put our finger on most of the referents of mathematics (where is the square root of a negative one?), nor poetry, nor logic, nor any of the virtues—we can't point to honor or valor or compassion or spiritual knowledge.

But the fact that most of the important issues in our lives do not have simple location does not mean they aren't real or do not exist. It only means that they cannot be found in physical space with simple location: they cannot be found in the sensorimotor worldspace.

But in addition to the sensorimotor worldspace, there is the emotional, the magical, the mythical, the rational, the existential, the psychic, the subtle, the causal, and the nondual worldspaces. *And all of those worldspaces have their own phenomenologically real referents.* A dog exists in the sensorimotor worldspace, and can be seen by any holon with physical eyes. The square root of a negative one exists in the rational worldspace, and can be seen by anyone who develops to the dimension of formal operational awareness. And Buddha-nature exists in the causal worldspace, and can be easily seen by anybody who develops to that very real dimension of their own structural possibilities.

In other words, *the real referent of a valid utterance exists in a specific worldspace.* The empiricist theories have failed in general because they ultimately recognize only the sensorimotor worldspace (and thus cannot even account for the existence of their own theories, which do not exist in the sensorimotor worldspace but in the rational worldspace).

In short, the *signifier* (e.g., the material word "dog," "negative one," or "Buddha-nature" as they are written on this page or spoken by a person) is the Upper-Right quadrant, the actual material mark. The *signified* (that which comes to mind when you read the word "dog" or "negative one" or "Buddha-nature") is the Upper-Left quadrant, the interior apprehension. This is what Saussure meant by the material mark (signifier) and the concept it elicits (signified), both of which are different from the actual referent. And the actual *referent* of a valid utterance, to the extent it is valid, exists in a given worldspace—in the intersubjective space, opening, or clearing within which all referents arise (the Lower-Left quadrant).

Because all signifiers are by definition material, they can be seen by any animal with physical eyes (my dog can see the physical marks on this page). But the *signified* can only be seen *if the appropriate level of interior development* has been attained. Thus, my dog can see the signifier "dog," but that word has no meaning for him, no signified for him, and thus he cannot know what the referent of that word actually is. Likewise, a six-year-old can read the words "the square root of a negative one," but those signifiers don't have any meaning (nothing is signified), and thus the six-year-old cannot grasp the actual referent (the mathematical entity that exists only in the rational worldspace).

Thus, because referents exist only in particular worldspaces, if you have not developed to that worldspace—if you do not possess the *developmental signified*—then you cannot see the actual referent. Thus, anybody can read the words (the signifiers) that say "Buddha-nature," but if the person has not developed to the causal dimension, then that word will basically be meaningless (it will not elicit the correct signified, the developmental signified, the interior apprehension or understanding), and thus that person will not be able to perceive Buddha-nature, just as the six-year-old cannot perceive the square root of a negative one.

Thus, all referents exist in worldspaces (the Lower Left); all signifiers exist in the material and empirical domain (Upper Right); and all signifieds are actually developmental signifieds, and exist in the Upper Left.

But signifiers (Upper Right) and signifieds (Upper Left) do not exist in a vacuum. They each have their collective forms. The *collective signifiers*—the form or structure that governs the rules and the codes of the system of signifiers (the Lower Right)—is simply *syntax*. And the *collective signifieds*—the actual meaning generated by cultural intersubjectivity (the Lower Left)—is simply *semantics*.

This gives us a chance to bring together the various semiotic schools I mentioned at the beginning of this summary. For example, by seeing that the signified (Upper Left) arises only in the space of the collective worldview or cultural semantic (Lower Left)—which will serve as the necessary background context for the individual interpretation—Peirce's triadic and Saussure's dyadic structure of the sign can be brought into close accord (Peirce's sign is Saussure's signifier; Peirce's object is Saussure's referent; Peirce's interpretant is Saussure's signified).

We can likewise find room in this integral approach for the important discoveries of postmodernism on the nature of the materialities of communication and the chains of sliding signifiers (Derrida), and on the importance of transformative codes in selecting which signifiers will be deemed serious and which marginal (Foucault). Even more important, I believe, we can honor Paul Ricoeur's "structuralist hermeneutics," a bold (and partially successful) attempt to integrate *formalist explication* (structural system or syntax of Lower Right) with *meaningful interpretation* (cultural hermeneutics and semantics of Lower Left). Ricoeur: "If, then, the intention is the intention of the text, and if this intention is the direction that it opens for thought, it is necessary to understand the deep semantics in a fundamentally dynamic sense; I will hence say this: to explicate is to free [or expose] the structure, that is to say, the internal relations of dependence which constitute the static of the text [the formalist syntax]; to interpret is to set out on the path of thought opened by the text, to start out on the way to the orient of the text [deep semantics]." Also, by emphasizing the fact that all signifieds are actually developmental signifieds, we can honor the important contributions of the developmentally oriented theorists (such as Habermas on the development of communicative competence).

In short, individual *signifiers* are Upper Right (material marks); *signifieds* are Upper Left (interior apprehensions); *syntax* is Lower Right (collective systems and structural rules of language accessed in an objective fashion); *semantics* is Lower Left (the actual referents of linguistic signs, referents which exist *only* as disclosed in particular worldviews or worldspaces). If we add ten or so levels of development in each of those quadrants, I believe we will have the beginnings of a truly comprehensive or integral theory of semiotics.

Finally, this integral approach—almost as a bonus—sets *spiritual referents* on precisely the same general footing as any other valid referent (sensory, rational, mathematical, etc.) To my mind, the grounding of spiritual referents is *the* crucial issue in this field, and so far virtually no work has been done in this area at all. But an integral semiotics puts both "dog" and "God" on the same footing.

This is why we can say that "Buddha-nature" is a material word (the *signifier*) whose semantic *referent* exists only in a *worldspace* (in this case, the causal worldspace) that is disclosed only as a *developmental signified* (the interior apprehension of someone who has actually developed or evolved to that worldspace). This is true of any signifier, signified, and referent, and thus, when coupled with the genuine methodology of spiritual knowledge (i.e., injunction, data, fallibilism), grounds spiritual knowledge in a justifiable and demonstrable fashion.

To my knowledge, this is a novel overall approach, with few precedents in the world's modern or ancient traditions, although what I have presented is a brutally simplified summary and outline. As I earlier indicated, a future work is devoted entirely to this topic.

13. Emerson, *Selected Prose and Poetry*.

Chapter 6: The Recaptured God

1. I have elsewhere presented a sustained critique of Michael Washburn's position (Wilber, 1990), and I will not repeat those arguments. I will here specifically address the revised, second edition of *The Ego and the Dynamic Ground*.

2. Other important enduring structures include what I call talents, such as artistic, mathematical, musical, dance, and so on. I have in mind Howard Gardner's important work on multiple intelligences, which I discuss in chapter 11. As we will see, each of these talents (as a relatively independent developmental line) unfolds through the same general levels of the spectrum of consciousness.

3. The self-needs, self-identity, and morals I call the *self-related stages* (other self-related stages include interpersonal, defense mechanisms, and object-relations). They are all generated, as we will see, when the proximate self-sense identifies with a particular level of consciousness.

   The basic structures of consciousness are the general (cross-line, cross-domain) levels or waves of development, through which almost two dozen developmental lines or streams proceed. The basic structures are mostly enduring structures (although they do have some transitional features associated with their phase-specific emergence). The developmental lines include both enduring and transitional structures, but they are mostly transitional. Examples of developmental lines include the self-stages, worldviews, affective development, various talents (music, art, dance), and so on. In this and the next few chapters, we will explore all of these topics in detail.

4. The distinction between enduring and transitional structures is not well known. Flavell (1963) is a rare exception; he points out this crucial distinction, only to note that almost nobody has done anything with it.

The difference between the enduring structures and the transitional structures can easily be seen in a comparison of, say, Piaget (cognitive) and Kohlberg (moral). With cognitive development in general, each stage is *incorporated* into subsequent stages, so that the junior is a crucial *component* of the senior. Once images emerge, for example, the individual has full and constant access to the capacity to form images. And images themselves will be an indispensable ingredient in the higher symbolic, conceptual, and formal thought. But with moral development, the process is quite different: higher structures do not so much incorporate as *replace* previous ones. Thus, a person at moral stage 3 does not have open access to moral stage 1, for those stages are mutually incompatible (a conformist does not simultaneously act as an egocentric rebel). In fact, a moral stage-3 person cannot even think in the terms of moral stage 1; those earlier structures have long ago dissolved and been replaced (barring fixation, repression, etc.).

At the same time, this is not a rigid and stark distinction, but more of a continuum between purely enduring and purely transitional (as idealized end limits). We see the distinction most clearly in terms of conscious access. Previous enduring structures are almost always fully present and available to consciousness (such as sensorimotor, images, symbols, etc.), but previous transitional structures are largely deconstructed and are not fully available to awareness, even if some of their core competences have indeed been differentiated-and-integrated. The need for food remains; the oral stage does not (barring fixation, repression, etc.). This will become more obvious as we proceed.

Since I first published an article on these two different types of development ("Ontogenetic Development: Two Fundamental Patterns," 1981), I have stressed the importance of this distinction, simply because the entire notion of *transcendence* depends upon it. Development might indeed follow the pattern of "transcend and include" or "negate and preserve." But what is negated, and what is preserved? What remains, and what is replaced? What endures, and what must go? Buddhas transcend the separate-self sense, but even Buddhas must eat. Some things go, and some things stay! And my point is that higher development (like all development) includes and incorporates basic structures but replaces and deconstructs transitional structures, and to confuse these two is effectively to abort development.

As I indicated, for the most part the basic levels are enduring structures—they are the waves in the Great Holarchy of Being. And the various developmental lines or streams are mostly transitional structures—they are replaced by their successors as consciousness continues its ever-expanding evolution. In the text I will focus on the basic levels and lines, but their respectively enduring and transitional natures might be kept in mind.

5. Wilber, 1984, 1996c; Wilber et al. 1986.
6. When describing it in Right-Hand (or it) language, I refer to the self as the self-system. In Left-Hand terms, I refer to it as the self-sense (and self-identity). Both are equally valid languages and equally important aspects of the holon that is the self.

As we will see, I divide the overall self-sense into the anterior self (experienced as I-I), the proximate self (experienced as "I"), and the distal self (experienced as "me" or even "mine").

So technically we say, when the proximate self-sense identifies with a particular basic structure, the exclusivity of that identification generates (or supports) the corresponding transitional structures of the self-stages (identity, needs, morals). Not all transitional structures are generated this way; only the self-related stages. Exactly what that means will become clear, I believe, as the discussion unfolds. [See *Integral Psychology* for a further discussion of this topic.]

7. Further, at each of those levels of pathology, there are specific subtypes, determined by the actual events in the phases of the particular fulcrum itself, because development can miscarry at any of those crucial phases. For example, a failure to leave the fusion phase of a fulcrum means that the self remains fully embedded at that level (developmental arrest, attachment, indissociation, fusion). A failure in the differentiation phase means that the self begins to differentiate and transcend that level but fails in crucial ways, and thus remains partially split and stuck to various aspects of that dimension (fragmentation, fixation), often with a consequently fragile self boundary (splitting). A failure in the integration phase means that the self refuses to include aspects of the previous basic structures in its makeup; it doesn't just differentiate, it dissociates (repression); it doesn't transcend and include, it transcends and alienates, denies, represses, distorts.

In *Transformations of Consciousness*, I suggest specific examples of each of those subtypes for each of the nine fulcrums (i.e., twenty-seven types of specific developmental pathologies). I also suggest the types of therapy that seem best suited to dealing with each of these pathologies. That is still a very introductory and generalized discussion, but I believe it is a useful step toward a more comprehensive overview of psychopathology. [See also *Integral Psychology.*]

8. Wilber, 1984, 1995, 1996d; Wilber et al., 1986. See also chapter 11, especially section "Integral Therapy." [See also *Integral Psychology*, chap. 8.]

9. In contrast to both the enduring and transitional structures of consciousness, states of consciousness tend to be discrete and temporary. This differentiates them from even the transitional structures in the developmental streams, because transitional structures, for as long as they are in place, are fully and continuously available, as are the enduring structures themselves; but states come and go, and rarely last more than a few hours.

Further, basic structures are inclusionary (they directly include their predecessors), but states are usually exclusionary (you cannot be drunk and sober at the same time), which is why all of the strict NOSC (nonordinary states of consciousness) models have proven incapable of conceptualizing the development and evolution of consciousness.

The three most important states are waking, dreaming, and deep sleep, said by the traditional psychologies to correspond with gross, subtle, and causal realms. The human being, beginning in the first months of prenatal life, is immersed in all three states (and thus has access to gross, subtle, and causal realms, although not in any permanent or adapted capacity). Growth will consist in a gradual conversion of these alternating and temporary states into enduring structures and traits. The mechanism of that conversion is the central story of the growth and development of consciousness in humans and evolution at large. [This topic is further discussed in *Integral Psychology*.]

10. This Plotinian approach can be directly applied to general Buddhist studies, thus securing one of the simplest and most durable integrations of East/West approaches. See *A Brief History of Everything* for an elaboration of this theme.

11. 1995, p. 38.

12. The *type of defense* depends upon the *level of development* at which the dissociation occurs (the hierarchy of defenses), even into the transpersonal domains with their own specific defenses and pathologies. In technical terms, almost any of the surface structures of the basic structures and the developmental lines can be dissociated, repressed, sublimated, or otherwise defended against; it is those surface structures, not the deep structures, that are repressed. The major *dynamic* of defense at any level is death-seizure; defenses finally drop only when all deaths have been died, all subjects have been killed, at which point only Emptiness reigns, which is not threatened with death because it was never born; the great Unborn, radiant to infinity, is radically undefended precisely because there is nothing outside it that could hurt it, harm it, push it, pull it. (For a further discussion of those themes, see *The Atman Project, Up from Eden, Transformations of Consciousness,* [and *Integral Psychology*].)

13. Here are the five:

1. *How central a role does pre-egoic conflict play?* According to Washburn, I give almost no importance to pre-egoic conflict. On the contrary, as we saw, the first four fulcrums of the pre-egoic period are in many ways the most crucial, and conflict in the subphases of those fulcrums is a central theme of early development. (As we will see, the real issue here is *what* is being repressed, not whether repression occurs.)

2. *Transition to the egoic stage: Are pre-egoic potentials lost or retained?* Washburn maintains that my model cannot accommodate the loss and repression of pre-egoic potentials. Once again, he is focusing merely on basic structures, which are incorporated, not lost. But the self-system is involved in extensive defensive measures, and thus many pre-egoic potentials are indeed lost.

(The real disagreement, again, is about the exact nature and characteristics of these pre-egoic potentials that are lost. For Washburn, these pre-egoic potentials are a form of the Dynamic Ground, which are originally in *full consciousness* in the infantile self but are then, in the first year or two, repressed and disconnected from awareness. For me, the pre-egoic potentials are general bodily vitality, sensual awareness, diffuse prana, and emotional-sexual energy in general—as we will see.)

3. *The egoic stage: Is the mental ego alienated from its sources and its foundations?* Washburn (1995) states that my model "sees the mental ego as remaining in touch with its foundations. Pre-egoic basic structures are preserved within the more inclusive boundaries of egoic life" (pp. 40–41). Once again, Washburn

focuses only on the basic structures and totally ignores the self-system and the self-fulcrums with their pathologies, repressions, dissociations. Of course the ego can alienate and repress aspects of its pre-egoic potentials (differentiation can go into dissociation at any of the fulcrums!).

4. *Transition to the transegoic stage: Straight ascent or spiral movement through origins?* By focusing on the basic structures alone, and ignoring the self-system and the many uneven developmental lines (not to mention altered states), Washburn can present a caricature of my model as a "straightforward ascending movement."

Not only does that ignore the entire movement of descending and involutionary energies, which I clearly described at great length in the sources cited by Washburn, it completely trivializes the dialectical and spiraling nature of self-development. (Once again, the real disagreement here concerns the nature of the infantile structure that is supposed to be the lost "source" and the "origin" to which the mature self *must* regress in order to gain spiritual awakening.)

5. *The transegoic stage: Are there two selves or none?* In this discussion Washburn seems to ignore everything I have written about the ego being *both* negated and preserved, and he simply presents his view as a correction to my errors.

Looking at those five points, which are supposed to be deficiencies in my model that then recommend Washburn's, it appears that none of them are very sound. As to the nature of the "dynamic ground," about which Washburn and I definitely disagree, see the text.

14. Wilber, 1979b. This view (that libido is a limited version of spirit) also makes sense from an involutional view, which derives the lower from the higher ontologically (in involution), not chronologically (in evolution), and therefore does not have to elevate the pre-egoic structure to transegoic God-consciousness. The involutional stance is my view, whereas Washburn (and my earlier stance) is essentially the Romantic orientation.

15. Wilber, 1978a, 1978b, 1978c, 1979a. I also published another article which summarized this overall position (Wilber, 1979b).

16. Wilber, 1982a.

17. Wilber, 1980.

18. 1995, p. 249.

19. 1995, pp. 48, 50, 49. I will discuss Stan Grof's view in the next chapter, but it should be noted that, despite certain vague similarities, the views of Washburn and Grof on the perinatal and neonatal state are often quite diametrically opposed. For Washburn, the real loss of the Ground doesn't congeal until around eighteen months; whereas for Grof, that drama is basically ended around birth. This is a crucial and altogether divisive wedge separating their views; if one of them is right, the other is very wrong.

Thus, in Grof's data, when people relive the agony of being born as a separate-self, they don't relive the events that occurred at eighteen months. But they would have to, according to Washburn's model. Likewise, Grof and Washburn do not agree on a common point that indicates the introduction of existential tragedy into human consciousness, and that would therefore accommodate both of their models. Grof and Washburn support each other only from a misty distance; up close, they are some of each other's greatest antagonists.

In my view, Grof is dealing basically with fulcrum-o and Washburn with fulcrum-1, and I believe the data from both of them strongly supports that conclusion. I will return to this in the next chapter.

20. These three great realms are exactly why Western philosophy has always had three broad currents: Sensory, Rational, and Idealistic, depending on whether emphasis was given to body, mind, or spirit.

And the pre/trans fallacy explains why Sensory/Romanticism and Idealism were always in strange and bizarre mixtures and alliances against their common "enemy," Rationalism. Schelling, in my opinion, did a fair job of integrating all three great domains, which is why he balances Romanticism and Rationalism and Idealism (and is claimed by all three movements); but subsequent Romantics all too often headed in a purely prerational and sensory-emotional direction, which is why Fichte and Hegel were forced to launch virulent attacks, not against reason, *but against the Romantics*, who were often busy elevating prerational infantilisms to transrational glory.

The entire German tradition itself is a study in the pre/trans fallacy, producing now a Hegel, now a Hitler. Precisely because the German tradition strove so nobly and so mightily for Geist and Spirit (which is to its everlasting credit), it was open more intensely to confusing prerational bodily and emotional enthusiasms with transrational insight and awareness. Blood and soil, return to nature, and noble savages flourished under the banner of a Romantic return to spirit, a recapture of the lost Ground, a return of the hidden God, a revelation written in blood and etched in the flesh of those who would stand in the way of this noble-savage, ethnic-blood purity, and the gas chambers waited as the silent womb of the Great Mother to receive all of those who corrupted this purity.

21. Of course, Washburn is too careful a theorist to actually believe his own two-pole reductionism, which is why he sneaks back the correct three-part model with his notion that Ground can appear as libido (gross), free psyche (mind), and spirit (causal). This is the correct three-tiered traditional view, and once we see that Ground is equally the Ground of all three, it drops out of the developmental equation, and the novel aspects of Washburn's presentation likewise disappear, leaving us with a Wilber-II type of model.

Failing to acknowledge this, the road is then wide-open for Washburn to follow through on his reductionism (and subsequent elevationism). Washburn states that in the "original embedment" of the infantile state, "the newborn is absorbed in the Dynamic Ground and in the numinous power resident in the Ground" (p. 48). The central characteristic of this state is "the unrestricted circulation of the power of the Ground within the newborn . . ." (p. 48). It is important that Washburn maintains this, as we saw, because if Ground is not fully present and *fully unrestricted* in the infantile state, then the spiritual awakening of the transegoic stage could *not* be an actual reunion with something lost in development (spiritual awakening would instead be an *emergent*, which is indeed a reunion, not with something lost in early evolution but in the prior movement of involution; which, of course, is the Plotinus/Aurobindo/Wilber-II view).

Given that the Ground supposedly exists "fully unrestricted" in the newborn, let us look at the actual characteristics of the infantile self in order to see what this Ground might actually consist of. Does the neonate have the capacity to cognitively take the role of other? No, that capacity doesn't emerge until around year six or seven. But without the capacity to take the role of other, there is no corresponding capacity for actual compassion, altruistic love, or intersubjective care; there is no concernful ethics or moral virtue, and no service to others. In fact, this infantile state is, by virtually unanimous agreement, a state of extreme egocentric and narcissistic involvement.

The ego then eventually emerges—especially, says Washburn, with concrete and formal operational thought—and this emergence, he maintains, *necessarily* involves the "primal repression" of the Ground (it is forced out of consciousness). Yet this is the very same period, researchers agree, that conventional and postconventional morality can develop—the period where the self learns to take the role of other, learns to develop intersubjective love, compassion, mercy, service, and care.

In Washburn's model, then, when the Ground is fully present and unrestricted, the self lacks love, lacks compassion, lacks virtue, lacks service. But when the Ground is repressed, the self develops love, compassion, virtue, and care. This is a very strange Ground. (It is, I suggest, a Ground shot through with pre/trans fallacies.)

Incidentally, Washburn's "ptf-3" is indeed a fallacy: it is simply another name for Washburn's refusal to recognize the Trikaya (the existence of gross, subtle, and causal realms). His collapse of tripartite into bipartite forces him to view any renormalization as a fallacy.

22. 1995, p. 171.
23. Ibid.
24. 1995, p. 201.
25. 1995, p. 74.
26. 1993, p. 67.

Chapter 7: Born Again

1. 1985, p. 16.
2. In Miller, 1993, p. 52.
3. Jungian "archetypes" are essentially monological, even if collective. That is, they are basically collective subjective, not collective intersubjective, structures. Thus, for example, the subjective image of the Great Mother arises within intersubjective patterns that are themselves found in none of the lists of archetypes ever given by the Jungians, precisely because these intersubjective patterns are not objects of monological phenomenology and are thus never disclosed by any of the techniques of Jungian or neo-Jungian inquiry. Jung and his many follow-

ers remain within the monological tradition, even if, as I indicated, they have fruitfully extended the content and range of that phenomenology. See chapter 11 for a fuller discussion of Jungian archetypes.

4. 1985, p. 435.
5. 1988, p. 9.
6. Ibid.
7. 1985, p. 99.
8. 1988, p. 9.
9. 1985, p. 99.
10. 1985, pp. 140, 99.
11. 1988, p. 10.
12. 1985, p. 99.
13. Smith 1976, p. 165.
14. Of course, the gross bodymind itself, and all of its competences and enduring structures, *will be included* in the higher organizations of the subtle and transpersonal domains. But the *exclusive* restriction and identification of consciousness to the gross bodymind must be released, and this is in every way a genuine and often brutal life/death struggle. Precisely because consciousness is leaving the biologically oriented worldspace (the gross bodymind in general), it is indeed a death to the extensive network of biological identifications—that is, a death to the *exclusive* identification with the gross mechanisms of life and vital force in general, not to mention the entire structures of conventional meaning and relationships that have developed around the gross bodymind itself.

 Grof maintains that my existential level is rather anemic because it doesn't contain a confrontation with biological death (which Grof, using his dual definition, tends to capitalize as Death, because he will insist that perinatal death is the only real death there is). But Grof's objection is clearly unfounded. Deconstructing the gross bodymind is altogether a biological death. When consciousness breaks the identification with the biological domain in general, this can be, on occasion, as dramatic and as physiologically intense as Grof maintains. The model I have presented is capable of accounting for that intensity and the genesis of that intensity. Furthermore, as we will see, my model fully accepts the possibility that this might involve a conscious reliving of the biological birth trauma. On both these counts, I do not believe that Grof's criticism is sound.

15. In *Eye to Eye*, and again in *Sex, Ecology, Spirituality*, I try to outline several ways in which "death" and the "death-instinct" have been used by different theorists. This is a semantic nightmare of unparalleled proportions. Let me here simply say that there are at least two very different types of "death" that have been recognized from Plato to Freud, East and West—and which I will call horizontal death and vertical death.

 Horizontal death is what I just described in the text: the death to any of the elements on any given level. This can have negative consequences (as in dissociation), but it can also be part of positive growth (the mechanism of disidentification and transcendence in general, which dialectically runs into vertical death).

Vertical death usually means—in Freud, for example—the regressive movement whereby a higher structure is lost altogether and there is a regression toward the lowest of all levels, insentient matter (and hence "death"). In this usage (Freud's final formulation, which is not in the least the way Grof portrays it), Freud contrasts the death instinct with Eros; the aim of Eros, he says, is to join together; the aim of the death instinct, to take apart or destroy. This shifting down to a lower level is one type of vertical death (this is Thanatos proper, the actual drive toward the death that is insentient matter, or total regression).

In that formulation, and as far as it goes, Freud was actually very much in the Neoplatonic tradition, which sees manifestation operating in a vertical ascending movement (Reflux, Eros) and a vertical descending movement (Efflux), which is not a linear notion but refers instead to spirals between shallower and deeper dimensions within the nested holarchy of being.

But I then pointed out that what Freud saw as Thanatos, the Neoplatonic tradition saw as Agape. And this allowed me to reach the following conclusions: Agape split from Eros appears as Thanatos; Eros split from Agape appears as Phobos. The repercussions of those formulations are carefully discussed in SES. Grof ignores all of them in his discussion of my views of death.

16. Grof protests that they aren't that similar, and therefore fulcrum-o will not in any fashion serve the same purposes as the BPMs. This strikes me as old-fashioned nitpicking. Fulcrum-o refers to the stencils surrounding biological birth; the BPMs refer to the stencils surrounding biological birth—how different can they be?

The fulcrums and their subphases, as I have described them, are general processes, simple milestones to help us orient ourselves in the overall developmental process. Moreover, they are based on significant amounts of clinical, therapeutic, empirical, and phenomenological evidence. In the general sweep of differentiation-and-integration, we can divide and subdivide that process in many fruitful ways. I have found that a fourfold division—which I usually shorten to the even simpler threefold fusion/differentiation/integration—works just fine as a theoretical summary of this extensive evidence (Wilber et al., 1986).

Grof's BPMs are based on the specific contours of actual clinical delivery, and so of course they will vary in specific details. But the fact remains: Grof's four stages of clinical childbirth and my fulcrum-o refer to *identical processes*. The very essence of Grof's criticism collapses under that simple fact.

Here are the correlations: Subphase 1 of fulcrum-o is the initial state of oceanic fusion, indissociation, merger, embeddedness; this is quite similar to the amniotic and oceanic oneness of BPM I (and refers in general to the entire prenatal period). Subphase 2 is the overall differentiation process, where the infant's body is differentiated and propelled from the mother's. At the beginning of this differentiation, there is "engulfment and no exit" (BPM II), eventually giving way to separation and differentiation through the birth canal (BPM III). The last subphase, that of resolution and integration, is birth itself and the neonatal state (BPM IV), which is then the *beginning* phase of fulcrum-1.

Stan maintains that fulcrum-o is an "ad hoc" addition on my part, hastily tacked on to my model to account for his data. Not so. When I first advanced the fulcrum idea fifteen years ago, not only was the perinatal fulcrum included (and yes, it was then included to acknowledge Stan's data, as well as other sources), but even earlier bardo realms were all described as fulcrums. I believe all of that is still very true, because a fulcrum simply describes any fusion-differentiation-integration sequence.

The reason that fulcrum-0 (and to some extent fulcrum-1) looks different from the other fulcrums is that they are the only physical-level fulcrums with *simple location*, whereas the other fulcrums are interior (such as emotions, concepts, existential dilemma, psychic occasions, and so on), none of which have simple location (and so they "look" different at first glance). But all of these fulcrums, first to last, are forms of Spirit and its developmental growth, a growth that occurs—in all domains, gross to subtle to causal—via the fulcrum (or transcend-and-include) process. There is nothing ad hoc about this.

All that remains, in terms of genuine disagreement, is the actual importance of these fulcrum-0 imprints as they play themselves out in adult development, transpersonal experiences, clinical pathology, and psychotherapy. I maintain that most of those events actually involve fulcrum-6, but that they might, under certain circumstances, involve fulcrum-0, just as Grof describes it. Grof, on the other hand, is locked into a perinatal/birth position, which recognizes only fulcrum-0, not also fulcrum-6.

17. This does not have to occur in a "linear" fashion, however, because the enduring imprints of past fulcrums are enfolded into the self-system—the compound individual—as complex nests of past actuals, holarchically available to present consciousness under specific circumstances, including LSD and holotropic sessions.

18. Aurobindo's overall model of consciousness consists basically of three systems: (1) the surface/outer/frontal consciousness (typically waking state), consisting of physical, vital, and mental levels of consciousness; (2) a deeper/psychic/soul system "behind" the frontal in each of its levels (inner physical, inner vital, inner mental, and innermost psychic or soul; typically dream state); and (3) the vertical ascending/descending systems stretching both above the mind (higher mind, illumined mind, intuitive mind, overmind, supermind; typically deep sleep state) and below the mind (the subconscient and inconscient)—all nested in Sat-Chit-Ananda.

I have sometimes been accused of omitting Aurobindo's system #2, the depth or soul system, but I do not (as the last chapter of *The Atman Project* makes clear). Nonetheless, I can certainly understand why a few Aurobindo followers believed I had, in that *Atman Project* is a simple outline of Wilber-II (and doesn't dwell on too many details), and in other outlines, such as *Transformations*, I do not mention it for space considerations. Nonetheless, from my first study of Aurobindo, it has been the very rare occasion that I find myself in disagreement. I generally accept all three of the above points of Aurobindo's model, and they have been fully incorporated into Wilber-II and its subsequent refinements.

For simplicity's sake, I sometimes use the "frontal" to mean not only system #1, but #3 if and when it breaks into frontal development in this life (in other words, my general use of frontal often means the entire vertical Great Chain as it might manifest in any individual's given lifetime: physical to vital to mental to higher mental to illumined mental to intuitive mental to overmental to supermental). Again, this does not imply any rigidly "linear" development; the deeper psychic being "behind" the frontal can often "peak" into the frontal; but developmental adaptation does indeed proceed holarchically on balance, because earlier competences form the platform on which higher ones will rest. This, too, is in general agreement with Aurobindo.

(This use of "frontal" should not be confused with Adi Da's use of that word, which usually means the descending spiritual force coming down the front line of the body; frontal in that sense means higher involutionary force that purifies the frontal line. I agree with that usage, but the two semantic meanings should not be confused.)

Finally, the soul (for Aurobindo and myself) is not to be confused with pure Atman. The ego is that which evolves in this lifetime; the soul is that which evolves between lifetimes (or, if you prefer, evolves to the superconscient in this lifetime; the entire "bardo" is occurring right now, moment to moment); but the pure Atman does not evolve or involve at all. The pure Atman is pure Witness, unmanifest, unevolving, unborn, undying. The *evolving soul* is superseded by the *Unborn Spirit* (pure Atman-Brahman). Technically, in my model, the soul is the psychic/subtle to low-causal, and thus, being of manifestation, it evolves; the pure Atman is high causal, and being unmanifest, does not evolve, is not born, does not die: it does not enter the stream at all, but embraces it fully as a mirror embraces its every reflection.

With reference to the Tibetan model and the "indestructible drop," I return to this topic yet again in *Sex, Ecology, Spirituality*, and discuss it at length (note 1 for chapter 14).

19. The existence of these prenatal, perinatal, and early infancy states, supported by Grof's data—should it be verified—is actually a severe blow to the Washburn/Wilber-I model, because that model rests entirely on the notion that the ultimate Ground is in some sense fully present in the infantile state. Yet, even in these models that are the most "far out" (such as Aurobindo and Vajrayana), the *highest level* that is present in the *pre-egoic period* is still just the psychic/soul, which not only is *not* Spirit, but is in fact the final dualistic barrier to Spirit.

This cripples the Washburn/Wilber-I model at its most crucial tenet: nowhere during the pre-egoic period is there anything that is in fact an unrestricted Ground of Being (nor Spirit-as-Spirit); there is at best the soul, at worst, chaotic impulses. Those two options—one "far out" (the soul) and one conventional (chaotic impulses)—are *both* equally and completely fatal to the Washburn/Wilber-I model, because spiritual realization, in that model, must be a *resurrection* and *recontacting* of something fully present in the pre-egoic period, and by both of those alternatives, that model fails; nowhere is there anything ultimate or nondual in the pre-egoic period. This, to my mind, is a strong argument against the viability of the Washburn/Wilber-I model.

20. [See *Integral Psychology* for a full elaboration of these sources, from premodern to modern to postmodern.]

Stan has a tendency to describe his research as being *the* clinical data. He has criticized my work for ignoring evidence, saying that it is necessary "to test theoretical adequacy against the clinical data." I agree totally. But by "the clinical data" Grof means basically *his* data (hallucinogens and hyperventilation), whereas the vast majority of researchers I have relied on are exactly those who pioneered direct clinical and experimental evidence—not to mention the vast phenomenological evidence presented by the contemplative wisdom traditions themselves. *The Atman Project,* for example, was directly based on the empirical, phenomenological, and clinical evidence of over sixty researchers from numerous approaches (and hundreds of others in an informal way)—the bulk of which cannot be adequately handled in Stan's model. And yet Stan keeps saying that my approach cannot handle "the" clinical evidence, a stance that certainly seems odd.

Because my model is evidence-driven, not theory-driven, I have not included astrology in it, which disappoints Stan. Or rather, I have completely included astrology, but in ways unacceptable to Stan. Namely, based on the total web of present evidence, I find that astrology is an accurate interpretation of the interior of the mythic-membership worldspace (i.e., the Lower-Left quadrant at its mythic level of development). This implies, of course, that astrology will fail in tests of accuracy when compared with methodologies derived from the mental (and higher) stages of development.

So far, as Roger Walsh has summarized the available evidence (*Gnosis,* Spring 1996), astrology has indeed repeatedly failed to pass experimental tests, even those arranged by astrologers themselves. Until astrology passes at least several such tests, I have no choice but to remain agnostic. And, in all cases, I believe it is still a *quite accurate hermeneutic of the interior of the mythic worldspace.*

Also, I believe that astrology can be very useful as an interpretive tool, rather like a Rorschach test; but that is rarely how it is presented, which is as a reading of an ontological reality with predictive capabilities, a claim that, the evidence to date suggests, is mythic-membership in its contours and its embrace. [See *One Taste,* July 29 and Dec. 21 entries, for recent studies on the validity of astrology and their disappointing results.]

Chapter 8: Integral Feminism

1. Peggy Wright has published two feminist essays about my work, which are unfortunately some of the most extensive distortions of my work that I have seen published. I can only warn readers that, in my opinion, she does not in any adequate fashion report my actual view, nor, therefore, does she offer a believable critique of it. Many other feminists have responded to my work with an appreciative, constructive criticism, which I value [see, for example, the contri-

butions of Elizabeth Debold, Kaisa Puhakka, and Joyce Nielsen in Jack Crittenden et al. (eds.), *Kindred Visions*, forthcoming from Shambhala.]

Wright's two essays were published in *ReVision Journal*. Because Jack Crittenden and I cofounded that journal, I am often asked my opinion of it, and unfortunately I must say that both Jack and I are disappointed in the course it has taken. We believe that it displays many deep-seated prejudices, and that a balanced, fair overview of alternative conceptions is rarely found in its pages (Wright's articles being typical). We are no longer associated with the journal.

When *ReVision* decided to run a three-volume series based on my work ("Ken Wilber and the Future of Transpersonal Inquiry"), I was perforce drawn back into its pages. A few of the essays were superb, but many were academically anemic and quite a few of them distorted my work in significant ways. The essays were later drawn together into a book, which purported to be a dialogue with my work, but which, most critics were quick to point out, was mostly a showcase for alternative conceptions, such as those of Grof, Washburn, various primitivists, and agenda-driven authors such as Wright. In presenting viable alternative conceptions such as Grof's and Washburn's, I believe the series and the book were a success. In presenting my own work, the series/book contained a host of misleading and damaging inaccuracies, as students of my work immediately noted. As one critic put it, "This is a model of how to treat a scholar unfairly." For those interested in a summary, presentation, or explication of my work, this series/book is not a reliable source.

The presentations by theorists such as Grof and Washburn I have responded to in the previous two chapters. In this endnote, I will address Wright's essays, and try to answer each of her misrepresentations. It is unfortunate that this has to happen, but I suppose it needs to be done for the record.

This is typical of a Wright argument: "Representing any theory as describing deep invariant human structures rather than culturally shaped experience involves the responsibility to identify the cultural assumptions inherent in the model itself" (1995, 3). But I do not portray, and have never portrayed, my model as describing invariant structures *rather than* culturally shaped experiences. I have frequently used the analogy of the human body; it has 206 bones, 2 lungs, 1 heart—those deep structures appear to be universal—but societies everywhere differ on the modes of play, sex, culture, and work engaged in by the body—those surface structures are contingent, historically molded, and culturally relative. I have consistently called for an understanding that carefully balances universal deep features with culturally variant surface features.

But Wright ignores this explicit balance in my work; she presents a very lopsided and at times ludicrous caricature of my views; and she then triumphantly corrects them with a "more balanced view" that is often nothing but a variation of my actual view before Wright distorted it. She simply reintroduces my actual conclusions, changing terminology if necessary to hide the sleight of hand, and then presents this as a "feminist" correction of my "androcentric" views.

Take, for example, her critique of my use of the terms "hierarchy" and "heterarchy" in SES. These terms have a long and established usage in the literature, which I represent carefully and fairly. I then add the understanding that each of these modes of governance has a *pathological* form. My entire discussion concerns all four modes: normal and pathological hierarchy, normal and pathological heterarchy.

I point out that "in a heterarchy, rule or governance is established by a pluralistic and egalitarian interplay of all parties" (chap. 1). Wright immediately claims that I am therefore "setting up heterarchy as incapable of establishing priorities," that I am in effect denying that heterarchy has *any* priorities at all. But of course "rule or governance" means a set of directions, guidelines, or priorities, or else there would be no rule or governance whatsoever (which would in fact be *pathological* heterarchy, as I make quite clear). But normal heterarchy's governance or priority, I point out, is based on "pluralistic and egalitarian interplay of all parties."

Wright will then "correct" my view by saying, No, heterarchy doesn't mean no rule or governance, as Wilber says, it really means "rule with," which is governed by "mutual relations and intercommunion of parts"—in other words, she defines heterarchy exactly the way I actually define it.

Wright thus totally caricatures my view as saying that natural heterarchy has no governance at all, and as examples of this, she gives what I clearly identify as *pathological* heterarchy, which is indeed a failure of priorities altogether. She then claims that I have ridiculed heterarchy by proclaiming it to be incapable of any governance or priorities or rules at all, and then she sets about to fix my faulty and demeaning (and "androcentric") thesis.

She does this by simply *renaming* my heterarchy (which I define as "mutual equivalence and communion of all parties") as "synarchy" (which she defines as "mutual relations and intercommunion of parts")—the same idea, but Wright will now claim it all for herself by simply giving it her own term. And then she will tie synarchy to females, so that all of a sudden we are on a strange Gilligan's Island where there all the nice linking and communion and healing connections belong to females and all the nasty ranking and dominance belong to males. Males will then be the major possessors of hierarchy—which Wright narrowly interprets, quite against the massive literature on the subject, as being power "concentrated in the hands of a few" (which is in fact *pathological* hierarchy)—and females are the main bearers of the wonderful synarchy. This is called correcting androcentrism.

My actual conclusion in that discussion was stated very clearly: "Beware any theorist who pushes solely hierarchy or solely heterarchy, or attempts to give greater value to one or the other in an ontological sense. When I use the term 'holarchy,' I will especially mean the balance of normal hierarchy and normal heterarchy. Holarchy undercuts both extreme hierarchy and extreme heterarchy, and allows the discussion to move forward with, I believe, the best of both worlds kept firmly in mind" (from the section "Pathology").

The fact that I point out that hierarchy originally meant "sacred rule" does *not* mean, as Wright claims, that I think heterarchy is *not* sacred (I was rehabilitating hierarchy from theorists such as Wright, and so I needed a more accurate historical reconstruction). My actual conclusion was that the sacred exists in and as a balance and partnership of hierarchy (traditionally male) and heterarchy (traditionally female).

But that conclusion, of course, Wright simply co-opts under the name synarchy, and so again she has simply taken my conclusion, presented it first inaccurately as androcentric, then added the gynocentric aspects of my view that she herself has ignored or distorted, and then presented my conclusion, renamed, as her contribution to the discussion.

Other of Wright's distortions: I do not, as Wright maintains, exclude children from transpersonal experiences (nor have I ever done so). The point, rather, is that as a rule children do not develop *enduring* structures of transpersonal adaptation (the bardo fades and the frontal structures are all pre-egoic). There has been no evidence whatsoever presented (by Armstrong or feminists or anybody else) for the assertion that children develop stable and enduring transpersonal structures, and so naturally I do not include it in my model. But children can have a variety of fleeting transpersonal *peak experiences* or altered states for a number of reasons.

As we saw in chapter 7, human beings, starting from the earliest months after conception, have access to the three broad states (of waking, dreaming, sleep), and they therefore have general access to the three great domains of gross, subtle, and causal (although not in any permanently accessible and continuous fashion). But influx from these states can therefore occur at any developmental (frontal) stage, simply because all individuals wake, dream, and sleep. Moreover, every individual, at almost any age, goes through an entire "round" every twenty-four hours, plunging from waking (gross) into dream (subtle) into deep sleep (causal), and then around again. The self can be "all over the place," and this is true for children as well. The question, rather, is one of stable frontal adaptation, which clearly proceeds from preconventional to conventional to postconventional to post-postconventional. (See chapters 9 and 10 for a further discussion of these themes.) Wright blithely ignores everything I have written on this topic.

Wright accuses me of "invidious monism," a stunning misreading. My "highest" reality, as I have often stressed, is not a stage set apart from other stages, but is rather the Suchness or Thatness or empty Ground that is *equally present* in and as all stages and all phenomena. The metaphor I have repeatedly used is that Suchness is not the highest rung in a ladder but the wood out of which the entire ladder is made. That is, when Spirit is realized as Spirit (what we called "spirit-as-spirit"), then what is realized is simply the entire Ground of Being, which is equally and fully present in every single thing and event in the entire Kosmos. It is radically all-inclusive and all-embracing, the primordial Emptiness that is one with all Form whatsoever. Wright's discussion of this issue (and her critique based on "invidious monism") is irrelevant because it misreports my view.

Wright maintains that I confuse the "permeable self" of females with preper-sonal structures, which she calls the "pre/perm fallacy." "Wilber has essentially taken the pre/perm fallacy . . . and carried it into transpersonal theory." As the following discussion in the text (under the section "The Permeable Self") makes obvious, I clearly distinguish between prepersonal permeable, personal perme-able, and transpersonal permeable, so that I do not in any fashion equate pre-personal with permeable, which is the entire crux of Wright's charge that I commit the "pre/perm" fallacy, the centerpiece of her implied charge of sexism. The fact that I clearly do no such thing does not stop Wright from making this bizarre charge.

(Incidentally, pathology in the prepersonal stages—in both male and female—involves self boundaries that, *within the context of their own gender standards,* are fragile, noncohesive, broken, and fused—not simply permeable, but frac-tured. A weak and noncohesive boundary in the permeable self is judged to be so within its own standards; it is not judged to be so with reference to the agentic self. This is all very clear in the literature, and Wright is rather badly missing some very important theory and research by her insistence on seeing androcentrism under every rock.)

Which she certainly seems to do. In SES I mention that Janet Chafetz has made the significant point that women who operated a heavy plow had higher rates of miscarriage, and therefore it was to their Darwinian advantage not to engage in such activity. Chafetz herself does not cite a source for this informa-tion. Wright leaps at this as evidence that I often use "unsubstantiated second-ary sources." But the fact that heavy physical labor in the third trimester increases the rates of miscarriage—sometimes dramatically—is a common med-ical fact. It is uncontested, and therefore Chafetz does not need to reference a source for this, nor do I. But Wright offers this as evidence that I don't cite sources well and that they are often "secondary."

Wright especially jumps on my use of the term "centaur." The meaning of a word, semanticists agree, is simply how you use it. Jane Loevinger's highest stage of development, for both men and women, is one that she summarizes (with reference to Broughton) as: "both mind and body are experiences of an integrated self." Hubert Benoit, Jane Alexander, and Erik Erikson had used the term "centaur" to describe such an integrated state, because the human (mind) is not a rider divorced from the horse (body) but one with it. I thought that was an interesting use of the term, and so I adopted it, and defined it precisely, using Jane Loevinger's summary. The way I define and use the term is, of course, precisely its actual meaning.

But Wright pounces on the fact that in ancient Greek mythology, the centaurs were male. Wright takes this as yet further evidence that my approach is andro-centric. But why not go all the way? In ancient Greek mythology, the centaurs were male, it is true; but many were also filthy, stupid, vulgar, and general idiots. Why not be consistent and accuse me of male bashing at the same time?

If it were widespread knowledge that centaurs were male, and if the use of that term could be shown to disenfranchise women in some significant ways, then its continued use might be sexist. But not only does the fact that centaurs were male come as news to most people, but to claim its use is sexist, based on archaic mythology, is like claiming that since Gaia is female, the very use of the germ "Gaia" is sexist, biased, and prejudiced.

Wright divides her overall critique of my position into three main sections. The first is her "hierarchy/heterarchy" discussion, which I dealt with above. The second she calls "ecological," and it concerns two main issues. One is her claim that, because I commit the pre/perm fallacy, my discussion of ecological issues is flawed. But I do not commit the pre/perm fallacy, as we just saw. This misconstrual is directly related to the other major ecological issue Wright focuses on. She feels, for example, that I underrate the contributions that rationality itself can make to world healing. But in truth, I make it quite clear that all of the positive contributions of all of the previous stages need to be honored, integrated, and incorporated, and this most definitely includes both prerational and rational modes. Wright incomprehensibly maintains that my view "overlooks, or at best minimizes, the importance of the positive, integrative actions [that can] take place within the cognitive levels of the rational. . . ." But in fact, after pointing out the extraordinary integrative capacity of rationality and reasonableness, here is my actual conclusion: "Thus, the single greatest world transformation would simply be the embrace of a global reasonableness and pluralistic tolerance—the global embrace of egoic-rationality . . ." (chap. 5, the section "Multiculturalism"). Once again, Wright has reached a similar conclusion—the importance of what can be achieved within rationality—claimed it for herself, denied it to me, and then presented my position as androcentric, outmoded, and fallacious.

Wright's third main area of critique is the claim that my anthropological sources are "outmoded." She points to my use of Habermas as an example. But I did not rely on Habermas as a main anthropological source. The bibliography of SES contains almost one hundred contemporary anthropological sources (and volume 2 contains over five hundred), all of which are listed for a reason. Thus, Wright claims that my earliest technological stage is hunting and gathering, and she says this conception is outmoded because scavenging was quite prevalent. Actually, my earliest technological stage is *foraging,* which includes scavenging, hunting, gathering. I clearly list the actual stages as "foraging, horticultural, agrarian, industrial, informational" (chap. 5, the section "Male Advantage and Female Advantage"), and I explicitly tie this discussion to Lenski, not Habermas (for a long discussion of these technological stages in my model, see Wilber 1996d). For Wright to claim that my approach is based on outdated anthropological research is irresponsible in the extreme.

Wright's biases, her extensive misrepresentations, and *ReVision*'s publication of them are perhaps their own comment: this is publishing with an agenda.

2. Gilligan's (1982) three hierarchical stages are what she calls (1) "selfish" (preconventional), (2) "conventional ethical" or "care," (3) "postconventional metaethical" or "universal care." They are hierarchical because they are invariant; none can be bypassed; each transcends but includes (differentiates and inte-

grates) the competences of its predecessor(s); each is thus ranked as more inclusive and more encompassing, capable of exerting power over its own lesser engagements; so that each stage is developmentally higher than its predecessor(s). Gilligan has also suggested a fourth stage that hierarchically integrates the justice and care perspectives (see below). Alexander et al. ("Introduction") have an excellent discussion of the centrality of hierarchy in Gilligan, and a contribution by Gilligan herself that highlights this importance.

3. C. Alexander et al. (1990), p. 10. Gilligan refers to this higher stage of moral integration as involving "a cognitive transformation from a *formal* to a *dialectical* mode of reasoning that can encompass the contradictions out of which moral problems often arise" (my italics, ibid., p. 223), which is what I have called the shift from formop to vision-logic, a vision-logic which Gilligan also calls "more encompassing," "dialectical," and "polyphonic"—a vision-logic that will "reunite intelligence and affectivity" (centauric) and, especially, integrate "the different voices of justice and care" (p. 224)—that is, achieve a balance within each individual of male and female, which Gilligan also calls a "paradoxical interdependence of self and relationship" (agency and communion) (p. 224). All of those points have been explicitly mentioned in my definition of centauric vision-logic, a stage that includes the beginning integration of masculine and feminine within each individual, and thus I am obviously in substantial agreement with Gilligan on these particular points.

Nonetheless, as Gilligan points out, this is never a simple, clean, and seamless integration; there still remains an (unresolvable) tension between these two voices, even though, relatively speaking, they are brought much closer together in vision-logic than in formal operational. This is why I believe that we continue to take the male and female dispositions with us even into the higher stages, although they increasingly find a relatively more harmonious stance within each soul. Spirit is neither male nor female; and as Spirit, we are neither. But as embodied and manifesting beings, we have roots in the bodily dispositions with their different value spheres, through which communication joyfully flows in any event, and those chords of the body still sing in different voices, all the way to God and Goddess, who are themselves manifestations of pure Emptiness.

Specifically, we might say that spirit-as-matter is sexless; Spirit has thrown itself outward into even the least sentient forms, too simple to reproduce themselves, untouched by sex. As Spirit evolves from matter to body, Spirit-as-body grows into its own sexuality in order to reproduce itself on that level. Spirit-as-body is thus profoundly sexed, male or female. As Spirit evolves from body to mind, the bodily differences, so pronounced, tend to influence the mind as well, so that Spirit-as-mind continues the sexual orientation (as seen in the different voices of moral orientation, for example), although with the higher mental stages (centauric) these voices are increasingly integrated. As the soul emerges through the mind, Spirit-as-soul contains the lingering "evolutionary traces" of the sexual dispositions found so heavily in the body and in a lesser degree in the mind; the soul is the last reach of sexual differentiation, which lingers as a faint but fine perfume. Finally, Spirit-as-spirit is again sexless—the pure Emptiness that, when it manifests, embraces (Agape) its own sexuality freely.

4. Even if we start *entirely* with Gilligan's model and with Jane Loevinger's model (which was originally developed using *women only*), we will still arrive at something very much like the model I have presented, because this model explicitly incorporates both Gilligan's and Loevinger's linking *and* ranking aspects and stages. (In fact, several aspects of my model were explicitly taken from Loevinger's early model, developed with women. I later "de-feminized" it—and "de-masculinized" it—to arrive at the gender-neutral basic structures of consciousness, through which men and women tend to develop with different emphasis.)

5. For an extended discussion of this theme, see chapter 1 of *Sex, Ecology, Spirituality*.

6. That is, the basic structures are essentially identical and gender-neutral, but the self-related stages tend to manifest with different orientations in the sexes, precisely because the self-system (which mediates between basic structures and self-stages) tends to operate with a different emphasis in male and female, namely, the self of males tends to operate more agentically, whereas the female self is constructed more relationally or communion-oriented. Thus, if we take the gender-neutral basic structures, apply the enzyme of self-system with its identification process (which itself is generally of the form male/agentic or female/communion), we will generate respectively the Kohlberg and Gilligan transitional moral stages. All of this is incorporated into the gender model that I have presented.

That is simply an example of what I believe is a larger process at work in development, namely: if you take the six or so major characteristics of the self-system, and allow each of them to work on the basic structures, you will generate the major lines of the self-related stages, such as morals, self-identity, self-needs, and so forth. Thus, the characteristic of the self known as identification, when applied to successive basic structures, generates the stages of self or ego development. The characteristic of defense, applied to the basic structures, generates the hierarchy of defense mechanisms. The characteristic of metabolism, applied to the basic structures, generates the hierarchy of self-needs, and so on. If, in each of these cases, the self takes a more predominantly agentic or communal voice, that will similarly color each of the translations.

7. Wright maintains this distortion in both of her essays.

8. I intentionally say "select from *male* and *female* value spheres" because different aspects of these biological givens are variably *selected* (e.g., plow societies select for male physical strength). I always refer to the male and female value spheres (not masculine and feminine), for these are biologically based and thus quasi-universal. "Masculine" and "feminine" are not so much "selected for" as "constructed from"—i.e., upon the selection from biological factors will be built culturally specific styles of masculine and feminine. Both cultural worldviews and techno-economic factors will play a hand in the selection from the male and female value spheres, which will then be elaborated and constructed in culturally specific ways to generate particular masculine and feminine styles.

Some of these masculine and feminine styles might (or might not) be fairly universal; those that are, are grounded more directly in the biological sphere.

9. In volume 2, I outline and summarize these various factors and the extensive evidence for each of these conclusions.

10. On the possible meanings of "Gaia" and its actual role in living systems, see SES, chapters 4 and 5.

Chapter 9: How Straight Is the Spiritual Path?

1. When I was doing research for *The Atman Project,* I was faced with a difficult choice: I had literally thousands of pages of notes, summarizing and cross-referencing the works of several hundred theorists, East and West. Should I try to publish all of this material, or simply present a brief outline?

At that time (*Atman* was written in 1976 and published in book form in 1980), I could find no publishers even vaguely interested in all this research material, and so I took the only available course: I presented several dozen tables that simply listed the stages given by some of the more prominent of these theorists, as well the overall correlations with the seventeen-stage "master template" that I had culled *from all of their combined efforts,* using all of them to fill in the gaps in the others.

I gave rather brief but fairly comprehensive summaries of each of the seventeen stages. I especially focused on the changes in motivation, cognition, sense of self, modes of space and time, affect, types of wholeness, self-control, socialization, morality, angst-guilt, perceptual clarity, and death-terror as they all developed and evolved through the seventeen stages. Using this summary approach, I brought the whole book in at two hundred pages, which was rather quickly accepted for publication in that "friendly" form.

My hope, in publishing this abbreviated outline, was that graduate students would pick this up, use the tables and the outlines, go to the original sources, and start cranking out the details themselves, which otherwise lay languishing in pages of research notes. This indeed began to happen, and many subsequent researchers went to the original sources and began filling in the details of this general template.

These seventeen stages, I suggested, dealt with the evolution of consciousness in the manifest individual human being (i.e., frontal evolution). In addition to those stages of evolution, there were the entire bardo (and involutionary) realms, according to the Tibetan model, which I adopted more or less in toto for those realms (since it is by far the most complete, and in some facets, the only, model of those states). I especially focused on the three bardo or "in between" states that start immediately postlife (with a direct immersion in the ultimate Goal and Ground that is Dharmakaya) and eventually end up in the conception or prenatal state—an overall trajectory that involves a stepping down from causal to subtle to gross, resulting finally in rebirth in the prenatal gross bodymind—thus covering the entire sweep of involution (ultimate to causal to subtle to gross).

According to the Tibetan model, each of these involutionary bardo "step-downs" is followed by a "forgetting" (amnesia) as the self steps down into increasingly denser forms, causal to subtle to gross. The early prenatal and neo-natal self thus does indeed come "trailing clouds of glory," but, I continued, these involutionary realms and sources are increasingly forgotten as evolution in the gross realm begins, moving through its seventeen stages. Each of these evolutionary stages "unfolds" that which was "enfolded" in the involutionary movement, and thus each developmental unfolding is a widening and deepening of consciousness via a "remembrance" (anamnesis) of the higher and transcendental realms "lost" in involution. This also means that the entire seventeen-stage sequence is driven by the overarching desire to recapture the Goal and Ground of Dharmakaya, which was experienced directly, not at the mother's breast, but in the prior Clear Light Emptiness. The entire evolutionary sequence was driven, in other words, by the Atman project.

But, I suggested, this involutionary bardo sequence is not simply (or even predominantly) something that happens after life and before rebirth. *It is in fact—and most importantly—the very structure of this moment's experience:* we are constantly contracting away from infinity into forms of grasping and experiencing and knowing and willing. As I put it in *The Atman Project:* "Not only did the whole involutionary series occur prior to one's birth, one reenacts the entire series moment to moment. In this moment and this moment and this, an individual *is* Buddha, is Atman, is the Dharmakaya—*but,* in this moment and this moment and this, he ends up as John Doe, as a separate self, as an isolated body apparently bounded by other isolated bodies. At the beginning of *this* and every moment, each individual *is* God as the Clear Light; but by the *end* of this same moment—in a flash, in the twinkling of an eye—he winds up as an isolated ego. And what happens In Between the beginning and ending of *this* moment is identical to what happened In Between death and rebirth as described by the *Tibetan Book of the Dead.*"

As we saw in chapter 7, we can also state this overall model using Aurobindo's terminology: there is what Aurobindo calls the deep self or psychic being, which transmigrates, and there is the frontal self, which develops or evolves in each manifest life. The seventeen stages are fundamentally stages of the frontal being (using "frontal" in the broad sense as overall evolution in this life [see note 18 for chapter 7]); they unfold in a developmental sequence over the course of a manifest individual life (although they also reflect enduring ontological levels of being—the Great Chain of Being, in fact).

Behind the frontal, and capable of "transmigrating" (in whatever sense you would like to give that, from microgenetic—in this moment—to actual life-to-life rebirth), there is the deeper or psychic being, which fundamentally partakes of the psychic/subtle level itself, and thus partakes of a profoundly (if still inter-mediate) transcendental and witnessing capacity (which is also the ultimate foundation of the self-system in manifest evolution). The Tibetans, as we saw, describe this deeper psychic being as an "indestructible drop" (the psychic/sub-tle level as it appears in each individual, which is also how I specifically use the term "soul"), an essence or "tigle" that carries karma from birth to birth, until reunited with the ultimate Clear Light Emptiness.

Thus, any "witnessing" memories from the prenatal and neonatal state are due, not to the actual structure of the infantile frontal consciousness embedded with the mother, but with the "trailing clouds of glory" that the psychic being might still intuit. The "glory" of this "recollection" is not the glory of the suckling infant and the "dynamic ground" of the mother/infant union, but the glory of the In Between through which it has just passed. In other words, as we saw, any trailing clouds of glory in the pre-eogic *period* are not due to pre-egoic *structures* (or "physicodynamic processes").

Likewise, this model (Tibetan/Aurobindo/Wilber-II) locates the *subject* of these memories in the psychic being, not in the frontal consciousness, which has little or no neuronal foundation at this stage anyway. According to the Tibetan model, access to this psychic being is increasingly lost as evolution in the gross bodymind gets under way (which, in my model, occurs via the basic waves and fulcrums of frontal evolution, during which, at the actual psychic stage— fulcrum-7—the deeper psychic being will begin to stand forth in consciousness, eventually standing as the causal Witness itself, which was *implicit* at every previous stage as the core of the self-system, its actual consciousness at any given level, but does not stand forth as a stable adaptation until the psychic/ subtle level of development, and does not stand as its own condition until the causal level, which is ultimately subsumed in the Nondual).

Likewise, the radical Unity which is lost and whose recapture is so fervently desired—the radical Unity that is the single and ultimate longing in the heart of every holon—is the prior Unity of the Dharmakaya, not the neonatal unity at the mother's breast (which, as we saw, is not one with the "whole" world at all). The Atman project is driven by the desire to actualize in evolution that which was lost in involution, and that actualization, via the frontal consciousness, fluidly unfolds in numerous waves—with all their ups and downs.

Such is a brief summary of the model (the Wilber-II model) presented in *The Atman Project*. During that period-II (whose books also included *Up from Eden, Quantum Questions, A Sociable God,* and *Eye to Eye*) I added the notions of peak experiences and altered states of consciousness, and I distinguished between levels of self (or waves of consciousness) and levels of reality (or realms of existence), so that this was a model of levels, states, and realms. Thus, a person at virtually any stage of development can have an altered state or peak experience of the psychic, subtle, causal, or nondual realms (which gives us a grid of numerous *types* of spiritual experiences, e.g., a magic-, mythic-, or rational-level peak experience of a psychic, subtle, causal, or nondual realm; this grid was outlined in *A Sociable God*). But, as always, for these altered states to become permanent traits, temporary states must be converted to permanent structures via development (so that, e.g., subtle states become subtle traits or permanently realized structures). All of those concepts were taken up and included in Wilber-III, with the addition of an explicit differentiation between levels and lines—as will be explained in the text.

2. Wade treats fulcrum-7 and fulcrum-8 as one stage, which she simply calls "transcendent," and she subdivides fulcrum-5 into two equivalent levels, Achieve-

ment and Affiliative, based on such items as hemispheric dominance (which often also means male and female versions of the same level, although some individuals experience both in sequence).

Wade does not clearly distinguish between basic levels and the self-stages traveling through those levels, nor does she distinguish clearly between levels and lines. But those are easily remedied [subsequent conversations with Jenny indicate that she is comfortable with such distinctions]. As presented in the book, her nine basic levels are thus an amalgam of those various items.

With regard to male and female, as I explained earlier, I believe that, for the most part, biological/constitutional factors predispose the male and female to develop through each and every stage with a somewhat different emphasis (agency and communion, achievement and affiliative), so I do not believe that this is a difference that jumps out at stage 5 and disappears at stage 7. The Graves model—and also that of Kegan and others—tends to see each stage as dialectically alternating from an individualistic emphasis to a collective or communal emphasis—e.g., stage 1 is self-assertive (or individualistic), stage 2 is self-sacrificing (or communal), stage 3 is self-assertive, stage 4 is communal, and so on. I believe there is some truth to that idea, but I believe it needs to be refined by taking into account the native dispositions of male and female (Upper Right), the cultural backgrounds in which individual development occurs (Lower Left), and the techno-economic mode of the social system itself (Lower Right), because all of those factors influence whether a stage is "individualistic" or "communal."

3. Many mystical and transpersonal models include at least four to six stages in the transpersonal domain, but Wade settles for two stages. She openly leaves room for other transpersonal stages, but it brings her account rather quickly to an end. As Daniel Brown, Jack Engler, and I attempted to show in *Transformations of Consciousness*, there is abundant cross-cultural material to construct at least a six-stage model of transpersonal-realm development (which I usually simplify to four stages: psychic, subtle, causal, and nondual). Still, these refinements are easily incorporated into Wade's model if she feels the evidence warrants it.

   Incidentally, Wade maintains that I do not recognize prebirth or postbirth states. This is incorrect.

4. The first summary of Wilber-II was published in 1979 ("A Developmental View of Consciousness," *Journal of Transpersonal Psychology* 11, no. 1 [1979]). The full-length *Atman Project* appeared in 1980. Work from period-II continued to be published for the next few years: *Up from Eden* (1981), *A Sociable God* (1983), *Eye to Eye* (1983), and *Quantum Questions* (1984).

   Wilber-III was first published in "Ontogenetic Development: Two Fundamental Patterns," *Journal of Transpersonal Psychology* 13, no. 1 (1981); this was followed by a two-part series in the same journal, "The Developmental Spectrum and Psychopathology: Part 1, Stages and Types of Pathology; Part 2, Treatment Modalities" (Wilber, 1984). These papers were then included in *Transformations of Consciousness* (Wilber et al., 1986). Wilber 1984 was probably the strongest statement of the difference between enduring and transitional structures; and Wilber 1990 was the strongest statement about the difference between levels and lines, although this present volume updates both. [See *Integral Psychology* for the most recent and comprehensive presentation of this model.]

5. With Wilber-III, I was once again faced with the choice of publishing pages of research notes or simply an abbreviated outline. This time, personal factors (my wife's illness) forced me to publish only the abbreviated outline (first as an article in the *Journal of Transpersonal Psychology,* then in *Transformations of Consciousness,* co-authored with Jack Engler and Daniel P. Brown; see note 4). And once again I did so with the hope that some bright grad student or subsequent writer would pick up the ball and run with it.

At the same time, it was becoming increasingly obvious that the "secret" to the psychological, noetic, or consciousness dimension could not be found in that dimension alone. In fact, the spectrum of consciousness only covered the Upper-Left quadrant, and thus my interest was increasingly drawn to the much more challenging issue: not just elucidating the states and stages of consciousness, but how those phenomena intermeshed with the other quadrants in an "all-level, all-quadrant" approach: in other words, Wilber-IV, which is the model presented in *Sex, Ecology, Spirituality* and *A Brief History of Everything,* as well as in this book. See chapter 11, section titled "An Integral Theory of Consciousness," for a summary of Wilber-IV. [See also *Integral Psychology* for the most recent overview.]

6. The need to distinguish between enduring and transitional structures becomes obvious when we attempt to correlate interior structures of consciousness with organic brain structures, because many of the former are transitional (and disappear), whereas most of the latter are permanent (and endure). The need to correlate interior (Left-Hand) with exterior (Right-Hand) structures is an important part of any integral approach, as Jenny Wade makes clear in her own terms, and this is one of the very useful aspects of her book.

As I would put it, brain structures are the exterior (Upper Right—brain stem, limbic system, neocortex, etc.) correlates of the interior structures (Upper Left—sensations, impulses, images, symbols, concepts, rules, and so forth). With reference to the interior stages, as consciousness evolves through the basic structures, it generates various transitional structures. Wade's nine stages are essentially stages of *transitional* structures (they are essentially the nine fulcrums of self development and associated worldviews), which is why when consciousness is at, say, her authentic level, it does not generally have simultaneous access to the naive level. But the correlative brain structures are still active and still fully functioning (they are enduring, not transitional). Wade's correlations between consciousness structures and brain structures are superb, I think, but she does not discuss why evolution deconstructs the former but not the latter, which becomes more apparent if we clearly distinguish between enduring and transitional structures.

Because Wilber-II is essentially consonant with Aurobindo, Wilber-III/IV constitutes my criticism and critique of Aurobindo (and Chaudhuri) as well. Again, this is not a repudiation but a refinement. Likewise, since the Great Chain of Being (the Great Holarchy) is essentially identical to Wilber-II, Wilber-III/IV constitutes a significant part of my overall criticism and refinement of the perennial philosophy itself (including the basic psychology of Vedanta, Mahayana/Vajrayana Buddhism, the Kabbalistic sefirot, Plotinus and the Neoplatonic tradition, and so on). I believe that these III/IV refinements (waves, streams, self, realms, and states, as they manifest in all four quadrants) are especially important as we begin the actual and specific details of integrating Eastern and Western models.

7. Confusions in these types of reductionistic models especially show up when they attempt to treat the nondual domain, which is often equated with "the Implicate Order." And precisely because the implicate order is in some sense different from the explicate order, this actually results in a hidden dualistic view. In other words, because of the implicate/explicate distinction, theorists like Bohm must assign *characteristics* to the implicate order, an order they also tend to identify with the *unqualifiable* absolute, Ground of Being, Emptiness, etc. Qualities that Bohm and others have assigned to the implicate order include: perpetual flux, parts merge and unite in a constant flow, an order of fluid energy, dynamic and holographic flux, a frequency realm, a seamless whole, and so on.

But, as Nagarjuna pointed out, as soon as you qualify the Absolute—in any fashion whatsoever, including "wholeness" and "nondual"—you in fact create a dualistic model. Washburn, for example, must *qualify* the Ground in order to *set it apart* from the ego, which immediately creates a strong dualism, which he then attempts to overcome with his "psychic whole," which makes the Ground a *subset* of something else, and thus not much of a Ground to begin with. According to Nagarjuna and the nondual mystics, all of this comes from the confused attempt to qualify Emptiness.

8. *ReVision*, Summer 1996.

9. The exact relation of these developmental lines to each other is a matter of empirical and phenomenological research. Most evidence to date suggests that, for example, physiological development is necessary but not sufficient for cognitive development, which is necessary but not sufficient for interpersonal (and self) development, which is necessary but not sufficient for moral development. (We return to this topic in detail in chapter 10.)

In my model, the major axis on which all of these are measured is consciousness (the levels of the spectrum of consciousness, the levels of basic structures). This "consciousness axis" is vaguely similar to cognitive development, but they are not simply the same thing, especially given the biases in cognitive research, which include: (1) an almost exclusive emphasis on it-knowledge, which is called "cognition," and which in fact leaves out the I and we aspects of consciousness; (2) a consequent overemphasis on the acquisition of scientific it-knowledge as the central axis of development, with a concomitant attempt to (3) define a central axis in terms of Piagetian logico-mathematical competence;

(4) a consequent failure to count emotions (and prana) as a mode of consciousness; (5) an almost total ignoring of the transrational structures of consciousness. This is why I do not simply equate the basic structures of consciousness with the cognitive line of development, although there is a closer overlap with this line than with most others. If I sometimes refer to the basic structures as cognitive, it is with all these major qualifications in mind; in almost all cases, I refer to them separately. [See *Integral Psychology*, chap. 1.]

10. P. 81. All quotes in this section are from Gardner et al. (1990).
11. Ibid.
12. Ibid, my italics.
13. P. 87, my italics.
14. P. 93.
15. P. 95. In my opinion, there is a "metaphysical" basis for the existence of levels and lines, or waves and streams, and the fact that their essential contours are universal (even if they often manifest with quite different surface features). The different lines of development are all variations on the four quadrants, each of which unfolds in levels of development or manifestation. All holons possess (at least) the four quadrants, or simply the "big three" of I, we, and it: subjectivity or self (self-expression, self-talents, aesthetics, self-identity, ego structure, self-needs, etc.); we or communal intersubjectivity (including moral development, ethics, justness and justice, care and responsibility); and it (or objective realities, cognition in an it-mode, object permanence, etc.). Each of those four quadrants unfolds through the basic levels of its own manifestation: thus, lines and levels, streams and waves. [See *Integral Psychology*, chap. 14.]
16. P. 95.
    We might also note that, following Aurobindo's lead, we can treat gross (frontal), subtle (psychic), and causal (higher and superconscient) development as three broadly distinct lines, which means that, within certain limits, they can each develop quasi-independently. This means that individuals (ontogenetically and phylogenetically) might make strides in psychic/subtle development while still being relatively undeveloped in frontal structures (ego, rationality, conventional verbal, etc.). This further points up why I believe these various streams are not stacked linearly on top of each other like bricks, but rather alongside each other like columns—and further, why progress in some lines might run ahead of, or lag behind, others.
17. P. 95.
    Two other similar approaches deserve mention. Diane McGuinness, Karl Pribram, and Marian Pirnazar (1990) agree with Piaget that there is a universal sequence of cognitive development from the sensory level to concrete schemas/operations to abstract subtleties, but they point out that research does not support the Piagetian notion that this logico-cognitive scheme occurs across all domains (nor always in an age-related fashion). Rather, that general progression *recurs with each new learning experience or developmental line (at any age)*. I quite agree. This "continuous state transformation model" is "nevertheless hierarchical in terms of microdevelopment in the acquisition of any specific

730 | THE EYE OF SPIRIT

skill. The states . . . form an invariant sequence, and each successor integrates its predecessor" (Alexander et al., 1990, p. 14). Note that the progression from sensory to concrete schema to abstract/subtleties is essentially preconventional, conventional, postconventional (although they recognize no post-postconventional).

Kurt Fischer, Sheryl Kenny, and Sandra Pipp (1990) begin by pointing out that the Piagetian notion of synchronous development across domains has not held up to further research. As we are putting it, different lines develop at different paces. The authors point out that a Piagetian stage is a *capacity* that must be fleshed out with *competency*, which varies with different skills, and which depends especially on actual *practice*. Although these skills differ, sometimes dramatically, they all nevertheless fall into three general hierarchical levels of acquisition, based on complexity, which the authors call: sensorimotor (cf. preconventional), concrete representations (cf. conventional), and abstractions (cf. postconventional).

The authors subdivide the abstract level into four more hierarchical stages: early and late formal operations (formal rational or formop), and then two postformal stages, that of systems and then systems of systems (i.e., two stages of vision-logic).

Fischer et al. also note the importance of biological/brain maturation schedules for these various cognitive developments, thus rightly emphasizing, I believe, the intimate connection of the Left- and Right-Hand aspects of each holon of human awareness.

Those important models are all consistent with the general notion of different streams progressing through the same general waves (for me, different developmental lines unfolding through the same general levels of consciousness, all held together, not by a single and synchronous Piagetian line, but by the self-system juggling the entire lot of quasi-independent lines, levels, stages, and states).

We should also note that, in addition to vertical or transformative developments, there are horizontal or translative developments. Any basic structure, since it remains in existence (even if subsumed), can be further exercised, developed, and trained within its own domain. The oral stage might emerge in the earliest months of life, but a great chef is a thing of adult wonder.

Thus, we can investigate the *horizontal* or *translative* developments of any number of lines, streams, or domains. Moreover, once major vertical transformations come to rest for any given individual, there remains only translative growth, if that. These translative unfoldings are both enduring and transitional; some are hierarchically integrated, others are more "the seasons of a person's (adult) life," which Daniel Levinson has so wonderfully documented.

One of the difficulties of studying higher vertical transformation is that society's force as a pacer of transformation drops out (at this stage in evolution) around the formal level, and thus with any postformal and post-postconventional developments, not only are you on your own, you are sometimes actively discouraged. Most studies, from Loevinger to Kohlberg to Piaget, show that major vertical transformations tend to end by late adolescence/early adulthood, and all that is left, from that point on, are variations on horizontal or translative development.

Thus, the center of gravity of a given culture tends to act as a "magnet of development": if you are below that average, the magnet pulls you up; if you try to go beyond it, it pulls you down.

At this point in evolution, it appears that there are only a relatively few practices that can act as higher and postformal pacers of development. These include most especially meditation and integral transformative practices; also a few forms of psychotherapy; intense artistic or athletic accomplishment (the intense exercise of any talent or developmental line); rare cases of psychedelics; holotropic breathwork and other yogic manipulations of the gross bodymind; life-threatening illness or accident; grace.

18. In *A Sociable God*, for example, I trace the spiritual/religion line through magic religion, mythic religion, rational religion, psychic religion, subtle religion, causal religion, and nondual religion (each of which is a level or wave of the spiritual line or stream). I further differentiated between translative spiritual *legitimacy* (on any given level) versus transformative spiritual *authenticity* (capacity for transformation to a higher/deeper level). [See *Integral Psychology*, chap. 10.]

19. The technical correlations (given in SES) for these various terms are as follows:

The *preconventional* realms refer specifically to the sensorimotor (the basic structures of matter, sensation, and perception), and in a more general sense to the overall preoperational realms (impulse, image, symbol, and concept, and early to middle conop)—and all of the developmental lines associated with those basic structures (e.g., protective needs, precon morality, impulsive self-sense, etc.). The associated worldviews include archaic, magic, and magic-mythic.

The *conventional* realms in general refer to the basic structures of late conop (rule/role), early and middle formop—and all of the developmental lines associated with those basic structures (conformist self, mythic-membership, belongingness needs, etc.). The worldviews include mythic and mythic-rational.

The *postconventional* realms in general refer to the basic structures of later formop and all of vision-logic—and all the developmental lines associated with those basic structures (formal, postformal, centauric, integrated, social contract and universal principles, etc.). The worldviews include rational and existential (integral-aperspectival).

The *post-postconventional* realms in general refer to the basic structures of psychic, subtle, causal, and nondual—and all the developmental lines associated with those basic structures (post-postformal, including the four corresponding moral stages in those realms [see SES, note 59 for chap. 8]). Worldviews include shamanic/yogic, saintly, sagely, and nondual (nature mysticism, deity mysticism, formless mysticism, nondual mysticism).

20. Fowler's empirical and phenomenological research, executed as a reconstructive science, found that individuals move through six or seven major stages of the development of spiritual faith (or spiritual orientation); his findings match very closely the map I am here presenting.

Briefly: Stage 0 is "preverbal undifferentiated" (our archaic); Stage 1 Fowler calls "projective, magical" (our magical), which he also correlates with preop.

Stage 2 he calls "mythic-literal," correlated with early conop, where faith extends to "those like us." Stage 3 is "conventional," which involves "mutual role taking" and "conformity to class norms and interests," late conop and early formop (stages 2 and 3 being our mythic and mythic-rational, respectively, with both stages being our overall mythic-membership).

Stage 4 is "individual-reflexive," as "dichotomizing formop" (and the ego) emerges, and involves "reflexive relativism" and "self-ratified ideological perspective." Stage 5 is "conjunctive faith," as "dialectical formop" emerges and begins to "include groups, classes, and traditions other than one's own"; this involves "dialectical joining of judgment-experience processes with reflective claims of others and of various expressions of cumulative human wisdom." (Postconventional, universal rationality and universal pluralism, mature ego, beginning of worldcentric orientation).

Stage 6 is "universalizing," which is "informed by the experiences and truths of previous stages" (centauric integration of previous stages, which Fowler also calls "unitive actuality" and "unification of reality mediated by symbols and the self"—that is, the integrated centauric self). This self is "purified of egoic striving, and linked by disciplined intuition to the principle of being," involving a "commonwealth of being" and a "trans-class awareness and identification," correlated with "synthetic formop" (our vision-logic, the fruition of the world-centric orientation, and the beginning of transpersonal intuition; the higher contemplative stages themselves were not investigated by Fowler, given their rarity, but the fit up to that point is quite close, often exact). Fowler, *Stages of Faith*.

21. There are, of course, many different definitions of "spiritual" (and "religious"); in fact, in *A Sociable God* I outline nine quite different but common uses of those terms. In this discussion we are focusing on the two most common uses that occur in this general discussion of the development of spirituality and its relation to psychological development.

In that regard, there is another usage of "spiritual" that is also fairly common, namely, spirituality is that which profoundly integrates all the other levels and lines. In this usage, it is quite similar to how I use the "overall self" (as the locus of integration), and readers who prefer this usage can make the necessary correlations. [See *Integral Psychology*, chap. 10.]

22. More specifically: In the transpersonal psychology textbook that I have been not-writing for fifteen years [*Integral Psychology*], I divide the "overall self" into two general aspects, the *proximate self* and the *distal self*. The proximate self is the intimately subjective self, the self that is experienced as an "I." The distal self is the objective self, which is experienced as a "me" or "mine." (There is also the *anterior self*, which is experienced as "I-I," which is whatever intuition of the Witness is present prior to its full causal unfolding.) The sum total of these (three) selves I call the overall self.

The proximate self is indeed *a separate developmental line*—it is the developmental line of the self-sense or proximate self-identity (often called "ego development"), but which in my model runs the entire spectrum, from the pleromatic self to the uroboric self to the typhonic self to the persona to ego to centaur to psychic/subtle soul to causal spirit. And for simplicity's sake, I often refer to this as the self or self-sense, without getting involved in further distinctions.

But the overall self is the proximate self plus the distal self (plus its own intuition of the anterior I-I), plus anything else that comes into the self's orbit: I, me, and mine, the great juggling act that is the overall self.

In the development of the proximate self-identity or self-sense line, the proximate self of one stage becomes part of the distal self of the next. That is, what is intimately *subject* at one stage becomes an *object* of awareness of the next ("I" becomes "me" or even "mine"), which is exactly how the basic structures are stripped of self-sense, how identification becomes disidentification, how attachment becomes detachment. Death to a proximate self converts it to a distal self, which is eventually dropped altogether in the Great Death of radical Enlightenment, where the I-I alone stands forth as the ultimate Self of all subjects and all objects.

That is the developmental line of the specific or *proximate self-sense*, which is indeed a developmental sequence of relatively invariant stages. *These stages of the proximate self-sense are exactly the fulcrums of self-development* (which I usually give as nine or ten in number).

But the overall self, which I sometimes loosely refer to as the "center of gravity" of consciousness, is an amalgam of the proximate self-sense plus distal self plus all the other items the overall self is juggling. This includes unconscious aspects split off in the development of the proximate self-sense (unconscious impulses, dissociated personae, etc.), as well as the balancing act of all the other transitional stages, traits, states, and talents. [See *Integral Psychology*, chap. 3, 8.]

Thus, when you have a sense of your overall self (simply as you exist right now), it is not just your I and your me, but also somehow all of the other concerns floating through your awareness at any given time—your possessions, your talents, your relationships, family, friends, your wishes, your goals, your fears, and so forth (including unconscious intentions that exert their own influence, whether consciously perceived or not).

And that is why the overall self does not follow an invariant (or universal) sequence of stages. Being an amalgam, it is indeed "all over the place." On the long haul, of course, the self, to the degree it continues to unfold, will show a broad progression through the major waves of consciousness, simply because all of the lines that it is juggling are themselves making their way through those waves.

Thus, this center of gravity, to the extent development in any of the lines continues, will show a slow and progressive developmental unfolding (but not in any set sequence). This means that *this overall-self development might therefore be initiated by any number of different lines during this process.* At one point, the overall self might develop—that is, increase its overall depth— through its cognitive growth; at another point, growth in the affective line might take the lead; at another, its artistic growth might explode and drag the self with it; at yet another, its spiritual growth; at yet another, it might be the proximate self itself that yearns for the light and drags everything it can with it. That overall growth will not follow a set sequence, even though almost all of the developmental lines within it will; and yet depth on the whole will increase, and increase in a specific direction (namely, toward spirit-as-spirit, pushed by the crane of Eros and pulled by the skyhook of Agape).

This is also why overall growth cannot be conceptualized as due primarily to cognitive structures nor to cognitive dissonance; nor to ego growth nor psychosexual growth; nor interpersonal growth nor emotional growth nor spiritual growth. At any point in development, in any given individual, any of those lines might take the lead in overall development, until that line lags and any other line or lines pick up the pace. None of this shows invariant (nor hierarchical) stagelike progression, and yet all of them have their eye on the same prize, namely, God.

23. Washburn raises the issue of whether vision-logic (and the centaur) is an ad hoc and perhaps unnecessary addition. Couldn't rationality simply integrate the body, since each level transcends and includes its predecessors? Why add the allegedly extra stage of vision-logic and make that necessary for the mind/body integration?

I have postulated each and every stage in my model based specifically, not on philosophical assumptions, but on substantial amounts of empirical, phenomenological, clinical, or contemplative evidence. The same is true for the centaur and its vision-logic.

A cognitive stage beyond Piaget's formal operational—a stage of "higher reason," as it were, or in some sense a generally *postformal* realm—has been suggested now by at least two dozen major theorists and researchers, whom I have carefully cited. When I was first pondering the existence of vision-logic (in "The Spectrum of Consciousness," *Main Currents in Modern Thought*, 1974), I could only find one or two mainstream researchers (such as Arieti) and a few philosophers (such as Schelling, Hegel, Gebser) who concurred. But those now proposing postformal stage(s) include Arlin; Cowan; Souvaine, Lahey, and Kegan; Koplowitz; Fischer, Kenny, and Pipp; Richards and Commons; Pascual-Leone; Kohlberg and Ryncarz; Habermas; Bruner; Cook-Greuter; Basseches; L. Eugene Thomas; Sinnott; Kramer; Gilligan, Murphy, and Tappen; Alexander et al.

Francis Richards and Michael Commons (1990) have given one articulation of this general postformal stage. They see vision-logic as consisting of four substages (systematic, metasystematic, paradigmatic, cross-paradigmatic); I recommend their work.

But whatever we decide on the fine details, the existence of something like vision-logic is now accepted by a very significant number of theoreticians and researchers, and is backed with a considerable amount of evidence. That, indeed, is why I present it; there is nothing ad hoc about this.

Likewise, I suggested the existence of the centauric self-sense based on various substantial research results, especially those of Loevinger, Broughton, Maslow, Rogers, Gilligan, Graves, and others, whose research shows that, beyond and quite distinct from the individualistic ego stage is a bodymind integrated stage. I have often used Loevinger's summary of Broughton's research: "At this stage, mind and body are both experiences of an integrated self."

Why do I say that it is only vision-logic that can integrate mind and body? This is, of course, a relative affair and a matter of degrees. One might even make the argument that the mind and body are not truly integrated until radical Enlightenment, and I would not argue with that. But generally speaking, I describe the centaur as the integration of mind and body because (1) this directly follows the evidence of Loevinger, Broughton, Graves, and others; and (2) the centaur, as the great transition from the gross bodymind to the subtle bodymind, represents the "final" integration of that gross bodymind.

More technically: because vision-logic is on the edge of the transmental, the self of vision-logic is increasingly disidentifying with the mind itself. Because vision-logic transcends formal rationality, it can more easily integrate formal reason and body.

It is true that each stage generally transcends and includes its predecessors, but that refers most specifically to the basic structures themselves (which are without inherent self-sense). But we must never forget that the basic structures are negotiated by the self, and the leading edge of self-development is the home of the death-terror. Thus, whatever the leading level of development with which the self's center of gravity is identified, just that level is the central nexus of the death-seizure. While the basic structures can be rather cleanly integrated, the self-stages, with their boundary of death-terror, cannot. Only as each basic structure is transcended and stripped of self-identify, can the self cease defending it against death. Thus, when the self is identified with formop, it cannot let go of formop and effect a "clean" integration with previous levels. This is nothing new with formop, but is true of every level appropriated by self-development (this is, in fact, the dynamic of the repression barrier at each and every level of development: the boundary of defenses, in their many forms and levels, is instituted from the embedded-unconscious of any level, with its inherent death-terror).

The first stage beyond identification with formop is, of course, vision-logic, at which point the formop mind, now basically stripped of self-sense, can be more cleanly integrated with the previous levels, including the bodily realms. And this, whatever the explanation, is what the actual clinical evidence shows at this level, where "mind and body are both experiences of an integrated self."

(One other contributing factor to the integration of the centaur is the significant loosening of the repression barrier that occurs at this stage. See chapter 7 for a discussion of this topic.)

The evidence, in short, clearly shows that this postformal integrated personal stage (centaur) is significantly distinct from the previous, formal, egoic stage. As I said, there is nothing ad hoc in any of this. [See *Integral Psychology,* chap. 8.]

24. 1990, p. 8.

Chapter 10: The Effects of Meditation

1. This is not to overlook what appear to be some valid criticisms of some of the TM research, including occasional bias in the researchers, inadequate methodology, and obliviousness to negative effects on practitioners. But even when those inadequacies are taken into account, what's left of the research is still quite impressive.

   For example, 1 percent of a college control sample scored at Loevinger's highest two stages (autonomous and integrated), whereas in a similar sample of regular meditators, 38 percent reached those stages. Moreover, "A review of over twenty published studies (involving approximately seven thousand subjects) indicated that the highest average ego development level obtained in any adult sample was the 'conscientious' stage [above which are individualistic, autonomous, and then integrated]. Furthermore, no interventions to facilitate ego development have succeeded in stimulating growth beyond the conscientious level." That 38 percent broke through this ceiling with meditation is quite extraordinary. Moreover, if the Loevinger test is slightly modified to be more sensitive to those at the higher stages, 87 percent in one meditating population broke the conscientious barrier, with 36 percent scoring autonomous and 29 percent integrated. Alexander et al. (1990), p. 333.

2. 1990, p. 339.

3. Alexander et al. refer to their seven or so basic levels of consciousness as "mental levels," which is perhaps not the best term, since there are submental and supramental levels in their scheme. They point out that "mental" in a broader sense means "the overall multilevel functioning of consciousness," and so I will usually refer to their basic levels as *levels of consciousness*; these, as I said, are essentially similar to my basic structures of consciousness.

   In the text I mention that this is more properly "Vedantic" rather than specifically "Vedic," because in the Vedas you actually find no mention of the koshas or sheaths of awareness; no mention of the three great realms (gross, subtle, causal); no doctrine of the three great states (waking, dream, sleep); no psychology of Atman and its relation to Brahman. Those are all tenets found in the much later Upanishads, which were then codified in Vedanta. It is common in India to claim "Vedic" authority for anything you want taken seriously.

4. P. 319.

5. The basic levels of consciousness are also their own lines, but not all lines come from those levels (in fact, the most important ones do not). That is, as each basic structure emerges, it remains in existence, and thus it can be developed indefinitely: as a level, it is also its own line. But the basic structures do not define the other major lines of development, nor in any way account for them (except by being necessary but not sufficient for their development).

   On page 296, Alexander et al. equate the "rows" on their diagram with "domains" (lines). But the rows are also the levels of consciousness—exactly the problem (i.e., levels used as the major lines). Of course, this by default leaves room for the other domains (such as moral, artistic, etc.), but there is no actual place for these domains on any of their rows. The authors therefore, at one point, are forced to put these domains into their "columns" or "faculties," but these are already *defined* as developmental *periods*, which in fact leaves no actual room for specific domains either.

6. Here is their central dynamic: "In accordance with the orthogenetic principle of development (Werner), the postrepresentational stages [post-postconventional] should become differentiated from and hierarchically integrated with the representational level. Thus, the capacity for conceptual thought would not be abandoned. Instead, the entire representational system . . . would take on the status of a subsystem within, rather than executor of, mental life" (p. 289).

I agree entirely—*but only for the enduring structures*; the transitional structures are *not* functional subsystems; their functionality comes precisely from their phase-specific *exclusivity*, and when that exclusivity is broken, that stage is broken with it.

It is precisely this confusion (of enduring and transitional) that forces the authors to list two of their six levels as "functional"—in their diagram they put these in "broken lines" to contrast them with the solid/structural nature of the other levels; but in fact all six levels are supposed to be structural—a move that effectively erases one-third of their model. Explicitly differentiating between enduring (solid lines) and transitional (broken lines) would rectify that problem, I believe.

7. P. 22.
8. P. 295.
9. Ibid.
10. The embedded-unconscious—created by the proximate self's exclusive identification with a particular basic structure of consciousness—plays an extremely important role in development and pathology, because the embedded-unconscious is the home of most of the self's defenses at any given level. Precisely because the self is identified with a level, it must defend that level against threats—and ultimately, defend it against death (until the self "dies" to that level, differentiates from it, disembeds from it, turns it from proximate to distal, from attachment to detachment). Prior to that point, the self-system will dissociate, repress, displace, project, distort, or otherwise alienate any aspects of self or other that threaten this identity, that threaten its life, that threaten its present level of development and adaptation. This is the "horizontal" battle of life and death that occurs on every level of development, until all deaths have been died, all subjects have been transcended, all selves disembedded, and there stands instead the radiant Self that is the Kosmos at large.
11. *The Evolving Self*, p. 31. Notice likewise that my point #5 in "The Form of Development" was: "What is *subjective* becomes *objective*." This ceaseless conversion of the subject of this moment into the object of the subject of the next moment is, of course, one of Whitehead's central contentions. This has always been one of the easiest entries into Whitehead's profound philosophy, and certainly one of the many points of my agreement with his views. In *Eye to Eye* (chapter 6), I gave a long appreciation of Whitehead's work, with several of its correlations with my own work. SES contains several endnotes doing the same.

My major criticisms of Whitehead are basically two. The first is that his essentially monological orientation severely limits the application of his metaphysics. In assuming an essentially subjectivist stance (the subject becomes the object of the next subject), he fails to grasp the extensive significance of intersubjectivity (his societies are interobjective, not genuinely intersubjective; that is, they are societies of monological occasions), so that he fails to see that actual occasions are not merely subjective/objective, but all-four-quadrant (holons). This is why Whitehead's stance, to give only one example, has never been able to generate a coherent and comprehensive linguistic theory, despite the claims to the contrary by his followers. Whitehead has taken the modern monological collapse of the Kosmos and made it paradigmatic for reality at large.

Second, although some theorists believe that Whitehead fits the bill as *the* great transpersonal philosopher, I believe Whitehead fails that task in the most essential respects (much as I admire him otherwise). To give only the most obvious example: in order to actually awaken to the nondual Kosmos, as we have seen, one must attain subject permanence (the unbroken continuity of awareness through waking, dream, and sleep states). Without that as an actual yogic or contemplative accomplishment in consciousness, *there is no corresponding mode of knowing that will disclose the Real.* This yogic injunction, exemplar, or practice is the real *transpersonal paradigm*, and without it (or something similar to it), you have no authentic transpersonal anything. At the very least, you must incorporate the necessity for this injunction into your system. Notice that Shankara, Nagarjuna, Aurobindo, Plotinus (and Alexander and Wilber) can pass this test; Whitehead does not. This is not a secondary issue; it is at the precise heart of the matter, a heart that Whitehead lacks.

Thus, the notion of "Whitehead as exemplary transpersonal philosopher" is based mostly on a translative language game, in my opinion, and not on transformative injunctions that actually disclose the transpersonal and post-postconventional domains. I myself have always found Whitehead's account to be an excellent place to begin, but it simply does not go nearly far enough. Certain of his notions are nonetheless indispensable, I believe, such as prehension and prehensive unification, actual entities and societies, creativity (as absolute and universal subjectivity), concrescence, presentational immediacy, causal efficacy, "the many become one and are increased by one"—the list is endless, and in that regard I am an enthusiastic Whiteheadian.

But all of those notions, without exception, take on dramatically different forms as you move from the gross domain (which Whitehead covers) into the subtle and causal domains, themselves disclosed only by higher yogic injunctions, and thus domains that, at best, are only vaguely postulated by Whitehead (e.g., eternal objects). Whitehead's philosophy remains a dilution of these principles as they appear, filtered and thinned, in the gross domain, where Whitehead first spots them (and quite accurately reports them at that level). But of their higher forms and functions, let alone the injunctions and exemplars that will disclose them, Whitehead has at best second- and third-hand intimations—and precisely no way, in his entire philosophy, to introduce you directly to those higher domains.

Nevertheless, Whitehead's beginning orientation is infinitely preferable to most other contenders, such as logical positivism, mere empiricism, scientific materialism, etc. This is why I continue to find myself sympathetic with so many Whiteheadians, including the wonderful John Cobb, Charles Hartshorne, and the many superb books by David Ray Griffin.

12. Summary by Alexander et al. (1990), p. 19.

13. In this book, Kegan addresses one of the limitations of *The Evolving Self*, namely, the exact nature and relation of line and level, or stream and wave, or specific domain and cross-domain principle. Here, he identifies the "general underlying principle" that similarly organizes the different lines (cognitive, affective, etc.) of "the same order of consciousness" (i.e., the same level or dimension of consciousness). His *three orders of consciousness* are essentially preconventional, conventional, and postconventional (readers are urged to consult his actual formulations), which, again, is quite consistent with my view, except that Kegan still is reluctant to acknowledge a post-postconventional wave, although his model can easily handle it.

14. P. 34.

15. P. 363.

16. Pp. 297, 295.

17. Note also that because they call their level 6 "the ego" (meaning the individual self), they cannot easily see that the self is instead that which navigates all levels, until it is subsumed in and by the Self (which was the implicit source of awareness or I-I in all previous levels, and the implicit core of the self-system at those levels), a Self which in turn steps out of itself and into the radiant Emptiness of the Nondual.

Their approach blocks them, in my opinion, from the more adequate conception of the self-system as that which balances all the various lines, and is not itself merely another line alongside others, which would leave the psyche an incoherent jumble of noncommunicating lines.

Thus, I believe the only viable view is this: (1) the proximate self (at whatever level) is the *locus of identification* ("the dominant locus of functional awareness," the "bounded I"); (2) the proximate self successively identifies with each emerging basic structure (or level of consciousness) and thus becomes embedded at that level (or at that wave); (3) which generates a stream of transitional self-related stages (self-sense, self-needs, morals) supported by the *exclusiveness* of the proximate identification; (4) these exclusivity structures, due to the "looseness" of the overall self, can develop in a quasi-independent fashion, though they tend to be held together in a bundle by the self; these remain in place until (5) the self de-embeds or dis-identifies with that level, (6) embeds at the next level, (7) which *integrates* the previous *enduring* structures but *negates* the previous exclusivity/transitional structures—and so on until developmental arrest (or Enlightenment, with its own post-Enlightenment dynamic).

Incidentally, Alexander et al. divide overall development into three very broad and major stages: the prerepresentational (the preconventional), the representational (conventional and postconventional), and the postrepresentational (post-

postconventional). I agree entirely; those are the gross, subtle, and causal realms. I also agree, as I said, with the authors' novel and important point that the transition from the first to the second is via object permanence, and from the second to the third via subject permanence. They would probably agree that the fourth (turiya) is yet another major transition, which we might call "nondual permanence."

18. I am in this book using "meditation" in a generic sense. Different types of meditation will produce different specific effects, and the generic conclusions can be adjusted accordingly.

19. The farther apart the developmental lines are in the "necessary but not sufficient" relations, the more independently they can develop. Thus, there can be severe disjunctures between cognitive and moral, with cognitive running quite ahead of moral, but interpersonal and moral tend to develop closer to each other. I maintain that the self-related stages (or simply the self-streams) tend to develop as a "bundle" held together by the proximate self-sense, but even these can develop somewhat independently because the self-sense can be all over the place, and can, in worst-case scenarios, interiorly dissociate and fragment, allowing the self-lines to splinter.

20. 1990, p. 289.

21. The integral psychograph can also include any horizontal typology the particular therapist finds useful. For example, a popular horizontal typing is the Enneagram, consisting of nine major types of personality with associated wisdom and defense. As I suggested in *Brief History*, those nine Enneagram classifications are not vertical levels but horizontal types, which can therefore appear on all levels (except the upper and lower reaches, where they fade out). Accordingly, if we wish to work with the Enneagram, we would have the spectrum of levels of each of the nine types. It is not enough to know that you are a "6" on the Enneagram. Are you a precon 6, a con 6, a postcon 6, or post-postcon 6? Thus, both horizontal and vertical analysis would be part of the integral psychograph. (The Enneagram as commonly used now does not foster transformation but merely translation.)

One of the reasons that I do not particularly emphasize horizontal typologies, whether Jungian, Enneagram, astrological, etc., is that empirical evidence for them is almost always lacking, because it is virtually impossible to demonstrate that *everybody* fits into the various types. (I am including astrology, not because I necessarily believe it, but because, even if it were shown to possess some sort of validity, it would still be a horizontal typology, which I maintain is intrinsically impossible to verify as characterology.)

The situation is quite different with vertical levels—such as the spectrum of basic structures—because, to the extent that those levels are accurate, virtually *everybody* passes through them, and this can be empirically demonstrated with a great deal of confidence. Thus, barring severe disturbances, everybody develops images, symbols, concepts, and rules. The vertical levels are precisely those universal structures through which virtually everybody passes, as cross-cultural evidence has consistently demonstrated. In order to develop concepts, you must first develop images, and there are no known exceptions.

Not so with horizontal typologies, because you may—or may not—fit into their stereotypes. This is why, as I said, I have not been much of an advocate of horizontal typologies, from astrology to Jungian to the Enneagram. At the same time, if you find them useful in an interpretive fashion, I have no objections whatsoever. Just do not suppose they are universal, comprehensive, or all-inclusive, because research does not support that claim.

Don Riso, in my opinion, is doing an excellent job of using the horizontal Enneagram with the vertical spectrum of consciousness. See *Personality Types* and *Understanding the Enneagram*.

22. Each of the nine or ten fulcrums of self development have a corresponding type or class of pathology. See chapter 4, The Spectrum of Psychopathology, in Wilber et al., *Transformations of Consciousness*. Bryan Wittine, in his review of SES (see chapter 11), presents my view as if it maintained clear-cut levels of pathology and clear-cut treatment modalities, which is not the case at all. Precisely because the self is "all over the place," so is pathology and its treatment. "Levels," as usual, are simply abstract landmarks that help orient us in the ongoing stream of consciousness unfolding.

23. I have left out a great number of types of therapies, including relational therapies (such as family therapy, group therapy, couples therapy, or sangha-oriented practices), simply because this is a list of individually oriented approaches. But I do not mean to exclude them from consideration. By definition, integral therapy is all-level, all-quadrant, engaging the intentional, behavioral, cultural, and social in all of their relevant dimensions.

24. Jack Engler, who first used the phrase "You have to be somebody before you can be nobody" (Wilber et al., 1986), was referring specifically to *the self-development line*, and I believe he is quite right in that regard. This is why Engler says that he is convinced that meditation increases ego strength, and I agree entirely ("ego strength" technically means the capacity for disinterested witnessing).

Engler's important point—a point I also suggested in "The Pre/Trans Fallacy"—has often been lost on his critics, perhaps because he did not clearly separate the spiritual line from the self line. Let us do so; his important point about the self line still remains (as the discussion in the text will make clear, I believe).

Nor can his point be dislodged by the ersatz feminist criticism of Peggy Wright. The permeable self *also* develops from precon to con to postcon to post-postcon modes of permeability, and Engler's point (and certainly my point) is that "You have to be con before you can be postcon."

25. I am referring to frontal development. If you map the ontogenetic development of, for example, "witnessing consciousness"—as Jenny Wade expertly does in *Changes of Mind*—you often find a U-shape development, reflecting (possibly) the "trailing clouds of glory" of the psychic/subtle soul-drop (see likewise Grof's data). But the first leg of that U is simply the *end* of the *involutionary* line, which is not to be confused with the evolutionary and frontal development line, which is just getting started and is here at its lowest and most primitive

level, where ultimate concern—the form of frontal spirituality—is oral: one's ultimate concern is food, survival, bodily safety, and so on. The ultimate concern of the "original embedment" is simply food, and that is exactly the form of the "dynamic ground" at that stage—God is oral, the spirit is all mouth.

26. When we use the second general definition of "spirituality" and maintain that spiritual development is a separate line of development that runs alongside the others (all held together by the self-system), that spiritual stream itself, evidence (such as Fowler's) suggests, runs from preconventional to conventional to post-conventional to post-postconventional waves. That particular stream is "linear" (which means nested), holarchical, and largely invariant, moving through those waves in a sequence that, according to available evidence, cannot be altered by social conditioning. Although that particular spiritual line, in my opinion, is composed mostly of transitional structures, those structures still build upon the competences and skills of the earlier structures, even as certain of their central elements are replaced. Gilligan's linear and invariant hierarchy, for example (which, as a hierarchy of care, is very close to the hierarchy of ultimate concern), runs from selfish (egocentric, preconventional) to care ("conventional ethical") to universal care ("postconventional meta-ethical")—to, I would add, transpersonal compassion (post-postconventional).

As Gilligan notes, none of those stages can be bypassed or fundamentally altered, and, as far as we can tell, that applies as well to any specific spiritual line, in *both* its more agentic/male modes and its more communion/female modes (because both of them progress through the same waves—the same gender-neutral basic structures of consciousness—but with a different emphasis or "in a different voice"). And, as I suggested, meditation can be expected to accelerate—but not alter—that sequence of spiritual unfolding, in both male and female modes.

The actual details will depend upon the specific type of meditation; upon the level to which the meditation aims; upon whether the focus is predominantly ascending or descending; and upon whether the practitioner is male or female. But as a generalization, this conclusion ("meditation can be expected to accelerate—but not alter—that sequence of spiritual unfolding, in both male and female modes") is quite accurate, I believe. The central core of meditative development consists of the unfolding of the gender-neutral structures of consciousness, so that the differences between the male and female modes, although very significant, are still secondary in this regard.

The major constraint on the relation of "psychological" and "spiritual" lines (considered as separate lines) would be the "necessary but not sufficient" relation that we find between the various lines themselves. For the most part, this is something that only empirical research can determine. [See *Integral Psychology*, chap. 10.]

Chapter 11: Heading toward Omega?

1. In the first printing of SES, several ellipses were incorrectly used in a handful of long quotes; this was corrected in subsequent printings. But even in the first

printing, the endnotes still listed all the different page numbers that the different quotes were taken from. Thus, for example, in one long Emerson quote, where the ellipses are missing, if you look at the endnote, it gives five different sources: in other words, nobody was trying to pretend that these quotes were all from one place. As I said, these ellipses were restored in subsequent printings.

2. My interpretation of Emerson included the notions that (1) nature is not Spirit but a symbol of Spirit (or a manifestation of Spirit); (2) sensory awareness in itself does not reveal Spirit but obscures it; (3) an Ascending current is required to disclose Spirit; (4) Spirit is understood only as nature is transcended (i.e., Spirit is immanent in nature, but fully discloses itself only in a transcendence of nature—in short, Spirit transcends but includes nature).

Since I had claimed these interpretations could be found in most college texts, and since Smoley and diZerega claimed otherwise, I decided to check the standard college *Cliffs Notes on Emerson* (Lincoln, Neb.: Cliffs Notes, 1975), known for their uncontroversial stances (they are written by a team of internationally recognized authorities—six of them, in this case), and found the following, point by exact point:

(1) "Emerson . . . used nature as a symbol of the realm of spirit. . . . Nature [is] a symbol of Spirit" (pp. 15, 16). Nature is a form or expression of Spirit, but is not Spirit itself in its fullness. The authors point out the essential similarity with Plotinus: "Here we have again Plotinus's idea of cosmic movement. There are two movements, one of out-going or descent [Efflux, Agape], the spontaneous creativity of the higher which generates the lower. This is the movement by which the various levels of reality are eternally brought into being. Then there is the movement of return, ascent [Eros, Reflux] by which Soul passes up through all the stages of Being [which Emerson often calls "platforms"] to final union with the First Principle [the nondual One]" (pp. 63-4). "So," the authors continue, "in Emerson's 1836 epigraph, nature is described as 'the last thing of the soul,' the last emanation from God" (p. 9). And thus the lowest expression of God, but an expression of God nonetheless. For Emerson, nature is the starting point of the soul's remembrance of Spirit, but not the stopping point! Nature worshippers and neopagans, of course, do not take kindly to this; they are welcome to their views, but they simply cannot claim Emerson in their camp.

(2) "Man's reliance on the senses and the unrenewed Understanding alone lead to a frustration of his spiritual desires" (p. 14). There is a "further knowledge, a knowledge not accessible by means of sensory experience or by the reflection based on this experience" (p. 40).

(3) "So, for Emerson the idea of ethical ascent involves the activity of man's higher powers" (p. 14). "Good and life for Emerson are realized in our ethical ascent toward Soul" (p. 11).

(4) "We see the unmistakable tendency of Emerson's mind to move to ever higher levels of reality" (p. 19), which occurs through "a hierarchy of faculties" (p. 24). "The central argument is one of ethical ascent: Nature teaches man the proper use of nature—to transcend it" (p. 16). Thus, nature is to be transcended (and included) in Spirit, since nature is simply a lower expression of Spirit, but

an expression nonetheless, and a fitting and sublime starting point for the return journey. But of anyone who remains at the level of nature worship, Emerson says: "His mind is embruted, and he is a selfish savage. . . ."

As I said, all of these Emersonian points are largely uncontested, and they are exactly the points I represented in SES.

3. A few scholars asked me about my choice of Inge's translation of Plotinus, and so perhaps a brief explanation is in order.

In presenting Plotinus's ideas, I consulted the works of Turnball, Brehier, Rist, O'Daly, Wallis, and Karl Jaspers (who was perhaps my favorite commentator), and I focused especially on three major translations of his works: A. H. Armstrong's seven-volume series in the Loeb Classical Library, Harvard University Press (published in 1966–88); William Ralph Inge's two-volume series, originally the Gifford Lectures of 1917–18, published in 1929 (and reprinted in 1968); and Stephen MacKenna's translations, which he undertook from 1917 to 1930 (now available in a Penguin Classics edition and the wonderful Larson Publication edition).

For various reasons, which I will explain in a moment, I decided that, of all these translations, William Inge's had certain advantages. The other translations seemed to understand better the letter, but not as well the spirit, of Plotinus, and so even where they excelled technically, they were sometimes rather thin in their interpretative sweep.

Nonetheless, Inge's translation is usually not listed among the various translations of Plotinus, simply because he included only large, representative tracts of Plotinus; he did not publish a complete translation. For that, I relied primarily on Armstrong. As O'Meara (1995) recently pointed out, "Armstrong's translation supersedes that of S. MacKenna . . . , which, although a work of great literary quality, is less reliable and less clear" (p. 127).

Many critics still love MacKenna's beautiful style, as do I. Inge actually consulted MacKenna's translations (except for the very last parts, which MacKenna had not completed at the time), and Inge spoke very highly of them. Nonetheless, where Inge's translations deviated from MacKenna, he had his own sufficient reasons, and these sorts of deviations are explained at length in Inge's extensive notes, which scholars can easily consult and adjudicate for themselves.

Instead of getting involved in this battle of technical details and technical debate, and instead of performing a mixing and matching and juggling act between three translations, I simply chose to go with Inge's translations. Since the main points—the identical main points—could be made with any of these three translations, why did I choose Inge? I already gave one reason: I found Inge to have a deeper spiritual resonance than the others. I love MacKenna's translation; it is often quite beautiful and always moving, and I don't mean to detract from his wonderful and loving effort; and Armstrong's is technically exquisite. Nonetheless, Inge seems to intuit a profound depth of realization that comes across clearly in his work, and I was drawn to this depth.

The second reason is that Inge was himself an accomplished philosopher, and it is often the case that such accomplishment can bring a greater depth and wider range of perceptions to an interpretive task, only one of whose elements is technical proficiency. Again, I do not wish to detract from MacKenna, but he was a bank clerk and a journalist; his sheer love of Plotinus is evident and altogether moving; but I also appreciated the background and commentary that Inge was able to bring to the task.

The third main reason I chose Inge is that, for a very long time, William Inge was the only respected academic scholar—or at least, one of the very, very few—who *actually believed in the truth of what Plotinus was saying*. He was not interested in Plotinus as a merely historical curiosity, but rather as the representative of a profound worldview that still possessed abundant truth and goodness and beauty. So respected was Inge that, when Bertrand Russell was writing his chapter on Plotinus in *A History of Western Philosophy*, Inge was the only decent philosopher Russell could think of who believed in Plotinus: "A philosophical system," says Russell, "may be judged important for various different kinds of reasons. The first and most obvious is that we think it may be true. Not many students of philosophy at the present time would feel this about Plotinus; William Inge is, in this respect, a rare exception." Russell goes on to refer to Inge's book as "invaluable," and points out that "it is impossible to disagree with what Inge says on the influence of Plato and Plotinus."

And that was exactly the topic of the section about Plotinus in my book; namely, the historical influence of Plotinus. Inge's undisputed expertise in this area was yet another reason I chose him.

And finally, I simply wanted to pay homage to this rather extraordinary man, who for so long kept the light of Plotinus burning when few, if any, were interested. So I chose Inge. I made it very clear that all quotes were from Inge, and thenceforth, I gave careful citations: the page numbers given in Inge contain the exact references to the specific Plotinus material (usually the *Enneads*). All that is required of a scholar who makes such choices is that he carefully indicate what his sources are, and I did so.

(In the first printing, several ellipses were omitted; these were restored in subsequent printings. And the "four satoris" versus "often" refers to Plotinus; this was also corrected in subsequent printings. But Karl Jaspers's conclusion remains precisely the same, which is why I quoted it in the first place: "What, according to Porphyry, would seem to have been a rare, anomalous experience, is, in the statement of Plotinus, the natural reality.")

There were two minor errors in the Emerson and Plotinus sections. With Plotinus, I indicated that all quotes were from Inge unless otherwise indicated, and then I gave Plotinus's last words as "the divine-in-us departs to the divine-in-all," which was actually Jaspers's translation, not Inge's, which is "the divine in me departs to unite itself with the Divine in the universe." With Emerson, I deleted a reference to "nature" in one quote because Emerson uses "nature" in several different ways, which becomes obvious only later in the narrative. Both errors were subsequently corrected, and neither of them affected the conclusions, which were exactly as outlined in note 2 above.

4. Walsh, R. 1995. The spirit of evolution. A review of Ken Wilber's *Sex, Ecology, Spirituality*. *Noetics Sciences Review*, Summer, 1995.

5. See also M. Commons, J. Sinnott, F. Richards, and C. Armon (eds.) *Adult Development,* vol. 1, *Comparisons and Applications of Adolescent and Adult Developmental Models* (New York: Praeger, 1990.)

  M. Commons, C. Armon, L. Kohlberg, F. Richards, T. Grotzer, and J. Sinnott (eds.), *Adult Development,* vol. 2, *Models and Methods in the Study of Adult and Adolescent Thought* (New York: Praeger, 1990.)

  J. Sinnott and J. Cavanaugh (eds.), *Bridging Paradigms: Positive Development in Adulthood and Cognitive Aging* (New York: Praeger, 1991.) Also J. Sinnott (ed.), *Interdisciplinary Handbook of Adult Lifespan Learning.* (Greenwich, Conn.: Greenwood Press, 1994.)

  Transcendence and Mature Thought in Adulthood: The Further Reaches of Adult Development, edited by Melvin E. Miller and Susanne R. Cook-Greuter, is an excellent and accessible anthology. Charles Tart's *Transpersonal Psychologies* is still a fine reference work, as is Seymour Boorstein's *Transpersonal Psychotherapy.* And *Transformations of Consciousness* (Wilber et al., 1986) remains a useful text in transpersonal developmental psychology.

  Perhaps the most accessible transpersonal anthology is *Paths beyond Ego,* edited by Roger Walsh and Frances Vaughan. (My only caveat is that the authors have continued to reprint the rough-draft version of my essay "Eye to Eye," which, for semantic reasons, denied that a higher or transpersonal "science" was possible—simply because "science" and "empirical" were so closely wedded. I subsequently decided this was a losing semantic quibble, and, in the published version of "Eye to Eye," defined exactly what we could mean by a higher, nonempirical science, which has remained my stance. Inexplicably, the editors are still using the original rough draft [pp. 184–89]). Aside from that, this anthology remains the finest introduction to the field, and is highly recommended. [See *Integral Psychology* for an extensive list of references to the field.]

6. Incidentally, as I always point out, I agree with Jung on the nature of these archaic images *qua* archaic images: I believe they are collectively inherited, a type of phylogenetic heritage (a point Freud also accepted); they are important in certain types of pathology; they can be found abundantly in the world's mythologies; they often appear in dreams; and so on. But those archaic images have little if anything to do with post-postconventional development. One of Jung's pre/trans fallacies was that he confused collective with transpersonal, whereas there are collective prepersonal, collective personal, and collective transpersonal structures.

7. There are many ways to describe the archetypes as used by the perennial philosophy. If you are in formless meditation (cessation or nirvikalpa samadhi), the first phenomena that you see as you come out of cessation are exactly the archetypes. They are subtle forms, sounds, illuminations, affects, energetic currents, and so on. Likewise, each night, as you come out of deep dreamless sleep and begin dreaming, the first forms you see are archetypes. In anuttaratantra yoga, as you descend out of black near attainment, the first forms you see are archetypes.

  What all of those have in common is that the archetypes are the primordial forms lying on the boundary between the causal unmanifest and the first subtle-level manifestation. They are thus the first and earliest forms in involution or manifestation (or movement away from causal Source), and the last or highest forms in evolution, or return to Source (and thus the final barriers as well).

These archetypes, as I said, are subtle forms, illuminations, energetic currents, sounds, extremely subtle affects, and so on—the first forms of being, on which all lesser being will be modeled; the first forms of affect, of which all lesser feelings will be a dim reflection; the first forms of manifest consciousness, of which all lesser cognition will be a pale reflection; the first forms of luminosity, of which all lesser understanding will be a hazy hint; the first forms of sound, of which all lesser sounds will be a hollow echo. And thus the archetypes, the true archetypes, are the Forms of our own highest potential, the Forms of our own true nature, calling to us to remember who and what we really are. And in their last action, they are set aside and deconstructed—the ladder that, having served its purpose, is discarded—and there stands instead the radiant infinity that was always already shining through and beyond those Forms altogether.

8. Most problematic is the fact that the mechanisms of inheritance are not even vaguely the same for these two types of "archetypes." Archaic images are inherited from common experiences of yesterday. But the higher deep structures (or higher archetypes) were never a common past experience, and thus do not have the same origin. (The reason is that the "high archetypes" are lost in early involution; the "low archetypes" or archaic images are lost in early evolution. I have seen no Jungian make that distinction, and this hobbles the entire thrust of "archetypal" psychology, constantly plaguing even its more sophisticated variants with pre/trans fallacies.)

9. *Essence*, p. 20.

10. For a discussion of this, see Anthony, Ecker, and Wilber, *Spiritual Choices*.

11. The Diamond Approach of Hameed Ali (who writes under the pen name A. H. Almaas) is, in my opinion, a superb therapeutic/transformative discipline. Within this broad appreciation, which I will reiterate in a moment, I have a few criticisms.

What is most interesting in Ali's theoretical development is his eventual move from a classic Romantic/Wilber-I model to an Aurobindo/Wilber-II model. But the problem, we will see, is that he nonetheless continues to wobble, in an often self-contradictory fashion, between these two models.

In his early book *Essence* (1986), we find a very strong Romantic/type-I presentation. The infant is born fully in contact with Essence or Being: "Babies and very young children not only have Essence, they are in touch with their Essence; they are identified with their Essence; they are the Essence" (p. 83; in his later books, Ali always capitalizes *Essence*; I have done so in these quotes as well). But then, through the emergence and development of the ego and its object constancy, Essence is lost. "So we can conclude that people are born with Essence but end up without it later on" (p. 84).

The various aspects of Essence, which Ali identifies as Platonic Forms (including Will, Strength, Joy, Self, Personal, Compassion, Merging, Love, Intelligence,

Peace) *are slowly lost as the ego develops*, because the ego is the great enemy, so to speak, of Essence and Being. "Because Essence has various aspects, and different aspects dominate at different times [of early development], Essence is lost aspect by aspect" (p. 89).

By the time of late childhood, Essence is for the most part thoroughly buried and rendered only vaguely available. In its place are various "holes"—the empty psychic spaces created by the repression or loss of the various aspects of Essence. Thus, early development (according to "Ali-I") consists of (1) the profound and widespread loss of Essence, aspect by aspect, leaving (2) various holes, inadequacies, or absences in the being of the individual, holes that (3) the individual then compensates for with various further defense mechanisms. Individuals, with virtually no exceptions, thus arrive at adulthood as a bundle of holes and defense mechanisms dedicated to the avoidance of Being and Essence.

Therapy, for Ali-I, thus consists in the actual *retrieval* of the aspects of Essence that were present in infancy but later repressed, denied, or abandoned. "This understanding of the loss of Essence is of paramount importance when it comes to the question of techniques of retrieval of Essence" (p. 89). By bringing non-judgmental awareness to one's present symptoms, distresses, inadequacies, or "holes," one ceases to defend against the lack, but instead simply experiences it. This direct awareness eventually discloses a sense of experiential emptiness, and if one stays with that emptiness and fully enters it, the corresponding aspect of repressed Essence will emerge and "fill" that hole. The retrieval of Essence thus allows postformal development to proceed apace.

That is obviously a very strong Romantic model. In many ways, it parallels Wilber-I; it even maintains that the infant is fully realized as Atman itself! "The Hindus call it the Atman. The child had it to start with, but its loss led to the development of the ego sense of identity . . ." (p. 169). We saw that not even the Tibetans (nor the Hindus, for that matter) believe that the child is fully realized or fully in touch with Atman, and that Atman is lost as one grows up. Rather, Atman is lost in prior involution, not in early evolution!

But at this point Ali is committed to a very strong Romantic model. "Our understanding of how Essence arises in children and then is put aside in favor of ego identifications is a new and rather surprising set of observations." Of course, it is neither new nor surprising, but the two-centuries-old Romantic developmental scheme.

Nonetheless, sensing a problem with this scheme, Ali begins to revise his stance toward the end of *Essence*, and we can see the start of the slow shift from a Romantic/Wilber-I to a Wilber-II type of model. He points out that there are two ways to look at the emergence of Essence, which he calls *uncovering* versus *development*, the former being the actual retrieval of something present in infancy but lost, the latter being the growth and development of something only minimally present in infancy. Ali says that he has been presenting an uncovering view, but he says that both views are probably true, and in fact, the most important part of the story is actually *development*. "Seeing the process as a development applies more accurately to an aspect of Essence that is in a sense more central" (p. 161). This central aspect of Essence "goes through a process of development, growth, and expansion. . . . This true personality [true Self, Atman, Personal Essence] grows, expands, and develops in a very specific sense" (p. 163). In other words, it primarily grows and develops rather than being lost and restricted.

Poised thus on the verge of a truly type-II model, Ali begins *The Pearl beyond Price—Integration of Personality into Being: An Object Relations Approach*, which is one of the genuinely superb contributions to East/West psychology and psychotherapy. The only major problem with the book, in my opinion, is that although it marks a shift from a type-I to a type-II model, Ali wobbles back and forth between them in some very self-contradictory ways.

On the one hand, Ali comes down decisively on the side of an overall developmental process (a strong Aurobindo/Wilber-II model), in which ego development is not a repression of Essence but a growth toward Essence, all part of a single overall developmental or evolutionary process. Thus, he says, Personal Essence "is the ultimate product of ego development. In other words, ego development and spiritual enlightenment are not two disjoint processes but parts of the same process" (p. 154). He makes that point time and again, and in very clear language. "It is more correct to consider ego development and spiritual transformation as forming one unified process of human evolution. . . . Inner evolution [moves] from birth, through ego development, to the realization of the Personal Essence. So it is one process of evolution from the beginning of ego development to the final stages of spiritual enlightenment" (p. 161). "This point is a radical departure from the understanding of both traditional spiritual teachings and modern psychology," he writes. "It unifies these two fields into one field, that of human nature and development" (p. 154).

That "unification," of course, was the central message of *The Atman Project*, and of Aurobindo, and before that, of Fichte and Schelling, among others. This shift to a full-fledged Aurobindo/Wilber-II orientation allows Ali to make some truly important contributions to the techniques of spiritual transformation (and postformal development) by working with the very early traumas to the self (particularly, as we will see, with fulcrum-2). If self development and spiritual development are part of the same spectrum of consciousness and not simply antagonists, then early damage to the former can cripple the emergence of the latter. That is the essence of the Diamond Approach (and of Wilber-II).

But throughout *The Pearl beyond Price* are scattered strong remnants of the "Ali-I" (Romantic/Wilber-I) approach. I want to give a few extended examples of these, both to show what is actually involved and to indicate why this issue is so important.

Start with the true Self or Atman or Essential Self. Is it fully realized in the infant? As we saw in chapter 6, the Romantic, neo-Jungian, Washburn, Wilber-I view is that the Essential Self is fully present in infancy, but the development of the ego denies, represses, or obscures this Ground. The ego becomes alienated from Ground, but later it can retrieve this Ground ("in a mature form" or "at a higher level") and so find a re-union with God, Ground, Being, or Essence. Thus, at the start of evolution, the self is one with Ground; in the middle of evolution, the self becomes alienated from Ground; at the further reaches of evolution, the self and Ground reunite, which is a retrieval of that which was fully present in the earlier stages of evolution but was subsequently lost. Such is the standard Romantic model in any of its forms.

The more typical perennial philosophical view is that the self becomes alienated from spirit during *involution*, not during anything that happens in *evolution*. Involution is the prior (but also timeless) movement whereby spirit goes out of itself to create soul, which goes out of itself to create mind, which goes out of itself to create body (prana), which goes out of itself to create matter. Each junior level is a restriction, manifestation, or stepped-down expression of its senior dimension, so that all waves are ultimately manifestations of the ocean of Spirit itself. But each lower wave "forgets" its senior dimension (amnesia), so that the end product is the world of matter, lying around all by itself and wondering how it got there.

. Evolution then proceeds to *unfold* and *remember* that which was *enfolded* and *forgotten*: out of matter arises life; out of life evolves mind; out of mind emerges soul; out of soul emerges spirit, which is both the Ground and the Goal of the entire sequence. The infant, in this view, is indeed born "trailing clouds of glory," because (to use the Tibetan version), it has just involved from spirit to soul to mind to take on a material body. But in no sense is the infant *fully* in touch with Dharmakaya or Spirit (except insofar as Spirit is the Ground of all things, including infants). Rather, the infant stands basically at the end of the involutionary line (the primary alienation has already occurred)—and at the beginning of the evolutionary line, which is now at its *lowest* and starting point: the infant is primarily a bodyself, instinctual, vital, impulsive, narcissistic, egocentric; living for food, its God is all mouth.

Precisely because the infant is at the lowest level in its *frontal* development and evolution, it is merged with and embedded in the lowest dimension of Spirit: it is one with the material and physical world (as Piaget put it, "The self is here material, so to speak"). This is the undifferentiated state of protoplasmic awareness that dominates the early infantile state (the fusion subphase of fulcrum-1). There are no differentiated emotions nor emotional object constancy; there are no mental concepts, symbols, or rules; no logic, no narrative, no poetry, no mathematics, no art, no music, no dance, no capacity to take the role of other, and therefore no genuine love, no compassion, no mercy, no tolerance, and no benevolence.

In other words, the Romantics' idea of Ground. Precisely because the Romantics lacked any genuine understanding of involution, they took this early infantile physical fusion state, and, simply because it was "undifferentiated," imagined that it was the great Ground of Being itself.

The self, of course, will very soon differentiate and transcend this crude physical fusion, in order to identify with the emotional body, then the mind, then the soul, then spirit itself, transcending all, embracing all. This transcendence of the physical fusion state is a painful awakening to the separate being of the bodyself (fulcrum-2). This awakening is not the loss of spirit or essence, but the bitter-sweet first step to the full awakening of spirit itself.

The Romantics, by contrast, reached the understandable but naive conclusion that the pain and alienation of the emerging ego occurs because God has just been lost (whereas the ego is simply the first painful step back to God). Thus we arrive at the *traditional* Romantic view, which is that (1) the infant self starts out one with the Ground but in an unconscious fashion; (2) that union is then necessarily lost or repressed by the emerging ego; (3) the ego, having necessarily crushed the Ground, can then return to, retrieve, or otherwise recapture the Ground, but now in a fully conscious fashion, thus effecting a spiritual reunion. Where the infant is one with Ground in an unconscious fashion, the mature self is one with Ground in a conscious realization.

But even the Romantics began to realize that their own scheme was incoherent, because the second step is inherently impossible. All things are one with Ground; if you lose that oneness, you cease to exist. Rather, you can either be conscious or unconscious of that union. If you are already unconscious of the union, you can't get any lower. And since the Romantics had already conceded that the infantile self is unconscious of the union, that actually meant that the infantile self is *already* fallen. But this put the Romantics in an untenable situation. If the early, primitive state is already fallen, then enlightenment *cannot* be a recapture of yesterday, and the entire impulse of the traditional retro-Romantic disposition was exploded at its roots.

(Historically, Romanticism then either evolved to a Hegelian/Aurobindo/Wilber-II approach, or it faded as a coherent movement, although, of course, retro-Romanticism continues to arise as a common pre/trans fallacy, which we will return to later.)

The only way to attempt to salvage a specifically retro-Romantic agenda is to take the course outlined by Washburn. If enlightenment is going to be the recapture of something present in the infant but lost, then that infantile state must be one with Ground and that oneness must be "unrestrictedly present" in some sort of fully conscious fashion. As I tried to show in chapter 6, this is untenable; nonetheless, it is the only possible way to proceed with the retro-Romantic agenda.

With that theoretical background, we return to Ali. Is the Essential Self or Atman fully present in the infant? And here Ali runs into the Romantic Waterloo. In order to make the model work at all, the infant must be conscious of the Self, must be genuinely Self-realized, else there is nothing worth *recapturing*. And so that is exactly what Ali does. "When the Essential Self is present then, in a sense, the child is born; he is self-realized. He is his true Self. . . . The child is self-realized, in some sense, at this early age. He is completely the Essential Self" (p. 266, 278–79). The young child, then, is completely Self-realized, and this enlightened child will then "lose" its Self-realization as the ego develops.

Let us then ask, is this Self-realized child motivated by compassion, or mercy, or selfless service, or tolerance, or benevolence? In fact, as Ali acknowledges, the self at this point is actually extremely egocentric, narcissistic, impulsive, utterly ego-absorbed—in many ways, the antithesis of all things spiritual. Up close and in fine detail, the young child is simply not looking very consciously Self-realized at all.

As a result, Ali begins the retreat from this Romantic confusion by reverting to the traditional Romantic oxymoron: the child is fully Self-realized but is *not conscious* of the Self-realization. "The child is not aware that he is being the Essential Self. He is not conscious of his self-realization" (p. 278). Oxymoron, because "Self-realized" means conscious of the Self; you cannot be unconsciously consciously realized.

To complete the reversion to the old Romantic model, all that is necessary would be for Ali to further claim that the child will then actually *lose the unconscious Self-realization* (an ontological impossibility, but the only route left open for the traditional Romantic agenda). Sure enough: "The perception of vulnerability, limitation and dependency, without the ability to separate these from the experience of the Essential Self, leads to the abandonment of identity with the latter. The child loses his unconscious self-realization" (p. 279).

(Of course, if it's actually unconscious, the loss has already occurred— namely, in prior involution, which Romanticism always confuses with the first steps in evolution.)

But Ali's own analysis shows that the Essential Self is never *actually* experienced by the infant. "There is a true and timeless Self, an Essential Self, a Self that is not constructed in early life" (p. 265)—all very true. "The Essential Self feels like a concentrated presence, a precious and pure presence of consciousness, with the characteristic sense of self. The self of definiteness, singularity, uniqueness and preciousness are lucid and complete. . . . It is a source of pure love and knowledge" (pp. 272, 277).

Does the infant then have all of that as a direct and undistorted experience? No, says Ali, the infant or young child does not. "Clearly, since he is not aware of the Essential Self in an objective way, he cannot but connect this sense of Self to the representation"—that is, the intuition of the Self is applied to the limited and separate bodyself. Ali says that in the infant the *grand* qualities of the Self appear distorted as the *grandiose narcissism* of the infantile self. "The grand qualities belong to the Essential Self, but they become grandiose when attributed to the body and mind. The delusion is in attributing them to the body-mind" (p. 278).

The central question then becomes, is the infant *ever* undistortedly aware of the grand qualities of the true Self, or is it always in touch only with the delusion? Ali answers that the grand qualities of the Essential Self are *always* confused and deluded by the infant self, that it has no choice but to do so. Thus at all times, "these feelings of grandeur and omnipotence are false" (p. 278). It follows that the infant is never undistortedly in touch with the Essential Self per se, but only with confused and deluded intuitions of that Self.

Moreover, it will do no good to say that the infant during the narcissistic (practicing) subphase intuits the Self but misapplies that intuition to its present and limited stage of development, because *all stages of development do exactly that*, in their own specific way (that's the "Atman project": the everpresent intuition of Atman mistakenly identified with the present and limited self).

It follows from Ali's own presentation that, either way, the infant is not undistortedly in touch with any of the grand qualities of the Essential Self—and thus, those grand qualities are not there to be "lost" in the first place. (They are lost in involution, not evolution, and thus their remembering is an emergence in evolution, not an uncovering in evolution.)

What *is* lost during childhood, or what might be lost, are any of the various forms of Essence-at-that-stage. As we put it in our discussion of Washburn, what is lost or repressed by the infant and young child is basically spirit-as-prana, not spirit-as-spirit. Just so, Essence manifests in various forms at each and every stage of its own development and growth (an overall growth that Ali has already agreed is the central axis of development), but any of the aspects of Essence-at-that-stage can be repressed, denied, lost, or distorted. This loss, not of Essence proper but of Essence-at-that-stage, does indeed leave "holes," against which the self will construct further defenses.

These defenses were originally instituted, in my opinion, not because of the actual loss of Essence proper, but because of malformations in the development of the self on the way toward Essence proper. These early defenses are often constructed to ward off dangerous impulses, desires, libidinal drives, élan vital (spirit-as-prana), emotions and feelings, and these defenses more often than not remain firmly in place well into adult development. Thus, as Essence proper (of the psychic level) begins to emerge in consciousness, *these defenses will defend against that as well*. A rigid boundary is a rigid boundary. A wall that keeps out id is a wall that can keep out God as well.

Thus, with regard to spiritual growth, understanding and deconstructing these early defenses is an important endeavor, not because we are then retrieving a pure Essence that was present in infancy but repressed, but because we are dissolving the same blocks that prevent the higher emergence of Essence per se.

Thus, these "holes" are a dual absence, so to speak, sealing out both the lower and the higher. They harbor the submergent as well as the emergent (generated by the embedded self and the embedded-unconscious at any of its stages of development). They are not, however, compensations for a pure Essence present but lost in infancy. As Plotinus used to say, most of our problems involve not a "no" but a "not yet." The holes are in part a "no" said to earlier feelings, emotions, desires, and impulses; but they are also, and most significantly, a "not yet" of Essence proper waiting to be born, a higher state struggling to come down, not an infantile state struggling to come up.

Thus, if one experientially approaches a hole with accepting awareness, one might initially be drawn to the repressed-submergent aspect of that emptiness or lack or absence; one might actually recover a specific memory of the earlier event(s) contributing to the repression or loss. But as that actual loss is negotiated, the emptiness gives way to some form of Emptiness itself, Essence per se, Essence proper, Essence of the psychic or subtle dimension (which was never, as Ali inadvertently demonstrated, directly present in the infantile structure). The hole contains, not simply a repressed past actual, but the emptiness on the edge of a future potential about to emerge in development for the first time. Analyzing the defenses against past actuals helps with the emergence of future potentials because the same defenses screen both (the embedded-unconscious, as we saw, hides both lower and higher from its narrow gaze).

This experiential aspect of the hole is thus not the emptiness of something once present but repressed, but of something new struggling to emerge. The experiential emptiness is a profound yearning for the greater tomorrow, not a lament at the loss of a lesser yesterday.

Ali says that, with enlightened awareness, you can see that the young child is radiating Essence. In fact, with enlightened awareness you can see Essence radiating from dirt; that's not the point. The point is, what is the actual form of Essence that can manifest at any given stage? If the infant *necessarily* experiences Essence as "grandiose," "faulty," "narcissistic," "delusional," and "deformed," then it is most definitely not "Self-realized," and thus development does not consist in its actual loss.

Ali can get caught in these confusions because, in a typical Romantic move, he covertly uses a dual definition of Essence, one horizontal and one vertical, as it were. Discussing the infant of the practicing phase (subphase 1 of fulcrum-2), Ali notes that, according to Margaret Mahler's superb research, the infant is "full of himself." As Mahler puts it, "Narcissism is at its peak!" She goes on to say that "The world is the junior toddler's oyster. . . . The chief characteristic of this practicing period is the child's great narcissistic investment in his own functions, his own body, as well as in the objects and objectives of his expanding 'reality'. . . . He is exhilarated by his own abilities, continually delighted with the discoveries he makes in his expanding world, and quasi-enamored with the world and his own grandeur and omnipotence."

Ali quotes those passages and then excitedly adds that "We could not have described the experience of the Essential Self more eloquently. Mahler here shows her exquisite perception of the manifestations of the true Self" (p. 271).

Actually, Mahler here is describing the subphase from which the narcissistic personality disorders originate. This subphase is actually the height, not of the true Self, but of egocentricity, the precise opposite of the true or essential Self. If this phase of development, just as it is, lasted into adulthood, the result would be a person absolutely incapable of taking the role of other, of showing any concern or care for other human beings or sentient beings in general, a narcissistic monster for whom others are mere extensions of its grandiose self, a person utterly lacking in compassion, love, care and concern. This is the formal opposite of Self-realization, not an "exquisite" example of it.

This is the constant danger in the merely monological approaches, here exemplified by the Diamond Approach. The I-me-mine becomes the central axis of reality, and then *anything* that radiantly shines in that line is actually perceived as "enlightened" or manifesting "Essence." If instead we track developments in all four quadrants (and especially in the Lower-Left or intersubjective domain), we would immediately see how impoverished the infantile awareness is.

Ali points out, correctly I believe, that "The capacity for integration exists on all levels of functioning: physical, mental, emotional, and on the Being level. But since the Being level is the deepest, when it is present it enhances all dimensions of integrative capacity" (p. 171). I agree entirely. There is horizontal integration—any integration of any particular level—and there is the vertical integration of the very highest level—that of Being or Essence per se, which can enhance all types of integration.

But Ali simply tends to confuse these two types of "fullness," and whenever he spots any sort of fullness on any level, he tends to immediately identify it with the Being level, when it usually is nothing but an exuberant horizontal fullness and integration. It is not Essence proper, but simply Essence-at-that-stage.

Thus, referring to the narcissistic and egocentric infant, Ali says that it exists in a state of pure Love and essential Being. "Babies exist in this state of Being a great deal of the time. It is this state that we are perceiving when we see a baby as cute and adorable. This aspect is experienced as a gentle and soft presence that feels fluffy, pure and sweet" (p. 320). But if sweet, cute, adorable, and fluffy are characteristics of pure Love and essential Being, then kittens are totally Self-realized. Again we see the confusion of Essence per se with any merely horizontal "fullness" (or Essence-at-that-stage).

In all of Ali's reversions to the Romantic model, we see the classic and defining Romantic confusion. The Romantics (past and present), to their everlasting credit, were looking for ways to transcend ego and discover Spirit or pure Being or holistic Ground. And in order to discover Being, one must surrender an exclusive identification with the ego or the separate-self sense. That is also what it experientially feels like: you relax the mind and let go of the ego, and more spacious, liberated, open, and spiritual modes of being become available.

So far, so good, and the Romantics made some very profound observations about all that. But then the Romantics made their characteristic mistake: they simply divided the world into Being versus ego. Anything that was ego (or rational, or analytical, or conceptual, or personal, or linear) was viewed as "bad," and *anything else*—anything that lacked ego—was thought to be God, or Ground, or Glory. Ego was sin, Non-ego was Being or Ground or God or Essence.

But the "Non-ego" world actually includes the pre-egoic and the transegoic, the former of which is infantile, the latter of which is highly evolved, and the Romantics simply lumped them both together. The result was most unfortunate. Nobly aiming for the transegoic, the Romantics ended up glorifying anything that was non-egoic, nonconceptual, nonrational—and this often included intensely prerational and preconventional modes: they were regressing in search of their God and Goddess.

Likewise, it was simply assumed that in evolution (whether ontogenetic or phylogenetic), prior to the emergence of the ego there *must* have been Essence, Being, Ground, Eden. Some sort of angels must have walked the earth prior to the nasty emergence of the ego. But developmentally prior to the ego was not angels but apes; and prior to that, worms; and prior to that, ferns; and to that, dirt. The ego was not a Fall down from Ground, but a major step up and toward the actual emergence of Ground as a superconscious state and realization.

In other words, the primordial Fall occurred in involution, not in early evolution. And the ego is not the extreme point of alienation and loss, but halfway back to the Source. The ego is a major increase in Essence, not a major loss of Essence. The glass is half-full, not half-empty.

But all of this was lost on the Romantics, because of their simple notion that "there is either ego or Being" (which opened them to massive pre/trans fallacies). And I mention all of this because, every time Ali regresses from his type-II model to his earlier Romantic/type-I model, he does so precisely under this "Being or ego" notion.

Thus, Ali will divide the world into "ego states" and "Being states," and anything lacking the former must possess the latter. "Being is always there. That it is not a conscious experience indicates the presence of defenses against it" (p. 138). But rocks do not have a conscious experience of Being, and they are *not* defending against it. Again, Plotinus was right on the money: the rock's problem is not a "no" but a "not yet." The rock is not repressing anything. The rock does not have to *undo* its defenses, *uncover* its Essence, and *retrieve* a oneness with it. Rather, in order to consciously realize Essence, the rock will have to grow and evolve into a plant, which will evolve into a horse, which will evolve into an ape, which will evolve into a human, which will take up the Diamond Approach and realize Essence. Not uncovering, but development.

Just so, most of the infantile pre-egoic states are not defending against Essence proper, but simply have not yet grown into a capacity to consciously contain Essence per se. But Ali constantly makes the assumption that there is ego or Being, and thus the pre-egoic states get a massive elevation to Essence proper (as we saw with his glorification of the narcissistic monster of the practicing subphase). His confusion is summarized in his technical statement: "To believe that one's boundaries coincide with the external contours of the body indicates that one has not only cathected [identified with] the body, but also decathected Being" (p. 398).

But that is not so. The choices are not ego or Being. The choices are pre-ego, ego, or Being. And the move from pre-ego to ego (and a cathecting of the body) is a move toward Being, not a move away from it. But once that pre/trans fallacy is made, then every step in the evolution of the self or ego will have to be interpreted as a destruction of Being: the oak is a violation of the acorn. The retro-Romantic slide.

If Ali were presenting a simple Washburn/Romantic/Wilber-I model, as he did in *Essence*, then he could at least be consistent. But, as I pointed out at the beginning of this review, in *The Pearl beyond Price*, Ali moves clearly and decisively to an Aurobindo/Wilber-II model, and he says so in unmistakable terms. But these terms contradict the remnants of his Romantic/type-I model.

Thus, in most of his presentation in *The Pearl beyond Price*, ego development is correctly seen as an increase in Essence, not primarily a loss of Essence. "The ego becomes less defensive as it grows and develops, acquiring more flexibility, pliability, and hence openness to essential [Essence] perceptions" (p. 136). "Of course [Essence] manifests more often as the child grows in years" (p. 159). "So it is one process of evolution from the beginning of ego development to the final stages of spiritual enlightenment" (p. 161). And there is his basic, Aurobindo/Wilber-II type model, with which I am in substantial agreement. (Of course, these can be refined into type-III and -IV models, but that is a secondary issue at this point.)

(As for the "trailing clouds of glory" that are increasingly forgotten as ego development or frontal development gets under way, that psychic/soul awareness will fade *of necessity*. Nothing the ego does, or can do, does or does not do, will stop or prevent that amnesia. In other words, that very specific loss is not due to the ego or to ego development. According to the Tibetans, that loss is foregone; as the Christian mystics put it, the infant is born in sin—it is not born in Essence and then has sin done to it by Mommy. Rather, this is a prior loss instituted in involution, by the separate self's contracting in the face of infinity. That contraction will play itself out right down to the material body in the prenatal period. Since there is *nothing* that can happen in ego development to stop this process, it is nothing that can be blamed on ego development itself. The frontal ego is part of the climb back to a recovery of Source. The ego becomes a "sin" only when it stays beyond its allotted time. That is, the ego is the *hero* from the pre-egoic to egoic leg of development. Only in the postformal and transegoic stages—starting in early adulthood—does the ego become "the problem." But to simply call the ego a "disease" is like calling an acorn a diseased oak. Its problem is not "no" but "not yet.")

I have a few other (but minor) criticisms, which I will briefly mention before turning to a positive assessment of the major strengths of the Diamond Approach.

- By focusing primarily on fulcrum-2 and the early separation-individuation phase of development, Ali tends to ignore or downplay the importance of the other intermediate fulcrums, in both individual and collective modes. By focusing on object relations, all the "major action" seems to be over by age three. But this overlooks the truly crucial fulcrums and developments still to come (especially fulcrums 3, 4, and 5).

- For a similar reason, the Diamond Approach seems to ignore the Piagetian revolution, which taught us that major psychological earthquakes keep occurring quite past age three. One of Piaget's classic experiments, for example, demonstrated that the young child cannot clearly take the role of other until around age six or seven. Genuine love, of course, involves caring and respecting the perspective of another. Ali might not have been so fast to equate the practicing narcissism of age two with Essential Love had he taken Piaget into account.

- Ali might be a little more generous in his recognition of the many transpersonal theorists who preceded him (Washburn, Engler, Alexander, for example). Many of Ali's major tenets were in print a decade or two before him.

That said, I would like to end with an appreciation of the Diamond Approach.

The modern West has made two profound discoveries vis-à-vis the unconscious mind and its relation to psychopathology and psychotherapy. The first runs in a line that starts with Plotinus and reappears in Fichte and Schelling, then Schelling's students Schopenhauer and Nietzsche, and was summarized in Eduard von Hartmann's *Philosophy of the Unconscious* (1869; it went into eight editions in ten years, an unprecedented popularity for an academic work), was brilliantly given clinical and theoretical grounding by Pierre Janet, and was eventually codified by Sigmund Freud. The insight, in its various forms, is simply that the mind can repress the body, that concepts can suppress instincts, that will can smash feelings, and the result of this interior civil war is emotional sickness, neurosis, inner division, and alienation. And the cure, by any name, is *uncovering*: relaxing the repression, recontacting the repressed feeling or emotion or drive, befriending that impulse, and reintegrating it with the self.

This first major discovery, in other words, was of the specific dynamics of fulcrum-3.

The second major discovery is more recent. It is much harder to discern and thus took longer to spot. It was the discovery of the even deeper dynamics of fulcrum-2, the actual process whereby the "protoplasmic" and "material fusion state" differentiates and individuates to produce a cohesive, unified, functional self. In other words, this is the beginning of the development from pre-ego to ego. The dynamic here is not that the ego represses the body, but that there is not yet an ego strong enough to repress much of anything.

The pathology at this early fulcrum therefore involves, not repression, not the Oedipus/Electra complex, not an interior civil war, but the very growth of a cohesive self to begin with. Problems with this fulcrum-2 therefore involve narcissistic personality disorders, borderline pathology, borderline psychosis, and other serious disturbances. Therapy aimed at this deep level does not attempt to *uncover* anything (there is little to uncover because the self is not strong enough to repress in the first place), but instead involves what is called *structure building*, or ways to help the self differentiate from the material fusion state.

This second major discovery runs in a line from Schelling to Jung (and his notion of individuation), but awaited the more precise theory and research of Edith Jacobson, D. W. Winnicott, Heinz Kohut, Otto Kernberg, and Margaret Mahler (to name a prominent few). It has revolutionized our understanding of the early development of the Upper-Left quadrant, and in its own way is every bit as groundbreaking as the first line leading to Freud and an understanding of fulcrum-3.

In Wilber-III, I included extensive references to this pioneering work, and indicated how absolutely crucial I felt it to be, not just for understanding ego development, but for the continuation of that development into postformal and spiritual domains. And yet, alas, apart from such important exceptions as Jack Engler, very little work has been done to integrate these pioneering insights with methods of spiritual development.

That is where the Diamond Approach excels, in my opinion. Hameed Ali (particularly in his "Ali-II" model in *The Pearl beyond Price*) has succeeded in powerfully utilizing the findings about fulcrum-2 to help individuals move into postformal and post-postconventional development. In my opinion, his understanding is precise, extensive, and accurate; and his use of this understanding to open access to the transpersonal domains is superb and in many ways unprecedented.

Ali has several stages of growth beyond the discovery of Personal Essence (but they all remain appropriately grounded in Personal Essence). These higher stages include Personal Essence proper, the discovery of which leads to realms beyond the personal, roughly in this general order: the impersonal Witness, cosmic consciousness, then pure Being manifested as dual unity with Personal Essence via Love; then Absence (or cessation), a Void within which Loving Presence spontaneously arises and takes the form of Personal Essence; the Nameless, nondual with Personal Essence in all realms; and the Absolute (which still spontaneously manifests as Personal Essence for appropriate, spontaneous functioning).

There is no indication in the writings of the Diamond Approach that subject permanence is achieved (which is a hallmark of stable causal-level adaptation); nor that permanent lucid dreaming constancy is reached (a hallmark of stable subtle-level adaptation). The Diamond Approach, in other words, seems to remain grounded in psychic-level adaptation, even as it powerfully intuits higher domains. This, nonetheless, is an extraordinary achievement, and certainly ranks it as one of the premiere transformative technologies now available on any sort of widespread scale.

The Pearl beyond Price is one of the truly great and pioneering books of the East/West dialogue. The criticisms that I have raised are all in the context of much admiration. It remains to be seen, of course, just what fate our culture will deal a postformal and post-postconventional approach. Historically—and in almost any country—postformal consciousness has been crucified. Once a group, grounded in such, starts to become "popular" and "noticed," a whole host of background cultural forces swing into play, even in pluralistic, tolerant societies that share the values of the Western enlightenment. It is thus with the very best wishes and encouragement, and slight trepidation, that I watch the future unfolding of the Diamond Approach.

12. This entire section is one summary of the Wilber-IV model, which is the model presented in *Sex, Ecology, Spirituality*; *A Brief History of Everything*; and this book. The Wilber-III aspects in this model are virtually unchanged, but they are set in a context ("all-quadrant, all-level") that renders their constitutive elements more visible. Neither consciousness, personality, individual agency, nor psychopathology can be located simply or solely in the individual organism.

The subjective domain is always already embedded in intersubjective, objective, and interobjective realities, all of which are partly constitutive of subjective agency and its pathologies: thus the shift from Wilber-III to Wilber-IV.

13. [A more complete version of this endnote is the article "An Integral Theory of Consciousness," contained in this volume.]

The Left-Hand dimensions are the realm of interior consciousness, it is true; but the Right-Hand domains are the exterior forms of consciousness, without which the interior forms do not, and cannot, exist. As for the "location" of consciousness, and for those who read chapters 4 and 5, it amounts to the same thing to say—and I do say—that manifest consciousness is "located" in exactly the same place art is.

In other words, the Upper-Left quadrant is simply the functional locus of a distributed phenomenon. Consciousness is not located inside the brain, nor outside the brain either: those are physical boundaries with simple location, and yet a good part of consciousness exists not merely in physical space but in emotional spaces, mental spaces, and spiritual spaces, none of which have simple location, and yet all of which are as real as (or more real than) simple physical space.

That is why we say that manifest consciousness is distributed across all quadrants with all their levels and lines. The Right-Hand domains all have simple location (location in physical spacetime) and can be "pointed to" with your finger; but the Left-Hand domains are located in spaces of intention, not spaces of extension, and so you cannot put your physical finger on them. And yet consciousness is anchored in those intentional spaces every bit as much as in the extensional spaces, whether those extensional spaces are of the external world or of the nervous system or anything in between. The Right Hand reductionists (subtle reductionists) attempt to reduce intentional spaces to extensional spaces and then "locate" consciousness in a *hierarchical network of physically extended emergents* (atoms to molecules to cells to nervous system to brain), and that, I believe, will never work. It gives us, more or less, only half the story (the Right-Hand half).

David Chalmers (1995) recently caused a sensation by having his essay "The Puzzle of Conscious Experience" published by *Scientific American*, bastion of physicalist science. Chalmers's conclusion was that subjective consciousness continues to defy all objectivist explanations. "Toward this end, I propose that conscious experience be considered a fundamental feature, irreducible to anything more basic. The idea may seem strange at first, but consistency seems to demand it" (p. 83).

Chalmers makes a series of good points. The first is the irreducibility of consciousness, which has to be "added" to the physical world in order to give a complete account of the universe. "Thus, a complete theory will have two components: physical laws, telling us about the behavior of physical systems from the infinitesimal to the cosmological, and what we might call psychophysical laws, telling us how some of those systems are associated with conscious experience. These two components will constitute a true theory of everything" (p. 83).

This attempt to reintroduce both Left- and Right-Hand domains to the Kosmos has been considered quite bold, a testament to the power of reductionism against which so obvious a statement seems radical. Chalmers moves toward a formulation: "Perhaps information has two basic aspects: a physical one and an experiential one. . . . Wherever we find conscious experience, it exists as one aspect of an information state, the other aspect of which is embedded in a physical process in the brain" (p. 85). That is, each state has an interior/intentional and exterior/physical aspect. My view, of course, is that all holons have not just those two, but rather four, fundamental and irreducible aspects, so that every "information state" actually and simultaneously has an intentional, behavioral, cultural, and social aspect. An "all-quadrant, all-level" view is much closer to a theory of everything, if such even makes any sense.

Chalmers goes on to point out that all of the physicalist and reductionist approaches to consciousness (including Daniel Dennett's and Francis Crick's) only solve what Chalmers calls "the easy problems" (such as objective integration in brain processes), leaving the central mystery of consciousness untouched. He is quite right, I believe. The funny thing is, all of the physicalist scientists who are sitting there and reading Chalmers's essay are already fully in touch with the mystery: they are already directly in touch with their lived experience, immediate awareness, and basic consciousness. But instead of directly investigating that stream (with, say, vipassana), they sit there, reading Chalmers's essay, and attempt to understand their own consciousness by objectifying it in terms of digital bits in neuronal networks, or connectionist pathways hierarchically summating in the joy of seeing a sunrise—and when none of those really seem to explain anything, they scratch their heads and wonder why the mystery of consciousness just refuses to be solved.

Chalmers says that "the hard problem" is "the question of how physical processes in the brain give rise to subjective experience"—that is, how physical and mental interact. This is still the Cartesian question, and it is no closer to being solved today than it was in Descartes's time, and for a simple reason: it is a dilemma that is solved only in the postformal realms. (See chapter 3 for an extended discussion of this theme [see also *Integral Psychology*, chap. 14, for an extended discussion of the mind-body problem].)

For example, in the simple hierarchy physical matter, sensation, perception, impulse, image, symbol . . . , there is an *explanatory gap* between matter and sensation that has not yet been satisfactorily bridged—not by neuroscience, nor cognitive science, nor neuropsychology, nor phenomenology, nor systems theory. As David Joravsky put it (in his review of Richard Gregory's *Mind in Science: A History of Explanations in Psychology and Physics*), "Seeing is broken down into component processes: *light*, which is physical; excitation in the neural network of eye and brain, which is also physical; *sensation*, which is subjective and resists analysis in strictly physical terms; and *perception*, which involves cognitive inference from sensation and is thus even less susceptible to strictly physical analysis." Gregory himself poses the question, "How is sensation related to neural activity?" and then summarizes the precise state-of-the-art knowledge in this area: "Unfortunately, we do not know." The reason, he says, is that there is "an irreducible gap between physics and sensation which physiology cannot bridge"—what he calls "an impassable gulf between our two realms." Between, that is, the Left and Right halves of the Kosmos.

But, of course, it is not actually an impassable gulf: you see the physical world right now, so the gulf is bridged. The question is, how? And the answer, as I suggested in chapter 3, only discloses itself to postformal awareness. The "impassable gulf" is simply another name for the subject/object dualism, which is the hallmark not of Descartes's error but of all manifestation, which Descartes simply happened to spot with unusual clarity. It is still with us, this gap, and it remains the mystery hidden in the heart of samsara, a mystery that absolutely refuses to yield its secrets to anything less than post-postconventional development.

I have repeatedly had people explain to me that the Cartesian dualism can be solved by simply understanding that . . . and they then tell me their solutions, which range from Gaia-centric theories to neutral monism to first-third person interactionism to systems theory. I always respond, "So this means that you have overcome the subject-object dualism in your own case. This means that you directly realize that you are one with the entire Kosmos, and this nondual awareness persists through waking, dream, and deep sleep states. Is that right?" "Well, no, not really."

The solution to the subject-dualism is not found in thought, because thought itself is a product of this dualism, which itself is generated in the very roots of the causal realm and cannot be undone without consciously penetrating that realm. The causal knot or primordial self-contraction—the ahamkara—can only be uprooted when it is brought into consciousness and melted in the fires of pure awareness, which almost always requires profound contemplative/meditative training. The subject-object duality is the very *form* of the manifest world of maya—the very beginning of the four quadrants (subject and object divide into singular and plural forms)—and thus one can get "behind" or "under" this dualism only by immersion in the *formless* realm (cessation, nirvikalpa, ayn, nirvana), which acts to dissolve the self-contraction and release it into pure nondual awareness—at which point, the traditions (from Zen to Eckhart) agree, you indeed realize that you are one with the entire Kosmos, a nondual awareness that persists through waking, dream, and deep sleep states: you have finally undone the Cartesian dualism.

As we will see below, the methodology of an integral theory of consciousness would thus have to include two broad wings: one is the simultaneous tracking of the various levels and lines in each of the quadrants, and then noting their correlations, each to all the others, and in no way trying to reduce any to the others.

The other is the *interior transformation of the researchers themselves.* This is the real reason, I suspect, that the Left-Hand dimensions of immediate consciousness have been so intensely ignored and aggressively devalued. Any Right-Hand path of knowledge can be engaged without a demand for interior transformation; one merely learns a new translation. (More specifically, most researchers have already, in the process of growing up, transformed to formop or vision-logic, and no higher transformations are required for empiric-analytic or systems theory investigations.)

But the Left-Hand paths demand, at some point, transformations of consciousness in the researchers themselves. You can master 100 percent of quantum physics without transforming consciousness, but you cannot in any fashion master Zen without doing so. You do not have to transform to understand Dennett's *Consciousness Explained*; you merely translate. But you must transform to actually understand Plotinus's *Enneads*. You are already adequate to Dennett, because you both have already transformed to rationality, and thus the *referents* of Dennett's sentences can be easily seen by you (whether or not you agree, you can at least see what he is referring to, because his referents exist in the rational worldspace, plain as day).

But if you have not transformed to (or at least strongly glimpsed) the causal and nondual realms, you will not be able to see the referents of Plotinus's sentences. They will make no sense to you. You will think Plotinus is "seeing things"—and he is, and so could you and I, if we both transform to those worldspaces, whereupon the referents of Plotinus's sentences, referents that exist in the causal and nondual worldspaces, become plain as day. And that transformation, it seems to me, is an absolutely unavoidable part of the paradigm (the injunction) of an integral approach to consciousness.

So those two wings—the "simultracking" of all quadrants and the transformation of researchers themselves—are both necessary for an integral approach to consciousness.

Thus, I do not mean for an integral theory of consciousness to be an eclecticism of the dozen or so major approaches I summarized in the text, but rather a tightly integrated approach that follows intrinsically from the holonic nature of the Kosmos.

The methodology of an integral approach to consciousness is obviously complex, but it follows some of the simple guidelines we have already outlined: three strands, four validity claims, ten levels of each. To briefly review:

The three strands operative in all valid knowledge are injunction, apprehension, confirmation (or exemplar, evidence, confirmation/rejection; or instrumental, data, fallibilism). These three strands operate in the generation of all valid knowledge—on any level, in any quadrant, or so I maintain.

But each quadrant has a different architecture and thus a *different type of validity claim* through which the three strands operate: propositional truth (Upper Right), subjective truthfulness (Upper Left), cultural meaning (Lower Left), and functional fit (Lower Right).

Further, there are nine or ten major levels of development in each of those quadrants, and thus the knowledge quest takes on different forms as we move through those various levels. The three strands and four claims are still fully operating in each case, but the specific contours vary.

Take, as an example, a specific researcher, whose individual consciousness is the Upper-Left quadrant, itself a spectrum of nine or ten levels, which we have sometimes summarized as matter, body, mind, soul, and spirit. As we saw in chapter 3, we can further simplify that as body, mind, and spirit, which is the traditional "three eyes" of knowing: the eye of flesh, the eye of mind, and the eye of contemplation. (This is just a simplification, and all of the points I am about to make apply across all ten levels, not just the simplified three.)

Now the eye of mind itself can, as it were, look up, look down, or look sideways. That is, the mind (reason and vision-logic) can accept data from the senses, data from the mind itself, or data from contemplation. In the first we get empiric-analytic knowledge (i.e., symbolic knowledge of presymbolic forms, whose referents exist in the sensorimotor worldspace); in the second we get hermeneutic, phenomenological, and mathematical knowledge (symbolic knowledge of symbolic forms, whose referents exist in the mental and formal worldspaces); and in the third we get mandalic sciences (symbolic maps of trans-symbolic occasions, whose referents exist in the postformal worldspaces).

All of those different modes of knowing (at all ten levels) nonetheless follow the three strands of valid knowledge accumulation, and thus each of them is anchored in a genuine and justifiable epistemology. (For an extended discussion of this theme, see chapter 3.)

The three strands, four claims, and ten levels thus present us with a fairly comprehensive methodology of knowledge acquisition, and this relates directly to an integral theory of consciousness. I'll run through some of the major approaches mentioned in the text and very briefly indicate what is involved.

The *emergent/connectionist* cognitive science models (such as Alwyn Scott's *Stairway to the Mind*) apply the three strands of knowledge accumulation to the Upper-Right quadrant, the objective aspects of individual holons. Statements about these are guided by the validity claim of propositional truth tied to empirically observable events, which means that in this approach the three strands will acknowledge only those holons that register in the sensorimotor worldspace (i.e., holons with simple location, empirically observable by the senses or their extensions). Nonetheless, all holons are holarchic, or composed of hierarchical holons within holons indefinitely, and so this emergent/connectionist approach will apply the three strands to objective, exterior, hierarchical systems as they appear in the individual, objective organism (the Upper-Right quadrant).

All of this is fine, right up to the point where these approaches overstep their epistemic warrant and try to account for the other quadrants solely in terms of their own. In the case of the emergent/connectionist theories, this means that they will present a valid Upper-Right hierarchy (atoms to molecules to cells to neural pathways to reptilian stem to limbic system to neocortex), but then consciousness is somehow supposed to miraculously jump out at the top level (the Left-Hand dimensions are treated as a monolithic and monological single entity, and then this "consciousness" is simply added on top of the Right-Hand hierarchy, instead of seeing that there are levels of consciousness which exist as the interior or Left-Hand dimension of every step in the Right-Hand hierarchy).

Thus, Scott presents a standard Upper-Right hierarchy, which he gives as atoms, molecules, biochemical structures, nerve impulses, neurons, assemblies of neurons, brain. Then, and only then, out pops "consciousness and culture," his two highest levels. But it appears that consciousness and culture are not levels in the Upper-Right quadrant, but significantly different quadrants each of which has a correlative hierarchy of its own developmental unfolding (and each of which is intimately interwoven with the Upper Right, but can in no way be reduced to or explained by the Upper Right). So in an integral theory of consciousness, we would include the Upper-Right hierarchy and those aspects of the emergent/connectionist models that legitimately reflect that territory; but where those theories overstep their epistemic warrant (and are thus reduced to reductionism), we might move on.

The various schools of *introspectionism* take as their basic referent the interior intentionality of consciousness, the immediate lived experience and life-world of the individual (the Upper-Left quadrant). This means that, in these approaches, the three strands of valid knowledge are applied to the data of immediate consciousness, under the auspices of the validity claim of truthfulness (because interior reporting requires sincere reports: there is no other way to get at the interiors). Introspectionism is intimately related to interpretation (hermeneutics), because most of the contents of consciousness are referential and intentional, and thus their meaning requires interpretation: What is the meaning of this sentence? of last night's dream? of *War and Peace*?

As we have seen (introduction, chapters 3, 4, 5), all valid interpretation follows the three strands (injunction, apprehension, confirmation). In this case, the three strands are being applied to symbolic/referential occasions and not merely to sensorimotor occasions (which would yield only empiric-analytic knowledge). As everybody knows, this interpretive and dialogical knowledge is trickier, more delicate, and more subtle than the head-banging obviousness of the monological gaze, but that doesn't mean it is less important (in fact, it means it is more significant).

The introspective/interpretative approaches (from depth psychology to phenomenology to contemplation) thus give us the *interior contours of individual consciousness*: the three strands legitimately applied to the interior of individual holons under the auspices of truthfulness. This exploration and elucidation of the Upper-Left quadrant is an important facet of an integral approach to consciousness.

Developmental psychology goes one step further and inspects the stages of the unfolding of this individual consciousness. Since it usually aspires to a more scientific status, developmental psychology often combines an examination of the interior or Left-Hand reports of experience (the *semantics* of consciousness, guided by interpretative truthfulness and intersubjective understanding) with a Right-Hand or objective analysis of the structures of consciousness (the *syntax* of consciousness, guided by propositional truth and functional fit). This *developmental structuralism* traces most of its lineage to the Piaget revolution; it seems an indispensable tool in the elucidation of consciousness and an important aspect of any integral approach. (It is rare, however, that these approaches clearly combine both the semantics and syntax of the stages of consciousness development, which is a pragmatic integration I am especially attempting to include.)

Eastern and nonordinary states models point out that there are more things in the Upper-Left quadrant than are dreamt of in our philosophy, not to mention our conventional psychologies. The three strands of valid knowledge are here applied to states that are largely nonverbal, postformal, and post-postconventional. In Zen, for example, we have a primary injunction or paradigm (zazen, sitting meditation), which yields experiential data (kensho, satori), which are then thrown against the community of those who have completed the first two strands and tested for fallibility. Bad data are soundly rejected, and all of this is open to ongoing review and revision in light of subsequent experience and further communally generated data. These approaches are quite right: no theory of consciousness can hope to be complete that ignores the data from the higher or deeper dimensions of consciousness itself, and this exploration of the further reaches of the Upper-Left quadrant is a central aspect of an integral theory of consciousness.

Advocates of *subtle energies* (prana, bioenergy) bring an important piece of the puzzle to this investigation, but they often seem to believe that these subtle energies are the central or even sole aspect of consciousness, whereas they are merely one of the dimensions in the overall spectrum itself (prana is sometimes subdivided into astral and etheric energies, but all of them are lower to intermediate levels).

For the Great Chain theorists, East and West, prana is the link between the material body and the mental domain (see chapter 1), and in a sense I believe that is true enough. But the whole point of a four-quadrant analysis is that what the traditions tended to represent as disembodied, transcendental, and nonmaterial modes actually have correlates in the material domain (every Left-Hand occasion has a Right-Hand correlate), and thus it is much more accurate to speak of the physical bodymind, the emotional bodymind, the mental bodymind, and so on. This simultaneously allows transcendental occasions and firmly grounds them. And in this conception, prana is simply the emotional bodymind in general, with correlates in all four quadrants (subjective: proto-emotions; objective: limbic system; intersubjective: magical; interobjective: tribal).

The investigation of these subtler pranic energies is hampered, of course, by the fact that, as a "step up" from the physical dimension, they cannot be empirically perceived in the sensorimotor worldspace (they exist in the emotional worldspace, and can be easily seen there—for example, any time you get angry, happy, or hungry; and these can be intersubjectively shared and confirmed, following the three strands). Moreover, the objective aspects of these energies are likewise open to investigation, first, in the standard empirical studies of the brain and limbic system using everything from PET to EEG (the three strands applied to the empirical correlates); and second, in the somewhat more delicate attempt to detect their field influences on the denser material domain, also following the three demands of instrumental, data, confirmation (e.g., by researchers from Tiller to Motoyama; see Murphy [1992] for an outstanding overview). What is not helpful, however, is to claim that these energies alone hold the key to consciousness.

Likewise with the *psi approaches*, which are clearly some of the more controversial aspects of consciousness studies (telepathy, precognition, psychokinesis, clairvoyance). I believe that the existence of some types of psychic phenomena is now beyond serious dispute. I have discussed this in the book *Eye to Eye* (along with the application of the three strands to psi events), and I won't repeat my observations here. I would simply like to emphasize that, once it is realized that the sensorimotor worldspace is merely one of at least ten worldspaces (the ten or so basic waves of existence from matter to body to mind to soul to spirit), we are released from the impossibility of trying to account for all phenomena on the basis of empirical occasions alone. At the same time, precisely because the sensorimotor worldspace is the anchor of the worldview of scientific materialism, as soon as some sort of proof of non-sensorimotor occasions (such as psi) is found, it can be excitedly blown all out of proportion. Psi events indeed cannot be unequivocally located in the sensorimotor worldspace, but then neither can logic, mathematics, poetry, history, meaning, value, or morals, and so what? There is still substantial evidence that some psi phenomena exist, and if there can be found no sensorimotor explanation, the conclusion is *not* that psi do not exist, but that we must look to other worldspaces for the phenomenology of their operation. I believe that any integral theory of consciousness would take seriously these phenomena and the substantial evidence of their existence.

Of the dozen or so major approaches to consciousness studies that I listed in the text, the *quantum approaches* are the only ones that I believe lack substantial evidence at this time, and when I say that they can be included in an integral theory of consciousness, I am simply holding open the possibility that they may eventually prove worthwhile. In *Eye to Eye* I review the various interpretations of quantum mechanics and its possible role in consciousness studies, and I will not repeat that discussion, except to say that to date the theoretical conclusions (such as that intentionality collapses the wave function) are based on extremely speculative notions that most physicists themselves find dubious.

The central problem with these approaches, as I see it, is that they are trying to solve the subject/object dualism on a level at which it cannot be solved; as I suggested above, that problem is (dis)solved only in *postformal* development, and no amount of *formal* propositions will come near the solution. Nonetheless, this is still a fruitful line of research, if for no other reason than what it demonstrates in its failures; and more positively, it might help to elucidate some of the interactions between biological intentionality and matter.

All of those approaches center on the individual. But the *cultural approaches* to consciousness point out that individual consciousness does not, and cannot, arise on its own. All subjective events are always already intersubjective events. There is no private language; there is no autonomous consciousness (short of spirit-as-spirit, which isn't individual anyway). The very words we are both now sharing were not invented by you or me, were not created by you or me, do not come solely from my consciousness or from yours. Rather, you and I simply find ourselves in a vast intersubjective worldspace in which we live and move and have our being. This cultural worldspace (the Lower-Left quadrant) has a hand in the very structure, shape, feel, and tone of your consciousness and of mine, and no theory of consciousness seems complete that ignores this crucial dimension.

In these cultural approaches, the three strands are applied to the intersubjective circle itself, the deep semantics of the worlds of meaning in which you and I collectively exist. These cultural worldspaces evolve and develop (archaic to magic to mythic to mental, etc.), and the three strands applied to those worldspaces, under the auspices of mutual understanding and appropriateness, reveal those *cultural contours of consciousness*, which is exactly the course these important approaches take. This, too, seems to be a crucial component of an integral theory of consciousness.

Likewise for the *social sciences*: the materialities of communication, the techno-economic base, and the social system in the objective sense also reach deep into the contours of consciousness to mold the final product. The three strands, under the auspices of propositional truth and functional fit, yield these social determinants at each of their levels. A narrow Marxist approach, of course, has long been discredited (precisely because it oversteps its warrant, reducing all quadrants to the Lower Right); but the moment of truth in historical materialism is that the modes of production have a profound and constitutive influence on the actual forms and contents of individual consciousness, and thus an understanding of these social determinants seems crucial for an integral theory of consciousness.

I hope that this outline, abbreviated as it is, is nonetheless enough to indicate the broad contours of a methodology of an integral theory of consciousness, and that it sufficiently indicates the inadequacy of any approaches less comprehensive. The *integral* aspect enters in simultaneously tracking each level and quadrant in its own terms and then noting the correlations between them. This is a methodology of phenomenologically and contemporaneously tracking the various levels and lines in each of the quadrants and then correlating their overall relations, each to all the others, and in no way trying to reduce any to the others.

Thus, as I mentioned above, an integral approach to consciousness has two broad wings: one is the "simultracking" of events in "all-quadrant, all-level" space; the other is the interior transformation of the researchers themselves. (This is the integral model that I have also been referring to as Wilber-IV.) And each of the dozen or so approaches that I listed in the text finds an important and indispensable place, not as an eclecticism, but as an intrinsic aspect of the holonic Kosmos. For an extended discussion of these themes, see Wilber, "An Integral Theory of Consciousness," in *Journal of Conscious Studies* 4, no. 1 (1997), pp. 71–92 [contained in this volume].

14. 1989, p. 173.

15. 1994, p. ix, his italics.
16. McDermott chastises me for several polemical endnotes in SES. For various reasons I did indeed decide that a certain polemical stance was required in a few cases. After consultation with several editors, publishers, and colleagues, I decided to include several endnotes with a polemical/humorous tone, sharply critical of perhaps nine or ten theorists (out of several hundred discussed). These theorists themselves often use polemical, and in some cases even vitriolic, prose. They aggressively condemn entire cultures and civilizations, or engage in unrelenting male bashing, or declare, without irony, that they alone boast the new paradigm. Those who disagree with them are often viciously dismissed. I simply chose in these endnotes to address their arguments by using a bit of their own polemical medicine.

   Specifically, from each of the dozen or so movements that are, in my opinion, particularly regressive or flatland—or that are merely Descended or merely Ascended—I chose one or two typical representatives. These fractious movements include some of the merely Descended aspects of ecofeminism, deep ecology, ecoholism, and eco-primitivism; some of the regressive aspects of Jungian, archetypal, and mythopoetic movements; astrology and astro-logic as mythic-membership; monological physics equals mysticism; monological systems theory; positivism; and merely Ascended gnosticism (East and West).

   I chose a representative example from each and responded polemically. McDermott laments this; I consider it an integral part of the book, without which it would have abdicated its duty. At the same time, I am more than willing to meet any of these theorists in dialogue, as witness the three-volume *ReVision Journal* discussion. *Sex, Ecology, Spirituality* has become a focal point for just this discussion, and the good in all this, as I see it, is that indeed the conversation has been jolted into high gear. This has also forced certain theorists to actually show their cards. McDermott opines that the tone of these endnotes has hindered the conversation, whereas exactly the opposite is the case. People have been galvanized, both for and against, pro and con, and this is a profound good, it seems to me.

Chapter 12: Always Already

1. Kunsang, 1986.
2. Most Nondual schools trace several stages of post-Nirvanic development leading to nondual Enlightenment, and then several stages of post-Enlightenment development, as ever-present awareness realigns the entire bodymind top down (rather like building a suspension bridge). Here is a typical classification of the post-Nirvanic and post-Enlightenment waves of development (I believe there is sufficient evidence for each of these waves to be included in an integral model):

   We start at the point of nirvana itself. Classical nirvana is permanent access to nirvikalpa samadhi or cessation—that is, to the pure, causal, formless, unmanifest realm (nirodh, nirvikalpa, nirvana: the prefix *nir* in each case means "without" or "absent" or "cessation"). But the Nondual schools claim this is actually a *conditional* state, set apart as it is from the entire realm of manifestation. This is why, for example, the state of conditional nirvikalpa samadhi is merely the eighth of the ten Zen ox-herding pictures depicting post-postconventional development (the eighth picture is an empty circle, "nir").

Beyond conditional nirvikalpa samadhi, the various Nondual traditions describe a series of stages or waves of development, leading eventually to a continuous and spontaneous recognition of the always already state (namely, the intrinsic, brilliant, simple, naked, ever-present awareness itself), a spontaneous and continuous recognition often referred to as sahaj samadhi.

These post-Nirvana developments move from conditional nirvikalpa samadhi to sahaj samadhi, usually in a series of three or so major waves, including (1) the recognition of subject permanence (continuous recognition through waking, dream, and deep sleep states); (2) the uprooting of the very subtlest of the subject-object tensions that surround the causal Heart and hold the separate-self sense in place; so that (3) the last remnants of dualism are illumined by ever-present awareness; and (4) the nondual state of sahaj is effortlessly recognized under all changes of state.

Sahaj itself is "nondual Enlightenment," beyond which lie the post-Enlightenment developments or waves leading to bhava samadhi, or the outshining and transfiguration of the entire manifest and unmanifest worlds. These post-Enlightenment developments are the events that unfold in the space of sahaj, in the nondual space of simple, ever-present awareness, once the bodymind is self-liberated from the tortures of the self-contraction; that is, once it is recognized that the self-contraction does not exist, never did exist, and never will exist. Under that realization, the bodymind is transfigured into its own primordial condition, the naked luminosity that is its own remark, self-evidently, eternally.

Bibliography

Alexander, C., and E. Langer, eds. 1990. *Higher stages of human development*. New York: Oxford Univ. Press.

Alexander, C., et al. 1990. Growth of higher stages of consciousness: Maharishi's Vedic psychology of human development. In Alexander and Langer (eds.), 1990.

Almaas, A. H. 1986. *Essence*. York Beach, Maine: Weiser.

———. 1988. *The pearl beyond price*. Berkeley: Diamond.

Anthony, D.; B. Ecker; and K. Wilber, eds. 1987. *Spiritual choices*. New York: Paragon.

Apel, K. 1994. *Selected essays*, vol. 1. New Jersey: Humanities.

Arieti, S. 1976. *The intrapsychic self*. New York: Basic Books.

Aristotle. 1984. *The complete works of Aristotle*, vols. 1 and 2, ed. by J. Barnes. Princeton: Princeton Univ. Press.

Arlin, P. 1975. Cognitive development in adulthood: A fifth stage? *Developmental Psychology* 11: 602–606.

———. 1990. Wisdom: the art of problem finding. In Sternberg (ed.), 1990.

Assagioli, R. 1965. *Psychosynthesis*. New York: Viking.

Aurobindo. n.d. *The life divine* and *The synthesis of yoga*. Pondicherry: Centenary Library, XVIII–XXI.

Austin, J. L. 1962. *How to do things with words*. Cambridge: Harvard Univ. Press.

———. 1979 (1961). *Philosophical papers*. Oxford: Oxford Univ. Press.

Barthes, R. 1982. *A Barthes reader*. Ed. by S. Sontag. New York: Hill and Wang.

Basseches, M. 1984. *Dialectical thinking and adult development*. Norwood, N.J.: Ablex Press.

Bataille, G. 1985. *Visions of excess*. Minneapolis: Univ. of Minnesota Press.

Bertalanffy, L. von. 1968. *General system theory*. New York: Braziller.

Birch, C., and J. Cobb. 1990. *The liberation of life*. Denton, Tex.: Environmental Ethics Books.

Bohm, D. 1973. *Wholeness and the implicate order*. London: Routledge.

Boorstein, S., ed. 1980. *Transpersonal psychotherapy*. Palo Alto, Calif.: Science and Behavior Books.

Broughton, J. 1975. The development of natural epistemology in adolescence and early adulthood. Doctoral dissertation, Harvard.

Brown, D. P. 1977. A model for the levels of concentrative meditation. *International J. Clinical and Experimental Hypnosis* 25: 236–73.

———. 1981. Mahamudra meditation: Stages and contemporary cognitive psychology. Doctoral dissertation, University of Chicago.

Brown, D. P., and J. Engler. 1980. The stages of mindfulness meditation: A valida-tion study. *J. Transpersonal Psychology* 12(2): 143–92.

Brown, L., and C. Gilligan. 1992. *Meeting at the crossroads*. New York: Ballantine.

Brown, N. O. 1959. *Life against death*. Middletown, Conn.: Wesleyan Univ. Press.

Bruner, J. 1983. *In search of mind*. New York: Harper and Row.

———. 1986. *Actual minds, possible worlds*. Cambridge: Harvard Univ. Press.

Buddhaghosa, B. 1976. *The path of purification*. 2 vols. Boulder: Shambhala.

Chafetz, J. 1984. *Sex and advantage*. Totowa, N.J.: Rowman and Alanheld.

———. 1990. *Gender equity*. Newbury Park, Calif.: Sage.

Chalmers, D. 1995. The puzzle of conscious experience. *Scientific American*, Decem-ber 1995.

Chaudhuri, H. 1981. *Integral yoga*. Wheaton, Ill.: Quest Books.

Commons, M.; C. Armon; L. Kohlberg; F. Richards; T. Grotzer; and J. Sinnott eds. 1990. *Adult development*, vol. 2, *Models and methods in the study of adult and adolescent thought*. New York: Praeger.

Commons, M.; F. Richards; and C. Armon. 1984. *Beyond formal operations*. New York: Praeger.

Commons, M.; J. Sinnott; F. Richards; and C. Armon eds. 1989. *Adult develop-ment*, vol. 1, *Comparisons and applications of adolescent and adult develop-mental models*. New York: Praeger.

Cook-Greuter, S. 1990. Maps for living. *Adult Development 2*.

Coomaraswamy, A. 1943. *Hinduism and Buddhism*. New York: Philosophical Li-brary.

Cowan, P. 1978. *Piaget with feeling*. New York: Holt.

Crews, F. 1975. *Out of my system: Psychoanalysis, ideology, and critical method*. New York: Oxford Univ. Press.

Culler, J. 1982. *On deconstruction*. Ithaca, N.Y.: Cornell Univ. Press.

de Man, P. 1971. *Blindness and insight*. New York: Oxford Univ. Press.

Dennett, D. 1991. *Consciousness explained*. Boston: Little, Brown.

Derrida, J. 1976. *Of grammatology*. Baltimore: Johns Hopkins.

———. 1978. *Writing and difference*. Chicago: Univ. of Chicago Press.

———. 1981. *Positions*. Chicago: Univ. of Chicago Press.

———. 1982. *Margins of philosophy*. Chicago: Univ. of Chicago Press.

Dewey, J. 1981. *The philosophy of John Dewey*. Ed. by J. McDermott, Chicago: Univ. of Chicago Press.

Douglas, M. 1982. *In the active voice*. London: Routledge.

Dreyfus, H., and P. Rabinow, 1983. *Michel Foucault: Beyond structuralism and hermeneutics*. Chicago: Univ. of Chicago Press.

Eccles, J. 1984. *The human mystery*. London: Routledge.

———. 1994. *How the self controls its brain*. Berlin: Springer-Verlag.

Edinger, E. 1992. *Ego and archetype*. Boston: Shambhala.

Eisler, R. 1987. *The chalice and the blade*. San Francisco: Harper.

Emerson, R. W. 1969. *Selected prose and poetry*. San Francisco: Rinehart Press.

Engler, J. 1984. Therapeutic aims in psychotherapy and meditation: Developmental stages in the representation of self. *J. Transpersonal Psychology* 16(1): 25–61.

Fischer, K.; S. Kenny; and S. Pipp. 1990. How cognitive processes and environmental conditions organize discontinuities in the development of abstractions. In Alexander et al., 1990, pp. 162–190.

Fish, S. 1980. *Is there a text in this class?* Cambridge: Harvard Univ. Press.

Flavell, J. 1963. *The developmental psychology of Jean Piaget.* Princeton, N.J.: Van Nostrand.

Flavell, J.; P. Miller; and S. Miller. 1993. *Cognitive development.* Englewood Cliffs, N.J.: Prentice-Hall.

Forman, R., ed. 1990. *The problem of pure consciousness.* New York: Oxford Univ. Press.

Foucault, M. 1970. *The order of things.* New York: Random House.

———. 1972. *The archaeology of knowledge.* New York: Random House.

———. 1975. *The birth of the clinic.* New York: Random House.

———. 1978. *The history of sexuality.* Vol. 1. New York: Random House.

———. 1979. *Discipline and punish.* New York: Vintage.

———. 1980. *Power/knowledge.* New York: Pantheon.

Fowler, J. 1981. *Stages of faith: The psychology of human development and the quest for meaning.* San Francisco: Harper & Row.

Gadamer, H. 1976. *Philosophical hermeneutics.* Berkeley: Univ. of Calif. Press.

———. 1992. *Truth and method.* 2nd ed. New York: Crossroad.

Gardner, H. 1983. *Frames of mind.* New York: Basic Books.

Gardner, H.; E. Phelps; and D. Wolf. 1990. The roots of adult creativity in children's symbolic products. In Alexander et al., 1990, 79–96.

Gebser, J. 1985. *The ever-present origin.* Athens: Ohio Univ. Press.

Gedo, J. 1979. *Beyond interpretation: Toward a revised theory for psychoanalysis.* New York: International Univ. Press.

———. 1981. *Advances in clinical psychoanalysis.* New York: International Univ. Press.

Geertz, C. 1973. *The interpretation of cultures.* New York: Harper & Row.

Gerson, L. 1994. *Plotinus.* London: Routledge.

Gilligan, C. 1982. *In a different voice.* Cambridge: Harvard Univ. Press.

Gilligan, C.; J. Murphy; and M. Tappan. 1990. Moral development beyond adolescence. In Alexander et al., 1990: 208–28.

Graff, G., and G. Gibbons, eds. 1985. *Criticism in the university.* Evanston, Ill.: Northwestern Univ. Press.

Gregory, R. 1982. *Mind in science.* Cambridge: Cambridge Univ. Press.

Grof, S. 1985. *Beyond the brain.* Albany: SUNY Press.

———. 1988. *The adventure of self-discovery.* Albany: SUNY Press.

Grof, S., with H. Bennett. 1992. *The holotropic mind.* San Francisco: HarperCollins.

Habermas, J. 1979. *Communication and the evolution of society.* T. McCarthy (trans.). Boston: Beacon Press.

———. 1984–5. *The theory of communicative action.* 2 vols. T. McCarthy (trans.). Boston: Beacon.

———. 1990. *The philosophical discourse of modernity.* F. Lawrence (trans.). Cambridge: MIT Press.

Hartman, G., ed. 1979. *Psychoanalysis and the question of the text*. Baltimore: Johns Hopkins.

———. 1970. *Beyond formalism*. New Haven: Yale Univ. Press.

Hayward, J., and F. Varela. 1992. *Gentle bridges*. Boston: Shambhala.

Hegel, G. 1993. *Hegel's science of logic*. Atlantic Highlands, N.J.: Humanities Press International.

Heidegger, M. 1959. *Introduction to metaphysics*. New Haven: Yale Univ. Press.

———. 1962. *Being and time*. New York: Harper & Row.

———. 1968. *What is called thinking?* New York: Harper & Row.

———. 1977. *Basic writings*. Ed. by D. Krell. New York: Harper & Row.

Hirsch, E. D. 1967. *Validity in interpretation*. New Haven: Yale Univ. Press.

———. 1976. *The aims of interpretation*. Chicago: Univ. of Chicago Press.

Hoy, D. 1978. *The critical circle*. Berkeley: Univ. of California Press.

Hoy, D., and T. McCarthy. 1994. *Critical theory*. Cambridge: Blackwell.

Husserl, E. 1970. *The crisis of European sciences and transcendental phenomenology*. Evanston, Ill.: Northwestern Univ. Press.

———. 1991 (1950). *Cartesian meditations*. Boston: Kluwer.

Inge, W. R. 1968 (1929). *The philosophy of Plotinus*. Vols. 1 & 2. Westport, Conn.: Greenwood.

Irigaray, L. 1985. *This sex which is not one*. Ithaca, N.Y.: Cornell Univ. Press.

Iser, W. 1974. *The implied reader*. Baltimore: Johns Hopkins.

Jackendoff, R. 1987. *Consciousness and the computational mind*. Cambridge: MIT Press.

Jakobson, R. 1980. *The framework of language*. Michigan Studies in the Humanities.

———. 1990. *On language*. Cambridge: Harvard Univ. Press.

Jantsch, E. 1980. *The self-organizing universe*. New York: Pergamon.

Jaspers, K. 1966. *The great philosophers*. New York: Harcourt.

Joravsky, D. 1982. Body, mind, and machine. *New York Review of Books*, Oct. 21, 1982.

Kant, I. 1949. *Kant's critique of practical reason and other writings in moral philosophy*. Trans. by L. Beck. Chicago: Univ. of Chicago Press.

———. 1951. *Critique of judgement*. New York: Hafner.

———. 1990. *Critique of pure reason*. Buffalo, N.Y.: Prometheus Books.

———. 1993. *Prolegomena*. Chicago: Open Court.

Kegan, R. 1982. *The evolving self*. Cambridge: Harvard Univ. Press.

———. 1994. *In over our heads*. Cambridge: Harvard Univ. Press.

Koestler, A. 1976. *The ghost in the machine*. New York: Random House.

Kohlberg, L. 1981. *Essays on moral development*. Vol. 1. San Francisco: Harper.

Kohlberg, L., and C. Armon. 1984. Three types of stage models. In M. Commons et al., 1984.

Kohlberg, L., and R. Ryncarz. 1990. Beyond justice reasoning. In Alexander et al. 1990: 191–207.

Kohut, H. 1971. *The analysis of the self*. New York: IUP.

———. 1977. *The restoration of the self*. New York: IUP.

Koplowitz, H. 1978. *Unitary thought*. Toronto: Addiction Research Foundation.

Kramer, D. 1983. Post-formal operations? *Human Development* 26: 91–105.

——. 1990. Conceptualizing wisdom. In Sternberg (ed.) 1990.

Kris, E. 1952. *Psychoanalytic explorations in art*. New York: International Univ. Press.

Kristeva, J. 1980. *Desire in language*. New York: Columbia Univ. Press.

Kuhn, T. 1970. *The structure of scientific revolutions*. Chicago: Univ. of Chicago Press.

Kunsang, E., trans. & ed. 1986. *The flight of the garuda*.

Lacan, J. 1968. *The language of the self*. Baltimore: Johns Hopkins.

——. 1982. *Feminine sexuality*. New York: Norton.

Laszlo, E. 1972. *Introduction to systems philosophy*. New York: Harper & Row.

——. 1987. *Evolution: The grand synthesis*. Boston: Shambhala.

Leibniz, G. 1990. *Discourse on method* and *monadology*. Buffalo, N.Y.: Prometheus Books.

Lenski, G.; P. Nolan; and J. Lenski. 1995. *Human societies*. New York: McGraw-Hill.

Levinson, D. et al. 1978. *The seasons of a man's life*. New York: Knopf.

Loevinger, J. 1977. *Ego development*. San Francisco: Jossey-Bass.

Lovejoy, A. 1964 (1936). *The great chain of being*. Cambridge: Harvard Univ. Press.

Lyotard, J. 1984. *The postmodern condition*. Minneapolis: Univ. of Minnesota Press.

Lyotard, J., and J. Thebaud. 1986. *Just gaming*. Manchester: Manchester Univ. Press.

Mahler, M. 1968. *On human symbiosis and the vicissitudes of individuation*. New York: IUP.

Mahler, M.; F. Pine; and A. Bergman. 1975. *The psychological birth of the human infant*. New York: Basic Books.

Maslow, A. 1970. *Religions, values, and peak experiences*. New York: Viking.

——. 1971. *The farther reaches of human nature*. New York: Viking.

Masterson, J. 1981. *The narcissistic and borderline disorders*. New York: Bruner/Mazel.

——. 1988. *The search for the real self*. New York: Free Press.

Maturana, H., and F. Varela. 1992. *The tree of knowledge*. Rev. ed. Boston: Shambhala.

McGann, J. 1985. *Historical studies and literary criticism*. Madison: Univ. of Wisconsin Press.

McGuinness, D.; K. Pribram; and M. Pirnazar. 1990. Upstaging the stage model. In Alexander et al., 1990: 97–113.

Miller, J. 1993. *The passion of Michel Foucault*. New York: Simon & Schuster.

Miller, M., and S. Cook-Greuter, eds. 1994. *Transcendence and mature thought in adulthood: The further reaches of adult development*. Lanham, Md.: Rowman and Littlefield.

Murphy, M. 1992. *The future of the body*. Los Angeles: Tarcher.

Murphy, M., and S. Donovan. 1989. *The physical and psychological effects of meditation*. San Rafael, Calif.: Esalen.

Murphy, M., and G. Leonard. 1995. *The life we are given.* New York: Tarcher/ Putnam.

Murti, T. 1970. *The central philosophy of Buddhism.* London: Allen and Unwin.

Naess, A. 1989. *Ecology, community and lifestyle.* Cambridge: Cambridge Univ. Press.

Neumann, E. 1954. *The origins and history of consciousness.* Princeton: Princeton Univ. Press.

Newton, J., and D. Rosenfelt, eds. 1985. *Feminist criticism and social change.* New York: Methuen.

Nietzsche, F. 1965. *The portable Nietzsche.* Ed. by W. Kaufmann. New York: Viking.

———. 1968. *Basic writings of Nietzsche.* Trans. and ed. by W. Kaufmann. New York: Modern Library.

Nucci, L., ed. 1989. *Moral development and character education.* Berkeley: McCutchan.

O'Meara, D. 1995. *Plotinus.* New York: Oxford Univ. Press.

Pascual-Leone, J. 1990. Reflections on life-span intelligence, consciousness, and ego development. In Alexander et al., 1990: 258–285.

Passmore, J. 1991. *Serious art.* La Salle, Ill.: Open Court.

Peirce, C. 1931–58. *Collected papers.* 8 vols. Cambridge: Harvard Univ. Press.

———. 1955. *Philosophical writings of Peirce.* Ed. by J. Buchler. New York: Dover.

Piaget, J. 1977. *The essential Piaget.* Ed. by H. Gruber and J. Voneche. New York: Basic.

Plato. 1956. *The works of Plato.* Ed. by I. Edman. New York: Modern Library.

Plotinus. 1966–88. *Enneads.* Vols. 1–7. Trans. by A. H. Armstrong. Cambridge: Harvard Univ. Press.

———. 1992. *Enneads.* Trans. by S. MacKenna. Burdett, N.Y.: Larson.

Popper, K. 1974. *Objective knowledge.* Oxford: Clarendon.

Popper, K., and J. Eccles. 1983. *The self and its brain.* London: Routledge.

Puhakka, K. 1996. Restoring connectedness in the Kosmos: A healing tale of a deeper order. *The Humanistic Psychologist,* Fall 1996.

Richards, F. and M. Commons. 1990. Postformal cognitive-developmental theory and research. In Alexander et al., 1990, 139–61.

Ricoeur, P. 1981. *Hermeneutics and the human sciences.* Cambridge: Cambridge Univ. Press.

———. 1992. *Oneself as another.* Chicago: Univ. of Chicago Press.

———. 1995. *The philosophy of Paul Ricoeur.* Ed. by L. Hahn. Chicago: Open Court.

Riso, D. 1987. *Personality types.* Boston: Houghton Mifflin.

———. 1990. *Understanding the enneagram.* Boston: Houghton Mifflin.

Robinson, L. 1986. *Sex, class, and culture.* New York: Methuen.

Rorty, R. 1979. *Philosophy and the mirror of nature.* Princeton: Princeton Univ. Press.

———. 1982. *Consequences of pragmatism.* Minneapolis: Univ. of Minnesota Press.

Rothberg, D. 1986a. Philosophical foundations of transpersonal psychology. *Journal of Transpersonal Psychology*, 18: 1–34.

———. 1986b. Rationality and religion in Habermas' recent work. *Philosophy and Social Criticism* 11: 221–43.

———. 1990. Contemporary epistemology and the study of mysticism. In R. Forman, ed. 1990.

———. 1992. Buddhist nonviolence. *Journal of Humanistic Psychology* 32(4): 41–75.

———. 1993. The crisis of modernity and the emergence of socially engaged spirituality. *ReVision* 15(3): 105–15.

Russell, B. 1945. *A history of western philosophy*. New York: Clarion.

Saussure, F. 1966 (1915). *Course in general linguistics*. New York: McGraw-Hill.

Schapiro, M. 1994. *Theory and philosophy of art: Style, artist, and society*. New York: Braziller.

Schelling, F. 1978 (1800). *System of transcendental idealism*. Trans. by P. Heath. Charlottesville: Univ. Press of Virginia.

Schopenhauer, A. 1969. *The world as will and representation*. 2 vols. New York: Dover.

Schwartz, T. 1995. *What really matters: Searching for wisdom in America*. New York: Bantam.

Scott, A. 1995. *Stairway to the mind*. New York: Copernicus.

Scotton, B.; A. Chinen; and J. Battista, eds. 1996. *Textbook of transpersonal psychiatry and psychology*. New York: Basic Books.

Searle, J. 1992 (1969). *Speech acts*. Cambridge: Cambridge Univ. Press.

———. 1995. *The construction of social reality*. New York: Free Press.

Shapiro, D., and R. Walsh, eds. 1984. *Meditation: Classic and contemporary perspectives*. New York: Aldine.

Sheldrake, R. 1989. *The presence of the past: Morphic resonance and the habits of nature*. New York: Viking.

———. 1990. *The rebirth of nature*. London: Century.

Showalter, E. 1985. *The new feminist criticism*. New York: Pantheon.

Siegler, R. 1991. *Children's thinking*. Englewood Cliffs, N.J.: Prentice-Hall.

Sinnott, J. 1984. Post-formal reasoning. In Commons et al. (eds.), 1984.

———, ed. 1994. *Interdisciplinary handbook of adult lifespan learning*. Greenwich, Conn.: Greenwood Press.

Sinnott, J. and J. Cavanaugh, eds. 1991. *Bridging paradigms: Positive development in adulthood and cognitive aging*. New York: Praeger.

Smith, H. 1976. *Forgotten truth*. New York: Harper.

Souvaine, E.; L. Lahey; and R. Kegan. 1990. Life after formal operations. In Alexander et al., 1990: 229–57.

Sternberg, R. (Ed.) 1990. *Wisdom: Its nature, origins, and development*. New York: Cambridge Univ. Press.

Strelka, J., ed. 1976. *Literary criticism and psychology*. University Park: Penn State Univ. Press.

Suleiman, S., and I. Crosman, eds. 1980. *The reader in the text*. Princeton, N.J.: Princeton Univ. Press.

Tannahill, R. 1992. *Sex in history*. Scarborough House.

Tannen, D. 1990. *You just don't understand*. New York: Morrow.

Tart, C., ed. 1992. *Transpersonal psychologies*. New York: HarperCollins.

Taylor, C. 1985. *Philosophy and the human sciences—philosophical papers 2*. Cambridge: Cambridge Univ. Press.

Thomas, L.; S. Brewer; P. Kraus; and B. Rosen. Two patterns of transcendence: An empirical examination of Wilber's and Washburn's theories. *Journal of Humanistic Psychology* 33(3): 66–82.

Tompkins, J., ed. 1980. *Reader-response criticism*. Baltimore: Johns Hopkins.

Trungpa, C. 1988. *Shambhala: The sacred path of the warrior*. Boston: Shambhala.

Vaillant, G. 1993. *The wisdom of the ego*. Cambridge: Harvard Univ. Press.

Varela, F. 1979. *Principles of biological autonomy*. New York: North Holland.

Varela, F.; E. Thompson; and E. Rosch. 1993. *The embodied mind*. Cambridge: MIT Press.

Wade, J. 1996. *Changes of mind*. Albany: SUNY Press.

Wallace, R. 1970. Physiological effects of Transcendental Meditation. *Science, 167*, 1751–54.

Walsh, R. 1989. Can Western philosophers understand Asian philosophies? *Crosscurrents* 34: 281–99.

———. 1990. *The spirit of shamanism*. Los Angeles: Tarcher.

———. 1995. The spirit of evolution: A review of Ken Wilber's *Sex, ecology, spirituality*. *Noetics Sciences Review*, Summer 1995.

Walsh, R., and F. Vaughan, eds. 1993. *Paths beyond ego*. Los Angeles: Tarcher.

Washburn, M. 1995. *The ego and the dynamic ground*. 2nd ed. rev. Albany: SUNY Press.

Whitehead, A. 1967. *Science and the modern world*. New York: Macmillan.

Wilber, K. 1974. The spectrum of consciousness. *Main Currents in Modern Thought*, November/December 1974.

———. 1978a. Spectrum psychology, part 1. *ReVision* 1(1): 5–29.

———. 1978b. Spectrum psychology, part 2. *ReVision* 1(2): 5–33.

———. 1978c. Microgeny. *ReVision* 1(3/4): 52–84.

———. 1979a. Spectrum psychology, part 4. *ReVision* 2(1): 65–73.

———. 1979b. Are the chakras real? In J. White, ed., *Kundalini, evolution and enlightenment*. Garden City, N.Y.: Doubleday Anchor, 1979.

———. 1979c. A developmental view of consciousness. *Journal of Transpersonal Psychology* 11(1).

———. 1980. The pre/trans fallacy. *ReVision* 3(2). Reprinted in K. Wilber, 1996c.

———. 1981a. Ontogenetic development: Two fundamental patterns. *Journal of Transpersonal Psychology* 13(1): 33–58.

———. 1981b. *No boundary*. Boston: Shambhala.

———. 1982a. Odyssey. *Journal of Humanistic Psychology* 22(1):57–90.

———. 1982b. *The holographic paradigm*. Boston: Shambhala.

———. 1983. *A sociable God: A brief introduction to a transcendental sociology*. Boston: Shambhala.

———. 1984. The developmental spectrum and psychopathology: Part 1, stages and types of pathology. *Journal of Transpersonal Psychology* 16(1): 75–118. Part 2, treatment modalities. *Journal of Transpersonal Psychology* 16(2): 137–166.

———. 1990. Two patterns of transcendence: A reply to Washburn. *Journal of Humanistic Psychology* 30(3): 113–136. [Reprinted in *The Collected Works of Ken Wilber,* vol. 4, under the title "A Unified Theory of Development."]

———. 1993 (1977). *The spectrum of consciousness.* Wheaton, Ill.: Quest.

———. 1995. *Sex, ecology, spirituality: The spirit of evolution.* Boston: Shambhala.

———. 1996a (1980). *The Atman project.* 2nd ed. Wheaton, Ill.: Quest.

———. 1996b (1981). *Up from Eden.* 2nd ed. Wheaton, Ill.: Quest.

———. 1996c (1983). *Eye to eye: The quest for the new paradigm.* 3rd ed. Boston: Shambhala.

———. 1996d. *A brief history of everything.* Boston: Shambhala.

Wilber, K.; J. Engler; and D. Brown. 1986. *Transformations of consciousness: Conventional and contemplative perspectives on development.* Boston: Shambhala.

Wimsatt, W. K., and M. Beardsley, The intentional fallacy, in W. K. Wimsatt, *The verbal icon.* New York: Noonday Press, 1966.

Wittgenstein, L. 1961 (1921). *Tractatus logico-philosophicus.* London: Routledge.

———. 1965. *Philosophical investigations.* New York: Macmillan.

Zimmerman, M. 1990. *Heidegger's confrontation with modernity.* Bloomington: Indiana Univ. Press.

———. 1981. *Eclipse of the self.* Athens: Ohio Univ. Press.

———. 1994. *Contesting earth's future.* Berkeley: Univ. of California Press.

SOURCES

A Brief History of Everything, 1st ed. Boston & London: Shambhala Publications, © 1996 by Ken Wilber.

The Eye of Spirit: An Integral Vision for a World Gone Slightly Mad, 1st ed. Boston & London: Shambhala Publications, © 1997 by Ken Wilber.

"An Integral Theory of Consciousness." *Journal of Consciousness Studies* 4, no. 1 (1997): 71–92. © 1997 by Ken Wilber.

BOOKS BY KEN WILBER

The Spectrum of Consciousness (1977)

No Boundary: Eastern and Western Approaches to Personal Growth (1979)

The Atman Project: A Transpersonal View of Human Development (1980)

Up from Eden: A Transpersonal View of Human Evolution (1981)

The Holographic Paradigm and Other Paradoxes: Exploring the Leading Edge of Science (1982)

A Sociable God: Toward a New Understanding of Religion (1983)

Eye to Eye: The Quest for the New Paradigm (1983)

Quantum Questions: Mystical Writings of the World's Great Physicists (1984)

Transformations of Consciousness: Conventional and Contemplative Perspectives on Development, by Ken Wilber, Jack Engler, and Daniel P. Brown (1986)

Spiritual Choices: The Problems of Recognizing Authentic Paths to Inner Transformation, edited by Dick Anthony, Bruce Ecker, and Ken Wilber (1987)

Grace and Grit: Spirituality and Healing in the Life and Death of Treya Killam Wilber (1991)

Sex, Ecology, Spirituality: The Spirit of Evolution (1995)

A Brief History of Everything (1996)

The Eye of Spirit: An Integral Vision for a World Gone Slightly Mad (1997)

The Marriage of Sense and Soul: Integrating Science and Religion (1998)

One Taste: The Journals of Ken Wilber (1999)

Integral Psychology (2000)

INDEX

785